Praise for

THE SECOND MOST POWERFUL MAN IN THE WORLD

"Phillips Payson O'Brien's *The Second Most Powerful Man in the World* is a beautifully written and thoroughly researched biography of Admiral William D. Leahy. In so many ways, Leahy was FDR's indispensable strategist. In these pages are magnificent stories about Pearl Harbor, Vichy France, and Winston Churchill. Highly recommended!"

—Douglas Brinkley, professor of history at Rice University and *New York Times* bestselling author of *Rightful Heritage: Franklin D. Roosevelt and the Land of America*

"O'Brien makes a compelling case that . . . [Leahy's] autobiography, published in 1950, [which] revealed little about his life and work . . . has led historians to miss Leahy's vital role in shaping U.S. grand strategy during the war and to exaggerate General George Marshall's part in consequence." —*Foreign Affairs*

"[A] first-rate biography . . . O'Brien recounts [Leahy's] astounding career in fascinating detail." —*The Christian Science Monitor*

"Whether it's the conferences at Tehran, Yalta, or Potsdam, Admiral Leahy stands out in the iconic photographs, in full uniform, just behind the Big Three. Why, though, was he there, and in so many other places that shaped the conduct of World War II and the early Cold War? As if more impressed by the uniform than by the man, historians until now have struggled to say. Phillips Payson O'Brien's biography at last gives Leahy his due, and in doing so shifts our understanding of the other great figures of that era. We're all going to have some serious rethinking to do."

—John Lewis Gaddis, Professor of Military and Naval History at Yale University and Pulitzer Prize–winning author of *George F. Kennan: An American Life*

"With his fascinating new biography of Admiral William D. Leahy, Phillips Payson O'Brien takes readers behind the closed doors of Franklin Roosevelt's White House to reveal how the biggest strategic decisions of World War II were actually made. *The Second Most Powerful Man in the World* greatly enriches our understanding of Washington wartime power."
—Former Secretary of State Madeleine K. Albright

"In the story of how Allied strategy was determined in World War II, there has long been a major gap. What made the relationship between Roosevelt and his Joint Chiefs actually tick? In this readable and revisionist biography of William D. Leahy, Phillips Payson O'Brien provides an answer that transforms our understanding of America's wartime decision-making. Leahy has been hiding in plain sight. Now that he has found his spotlight, we shall need to rethink some of our most cherished assumptions."

—Hew Strachan, Emeritus Fellow of All Souls College, Oxford, and author of *The Direction of War*

"A welcome biography of Franklin Roosevelt's closest adviser . . . A lucid, opinionated life of a man who exerted far greater influence than historians give him credit for—and a book sure to invite spirited argument from historians who disagree." —*Kirkus Reviews* (starred review)

"Engaging . . . Excels at relating the political maneuvering that allowed [Leahy] to repeatedly upstage better-known historical figures including George Marshall and Douglas MacArthur. . . . This is a solid and informative account of a relatively underdiscussed influence on Cold War policies, worldviews, and relationships that still matter today."

—*Publishers Weekly*

"An excellent biography of perhaps the most notable navy officer in American history, and one of the most important, if neglected, figures in World War II history." —*Library Journal*

THE SECOND MOST POWERFUL MAN IN THE WORLD

The Life of Admiral William D. Leahy, Roosevelt's Chief of Staff

Phillips Payson O'Brien

CALIBER

CALIBER

An imprint of Penguin Random House LLC

penguinrandomhouse.com

Previously published as a Dutton hardcover edition in 2019

First trade paperback printing: March 2020

THE LIBRARY OF CONGRESS HAS CATALOGUED THE HARDCOVER EDITION AS FOLLOWS:

Names: O'Brien, Phillips Payson, 1963– author.

Title: The second most powerful man in the world : the life of Admiral William D. Leahy, Roosevelt's chief of staff / Phillips Payson O'Brien.

Description: New York, New York : Dutton, [2019] | Includes bibliographical references and index.

Identifiers: LCCN 2018016899| ISBN 9780399584800 (hardcover) | ISBN 9780399584817 (ebook)

Subjects: LCSH: Leahy, William D. | United States. Joint Chiefs of Staff—Biography. | Admirals—United States—Biography. | LCGFT: Biographies.

Classification: LCC E748.L44 O37 2019 | DDC 359.0092 [B]—dc23

LC record available at https://lccn.loc.gov/2018016899

Dutton trade paperback ISBN: 9780399584824

Printed in the United States of America
1 3 5 7 9 10 8 6 4 2

BOOK DESIGN BY AMY HILL

For Mathilde,
who has changed everything
for the better

Contents

Prologue   1

Chapter 1   **The Education of a Naval Officer**   5

Chapter 2   **Building a Career and Family**   24

Chapter 3   **Enter Franklin Roosevelt**   40

Chapter 4   **The Roaring Twenties**   53

Chapter 5   **Depression**   70

Chapter 6   **Nearing the Top**   84

Chapter 7   **Rising in Roosevelt's Court**   100

Chapter 8   **Leahy's Navy**   111

Chapter 9   **The First Retirement**   124

Chapter 10   **Governor of Puerto Rico**   131

Chapter 11   **Ambassador to Vichy France**   143

Chapter 12   **Dark Days**   161

Chapter 13   **Chief of Staff to the Commander in Chief**   177

Chapter 14   **Chairman of the Joint Chiefs of Staff**   188

Chapter 15   **The Grandest Level of Strategy**   201

Chapter 16   **From Casablanca to Trident**   211

Chapter 17   **Difficult Friends**   230

Chapter 18   **Top Dog**   241

Contents

Chapter 19   **Cairo and Tehran**   249

Chapter 20   **Acting President**   266

Chapter 21   **Leahy's War**   279

Chapter 22   **Atomic Bombs and Elections**   291

Chapter 23   **Yalta and Death**   307

Chapter 24   **Truman**   328

Chapter 25   **The End of the War**   344

Chapter 26   **Two Speeches**   360

Chapter 27   **Personal Snooper**   375

Chapter 28   **Priorities**   386

Chapter 29   **Cold War**   396

Chapter 30   **Key West**   409

Chapter 31   **On the Outside**   417

Chapter 32   **Fading Away**   427

Chapter 33   **The Forgotten Man**   437

Epilogue   447

Acknowledgments   449

Appendices   451

Select Bibliography   461

Notes   469

Index   511

Prologue

On the morning of March 3, 1946, an overnight train from Florida pulled into Union Station in Washington, DC. On board was one of the most famous men in the world, Winston Churchill. The former British prime minister and wartime leader had spent the previous six weeks lounging in the Miami sun, battling vertigo and a chest infection while writing one of the most consequential speeches in history. Properly titled the "Sinews of Peace," it was to become better known as the "Iron Curtain" speech. If Churchill could not have known how famous this speech would become, he did know that it could be political dynamite. He intended to address the growing split between the Anglo-American allies and the Soviet Union, a division that threatened another catastrophic world war on the heels of Germany's defeat, and he knew his words would garner attention around the globe. In two days he was set to deliver his speech before President Harry S. Truman at Westminster College in Fulton, Missouri, Truman's home state. Churchill knew that his call for a dramatic change in policy could succeed only if he had the wholehearted support of the president. And he knew that there was only one man who could let him know all would be OK.

Churchill's first destination in Washington was the British embassy on Massachusetts Avenue, where a bedroom had been put at his disposal. Next was a telephone call to the White House, with a request not for Secretary of State James Byrnes, nor even President Truman himself, but for Adm. William D. Leahy, a salty seventy-year-old sailor whose military career extended back almost as far as Churchill's own.

Leahy arrived to find Churchill in bed, but the former prime minister roused quickly and handed over a manuscript of his speech. The two men went through it methodically, reading each line aloud as Churchill puffed on a long cigar, scattering ash all over his bed and sprinkling the papers they passed back and forth.[1] They made an odd pair: the orderly sailor and the disorderly politician. It is not hard to imagine Leahy, relatively trim for a man his age, with only the slightest hint of a potbelly, dressed as always in a crisp, clean uniform, speaking in his clipped tones while the portly Churchill, all energy and eloquence, rehearsed the speech in his dressing gown.

Leahy listened intently to Churchill's words, knowing full well their gravity. Earlier that morning, he had provided Truman a briefing on the state of the world and American security, as he did every day, and knew, as much as anyone, what was on the president's mind. As Churchill spoke, Leahy did not hesitate to interrupt, suggesting changes in both content and emphasis. These Churchill were quick to note and incorporate, and for which he would remain grateful for the rest of his life.

This was not the first such consultation between the renowned British hero and the relatively obscure American naval officer. Indeed, Churchill had stopped briefly in Washington back in February to discuss the speech with Leahy, understanding the man's outsized influence on the workings of the highest level of the US government. He knew that Leahy was the one man in DC who could approve the speech on behalf of the president. What's more, he respected Leahy's opinion of international affairs, having worked with the man, sometimes tempestuously, sometimes affectionately, during the great strategic conferences of World War II. Churchill had taken the measure of William Leahy, and vice versa, and each liked what he found—mostly.

Only after the speech had been thoroughly vetted by Leahy would Churchill allow anyone else to see it. Byrnes was given a copy only later that evening. The speech itself proved to be momentous. Churchill spoke of Europe being divided into two armed camps, a Communist Eastern Bloc and a Capitalist West. He made an explicit call for the United States to toughen up its policy toward the Soviet Union, to protect Europe against any further increases in Communist power. In a line that has echoed down the decades, and will echo down the centuries, he spoke: "From Stettin in the Baltic to Trieste in the Adriatic, an iron curtain has descended across the Continent. Behind that line lie the capitals of the ancient states of Central and Eastern Europe. Warsaw, Berlin, Prague, Vienna, Budapest, Belgrade, Bucharest and Sofia, all of these famous cities and the populations around them lie in what I must call the Soviet sphere . . ."[2]

An examination of history books, however, will show no mention of William Leahy's role in shaping Churchill's world-changing address, and that is typical of the man and the way he has been remembered. Churchill understood what subsequent generations of historians have not: William Leahy had influence in the US government in ways that almost no other individual has had in American history. For almost seven years Leahy was the closest policy-making individual to the president of the United States. Between 1942 and 1949, America was the globe's unchallenged superpower, possessing almost half the world's product, sucking up almost all the world's gold, building up an air force and navy without parallel and, finally, becoming the sole possessor of the atomic bomb. American air and sea power determined the outcome of World War II and American policy choices established the contours of the Cold War in Europe, Asia, and around the world. Every other power in the world was "reactive" to American decision-making. As Leahy had more influence over those decisions than anyone not named Roosevelt or Truman, he was even more powerful than leaders of other nations, such as Winston Churchill or Joseph Stalin.

That he is hardly known today says both a great deal about him and about how he accumulated power. We often confuse celebrity with authority. Leahy never wanted to be famous, or known to be important, or even rich. He wanted to serve the president of the United States, and in doing so shape American policy and guarantee American security. He realized, instinctively, that it would help him immeasurably in this task if he remained in the background, unknown and undiscussed. He was the substance of power, not the style.

CHAPTER 1

The Education of a Naval Officer

William Daniel Leahy died with a crooked nose and little money. The two were related, and it's best to start with the money. Upon his death in 1959, his net worth was shockingly small, considering he had spent more than a decade as one of the most powerful men in the world, shaping America's military and diplomatic policy while hobnobbing with the rich and famous. His property, savings, and investments combined were valued at only $113,903, a sum worth just over $900,000 today.[1] This would mark his economic status as lower middle class. This surprisingly small figure was mostly the result of choice, with a dash of bad luck. Throughout American history, senior military and political figures have used their positions and influence to enrich themselves, becoming high-paid lecturers, media personalities, business executives, or lobbyists. Leahy could have done so as well, yet he chose not to.

Economically cautious, he learned early to get by with little in the way of luxuries, a lesson that held for the rest of his life. He was born in Hampton, Iowa, on May 6, 1875, to Michael Arthur Leahy and his wife, Rose Mary Hamilton, both first-generation Americans of Irish-born parents. Like many a son of Irish immigrants, William was told by his paternal grandmother, Mary Eagan Leahy, a native Gaelic speaker from Galway, about how his family had been great chiefs in the west of Ireland before being dispossessed by the hated British. The last Leahy chief had supposedly fought for the Catholic king James VII at the Battle of the Boyne in 1690, the loss of which spelled the end of the family's prosperity. Mary Eagan had immigrated to America with her husband, Daniel Leahy, in 1836, and they had moved steadily westward from New England to Wisconsin, where they raised their four sons, including Michael.

Michael was one of those second-generation Americans who lived on the edge of success without ever reaching the Promised Land. At the age of twenty-four, he graduated from the University of Wisconsin with a law degree. With the Civil War raging, he enlisted in the 35th Wisconsin Regiment and was commissioned a captain, a sign that he had achieved a certain level of educational and social attainment. After the war, he embarked on a career in law and politics. In 1868, he decided to move to Hampton, Iowa, a farming community, to start a new life. There he married Rose, opened his law practice, and entered politics, being elected to the state legislature in 1872.

Little today is known of Rose. Three years after her husband's electoral victory, she gave birth to their first son, William Daniel Leahy. From William's birth certificate we know that she was twenty-four years old when he was born, thirteen years younger than her husband, but little else. Her son's diary leaves the impression he was emotionally distant from his mother—the detached, formal nature of the diary was indeed a reflection of his character—but in fact he loved her dearly.

Michael gives the impression of treading water in Iowa. He and Rose continued producing children—they would have five more sons and a daughter—while Michael continued getting reelected to the state legislature.[2] Yet he could rise no further, and in 1882 he packed up his large family and moved back to Wisconsin. The Leahys settled first in Wausau, in the middle of the state, where Michael's brother had established himself as a prominent lumber merchant. Once again, success eluded Michael, and in 1889 he moved the family to Ashland in the far north of Wisconsin.

Ashland was the city with which William Leahy would most identify his youth, and one can see why Michael chose it. By 1890 Ashland had grown into a bustling little transport hub, servicing America's burgeoning industrial economy. Situated on an excellent harbor on Lake Superior, Ashland expanded because of its access to the rich iron ore veins, timber stores, and copper mines of northern Wisconsin and the Upper Peninsula of Michigan. Rail lines were built linking Ashland to these resources and they poured into the city, where they were put on ships and moved to the factories of the lower Midwest. Ashland grew from almost nothing in 1880 to more than 13,000 people by 1900— more than 50 percent larger than it is today.[3]

When the Leahys arrived, Ashland still had a whiff of the frontier. The Chippewa Indian Nation, which had dominated the area before whites piled in, remained a significant presence, and for the rest of his life Leahy felt a connection to the tribe. Though we might scoff at it now, he felt proud to be made a member of the Chippewa in the 1930s. Ashland itself was ramshackle, a jumble of new, ever-changing buildings linked by dirt roads and wooden walkways. Leahy's time there seems completely ordinary. He went to high school, where he did enough work to get by but was not a standout student. He developed his lifetime interests in fishing, hunting, and football.

While playing a rowdy game of football one day, Leahy's nose was broken. As he could still breathe through it, and the family had little spare money, he left it untreated. Sixty years later, Adm. Chester Nimitz noticed the defect for the first time when his eye was drawn to the crooked nose in a portrait of Leahy being painted by well-known naval artist Albert Murray. "You fellows have known me ever since my late teens and never seen it any other way," Leahy responded when Nimitz asked about his nose, "so you thought it was normal and it never even occurred to you that it was bent out of place like it really is."[4]

His family's lack of money helped to shape Leahy's desires. It certainly made him resourceful and at the same time able to cope without many possessions. On the other hand, it also made him want to get the hell out of town. Though Leahy would later remember Ashland fondly, when he graduated from high school, he wanted to experience something new. Michael hoped that his eldest son would follow in his tracks and study law at the University of Wisconsin, but for William that option held little appeal. His great hope was to secure admission to the US

Military Academy at West Point, but there were no appointments available from local members of Congress. One did, however, have an open slot for Annapolis, as naval positions were less prized by the boys of the Midwest. Leahy jumped at the chance, hopped on a train to Maryland, and never looked back.

Later in life Leahy would reminisce about having developed a love of sailing ships by watching them cruise in and out of Ashland's port, but that seems to have played only a minor role in his choice. Going to Annapolis provided three things that suited his nature. First, it offered the opportunity for adventure. Though Leahy would later be seen as a grumpy, parochial exemplar of Middle America, as a young man he wanted to see the world, and the navy allowed him to spend many exciting, interesting years living outside the United States. Second, it allowed him to live a life of national service. Michael Leahy had raised his children to see themselves first and foremost as Americans, not Irish Americans. In the Leahy household, there were no divided loyalties or identities, and this had a huge impact on young William. Finally, a career in the navy held the possibility of service with financial security. William Leahy, not a natural businessman, always seemed uncomfortable dealing with money and investments. A career in the navy meant he could combine love of country and the values for which he believed it stood in a career that provided stability. That he eventually liked being at sea was gravy on top.

When he boarded the train to Annapolis in 1893, the trip alone was a gamble. Those who were offered appointments were still required to take an entrance examination, and that was only on offer at the academy itself. If a student failed, he typically returned to his hometown in disgrace, sometimes suffering the indignity of having to pay for his own transportation. Fortunately, Leahy, somewhat to his surprise, made it through the exam process and was welcomed into the United States Naval Academy as a new midshipman.

The first thing he had to learn was how to sail. It is an interesting side note to history that the highest-ranking American military officer when the first atomic bomb was dropped had learned to sail on the USS *Constellation*, a ship of wooden walls and cloth sails that had been commissioned in 1855 and had seen extensive service during the Civil War.[5]

A sailor's life on board the *Constellation* was closer to that of the Napoleonic era than to the days of steam and iron, much less the atomic age. Leahy remembered standing night watch in a masted crow's nest high up in the rigging. Yet his time on the ship was no romantic adventure. The cruise was supposed to last all summer, taking the young crewmen to Europe and back to learn their craft. Yet the *Constellation* was in a sorry state, smelly and leaky, and she broke down before reaching Europe. The crew had to stop in the Azores before the old ship could be made right to sail back to America.

Once back, the real naval education commenced. Leahy was one of the last midshipmen to pass through an unreformed Naval Academy. His small class was educated in the unforgiving environment of the nineteenth century. Annapolis was famous for its hazing and harsh discipline, and its education was geared toward creating assimilation and cohesion.[6] An entire class could be punished for one midshipman's mistake. Once, when a slop jar (or piss pot) was rolled down the stairs after taps, every member of the class was forced to stand at attention in the middle of the night until the guilty prankster confessed.[7] Normal hazing was done by upperclassmen to underclassmen, and could involve humiliations, physical tests, and even beatings. When the academy's hazing became public in a 1921 scandal, Leahy forcefully called for the practice to be "stamped out."[8]

Hazing could be particularly brutal when directed at those considered different. The US Navy was a monoculture, one of the least inclusive organizations of its day, overwhelmingly white, middle-class, and Christian. The first African American midshipman to enter the academy, twenty years before Leahy, was hazed so cruelly that he was forced out.[9] He was beaten regularly and at one point his classmates even tried to drown him. From there on out, African Americans were practically nonexistent and Jews extremely rare.

The punishments were harsh, but the system created close-knit groups, and Leahy's class was one of the best examples. The class of 1897 was one of the most distinguished in American history and arguably the most successful that Annapolis ever produced. It included many of the admirals who dominated the service in the 1930s, including Leahy,

Thomas Hart, Harry Yarnell, and Arthur Hepburn. To this day the class is the only one to have five members reach 4-star rank while on active duty (and one to reach 5-star). Four other classes have had four members reach the 4-star rank, but these all came many decades after 1897, when the Naval Academy, and the navy as a whole, was far larger.[10] The class of 1897, perhaps for this reason, remained very tight, and Leahy paid close attention to the lives and careers of many of his classmates. In return he received continuous, lifelong support.

Leahy stood out to his classmates for his level-headedness. He grew a mustache that made him look like a judge, and his classmates treated him accordingly.[11] The best description of Leahy at Annapolis came from his classmate and lifelong friend Thomas Hart, who would go on to serve as one of the leading submariners of his generation, commander of the Asiatic Fleet in World War II, and a US senator from Connecticut. "As a student at the Academy [Leahy] was not good, a little lazy," wrote Hart. "But when his classmates had a problem, a dispute about it, someone would say, 'Let's go ask Bill Leahy. He's got a better sense than all of us put together.' That was always true for his common sense, his wisdom, was profound all through his life."[12]

Though he would have been loath to admit it, Leahy's political skills were apparent even at this young age. He possessed the ability to judge the person with whom he was interacting, decide the best way to appeal to or motivate him or her, and adjust his behavior accordingly. "Leahy was a born diplomat," Hart remembered, "and the sort of man that always gets on with others. . . . That's always been Leahy: fundamentally wise, quick to pluck the right answer out of the air, without any powerful cerebration; intuitive, instinctive, smart."[13] Despite this intelligence, Leahy was a mediocre student. He studied French (which he would speak with an atrocious accent for the rest of his life) and played tackle on the football team's B squad. His academic results put him in the bottom third of his graduating class, 35 out of 47. When he graduated from Annapolis, he was hardly marked for greatness.

His first assignments, however, showed that there was more to him than a below-average academic. After graduating, an Annapolis midshipman was required to serve two years at sea before being permanently commissioned into the navy. For Leahy, that meant going to war. He came of age during the Spanish-American War and the Philippine Insurrection that followed, and he was thrust into the center of both. His first ship was one of his favorites. In the summer of 1897 he was ordered to join the crew of the USS *Oregon*, one of the newest and most powerful battleships in the US fleet. In those days, even getting to your ship could be a test of resourcefulness. Leahy was told to report to the *Oregon* in "whatever port that vessel might be."[14] Checking around, he discovered she was supposed to be in Seattle at the time he was to board, so after a night of celebrating with his fellow graduates, he headed across the country, undoubtedly worse for wear. When he reached Seattle, he found that the *Oregon* had already left for Victoria, British Columbia, to help the Canadians celebrate Queen Victoria's Diamond Jubilee. Hopping a steamship north, he landed in Port Townsend, Washington, where he found the one hotel was closed, forcing him to spend the night outside in the freezing rain. When he finally reached Victoria, he was told that the *Oregon* was berthed in the port of Esquimalt, a few miles away, reachable by streetcar. Thus, after a cross-country train trip and two boat journeys, Leahy arrived at his first assignment by trolley.

He was delighted that he did. Being on the *Oregon* provided a great lesson about the power of command. The ship's captain, A. W. Barker, was an excellent seaman who impressed his men with his ability to handle such a large vessel in the fog and mist that regularly shrouded the Pacific Northwest.[15] Yet, according to Leahy, Barker did "not possess an attractive personality" and could be very hard on junior officers. It gave the vessel a gloomy air. In early 1898, Barker was transferred and a little while later the *Oregon* was taken over by Capt. Charles E. Clark, whom the men worshipped. Leahy was impressed by how the change in captains completely changed the mood of the ship. It helped make the *Oregon* both a happy and a good ship, transforming his experience. For the rest of his life, Leahy would look to Clark as an inspiration on command.

The battleship spent most of late 1897 and early 1898 cruising up and down the west coast of North and South America, allowing Leahy to engage with some of the wider world. After a bumpy start he grew comfortable in San Francisco, and for a while it became a second home. He enjoyed its cosmopolitan nature as well as its rough-and-ready atmosphere. In early 1898 the *Oregon* paid a visit to Peru, which permitted Leahy to experience a truly different culture for the first time. He found it fascinating. He was captivated by the women, finding them dark-eyed and graceful, with the "unnerving" habit of staring directly into the eyes of strangers. On the cruise to Peru Leahy crossed the equator for the first time, and he experienced one of the stranger naval customs, paying homage to King Neptune's court. Those making their first crossing were labeled pollywogs, and the veteran sailors were called shellbacks. The pollywogs were made to pay a penalty to calm the wrath of the sea god for having disgraced his domain by appearing for the first time. One of the older noncommissioned officers would get dressed up as Neptune. In Leahy's first experience this sailor used manila rope to simulate a wild head of hair. He would be accompanied by other shellbacks in different wild getups, making up his "court." The pollywogs would then be presented to Neptune and ritually humiliated. For the enlisted pollywogs of Leahy's day, it could be a rough initiation. In this instance they were placed in a barber's chair and covered from head to toe in a grotesque mixture of molasses, salt water, oil, and flour. They were then "shaved" with a three-foot wooden razor before being catapulted down a large chute into a pool of water where they were beaten by another group of shellbacks. The officers were often exempted from the most humiliating treatments, and in this case were allowed to calm Neptune's wrath through a large offering of beer. Neptune indulged so much in the generous offering that he was incapable of delivering his closing speech. He sat there, a smile on his face, repeatedly mumbling, "I am satisfied."

The real excitement of the cruise began in April. Whipped up by a feverish press, the population of the United States had become increasingly agitated by what it saw as Spanish brutality and incompetence in its rule of Cuba. In February 1898 the battleship USS *Maine*, which President McKinley had dispatched to Cuba as a sign of American interest, exploded in Havana Harbor. Popular wrath turned on the perfidious Spanish, and the navy fed this paranoia rather than admit the truth. The *Maine* exploded because it was a poorly designed ship and did not have enough protection between the highly explosive propellants needed to launch its large shells and the shells itself.

After the explosion of the *Maine*, it was thought prudent to send the *Oregon* to the Atlantic in case war broke out. As the *Oregon* was still in the Pacific, this meant that the ship had to cruise all the way around the Strait of Magellan, almost 14,000 miles, to reach its destination. While the ship was en route, the US government declared war on Spain, making the *Oregon*'s cruise a minor sensation: a naval vessel of the time steaming for such a distance was a serious undertaking, and the *Oregon* had to keep its engine functioning at close to full capacity for more than two months.[16] Fresh water had to be strictly rationed, as power was needed to propel the ship, leaving only a little for the onboard distillation system. By the time the *Oregon* took its place off Cuba on May 30, 1898, it had become the most famous vessel in the US Navy. Leahy, for one, was immensely proud of what they had achieved.

Yet Leahy was conflicted about the war itself. He held decidedly mixed opinions about both the value of American intervention in Cuba and the way certain commanders fought the war. These doubts crystallized a few weeks after the *Oregon* arrived on station, when he saw American troops heading ashore and witnessed the American navy bombarding the Cuban coast.

> These splendid young Americans that I saw marching their sentry posts ankle deep in hot sand with a deadly tropic sun beating down upon their heads, could have been spared much hardship if our country had been willing to let the occupants of Cuba fight it out without assistance. Our intervention may shorten the contest but it is not likely to improve the quality of the survivors.
>
> In the evening we fired four thirteen inch shells into the town of Guantanamo, which I thought unnecessary and cruel, and then steamed back to blockade.[17]

Despite his reservations, Leahy was soon caught up in the great naval engagement of the war, the Battle of Santiago de Cuba in July, which saw the destruction of the Spanish Fleet in Cuban waters. Leahy served as the officer in charge of the *Oregon*'s forward turret during the battle, which gave him a great vantage point from which to watch the action unfold.[18] During the fighting, the *Oregon* steamed out in front of the US force, distinguishing itself for its aggression and effectiveness.[19] To the young officer it was a confused, chaotic affair, though he was sure that the *Oregon* had performed the best of all the American vessels. Leahy believed that it engaged four different Spanish warships and came away almost unscathed.[20] He was also to be seen celebrating wildly with his crewmates when the Spanish surrendered, though from reading his diary one would get no idea that it mattered to him much at all.

The victory allowed Leahy the chance to go ashore in Cuba, and once again his doubts crept in. He was saddened by the deprivation and sickness he encountered. With food and medicine in short supply, the Cuban people had endured enormous hardships. "The suffering of these fever stricken and shot torn patients made a sad picture of the cruelty of war," he wrote. "There is glory enough for those of us who return safely or who are killed in the discharge of hazardous duty, but to a wreck of a man lying in a hospital tent, and to his mother, there is little glory in war."[21]

This tonal change between the enthusiastic Leahy celebrating the victory and the somber Leahy wondering if it was all worthwhile can be seen differently. One could say that his protestations were a little staged, predictable clichés about the brutality of war.[22] That might have been part of his reaction, but it was not all. In the first case, war was not seen in the late nineteenth century as an intrinsically awful thing. Many, including Theodore Roosevelt, believed that war was a positive, the ultimate test of human beings, one that could purify or strengthen the soul. Secondly, Leahy's expressions, as hackneyed as they might sound, represent a lifelong outlook. He would remain skeptical of the value of US interventionism for the rest of his life. He was also adamant that civilians not be targeted in war. He would argue strongly for both these positions when he was at the top of the US decision-making structure.

Leahy's dual reaction was seen right after the Spanish-American War, when he was sent on what turned out to be a formative assignment, his dispatch to the Western Pacific. When he looked back on his life as an older man, this journey was one that he returned to often. The reason was the establishment of the American empire in the Philippines. That famous archipelago, which the United States had seized from Spain, had a nationalist independence movement that did not want to merely exchange Spanish rule for American. President William McKinley, however, decided that the Filipinos were not up to the task of ruling themselves, and that it would be much better if they were made wards of the United States. A war was required for the United States to begin the process of betterment.

Leahy was desperate to get into the action. While he was still in Havana in late 1898, the US gunboat *Castine* passed through. Hearing that it was on its way to the Pacific, Leahy volunteered to join its crew. He was taken on by the grateful captain, who was pleased to have an Annapolis-trained sailor on board. The *Castine* was a shock to Leahy. A small gunboat with cramped quarters, it was a world away from the large battleship to which he had grown accustomed.

Furthermore, it was a long way to the Pacific. The *Castine* headed east, across the Atlantic, through the Mediterranean and the Suez Canal, before reaching the Indian Ocean. There she docked at Ceylon (modern-day Sri Lanka), where another shock was waiting for Leahy. After having cruised ten thousand miles, the navy in its wisdom sent him an order to return to the United States to complete his final examinations. He was therefore left behind when the *Castine* sailed for the Philippines and had to wait until a steamer appeared that would take him back to America. He did not reach Annapolis until late June 1899, having spent six months sailing around the world and going nowhere.

In late 1899, he tried again to go to war. He was assigned to the USS *Nevada*, reputedly an unhappy ship that lived up to its reputation. His voyage across the Pacific was gloomy, enlivened only by stops in Hawaii and Guam. Guam, which Leahy reached in November, gave the young man particular pause. Another island seized from the Spanish, Guam was as close to a tropical paradise as Leahy had ever encountered. The near nudity, open sexuality, and nonacquisitive lifestyle of the islanders sparked the censoriousness that was never that far below Leahy's surface. His first impression was that of a bigot: "The natives are indolent and worthless, having no idea of the value of time or money. Living as they do on the fruit provided bountifully by the tree used in the construction of their simple house, they do not need to work and are therefore happy in idleness. Morality as we know it is unknown to them, they consider falsehood entirely justified, marriage entirely a matter of option before the arrival of Americans."[23]

Yet, after a few days in Guam, something unexpected happened: the reflective Leahy appeared, and all of a sudden a quiet life of fruit and sex did not seem so bad. "It seems to me that one might learn something about human happiness by watching these people," he wrote. "They have little and want nothing. Living in little grass huts one storey above the pigs and chickens; wearing what clothes they can find, or none at all, and subsisting on whatever fruit happens to grow near, they appear to be happy and contented beyond the usual lot of humans."[24]

Paradise could not hold him, and Leahy soon arrived in Manila, back at war. At first he had a lucky break. The *Oregon* appeared, and he was able to transfer to his favorite vessel. After a few days, though, he was transferred back to the gunboat *Castine*, which he had left more than a year earlier in Ceylon. It was at least preferable to the troubled *Nevada*. He was able to visit Manila, attend a dance (he thought the "white" women in attendance were very unattractive compared to the Filipinas), and tour the city. He also tried to find out as much as possible about the local culture. He visited Manila's oldest cemetery, so cramped that older bodies had to be dug up to make way for the new. On Christmas Day he was even taken to a cockfight.[25] The cocks had thin, sharp blades strapped to their bodies with which they had been trained to attack. Though Leahy was undoubtedly a warrior, he was never cruel, and he found the spectacle grotesque as the birds sliced into one another and the smell of fresh blood permeated the room. Each fight ended only when one of the birds died or ran out of the ring. Leahy made it through only three fights. During the third, which was "long and savage," the more aggressive bird started pecking out the eyes of its opponent. As the crowd roared with excitement and money changed hands at an ever more frantic pace, Leahy got sick. He staggered out of the hall for fresh air and never went back to anything like that again.

Leahy expected to see action not long after this, but the nineteenth-century American navy being what it was, he was soon ordered to China and Japan. This trip set in motion a series of impressions that would have a huge influence on US policy in World War II and the early Cold War. Leahy loved and was fascinated with China. Many of his impressions we might consider today parochial or romantic, but for him they were intense and long-lasting. He paid close attention to the physical shape of Chinese cities and the topography of the countryside, the noises, flavors, and smells of the markets, the customs of the people. He was fascinated by China's cultural peculiarities, such as the reburial of what were considered unlucky ancestors. He was so taken by the decorations at a cemetery in Amoy that he tried to buy a number of sketches that adorned the walls of a temple, but could not communicate his intentions clearly enough to the local priest.[26] He was even fascinated by the Chinese use of slow strangulation to execute criminals. He heard of one unlucky prisoner who was supposed to be strangled horribly over a four-day period, his throat being ever so slowly constricted by two boards being pressed together. The prisoner died after two days, and it was guessed that he had been poisoned by his own wife to end the torture.

Of everything in China, he most loved Shanghai. He found the urban life there intoxicating, applauding its tolerant atmosphere. He spoke approvingly of the Western women in Shanghai being able to smoke and drink in public, a deliberate snub to the many American missionaries in the country who were preaching abstinence. For a young American officer, Shanghai offered a privileged existence, with special protected districts set aside for foreigners where lives of great luxury could be lived on small salaries. He wanted to stay longer.

Leahy's early perceptions of China stayed with him for the rest of his life. When a navy friend wrote to him twenty years later during an assignment in the country, Leahy replied with an uncharacteristic touch of poetry: "Your word picture of the streets of Peking takes me back across the years to long ago and I can now, with closed eyes, see the swarming horde along the bund, hear the song of the stevedore coolies, and feel the heavy, mysterious leisure inducing pressure of the summer atmosphere of that fascinating world. One wonders if at the half century mark, it is like it was when only a quarter of the cycle had been run, and would like to know by personal trial."[27]

His Chinese experiences allowed Leahy once again to express doubts about foreign intervention. He was in China during the high point of the Boxer Rebellion. The Boxers were a determined Chinese resistance movement, dedicated to removing foreign, and particularly Christian, influences from within China. An understandable reaction to the constant humiliations that Westerners had forced on the Chinese, the Boxers in 1900 converged on Beijing. They drove European and American nationals out of the capital and threatened to throw them out of much of northern China. Unsurprisingly in this era of imperialism, their threats brought a harsh, united response as British, Japanese, Russian, French, German, Austro-Hungarian, Italian, and American troops were brought together to crush the uprising.

When Leahy first became aware of the seriousness of what was happening, he was still in Shanghai, very much enjoying himself. When it was thought the Boxers were going to attack the city, however, he prepared to mount the city walls and fight.[28] At another time, he heard that a messmate from the *Oregon* serving in the marines was killed fighting the Boxers in Tianjin.[29] As such, Leahy had little sympathy for the Boxers, and if he had been asked to kill, he would have done it without hesitation. Yet he also wondered whether any of this mattered for the United States. "The political situation is quite beyond my understanding," he wrote in his diary, "but this turning up of the powers is likely to end in a noisy concert before China settles down to business again. The newspapers are attacking everybody who might be responsible for the failure of British troops to land, and the French and American Consuls General are getting most of the hammering. I do not see any reasons for us to get mixed up in the row."[30]

This combination of skepticism but a willingness to do his duty became even more intense when he returned to the Philippines. When he arrived back in the archipelago in September 1900, the war was entering a particularly nasty phase. Thousands of American troops were being deployed around the islands, undertaking a brutal pacification campaign against the Filipino nationalists. The US Navy played a major role in these operations, conducting amphibious landings up and down the Philippine coast.[31] Leahy was thrust into the heart of these from the moment he returned, often under the guise of surveying the Philippine coastline.[32] Such a survey, Leahy believed, would take many lifetimes, but he did find the landing of troops under fire to be exciting. He rarely saw the insurgents but could hear the crackle of their rifles as he moved ashore. He was even given his first command, probably the least glamorous ship in the navy, the USS *Mariveles*. She was a small gunboat of 250 tons, captured from the Spanish and then refitted. She had two-screw propellers supposedly capable of generating 8 knots and mounted two 3-pound guns and two machine guns. The little ship smoked, sputtered, and regularly shed parts. Leahy loved her. "We had a crew of 25 men, and three very ancient guns, which would have just been fit for shooting at sea-gulls," he later fondly recalled. "But she was a fine boat because she was my first one."[33]

Command suited Leahy. He had to learn to control the rough-and-ready group of sailors. When the Chinese cook on board was tormented by another crewman, Leahy eventually slapped the tormentor into solitary confinement—though that did not stop the cook from jumping ship. Leahy also had to learn to get by with limited supplies, and how to handle a naval vessel in shallow waters. These were all lessons that would serve him well later.

If Leahy gained satisfaction from his professional success, he was deeply troubled by much of what he discovered about the war in general. Impressed with the insurgents' determination and military bearing, he was troubled by widespread cases of torture being committed by US troops.[34] The pressures of war had become so intense that American soldiers regularly resorted to torture or even summary execution of captured or suspected insurgents.[35] At one point Leahy witnessed the shooting of a young Filipino insurgent prisoner.[36] In his diary, Leahy pulled no punches. Recounting a story about the death of a local priest who died while being tortured by American soldiers, Leahy wrote:

> Such things make one doubt that this is the beginning of the twentieth century. What has become of the knights of our childhood stories, who delighted in battling with foemen worthy of their steel, who treated vanquished enemies as honored guests and who away from battle were gentle souls[?] One used to wonder why all the fuss about Chevalier Bayard, "sans peur et sans reproach [*sic*]," who when dying gave half his cup of water to a wounded soldier. I have been taught from childhood that it is the duty of every soldier to forget his own troubles in those of his comrades, to fight with courage while the fight is on, and when it is finished, to make less bitter the defeat of the vanquished. My father was just that kind of a soldier, but in this war there are few sans peur and fewer sans reproach.[37]

Doubts, of course, would not keep him from fulfilling his duty. In June 1901, the *Mariveles* gave up the ghost. One of its two propellers disappeared into the deep, and the hobbled little ship needed so much work that it was thought better that Leahy be transferred elsewhere. He was put on the USS *Glacier*, which had the unexciting job of ferrying supplies between the Philippines and Australia. This would be Leahy's life for the next fifteen months.

It was perhaps the most relaxing assignment of his career. Once the *Glacier* reached Australia, it could take many more weeks for the vessel to be repaired and loaded up with supplies for the return to the Philippines. Once again, Leahy played the tourist. He was fascinated by the vastness and variety of Australia, believing that the country had a great future ahead of it. Many of his impressions were completely conventional. He loved Australian beaches and hated Australian sharks. He voiced the common American view that cricket, which the sports-mad

Australians played religiously, was too slow. He also made one journey deep into the outback to take part in a kangaroo hunt. The huge, empty countryside enthralled him with its sense of isolation.

Maybe because he had so much spare time on his hands, Leahy began to discuss politics. The results were surprisingly non-doctrinaire.[38] Often Leahy is described (and he described himself) as ideologically a "conservative." Quite what this means is never clear, but it is assumed that he was a small-government, fiscal-responsibility man. A close reading of Leahy's life, starting with his Australian reflections, reveals a more complex mind-set. Here, and much later in life, Leahy would argue for an activist role for the state and wanted to balance free enterprise with a government that could regulate and protect the citizenry.[39] At one point in Australia he remarked that the country would grow faster if it had its own version of Richard "Boss" Croker, the Irish American Democratic politician who ran New York's notorious Tammany Hall machine and who enriched himself by millions from different state enterprises.[40] He also approved of some of the more democratic elements in the Australian system. While he believed that Australian labor unions had too much power to set wage rates, which made Australian goods too expensive for world trade, he also saw the benefit of the Australian system by which the state seized all unoccupied land. In 1904, once back in America, he commented that California's Sacramento Valley would be greatly improved if the state broke up many of the massive private estates that dominated landholding in the area.[41] It was the first sign that Leahy's views on politics were far more pragmatic than one might assume.

It was also in this phase that Leahy received his first exposure to real political power. He was careful during his career to pretend he had no political identification. For the first part of his life, that was probably true, as he spoke positively and negatively about both Republicans and Democrats. What he had, however, was a real reverence for the office of the presidency. In return he expected a president to behave with dignity. When he heard in 1901 that President McKinley had been shot and killed by Leon Czolgosz, a "cowardly foreign assassin," Leahy believed it would have been better if the shooter had been turned over to the crowd for summary execution.[42] Leahy likely approved of McKinley due to the president's lack of showiness. His successor, Theodore Roosevelt, brought out more mixed emotions. Like most naval officers of his generation, Leahy believed that Roosevelt had been a good assistant secretary of the navy, yet he thought this rambunctious new president could act without the necessary gravitas at times.

On his final trip to the Philippines in September 1902, Leahy met Roosevelt's new choice for governor of the Philippines, William Howard Taft. Invited to a reception held by Taft, Leahy walked into a gala affair in the old Spanish palace, with the crème de la crème of Filipino society and the upper echelon of US imperial rule in attendance. Leahy betrayed his almost total ignorance of religion by not being aware of the rank of the senior Roman Catholic churchman, quite possibly the first bishop ever appointed in the Philippines, Jorge Barlin.[43] Leahy looked at Barlin in his bright vestments, surrounded by a crowd of Filipinos, and thought he looked like a "fat, brilliantly colored beetle."[44] He was also intrigued, but not entirely impressed, that it was a racially mixed reception. The young officer had doubts about whether the Filipinos would ever be reconciled to US rule, partly because of the oafish behavior of the Americans themselves:

> The natives are proud, ambitious, and sensitive and our people will not actually admit to social equality any large number of an alien race. . . . Some of [Taft's] guests of full equality in the palace may be pushed off the sidewalk on their way home by a high private from the rear rank and told "You may be a brother of William H. Taft, but you ain't no brother of mine."[45]

That being said, Leahy did have a touching faith in Taft's ability to get things done, even if he could muster little enthusiasm for US rule in the islands. "It is . . . safe to assume that Governor Taft knows what he is doing and will in the end accomplish his purpose, whatever it is."[46]

Leahy's detachment indicated that it was time to go. In a transformative three years in the Pacific, he had seen more war, visited cultures quite different from those of northern Wisconsin, commanded his first vessel, and learned how to cope under the most trying of circumstances. He had even been promoted. One of the last tasks he had to do in the Philippines was take the examinations needed to rise to junior lieutenant. He passed with flying colors and was allowed to read all the fitness reports filed by his different commanders.[47] They were unanimously positive, even from the commanders with whom he had disagreed strongly. He had every reason to feel confident about his future prospects.

CHAPTER 2

Building a Career and Family

In 1900, while William Leahy was serving in the western Pacific, Rose Leahy died. In his diary, he did not mention his mother's passing until early 1903, after his return to America, and even then only elliptically. He wrote about going to Wisconsin to spend a few days with his father in a "sad" house because of his mother's "absence."[1] Michael Leahy figured only slightly more often in his son's diary, but again details were sparing. In 1921, having received word that his father was ill, William made a special trip to Chicago to see him. He found Michael to be feeble, though pleased to see his son. After a short visit, Leahy promptly left for his next command, and his father promptly died.[2] Leahy rarely mentioned his father again.

There were many reasons for this notable void, and lack of emotion was not one of them.[3] Propriety was. As a formal man of the Gilded Age, Leahy did not believe it seemly to discuss or even record emotions—at least until he was older. Furthermore, he was by nature discreet. His ability to appear unemotional, when allied with his competence, drew people to entrust him with their secrets. Discussing his mother's death was not something in which he would have seen any value. He was, as always in his life, looking forward.

Back in America, he thought it was time he found a wife. Now in his late twenties and promoted, he felt he could both afford to support and benefit from a family. In finding a spouse he naturally turned to the US

Navy. While serving in the Pacific he had formed a bond with Albert Niblack, an officer who was sixteen years older.[4] Niblack eventually reached the upper echelons of the fleet. During World War I he would command the first battleship force of the Atlantic Fleet and be promoted to rear admiral.[5] Leahy looked on Niblack almost as a surrogate father. In the 1920s his letters to the older man were some of the most revealing that he would ever write. Having a successful senior confidant undoubtedly helped Leahy's career. While there was no hint that the friendship was anything but genuine, it was an early sign of Leahy's propensity to identify and impress the coming powers in the navy. In this case, it helped him get married. When Leahy returned to America in early 1903, he was stationed on the West Coast, much of the time in San Francisco. It was there that he met Louise Harrington, the sister of Niblack's wife, Mary. He quickly decided she was the perfect person to become Mrs. William D. Leahy.

It is easy to see why he was drawn to Louise. She was well-mannered and educated, and had experience of the world, having gone to school in both France (she spoke the language much better than Leahy) and Baltimore. The Harringtons were a respectable Northern California family who owned the local bank and a large parcel of land in Colusa, an agricultural area about fifty miles north of Sacramento. They were also well established in San Francisco social circles. Louise had other characteristics that would have appealed to Leahy. She was level-headed and, crucially, ambitious in her own right. Emotionally they were very well suited.

Leahy courted Louise quickly and efficiently, demonstrating the competence that he showed whenever something really mattered to him. They were married in February 1904, after Leahy had been stationed in San Francisco for less than a year.[6] The ceremony was a subdued affair, as Louise's father had died just weeks before. As befitting a young couple with some prominence, the *San Francisco Call* published a report of the event in its society column.

> A notable wedding was celebrated yesterday at 3 o'clock when Miss Louise Harrington, daughter of Mrs. W. P. Harrington, became the bride of William D. Leahy.

Owing to a recent bereavement, the affair was celebrated in the quietest manner possible, the bride being attended solely by Miss Marie Louise Harrington, a tiny niece; Lieutenant Hanrahan, USN, serving the groom as best man.

The bride, a Junoesque girl of fine style, never appeared more lovely than in her nuptial robe of white Chantilly over ivory silk.

It is a matter of regret that Mrs. Leahy must be lost to local society, but such is the chosen lot of naval brides.[7]

The newlyweds set off for a honeymoon and, for the first time since Guam, Leahy mentioned sex, albeit subliminally: "Ten days were spent in Santa Barbara, where everything is beautiful."[8] Eight months later, their first and only child, William Harrington Leahy, was born. From the moment they were married, Louise showed herself to be a real asset to her husband's career. When possible, she would accompany Leahy on his different assignments, eventually living with him on both coasts, in Europe, and in Puerto Rico. Being the repressed writer that he was, Leahy offered a rather dull and unformed picture of his wife. During the rare diary passage when he mentioned her, she was described as the supportive, maternal wife of an early twentieth-century American man. Yet, in reality, Louise was a forceful and intelligent woman, and definitely no wallflower. The reporter who described her on her wedding day as "Junoesque" was perceptive. She was a determined and politically minded hostess who helped drive Leahy to the top. Thomas Hart recalls Louise bristling when Leahy was once described as the perfect second-in-command.[9]

Her influence over Leahy can be seen in a number of ways, not least in her persuading him to become an Episcopalian. In his early life Leahy showed no interest in theology, the Bible, or religious doctrine. The first mention of religion in his diary was uncharacteristically subversive. While he was serving on the *Oregon*, the ship's chaplain was sent home for illness (it was believed by the crew that he became sick from overeating).[10] In his place, divine services were conducted by the ship's paymaster. Leahy and the other junior officers much preferred the new arrangement and wanted to keep the *Oregon* from getting a new chaplain, not least because it gave them an extra stateroom. That being said, Roman Catholicism was clearly part of the Leahys' family identity. Both of his parents and a brother who died young were buried in a Roman Catholic cemetery. It is unlikely that his Gaelic-speaking, British-hating grandmother would have had much truck with the transplanted faction of the Church of England in America. Yet Louise was a churchgoing Episcopalian and would have their son baptized into that faith. From that moment, Leahy began taking basic instruction in Episcopalian doctrine. Though he would not formally be baptized for decades, it is inconceivable that he would have headed down that road without his wife's influence.

Had the Leahys not eventually discovered the more intense political pleasures of Washington, DC, Louise would also have led Leahy to making San Francisco his permanent home. By the time their son had arrived the young couple was comfortably settled there. Louise's skill at entertaining became apparent immediately, and a number of her parties ended up in the society pages.[11] Not only did San Francisco have a large naval base, it was a booming city of more than 400,000. It had become the ninth-largest city in America and seemed to be destined for even greater things as the country moved westward. Though this might surprise some, considering his curmudgeonly nature, Leahy loved big cities. Being raised in a series of small, isolated communities had not endeared him to the quiet life. He would occasionally be forced into the wilderness by family vacations or even Franklin Roosevelt, but it was never his natural environment.[12] From the moment he started visiting large cities he was powerfully attracted, commenting on their architecture, their atmosphere, and their economic prospects. He saw cities as an indicator of a healthy society and economy. He also liked going out, to dinner parties, bars, restaurants, even the occasional concert or theater production. Leahy even appreciated the temperate Northern California climate as only someone raised in northern Wisconsin could. When Leahy visited his father in Wisconsin in January 1903, he was shocked by the cold and could not wait to get back to his new home.

The Leahys saw themselves as important members of San Francisco's better class. In 1906 this governed their behavior during a few of the most remarkable days of their lives. Early in the morning of April 18, Leahy, in bed, was dreaming about a train wreck.[13] He was jolted awake by the clatter of the desk next to his bed flipping over. It was the first rumblings of the San Francisco earthquake. Like most of his neighbors, he rushed out of the house and was quickly covered in a fine white dust—particles from the many buildings that had toppled over. From their house's perch on California Street in Pacific Heights, overlooking the old city, the family had a perfect vantage point from which to witness the unfolding disaster. Looking down, Leahy saw many fires glowing in the darkness, small at first, then growing in intensity. With the water mains into the city having been broken by the quake, nothing could be done to contain the blazes. Soon the fires were marching inexorably toward one another, threatening to unite in one giant conflagration that would consume the entire city.

Leahy reacted decisively. He ordered that all the tubs and large containers in his own house be filled with water while there was still time to get some out of the pipes. The Leahys collected so much water that they not only provided for themselves for a week, they were able to support many of their neighbors as well. Then Leahy headed off into town to see how he could help. What he found was surreal: crowds of people milling around, their homes destroyed, unsure what to do as smaller aftershocks shook the city. Leahy had believed his own home was safe, but as the fires converged and the wind blew in, flames began to creep up Pacific Heights. The inferno continued through the day and into the night, at times consuming a city block in an hour. Finally, at two a.m. the next morning, Leahy told Louise to get their infant son ready to flee at a moment's notice. They quickly packed as many of their valuables and essentials as they could. A few hours later, when he received word that the Mare Island Naval Shipyard was still functioning, he escorted Louise and his son through the madness, pushing their belongings in an overstuffed baby carriage. They eventually reached Fort Mason, from where mother and son could board a tug to safety. Leahy returned to the ongoing disaster.

By six p.m. on the nineteenth, Leahy had given up hope of saving the house. Told by the police to evacuate, he took his mother-in-law (who had refused to abandon her home and property), along with what could be carried, and moved a few blocks south of the fire, where he collapsed, exhausted. He fully expected to return the next day to find burned-out ruins, but was amazed to discover that the fire had changed course in the middle of the night, just before reaching the house. It had not even been singed. With his home preserved, Leahy went down to the port to see what he could do to help. He was able to make contact with the USS *Chicago* and was put in charge of evacuating the refugees. For the next three days and nights he barely slept as he shepherded much of San Francisco's population to safety.

Surveying the wreckage of the city, Leahy's mind turned toward renewal—with a particularly hard edge. He saw hope in the united effort of those around him that San Francisco might rise to become greater and more beautiful than before, and despised the weak who would abandon their erstwhile home.

> The same self-reliance that was needed in the discovery days is needed now, the same weeding out of incompetents is going on, people who can not live without luxuries will move out, new strong men will come to the front, and out of the universal wreck of an established social order should emerge a new and better people.[14]

Leahy stayed at his post until May 10, when he was relieved and allowed to leave the smoking ruins to meet up with Louise. It was many months until the family could return to their home, and they ended up staying in a miserable hotel in Vallejo on the other side of San Francisco Bay. In contrast to the extraordinary tension of the month before, there the only excitement occurred when little William swallowed a needle and the parents had to wait nervously until he safely passed it.

It was a lucky break for Leahy's family that he was home when the earthquake had hit. For much of the previous three years he had been at sea. That was the period in which Leahy had begun to specialize in the large naval vessels, particularly cruisers and battleships, in which he would make his name. Battleships, of course, were the biggest, most well-protected, and heavily armed warships afloat. Cruisers were smaller and faster, though still relatively well armed. The nimble vessels acted as the eyes and ears of the battleships, sent ahead of the main force to scout the enemy. They also could operate independently, dispatched to destroy enemy commerce on the high seas.

In January 1904, just before he was married, Leahy was assigned to the first of a series of cruisers, the brand-new USS *Tacoma*. Much of his time on board was spent on a pointless mission: the *Tacoma* cruised for months off Hawaii trying to find a reef that Leahy was firmly convinced did not exist. In the summer he had a momentary panic when the *Tacoma* was ordered to the East Coast. Operating quickly, he arranged a swap with a lieutenant on the USS *Boston,* which was to stay in the Pacific. He considered it a lucky break, though it came with one downside. The *Boston* was ordered to cruise down to the Pacific coast of Mexico, Central America, and South America. Leahy, not wanting to be away from his pregnant wife, grumbled that the whole affair was a waste of coal.

It was just after this cruise commenced that Leahy received a telegram announcing the birth of his son. The new father did not see William H. until five months after he was born. Completely keeping in character, Leahy expressed few emotions about his son at first, even referring to him a few times in his diary simply as "the boy." Despite his reticence, he was a devoted father, and would fret terribly when his son became sick.

When he learned of his son's birth, the *Boston* was docked in Acapulco, Mexico, allowing Leahy to witness one of the most colorful sights he would ever see: the gambling festival that occurred every time the local workers received their pay. The main streets of Acapulco were filled with rows of tables offering a variety of games of chance. Many involved the rolling of dice out of tin cups. Those running the games prominently sported silver revolvers to scare off those contemplating robbery. To Leahy, it looked like the Wild West of lore. His visit also prompted one of the few imperialist notions he ever displayed: in his diary, he mused on a future when the United States might "own" Mexico, and Acapulco would change from the wild place it was then to a prosperous, orderly version of an American town."[15]

His vision of a US-dominated Western Hemisphere returned at the next port of call, Panama, where he fumed at what he saw as the timidity of US policy makers in pushing for a transisthmian canal. The United States, he asserted, should simply seize the land it needed to build the waterway. Leahy believed that such a canal would not only become the single most important thoroughfare for world trade; it would require an even more powerful US Navy. That it might offend the government of Panama was irrelevant.[16]

Not long after, Leahy almost died. In January 1905, he came down with what he thought was a severe case of malaria, but it turned out to be yellow fever. The first symptoms were innocuous: a slight fever and pain in his back and legs. He became dangerously ill. His fever shot up to almost lethal levels; he was gripped by severe nausea and had difficulty seeing. The ship's doctor misdiagnosed the case, telling Leahy he had malaria and pumping him full of quinine. Luckily, that doctor too became sick and the *Boston* was put under the care of Dr. William Gorgas, whose ingenuity at eradicating the threat posed by tropical diseases would make the building of the Panama Canal possible.[17] Gorgas diagnosed a major yellow-fever outbreak and started Leahy on the best treatment available at the time.

Though he was soon out of immediate danger, he was still so sick that it was thought prudent to keep him hospitalized in Panama. There he waited for weeks, recuperating, while the *Boston* sailed off to complete its cruise. Getting back to his family was no easy feat. Leahy had to be transported by a rickety old railroad to the Caribbean side of Panama, where he was put on a vessel bound for New York. He did not disembark in the United States until March. To aid in his recovery, the young officer was given a month of leave. On the way back to the West Coast he decided to stop and visit Annapolis. What he discovered was an institution vastly different from the one he had left a few years prior. It had almost quadrupled in size, from 200 midshipmen to 800, and a series of new, modern buildings were being built. He did think that the expansion had led to a loss of some of Annapolis's special character, but on the whole he viewed that as a price worth paying for the growth of US naval power.

It was not until April 1905, when he was back in San Francisco, that William Leahy saw his son for the first time. The next few years passed promisingly enough professionally. Another year and a half on the *Boston* was followed by a two-year stint at the Naval Academy. In 1907, he was sent to Annapolis as an instructor in electrical engineering. This assignment was less enjoyable than expected because of the inferior state of the family quarters offered to faculty. In fact, he most enjoyed getting away for the summers, when he acted as an instructor for the navy rifle team, which practiced in New England. It was an experience that revealed another talent that people might not have suspected: Leahy was a crack shot.

In August 1909, Leahy was sent back west to serve on the USS *California* for what turned out to be the longest stint he would have on one ship, more than three years and three months. It was on the *California* that he first encountered another of his great patrons, Capt. H. T. Mayo.[18] Mayo would later rise to public prominence in 1914, playing a leading role in the "Tampico Incident," which occurred when naval forces under his command were ordered by Woodrow Wilson to intervene in Mexican domestic politics.[19] In 1915 he was the first officer in US naval history to be raised to the rank of vice admiral.[20] During the First World War he was elevated to the most important command in the navy.[21] When the United States entered the war in 1917, Mayo was the commander of the Atlantic Fleet and in charge of the large majority of major warships that the United States deployed against Germany.

When he took command of the *California* in 1909, Mayo was already a legend. He was everything Leahy believed a commanding officer should be: a great seaman, a strong commander, and a considerate human being.[22] Leahy worked hard to be noticed by Mayo and was soon taken under the older man's wing. One of the most important opportunities Mayo offered was to make Leahy into a gunnery officer on the *California*.[23] Over the coming two decades, Leahy would establish himself as one of the finest gunnery officers in American history.

In 1909, the world's great navies, including the British, German, Japanese, and American, were based around the construction of big-gun battleships, known as dreadnoughts. These behemoths changed the ranges at which ships were expected to engage, from a few thousand yards to five miles or more. Dreadnought battleships put a premium on gunnery ability, and the skill became prized in all advanced navies.[24] Leahy thus started specializing in the right skill at the right time. And work hard he did. From the moment he became a gunnery officer he tried to raise standards, both on the ships on which he served and in the fleet as a whole. He chafed at those he thought did not understand the importance of gunnery practice. In late 1911, while still on the *California* and after Mayo had left the ship, he complained that senior officers were not letting him make needed gunnery improvements.[25] He tended to judge senior officers by whether they worked hard enough to improve gunnery on their ships.

The *California* spent a great deal of time on international visits, and took part in one military intervention while Leahy was on board. Two of the cruises—one in the winter of 1909–1910 and the other in the summer of 1913—were into the western Pacific, allowing Leahy the chance to revisit locales from a decade prior. The trips reconfirmed one of the foundations of his international outlook: his skepticism toward Japan and his affection for China. During the first cruise the *California* stopped at Hawaii, the Admiralty Islands, and the Philippines on the way to Japan. Leahy was told the Admiralties were populated by cannibals, but he did not have time to explore and find out. The real highlights of the journey, however, started when the ship pulled into Yokohama, the great port of Tokyo, in January 1910.

In the years since Leahy had returned home from the Philippine War, the Japanese Navy had fought the Russians at sea, and won. In one of the most lopsided victories in naval history, the Japanese had destroyed almost the entire striking power of the Russian Baltic Fleet. For many Americans, the 1905 Battle of Tsushima had transformed their view of Japan from a slightly comic, inscrutable country populated by short people to a formidable, feared, and growing power. Leahy was particularly affected by Japanese successes, and they led him to see Japan as a much greater rival to the United States than he ever had before:

The Japanese are the most patriotic people in the world today, they are intellectually equal, and physically superior, to most other people; and their undeclared but unmistakable policy is Asia for the Asiatics. Being the dominant Asiatics they will rule Asia, a continent as rich as North America, with two men to our one, and already over populated. Ruled by a people with a high order of military talent and an intense nationalism, it will be a menace to our institutions.[26]

Leahy's hostility toward Japan was evident from the moment he arrived, even when he and his fellow officers were treated with great hospitality. After a traditional Japanese duck hunt—during which Leahy caught a fowl, which he found delicious when roasted on an open fire—their hosts provided an assortment of alcoholic beverages. Leahy's one substantive comment was that he did not like the sake. Though seemingly small, this disapproval extended to much of Japan. When he met Admiral Tōgō Heihachirō, the famous victor at Tsushima, Leahy claimed to be underwhelmed, describing him as "a very ordinary looking Jap."[27] Shopping for souvenirs, he complained that anything nice was made in China.

His affection for China, in comparison, remained undimmed by time. When the *California* sailed into Woosung Harbor, the port outside Shanghai, he made a special trip to the Old Town "for old times sake." He was delighted to find that modernization had gone only so far. "There is an electric car line, some new hotels and European suburbs that did not exist before," he observed, "but the people seemed to be the same old type that one associates with Tangiers, Melbourne, and Shanghai, who will probably have to jump off the edge when their few remaining places of refuge are taken from them."[28]

Two years later he returned to Japan and China on the *California*, and repeated the same emotional process. His discussions about Japan were perfunctory and often negative. He did admit to being impressed with one Japanese country hotel he stayed in, calling it the best he had ever experienced, but also went out of his way to criticize the shoddy goods and souvenirs on offer. China, even with some noticeable changes, was still a place after his own heart.

At the time of my first visit nobody ever saw a Chinese man without a queue. Now nearly all of them wear their hair short though I did see some with queues. I also saw some women wearing their hair in braided and some in skirts. A great change has certainly come to outward appearances of the supposedly unchangeable customs of the Chinese. The rickshaw men are still boisterous, the street odors have not improved, the hotels are terrible, and the money counterfiet [*sic*], so I felt quite at home.[29]

In between Leahy's journeys to the western Pacific, the *California*, in the fall of 1910, cruised down the Pacific coast of South America. The stated purpose was to take part in Chile's centenary independence celebration, but the real reason was to entice the Chilean government to purchase American-built warships. When the *California* arrived, it was discovered that the Chileans had already promised the British the contract. It was indicative of what Leahy saw as a real problem for the United States: British and German influence in South America. While the British had a dominant influence over the Chilean Navy, the Chilean Army was very pro-German, leaving the United States completely shut out. This led Leahy to the same kind of nationalist outburst he had displayed over the Panama Canal. He wanted his country to be the dominant power in the Western Hemisphere.

That being said, he also developed a fondness for Chile that would last for the rest of his life. Leahy had a fabulous trip to the capital, Santiago.[30] With his brother-in-law Albert Niblack in the city serving as the US naval attaché, Leahy was able to take part in most of the high-level celebrations for Chilean independence. He attended balls and banquets, and even enjoyed the opera. He was bowled over by the jewels the ladies wore, as well as the quality and variety of wine. He so much enjoyed Chilean wine that he felt a little embarrassed handing over some cases of Californian wine that his ship had brought as a commercial gift for their Chilean hosts. The American vintage, he believed, was of a noticeably inferior quality. When it was time to leave, he remarked that he was the only one of his comrades who wanted to stay.

Combined, these trips helped to sum up his international outlook.

Leahy had developed a distinct vision of the role that he wanted the United States to play in the world, and he believed that when it came to the Western Hemisphere, his country should become the dominant power and do everything possible to displace European influence. Europe itself, on the other hand, was something for the United States to avoid if at all possible. Its rivalries were foreign and unpredictable, holding out the possibility of real danger for America. As for Asia, Leahy's affection for China and skepticism toward Japan were more than prejudices; they were embedded in his international outlook. He was worried that Japan would try to dominate China while the latter was in political chaos. To help forestall this, he wanted the United States to become China's firmest friend. He would hold this vision, in only a slightly altered form, for the rest of his career.

These trips also gave Leahy his last taste of real combat, though it took place a long way from the sea. Whilst serving on the *California*, Leahy was one of the first American military officers to enter Nicaragua as part of the 1912 American intervention. In August, just after returning from China and Japan, the *California* was ordered to Nicaragua to take part in what came to be known as the Banana War. It was a typical intervention by the United States, done to support a pro-American faction in a struggle to control the Nicaraguan government. Of course, the original justification for the landing was the need to protect American citizens (and their property) who were threatened by the fighting.

As one of the first Americans ashore, Leahy was transformed into a soldier.[31] The *California* landed its expeditionary force at the port of Corinto, with instructions to make its way inland. Leahy was given the unenviable task of organizing the defenses of the town with only ten sailors. Once again it was clear he doubted both the ethical and strategic value of what he was being asked to do. He remarked in his diary on the second day ashore that sentries under his command had shot and killed an innocent peasant, who, Leahy guessed, simply didn't know how to respond properly when halted by a military patrol.[32] A few days later, his frustration became even more acute. On September 1, US personnel were ordered to take sides with the Nicaraguan government and use violent measures to make sure that the rebellion was crushed. It all seemed pointless to him. He remarked that this order from Washington "directed us to take a definite stand on the side of the government which has resulted in disarming the rebels and supporting a weak, unpopular tyrannical government, against which the people will in self-defense take up arms again as soon as we leave the country."[33] Later, when he came across the captured leader of the rebel forces, Gen. Luis Mena, he considered him "not much better or worse than other leaders on both sides in this war."[34]

Once Corinto had been secured, Leahy had to get through to the town of Leon, fifty miles away by train and continually under threat of rebel attack. For the next few weeks he was constantly up and down the train line, occasionally under fire. It was the last time that he was directly targeted in a combat situation. The most interesting thing for Leahy was to observe the operations of Smedley Butler, the most famous Marine Corps officer of the time. Leahy was full of admiration for how Butler and the marines behaved. Yet the longer he was in Nicaragua, the more he not only thought the intervention pointless, the more he believed that the US government was backing the wrong side. Leahy felt that the United States was propping up the rich conservatives who were guilty of abusing the large majority of the Nicaraguan people.

> Political parties in Nicaragua are the conservatives now in power and the Liberales who were in revolt. . . . To me it appeared that the Liberals counted in their ranks a large majority of the inhabitants but the U.S. Minister says not. At any rate the government is not in any sense representative but is an undisguised military despotism, control being in the hands of those who have the rifles and ammunition. Those in office rob and persecute those who are not and the people generally are poor beyond our understanding. An impossible condition of semi civilization exists that is almost unbelievable in this year of our Lord 1912. It would seem that a right to revolt against such conditions is inherent.[35]

Yet for all his skepticism, he was also as determined as always to do a thorough job—and to make sure that his superiors were aware of his efforts. While the intervention was ongoing, Leahy reached the formal end of his cruise, and was ordered back to America for reassignment.[36] Instead of taking the easy way out, he wrote to the commander of the Pacific Fleet, Adm. William Southerland, asking if he could remain on duty in Nicaragua until his mission had been completed. This request was gratefully accepted.[37] Leahy now had another supporter in the fleet.

A sign of his growing reputation occurred not long after, in October 1911, when he was selected to be a special naval aide to President William Howard Taft during his visit to the West Coast to inspect the navy.[38] Leahy was with the president for four full days, attending receptions, fleet demonstrations, and all meals with Taft. It was invaluable exposure to the logistics of a presidential trip, though Leahy feigned indifference, saying he would never want a similar assignment in the future. For all the faux nonchalance, Leahy showed that he had a shrewd understanding of American politics. He criticized Taft's staff for keeping the press at arm's length, saying it would be better for all concerned if photographers were given better access to record the different events. He even demonstrated an understanding of the political dynamic of the Republican Party, which was on the verge of splitting into two, one wing backing Taft and the other the former president, Theodore Roosevelt. Leahy hypothesized that the relative lack of enthusiasm shown to Taft by the crowds was because most of them supported Roosevelt.

The perceptiveness that Leahy displayed in his political evaluation is the kind of trait that appealed to his commanding officers and one of the reasons they chose him for the assignment in the first place. They believed that he would discharge the responsibility with skill and tact. It was striking how often a senior commander, once he had Leahy serve beneath him for the first time, tried to co-opt the younger officer in the future. This is what happened with Mayo. In October 1912, news of Leahy's success as a gunnery officer made it to Washington and he was offered the chance of being the navy's assistant director of target practice. He leapt at the opportunity.[39] It was an extremely important position, one that put him in the heart of the naval bureaucracy and marked him as an officer on the rise. But it was a position he would not hold for long.

Mayo, who was in Washington in charge of naval personnel, wanted Leahy to be transferred to his command. The head of personnel was one of the trickiest and most politically sensitive jobs in the fleet, and Mayo judged Leahy to be the perfect officer to help him. In August 1913, Mayo formally requested that Leahy be made his chief aide, and as the head of personnel he was able to make it happen. It ended up being the most important development in Leahy's professional life, the necessary precondition to making him the second most powerful man in the world. When Leahy sat down and looked across his new desk, he stared directly at the handsome figure of Franklin Delano Roosevelt.

CHAPTER 3

Enter Franklin Roosevelt

William Leahy first met the man who would forever change his life while doing a job he should never have done. Not long after he had been assigned as Admiral Mayo's aide in the personnel division, he lost his boss. Wanting to return to sea as soon as possible, Mayo reassigned himself as commander of a division of the Atlantic Fleet. He was replaced by Adm. William Fullam, who was promptly reassigned as the new superintendent at Annapolis. With no new head of personnel named, William Leahy was by default in control of one of the fleet's most sensitive offices. With a rank of only lieutenant commander, he was performing the job of an admiral, and he rose to the challenge. Without the aid of an assistant or a secretary, he acted as the personnel director of the entire US Navy, handling the assignments and paperwork for all officers at sea or onshore. He was also responsible for overseeing all disciplinary courts and procedures.

The fact that no new director was named undoubtedly had a great deal to do with the spark that had been lit between Leahy and the new assistant secretary of the navy. In March 1913, Franklin Roosevelt was a young politician who possessed a good deal of drive and an attention-grabbing last name. Appointed by President Woodrow Wilson, Roosevelt dove headfirst into his role, taking a great interest in personnel questions. Had he wanted a more senior replacement for Fullam, he could easily have had one appointed. Instead, after only a few months working with Leahy, Roosevelt was happy to keep things as they were.

Sharing a similar outlook on the world, Leahy and Roosevelt melded from the start. Both were convinced of the need for a large and efficient US Navy.[1] Roosevelt had manifested a love of the sea since boyhood and was fascinated with the importance of sea power. He was a believer in the historical theories of Alfred Thayer Mahan, the American naval officer who argued in the late nineteenth century that sea power was the greatest determinant in world politics.[2] Mahan's ideas became fashionable and spread across the globe, influencing thinking not just in America but in Europe and Asia as well. In a series of books on various periods of history, he posited that control of the seas was practically an immutable law of international relations; that nations such as Great Britain, which could exercise dominance on the world's oceans, would inevitably triumph over other countries that could not. For Americans like Roosevelt and Leahy, Mahan helped codify an instinctive belief that the United States needed a much stronger fleet. When Roosevelt became assistant secretary, he engaged in a correspondence with Mahan about sea power, and, with war looming in Europe, the need to popularize its value.[3] Yet Roosevelt, like Leahy, did not believe in sea power as part of some imperialist drive to conquer. He saw sea power as something vital to the United States' security, regardless of whether an American empire existed or not.[4]

It was not just a shared strategic outlook that brought the two men together. Their personalities meshed. Roosevelt was everything Leahy wanted in an American political leader.[5] Energetic and dignified, he was bold in achieving what he believed best, but extremely well-mannered and capable of inspiring great loyalty. The Franklin Roosevelt who strode into the Navy Department in 1913 was tall and thin, and still had the use of both legs. He could be found clambering up the rope rigging of old naval vessels, or walking with purpose, top hat on, to high political meetings. His patrician air and charm were legendary—the Roosevelt stardust. He came from privilege, the product of the New York Dutch Roosevelts and the Delanos, a family who traced their lineage back to the *Mayflower*. His early schooling was at Groton, an elite Massachusetts establishment that espoused a version of muscular Christianity. He attended Harvard and then Columbia Law School before embarking on a career in public service. William Leahy was wowed. The force of the young Roosevelt was something that never left him. Forty years later he looked back on the young FDR as "a handsome, companionable, athletic, young man of unusual energy and decision."[6]

Roosevelt realized early that Leahy possessed a valuable combination of different personal characteristics. Leahy was good at his job, efficient and thorough, and not overawed by the responsibility of handling a post many times higher than his pay grade. In Leahy he found a calming and sensible presence, and he grew to trust the young officer's instincts and steadiness—the bedrock of their relationship. Moreover, he understood that Leahy was loyal and discreet, and Roosevelt could collaborate with him knowing that all confidences would be kept. They were even slightly devious together, such as in their handling of Josephus Daniels.

Daniels was a strange choice to be secretary of the navy. A genial and pious white supremacist from North Carolina, he was practically a pacifist and had no previous interest in or experience of naval policy. Yet as an important political ally of Woodrow Wilson, he was rewarded for his support with a cabinet post. A "progressive" in the language of the time, Daniels seemed more interested in the moral than the material well-being of the fleet. His most famous intervention into naval policy was General Order 99, issued in 1914, which banned the consumption of alcoholic beverages aboard US naval vessels. Both Leahy and Roosevelt, who enjoyed a cocktail or two, hardly considered this a priority.

Leahy was of two minds about the navy secretary. While he admired Daniels's dedication to his task and his loyalty to President Wilson, he judged the secretary to be "not in sympathy with the navy." He lamented in his diary that Daniels's "feelings toward [naval] officers as a class is that which would be naturally expected of a clerk. It is more than unfortunate that he was not sympathetic, as with his energy and his powerful influence with Congress and with the President he could have commanded the full loyalty of the Naval Service and accomplished much for its good."

Naturally, Roosevelt considered himself more suited than the secretary to make the big decisions affecting the fleet, and often acted accordingly.[7] He was known to issue orders or call for plans without consulting Daniels. Through it all he came to realize that Leahy would help him get his way. In personnel terms this was important, and the two men seemed to share responsibility, Leahy playing a large role in choosing assignments for the service personnel and Roosevelt for the civilians. Leahy was obviously happy to play along with Roosevelt to subvert Daniels.

Leahy and Roosevelt not only worked together in the office, they socialized after business hours. The Roosevelts and the Leahys lived only three blocks apart in Washington. As assistant secretary, Franklin and his wife, Eleanor, regularly threw receptions, garden parties, and the like for different naval personnel, and the Leahys were often invited.[8] This was an important test for Leahy to pass. Roosevelt could be a snob, expecting people to behave properly, but also with a pleasant sense of bonhomie. Leahy, clubbable considering his rather austere image, knew exactly how to handle himself. He had an ability, commented on by Thomas Hart, to insert himself into a social situation and be "as comfortable as an old shoe."[9]

Having Louise by his side was a huge support. Not long after Leahy was posted to Washington in 1912, she moved across the country with William H., and the family set up house at 1751 Q Street (Northwest). Life in the nation's capital suited them both. Leahy realized that Washington was where the important decisions were made, where his career would be determined, and where he had the best chance to influence high policy. For Louise, Washington offered access to cultural events not yet regularly available on the West Coast. Foundations were being laid for new museums and galleries, and important performers of global renown often passed through town. Leahy, sometimes to his regret, was often brought to both.

Engaged in an emerging cultural center, Louise became an assured hostess and noted member on the Washington social scene. She enter-tained the wives of some of the capital's movers and shakers, not an in-considerable achievement, as her husband was still relatively low on the Washington food chain. Much of her socializing involved Josephus Daniels's wife, Addie Worth Bagley Daniels, and some of Louise's for-mal events made it into the society pages. In February 1917, Louise hosted a luncheon party at the new Shoreham Hotel.[10] The guest of honor was Addie Daniels, and other guests included the wives of Sen. James H. Lewis from Illinois; the former attorney general, Richard Olney; and the present chief of naval operations, William Benson. Later, when the United States joined the First World War, Louise paid promi-nent visits to the mothers and widows of those naval officers and men who died fighting.[11] Of course, the Leahys also had their own friends. Fortuitously, the Niblacks were in town, and the two couples spent as much time together as they could manage.

In 1915, Leahy was set to leave Washington. Naval officers were re-quired to cycle between positions ashore and at sea, and Leahy's sea duty was coming due. For the first time since the Philippine War, he could expect to be given his own vessel, and one considerably grander than the *Mariveles*. He wanted a ship that would be assigned to a main fleet, and maneuvered to command the USS *Melville*, the navy's newest destroyer tender. The ship was just finishing its trials, and Leahy, think-ing his command all but assured, began to visit the vessel regularly and even selected its officers. At the last minute, Daniels stepped in and or-dered that Leahy be made the captain of the secretary of the navy's own dispatch vessel, USS *Dolphin*.

It was a blow, but one that helped his career, and it spoke to his po-litical skills. One of the *Dolphin*'s first duties under Leahy's command was to serve with another powerful officer in the navy, Adm. William Banks Caperton. During World War I, Caperton would have the Amer-ican navy's second most important combat command, commander in chief of the Pacific Fleet, and would be highly decorated for his war ser-vice. In January 1916, he was commander of the Atlantic Fleet's cruiser squadron, and needed a vessel to serve as his flagship. The *Dolphin* was sent, which meant that Leahy lived at close quarters with the admiral for the next few months, once again giving him the opportunity to shine.[12]

Most of their time together was spent off Haiti, during what would turn into one of the longest interventions in US history. It started when President Wilson decided that, after the assassination of Haiti's president in 1915, the Haitians could not survive without American military power enforcing stability. For Leahy, it was a diplomatic as much as a military assignment, and he was required to work with the local population to gain their acceptance for the presence of American forces. He was more supportive of this operation than the one in Nicaragua, believing that American power was being used to help the poor and disadvantaged while at the same time weakening the power of the wealthy "ruling class."[13]

Leahy was impressed with Caperton's decisiveness and believed that the admiral was personally responsible for much of the success of the mission. His approval was reciprocated. After working with Leahy just a short time, Caperton asked him to step in as his chief of staff.[14] Afterward, Caperton wrote a particularly fulsome commendation of the young officer. "I have found [Leahy] in every instance to be of excellent judgement, strong convictions, very energetic, and ready for any duty," Caperton wrote. "His fairness, firmness, and just decisions were a great factor in winning the good will of the Haitian officials. I feel that he is loyal to a degree unusual in a service where loyalty is a rule."[15]

So impressed was Caperton that when he was made commander in chief of the Pacific Fleet, he tried to have Leahy once again appointed as his chief of staff. Yet the chief of naval operations, the gruff Adm. William Benson, objected. In a long letter to Caperton relaying this decision, Leahy demonstrated another talent he used to ingratiate himself with senior officers—he could kiss ass: "I regret more than I can express that it was not possible for me to make the Pacific cruise with you. . . . I never expect to again have as interesting or as satisfactory a cruise or to again have an opportunity to acquire so much information that will be of value in case I should be fortunate enough in later years to be entrusted with such a difficult political task as you brought to a perfectly satisfactory conclusion."[16]

Kissing ass has been and continues to be a regular part of advancement in military life. When Leahy reached the height of his authority as the most senior five-star officer in the military, his ass would be kissed shamelessly by otherwise egocentric and self-assured three-star officers in both the army and navy. It is unsurprising to see Leahy doing it as a more junior officer, therefore, but it also must be recognized as one of his political skills.

After the Haiti intervention, the *Dolphin* was sent to Santo Domingo and then Mexico for short stays before returning to the United States in July. Back to duty serving the navy secretary, the ship resumed its role as a perk of the higher-ups in the Navy Department. Originally built as a presidential yacht for Chester Arthur, the *Dolphin* during its lifetime was used regularly to undertake official trips. Never intended to be a warship, it was armed with two small guns, so occasionally did duty as a cruiser. It was much more comfortable than a normal warship, with wider decks on which to stroll and comfortable staterooms. As Josephus Daniels had only a passing interest in the sea, Franklin Roosevelt was able to indulge himself with use of the *Dolphin*. It gave Leahy and Roosevelt many more days together. FDR, a keen sailor, would even ask to take command of the *Dolphin*, so Leahy would let him grasp the wheel.[17] In the summer of 1916, it served as a Roosevelt family yacht.

Wealthy New York families, such as the Roosevelts, were in the habit of sending their wives and children away for the summer, to protect them from the unhealthy urban climates of the day. The Roosevelts did this in style, possessing a large house on Campobello Island, just over the border from Maine in the Canadian province of Nova Scotia. FDR trusted Leahy enough to shepherd his growing family from Campobello back to New York and up the Hudson River to the Roosevelt family estate at Hyde Park.[18] Through this, Leahy became well-known to the Roosevelt children. They would scamper madly around the deck, "sticking their noses" into places they shouldn't. Leahy would scold them, but not in a serious way. Roosevelt's daughter, Anna, of whom Leahy was particularly fond, was one of the few people in the world who felt confident enough to tease Leahy, and would do so for the rest of her life. As a sign that Roosevelt not only trusted Leahy with his family but also liked having him around, he invited the sailor to spend some of the vacation with him at Hyde Park. Something was growing between the two that was deeper than a normal Navy Department professional relationship. Leahy's fondness for Roosevelt helped shape his perception of the entire Wilson administration. In a letter to Admiral Caperton in 1916, he stated, with an election looming, that the Wilson administration had been very good for the navy. Clearly, he was talking about Franklin Roosevelt and not Josephus Daniels.[19]

After his summer and fall of "usual duties" on the *Dolphin*, matters became much more serious. A sharp deterioration in relations between the United States and Germany made the possibility of war far more likely. Since the outbreak of war in 1914, German-American relations had moved from crisis to crisis. The most important issue, from the US point of view, was freedom of the seas. The American government claimed that, as the United States was neutral, American ships on the high seas should be able to sail without fear of attack. The Germans, on the other hand, felt that, as the British had cut off all of Germany's oceanic trade with the outside world, they should be able to use the submarine, the one weapon open to them, to cut off British trade as well. The fight between the Germans and Americans focused on the question of unrestricted submarine warfare, or the German policy of attacking non-warships on the high seas without warning.

In 1915 the first crisis erupted when the Germans sank a series of commercial vessels, including most famously the RMS *Lusitania*. Yet the prospect of antagonizing the United States was too terrible for the Germans, and they backed down. In early 1917, in one of the most disastrous decisions in the history of international relations, the German government, under pressure from its armed services, decided to restart unrestricted submarine warfare. They were calculating that they could stop all trade across the Atlantic before American power could be employed against them. They dared the United States to enter the war, and Woodrow Wilson took up the challenge.

In April 1917 the *Dolphin* was dispatched to assert US control of the Virgin Islands, previously known as the Danish West Indies. With war raging in Europe, the United States had recently forced the Danes to hand over the islands. The ambitious young Commander Leahy, freshly promoted, was desperate for action. A rumor went around that the Danish-flagged cargo ship the *Nordskov* was actually a camouflaged German raider, and Leahy set out to track it down.[20] Sailing Caribbean waters in search of his elusive quarry, he finally cornered the *Nordskov* in St. Lucia, where he discovered after close inspection that her papers were in order. Years later, he admitted that he was lucky that the *Nordskov* had not been a camouflaged raider.[21] If it had, it would have seriously outgunned Leahy's lightly armed pleasure boat. The *Dolphin* had such little firepower that Leahy was planning on taking his prize with a boarding party like some swashbuckling Napoleonic-era naval adventurer.

When he returned to Washington in July 1917, Leahy was hopeful of seeing more action. He was given what seemed to be another plum assignment, named the executive officer of USS *Nevada*, the newest, most technologically advanced, and most powerful battleship in the US Navy. She was heavily armored, used oil-fired engines instead of coal, and was the first American ship with three-gun turrets. She should have been the pride of the US fleet sent to Europe. Instead, the *Nevada* suffered from teething problems and was in many ways too advanced. The British, with whom she would have been stationed, were suffering from a shortage of oil and wanted the United States to send only older, coal-burning ships. Thus the *Nevada* remained in American waters while its less-advanced sister battleships steamed off to war.

Leahy chafed. Arranging a transfer to another ship in hopes of reaching combat, he was given command of the USS *Princess Matoika*, a captured German steamship that had been converted into a troop transport. He was slated to take five thousand American soldiers across the Atlantic as part of the massive US buildup on the western front. It was hardly a glamorous assignment, but at least it offered him an opportunity to join the war effort. Just before Leahy was to leave, he was summoned to Washington and offered what should have been his dream job, the navy's director of gunnery. Instead of being pleased, he felt let down at being deprived of the chance to serve in a war zone. In a sign of his growing assertiveness, he went right to the top.[22] He told Admiral Benson that he wanted to stay on the *Princess Matoika*. The chief of naval operations, who did not particularly like Leahy, grumbled and replied that, in war, officers could not choose their assignment.[23] Yet Leahy stood firm, and, in a telling sign of Leahy's standing, Benson blinked first, issuing orders that the commander would be allowed to cross the Atlantic one time before taking over gunnery.

In May 1918, Leahy finally crossed the Atlantic aboard the *Princess Matoika*, fully laden with troops, many of whom were seeing the ocean for the first time in their lives. He was part of a convoy of twelve ships that zigzagged their way across the sea to avoid torpedo attacks from German submarines. There was an outburst of activity once when an escort vessel started firing rapidly into the water in front of the convoy, but Leahy never saw a submarine and no ship was attacked. The convoy reached France on May 23, docking in Brest, where the troops were disembarked. Though he had seen no action, Leahy had discharged his duty, and that was important to his career. At the end of the war he was given the Navy Cross, partly because he had captained a ship in a war zone.[24]

When he returned to Washington in June he was able to take up the position of director of gunnery without regrets. Once again, Admiral Mayo, now back in the Navy Department, was there to look out for him. After a few weeks of consultation, it was decided to send Leahy back to Europe, particularly to meet with British naval representatives to investigate their most up-to-date practices.[25] The trip itself was revealing in many ways, not least for lifting the lid on Leahy's views of Great Britain and the Royal Navy. US naval officers at the time often fell into two diametrically opposed camps. Many, like Admiral Benson, hated the British. They resented what they considered British arrogance and the assumption that Britannia should continually rule the waves. For them there was no "special relationship" between Britain and America, merely a fierce determination for the United States to seize the mantle of the world's greatest naval power. On the other hand, there were those who saw Britain as America's natural ally, a country with similar values and traditions, and believed that the United States should learn as much as possible from its friends in the Royal Navy.

Leahy fell in between. While he was certainly no Anglophile, he remained open-minded when it came to working with the British. By July he was in London, where he met his Royal Navy counterpart, the famous gunnery officer Capt. Frederic Dreyer. Leahy was struck by the uselessness of this meeting, feeling that Dreyer was unwilling to share information of any value. Indeed, in London the British met with him so infrequently that he spent much of the time playing tourist.

After London, Leahy headed up to Edinburgh, where the Royal Navy's Grand Fleet and its squadron of US battleships were based. The British officers there were far more open, and Leahy was allowed to observe exercises and have an afternoon's discussion with Ernle Chatfield, the fleet's chief gunnery officer, with whom Leahy would work again in the 1930s. He even had a day to look around "old" Edinburgh, which fired up his boyhood memories of tales of Scottish heroes. The final part of his visit was to Ireland, and this brought out some strongly conflicting emotions. Boarding a train en route to the US destroyer force based out of Cork (named Queenstown at the time), he was appalled at the poverty he glimpsed from his carriage window. The south of Ireland seemed to Leahy to be an occupied, oppressed military camp, with soldiers at every station, bridge, and railway crossing. It reinforced his natural anti-imperialist beliefs. When discussing the sad state of Ireland, he made a point of not identifying himself as an Irish nationalist but instead as an American first and foremost. Though his sympathies were with the Irish, he could not support an uprising against the Allied cause (and hence the American cause) in the midst of a war of such international importance.

Leahy's antipathy toward British rule in Ireland is important, as it heralded how he would view Anglo-American cooperation later in his career. He held no romantic notions about the special relationship, or the historic ties between the United States and the United Kingdom. In truth, he despised the British Empire. On the other hand, he was liked by and was willing to work with many British officers. Leahy believed that Anglo-American relations should be determined by the United States without sentiment, based on the idea of American national interest. If Britain was helpful to the United States and they had shared goals, then they should work together closely and for each other's benefit. If Britain was out simply to protect the British Empire, then the United States should not come to its aid.

Leahy's last port of call before heading back to Washington was Paris. He found a city on edge. In the spring of 1918 the Germans had launched their last great offensive, which had temporarily broken Allied lines and threatened the French capital. By the time Leahy arrived, the situation had stabilized, and the Allies were close to driving the Germans back. Yet after four years of war on their doorstep, Parisians could not yet grasp that the tide was about to turn dramatically in their favor. Leahy found them nervous and jumpy, fearful that the Germans might be able to conjure one final act of military magic.

Some historians portray Leahy as a Francophobe because of his irrepressible disdain for Charles de Gaulle, yet nothing could be further from the truth. While he enjoyed London, he could be emotional about Paris. His diary descriptions about the French capital were usually more detailed and involved. When he arrived in Paris, even with the war raging, he visited as many historic landmarks as he could find open.[26] He drove out to Versailles and the château of Malmaison, and in the city toured the medieval abbey church of Saint-Germain-des-Prés. He considered his five-day visit far too short.

Militarily he visited French antiaircraft defenses and studied the impact of German long-range gunnery. Pushing the boundaries of industrial and ballistic technology, the Germans in 1918 developed an artillery piece that could fire a shell an extraordinary seventy-five miles, using it to bombard Paris. The range was so great that any hope of hitting a specific target was gone, and the shells, which could land two or three per hour, fell indiscriminately. While Leahy was in the city, one hit a market stall, killing a few people and two horses. He was appalled at this blind targeting of civilians, which he viewed as morally retrograde and militarily useless.

When Leahy boarded the USS *Leviathan* at Brest on August 12 for the return voyage to the United States, he quickly put the nervousness of Paris behind him. No one would have blamed him for being in a confident, even cocky mood. He had captained a ship in a war zone, gained valuable experience working with America's allies, and was heading back to take over his perfect desk job. He knew he could handle himself in the political bear pit that was Washington, DC, and though he had no idea how decisive this would be, he had also secured the friendship and trust of Franklin Delano Roosevelt.

He had even been promoted. After one day at sea, a cable arrived saying that he was now *Captain* William D. Leahy, an important milestone for any naval officer. On board this was big news. Before the war the *Leviathan* had been one of the most luxurious liners crossing the Atlantic, the Hamburg Lines's *Vaterland*. The United States had seized the vessel as a trophy of war when America entered the conflict. The newly promoted captain was soon upgraded by fellow officers and given the Kaiser suite, complete with two bedrooms, a private library, and its own dining room, all done up to the most luxurious standard. As he sat in such unexpected splendor, Leahy had to feel pleased.

CHAPTER 4

The Roaring Twenties

On the evening of September 21, 1921, Capt. William D. Leahy stood on the bridge of the USS *St. Louis*—a 9,500-ton cruiser with a crew of 650 officers and men—and pondered an unfolding humanitarian catastrophe. His ship, in a poor state of repair, its engines operating far below capacity, was part of a US task force sent to observe one of the most horrific conflicts in the postwar era, the struggle between the Greeks and Turks for control of the remnants of the Ottoman Empire. On that evening, Leahy, the senior commander of all US vessels in the area, was patrolling along the Black Sea coast of Turkey, just offshore of the town of Samsun.

At first, the war had gone well for the Greeks, then had devolved into a bloody stalemate. In the regions they controlled along the coast, the Turks began to deport the Greek populations from lands that had been their home since the time of the Roman Empire. Deportation often meant death, as women and children were forced to march to the interior of the country without food or warm clothing, easy marks to succumb to the forces of nature. Leahy's orders were to not intervene under any circumstance. The Americans were there only as observers, to protect US nationals and their property. But Leahy, a man of strong conviction, was not the type to sit back passively as disaster loomed.

Who was the man walking the decks of the *St. Louis*? At forty-six, he was just entering middle age, and no one would have described him as beautiful: the first deep wrinkles had opened around his eyes, and though he worked hard to maintain a constant weight, the hint of jowls had appeared below his jawline.[1] This extra flesh started to diminish what was already not a strong chin and accentuate his large, crooked nose. He was of medium height, but his narrow shoulders and large head made him seem smaller than he was. Though hardly a handsome man, he stood erect, and his blue eyes, framed by bushy eyebrows, remained penetrating. If pleased, they could be mirthful; if angry, "freezingly cold."[2] The aging of his face, if anything, accentuated the strength of his stare, making him appear even more owl-like.

Physically vigorous, he was also decisive and confident when it came to his profession. Doing his best to live up to the masculine ideal of his era, he was, for want of a better cliché, a man's man. He drank, smoked, and gambled. He spoke with a staccato rhythm and, if the situation was right, used the saltiest language overlaid by a wide range of phrases that would be considered either macho or horrifying today. In his diary or letters, the profanities were absent; his writing was formal and non-ornamental. Yet when he spoke with those he trusted, he used a completely different, animated vocabulary.

Now faced with a situation that meant life or death for countless people, Leahy was tasked with arguably the trickiest assignment in the US Navy. Earlier that day, he had heard that there were hundreds of Greek women and children imprisoned in a warehouse and about to be deported. He went ashore and pleaded with the Turkish officer in charge to show mercy. His entreaties worked, at least temporarily. The officer made a pledge "on his honor" not to deport the Greeks to an almost certain death. Leahy, a man of honor himself, believed that in securing this vow he had given the Greeks a chance at life.

Once back on board, he faced another dilemma. That evening a Greek boy from the countryside outside of Samsun swam out to the *St. Louis* to escape capture. To Leahy he looked to be fourteen years old, which was considered military age by the different sides of the conflict. Leahy had orders not to interfere, and though he should have sent the boy back to shore, he quickly decided not to. "Our plain neutral duty was to turn the boy over to the Turks who would probably have shot him as a spy," Leahy wrote. "We might have compromised by telling him to again take his chances in the sea, but that would have been almost as certainly fatal as a firing squad." Giving him a naval uniform and a meal, Leahy "in plain but very secret violation of all the rules of neutrality made him an honorary member of the crew until it was possible for him to make contact with his countrymen in a safe area."[3]

Leahy's decisiveness and moral bravery in quickly deciding to contravene orders to do what he believed was right was typical of his professional behavior in the 1920s. When he returned from Europe after the war and took up the Gunnery Practice Department, he had already been marked out as one of the most self-confident and successful officers of his generation. Over the next decade, his performance would only add to his reputation within the fleet. Leahy's ability to swing powerful appointments in Washington became an open and envied secret among other naval officers.[4] A certain smugness entered into his language when he discussed navy politics. In 1919, when Chief of Naval Operations Benson retired from the fleet, Leahy let out a squeak of satisfaction, remarking that the new chief, Adm. Robert Coontz, was "much brighter."[5]

The end of World War I was the ideal time to be the director of gunnery, as the US Navy was preparing to possess the most powerful battleship fleet in the world. In 1916 the Wilson administration, worried about the prospect of either the Germans or the British winning the war, had unexpectedly pushed for the construction of a large fleet of advanced battleships. Congress eventually approved funding for nine of the most powerful dreadnoughts designed up to that time.[6] If completed, they would have given the United States an unparalleled striking force at sea. Such a fleet of super-dreadnoughts put an even greater emphasis on gunnery, as the ranges at which they could engage an enemy were considerably greater than any ship yet built.

Once the United States joined the war, construction on these huge ships was put on hold so that the American shipbuilders could concentrate on building antisubmarine vessels and merchant ships to transport the US force safely to Europe. At the war's end, work on the battleships recommenced, and the first ones were slated to be ready to go to sea in 1922. Leahy was centrally positioned to take the gunnery lessons learned from the war and apply them to the preparations for this grand new force. He became a key officer in what was known as the US Navy's gun club, which dominated much of the fleet until 1941.

Leahy's work was noticed. In 1919, the new head of the Pacific Fleet asked for Leahy to be made his chief of staff.[7] With the end of the war, the Pacific Fleet was now the focus of US naval strength, as the Japanese were seen as America's greatest naval competitor. Leahy had no desire to leave Washington and fended off the request. He still got around, however.[8] He made one long trip out to the West Coast to observe the Pacific Fleet undertake target practice. He also helped entertain two of the most senior British representatives who visited the United States, the Prince of Wales (the future Edward VIII) and Admiral Lord Jellicoe, the commander of British naval forces during the Battle of Jutland.

In early 1921 he was sent back to European waters to take command of the cruiser USS *Chattanooga*. After crossing the Atlantic in March, his first few weeks were a combination of holiday and low-key duties. He toured Holland, then made a trip to England to discuss British advances in using aircraft to spot naval guns. In an echo of his first assignment, he was required to find his own way to his new ship, and while in England he heard that the *Chattanooga* was about to sail to Lisbon to represent the United States at the dedication of the Portuguese Tomb of the Unknown Soldier. Rushing south to meet his ship, he arrived in time to be the official American representative at the solemn ceremony. In April, Louise and William H. arrived from America to stay with him. The small family took a holiday in Antwerp and Paris. As always, he found his time in the French capital too short. He kept up a frantic pace seeing as many of Paris's "wonders" as he could.[9] He visited the Louvre, the Bois de Boulogne, and Versailles, to name just a few. He took a particular interest in learning about Napoleon, visiting not only the emperor's tomb in the grand Hôtel national des Invalides, but also being given a special tour of Napoleon's "relics" that had not yet been made available to the public. The only thing he was unimpressed with was the new Parisian tendency to automatically include a tip in all hotel and restaurant bills.

Circumstances changed markedly in May when Leahy was transferred to the command of the *St. Louis*, in the waters off Turkey. He hopped aboard the *Orient Express* for the train journey from Paris to Constantinople, and when he arrived he entered into a world of intense heat, chaos, despair, and beauty. The city, under occupation by British and French forces since 1918, had been turned into a transit point for people fleeing in every direction. There were Russian émigrés who had escaped from the Bolsheviks, Armenians who had survived the brutal pogroms unleashed against them by the Ottomans, and large Turkish and Greek populations who mostly kept to themselves. The former resented what they saw as a Western invasion of their capital city.

The assignment made a large impression on Leahy, and he was considerably more descriptive than he had been for a decade, discussing scandal and intrigue. The desperation and instability of the city made it particularly sexually charged. The British high commissioner in Constantinople, Leahy recorded, complained that other diplomats were shunning him because he went out in public with his young Greek mistress.[10] Leahy personally received an offer of marriage from the already married wife of a Turkish interpreter; having seen her husband, he commiserated but decided to stay with Louise. She then offered to marry any other officer on the *St Louis* who was in need of a spouse. In his writing, Leahy was more open than ever before about being drawn to other women, paying particular attention to the plight of Russian émigrées. There were many around, often claiming to be princesses, trying to survive by selling what they could, including family heirlooms or their bodies. Many were forced to become mistresses of men of authority, such as Leahy, who enjoyed a safe income and could offer protection. While there is no indication that Leahy ever had an affair, he was clearly attracted to a number of different women. When attending a late-night dance at the Dutch mission, he was engaged in conversation by the charming wife of the Dutch minister.[11] She spoke of her shock at seeing some Russian women living openly as concubines, while Leahy replied enigmatically that he found that many of them were easy on the eye, but that none had so far shown an interest in him.[12]

He might have been referring to an odd event that was retold by the American journalist Constantine Brown. Brown, whom Leahy first met in Constantinople, would become his most important conduit to the press during World War II.[13] In 1921 Brown also found the Russian women alluring, developing an attraction to one who called herself Princess Tamara from Tiflis. He suggested to Leahy that the two of them escort Tamara and another self-styled princess for a night at the cabaret. Leahy agreed, but being the Annapolis-trained stickler for propriety that he was, he believed he should bring flowers to present to his date. He spent the day searching high and low throughout the city, finally scrounging up a rather homely bouquet, which he had tied up with masses of ribbons. When he presented it to his princess, she turned her nose up at the pitiful offering, saying, "In Russia . . . when a gentleman invites a lady to dinner, he always presents her with an armful of roses." Leahy snapped, "Then why in the hell didn't you stay there?" He turned to Brown and said, "Come on, Brownie, let's get out of here," and dragged the reluctant journalist away. This experience did not, however, sour Leahy on distressed Russian women. Twice more he recounted the stories of beautiful émigrées who had escaped from the Bolshevik terror with bravery and ingenuity.[14]*

The Russians in Constantinople sparked Leahy's first comment on communism. During the origins of the Cold War, Leahy is normally described as being a hardliner, afraid of the threat that communism posed to the United States. Actually, from the beginning his views on communism were more nuanced. He believed that Communist efforts

---

* Interestingly, once he left Constantinople, Leahy would revert to being repressed. Later that year, 1921, he visited the ruins of Pompeii, the Roman Empire town near Naples buried in ash during the eruption of Mount Vesuvius in 79 CE and almost perfectly preserved. Like many visitors, he commented on the open and energetic sexuality that was expressed in Pompeii, with its large, centrally located brothels and houses with pornographic mosaics. He affected disapproval. "Judged by their pictures and statues," he wrote, "the Pompeiians must have had what in these days we might term a sex complex, and it is surprising that the city's destruction was not recorded in our religious history as example of the vengeance of the offended Deity" (Leahy Diary, October 15, 1921).

to infiltrate Constantinople and unleash mayhem were more comical than threatening.[15]

Beyond his fascination with all things Russian, Leahy was culturally engaged in Constantinople. He visited mosques and churches, was enchanted by Justinian's great creation the church of Hagia Sophia and was impressed by a performance of the whirling dervishes.[16] He considered the fourth-century BCE Sarcophagus of Alexander the single finest piece of carving he had ever seen. He also visited the famous bazaar, where he threw himself into the local custom of haggling. He purchased a pair of German binoculars for $15 and, perhaps in a genuflection to his attractions, two Russian-made silver serving trays.[17] Constantinople struck him as a vibrant and exciting city, a place to which he would want to return. He paid it a great compliment when he said that it reminded him of China.

It also had a surreal atmosphere, something Leahy encountered when, of all things, a bear stowed away on the *St. Louis*. One day, when working in a cabin, Leahy's orderly appeared to tell the captain that a bear was coming up the starboard gangway. Leahy, who thought for a second that his orderly had lost his mind, rushed to the deck to behold a gigantic bear "as big as an ox" lumbering around like he had not the slightest care in the world. The sailors of the *St. Louis* scattered, while "Mr. Bear" eventually entered the crews' quarters, where he settled down, most content. A short while later, a delegation from the famous British dreadnought HMS *Iron Duke* came alongside and reported that one of their crew, a badly disciplined bear, had gone AWOL. Leahy let them board to find the deserter. While Mr. Bear was delighted to see his British crewmates, he had no desire to get in their boat, so he plopped himself down and refused to move. It took a dozen British sailors, and an extensive rope rigging, to propel the creature across the deck and down the gangway into the waiting launch, where, resigned to his fate, he sat compliantly as he was brought back to his dreadnought home.[18]

This one amusing story aside, Leahy's assignment in Turkey was a real test of his diplomatic skills. He was there not to make war but to look after US interests.[19] He claimed that his position required him to attend diplomatic parties and receptions on a regular basis, but then admitted that he also enjoyed the socializing a great deal.[20] He assisted the American commissioner, Adm. Mark Bristol, with organizing American events.[21]* The most lavish took place on July 4, 1921, when the Americans celebrated Independence Day with a series of parties and a sponsored boxing match between British and US naval personnel. As a sign of the relaxed atmosphere, the enlisted men were allowed to bring their new "girlfriends."

Leahy identified the largest American economic interests as the Standard Oil Company and a number of large tobacco farms in the interior. The latter were particularly vulnerable, as the war had led to much of their workforce running away. This reconfirmed his general anti-imperialist credentials. He believed that most of the diplomatic representatives of the Great Powers were there to try to grab "their pound of flesh" from Turkey, and he wanted the United States to stand aside from all that.[22] For instance, Leahy believed that the British and French had inserted themselves so prominently in the war to try to dominate the area, preferably through the imposition of a Greek government that they could control.[23] Leahy wanted the United States to play no political role in the region—a position he maintained for the rest of his long career—and worked very hard to be seen as an honest broker by all sides. He was convinced that in doing so, the Americans were the only power seen as even-handed by the Turks. This allowed him and the other US officers to provide protection for US nationals, such as the tobacco farmers, who had to travel to the interior of the country to look after their assets.

Leahy's experience in Turkey showed an interesting evolution. When he first arrived, he wrote a rather flippant letter to Albert Niblack describing Greeks and Turks "merrily burning each others villages and shooting each other throughout the western part of Asiatic Turkey."[24] Soon, the tragedy of what was happening in the country changed his tone. The cruelty of what he witnessed led him to write one of the bleakest reports of his entire career. When he left he

* Admiral Bristol was known to be one of the most diplomatic officers of his generation and became another one of Leahy's patrons. In the late 1920s and early 1930s Bristol chaired the navy's General Board and Leahy was the director of the Bureau of Navigation. The two worked very well together.

prepared a report to the chief of naval operations that spoke of the great atrocities committed by both sides and the historic suffering of the civilian populations. It was a situation of such great cruelty that it surpassed the horror stories he had heard about World War I.[25] He guessed, rightly, that the Greeks would end up losing this war and the result would be a biblical level of suffering.

Though Leahy served off Turkey for only a little more than half a year, the experience had an outsized impact on both his emotional responses and international outlook. When he sailed the *St. Louis* back to America in November 1921, he was returning to a country with rather different issues. The strategic changes for the US Navy were many, and potentially destabilizing. In December an international conference commenced in Washington to discuss ways to regulate the world balance in naval power.[26] Known as the Washington Naval Conference, it included representatives of all the great sea powers: the United Kingdom, the United States, Japan, France, and Italy. The meeting began with a dramatic proposal by the US Secretary of State, Charles Evans Hughes, offering to scrap every large battleship being built under the terms of the 1916 program if all other major powers ceased battleship construction as well. With building stopped, and all future battleship building frozen for a decade, Hughes proposed that battleship strength then be controlled through a ratio, giving the United Kingdom and the United States equal forces, and Japan 60 percent of this. The ratio as agreed is sometimes known as the 5-5-3 agreement.

The Washington treaties that emerged from this conference are some of the most famous and controversial of the twentieth century.[27] For a while they seemed to herald a new era of peace. Not only did they lead to a halt in battleship building, they froze base construction throughout much of the Pacific Ocean. In a swipe, the possibility of the United States building up the world's largest fleet was ended. For many in the US Navy, the whole process left a bitter taste. For officers of Leahy's generation, it significantly lessened the possibilities for major command, making further advancement in the fleet that much more difficult. They saw a United States, with the world's largest and strongest economy, and possessing the raw materials to construct the greatest fleet in the world, abrogate that ability to an international system that both gave the resented British Navy parity and the Japanese Navy too much relative strength.

Leahy was not one of these officers. Unlike many of his contemporaries, he judged that the offer was a good deal for America, even if it could harm his own career. His honorable stand may have been made easier by the fact that he continued to excel in the commands he was given. Even with fewer jobs available, he had a high chance of getting the best ones. When he returned to America he was still slated to remain at sea a little while longer and was given his first flotilla command. He was put in charge of a squadron of minelayers, raising his flag on the USS *Shawmut*. He spent most of 1922 cruising up and down the East Coast with his squadron, training and attending ceremonial events. He did his customary thorough job, so that another senior officer, Adm. Newton McCully, who was serving as the chief of the Bureau of Navigation, the second most powerful position in the Navy Department after chief of naval operations, asked for Leahy to be his chief of staff. Once again, Leahy got himself out of a job he did not think would help his career. He was no longer interested in being anyone else's chief of staff. He spent his time drilling the squadron to be as effective as it could be. In his expertise of gunnery, he was particularly successful. Under his direction the *Shawmut* produced some of the best long-range gunnery results in the fleet.[28]

The ship also took part in a number of exercises involving a controversial new weapon: aircraft. In the 1920s Leahy was one of the more cautious American naval officers when it came to the power of aircraft. Before the war, he had thought little on the subject. He had been introduced to the notion of military airpower in 1911 by Glenn Curtiss, among the most famous pioneers in US aviation history.[29] Stationed on the West Coast at the time, Leahy watched Curtiss, who operated a pilot school near San Diego, make many flights that year, and heard him discuss the future of airpower. Curtiss insisted that while aircraft could do little presently, it possessed real potential for future development.

In the years following the war, Leahy seemed to be put off by what he saw as the overblown claims of the aviation lobby. Within the navy he was particularly irritated by the special treatment demanded by the new class of naval aviators. He did not like the idea of separating out naval aviators from other naval officers, and was particularly irritated by the demands of the aviators (who had a very dangerous job) for extra pay.[30] Leahy was also more than a little miffed with what he saw as the grandstanding of the most famous American airman of the 1920s, William "Billy" Mitchell. An army officer who had gained public prominence in France during the world war, Mitchell returned home determined to show the superiority of the aircraft over the naval vessel when it came to defending the United States. He orchestrated, sometimes dishonestly, a series of tests in which aircraft sank a captured German vessel or obsolete American naval vessel.[31] The navy, on the other hand, was hardly blameless itself, as it held some less-than-straightforward tests to show that its ships could survive air attack, but were under much greater threat from battleship attack.

As a gunnery officer, Leahy took part in a number of these tests, and was obviously motivated by a desire to thwart Mitchell. In March 1923, he participated in an exercise to sink the obsolete battleship *Iowa* with naval gunfire. After the vessel was relatively undamaged following a day of bombardment, Leahy guessed that the special ammunition being used in the test was too weak. The next day the ship was attacked with full-charge projectiles. Leahy admitted that the decision was made "because of a fear that the Army air service General Mitchel might broadcast a statement that modern Naval guns are unable to sink a twenty five year old ship."[32] Thankfully for Leahy, the *Iowa* was quickly obliterated.

Leahy had returned to the United States at a time when a great social change was reshaping the country. In 1919, the eighteenth amendment to the Constitution, prohibiting the manufacture, supply, and consumption of alcoholic beverages, had been passed, and the next year strong enforcement efforts commenced.

Like many a navy man, Leahy was a lifelong drinker. As a young officer in 1905, he went out for a night of carousing in Panama City with a group of his fellow junior officers.[33] The drinks flowed until Leahy made a late-night call on Panama's president and his wife. The Americans ended up, appropriately lit, at a party in the US legation. Once Josephus Daniels made the navy dry, Leahy could find long sea journeys trying. In 1923, after completing one of his last legs on the *Shawmut*, he admitted to being delighted to come ashore and have a drink.[34] His drinking habits could be idiosyncratic: if he wasn't given a swizzle stick with his cocktail, he was known to stick his forefinger into the glass and stir.[35]

Leahy believed strongly that both men and women were entitled to drink, and Prohibition was not going to stop that. Despite the law, he continued to drink at navy functions, dinner parties, picnics, in public, and in private, whenever it seems that alcohol was on offer. In 1922, when Leahy was exploring the possibility of taking a course at the Naval War College in Newport, Rhode Island, he was delighted to find alcohol being served and consumed everywhere, even directly in front of the town officials.[36] A few weeks later he represented the navy during a yachting competition held off Long Island. Again, alcohol was ubiquitous and Leahy remarked approvingly that drinking was a "usual and necessary" part of every dinner.[37] He even went on a tour of a particularly extensive wine cellar that had been established before Prohibition, and bemoaned the fact that he had neither the farsightedness nor funds to have set up something similar for himself.[38]

If Leahy had some fixed ideas on drinking, by this time in his life he had clear ideas on other vices as well—and mentioned them all in the 1920s. He was a committed smoker and would be for the rest of his life. In 1923, the crew of the *Shawmut* gave him a silver cigarette case when he finished his command.[39] It was one of a number of different cigarette cases he would receive in his career. He also liked to gamble, though, as always, in a controlled fashion. In 1923, while passing through Key West, he dropped by the Duval Club, where craps and roulette were played and drinks were poured. Leahy seemed more than happy with what he found, and even contrasted the experience with visiting casinos earlier in his career—with the only problem being that Prohibition meant that the casinos could now charge for drinks, instead of offering them for free to attract customers.

While Leahy enjoyed his vices, he made sure to keep them under control. He never seemed to get too drunk or gamble too much. Later in his career, this restraint helped him win over Franklin Roosevelt and Harry Truman and become a valued member of their social circles.

While Leahy was more than comfortable at a bar or casino in the 1920s, he was less at home in church. Even though he was taking baby steps toward becoming an Episcopalian, he spent little time thinking about God. While in Constantinople, he was impressed with the seriousness with which the Turkish men took their Islamic obligations, contrasting them with the lax habits of modern Christians.[40] As a middle-aged man he seemed unfamiliar with the proprieties of different religious faiths. In 1922, when he was forty-seven, he attended a funeral in Honduras as part of a diplomatic mission. Leahy admitted to almost total ignorance of proper church services. "I am informed that there were two separate services, but to one unfamiliar with church procedure, there was no appreciable interval and the performance seemed continuous."[41] Once the service was over, drinks were served, including brandy, whiskey, claret, and Champagne. Leahy was much happier.

After Leahy became captain of the *Dolphin* in 1915, he had moved Louise and William H. from their house on Q Street to an apartment. Now back in Washington, the Leahys bought a new home on Connecticut Avenue. Settling down into the middle-class life of a conventional American, in 1923 he bought a prestige car, a Buick Coupe, for which he paid the princely sum of $2,045. After a few weeks it was stolen off the street in Washington, and turned up later, abandoned and wrecked, in Virginia. Leahy being Leahy, he had had it fully insured, and was able to restore the Buick to perfect condition. A few years earlier he had purchased a Boston terrier, whom he named Patriot. He fretted over Patriot as if he were another child. When the dog broke his leg on board *Shawmut*, Leahy had the best medical personnel from his squadron operate. Leahy, worried, stood holding Patriot's paw throughout the entire operation. He was particularly pleased that his pet endured the pain with only an occasional whimper.[42]

When it came to his son, William H., things were up and down. Leahy was definitely the proud naval father when William H. secured a nomination for and then passed the examinations to enter Annapolis. When it came to his son's tastes, Leahy was the predictable traditionalist. The jazz craze mystified him, as it did many parents in the 1920s when their children adopted the music as their own. He remarked in 1925 that William had decided to take up the saxophone and was learning "to blow most of the general junk that one hears nowadays."[43]

In 1923, William H. caused his father a great deal of worry. That summer, during a vacation to Squam Lake in New Hampshire, William H. suffered from a series of serious lung and chest infections. Leahy was beside himself and brought his son at once to Massachusetts General Hospital, and then to the best navy doctors in Washington, to see if they could help. At particularly dangerous moments William H. ran high fevers and hallucinated. He was hospitalized for months, even spending Christmas in the hospital. In a sign of the inner turmoil that existed under his crusty exterior, Leahy admitted in his diary that the anxiety surrounding his son's illness, which was compounded by the death of his brother Stephen, led him to experience a serious psychosomatic reaction. One December evening Leahy was awoken by stomach pains and indigestion so intense he also had to be admitted to the hospital for days of tests.[44] A thorough examination revealed nothing but a few infected teeth. Leahy decided to diagnose himself, with unusually revealing results. "My diagnosis of my own trouble is nervous indigestion, caused by long continued and constant worry about the boy."[45]

William H. was unable to return to Annapolis until the fall of 1924, and would be plagued by ongoing lung issues for the next few years, which his worried father often noted in his diary. Despite his nervousness over his son's health, Leahy was not a domineering father. Even when he disagreed strongly with his son's life choices, he did not try too hard to change them. When William H. fell in love and proposed to Elizabeth Beale in the summer of 1927, Leahy was "acutely disappointed."[46] He liked Elizabeth very much, viewed her as "acceptable . . . by any standard," but he believed that getting married so young would adversely affect his son's career. Leahy's strong reservations made no difference. William H. and Elizabeth married less than a month after informing his father.

When Leahy finally left the *Shawmut* in mid-1923 he was reassigned to a desk job in Washington, being, once again, put in charge of the personnel division. Now, though, he was an appropriately high rank to do the job. For three years he held the assignment, one of the least eventful periods of his life. In the world of the Washington treaties, personnel changes slowed.[47] He grumbled about a plan for aviator pay, and did his best to scupper it. While he was building even more political experience, he also seemed to miss the world. He wrote a series of wistful letters to friends on overseas assignments, reminiscing about his earlier trips. He thought back on his first overseas voyage, to Peru, and, as always, spent time thinking about China. He also made a great friend in this period, the famous Antarctic explorer Richard Byrd, with whom he would remain close until death.

After three years of relative quiet, Leahy ended up with one of the most successful single ship commands in the entire interwar period. In May 1926 he was given one of the great commands about which every naval officer of his generation dreamed—his first battleship. The USS *New Mexico* was one of the newest and most powerful battleships in the fleet, armed with twelve 14-inch guns in three-gun turrets and considered a marvel. Everything on board was electrically powered. Nicknamed "the Queen," a moniker that referred to her striking lines, she was beautiful in profile and rakish, with a jutting bow. Leahy claimed not to have been particularly concerned with which battleship he was given, but he could hardly have been upset to get such a plum assignment. As head of personnel one has to wonder if he played some role in arranging such an excellent command.

Leahy drove the *New Mexico* hard, not just in its gunnery practice but in all areas under his control. The results were remarkable. He made her unarguably the best-performing ship in the fleet. The battleships of the US Navy ran a biannual competition in three areas: gunnery, engineering, and battle efficiency. During the competitions of 1927–1928, the *New Mexico* topped all three categories.[48] Leahy considered this result, known as the "meatball," as one of his finest moments, and he had been willing to run great risks to achieve it. During one of the high-speed cruises as part of the engineering competition, the *New*

Mexico developed a worrying shudder, almost certainly a major propeller problem. Leahy threw caution to the wind and continued to run the engines at full capacity. He won the trophy, but it was discovered in port that two of the propellers had badly damaged blades. Twenty-five years later, Leahy claimed that a more "cautious" commander would have slowed the ship down.[49]

The *New Mexico* was a happy ship under Leahy's command. According to a junior sailor there was only one unpopular officer, a Lieutenant Commander Bode. Bode brought a cat with him and forced the men to build a crate big enough to accommodate a horse so that his pet could be transported in comfort.[50] One irritated sailor threw an egg at Bode when the officer's back was turned, and it splattered all over the officer's uniform. Bode, irate, tried to goad the unseen miscreant into a fight, but the egg-thrower refused to identify himself. Leahy, who only heard of this story years later, had many fond memories of the cat, if none of Bode. He recalled Bode's pet as a kitten that grew into an enormous friendly beast that, unafraid of rank, would sneak into Leahy's cabin and snuggle up with him to sleep.

Leahy's achievements while in command of the *New Mexico* were so emphatic that he received a special letter from President Calvin Coolidge congratulating him on the results. He was also the first member of his class to be raised to the flag rank of rear admiral.[51] Furthermore, he once again received the best possible desk job available for someone of his standing. In late 1927, he was made the new chief of the Bureau of Ordnance, the second most important bureau in the navy and the one in charge of procuring all the weapons and shells for its vessels. It marked him out as one of the few officers of his generation who had a legitimate chance of reaching the position of chief of naval operations.

Leahy's professional success was matched by what seemed to be financial security. The "richest" that Leahy would ever be was in the late 1920s. Not only did he have his naval pay, he had two significant assets that he had acquired through marriage to Louise: stock in the Colusa County Bank, where he also kept some family savings, and agricultural land in the Sacramento valley.[52] Interestingly, Leahy was not particularly comfortable handling investments. He was clearly concerned with both the bank and the yield from the land, sharing his worries with Niblack.[53] Like many Americans in the roaring 1920s, Leahy both wanted to believe that the good times were never going to end, yet had a nagging suspicion that the prices of these assets, because of the debts that were held against them, were overvalued. Part of Leahy really wanted to sell up and realize a profit, but he refused to act. He continued waiting for the even better times that were supposedly just around the corner. He kept spending. In 1928 the Leahys purchased a town house on Florida Avenue, near Dupont Circle in the center of Washington, for $20,000. Life was good, but tougher times lay ahead.

CHAPTER 5

Depression

Nineteen twenty-nine started as another promising year in the life and prodigious career of William Leahy. After the failure of the Geneva Naval Conference of 1927 to extend building limits to auxiliary vessels, the US Navy had commenced construction of the most powerful cruisers in the world. As the chief of the Bureau of Ordnance, the body responsible for the production of new naval vessels and the stockpiling of weapons and ammunition, Leahy held a great deal of influence over this process. Weighing in at 10,000 tons and armed with 8-inch guns, these nimble greyhounds represented a leap forward in technology for the class, boosting America's fighting prowess at sea. Moreover, under Leahy's direction, a number of battleships were modernized, their horizontal armor strengthened, their antiaircraft batteries augmented, making them more resistant to air attack.

Overseeing one of the larger budgets in the US government, Leahy estimated that his office was set to spend $20 million annually. So much money sloshed around the Bureau of Ordnance that he began to fear that much of it was being wasted. That year he crossed the continent to visit a new ordnance-storage facility located in the desert outside Hawthorne, Nevada. A classic example of pork-barrel politics, the new depot cost $3 million. Leahy thought it would have been more economically sound to throw the explosives into the sea—which, incidentally, lay more than 200 miles to the west. Despite his frustration over the

project's wastefulness, he was remarkably understanding about its political purpose, admitting that the poor district obviously needed the
financial support that came with the facility.[1]

Leahy's relaxed attitude may have been due to a happy development
in his home life. The previous year, William H. and his wife, Elizabeth,
had welcomed a daughter, whom they named Louise. Leahy quickly became a doting grandfather. He eventually nicknamed her "Louisita,"
and the joy she brought would become one of the great constants of
Leahy's life. Unfortunately, his joy was soon to be tested.

The stock-market crash of October 1929 hit the United States like a
full dreadnought broadside. As the American economy sputtered and
then failed, prices on goods plummeted; across the nation, workers
were laid off and industrial production crumbled. Eventually the stock
market lost almost all its value, and bankruptcy, both personal and corporate, spread across the country. Within a few years, government tax
revenues dropped by more than half.[2]

For the navy, the productive years of the late 1920s were brought to
a halt. President Herbert Hoover, who assumed the Oval Office in 1929,
was not a believer in a big navy to begin with; facing collapsing government revenues, he singled out the fleet for economy. The first thing he
did, in 1930, was agree to a new naval arms-control treaty. During what
is known as the first London Naval Conference, Hoover's representatives worked out a deal with the British and Japanese that extended the
Washington ratios to most classes of auxiliary vessels.[3] Having placed
limits on his nation's fleet, the president then brought an ax to the navy's budget, ordering that naval spending, which had peaked at more
than $400 million in the fiscal year of 1930–1931, be cut to $340 million
in 1931–1932, a reduction of 15 percent.[4]

Most of the cuts fell on the naval construction budget and salaries.[5]
The Hoover administration stopped the construction of two aircraft
carriers, three cruisers, one destroyer, and six submarines.[6] Leahy, in
charge of enforcing the cuts, was devastated by their human cost. He
discovered that because of the canceled ships, the Bureau of Ordnance
was directly responsible for 5,000 industrial workers losing their jobs.
Leahy was no fool and knew that these shipyard workers, who had

some of the best-paid industrial jobs in the country, would find it practically impossible to gain employment elsewhere in the midst of the economic tsunami.[7] He also knew whom to blame: Herbert Hoover.

Even before the Depression, Leahy had been no fan of Hoover.[8] He believed the president, a Quaker and a rumored pacifist, had no understanding of naval power, nor sympathy for the fleet. He also believed, perhaps unfairly, that Hoover had made his fortune not as an honest businessman but more out of a talent for self-promotion. Once the economy tumbled, his doubts about Hoover became pathological. Leahy came to dislike everything about the president: his speaking voice, his foreign policy, his naval policy, and most important his supposedly supine response to the Depression.[9] While Leahy would never have criticized a president publicly, and disapproved of those who did, in private he was scathing. In October 1931, he attended the four-day gala held by the US government celebrating the 150th anniversary of the Battle of Yorktown, which decided the American Revolution. It was a lavish affair, attended by the likes of French field marshal Philippe Pétain, German general Kuno von Steuben, and America's own John J. Pershing. Mingling with some of the most influential and powerful men in the world, Leahy was happy to see that Prohibition rules "did not apply" during the celebrations. Yet his irritation rose at the appearance of Herbert Hoover. "At the forenoon exercises, Mr. Hoover read a very mediocre address that referred lightly, if at all, to the combatants of Yorktown," Leahy vented in his diary. "During the reading, a puff of wind blew away some of the President's prepared address and he stood mute and apparently uninterested while aides secured the disturbed manuscript, after which he proceeded with his reading. A more vigorous wind would not have annoyed spectators. . . . The paper read by the President did not impress me or any person to whom I talked."[10]

His hatred of Hoover led him to fall out with the chief of naval operations. Adm. William Pratt, who had served as CNO since 1930, was in Leahy's eyes a political schemer too closely identified with Hoover.[11] Relations between the two officers were made worse when the CNO supported the building of a new class of cruiser that Leahy considered pointless. Pratt reciprocated Leahy's disdain. Eventually the CNO tried to sideline Leahy with an unsatisfactory posting. Without consulting him, Pratt assigned Leahy to be the chief of staff to the commander of the Pacific Fleet.[12] Leahy smelled a rat and went straight to the chief of the Bureau of Navigation, which oversaw such transfers, and blocked the move. As he explained in a letter, he was more than happy to use "strong-arm methods" to thwart Pratt.[13] Still, Leahy thought it best to get out of Washington for a while, and in 1931 he accepted the command of the navy's scout destroyers.[14]

First based out of Brooklyn, the scout destroyers were redeployed to the West Coast for much of Leahy's command. When Leahy headed west, he was clearly suffering from anxiety brought on by his personal experience of the Depression. Though it might not have been apparent to those on the outside, his finances were slowly collapsing. Federal budget cuts had meant reduced pay for all naval personnel, which in and of itself was not too devastating, as the cost of most items had fallen as the economy contracted. Yet having purchased a new town house at the height of the boom, Leahy was now forced to sit by and watch its value crater. The Florida Avenue property, which he had purchased for $20,000, soon became a millstone around his neck. Not long after Leahy took command of the scout destroyers, he moved Louise into an apartment and rented out the town house. Yet he could only find a tenant willing to pay a rent that would not even cover the cost of repairs needed to keep the house habitable. He felt the pinch so much that he even referred to it when responding to a letter from an admirer asking whether he would recommend a career in the navy to a young man. Leahy was mostly enthusiastic, yet admitted that "a military and naval career has always given and now offers very little material reward for success."[15]

Even more worryingly, his two largest investments were in the exact sectors of the economy most threatened by the Depression. His large piece of agricultural land in Colusa County became almost worthless. The collapse in food prices made the value of the land plummet, and even raising enough money to pay his annual land tax bill became a struggle. The decline of the property's value unsurprisingly also made his part ownership of the Colusa County Bank a risky proposition. In an era before federal insurance, banks were uniquely vulnerable to collapse if their depositors either lost faith in their liquidity or fell on such hard times that they started taking their money out of the bank at too fast a pace. Ominously, both were happening in Northern California.

At this time, Leahy began to suffer from some of the same stress-related psychosomatic conditions he had first experienced during his son's illness in 1923. In 1932, as he was passing through California, Leahy took time to stop at Warner Springs Spa, just outside of San Diego. There guests were given splendid sleeping cabins, good food, and access to a large swimming pool. They could also drink the heavily sulfurous mineral water, which bubbled out of the ground at a constant 120 degrees Fahrenheit. Leahy loved the spa, admitting that it was the perfect place to recover from "nervous exhaustion."[16] Yet the trip was no panacea. Later that year he was hospitalized for two days due to a stress-related stomach complaint.[17] After a thorough examination, his doctors told him there was no physical reason for his distress.

Watching the unfolding national and personal disasters, Leahy became increasingly reflective on the ghosts of his own past. In 1931 he made two trips to visit the USS *Constellation*, the sailing ship on which he had made his first cruise in 1893. She had been turned into a museum, and Leahy was struck by just how primitive living conditions had been back in the day. He decided to preserve a typewritten copy of the diary he had sporadically kept by hand since leaving Annapolis in 1898. After rereading his own words, he judged that the diary had "no merit in composition" and was "lacking in interest."[18] Assuming the diary would stay in the family, he composed a handwritten note for William H. in which he passed on all the information he had about his parents' families and discussed how one could best succeed in life. He was trying to use family as a lesson; in fact, he was frustrated at what he considered his son's meek career choices. William H. had decided to concentrate on naval engineering, and in 1931 he applied to join the Corps of Naval Constructors, limiting himself to a career based ashore.[19] In doing so, his father believed, William H. was disqualifying himself from ever reaching the top jobs in the fleet. So disappointed was Leahy that, in an unusually revealing move for such a private man, he made his displeasure known to a reporter seventeen years later.[20]

As Leahy composed his version of the Leahy family history, what impressed him, and what he wanted to impress on his son and grand-child, was that the family came from "racially good ancestry" that had demonstrated "qualities of leadership and high-standing in the ancient world." In and of itself, that would mean relatively little in the future. "Laws of heredity beyond our control, and at this time only vaguely discerned," he wrote, "will probably produce a correct proportion of high and low order descendants regardless of what we may think or do, but pride of ancestry has been and is of value to us in that it makes repugnant any deviation from traditional ideas and gives strength with which to resist temptation to drift into a lower order of human society."[21]

Of course there is a basic contradiction in that quote, which summarizes a constant tension in Leahy's own nature and outlook that had become accentuated under the pressure of the Great Depression. On the one hand there was the fatalist, one could even say cynic, believing that his descendants would become what they would become, with little that anyone could do to shape the process. On the other hand, there was a desire to believe that hard work and commitment to ideals must matter, or at least should matter. Leahy certainly believed that his own career success was down to such factors. As he summarized his views to his son at that time: "The present changing social order stimulates appreciation of the fact that circumstances, customs fortunes families, and everything in history except people, change, and that those individuals who succeed are the ones who take advantage of the environment in which they find themselves."

One reason he had the time to indulge his interest in family history was because the Great Depression made a material difference in his command of the scout destroyers. These ships were considered a vital part of the main battle fleet, a group of fast, small vessels that would range far out in front of the battle line to provide protection to the large battleships and, if possible, launch surprise attacks on the enemy's large warships. In 1932, Leahy's command was expanded to take in all the destroyers attached to the battle fleet, including those that were assigned to shadow the battleships to protect them from submarine attack. It should have been an exhausting command. When he was able to conduct drills, he pushed his destroyer crews hard, trying to guarantee that the exercises were as realistic as possible.[22] But budget cutbacks sidelined the ships to port for long stretches, leaving Leahy ashore, living in hotels, fretting and wondering what was happening back in Washington. He did get to work with Capt. William Halsey, who would become famous in the coming war and given the nickname "Bull." Halsey commanded one of the destroyer divisions below Leahy.

Strategically, the most important part of the post was his growing acceptance of the influence of naval airpower. The Leahy of the 1930s was far from being the blind leader of the navy's gun club that some would have us believe. As technology changed, he adjusted his view. The aircraft of the 1920s were primitive devices that would have had real difficulty attacking modern warships at sea. By the early 1930s, however, while aircraft technology still had a long way to go, Leahy was quick to note improvements. Aircraft were faster, could carry heavier bomb loads, and were made more robustly. To protect against air attack, Leahy became a driving force in the US Navy's push for greater air-defense efforts and to make sure that the navy could control aircraft flown from ground bases as well as aircraft carriers. He did this as the head of the Bureau of Ordnance, a position that normally connects Leahy to a big-gun ideology. His passion for increasing the US Navy's antiaircraft protection even made it into a large story in the *New York Times*.[23] Behind closed doors, he argued strongly for his ideas on airpower during meetings of the General Board. On February 3, 1931, the General Board (chaired by one of Leahy's mentors, Admiral Bristol) met to discuss the future design of American destroyers. Leahy argued strongly and successfully for linked, double-mounted antiaircraft guns as opposed to single mounts.[24] It was a prescient and important interjection. The United States was "unique" in providing its destroyers from 1932 onward with dual-purpose antiaircraft weapons, an important step in helping the USN develop the right antiaircraft weaponry to fight and win the Pacific war.[25]

On May 1, 1931, the General Board engaged in a wide-ranging discussion over the navy's future. Leahy spoke before anyone else about the importance of the navy maintaining a ground-based air force, as he was terrified that the US Army Air Force would be given control over all aircraft not directly flown from naval vessels.[26] This showed one area where he was a leader in the 1930s, in making sure that the US Navy was able to maintain and operate its own ground-based aircraft. This decision was not as straightforward as it seems. The British at the end of World War I had given control of all aircraft operations to the new RAF and its Air Ministry. Thus the Royal Navy had no control over any of the aircraft either flown from its bases or even launched from its aircraft carriers. There were many people in the US Army Air Force (and some in Congress) who believed likewise and thought that the USN should give up its independent air arm. Leahy opposed this with his usual ruthlessness.

Leahy also saw firsthand the growing effectiveness of aircraft attacks on surface ships. He was appointed the senior officer in charge of overseeing the bombing attacks on the USS *Pittsburgh*, an old armored cruiser being decommissioned. These air attacks, which occurred in September and October 1931, made it more apparent to Leahy that with heavier ordnance, naval vessels were now under increasing threat. Destroying the *Pittsburgh* was also a bittersweet affair. She was the spitting image of the USS *California*, on which he had had the most important cruise of his early career. As he walked her decks before her destruction, he was seized by a great sense of sadness.

As Leahy honed his command skills in charge of the navy's destroyers, the United States was watching the most worrisome international developments since the end of World War I. In 1931, the Japanese Kwantung Army had launched an invasion of Manchuria in what turned out to be its first attempt to colonize most of China. It was seemingly a case of a military unit running out of control, but the Japanese government, led by men worried that they could be assassinated if they tried to interfere, eventually approved of their army's invasion. Throughout 1932, the Japanese expanded their control of northern China, eventually reaching the outskirts of Beijing.

For the United States this represented a challenge to one of its basic assumptions of the last three decades. America had claimed that it stood for the "Open Door" to China, the policy by which no other nation would be allowed to colonize that vast country. It was part of a partly patronizing, partly genuine belief of many US policymakers that America could play a positive role in limiting the growth of European and now Japanese imperialism in the region. For most of his career, Leahy would have supported the idea of the Open Door with gusto. Now, however, even despite a hostile Japan on the march, Leahy was at his most isolationist. He wanted nothing to do with foreign adventurism, even if it was to defend Chinese independence. From the moment the Japanese crossed the border, he worried about the possibility of a war involving the United States.[27] To Leahy, the problem was not the American people, whom he was convinced did not want war, but rather "foreign interests." By this he meant the large European powers that would want the United States to fight the Japanese for them.[28] His international outlook, shaped as it was by the Great Depression, verged on the paranoid. He claimed that if the United States had to fight Japan during the economic crisis, it might "destroy the existing social order," and yearned for a foreign policy of international disengagement.[29]

In some ways Leahy's paranoia was understandable and forgivable. While the nation was in the throes of the Great Depression, Leahy was experiencing a deep, personal melancholy. Attending a Shriners dinner in San Francisco in April 1932, he was unamused to find that the entertainment included the 1930s version of strippers. The sailor who had once indulged in rowdy nights out grumbled of "alleged entertainment that included some singing by a Russian woman . . . a lot of terrible 'jazz' music by a large orchestra, and a number of dances by a dozen or so almost completely naked women."[30] A few days later—his birthday, in fact—his indignity was compounded when he was invited to attend a dinner for Annapolis graduates where, once again, dancing girls were on display. He tutted that exposing older men such as himself to sexually explicit entertainment was degrading. "Entertainment provided by some kind of theatrical troupe consisted of dancing by almost naked females. That part of the evening was not interesting on ones 57th birthday, if it would have been at any age."[31]

Leahy's sour disposition was doubtlessly caused by the fact that he was about to lose his fight to avoid bankruptcy. In May he made a trip to his land in Colusa County and came face-to-face with an economic and social catastrophe. His fields and those of his neighbors were lush with crops, yet the price of food had fallen so low that all this bounty could not generate enough income to pay the land's running costs.[32] The farm laborers, whom the ranchers had no money to pay, were so desperate that they often offered to work in exchange for food. Leahy realized that his land was as good as lost and would be seized by the government because of unpaid taxes.

Leahy's sympathy for his fellow Americans suffering from the Great Depression led him to take some surprisingly radical positions. In March 1932 tens of thousands of World War I veterans descended on Washington, DC, and set up a shantytown on Anacostia Flats, only a few miles from the Capitol. Nicknamed the Bonus Marchers, they called for the early payment of government bonuses for their military service and planned to stay in their makeshift town until they received help. In late July, they were forcibly evicted by the head of the army, Gen. Douglas MacArthur. Using tanks and cavalry, MacArthur brutally pushed the veterans from their new town before burning it to the ground. To many military officers, the Bonus Marchers represented a threat to domestic order, yet Leahy exhibited remarkable sympathy toward the downtrodden men, writing that they were "undoubtedly entitled to much more than they will ever get" from the Hoover administration.[33] Though personally his own straits were not so dire, he empathized with their condition, noting that naval officers had just had their pay cut by another one-twelfth, as they were forced to take an extra month of unpaid leave every year. As he reflected on the future, this further pay cut made things look very bleak indeed: "This added to the failure of income from nearly all investments and increased taxes will be a difficult burden for most of us. I have a fear that the next year will be worse instead of better."[34]

October 1932 brought even more turmoil. For four days, Leahy sat on the court-martial board of an old friend, Capt. George W. Steele. A decorated thirty-year veteran of the fleet, Steele had been in command of the aircraft carrier USS *Saratoga* that August when she ran aground not far from Los Angeles.[35] Though Leahy thought there were some extenuating circumstances, and tried to understand what had happened to his friend, it is clear that Steele had made significant mistakes while in charge of one of the United States' largest warships.[36] Steele was eventually allowed to resign instead of being fired, but his career was over.[37] Two days after the end of this most unpleasant duty, Leahy left the opulent El Cortez, San Diego's landmark Spanish Renaissance hotel that had opened in the late 1920s during the economic boom that would seemingly never end. As he opened the door to his car, parked just outside the hotel, he was greeted by the barrel of a pistol. In the backseat sat a masked man who had been lying in wait. The man, his gun aimed at Leahy's head, quietly ordered Leahy to get into the car and close the door. Leahy's military training kicked in. He immediately slammed the door shut, ducked low, and took cover behind a neighboring vehicle. Once out of the direct line of sight of his assailant, he retreated into the hotel and called for the police. It was a lucky escape. Leahy heard later that this was one of a series of armed robberies being carried out at the time.

Yet in the midst of this chaos and despair, Leahy saw one sign of hope, his old friend Franklin Delano Roosevelt. Over the previous decade Roosevelt had undergone an extraordinary rise and fall in political fortunes, only to rise once again. In 1920 he had been selected as the Democratic nominee for vice president. Though he performed impressively on the campaign trail, the Democrats were swamped by the Republican landslide led by Warren Harding. Not long afterward, Roosevelt's life took a particularly dark turn when he contracted polio, one of the most frightening diseases of the time. In 1921, as he was vacationing with his family on Campobello Island, Roosevelt started complaining of chills. Less than two weeks later he was completely paralyzed from the waist down. Polio was incurable and mysterious, and Roosevelt could easily have wallowed in his misery, using his money to allow for a long and comfortable period of reclusion. Instead, his disease, if anything, provided motivation for him to move forward—a resoluteness Leahy would have appreciated as much as anyone. After a few years of emotional recalibration, Roosevelt reentered politics. In 1928 he was one of the few positive signs for the Democratic Party when he was elected governor of New York. When the stock market crashed a few months later, the fortunes of the Democrats were transformed as Hoover and the Republicans seemed unable to cope with the unfolding disaster. Roosevelt went to work, and in 1932 he had secured enough support to make himself the Democratic nominee for the presidential election.

Leahy followed the 1932 presidential race with greater interest than any previous contest. Like millions of other Americans, he saw FDR as the last chance to stave off total collapse. He was elated when Roosevelt secured the nomination in July, and not because he expected Roosevelt to start lavishing money on the navy. Roosevelt had publicly supported the naval arms-control process in the 1920s.[38] As a presidential candidate he continued to call for restraint in military spending.[39] What pleased Leahy was his view of Roosevelt as an honest man, a "gentleman by all standards of comparison" with politically progressive views.[40]

During the last few months of the campaign, Leahy's bitterness toward Hoover, indeed toward the entire Hoover administration, grew as the president seemed powerless to stop the nation's slide into even more disorder and poverty. In addition, he believed that the administration's foreign policy, which was being run by Secretary of State Henry Stimson, was dangerously naïve. After having gutted US defense capabilities over the last four years, Leahy saw Hoover and Stimson making pious, inflammatory remarks criticizing the behavior of other nations, particularly Japan. In his diary, he noted that Stimson's statements had "failed to deflect Japan from its predetermined course of action." The president and secretary of state, Leahy believed, would be well-advised to just shut up and stay out of the international crisis: "There is some danger of America getting involved with Japan if our State Department continues to take an active interest in Oriental affairs. We will probably not continue to interfere in the Orient if the present administration is thrown out of office by the November election."[41] Leahy's opinion of Stimson as an ineffectual prig never abated.

Leahy's joy at Roosevelt's landslide victory in November 1932, as well as the subsequent New Deal, revealed that Leahy was never quite the economic conservative that he liked to pretend he was. For a while he praised the new president precisely because of Roosevelt's strong left-wing economic credentials. In one of the more remarkable outbursts in his diary, Leahy wrote that the new president would not kowtow to the interests of "bankers and stock promoters" like the Republicans.[42] This rage against bankers was personal, for Leahy had suffered in the months before Roosevelt's inauguration due to what he saw as Republican inactivity to save the national banking sector.

Starting in January 1933, during the transition between Hoover and Roosevelt, the United States experienced an unprecedented run on its banking system. Panicked savers besieged their local savings institutions trying to withdraw as much money as they could. In doing so, they wrecked the viability of many small banks, such as Leahy's. On January 26, he was told that the Colusa County Bank would be forced to shut down. He remarked, matter-of-factly, that this "destroys the remainder of my life-time savings."[43] It turned out to be worse. The collapse of the bank not only left Leahy penniless—as a part owner, it left him with a large debt. He would not be able to get out from under it until 1941, when he made a final large payment to help settle his outstanding obligations.[44]

For a man like Leahy, who had built his life on confidence, success, and a sense of machismo, it was all extraordinarily humbling. His humiliation was made worse when rumors of his bankruptcy spread amongst members of his Annapolis class.[45] For Leahy, Roosevelt's promises of economic relief had become crucial to his own life. After listening to Roosevelt's inaugural address on the radio, he wrote in his diary that while he was concerned FDR might prove too radical, he was strongly supportive of the president's anti-banking rhetoric and applauded his call for a change from Hoover's Republican Party policies. Roosevelt, he wrote, had delivered an "indictment of every basic principle accepted by his predecessor," and he pondered "perhaps this Roosevelt is the American we have been wishing for."[46]

Even though it was too late to save the Colusa bank, one of the first things President Roosevelt did was save the American banking system. A few hours after taking office, FDR ordered all American banks shut. This banking "holiday" allowed for the nation to take a deep breath and calm its passion. By the time the banks reopened, Congress had passed Roosevelt's Emergency Banking Act, which provided support for the banks and insurance for America's panicked savers. On the first day that they were reopened, more Americans deposited money in their local banks than made withdrawals. The crisis had been surmounted.

Leahy applauded Roosevelt's efforts like this to interject the government into the economy, believing that national survival was at stake. A few weeks later he had seemingly dropped even his small doubts about Roosevelt's moves being too left-wing, writing, "It is the universal hope of all Americans that the President's radical efforts to improve the industrial and financial condition of the country will be successful, and a certainty that if they fail the continued existence of our American Democracy will be doubtful."[47]

After less than a year with Roosevelt as president, Leahy's support, if anything, deepened. When he started his diary for 1934, he opened, for the first time in years, with an optimistic outlook: "The year started auspiciously with promise of improvement in the distressing condition of industrial and financial depression by the radical and original relief measures inaugurated by President Roosevelt."[48]

Leahy had hope.

CHAPTER 6

Nearing the Top

When Franklin Roosevelt was sworn in as the thirty-second president of the United States in March 1933, naval policy ranked among his lowest priorities. So low, in fact, that his first instinct was to continue with President Hoover's policy of spending little on the fleet. Facing an ongoing economic crisis, Roosevelt in one of his first moves in office further reduced naval pay by 15 percent across the board. He planned to spend the money Congress handed to him to reflate the American economy by starting new domestic projects. Soon, however, advisers argued that he should use a large slice of the funds to put ship workers back on the job building naval vessels.[1] In an abrupt turnabout, Roosevelt announced in late June that $238 million had been allocated for the construction of new ships. Using money given to him under the Public Works Administration, he ordered work to commence immediately on two aircraft carriers, four cruisers, and twenty destroyers.[2]

Though it was not realized at the time, Roosevelt had begun the process that would eventually—and in the minds of many American naval officers, finally—make the US Navy the most powerful in the world. For William Leahy, the president's move had dramatic professional repercussions, shaping how he would spend the next two years. During FDR's first term Leahy would hold two important commands that allowed him to demonstrate both his political skills and strategic ideas as

84

he approached the peak of his career. From June 1933 until July 1935, Leahy held the second highest administrative post in the fleet: chief of the Bureau of Navigation. His role was to prepare the fleet to man all the vessels that would be built during Roosevelt's presidency. Though the president had put Leahy forward for the job, there is no evidence that Leahy used any influence he had with Roosevelt to get it.

The US Navy's organizational system in these years was more than slightly schizophrenic. At the top of the chain sat the chief of naval operations, the most senior officer in the Navy Department. A position created in 1915, the CNO was the chief adviser on naval issues to the secretary of the navy and the president. His actual authority over the branches of the fleet, however, was limited.[3] For instance, the CNO did not have direct control over ships, as that was the responsibility of the CINCUS (commander in chief, US Fleet). More immediately, the CNO did not have the ability to issue orders directly to the heads of the different bureaus, such as Navigation, Ordnance, and Aviation, that oversaw the technical and bureaucratic parts of naval administration.[4] Instead, the bureau chiefs received their orders directly from the secretary of the navy. There could thus be great tension between the CNO and the different bureau chiefs if they disagreed on policy or personality. At the same time that Roosevelt nominated Leahy for Navigation, he pushed William Pratt aside as CNO and in his place nominated Adm. W. H. Standley. Getting rid of Pratt pleased Leahy to no end, but in appointing Standley, Roosevelt had set the stage for one of the nastiest fights in the administrative history of the US Navy, with Leahy as the chief protagonist.

Before that happened, Leahy had to take over the reins of this tricky post. He arrived at a particularly fortuitous time. Not only did he have his connection to Roosevelt, Leahy thought very highly of the president's appointments to head the navy.[5] He considered former Virginia senator Claude Swanson, the new secretary of the navy, to be a "strong" man.[6] Perhaps even more important, the new assistant secretary of the navy, Henry Latrobe Roosevelt, was a personal friend of many years' standing.[7] This Roosevelt was an Annapolis graduate who had served with distinction in the Marine Corps before entering business after World War I. As Swanson ended up being, physically, less strong than

Leahy had hoped, having a personal connection to the assistant secretary was particularly useful. Overall, Leahy could take office with confidence that he would receive political backing.

He would need it. As the head of the Bureau of Navigation he held in his hands the careers of his fellow officers. The personnel office, which Leahy first worked for in 1913, was housed within the bureau. Later the post would be renamed the Bureau of Naval Personnel. It required the kind of political tact and discretion that Leahy possessed in spades, as well as playing to his career-long strengths in what is today termed "human resources." Basically, Leahy personally selected the captains of all major warships, and this involved working with some of his oldest and dearest friends—and in some cases disappointing them with tougher assignments than they would have liked.[8]

Tricky cases regularly arose. While Leahy was head, Adm. E. B. Larimer, who had succeeded Leahy as chief of the Bureau of Ordnance, began manifesting a serious mental illness that culminated in a major breakdown.[9] He was hospitalized in Newport, and asked to be retired immediately from the service on medical grounds. He wrote a personal letter to Leahy, pleading his case. Larimer thought it best to be discharged from the hospital as soon as possible. Though Leahy would have been well within his rights to let this happen, he prevailed on Larimer's doctors and lawyer to hold off a few weeks, until Larimer reached his scheduled retirement date. This protected Larimer's pension and provided for his wife for the rest of her life.

Leahy showed such tact regularly, to the benefit of some of the most famous Annapolis graduates. It was a strict policy at the time that to enter the US Navy one needed to be at least five feet six inches tall. A candidate could be accepted into Annapolis if he was shorter, but on the assumption that he would continue growing during his four years at the academy. Two midshipmen of the Class of 1934, John Hyland and Victor "Brute" Krulak, were accepted on exactly those terms.[10] As graduation approached, Hyland had only reached five feet five and three-quarters inches. Poor Krulak had not grown at all and was thought to be only five-two. In the past both would have been out. When their predicament was brought to Leahy's attention, he noted that the young men were near the top of their class and allowed them to join the fleet. Both went on to have stellar careers. Hyland ended up in command of the Pacific Fleet in the 1960s, and Krulak became one of the most famous Marine Corps officers in US history.

Even more sensitively, Leahy as chief of the Bureau of Navigation had to work closely with Congress. When Leahy took over the bureau he had to start preparing the fleet for the immediate expansion that loomed after Roosevelt's first call for extra naval construction. In one case he established an important relationship that would help shape US naval policy throughout the 1930s and into the Cold War. At this time the two most important congressional bodies for authorizing funding and legislating administrative changes were the House and Senate Naval Affairs Committees. If there was any hope of getting a bill through Congress, it had to be reported positively out of these committees. This gave their respective chairs a huge amount of influence.

In the case of the House committee, it helped create a platform for the greatest supporter of the US Navy in the history of Congress, Rep. Carl Vinson from Georgia's tenth district. A blue-dog, segregationist Southern Democrat, Vinson was the longest-serving member of Congress in American history, elected continually from 1914 until he retired in 1965. Vinson's impact on US naval development was both powerful and unexpected. Hailing from a rural, landlocked Georgia district, Vinson entered the House with little interest in naval policy. Usually members of the Naval Affairs Committee came from districts with a large naval base or some kind of financial interest in naval spending. Vinson had neither and had originally wanted to serve on a more prestigious committee, such as Judiciary. Not long after arriving in Washington, a seat on the Naval Affairs Committee became available when another member of the Georgia delegation died. Vinson took up the challenge.

Both he and the navy were pleased that he did. Though Vinson, with his slow mid-Georgia drawl and his habit of chewing on cheap cigars, looked very much the country bumpkin, he had an innate understanding of how to build political support and quickly married this to what became an obsession with strengthening American sea power. He believed that the United States, as the largest economy in the world, had to maintain a correspondingly strong fleet to protect its security. Scrimping on national defense was, to him, an expensive risk. In 1931, after the Democrats had captured the House during the first midterm election following the stock-market crash, he became chairman of the Naval Affairs Committee and set out to rectify what he believed to be a severe neglect of American defenses since the Washington Conference.

Vinson in many ways was the driving force behind the specifics of the Roosevelt administration's naval buildup. He conferred with Roosevelt not long after the 1932 election and was one of those who pressed the president-elect to spend more on the fleet. While Vinson was obviously pleased with the initial $238 million Roosevelt directed to the navy, to him that was only the beginning. What he wanted was to allocate funding so that the US Navy could possess every ship in every category allowed under the Washington and London naval arms-control agreements. At the beginning of the 1930s the United States maintained only 65 percent of the vessels to which they were entitled, and Vinson made the construction of a full "treaty" navy his great crusade of 1933 and 1934.[11] He was completely successful, brilliantly shepherding his bill through the House.[12] In January 1934 Vinson secured unanimous approval for what has come to be known as the Vinson-Trammell Act (Sen. Park Trammell was the chair of the Senate Naval Affairs Committee) authorizing not only a full-treaty navy but a regular schedule of replacement vessels that would keep the US Navy at its full strength in the future. Passage of Vinson-Trammell meant that between 1934 and 1936 the United States undertook the largest naval building program in the world, outpacing the British and Japanese. The United States started three aircraft carriers (the famous WWII flattops *Yorktown*, *Enterprise*, and *Wasp*), eleven cruisers, and forty-two destroyers.[13] During the same years the British laid down one aircraft carrier, twelve cruisers, and forty-two destroyers, though British tonnage was less than American, as they had accepted lower per-ship tonnages for cruisers to allow them to build more numerically.[14] The Japanese, meanwhile, were able to build only two aircraft carriers, seven cruisers, and seventeen destroyers.

A grateful Leahy watched while all this unfolded.[15] His specific role in the process was to adjust personnel policy to cope with the growing fleet. He needed more and better men and spent a good deal of his time lobbying Congress to increase the overall size of the navy. Beyond that, he wanted to make sure that the navy developed and kept the best personnel possible. His reaction to this problem showed once again that he could be surprisingly non-conservative if the situation called for it. The US Navy, not being the most daring organization in the world, often ran its promotion policy based on strict seniority. Officers could be slotted into roles depending on their years of service on the assumption that it was now their turn. This left many ambitious, highly skilled younger officers champing at the bit as they were forced to wait for plum assignments. This became a real problem in the interwar period as shipbuilding almost completely ceased at different times. Leahy wanted to set up a system whereby low-performing older officers were pushed aside for higher-performing younger ones. He also wanted to infuse the fleet with much-needed younger talent by significantly increasing the intake every year at Annapolis and then to nurture this talent by having promotion boards handle cases all the way down to the lieutenant level. Moreover, he wanted to keep high-performing talent in the fleet by reversing some of the salary cuts and freezes that were brought in by both presidents Hoover and Roosevelt.

The first thing Leahy did was secure the strong backing of Swanson and Henry Roosevelt.[16] Then he was presented with the trickier task of getting Congress on board. This is what led him to first work closely with Vinson particularly and both naval affairs committees in general. For days at a time he would either testify to the committees about the changes he wanted or negotiate privately with their members.[17] It was maybe the greatest test thus far of his highly developed political skills. By the end of the 73rd Congress, in June 1934, he had secured most of the important steps that he had set out for himself.[18] By the time he gave up the bureau, Leahy had been able to secure congressional support for a 15 percent increase in the numbers of officers and enlisted men in the fleet from 87,500 to more than 100,000.[19]

In the way that Leahy was usually able to impress those who had power above him, or had power from which he could benefit, he bent over backward to please Vinson.[20] One can see the two getting along, both men who, on the surface, could be underestimated and yet both in possession of innate political skills. They eventually formed a mutual admiration society that lasted for years. Leahy was impressed not only by Vinson's general vision of the importance of sea power but also by the Georgian's political tenacity on behalf of the fleet. He started praising Vinson regularly in his diary and ever so subtly expressed a growing solidarity with the Democrats as a party over the Republicans. In early 1935, after Vinson had waged another successful campaign in support of naval funding, Leahy described him as "particularly able," "attractive," and "devoted to the cause of national defense."[21] The Republicans on the committee, by comparison, were nefariously "collecting data with the purpose of making a political attack" on the naval budget.

Vinson, in return, was very impressed by how effectively Leahy worked with the Naval Affairs Committee. After almost two years of close cooperation, the chairman sent a special letter of commendation about Leahy to Swanson, relaying "not only my personal appreciation but also the appreciation of the entire Committee on Naval Affairs on the efficient and splendid manner in which Admiral Leahy has cooperated with and rendered valuable assistance to the Committee on all matters pertaining to legislation for the personnel of the navy." He went on to add that Leahy "has the admiration and high esteem of the members of this Committee for his admirable service to us on account of his thorough understanding and complete knowledge of the needs of the navy."[22]

The secretary of the navy responded with just as strong a statement of admiration, describing how Leahy had won "to the fullest extent the esteem and confidence of his fellow officers."[23] This show of confidence in Leahy was indicative of not only his political skills but the fact that both Vinson and Swanson realized that Leahy, by the end of his time as chief of the Bureau of Navigation, had an excellent chance of becoming the professional head of the fleet two years later. The most important sign of his imminent rise was the fact that he had just emerged triumphant from a vicious confrontation with the CNO.

Though Leahy was first happy with Standley, not long after the two men took office their relationship began to fracture. It was all about control. Standley, an officer who operated with a large chip on his shoulder, was convinced the fleet needed more centralization.[24] He asked Roosevelt to make sure that the CNO was given direct-line control over the different bureaus, Leahy's included.[25] The president demurred, ruling that the secretary of the navy was the only position that could issue direct orders to the different chiefs. Standley refused to give up and continued to argue that his position needed more direct authority.

Leahy came out as the leader of the opposition, working with other senior officers against Standley's plans. An early sign of tension between the two was their disagreement over the CINCUS, Adm. Joseph Reeves. Standley also wanted to make the CNO the direct-line commander of all US warships, and therefore wanted to place the CINCUS under his authority. He particularly wanted to get rid of Reeves, who had angered him with his independence.[26] Leahy, who was close to Reeves, used his position in the Bureau of Navigation to block any change. Leahy also combined forces with the head of the Bureau of Aeronautics, Adm. Ernest King, who wanted to protect his independence as well. It was a small indication of how Leahy and King, quite different in nature, could work productively, as they would in World War II. Eventually the atmosphere at the top of the fleet became toxic as these different alpha males continued to circle one another warily in their struggle for power.

Leahy's strong opposition to Standley's gambits emerged from two parts of his nature. As someone who had built his career through thriving in the decentralized bureau system, Leahy felt that the ability of officers to show independence and initiative should not be frittered away. From a more catholic point of view, Leahy was also opposed to Standley's plans because he disliked concentrating too much power in the hands of individual military officers. He hated anything that would have created a rival to civilian authority and approved of collective decision-making. He was a big supporter of the General Board concept, which saw the bureau chiefs and other important officers brought together to discuss different strategic and technical questions before decisions were reached. His support for such a collective approach, and his ability to get his own way within it, also pointed the way to another reason for his bureaucratic success during his career.

The tensions between Leahy and Standley simmered throughout 1934 before eventually boiling over. The CNO, in the end, decided to try to drive Leahy out of the fleet. The key issue was Leahy's next sea command, scheduled to start in the middle of 1935. If he did not receive a major assignment, it would mark the end of his career, with retirement following soon after. Perhaps, Standley thought, with his direct line to the president and Swanson, he would prevail. If so, he was badly mistaken.

Leahy was far more politically connected and astute than Standley and crushed the efforts of the CNO. What Standley did not seem to understand was the wide base of support Leahy had established in the Navy Department, Congress, and the White House.[27] Leahy's friendship with Roosevelt, for instance, was reasserting itself. Between 1921 and 1933, it seems that the two men had not met in person. On December 6, 1933, Leahy and Louise were invited to attend a speech by Roosevelt at the National Council of Churches.[28] Not Leahy's natural milieu, it was a meeting of pacifistically inclined Protestants, and Roosevelt gave a subpar speech. However, what most surprised Leahy were the heavy leg braces that the president was wearing. He admitted that it was the first time he had seen Roosevelt up close since FDR had contracted polio, and he'd had no idea that the president's disease had left him so completely crippled.

As chief of the Bureau of Navigation, Leahy started attending White House conferences, presidential speeches, and even football games and other sporting events with Roosevelt. It became clear that the two men had a much closer relationship than would normally have existed between a president and the fourth-ranking member of the Navy Department.[29] In late December 1934, for instance, Leahy went to the White House for a conference about military education. He was one of the most junior people in the room, which included the secretary of war, Henry Roosevelt, and Gen. Douglas MacArthur, chief of staff of the army. Regardless, Leahy was the one who afterward chatted informally and swapped jokes with the president.[30]

Standley, who seemed unaware of Leahy's standing, made his move in early 1935. Leahy was angling to take over as the commander of the fleet's battle force that summer. Most of the US Fleet in the mid-1930s was divided up into "forces": a smaller, lighter scouting force, made up primarily of destroyers and some cruisers, whose job it was to discover the enemy, and the heavy fist—the battle force. This latter force included all the battleships and most of the best aircraft carriers, destroyers, and cruisers in the fleet.[31] Its job was to annihilate the enemy in a pitched battle. Though placed below the CINCUS, the commander of the battle force was the premier combat command position in the fleet. Had the US Navy gone to war, the commander of the battle force would have called the shots in any great sea battle. Leahy was desperate to get the post, and Standley was just as desperate to deny him it.

Standley lobbied hard to keep Leahy from becoming battle-force commander, but in doing so he ran into a brick wall composed of Swanson and Franklin Roosevelt. The president had always taken a keen interest in senior naval appointments and had made sure that the secretary of the navy continued to call the shots over the CNO. Even though Standley tried to persuade them otherwise, Swanson and Roosevelt supported Leahy's promotion. Leahy, who watched all of this unfold, understood the power of his political backing, and in one of the most illuminating and cocky entries in his diary made it clear that he was confident that the secretary of navy, and therefore the president, had his back.

> Admiral Standley is now persistently and vigorously opposing this nomination [Leahy to take over battle force] with the purpose of eliminating me from any prospect of promotion in the Fleet or of succession to his office when he retires.
>
> Secretary Swanson wants me to succeed Admiral Standley which is undoubtedly the cause of the latter's attitude.
>
> In view of the fact that Admiral Standley has officially questioned my professional competency, it is pleasing that a decision as to future prospects will not be made by him, and that he will not find it easy to remove me from the picture. It is my present intention to obtain appointment as Vice Admiral in the Fleet.[32]

And that is precisely what happened. In March 1935, Roosevelt confirmed that Leahy would command the battle force and authorized his promotion to vice admiral.[33] Standley had to accept the humiliation. Roosevelt then paid Leahy a particular sign of favor. Right before he was to head out to the West Coast to assume his new post, Roosevelt called Leahy into the White House for a private chat—two old friends shooting the breeze.

> The President asked me to see him at 4pm, at which time we had a half hours talk about the Navy, Naval affairs, and things in general. He had nothing of importance to tell me, but apparently just wanted to have an informal talk and to wish me good fortune in my new command.[34]

Two days after this chat, Leahy boarded a B&O train for the trip to California and his new command. He was mostly excited, though the moment was also bittersweet. He was heading for what would be his last sea duty. Reflective, he decided to revisit his past. Not long before he left, he received news that his aunt had died. This represented the severing of the last living link to his mother's family. Perhaps for this reason he decided to make a special stop. As his train traveled from Chicago to Minneapolis, Leahy disembarked for a day in Wausau, Wisconsin, the city where he had spent much of his adolescence and where his parents were buried.

He found the Rust Belt, and it depressed him. When his father had moved the family to Wausau in the 1880s, it was a prosperous town of noisy lumber mills and hope. Now the lumber business was gone and the Great Depression was very much alive. The mill areas were silent, overgrown with bushes. The river, which had been choked with felled logs when he was young, was taken over by dams and bridges. Almost all traces of the Leahys had been expunged. The house in which he had lived with his parents had been torn down and was now someone's backyard, while that of his uncle John had been replaced by an office building. It all felt alien, and as he left he wondered if he should ever "again feel a desire to return to that city of my childhood."[35]

Leahy served in command of the battle force from the late summer of 1935 until early 1937. During that time he was stationed mostly on the West Coast, as Japan was seen as the most likely naval enemy. In October 1935, not long after Leahy took command, Roosevelt headed out to California to watch the battle force in action. The president was ostensibly there to address the opening of the San Diego World Exposition (modeled on the Chicago World's Fair), but Leahy used the opportunity to lay on a spectacular show—the largest tactical maneuver the US Navy had ever done to that time.[36] Pulling out all the stops, he assembled 129 warships, including 12 battleships, 17 cruisers, and all the destroyers he could get his hands on.[37] The president, from the deck of one of his favorite warships, the cruiser USS *Houston*, watched intently as this armada deployed into its threatening battle formation. The president's ship was the intended target of attack. However, instead of bombarding the *Houston*, each ship in turn fired a proper twenty-one-gun salute as they passed the president. Then, for a little extra flair, Leahy used his destroyers and all available aircraft to lay down a thick cover of smoke, which was used to obscure a mock destroyer attack against the *Houston*. The festivities culminated with a mass aerial display, with almost five hundred naval aircraft putting on a great show directly over the president. Leahy claimed in his diary that preparations for this show were an important part of fleet training—but one has the feeling that impressing the president mattered a little more. Certainly Leahy did his cause no harm in Roosevelt's eyes. In December 1935, when the admiral was visiting Washington, Swanson took him aside and told him, confidentially, that he would be named chief of naval operations—as long as Franklin Roosevelt was reelected.[38]

Leahy still had more than a year to go before the next presidential election, and in that time he did his best to make the battle force a potent weapon of war. When Leahy surveyed the world as battle-force commander he still favored a form of isolationism, especially toward Europe. The rise of Hitler and Stalin left him worried that Europe was heading for a war between fascism and communism. He prophesied that if things continued, the war would involve Germany and Italy on one side, with the Soviet Union and France on the other—the British remaining neutral until they saw which was most likely to triumph. Leahy wanted the United States to stay out, believing that unless the State Department screwed up, US neutrality should be maintained.[39] In the Pacific, however, Leahy was more likely to contemplate a war than he had been a few years earlier. When Japan, in 1936, repudiated the naval arms-control process and called for equivalent naval forces for itself, the United Kingdom, and the United States, Leahy was worried. He believed that Japan would keep expanding and would eventually provoke a war, and in this case wanted the United States to work in tandem with the British.[40] He thus drove the battle force with the idea of a war with Japan in mind.

His final sea command revealed Leahy as both confident and a stickler for routine. He had a rigid work schedule when the ships were in port. Living onshore much of the time, Leahy would drive out to the force, based at Long Beach, earlier in the morning than his staff would have wanted. Having roused his men from bed so early, he usually took a nap after lunch, during which the quarterdeck had to be very quiet indeed.[41] Leahy appeared to many enlisted men as a demanding, somewhat forbidding figure. At one point word went out that he needed a new yeoman. William Rigdon, who would later work with Leahy in the White House, was offered the position—but could not say no fast enough. Leahy's reputation as an old-school navy man, a "sea dog," was enough to keep Rigdon from coming forward.[42]

Leahy hated the present organizational structure and division into different forces. His first report as commander began with the claim that the present organization of the fleet left it inadequately prepared to fulfill its mission in war.[43] He acted as if war were imminent and wanted the force to train as such. He called for the political visit of warships to American ports to be cut back significantly, to allow for more realistic combat maneuvers.[44] Remarkably, this occurred, and the following year Leahy was able to report that port visitations had been "consolidated."[45]

Leahy prioritized preparing for a great naval war in the Pacific when it came to battle-force training. He used his exercises to make points about fleet concentration. In one of the first maneuvers he oversaw he divided the fleet into two parts, one significantly larger and stronger (white) and a weaker force (blue). He took command of the blue force and tried to escape from the white force and reach the Panama Canal without being destroyed.[46] He was making a point about how stupid it would be for the United States to divide its fleet between the Atlantic and Pacific, leaving the two halves to rush to combine after hostilities started. It showed that he remained a believer in many of Admiral Mahan's precepts, fleet concentration being foremost among them.

Not surprisingly, considering his past experience, Leahy spent much of his drill time on gunnery. He improved results almost from the moment that he arrived.[47] By the time he was done, every category of ship in the force was shooting better than before he took command.[48] That being said, he also put a surprising amount of effort into the development of carrier-based aircraft attacks.[49] Leahy remained convinced that battleships at sea would still be very difficult for aircraft to sink, but he was becoming aware of the growing power of both torpedo and dive-bomb attacks, which he practiced regularly.[50] It was part of a process whereby the United States probably led the world in naval air developments in the mid-1930s.[51] One of the last acts that he performed when he gave up command of the battle force was to switch his flag onto the aircraft carrier *Ranger*—the most useless aircraft carrier ever designed by the United States.* He did this as a strong statement of his belief in a navy-run air wing, and a sign that he was now accepting of the fact that aircraft technology had developed to the point that airplanes were far more formidable weapons of war.[52]

Before departure I shifted my flag to the airplane carrier RANGER . . . and made the return journey on that ship with the purpose of observing the tactics and operation of our seaborne air arm. There is no doubt whatever that America's carrier based naval airplanes have reached a marvelous efficiency considering the short time that has elapsed since their introduction into the navy. I believe that their present efficiency is largely if not entirely due to the

---

* The *Ranger* was an attempt to build a small, light aircraft carrier. As it turned out, it was too light to be of much use in battle and spent World War II serving in the Atlantic to keep her away from the deadly carrier battles in the Pacific.

fact that they are operated exclusively by seagoing naval personnel instead of by a separate air force as is the case in England.[53]

When he made this cruise, Leahy was in a particularly good mood, because he was heading back to Washington to work with Roosevelt. Leahy had spent 1936, after Swanson told him of his personal stake in the election, closely following the political scene. When Roosevelt was renominated by the Democrats in June and gave a rousing speech in front of 100,000 supporters, Leahy believed that the president's reelection was almost certain. By October, Leahy was so confident that he already started putting in place plans that he wanted to implement as CNO.[54] Roosevelt's reelection also allowed Leahy to revisit his vision of the New Deal and his place in US politics.

Once again, Leahy revealed himself to not be as doctrinaire as most would assume. He was worried that some "radicals" were pushing FDR too far, but he had also become quite fond of a number of progressive Democrats. He remarked favorably on several, including Rep. G. H. Cary of Kentucky, Sen. Joseph Robinson of Arkansas, and Mayor William B. Hartsfield of Atlanta.[55] Leahy also astutely prophesized where American politics were heading in the coming decades. He understood that Roosevelt's New Deal would reshape American politics into one in which a liberal Democratic Party faced a conservative Republican one.

The political contest this year definitely points to a future separation of the electorate into Liberals and Conservatives, whether or not the parties retain their present designations as Democrats and Republicans.

Roosevelt at the present time is definitely a Liberal, and it is the hope of many of his friends that he can detach himself from radical members of his present entourage and incline his efforts more toward conservatism.[56]

It was an important statement. Leahy's view of himself as a "conservative" was not that of a classical free marketeer—but as a conservative within the political and policy world constructed by Franklin

Roosevelt and infused with New Deal values. If categorization is necessary, Leahy would best be described as a conservative New Dealer. He applauded the president's daring attempts to resuscitate the economy, believed that the state could play a positive role in helping the disadvantaged, and was not a believer that business concerns had either the national or public interest at heart. On the other hand, he did not want to fundamentally reorder American society. He would get concerned when he thought Roosevelt went too far, such as in his plan to "pack" the Supreme Court in 1937, but he was an enthusiastic supporter of the president and his policies in general.[57]

Of course the reason Leahy was pleased as he cruised back in the *Ranger* was that he had reached the top and was going to work for the president he respected more than any other. Only a few days after winning reelection in November 1936, Roosevelt had done what he had promised and announced publicly that on January 1, 1937, he would be recalling Leahy to Washington to be the new chief of naval operations.[58]

It was what Leahy assumed would be the high point of his already distinguished career.

CHAPTER 7

Rising in Roosevelt's Court

On January 5, 1937, William Leahy attended his first state dinner as Franklin Roosevelt's chief of naval operations.[1] It would prove to be a fateful affair. A strict protocol was enforced for such ceremonial events: when guests arrived, they were escorted to the White House's East Room, where their names and titles were announced before they were placed in a line, based on the rank of his or her position. There they waited, the line snaking around three sides of the room, until Franklin and Eleanor Roosevelt were brought in for official greetings, beginning with the most senior. Leahy was standing among cabinet members, senior politicians, and their partners when Secretary of the Navy Claude Swanson fainted.

Swanson's health had been delicate ever since taking the post at the start of Roosevelt's first term. Forced to remain on his feet for longer than the older man's weak constitution could bear, he collapsed onto the floor. Though he officially retained his role as secretary, he was soon forced to give up work for long periods as his health continued to deteriorate.[2] According to procedure, the assistant secretary of the navy should have taken up much of the slack. Yet the prior assistant secretary, Leahy's friend Henry Latrobe Roosevelt, had died the previous year, and the role was filled by the ineffective Charles Edison. Technically minded like his father, the famous inventor Thomas Edison, the new assistant secretary was a political neophyte who, in the president's eyes, revealed himself to be unequipped to represent the navy in political meetings.

With no effective leader in place at the Navy Department, Leahy quietly took over many of the sensitive roles that should have been done by either Swanson or Edison. His assumption of another makeshift role brought him a step closer to Roosevelt's inner circle, where he became acquainted with Undersecretary of State Sumner Welles, whom the president considered a friend and confidant. Welles hailed from a social milieu in which the president felt at ease—Northeastern money and snobbery. He had received his prep school education at Groton, the same school attended by Roosevelt, and as a boy served as a page at Franklin and Eleanor's wedding. Intelligent, well-bred, and rich, he was an open alcoholic and repressed homosexual. With his second wife (in the end he married three times), the even wealthier railroad heiress Mathilde Scott Townsend, he lived in aristocratic splendor in a forty-nine-room Maryland estate, Oxon Hill. Roosevelt, an aristocrat himself, grew to both like and trust Welles greatly. When Roosevelt was assistant secretary of the navy, he helped Welles get his first appointment in the State Department.[3] Welles's early career was spent building up an expertise in the Americas and Asia, and he gained a small amount of notoriety when he wrote a history of the Dominican Republic in which the United States is portrayed as the biblical queen Jezebel, leading the poorer nation astray.[4] When Roosevelt was elected president, Welles rose meteorically. In April 1933 he was made assistant secretary of state, and when Roosevelt was reelected in 1936, Welles was appointed undersecretary of state, the second highest position in the American diplomatic corps. In response, Welles looked on the president with a hint of hero worship and, very possibly, sexual attraction.[5]

Welles's place in Roosevelt's policy-making circle was ironclad; in fact, the president's only comparable confidant in his final seven years of life was Leahy. Not even Roosevelt's relationship with Harry Hopkins, which was practically codependent between 1940 and 1942, was as consistent. The president almost always consulted Welles first on tricky foreign policy questions and, crucially, welcomed him into his personal space. By contrast, his secretary of state, Cordell Hull, was kept at arm's length. Roosevelt's preference for Welles over Hull created real animosity within the State Department. To the young diplomat Charles Bohlen, who would later serve as the department's liaison with the White House, it was clear where the real power to affect policy lay. He wrote that Roosevelt's favoritism for Welles, "who was cut from the same cloth of Groton, Harvard, and the Eastern Establishment," led to a sense of malaise among American diplomats.[6] Members of Roosevelt's cabinet, such as Harold Ickes and Harry Hopkins, were likewise jealous of the prominent role that Welles played in Roosevelt's foreign-policy life.[7]

Welles and Roosevelt shared a similar foreign-policy outlook, supporting a more aggressive line against Germany and Japan than the more indecisive Hull. Leahy, well aware of the undersecretary's influence with the president, either consciously or unconsciously mimicked FDR in his view of the man. From early on he praised Welles's foreign-policy vision.[8] On the other hand, Leahy, who first expressed doubts about Cordell Hull in 1935, grew even more critical of the secretary. He became damning of Hull's inability to communicate his ideas coherently as well as his general ineffectiveness.[9]

A few weeks after Swanson's collapse, Leahy was summoned to the White House for a meeting with Roosevelt and Welles. The topic of this early meeting was the "loaning to South America of a group of American destroyers to be used for training purposes by South American States . . . also the feasibility of utilizing a naval surveying ship for the purpose of investigating possible port facilities on the coast of Brazil north of the Amazon River."[10] The meeting of Roosevelt, Welles, and Leahy was the start of the establishment of a new axis of policy-making in the Roosevelt administration. From then on, Leahy could meet regularly alone with Welles to work through sensitive issues for Roosevelt, confident that they were in high standing with the White House. The two men, for instance, continued to determine policy on the loaning of warships to South American countries.[11] In June the two even had to meet to handle a small diplomatic embarrassment set off by something Leahy reportedly said to the press. A newspaper quoted Leahy describing Soviet citizens as "slaves" to their totalitarian system.* Right away Leahy went to Welles to discuss how to handle the incident.[12] Cordell Hull had to make an official apology to the Soviets on Leahy's behalf, but the sensitive part of the discussions was handled by Leahy and the undersecretary.[13]

Leahy also started handling other tricky questions by himself, often acting as de facto secretary of the navy. One was naval relations with the Soviet Union. On January 25, Leahy sat down with a Mr. Wolf, a Soviet agent of "apparently Jewish origin," who asked for access to the design plans for US battleships.[14] It was the first of many meetings he would have with Soviet representatives during his time as CNO. The Soviets, who lacked the technology and experience to construct large battleships of their own, were keen to have US shipyards build some for them.[15] They made extensive contacts with Bethlehem Shipbuilding to start arranging for this. To get these ships built in US yards, they needed the support of the US government, which put Roosevelt in a quandary. He did not want to say no, but he had no interest in saying yes. With his eyes fixed on the rise of Hitler, Roosevelt did not want to do anything to antagonize the Soviet Union. So Roosevelt let Leahy do the dirty work. He told the admiral that the United States should not forbid the Soviets from ordering the vessels, but on the other hand the US Navy should not help them in any way.[16]

From the beginning, Leahy handled these meetings with his trademark political skills, albeit with a sense of growing exasperation. He had to be polite, nonargumentative, and nonconfrontational, but remain resolute that the US Navy would neither forbid nor support Soviet efforts. With a slight smile he told the Soviet representatives that he had no problem if they chose to build warships in American yards, but he simply could not allow them access to the most up-to-date plans and technologies for America's own warships.[17] Behind the scenes, he worked diligently to spike their plans. In March 1937, when some

---

* Leahy claimed that he had been misquoted, but considering his general view of communism, there is a good likelihood that he said this. It is one of the few instances when he allowed something controversial to end up in print.

representatives of US shipyards (with whom Leahy had a close relationship, having served as the head of the Bureau of Ordnance) reported
that the Soviets were going to different firms to try to purchase the separate parts of a warship to presumably assemble on their own, Leahy
went right to the State Department to block their plan.[18] When the Soviets gave up on a battleship purchase, they switched to trying to buy a
destroyer. Once again, Leahy was there to stop them.[19]

Closer to home, much of Leahy's time as CNO was spent trying to
please or at least mollify American politicians. The most difficult, by
far, was the congressional delegation from Oregon. Starting in March
1937, Leahy met regularly with Oregon's senators and representatives,
who were pressing for more Navy Department funding. The particular
bee in their bonnet was the small naval facility at Tongue Point. A
World War I–era facility, the Tongue Point base, which sat at the mouth
of the Columbia River downstream from Portland, had been moth-
balled in the 1920s after the naval arms-control process. The Oregonians came by Leahy's office begging, cajoling, and even threatening to
get his support for reopening and expanding the facility. At first Leahy
rebuffed their efforts, convinced that spending money on Tongue Point
would achieve little. He even told Roosevelt as much.[20]

In letting Leahy act as a buffer between himself and the Soviets and
Oregonians, Roosevelt was putting a great deal of faith in Leahy. He
trusted the admiral to act prudently yet effectively, and at all times
to put the interests of the administration first. Moreover, he enjoyed
Leahy's company, and the lengths and frequencies of their private
meetings began to increase. One of their first private lunches occurred
on April 15, 1937.[21] Over cream soup and scrambled eggs, the two men
talked shop, the president indulging his love of all things navy by pondering the question of how large a gun should be placed on the next
generation of American battleships. They also discussed relations with
the Soviet Union and naval personnel policy. Roosevelt often held private lunches with different members of his government, but when it
came to those who were in charge of the army and navy, his hour
alone with the admiral was a sign of a special relationship. During
Leahy's tenure as CNO—January 1937 to August 1939—he is recorded as

meeting with Roosevelt in the White House fifty-two times. In comparison, Gen. Malin Craig, Leahy's army counterpart, showed up twelve times, and none were private lunches.[22] Even more remarkably, Leahy enjoyed more face time with Roosevelt than the civilian heads of the armed services. Swanson and Secretary of War Harry Woodring met with Roosevelt a combined forty-two times during the same period, and many of the meetings were short and involved groups.[23] Leahy probably had more actual time with Roosevelt than the secretary of war, secretary of the navy, and chief of staff of the army—combined. The range of Leahy's different meetings with Roosevelt also went far beyond the normal ones between a president and a senior military officer. They often went on for hours.[24] Sometimes the president wanted their meetings to be inconspicuous and asked for Leahy to be ushered secretly into the White House through a back door.[25] During other meetings, Roosevelt would often ask to be left alone with Leahy to discuss highly sensitive issues. With such an intimate relationship with the president, Leahy was arguably the most powerful CNO in American history.

Roosevelt prioritized meeting with Leahy for a few reasons. He remained, as always, invested in the minutiae of naval policy. He cared about ship design, naval bureaucracy, and the worldwide naval balance. The army never held his attention in the same way. Having Leahy come by was a form of fun. What's more, Roosevelt trusted Leahy with his foreign and strategic ideas. Using him as a sounding board, the president would bring up sensitive issues, such as relations with the Soviet Union, confident in Leahy's advice, and, once a decision was made, confident he would receive the admiral's unreserved support. Perhaps most important, Roosevelt increasingly grew to enjoy Leahy's company. He found that he could relax with the admiral. Leahy understood how to act around the president, to strike the right balance between deference and independence.

A few weeks later, in a sign of Roosevelt's growing level of comfort and confidence in Leahy, the president invited the admiral along for a political trip with a powerful cast of Democratic grandees.[26] It was a cruise on the presidential yacht *Potomac*, an old side-wheel steamer with hand-operated engine valves. The other men involved reeked of Washington, DC, political power. From the administration, there was Vice President John Nance Garner and Harry Hopkins, the director of the federal government's Emergency Relief Program. From the Senate were men such as James Byrnes of South Carolina, Morris Sheppard of Texas, Clyde Herring of Iowa, Edwin Johnson of Colorado, and Claude Pepper of Florida. Byrnes was a rising star in the party and would soon be selected by Roosevelt to serve on the Supreme Court. Also included was Rep. Sam Rayburn of Texas, who would become Speaker of the House in 1940. The purpose of the cruise was partly to relax while traveling down to Quantico, Virginia, to watch a baseball game between congressmen and members of the press.

In the summer of 1937, Leahy began to represent the navy during many of the president's cabinet meetings. He was an unusual inclusion—in a gathering of civilian officials, an active-duty military officer was present when the most politically sensitive domestic issues were discussed, though he did almost always limit his comments to naval or foreign-policy questions. He handled himself with such skill that the veteran Washington operators came away impressed. The meetings were another important step in the political education of William Leahy.[27]

The biggest issue the cabinet confronted that summer was how the United States should react to the Japanese invasion of China. On July 7, from across the expanse of the Marco Polo Bridge, which separated China proper from the Japanese Manchurian puppet state known as Manchukuo, Japanese soldiers exchanged gunfire with Chinese forces. Nationalist fanatics in Japan's Kwantung Army used the skirmish as a pretext to launch a full-scale invasion of China, unleashing one of the most horrible conflicts in history and, for some historians, the true beginning of World War II. During the following months the Japanese would run wild first in northern China, then along the coast, plunging deeper and deeper into the country's interior. America's response was the greatest strategic question the Roosevelt administration had yet to face.

Leahy was more than willing to argue his case before the nation's political elite. He counseled that US forces in China should be deployed in more defensible, practicable positions—in particular in areas where they could be given some air cover.[28] Secretary of the Interior Harold Ickes recalled that Roosevelt "asked Leahy to explain where our Marines were located with reference to the Sino-Japanese line-up and Leahy reported that they were nearest the point of danger. The President wanted to know why they were there instead of the British or some other marines and Leahy's answer was that the British are smart."[29] In his deadpan way, Leahy was making a deadly serious point. While the Japanese invasion had begun to erode some of his innate isolationism, he did not want the United States to get dragged into a war because of the careless placement of their armed forces.

Roosevelt was obviously listening to what the salty admiral was saying. On August 14 Leahy left Washington for a vacation with Louisita in rural Pennsylvania. Kept constantly informed of developments in China by telephone and air mail, he was called back to Washington early to take part in a cabinet meeting on August 20. Shanghai was close to being seized.[30] The Japanese had bombed the city, killing thousands of civilians, and were extending their control over different urban areas through street-by-street fighting. Leahy made it clear that he felt it would be a tragedy if Shanghai fell to the Japanese. That being said, he did not want to provoke a war and felt that the US commander on the ground, commander in chief of the Pacific Fleet Adm. Harry Yarnell, an old classmate, should be allowed a great deal of latitude in control of his forces. Roosevelt clearly valued Leahy's counsel: when the cabinet meeting ended, he had the admiral and Hull stay behind to discuss US policy in more detail.[31]

By the end of August, the State Department was floundering on an appeal from Admiral Yarnell for four additional cruisers to help evacuate the large number of American citizens caught in the Shanghai crossfire. Leahy supported Yarnell's request and counseled Secretary Hull on the issue throughout late August. Still, Hull remained paralyzed by indecision. It was eventually decided that Leahy should make a special trip to Hyde Park, where Roosevelt was vacationing, to discuss the issue privately with the president. Thus, at fifty-five minutes after midnight on September 1, Leahy boarded a train bound for New York

City, where he switched to a local rail line heading north, along the Hudson River.[32] In doing so, he left modern America behind, speeding through a pastoral land toward the small town of Hyde Park, New York.

Hyde Park, of course, was the site of Franklin Roosevelt's family home. It was where his father, in 1866, had bought a large parcel of land and a house named Springwood. The house stood on a bluff along the east bank of the Hudson River, where the land stretched up a series of hillsides. Surrounded by green forests and immersed in family lore, Roosevelt could relax there more than almost anywhere else in the world. Springwood was a rambling neocolonial mansion with all the rooms a Gilded Age gentleman and his family could ask for. During his stint as assistant secretary of the navy, he began to have the house enlarged. Yet though he considered Springwood his home, it remained his mother's residence, and he cast his eyes to other parts of the estate for structures of his own. By the time of Leahy's visit, Roosevelt was planning a one-story, wheelchair-friendly home that he intended to use as his private retreat once he retired from the presidency. He named the future house Top Cottage. His wife, Eleanor, was planning her own house on another parcel of Roosevelt land quite far from Top Cottage. All this was made possible because Franklin had busily acquired more and more property over his career.

Having first visited in 1916, Leahy knew Hyde Park well. When he arrived at Springwood a few minutes after ten in the morning, the estate was still blanketed in the intense heat of late summer. He found the president in a relaxed mood, his shirtsleeves rolled up, surrounded by papers as he worked in a small, dark study to escape the muggy weather. Roosevelt was well briefed on the crisis in Shanghai and had made his decision. No new American warships would be sent to China. Yarnell would be allowed to charter merchant vessels, if he could find some, to evacuate Americans, but the risk of losing naval vessels was too high to send them into such dangerous waters. There was also the political problem of offending American isolationist sentiment. A large part of the American population was seething at the prospect of involvement in the deteriorating international situation in Europe and Asia. To appease them, Roosevelt and Leahy discussed the possibility of issuing a general neutrality proclamation.

Leahy, as always, accepted the president's decision even when he disagreed. Immediately upon his return to Washington, he telegraphed Yarnell that no additional cruisers would be sent at this time. There would never be any criticism, backbiting, or dirty dealing by William Leahy. So, by the late summer of 1937, Leahy was entrenched as the most powerful CNO in US history. He had the trust and friendship of the president, with arguably more access to the Oval Office than any other military officer previously. His ease of interaction with the president had grown steadily since January, to the point that Leahy and Roosevelt started exchanging joking letters with each other. In August, Leahy sent the president a faux apology for underestimating the size of the Soochow Creek in Shanghai.[33] He was invited to personal events, such as Roosevelt's birthday party, and the president's trust grew so strong that he asked the admiral to stand in for him during official events, including delivering a speech in FDR's stead at the Mayo Clinic in Minnesota.

Leahy understood his support in the White House and could come across to others as self-confident, secure, and more than a little cocky. Someone who was unimpressed with Leahy's growing authority was Charles Edison, who felt increasingly impotent in Leahy's presence. "Edison was constantly annoyed by the presence of Admiral Leahy," recalled Comm. Robert Bostwick Carney, who would later become an admiral and CNO in his own right. "I remember one day he told me to do something and I said, 'Well I talked to Admiral Leahy about that the other day.' He said, 'Leahy, Leahy, Leahy—God Damn it all I ever hear is Leahy and I'm getting tired of it!' Which had no effect on Admiral Leahy whatsoever."[34]

Interestingly Leahy, who had accumulated so much authority, was more than happy to allow the bureau system to function as it had been and, unlike Standley, never tried to turn the CNO into an overall naval commander in chief.[35] His press officer for much of this time, Bernard Austin, found Leahy refreshingly non-domineering and nondogmatic.[36]

Not long after becoming his press officer, Austin was ordered by Leahy to discover the source of a leak in the navy. Someone had passed to the press the complete details of a confidential naval building program, and Leahy wanted to find the culprit. Austin learned it was someone quite senior in the navy, the judge advocate general, Adm. Walter Woodson. Woodson confessed to Austin, who thereupon returned to Leahy.

> I said "Admiral, I know who gave out the information which appeared in the POST on the navy's legislative program for next year. Admiral, he will never do such an indiscreet thing again. I have been given this assurance by him. I don't think you want me to tell you the name of the person involved."
>
> Admiral Leahy was a wonderful man to work for. He looked at me for a few minutes. He said "Are you certain that he will remember this and that he's had his lesson?" I said "Yes, sir, I think I'm certain enough to assure you that it won't happen in that particular office again." He said, "All right, don't tell me."[37]

Later, Austin would be even more impressed with Leahy's self-assurance. It happened because Austin, innocently in his mind, supplied to the United Press a series of speeches by a serving naval officer and said that they could quote from them in any way they saw fit. It resulted in an article entitled "Admiral Predicts War," which caused a real stir. Austin went to Leahy to apologize for the faux pas and instead found the admiral to be philosophical about the situation, even willing to see the positives. At the least, Leahy thought, it might open some people's minds to the threat of Nazi Germany.

Leahy had judged his situation correctly and could afford to be confident.

CHAPTER 8

Leahy's Navy

The Japanese invasion of China represented an important watershed in William Leahy's strategic and ethical outlook. A consistent noninterventionist, he had long argued that the United States should take no aggressive action that might ensnare the country in a war outside of the Western Hemisphere. Yet the possible subjugation of China led him for the first time to press for steps that could result in war. China had mattered to him, both strategically and emotionally, since his first experience there in 1900. Unlike many of his contemporaries, he believed the country would eventually emerge from its period of chaos and uncertainty to become a great force on the world stage, and he was convinced that the United States had an important role to play, to prevent other powers from taking advantage of China's present weak state by attempting to colonize it. He therefore saw Japan's move as in many ways more threatening to the United States than anything happening in Europe.

A few weeks after Leahy's trip to Hyde Park, the Japanese announced that they would commence the bombing of Nanjing, which was serving as the Chinese capital. Japan warned all neutrals to withdraw their civilian populations. Leahy was appalled, for reasons both ethical and national, and contemplated military action.

This threat by Japan to conduct a bombing raid against the civil population of China is another evidence, and a conclusive one, that the old accepted rules of warfare are no longer in effect. It establishes another precedent that will be seriously destructive of the rights and privileges of neutrals and combatants. Compliance of the American Government with the demands of Japan in her undeclared war of aggression against China will almost certainly lose for Americans much of the high regard in which they have heretofore been held by the Chinese. . . . Some day Japan must be called to account for its abuse of power in this instance.[1]

For Leahy, someday came sooner than expected. On December 12, 1937, while attending a dinner party thrown by Secretary of War Henry Woodring, Leahy was telephoned with news that a small American gunship, USS *Panay*, patrolling on China's Yangtze River, had been attacked by Japanese aircraft.[2] In the coming hours he learned that not only had the gunboat been sunk and some accompanying American tankers hit, but also a number of crewmen had died and many more had been injured. The reasons for the attack are still debated, but for Leahy the significance was crystal clear.[3] Now was the time to stand up to the Japanese and help China.

Once the dinner party ended, Leahy went to meet with Cordell Hull to discuss American policy in light of the attack. At 11:30 p.m. he arrived at the secretary of state's apartment in the Carlton Hotel. There Leahy, Hull, and two other senior State Department officials tried, without success, to craft a response. The meeting meandered on until 1 a.m., with Hull seemingly more concerned that he receive no blame for the incident than in articulating a coherent plan. All that was agreed was that Leahy had to take the superfluous step of messaging the fleet to request more information.

Hull's behavior helped crystallize Leahy's doubts about the secretary of state. A longtime Tennessee representative and then senator with a distinctive lisp and a vocabulary shaped by his Appalachian roots, Hull had strong influence over many Southern Democrats.[4] Yet for such a successful domestic politician, Hull was oddly passive, one could even say weak, when it came to foreign policy.[5] He could neither express his notions well nor build a bloc to support what ideas he had. The president usually allowed Hull to act important by indulging him with the style of foreign policy–making—speaking with foreign diplomats and traveling overseas, presiding at unimportant but well-covered international events, and giving interviews—while keeping the substance of power for himself. Leahy found Hull's vacillating annoying and believed that the secretary was obsessed with his own image.

December 13, if anything, made matters worse. The day started well enough, with a visit to Leahy from the Japanese naval attaché. In a sign of just how panicked the Japanese government was about the attack, he was offered unreserved apologies.[6] This did little to mollify the admiral. Later that day he met again with Hull and was further frustrated by the secretary's continuing paralysis. "Personal contact with the Department of State is convincing [me] that everything which can be done by the English language to protect Americans has already been done," wrote Leahy. "It is, in my opinion, time now to get the Fleet ready for sea, to make an agreement with the British Navy for joint action, and to inform the Japanese that we expect to protect our nationals."[7] Leahy's outlook was so hard-line that Hugh Wilson, the assistant secretary of state, became worked up to the point that he developed a migraine, and Hull was forced to personally prepare a cold pack to provide him some relief.[8]

The next day, Leahy and Roosevelt had their first private conversation about the *Panay* attack.[9] Leahy argued that the navy should be made ready for action. He wanted all warships to be sent to port to have their hulls cleaned, their fuel tanks filled, and their stores packed with provisions. The president was more circumspect. Politically cautious, Roosevelt was unwilling to take any step that might end up in a shooting war, and while he strongly condemned the Japanese attack, he wanted to negotiate a settlement. Eventually the Japanese government, searching for a way out of the crisis, paid the American government $2 million in blood-money compensation, and that ended the whole affair.

If Leahy's aggression did not win out in this instance, the *Panay* crisis did drive home an important point to him and the president. A war involving the United States was now far more likely than it had seemed only six months earlier. Even before the crisis, the two men had dwelled on serious questions about the present and future strength of the US Navy. On November 26, Roosevelt had called Leahy to the White House, and the two settled into the president's office for an hour-long chat covering the increasingly uncertain world situation and the balance of global naval power. America's best course, they decided, was to press ahead with the construction of four large battleships.[10] It was the start of the process that determined the shape of the US Navy in late 1941 and early 1942, and therefore what the United States could or could not do once the Japanese attacked at Pearl Harbor.

In making their choices Roosevelt and Leahy were given greater flexibility than any US president and CNO in the interwar period. For the first time since 1920, the United States had complete freedom of choice about what to build. The naval arms-control process, which had dominated interwar fleet construction since the Washington Conference, had come to a shuddering halt in 1936. At the Second London Conference, the Japanese delegation had made a pitch for naval parity between itself, the United States, and the United Kingdom.[11] When the Americans and British refused, Japan withdrew from the arms-control agreements. All bets were now off.

Starting with their November 1937 conversation through the end of June 1938, Leahy and Roosevelt decided on a new naval building plan and then laid the groundwork for congressional approval. The plan they devised reveals a lot about their strategic beliefs. When it came to naval construction, they favored an orthodox, balanced force. This meant continuing with the present American fleet structure, only building bigger, faster, and more heavily armed vessels. In other words, the United States would continue to prioritize the battleship over the aircraft carrier. Leahy and Roosevelt were so entwined when it came to battleship building that they had only one significant difference of opinion between 1937 and 1938. Roosevelt wanted to limit all new battleships to 14-inch guns to save money and preempt any new naval race in gun size.[12] Leahy pressed for 16-inch guns, and in the end the president gave way. This was an important victory, as the war would show.

The firepower of 16-inch guns was significantly greater than their 14-inch counterparts, and they provided important benefits in both ship-to-ship combat and in supporting US landing forces in the Pacific. Leahy did not know it at the time, but the Japanese were secretly preparing to build battleships armed with guns of more than 18 inches.

Leahy's continued focus on battleship construction only reinforced his reputation as the preeminent member of the US Navy's "Gun Club," leading to criticism that he failed to realize that the battleship was about to be replaced by the aircraft carrier as the defining weapon of sea power.[13] There is a certain truth in this. Leahy, like his Japanese, German, and British counterparts, never wavered from his basic position that his nation must maintain battleship dominance. When in the wake of the *Panay* crisis the president suggested extra aircraft carriers be added to the US building program, Leahy, who believed that the United States was already the world's leader in this category, demurred.[14] The president accepted Leahy's judgment.

In January they brought Congress into the discussions, a sign of how assertive the president now was about naval policy. Whereas Roosevelt had in the past often let Carl Vinson be the driving factor in deciding what would be built, now the president pushed on Congress the plan that he and Leahy had developed. On January 5, 1938, Roosevelt sat down with Leahy, Assistant Secretary Edison, and Vinson to discuss naval needs.[15] The president proposed a flat 20 percent increase in all vessel categories above the naval arms-control limits.[16] The next day, Leahy met alone with Vinson to craft a strategy to gain congressional approval.[17] Leahy soon returned to the White House to meet with Roosevelt and Claude Swanson, who was temporarily back in the office, to further refine the 20 percent plan.[18] Finally, on January 29, Leahy met for more than two hours with the president, discussing naval building and the possibility of a naval war.[19] It capped an extraordinary month of close cooperation between the two men. Harold Ickes, who watched it unfold from his place in the cabinet, was once again impressed. Roosevelt informed his cabinet that he was going to press ahead with a huge peacetime American naval expansion and prepared a public statement to that effect. He held off on releasing the statement, according to Ickes, because Leahy told the president that the time was not right.[20]

In February 1938, Leahy and Vinson reprised their double act and worked together to shepherd the plan through Congress. Over a period of months, they proved to be a political juggernaut. Testifying before congressional committees, Leahy often spoke lines he had scripted ahead of time with Vinson, and the two huddled in the admiral's office to select which shipyards should build which ships.[21] As time was running out before Congress's June adjournment, Leahy made a personal call on the Speaker of the House, William Bankhead of Alabama, to make sure that the Speaker called on Vinson first the following day during one of the House's last sessions.[22] Coordinating action and employing all the levers of power at their disposal, they pushed through a number of different naval appropriations bills, as well as other naval measures.

They were historically successful. In May, Congress approved the entire building plan in what has come to be known as the Second Vinson Act (HR 9218). The measure included Roosevelt and Leahy's flat 20 percent building increase. Among the vessels slated for construction were four battleships with 16-inch guns, which were to be some of the most famous US warships of all time, the *Iowa* class.* In addition, more than 60,000 tons of new cruisers and 30,000 tons of new destroyers were also approved, vessels that would prove crucial to the US Navy in the months after Pearl Harbor. Yet the Second Vinson Act was but one of many major pieces of naval legislation the two helped pass. The number of naval personnel was increased significantly, so that the navy and Marine Corps combined were now more than 125,000. In moves that would pay great dividends to the carrier wars in the Pacific a few years later, the *Saratoga* and *Lexington* were modernized and a great deal of money was spent on improving US base facilities and building support ships, such as another fast tanker.[23]

Leahy and Roosevelt's focus on the battleship continued even after all these legislative successes. In July 1938, when the navy began

---

* In the end only three of the *Iowa*-class battleships were ever built: *Iowa*, *Wisconsin*, and *Missouri*.

putting together a proposed ten-year building plan, it was decided to ask for fourteen new battleships and five aircraft carriers.[24] This was the genesis of what would result in the "Two-Ocean" naval bill of 1940. Regardless of Leahy's continuing love for the battleship, he was determined that the United States have the best carrier force in the world. He always operated on the assumption that the United States did and would continue to possess the world's most powerful naval air force. During Leahy's time as CNO, the navy made significant strides in the development of its aviation abilities. The range and striking power of US aircraft carriers markedly increased.[25] Large mobile dry docks were also built, thanks to Leahy.[26] The admiral's greatest role in transforming the navy into a force that could project airpower across the Pacific might have been the emphasis he placed on fast fleet tankers. Working closely with Democratic senator Josiah Bailey and Rep. S. Otis Bland, Leahy helped gain approval for the construction of twenty-four high-speed tankers for the fleet.[27] Adm. Emory Land, who ran the Bureau of Construction and Repair from 1932 until 1937, and would run the Maritime Commission (which oversaw the construction of merchant vessels) during the war, believed that, without Leahy's push, these ships would never have been built. Having access to these mobile dry docks and fast tankers meant that the navy could develop its fleet train concept earlier than any other power, allowing it to project aircraft carrier strength far into the Pacific for what would have seemed extraordinarily long periods of time by the perspective of the 1930s.* Leahy's dogged determination and political prowess made sure that the navy was able to fight effectively in the Pacific war.

Leahy's understanding of the importance of air superiority for the application of sea power had been revealed during the *Panay* crisis, in a way that foreshadowed many of his strategic plans during World War II. But perhaps most telling was his support of a distant blockade against Japan. Though he had called for action, he believed that the best way to fight was not by charging across the Pacific to engage the

---

* The fleet train was a large force of merchant vessels devoted to the constant resupply of naval task forces at sea. It was what allowed the US Navy to operate for such long periods so far away from their main bases in the Pacific during the war.

Japanese but by obstructing Japan's access to world markets. "Send the Japanese a strong note, demanding not only their apologies and indemnities but also their withdrawal from Manchuria," he told his old friend Constantine Brown. "If they refuse these demands, we should blockade the Japanese trade routes by placing destroyers at the entrance to the Indian Ocean."[28] Leahy knew that the United States could not yet guarantee air supremacy in the western Pacific. Without air control, he did not want the navy to take the unnecessary risk of search of the Japanese Fleet at the opening of hostilities.[29] He first wanted to sever Japanese trading lines to such vital raw materials as oil and various metallic ores. "We should assign two destroyer divisions to intercept Japanese shipping to South America," he said to Brown. "We can do this successfully now because it will take the Japanese Navy three to four years to complete its building program."[30] Having stepped on Japan's economic windpipe, Leahy believed that American naval power could bring the enemy to heel without risking a major engagement; at the very least, the navy could force the Japanese to fight on American terms. It was part of his growing understanding of the coming air-sea war, which he made explicit during one of his congressional testimonies. In front of the Senate Naval Affairs Committee, during his advocacy of the Second Vinson Act, Leahy was asked by the committee chair what he wanted out of any naval buildup. Leahy was unequivocal that controlling movement was essential, and that the United States needed to be able to impose a blockade and at the same time not allow another power to control the movement of American goods and supplies.[31]

His faith in the supremacy of air-sea war was reinforced during the internal American struggle over the future of the US base on Guam. This famous island in the Mariana chain was the focus of a great deal of political debate during Leahy's time as CNO.[32] The closest major American-controlled island to Japan, Guam was a vital strategic location. Yet Leahy argued that developing a large naval base there was pointless unless a large air component, including airstrips, hangars, and repair facilities, was included. Without the ability to launch significant airpower from the island, Leahy believed that it would be far too risky for the United States to deploy the Pacific Fleet to Guam.

The fight over approving the funds needed to build up Guam started in late 1938 and extended into early 1939. Leahy was so worked up that he asked for a private meeting with FDR in January 1939 to press his case for an integrated air-sea facility.[33] Though he was able to get the president's backing, in this one case Congress demurred under the strength of isolationist sentiment and the desire not to spend such sums. The legislature would support the building of certain naval facilities but opposed a large air-support plan. Deciding that developing a smaller facility on the island would be pointless, Leahy pulled the plug.[34] Though this move was criticized at the time, in light of what we now know about World War II, Leahy's instincts were proven correct. It was impossible to defend any Pacific island without air control, as the course of the war demonstrated.

The fight over Guam represented the only setback that Leahy and Roosevelt experienced when it came to preparing the US Navy for the coming war in the way that they most wanted. Indeed, their work together over the previous year and a half had further reinforced their friendship. Their interactions grew more relaxed, even when they had different perspectives on a particular question, and their correspondence more informal and friendly. One of the most illuminating of these gentlemanly disagreements was in an area that became increasingly important as the world crept ever closer to war: the exchange of intelligence. With access to reports from US naval attachés deployed around the globe, Leahy controlled a great deal of America's secret intelligence, and he forwarded reports to the president that he felt were worthy of concern. Roosevelt, by contrast, often sent the admiral intelligence reports he had received that appeared dubious at best.

Roosevelt favored stories of cloak-and-dagger activities on the part of devious foes. In August 1937, as the Japanese were plunging ever deeper into China, the president passed to Leahy a report that Japanese crab-fishing boats were appearing off the coast of Alaska in suspiciously large numbers.[35] These sneaky Japanese fishermen, Roosevelt believed, might very well be scouting for invasion sites in case of war. Leahy, dismissive of alarmist reports and conspiracy theories, tried to calm the president's nerves about the crab fishermen instead of feeding his suspicions. He promised he would send the navy to investigate but told

Roosevelt, politely, to relax: "The specific fishing activity referred to . . . are carried on north of the Alaskan Peninsula and in an area that would not be of much use in war except for such airbase activities as might be permitted by the arctic weather conditions."[36] The rational application of airpower mattered far more to the admiral than any tales of derring-do.

Leahy, in comparison, would usually send Roosevelt either data-driven analyses or larger geopolitical reports. A few weeks after Roosevelt got worked up over the crab fishermen, Leahy passed to the president intelligence that Japan and Russia had significantly increased their stockpiles of oil.[37] In October 1937, he sent Roosevelt a detailed report he had received from a US naval officer in China about the different domestic pressures being placed on Chiang Kai-shek's Nationalist government and how these pressures might lead to a Chinese collapse in the war against Japan.[38]

Leahy was not one-sided in the intelligence he passed along. He sent Roosevelt different reports that he thought were relevant, regardless of their implications. In early 1938, Leahy sent Roosevelt intelligence gathered from the US naval attaché in Fascist Italy. The attaché had sources in the Italian Navy, who had recently met with members of the Japanese Navy. Far from painting the Japanese Navy as a threat, these Italian sources claimed (falsely, as it turned out) that Japan would not try to build battleships with 18-inch guns.[39] The entire thrust of the report was to minimize the idea that Japan was planning on entering a naval race with the United States. There was no sign that the report was a deliberate distortion by the Italians, and Leahy did not try to undermine its credibility to the president.

Another area where Leahy and Roosevelt differed was on the possibility of war in Europe. Focused on the threat posed by Japan, Leahy took longer than the president to become truly worried about Nazi Germany. When the Nazis first rose to power in 1933, Leahy was skeptical of their intentions but spent little time considering their impact. Germany's navy was so small that it hardly concerned a man obsessed with sea power and naval threats to the United States. He rarely discussed the Nazis or Hitler. He did mention once some severe criticism of Hitler's anti-Semitic policy and looked on the German dictator as a typical thuggish nationalist who was trying to rebuild Germany—in a brutal manner, at the expense of other nations.[40]

Not until 1935 did his worries about the Nazis start to grow. In March of that year Hitler repudiated the conscription clauses of the Versailles Treaty, which meant that Germany intended to build up their armed forces in any way it saw fit. Though Leahy deemed the development "alarming," he remained committed to keeping the United States out of any European crisis.[41] The United Kingdom, France, and the Soviet Union together, he believed, should be able to keep Hitler in check. He held on to this detached view until 1938. While he was working to secure the passage of all that naval legislation in the spring of that year, the Nazis seized and incorporated Austria into the Third Reich. This was another direct contravention of the Versailles Treaty and represented the first serious expansion of German power. Leahy lamented the disappearance of the Austrian state but showed no interest in having the United States do anything about it.[42] In Leahy's mind that was something that Britain and France could object to if they wanted.

In September 1938, Hitler made his infamous move on Czechoslovakia by demanding the transfer of the German-populated Sudetenland from the Czechs to the Reich. In what is often seen as the high point of the policy of "Appeasement," British prime minister Neville Chamberlain and his French counterpart, Édouard Daladier, agreed during the Munich Conference with Hitler and Mussolini to hand the Sudetenland to the Nazis. Leahy's reaction was highly critical, though more than a little tinged with hypocrisy. He complained that the British and French were cravenly surrendering to Hitler's dangerous demands and in the process threatening to overturn the European balance of power. For the first time he seemed worried that Germany might dominate the Continent. His rhetoric about the Nazi state hardened markedly. Now the Germans were a "bandit" state.[43] However, he still hesitated to have the United States stand shoulder to shoulder with Britain and France. A few months after the crisis had passed, Leahy applauded an address given by his friend and committed isolationist Sen. David Walsh that called for America to stay out of European affairs.[44]

Interestingly, Leahy's reaction to the Munich crisis did reveal that he remained reluctant to send warships into areas where air control could not be guaranteed. On September 17, 1938, Leahy made a special visit to the White House to discuss with Roosevelt what the United States should do in case Britain and France went to war with Germany. They also discussed sending American warships to European waters to help evacuate American citizens and treasure (specifically gold). Leahy opposed sending battleships, as air supremacy could not be guaranteed, instead suggesting cruisers with the best possible antiaircraft defenses.[45] Roosevelt also wanted to send only cruisers, though smaller ones than those Leahy favored.

While Leahy was worried about war with Nazi Germany relatively late in the day, he seemed even less concerned with the Soviet Union. The Soviet Navy was far weaker than even the German Fleet, and it made little or no impression on Leahy, even when he continued to doubt whether capitalism and communism would ever coexist peacefully. In July 1938, Leahy was invited to a dinner at the Soviet embassy to celebrate Howard Hughes's round-the-world flight, which had included a Russian stopover. Guests were shown a Soviet film of a huge military parade in Moscow. Leahy watched as thousands of well-drilled soldiers marched by Stalin, impressed at their military bearing. He remarked that all those soldiers were in service to "a government that completely disagrees with our ideals" and an ideology that was "an impressive menace to the continued existence of Democratic Governments."[46] Yet he hardly seemed worried about the military capabilities of the Soviet Union.

By the end of 1938, Leahy had stamped his authority on the US Navy and the Roosevelt administration—and his naval career had stamped him with certain strategic ideas. From the time he served as the head of the Bureau of Ordnance through his time as CNO, he had wielded more power over deciding not only what types of vessels the United States would build but how each class should be configured. American battleships, cruisers, destroyers, and even aircraft carriers were all shaped by his preferences. Further, he had crafted much of the fleet's personnel policy, a particularly important development, as the fleet was expanding rapidly in the late 1930s.

The US Navy was more Bill Leahy's navy than that of any other officer of his generation. Strategically, he had refined his ideas in surprising ways to take into account the growth of air-sea power. He had developed a strong faith in the economic power of sea control, believing that the United States should first and foremost be able to cut off any potential enemy from world trade. As such, he saw no need for his nation to wage risky campaigns or fight grand battles it was not certain to win. He saw war as a methodical business, wanted to keep American casualties to as minimal a level as possible, and believed that even distant blockade resource control should form the foundation of American strategy until the United States had built up such an overwhelming force that it could guarantee victory. It meant that when the war did break out, America would have to fight Bill Leahy's war.

CHAPTER 9

The First Retirement

On May 6, 1939, Bill Leahy arrived home after another long day at the Navy Department and was surprised by a party.[1] For his sixty-fourth birthday, Louise had gathered all the officers she could find who had served under his command to help him mark this milestone. It was more than just a birthday—Leahy had reached the navy's mandatory retirement age. Though neither he nor President Roosevelt had any desire for him to stop being chief of naval operations, nothing could be done to sidestep the rule. In three months, he would have to step down and leave the fleet.

Retirement held no appeal for Leahy. Still physically robust and mentally alert, he was confident in his own skin, seemingly over the doubts and insecurities that had plagued him during the early years of the Great Depression. After two years as CNO, he had a firm handle on all facets of the job and had shown himself to be a superb and politically sophisticated administrator. What's more, he had become the public face of the US Navy. He had first stepped into the national spotlight in 1937 when famed pilot Amelia Earhart, along with her copilot, went missing over the central Pacific. Leahy placed the navy on alert, dispatching the aircraft carrier *Lexington* to assist in the search. For weeks he was widely quoted in newspapers across the nation as expectant Americans waited impatiently for the latest updates. The media exposure taught Leahy how to shape news stories in such a way as to reflect positively on the navy and the Roosevelt administration, a skill that would prove useful in his role as the president's chief of staff.

Leahy's fame grew as he worked with Congress to secure passage for naval appropriations and other fleet legislation. Moviegoers began to recognize him from newsreels: the long-faced admiral speaking slowly and carefully about naval preparedness in a low, rather dull voice. He hardly cut a dashing figure, but he carried himself with an air of gravitas and a no-nonsense demeanor that left an impression on audiences. On Navy Day in 1938, in an event broadcast on NBC radio throughout the country, Leahy gave a speech before a crowd at Radio City Music Hall in New York City, addressing the power and readiness of the US Navy.[2]

As Leahy honed his media abilities, he was also sharpening his political skills. The fight over the future of Tongue Point continued to rumble on even as Leahy stood fast against wasting money building up the facility.[3] In December 1938, Oregon Republican Charles McNary, the Senate minority leader, dropped by Leahy's office and made an unveiled threat to cut the naval budget if Tongue Point was not funded. Leahy was irritated, but he knew when a fight was lost.[4] When a congressional report recommended an enlarged naval facility at Tongue Point, Leahy gave in gracefully, even testifying in favor of funding.[5] McNary soon returned to Leahy's office, acting as if the two men were the best of friends.[6] Leahy diplomatically held his tongue, though he could not have been impressed with the senator's behavior.

Leahy's distasteful interaction with McNary indicated a change in his political outlook. Though he clung to the idea that he was politically independent, happy to work with Republicans and Democrats alike, he was, unconsciously or not, beginning to identify with the latter. Schmoozing with the Washington establishment as CNO, he had in fact become a member of that establishment, which was overwhelmingly Democratic. He dined with Roosevelt officials like Cordell Hull and Sumner Welles, as well as sympathetic newsmen such as Walter Lippmann. He was friendly with a range of Democratic politicians and frequented parties alongside DC's powerbrokers. As a man who had the president's ear, he was courted by officials who needed the administration's support for efforts normally removed from the CNO's remit.[7]

Indeed, Leahy was at home in Washington. He and Louise were slowly recovering from the loss of their life savings and even indulged occasionally, such as when they purchased a new Buick Roadmaster. They needed it, as their family was growing. A second grandchild, Robert Beale Leahy, was born in 1936, and the admiral continued to dote shamelessly on his granddaughter, Louisita. Leahy's modest public celebrity extended to his wife: Louise launched ships, attended state dinners and receptions, and hosted foreign diplomats. She was an enthusiastic patron of the Naval Relief Society and the Red Cross.[8] In 1939 she was even named to the advisory committee of the New York World's Fair.

Having reached the top of his profession, Leahy found himself once again revisiting his past. In 1938, he returned to Wisconsin during a tour of naval facilities on the Great Lakes. In his boyhood hometown of Ashland, he addressed an American Legion convention and looked up all the old friends he could find. Receiving an honor he would cherish for the rest of his life, he was inducted as an honorary member of the local Bad River Chippewa tribe. An eagle headdress was placed atop his head while four "medicine" men with tom-toms and twenty "braves and squaws" performed a ceremonial dance of welcome. He was presented with a pair of beaded moccasins, a peace pipe, and two birchwood food plates and given the tribal name "Kitchi-Be-Ba-Mash," which meant "Great Man Sailing Around."[9]

Leahy's sense of satisfaction never spilled over into self-aggrandizement, or, crucially, a desire to make himself into too prominent a personality. Serving the president was his highest priority, and this is what led Franklin Roosevelt in 1939 to decide that Leahy would be the man who would help him win the next world war. The old sailor was on the path to becoming the second most powerful man in the world.

Leahy had become one of the few people with whom Roosevelt felt he could escape the pressures of office. In February the president decided to observe the navy's fleet exercises in the Caribbean. Recognizing an opportunity to relax and flee the dreariness of a Washington winter, he invited his CNO to join his entourage aboard the USS *Houston*. Leahy was given the cabin next to the president's. For two weeks the party cruised at leisure, visiting Cuba, Haiti, the Dominican Republic, and a number of smaller ports. Roosevelt and Leahy fished and chatted under a tropical sun, becoming so sunburnt they had to be covered in Noxzema. Over cocktails and cigarettes, the admiral bonded with the men who made up Roosevelt's inner circle, including aides Edwin "Pa" Watson and Capt. Daniel Callaghan, and Roosevelt's personal physician, Dr. Ross McIntire.

When the *Houston* finally joined the rest of the fleet for maneuvers, Roosevelt and Leahy watched as the ships steamed in various antiaircraft formations and conducted a classic battle-line engagement. One exercise that captivated the president was when the US fleet was divided into two parts. The larger force, acting as an unnamed European aggressor, attempted to seize a Caribbean naval base to establish a forward facility in the Western Hemisphere. The smaller force, representing the limited naval power the US could deploy in the area if most American ships were in the Pacific, tried to thwart them.[10] As they looked on, Roosevelt stunned his friend by telling him that there was a strong likelihood that Leahy, upon retirement, would be named the next American governor of Puerto Rico.[11] He wanted Leahy to help make the Caribbean more secure for American interests.

Not long after Roosevelt and Leahy returned from the Caribbean an event occurred that set the stage for the outbreak of World War II in Europe. On March 15, 1939, Adolf Hitler ordered the German Army to seize what remained of independent Czechoslovakia.* This was an open repudiation of everything the Nazi dictator had agreed to during the Munich Crisis of the previous October, and it destroyed the foundations of the appeasement policy that Britain and France had followed to that time. It was now clear that Hitler wanted more than just a large national German state. He was set on seizing new lands and oppressing other peoples. When almost immediately afterward Hitler made his next move and started agitating for control over German-populated areas of Poland, the British and French governments decided to take a much tougher line. Poland would not be sacrificed like Czechoslovakia.

---

* The Czech portion of Czechoslovakia was taken over by the Germans, while the Slovak part was allowed to form an independent Slovak state, which became a close Nazi ally.

Though neither Roosevelt nor Leahy were in favor of America jumping into any European conflict, and Leahy judged that the seizure of Czechoslovakia itself would not be enough to trigger a war, they both understood that if one did break out, the United States might be pulled into the fight. Leahy's rhetoric about the Nazi state became noticeably harsher, even in his usually dispassionate diary.[12] He also took a particularly trenchant line during cabinet meetings, much to the president's delight. During the meeting on March 16, Roosevelt asked Leahy what he would do if the navy were ordered to seize the German liner *Europa* and that ship refused to surrender. Leahy replied without hesitation, "I'd sink her."[13] Roosevelt, pleased, told Harold Ickes a few hours later of his plan to send Leahy to Puerto Rico.

By early April the European situation had deteriorated further. The Polish government said that it would fight any attempt by the Nazis to seize their territory, while Hitler's Italian ally, Benito Mussolini, invaded the small independent state of Albania, which lay across the Adriatic. With the sense of crisis growing, Leahy met with Roosevelt on April 11 to work out American policy. Cordell Hull was with them at first, but after the secretary of state left, the president turned to the admiral and said that if war did break out, Leahy would be recalled to the White House to serve the president as "an aide and an advisor."[14] The threat of war had concentrated Roosevelt's mind and, faced with great peril, he had concluded that Leahy was the one person in the US government whom he wanted by his side. It was this foundation of a special role in Roosevelt's life that would make Leahy the second most powerful man in the world during World War II.

For the next few months, it almost seemed like the president was preparing Leahy for his future post. Leahy became one of the first informed when Roosevelt made important foreign-policy decisions. For instance, on April 14, FDR told Leahy, along with Cordell Hull, that he was about to issue his soon-to-be-famous, and somewhat derided, statement to Hitler and Mussolini, asking the dictators to state publicly that they had no more territorial ambitions.[15] In addition, he began tapping the admiral for jobs almost entirely removed from naval policy. In late April he asked Leahy to meet personally with Secretary of Labor Frances Perkins to discuss prospects for ending an ongoing coal strike and report back. Leahy took on these extra responsibilities while continuing his job running the navy.

Roosevelt was so pleased with the admiral's performance that when Claude Swanson died suddenly in early July, the president contemplated appointing Leahy as the new secretary of the navy.[16] In the end, he opted for a political appointment, Frank Knox, a Republican who could help gain bipartisan support for Roosevelt's foreign policy. Having Leahy in Puerto Rico meant that he would be close enough that he could be recalled quickly if needed. To make such a recall simpler, Roosevelt told Leahy to ask the chairs of the House and Senate Naval Affairs Committees (Leahy's friends Carl Vinson and David Walsh, respectively) to speed up a measure that made it possible for Leahy to be kept on the active navy list for an additional two years.[17]

Leahy's last few weeks in office were taken up with preparations and celebrations. Much of his time was spent getting ready to take over in Puerto Rico, a job that appeared more daunting by the day, and he continued to look after the fleet, with one of his last moves to further augment the navy's shore-based air arm.[18] Meanwhile, the great and good of Washington, including the incoming chief of staff of the army, Gen. George C. Marshall, came by Leahy's office to pay their respects. The navy threw a gala dinner in Leahy's honor, attended by three hundred officers. On July 28, the president threw a surprise party for the admiral, awarding him the first of his Distinguished Service Medals. Two days later Roosevelt had Leahy come by the White House for a private conversation, stressing once again that he wanted Leahy by his side if the United States went to war.

On August 1, Leahy formally left office and Adm. Harold Stark became the CNO. Deciding he needed to get out of Washington for a few days, he and Louise hopped in the Roadmaster for a trip through Pennsylvania and New York, stopping off to visit friends along the way. Laconic as usual, the final duty entry in his diary was: "This brings to an end forty six years of active service in the Navy of the United States."

The president was more emotional. In the formal letter he sent to Leahy announcing his retirement, Roosevelt included in his own handwriting: "I just HATE to see you leave."[19]

He meant every word. On August 30, as Leahy was about to board a ship for Puerto Rico, the war clouds had fully gathered over Europe. Nazi Germany was poised to invade Poland, and this time France and Britain were determined to fight. Roosevelt wanted one more strategic discussion with his friend and called Leahy in for a private, hour-long chat. They analyzed the coming war and what the US could or should do as a neutral power. Roosevelt once again told the admiral explicitly that he would be brought back to the White House if the country went to war. This time he was more specific, describing how he wanted Leahy to chair something similar to the Joint Chiefs of Staff. "He informed me that if the United States becomes seriously involved in the European difficulty, it will be necessary for him to recall me from Puerto Rico and assign me to membership on a Four-Man-War Board, with the duty of coordinating the work of the State, War and Navy Departments."[20]

Franklin Roosevelt was a man constantly surrounded by courtiers, flatterers, even potential rivals, all asking for favors or advantages. Often he would promise them positions or dazzle them with the possibility of future greatness. For Roosevelt, such offers were excuses, said to get himself out of sticky situations or to keep an ambitious person at bay. In the end, he typically left these courtiers disappointed or passed over. Leahy was different. Over the previous few months Roosevelt had gone to great lengths to prepare him to be his most important strategic wartime adviser. Leahy requested no favors, yet Roosevelt continually promised that a great position was on offer—and it would be Roosevelt who made sure that it happened.

With Bill Leahy, Franklin Roosevelt would always be true to his word.

CHAPTER 10

Governor of Puerto Rico

Puerto Rico was no sunshine-filled retirement job. Indeed, the island was at both a critical and a dangerous moment in its political development. The previous governor, Blanton Winship, had been a disaster. Behaving more like a party boss than an administrator of justice, Winship had antagonized much of the population, particularly the nationalists, by clamping down on political dissent and using the police in an aggressive, bloody manner to assert American rule. Under his heavy-handed leadership the police had killed a number of nationalists, while the nationalists had killed a number of government officials and tried, at least once, to assassinate Winship himself. Winship made common cause with the Coalición, a politically pro-American group that represented the island's entrenched economic elite, including the wealthy sugar interests.[1] He rewarded his favorites with hefty pay raises and lucrative contracts while doing little for the poor. Unwilling to ignore the corruption, Roosevelt and Interior Secretary Harold Ickes put intense pressure on Winship to resign.[2] Yet Winship and the Coalición resisted as long as possible before realizing that a change had to happen.[3]

Roosevelt had complete trust in Leahy. He thought the admiral was the right person for the job, maybe the only one he could trust to take on two ambitious tasks in Puerto Rico, one strategic and one economic/

social. Strategically, Leahy was sent to improve the military installations throughout the island, to turn Puerto Rico, in his own words, into an American Gibraltar.[4] Socially, Leahy was sent to alleviate the extreme poverty and inequality that beset the island. The reality of the appalling living conditions of the Puerto Rican poor and the disparity between them and the wealthy was apparent from the moment he arrived. Leahy found that "practically all of the wealth of the island" was owned by a small number of families who controlled sugar production and worked closely with American corporations.[5] In comparison to these wealthy few, Leahy saw that most Puerto Ricans lived in abject poverty (the only thing to which he could compare it was the condition of some African Americans in the poorest parts of the South), forced into either squalid urban slums or trying to eke out a precarious living on the worst agricultural land. Roosevelt told Leahy to do everything possible to change this economic imbalance and deprivation, and the admiral was determined to try.[6]

Leahy spent much of the spring and summer of 1939 learning as much as he could about his new job, enjoying the full support of Harold Ickes, who even handed over some of his authority to Leahy.[7] "Practically everyone who has come in contact with Admiral Leahy," Ickes wrote in his diary, "is greatly pleased with him and his attitude. I believe we have a good man in him."[8] Having such access to the president and the secretary of the interior meant that Leahy could go right to the top to get what he needed. Before he even departed Washington he had asked Roosevelt for an additional $10 million in funding for Puerto Rico. More than simply money, however, what made Leahy's governorship special was the amount of authority the president placed in his hands. Roosevelt made Leahy the most powerful appointed governor in Puerto Rican history. Crucially, Leahy was named head of the Puerto Rican office of the Works Progress Administration (WPA), making him the guardian of almost all of the New Deal's funding on the island. Soon his offices were expanded further.[9] In October 1939 he was made head of the Puerto Rico Cement Corporation to help the institution secure a $700,000 loan from the federal government's Reconstruction Finance Corporation.[10] In December, he was named the head of the Puerto

Rican branch of the corporation itself, taking the post from Ickes. For all intents and purposes, William Leahy was the US government in Puerto Rico. He had considerably more funding under his control than was available to the Puerto Rican government itself.[11]

Therefore, when on September 11 Leahy and Louise arrived on Puerto Rico, he had a chance to make a difference. One of his first meetings revealed how tricky the new assignment would be. The Puerto Rican legislature was dominated by Sen. Rafael Martínez Nadal, a leader of the Coalición. Nadal was viewed by himself and others as a classic "caudillo," a strongman who expected Leahy to behave like Winship by cutting deals to run affairs with the conservative and wealthy. Nadal learned quickly that Leahy would choose people for the positions under his control based on the wishes passed down to him by Franklin Roosevelt, not by those of the island's elite. This was an extremely important change. Controlling patronage was how different factions in Puerto Rican and American politics stayed in power. They could offer their supporters well-paid government posts or contracts in exchange for continuing support. By telling the Coalición that they could not simply appoint the people they wanted, Leahy was taking aim at one of their fundamental sources of power. His relationship with the Coalición quickly spiraled downward from unease to outright hostility.

Leahy was never going to permanently overturn Puerto Rico's political and economic culture in the fifteen months that he spent in office, but he did try to make a difference. He enthusiastically brought the New Deal to the island, devoting more than half of the WPA's efforts on non-military projects designed to transform Puerto Rico's infrastructure or public health. These included building or improving roads, bringing proper sanitation facilities to rural parts of the island, and working on different health initiatives such as the eradication of hookworm.[12] He used state power to regulate certain prices and production, such as in the coffee industry.[13] He was not shy in using his military contacts to bring in more work. With the United States spending a great deal of money widening the Panama Canal, Leahy pressed George Marshall to divert the project's ships passing back and forth from the United States to Panama to Puerto Rico if they needed supplies or work.[14]

Leahy was particularly successful in employing his political connections to get money for as many new jobs as possible. Much of the lobbying occurred during his trips back to Washington. In late December 1939, he met with Roosevelt three times and lobbied his friends in Congress, advocating for more money for the WPA and legislative changes to hiring laws that he hoped would improve Puerto Rico's unemployment problem. He quickly achieved more than any previous governor. President Roosevelt pledged an additional $100 million for an insular reconstruction authority (taking in Puerto Rico and the US Virgin Islands).[15] This and other support allowed Leahy to hire an additional twenty thousand workers for the WPA. In October 1940, he returned to Washington and once again had a long private meeting with the president, this time leaving with an even greater haul—a promise for an additional thirty thousand jobs for Puerto Rico.[16]

During these trips back to Washington, Leahy did his best to publicize the extent of poverty that existed in this protectorate of the United States. In December 1939, he tried to shame his countrymen by letting them know that half a million Puerto Ricans were living lives of deprivation, three hundred thousand of whom were in such poverty that they needed emergency relief.[17] He had to walk a fine line in doing this, because he was also Puerto Rico's most prominent booster within the United States, wanting to attract investment and favorable publicity to the island. Once, he let it be known that he had telegraphed Leopold Stokowski, the renowned music director of the Philadelphia Orchestra. The orchestra was set to make a tour of the Caribbean, and Leahy wanted to make sure that they came to Puerto Rico. "I understand that [Stokowski] is a pretty fair fiddler," Leahy told the press.[18] The world-famous conductor might not have been elated to hear himself described as such, but Puerto Rico was included in the tour.

As the president's man in San Juan, Leahy came to identify himself so closely with the role of a Roosevelt appointee that he crossed the nonexistent line between his career and politics, which he had always tried to pretend was in place. In the summer of 1940, with the US presidential election looming, Leahy met at least twice with R. C. Durham, a senior figure from the Democratic National Committee.[19]

Leahy advised Durham about how to best raise money for the party's campaign. Durham must have found the advice useful, because he spent more than a week in Puerto Rico collecting funds, making sure to pay his respects to Leahy before leaving. In October, Durham telephoned Leahy to discuss the state of the campaign, a rather unusual consultation, as Puerto Rico had no votes in the Electoral College.[20] There was no sign that the head of the Republican Party ever called him for advice. On November 6, the night of the presidential election, Leahy stayed up until 1:30 a.m., waiting to make sure Roosevelt had been reelected. He would not go to bed until the Republican candidate, Wendell Willkie, had formally conceded. Leahy was pleased to note that Roosevelt had won in a bigger landslide than many had expected.[21]

November 6 also saw an election on Puerto Rico for control of the island's bicameral legislature, the culmination of an important chapter of Leahy's governorship. It involved one of the great political figures in Puerto Rican history, Luis Muñoz Marín. A poet as well as a politician, Muñoz had founded the Popular Democratic Party in order to challenge the power of the Coalición. Strongly influenced by Socialist ideals and someone who had flirted with the idea of Puerto Rican independence, he worked to mobilize the support of the rural poor.[22] After only a few months of Leahy's governorship, Muñoz was calling him the "best governor" the United States had ever sent to the island.[23] During the election he also showed his confidence in Leahy's probity by turning to the governor regularly to make sure that the election was run honestly.[24]

Leahy repaid this mostly unknown faith by overseeing a fair 1940 election. Throughout his time in office, he had continued to appoint people from across the political spectrum to open positions and showed himself willing to veto bills that the Coalición had passed to benefit their supporters.[25] By the time of the campaign, the Coalición's relations with Leahy had grown hostile.[26] With the faction determined to do everything possible to ensure their continued supremacy, the Coalición-supporting press regularly lambasted Leahy as incompetent or meddlesome.[27]

As the vote neared, the contest came down to a three-way competition between the Coalición, the Tripartismo (a grouping of anti-Coalición forces partly identifying with the Roosevelt administration), and Muñoz's Popular Democratic Party—with the latter the most left-wing.[28] It was assumed that the Coalición would win, with the Tripartismo coming in second. As Election Day crept closer the situation grew more tense. Violence was in the air, and there were even rumors that an attempt would be made to assassinate Leahy. In October 1940, with the vote only weeks away, Leahy made another trip to Washington to consult with Roosevelt and Ickes. Leahy told the interior secretary that things could get messy. "Leahy thinks that there might be an attempt on his own life," Ickes recorded, "but he seems prepared for it and I don't believe that he would hesitate to shoot down anyone who might attack him."[29]

After Leahy's return to the island, Muñoz came by the governor's office on October 31, warning that the Coalición might use fraud to steal the vote. The next day, Leahy called all the leaders of the main political parties to a meeting and declared that this would be a clean election.[30] On polling day three people were killed and fifteen injured, and there were reports of missing ballot papers. However, when the dust settled the vote was judged to be relatively fraud-free, and the result was completely unexpected. The Popular Democrats and the Tripartismo together gained a significant majority over the Coalición, with Muñoz's party the larger of the two. Muñoz eventually became president of the Puerto Rican Senate, which began his march to the governorship. If pressed, Leahy would probably have preferred a Tripartismo victory, as they were most closely identified with the Roosevelt administration, yet he was more than happy to give Muñoz a chance.[31] The two men worked out an agreement covering the next two years, whereby Muñoz would promise not to bring up independence and the Roosevelt administration would support his efforts to bring change.[32]

This agreement highlights one of the most interesting questions of Leahy's governorship: How did an anti-imperialist and isolationist view his running the second largest colonial possession of the United States? As CNO, Leahy had happily supported the notion of independence for the United States' largest possession, the Philippines. When it came to

Puerto Rico, he was never particularly clear. He seemed content for the present political relationship to continue for a few reasons. First, the Puerto Rican people continued to give a large majority of their votes to parties that did not want independence. Second, during the time of his governorship he was thinking strategically. He viewed Puerto Rico as a vital cog to protect all of the Americas in case Nazi Germany conquered all of Europe. That was probably why he cut the deal with Muñoz to take independence off the table for at least the next two years.

Leahy was generally happy living in Puerto Rico, and not just due to the warm weather, of which he was growing increasingly fond. He and Louise operated, as always, as an effective team, even when they were denied the opportunity of living in the governor's official palace, La Fortaleza. When they arrived, La Fortaleza, an early-modern Baroque palace and fortress, was in such a poor state of repair that it had to be completely modernized—another one of Leahy's WPA projects, as it turned out. The couple moved into a small guesthouse in La Fortaleza's gardens, while Leahy's office was put in a building across the street. Living in the less sumptuous surroundings seemed to suit the couple. It certainly did not stop them from being hospitable, and they spent a good deal of their time hosting a wide array of different social events. Louise also devoted much of her time to different charitable obligations.

For the rest of his life the friends Leahy made in Puerto Rico would matter to him a great deal, entertaining many who passed through Washington and even in the late 1940s paying a number of visits to the island to reconnect with others. The ease with which Leahy made friends of a Hispanic background points out one of the strange contradictions in his nature, his views on race and culture. Leahy's career to this point showed both a capacity for extreme prejudice as well as a regular ability to take individuals at face value. He used some of the most common, unthinking generalizations of his time, class, and background. Natives could be shifty, Jews good at business, black people sullen, Arabs mysterious, and many different Asians inscrutable. He also used racial epithets often when talking with friends and those with whom he felt comfortable, and even at times in a professional environment. There was also a built-in assumption in Leahy's view of the world that the white, American, Christian community from which he sprang was the best. It was what he knew and what he trusted.

Yet throughout his career he developed close, personal friendships with people from many different backgrounds, including not only Puerto Ricans but Chinese, Japanese, Filipinos, and Jews. Moreover, examples can be found of Leahy in his diary referring to a member of every racial group possible as being "attractive." For Leahy this was not a word used to describe a physical attribute, though being physically appealing helped. "Attractive" to Leahy meant something more holistic: good manners, pleasant conversation, a strong moral code, as well as a dignified bearing. If you were attractive, you passed an important test.

Leahy could make a prejudiced comment about a certain race or ethnicity while at the same moment finding someone of that background attractive. It happened right before he went to Puerto Rico, when he was still serving as chief of naval operations. During his protracted negotiations with different Soviet representatives about the possibility of building warships in US shipyards, Leahy made some stereotypical remarks about Jews. He described the Soviet representatives, a Mr. Woolf and a Mr. Carp, as "Russian Jews, the former a typical argumentative, plausible advocate, and the latter a sinister-appearing person who looks exactly like the conventional international villain of the stage."[33] Yet, just a few weeks after writing this, Leahy was invited by Roosevelt on the political cruise down to Quantico. At the end of the cruise Leahy gave a ride back to three men who were in need of a lift. One of them was described by Leahy as being Jewish and "attractive."[34]

Coming to a conclusion as to whether Leahy was a racist is facile. It would be better to compare him to two of the most famous presidents of his lifetime: Woodrow Wilson and Franklin Roosevelt. Roosevelt regularly used racial epithets and clearly believed in the superiority of white, Anglo-Saxon, Protestant Americans. Yet he was also capable of taking individuals on their own merits and at times did his best for people of all races. Wilson, on the other hand, was a clear segregationist who believed that blacks and other races were inferior, and he legally sanctioned treating them as such. Leahy was much closer to Franklin Roosevelt than to Woodrow Wilson.

Leahy's stint in Puerto Rico did little to interfere with his friendship with President Roosevelt. Though they could not get together as frequently as before, Roosevelt made time for Leahy whenever the admiral was back in Washington. Leahy said little about what was discussed, except that it involved the war. The only time he revealed anything of interest was in regard to their meeting on June 28, 1940.[35] This was the first time that the two had met since Germany had seized France, an event that had shaken Roosevelt badly. Sitting in his office, analyzing the question of national defense in light of the rapidly changing world situation, a worried Roosevelt reminded the admiral of his earlier promise if America went to war. Leahy wrote that he needed to be in a constant state of readiness, the president warned, to get back to Washington "at any time, in case he should recall me."

Without a doubt, Leahy was President Roosevelt's closest military adviser. Between January 1 and November 1, 1940, Leahy is recorded as having six meetings with Roosevelt, three of which were one-on-one.[36] Yet, curiously, historians have crowned George Marshall as the president's most trusted military adviser. The record of their meetings paints a very different picture, one of a distant, formal relationship. January through November of 1940 was one of the most militarily fraught times in history. Nazi Germany conquered Poland, Norway, Denmark, Holland, Belgium, and France and launched the Battle of Britain, raising fears that all of Europe would soon fall under Hitler's sway. Yet Roosevelt's private time with Marshall during this crucial period amounted to a single meeting for a total of fifteen minutes.[37] In his twelve other meetings on record with the president, Marshall shared time with at least one other person, usually many more. Even though Leahy was no longer based in Washington, Roosevelt sought out his advice more often than the chief of staff of the US Army.

One reason was because much of Leahy's time on the island was spent preparing for war. Roosevelt and Leahy were convinced that Puerto Rico would be an important naval base if the United States ended up involved in the European conflict. Located in the center of the Caribbean, halfway between the coasts of North and South America, Puerto Rico looked like the perfect pivot point from which the United

States could protect the Atlantic coast of the entire Western Hemisphere.[38]

When Leahy arrived, however, there were few modern military facilities on the island. The navy had only a small radio station and a hydrographic office.[39] Starting from scratch, work commenced on a number of modern facilities, often in a brutal fashion. A few days before Leahy arrived two prosperous Puerto Rican communities were forcibly evicted to start work on the expansion of the Borinquen Airfield.[40] Another new facility that took a good deal of his time was the construction of an air base near San Juan on Isla Grande.[41] Much of Leahy's WPA funding was spent linking these two facilities with better roads.[42]

This was all dressing for what came next. Leahy eventually conceived of constructing an integrated air-sea facility on a much grander scale, taking in not just Puerto Rico but many of the European-owned islands to the east. With France about to fall to the Nazis, Leahy publicly called for the United States to seize both French and British islands to create this network of bases that would control all sea and air movement in and out of the Americas.[43] It is worth noting that only a few months after Leahy's public call for the United States to control British facilities in the area, Roosevelt concluded his famous lend-lease deal, whereby the United States sent the United Kingdom fifty World War I–era destroyers and in return received leases to the exact naval bases Leahy had in mind, including St. Lucia and Antigua.

The final step in the process, which was taken just as Leahy was leaving Puerto Rico, was when Roosevelt decided to create a huge military base on the far east of the island, centering on the island of Vieques. It was an area that Roosevelt and Leahy had studied well in early 1939, during their Caribbean cruise.[44] This facility, which came to be known as Roosevelt Roads Naval Station, was to be one of the largest naval bases ever built outside the continental United States, capable of basing and repairing the largest warships in the US Navy and of projecting American airpower throughout the Caribbean. Almost all the work was completed after Leahy left Puerto Rico, but the facility became something similar to the American Gibraltar he wanted.[45]

While Leahy spent most of his strategic time thinking about US security in the Caribbean, he also continued to work with Roosevelt (and Vinson and Walsh) on the nuts and bolts of US naval policy. Rumors went around the fleet that Leahy remained so powerful in Roosevelt's eyes that he could still choose the most senior commanders.[46] Structurally, Leahy remained committed to the naval buildup he had started when CNO. He was aware that airpower was showing itself to be more effective, but he refused to abandon the battleship. In late May 1940, as France was entering its death throes, Leahy told a reporter from the *New York Times* that while he still considered the battleship the "backbone" of the fleet, he believed that they needed to be redesigned to protect them from air attack.[47]

Leahy's continuing role in US naval policy, as well as his finely honed political instincts, were most interestingly revealed on October 8, 1940, when Roosevelt invited him for lunch at the White House with Adm. James O. Richardson, the commander of the Pacific Fleet. Casual conversation soon turned to a serious issue: Should the Pacific Fleet continue to be based at Pearl Harbor? Richardson had been lobbying to move the fleet to America's West Coast, believing that Pearl Harbor was too vulnerable to Japanese attack.[48] Roosevelt, determined to keep the fleet in Hawaii, argued that having the fleet at Pearl Harbor was a deterrent on Japanese behavior.

Leahy was in a bind. His doubts had grown about the safety of Pearl Harbor; indeed, a few months later he would tell close associates in France that he would not be surprised if the Japanese launched a surprise attack there. He also greatly respected Richardson, who had been one of his chief assistants when he was CNO, and believed him to be one of the most level-headed officers in the fleet.[49] However, Leahy could sense that Roosevelt was not going to be persuaded on the point, and having a much better understanding of how to work with the president than Richardson, he decided not to press the issue. Richardson refused to back down. The result was a nasty disagreement between him and Roosevelt, which permanently damaged their relationship. When the meeting broke up, Roosevelt and Leahy had a private conversation. "What's the matter with Joe?" Roosevelt fumed. "He has got yellow." Leahy leapt to Richardson's defense: "Joe is not and never will be yellow. He is dead right." Roosevelt, unmoved, replied, "I want him fired."[50]

It was a textbook example of how Leahy's political understanding set him apart from others, for either good or ill, depending on one's perspective. Richardson was more than aware of this, describing Leahy as "a successful student in human nature . . . skilled in the Washington scene."[51] While Roosevelt was alive, Leahy refused to mention the dispute, though after he died, the admiral testified about it in front of Congress.[52] In his testimony he walked a fine line between Richardson and Roosevelt. He supported Richardson's claim that he had argued that the fleet was too vulnerable at Pearl Harbor and should be withdrawn. On the other hand, he claimed that he did not remember something that Richardson said was vital, that Roosevelt had claimed he would not go to war against Japan even if the Japanese attacked Pearl Harbor. Even after Roosevelt's death, it was clear where his first loyalty lay.

If anything, the lunch convinced Roosevelt that he could trust Leahy more than almost anyone else in the armed services, and maybe in all of Washington. It made the next step in his remarkable career a natural one. It started with a telegraph call one morning at breakfast.

CHAPTER 11

Ambassador to Vichy France

On the morning of Sunday, November 17, 1940, William and Louise Leahy were having breakfast in their small guesthouse in the gardens of La Fortaleza, when an aide approached with an official telegram from Franklin Roosevelt.[1]

We are confronting an increasingly serious situation in France because of the possibility that one element of the French Government may persuade Marshal Pétain to enter into agreements with Germany which will facilitate the efforts of the Axis Powers against Great Britain and there is even the possibility that France may actually engage in a war against Great Britain. . . . We need in France at this time an ambassador who can gain the confidence of Marshal Pétain . . . I feel that you are the best man available for this mission.[2]

Ambassador to France, a nation just conquered by Nazi Germany, with a government in chaos and a population ground down by defeat—Leahy had never imagined himself in such a role. Yet Franklin Roosevelt was asking, and the admiral did not hesitate. On the back of the telegram he scribbled a note saying that he could be ready to leave Puerto Rico in a week, and had the message relayed immediately by navy radio. It actually took him ten days to prepare. He and Louise hurriedly packed their possessions, taking their pets and a few mementoes from their time on the island. Leahy was particularly fond of a cane made from a shark's spine, and he was given a going-away present of a Spanish sword. In between packing he held final meetings with staff members and friends, including Edward Flynn, the head of the Democratic National Committee, who made a point of stopping off in Puerto Rico on holiday to pay his respects to the supposedly non-political Leahy.[3]

When Leahy left Puerto Rico, no one was neutral. The Coalición celebrated.[4] Many Puerto Rican newspapers expressed regret, some even hoping that Leahy would be sent back to the island after his job in Europe was over. Secretary Ickes was downright depressed. Having finally found a governor who could make a difference, he worried about the future: "I told the President that in taking Leahy away from Puerto Rico he was depriving the island of the best Governor that we had ever sent down there. . . . Leahy has done an upstanding job. He hasn't played favorites and he hasn't allowed the politicians to kick him about, although he hasn't mixed in politics."[5]

The selection of Leahy for France sheds light on Roosevelt's mindset at this point in the war. The serving ambassador to France prior to Leahy was William Bullitt, a wealthy, volatile, and charming egomaniac from Pennsylvania. Over his lifetime Bullitt used his money to indulge a range of interests; in the 1930s, he teamed up with Sigmund Freud to write a psychological study of Woodrow Wilson, concluding that Wilson's great love interest was his father, which in turn led Wilson to view his father, an evangelical minister, as God, and Wilson himself as Jesus Christ.[6] Naturally, Bullitt believed he was the right man to shape American foreign policy and used his wealth and connections to become a diplomat. First named the ambassador to the Soviet Union, Bullitt moved from Soviet sympathizer to a hard-line opponent of communism. At the same time, he steadily declined in Roosevelt's eyes, having committed two significant sins. The first was that he had started a romantic relationship with Missy LeHand, the president's personal secretary, confidante, and rumored lover.[7] By interposing himself emotionally and physically between the president and one of the few people

Roosevelt relied upon, Bullitt had become a threat. This was compounded by Bullitt's behavior during May and June 1940, when the German Army poured into France. During these fraught months Bullitt, an extreme Francophile, crossed some deep psychological threshold. No longer simply seeing himself as the American ambassador, he began casting himself as a physical rebuke to the Nazi invaders. As the French capital was about to fall to the Germans, and while the French government was relocating to Bordeaux, Bullitt proclaimed to Roosevelt that he planned to stay in Paris as an international sign of defiance and a beacon of hope for those left behind. He even proposed to announce over the radio that he would personally confront the German invaders so that they knew the world was watching.[8] This grandiose step was the kind of posturing Roosevelt detested, and he cabled back to Bullitt to go to Bordeaux and continue representing the government to the French government.[9] Yet Bullitt remained in the French capital. From that moment Roosevelt decided that Bullitt was not to be trusted to act calmly or keep his mouth shut.[10] A few months later, when Roosevelt was able to recall Bullitt to Washington for consultations, he was determined to appoint someone he could trust to replace him.

The question was: Who? Whomever he sent to Vichy, Roosevelt believed, would have the most difficult and important American ambassadorial job in continental Europe. Some suggested Gen. John J. Pershing, America's World War I commander, yet at more than eighty years old and in poor health, the notion was impractical. It was Sumner Welles, Roosevelt's most trusted State Department adviser, who first came up with the idea of sending William Leahy. In Welles's memoirs he describes the admiral as someone deeply valued by Roosevelt "as a close friend and as a man of exceptional character, wide knowledge and incisive mind."[11] He recalled the moment in November 1940 when he first suggested Leahy as the next ambassador to France.

When I was shown to the President's bedroom I found him eating his usual hearty breakfast of grapefruit, coffee, cereal and eggs. He was sitting up in bed with a brown knitted sweater pulled over his pyjamas. The morning was grey and raw, and as an added protection his blue cloak was thrown around his shoulders. Over the bedspread were scattered the *New York Times,* and the *Herald Tribune,* and the *Washington Post,* which constituted his early morning reading.

"Have you any ideas," he asked.

When I suggested Admiral Leahy, the President's face lit up as it always did when a new idea appealed to him. Without further ado he seized the telephone at his bedside and asked the operator to get the Admiral on the long-distance telephone.[12]

On the morning of December 2, 1940, Leahy arrived in New York Harbor aboard the SS *Borinquen,* the same ship that had brought him to Puerto Rico fifteen months before, and was soon on a flight en route to Washington, DC. Within three hours of his arrival on the East Coast he was sitting in the White House with Franklin Roosevelt.[13] Louise, complete with dog, canary, and luggage, did not reach Washington until five hours later.

Roosevelt, scheduled to leave Washington later that day until after Christmas, was determined to have as much time as possible with his friend. For the remainder of the morning, more than two hours, the two men talked, the president laying out his hopes and priorities for American policy toward France.[14] Leahy was to be Roosevelt's official representative, and knowing that the president valued loyalty, he was determined to follow Roosevelt's instructions to the letter—literally. Before departing for France a few weeks later, Leahy asked for a document spelling out exactly the president's priorities. The letter he received—which was drafted by the State Department, which probably meant Welles—was heavily detailed and more than a little daunting. Leahy was supposed to convince the French to cooperate with their conquerors as little as possible.[15]

The specific points of the letter give an important indication of Roosevelt's views of France and the war. To begin with, France was still considered a significant source of power, for either good or ill. For that reason, the number one priority in Roosevelt's mind was for Leahy to establish as close a relationship as possible with Marshal Pétain. The famous World War I commander Pétain had an extraordinarily high opinion of himself (not uncommon in field marshals) and came to view himself as some sacred father to a French nation of louche teenagers. Roosevelt believed that Pétain was opposed to succumbing completely to Germany, and he wanted Leahy to do everything possible to drive a wedge between the marshal and the real bogeyman in American minds, Pierre Laval.[16] Roosevelt, astutely, judged Laval to be the most motivated political force for French collaboration with Germany, describing him as an "evil genius" as early as November 1940.[17] Short, ambitious, and far too clever for his own good, Laval would come to dominate the French collaborationist government for most of the war. He was strongly supported by a number of Germans, including the Nazi ambassador to France, Otto Abetz. Pétain, however, had fired Laval in December 1940, and keeping him away from the levers of power was one of Leahy's greatest preoccupations.

The second point, and geopolitically the most important, was that Leahy should make it perfectly clear to the Vichy leaders that Roosevelt was going to use the immense resources of the United States to support Great Britain and all other powers willing to fight Nazi Germany. In other words, the United States was not going to let the Germans win. The following points built upon this, and Leahy was to make it clear that any extra aid that France gave to Germany or Italy would be considered an unfriendly act by the United States. Finally, if the United States felt at any time that a French act would endanger American security, the country would not hesitate to act, even to the point of seizing parts of the French Empire.

Roosevelt was aware that France was obligated to provide certain support to the Nazis because of the harsh terms imposed by the Germans under the June 1940 armistice. However, he wanted the French to provide only the minimum possible aid consistent with those terms. If there was one area of French support that most obsessed Roosevelt, it was the French Fleet. More space in the letter was devoted to discussing this than any other question. Both Roosevelt and Leahy were convinced that sea power would ultimately determine the outcome of the

Second World War.[18] Their long-standing vision of sea power as the determinant of global power had remained undimmed even with all the conquests of the German Army in 1939 and 1940. Both felt completely comfortable in saying that the British (with American aid) would win the war in the end if they maintained naval supremacy. Roosevelt even lectured his cabinet about the value of sea power while Leahy was in Vichy. In April 1941, he turned one cabinet meeting into a history class, outlining American naval developments from the Revolution to the present day, putting particular stress on the need to protect commerce on the high seas.[19] A few weeks later, when the United States was in the midst of its first major crisis with the Vichy government over collaboration, Roosevelt once again returned to the importance of sea power during a cabinet meeting, saying that "it looked as if we would have to go back and found our military policy on the sea-power theory of Admiral Mahan. As he saw it, the determining thing at present is control of the seas."[20]

As such, the French Fleet mattered to Roosevelt more than any other single element of French power. It had been built up considerably between 1935 and 1939 and had some strong and excellently designed warships under its control, including the *Dunkerque*-class battleships. The Germans left them under the control of Vichy, worried that if they tried to take them for themselves the British would step in and grab them first.[21] Even though the British had destroyed or heavily damaged some of these vessels during their controversial surprise attack on the French Fleet at Mers-el-Kébir, the French Navy remained a real prize in both Roosevelt's and Leahy's eyes. Welles referred to it as the president's "paramount" concern, and Leahy was to make sure that the Germans were not allowed to make use of it.[22]

Another element of concern in the letter was the fate of the French Empire, almost all of which remained under Vichy control. French North Africa, including modern-day Tunisia, Algeria, and Morocco, caused the most worry. If the Germans could exert control over this region, it was feared they could deal a devastating blow against British air- and sea power in the Mediterranean and open new ways to attack trade in the Atlantic. Secondly, French Indochina—modern-day Vietnam,

Laos, and Cambodia—was considered a vital block to the southward expansion of Japan. It is notable that the anticolonialist Roosevelt was more than happy to guarantee continued French rule in their empire, if the French were willing to keep out the Germans and the Japanese.

It was a formidable list that Roosevelt had constructed, particularly considering the relative lack of power Leahy could hope to deploy on the United States' behalf when compared to that of the Nazi invaders. That was not to say that Leahy was entirely without influence. He could attempt to modify Vichy behavior using both the carrot and the stick. The United States was providing the French people, economically crippled and paying enormous occupation costs to the Germans, with food aid in various forms. The withdrawal of this support would make an already deplorable situation in France even worse.[23] The United States also stood willing to send aid to French North Africa. Keeping the empire intact was one of the great goals of the Vichy regime, and yet, being a conquered power itself, it would find it almost impossible to maintain control if others wished to seize parts of it. Leahy could also point to the reality of American economic might and the fact that when the dust settled, the United States would still be left standing as a Great Power. Finally, there was the legitimacy offered by the physical presence of the American ambassador. The Vichy regime, always aware of the cataclysmic source of its origin, craved international recognition. The American ambassador was perhaps the most powerful symbol of its legitimacy, and Leahy's removal would make Vichy seem even more of a puppet state than it already was. Leahy could also use the press to put pressure on Vichy. In his diary, he mentions regular meetings with American reporters based in Europe. One that he praised as particularly effective (and whom he used regularly to plant important stories) was G. H. Archambault of the *New York Times*.[24] It was certainly no accident that the first major story that Archambault published after Leahy's arrival in France was a loud declaration by the admiral that the British would win the war.[25]

So Leahy did have some sources of influence, though they were rather esoteric when contrasted with the enormous German boot placed squarely on the French windpipe. From the perspective of those in Vichy, the United States was a long way away and out of the war. Germany was in control of almost all of Europe, had defeated the French Army, held more than a million French military personnel as hostages, and could invade Vichy at any time. If Leahy was preaching to them about eventual victory, those in Pétain's regime could point to more immediate concerns.

Armed with his written instructions, Leahy and Louise departed for Vichy on December 23, 1940.[26] It was one of the worst journeys of their lives. Winter storms over the Atlantic raised huge swells, and Christmas was spent clinging to a couch in the captain's cabin. They had a brief respite when they arrived in the Portuguese capital of Lisbon. Having been warned, they then stocked up on food to bring to Vichy, which was suffering from severe shortages. The trip from Lisbon to Madrid went smoothly enough, but the train from Madrid to Barcelona was dreadful. The Leahys elected to take the day train, thinking they would have wonderful views of the Spanish countryside. What was supposed to be an eleven-hour scenic break became a chaotic twenty-five-hour expedition. "Unspeakably dirty," the Leahys' unheated carriage was crammed with so many people that many had to lie on the floor to sleep. After a quick rest in a mediocre Barcelona hotel, the couple set off for France by automobile, their luggage following in a truck. An hour from the French border, they discovered that a bridge they'd expected to cross was gone, destroyed during the Spanish Civil War. Rashly, they tried to ford the river in their little car, but it broke down, leaving them stranded and surrounded by water for more than an hour until rescue arrived. Once they finally crossed the border into France, things improved. Pétain, understanding the importance of the American ambassador's arrival, arranged for an escort to bring the Leahys to Montpellier. There they were served an excellent meal in the Hôtel Métropole and then put on Pétain's private train for the trip to Vichy. When they arrived, Leahy noted how cold everything was.

Vichy was a strange town for a nascent state, and not one that Leahy found particularly genial. A relatively successful spa town before the war, favored by wealthy hypochondriacs with rheumatism and stomach complaints, Vichy was chosen as the temporary capital of the

French government because it had a large number of hotel rooms and a modern telephone service and was far enough inside unoccupied France that the Germans would not fear that the French government would flee. There wasn't much to do in terms of recreation. One could attend the opera or take the water cure—both of which Leahy did, but neither of which he particularly enjoyed.

The real entertainment in Vichy came in the form of limitless servings of gossip and intrigue. A government that wasn't fully sovereign, in a small city that seemed permanently on the edge of a nervous breakdown, Vichy struck Leahy as part soap opera, part asylum, part tragedy. The unstable nature of the place was made clear during his first two meetings with Pétain. On January 8, two days after arriving, Leahy was ushered in for his formal reception with the marshal and found himself impressed by the Frenchman's physical strength and mental acuity. Yet when the two had their first proper conversation the next day, Pétain struck Leahy as a tired old man unwilling to take any significant steps to stand up to Nazi Germany. It was the beginning of a schizophrenic relationship. As Roosevelt wanted, Leahy developed (for a while) a strong personal relationship with Pétain.[27] Pétain obviously believed that Leahy was worth cultivating and used his own brand of charm to convince the American that he wanted the Germans to lose the war and that he saw the United States as France's greatest hope in the future. Leahy, in return, developed some sympathy for Pétain, believing him to be an honest patriot who was doing what he thought was best to protect the French people. Leahy believed that there was no one else capable of holding the French government together at the time. The caveat to all this was his view that Pétain (and with him the vast majority of the French people) had been so psychologically traumatized by their defeat that, even had they wished to, they lacked the strength to take any step that would have antagonized their German masters. The depth of despair that Leahy discovered in France went beyond what he had expected. Less than a month after arriving he wrote in his diary that the "total defeat of the French Army has left the people with a sense of shame, helplessness, and loss of self-respect that inclines them toward any compromise with the Germans as the least harmful of many possibilities."[28] For Leahy, a convinced Democrat, the most worrying political aspect of this loss of self-respect within the Vichy regime was its openly authoritarian direction. It seemed to him that military defeat was being used to discredit the entire notion of representative government and France seemed to be drifting toward becoming something close to the Italian form of a Fascist state.[29]

If there was one man in Vichy who seemed convinced of the inevitability of German victory, it was the dominant political actor at the time of Leahy's arrival, Adm. François Darlan. Even today he is a man who divides opinion, particularly when it comes to the depth and enthusiasm of his collaboration policy. One view is that Darlan was more a willing collaborator who pushed the policy further than needed (both for his personal benefit and that of the glory of France) and had some sympathy with a number of Fascist domestic policies. The other view of Darlan—that he was caught in an impossible situation that would have overwhelmed almost any political operator, and chose the collaboration policy because it was the only thing he could do—is more sympathetic.

Darlan was the frantic instigator of the Vichy government, serving Pétain as not only the government's vice president but also eventually as foreign minister, interior minister, navy minister, and minister for national defense. For a while he was even referred to as Pétain's heir apparent. He was suspicious of everyone, including Leahy, and made sure to limit the time Pétain and Leahy could spend together alone. In some ways Leahy tried hard to cultivate warm relations with his fellow naval officer. While he viewed Darlan with deep skepticism, he considered him infinitely preferable to Pierre Laval. As keeping Laval from returning to power was such a high priority, it was in Leahy's interest not to subvert Darlan's position.

Darlan also struck Leahy as emotionally unstable, dangerously impulsive, and devious. He tried hard to understand the French admiral, recognizing that as long as Pétain had faith in Darlan, the latter would be the most important political actor in Vichy. Therefore it was important to try to work with Darlan to achieve Roosevelt's goals. Yet there were two main problems that would have to be faced. The first, as Leahy saw it, was that Darlan had a "psychopathic" hatred of Britain and the British Navy and seemed pleased that British influence on the Continent had been, in Darlan's mind, broken. While Leahy felt Darlan's anti-British sentiments were misguided (though psychologically comprehensible, considering what he had experienced), he was mystified by Darlan's analysis of the world situation. He believed that Darlan "definitely underestimates British Sea Power" and might even be willing to use the remaining units of the French Navy against the British if the Royal Navy continued blockading trade with France. It was as if Darlan had taken all the shame he felt about French defeat and translated those emotions into a black loathing of France's former ally. During some of his anti-British rants, Darlan would become unhinged.[30] His eyes would bulge out with anger and his face would redden, one of the reasons, perhaps, that his American code name in diplomatic cables was "Popeye."[31]

Leahy was not only worried about Darlan's Anglophobia. He was depressed to see that Darlan "expresses himself very freely as being in favor of economic collaboration with Germany."[32] That Darlan was willing to tell Leahy straight out that he favored greater collaboration might seem foolhardy but was indicative of one of the profound splits in Vichy. Darlan, like most in the upper echelon of Vichy politics, had decided by this point that the United States, for all its fine words, would never intervene decisively in the European war. The assumption was both that Germany was too strong and would impose a new European order, whereas the US was too soft and unwilling to make the necessary sacrifices. Darlan made an explicit comparison between the United States in 1941 and France before the war when he claimed that America was in a greater state of "decomposition" than the Third Republic.[33] In comparison, the French admiral seemed dazzled by German manliness. He told Leahy that while the American soldier was too used to luxury, and demanded to be fed steak for dinner, German soldiers could survive on the nutrition supplied by a handful of pills.[34]

This respect from Darlan, and others, for Nazism/Fascism over democratic systems seemed to grow throughout the spring of 1941. The successful and rapid German invasions of Yugoslavia and Greece once again made Germany seem unstoppable. Up through April, Leahy seemed to be achieving his fundamental goals in Vichy. He had lobbied successfully to keep the Vichy government from moving the battleship *Dunkerque* from Algeria, where it had been damaged during the British attack on Mers-el-Kébir, back to France—where it would have been much easier for the Germans to seize.[35]

In April, things changed significantly as information was passed to Leahy that Darlan was trying to push ahead and force a new collaborative partnership with the Germans. It was typical of how Leahy and the American embassy found out information. If the upper echelon of Vichy leadership was loyal to Pétain, there was a whole faction of mid-level functionaries who were unconvinced that Germany would win and were willing to help the American government by providing as much information as possible. In this intelligence endeavor and all other efforts, Leahy was helped by an excellent diplomatic team. For the rest of his life Leahy remained fond of three members of the embassy staff, H. Freeman Matthews (his chargé d'affaires), Comm. Roscoe Hillenkoetter (his naval aide), and Douglas MacArthur II (third secretary in the embassy).[36] They all developed contacts within Vichy and, with the information Leahy was getting himself, provided Washington with practically real-time knowledge of developments inside Pétain's government. All three were exceptionally skilled and went on to have excellent careers, often helped along by Leahy. Matthews, who was the senior diplomat under Leahy, became the head of the European desk of the State Department in 1944 and later the undersecretary of state. Hillenkoetter became the head of the CIA in 1947, with Leahy instrumental in his selection. MacArthur, the nephew of the famous general—who was himself a long-standing friend of Leahy's—would eventually serve as US ambassador to Japan, Belgium, Austria, and Iran.[37]

Enough people inside the Vichy government were willing to provide intelligence that Leahy divided French officials into three groups to attempt to understand their motivations.[38] There were the out-and-out collaborationists, anti-democrats, and anti-Semites who saw much to be admired in the Fascist way of life and who were quite eager to secure for France a prized position in the new German order. There was the "France Must Live" group, who were not pro-German but who believed an overall German victory was almost certain and that the Vichy government must protect France by gaining favor with the Nazis. Finally there were those Leahy, rather parochially, called the pro-Americans. They did not believe Germany would win the war, had faith that American power would prove decisive in the end, and were willing to be as helpful as possible to the United States. This the last group did by feeding as much information as possible directly to the American ambassador or those working with him. At times the real problem that Leahy and the American diplomatic corps had was trying to sift through the huge mass of intelligence they were being fed.

Many of these sources would play major roles in postwar France. One, Maurice Couve de Murville, would be the foreign minister and then prime minister under Charles de Gaulle. Serving in the Finance Ministry in 1941, he was a regular source of confidential information for Leahy, who grew to trust him implicitly.[39] Another important source, particularly early in Leahy's tenure, was the poet and diplomat Jean Chauvel, who led the Foreign Ministry's Far Eastern Affairs section.[40] By the end of the war Chauvel was working as secretary-general of the Foreign Ministry in Charles de Gaulle's government and later he would be the French ambassador to the United Nations.

Chauvel handed over to Leahy all the confidential information he could sneak out of the Foreign Ministry. On June 13, 1941, for instance, he informed Leahy that the French had discovered from German sources that the Nazis would soon launch their invasion of the Soviet Union, Operation Barbarossa.[41] Leahy quickly passed the intelligence to Washington. Chauvel was partly motivated to commit such brazen if honorable treason against his own government because he wanted the United States to work with France to resist Japanese encroachments against French Indochina and saw the war in Europe as part of this global struggle.[42]

It was Chauvel who first passed to Leahy information that contributed to one of the most fateful decisions of World War II, Franklin Roosevelt's July 1941 decision to embargo oil shipments to Japan, a move that led directly to the Japanese attack on Pearl Harbor. Roosevelt's embargo, almost always seen as emerging from a bilateral dispute between the United States and Japan, has never been properly understood. As such, his decision strikes some as confusing, unprepared, or even unintentional—an extremely harsh if mysterious overreaction that resulted in war.[43] However, this decision was not confused at all, but built upon a dialogue between Leahy, Welles, and Roosevelt that had been going on for months. Indeed, it only makes sense if the role of Leahy and Vichy France are added to the equation.

It was part of a process of placing what happened to French Indochina for Roosevelt into the context of the world war. The Japanese Army, in the typically reckless manner that characterized its actions in these years, had occupied parts of northern Indochina in 1940 after the fall of France. However, they created a figment of legitimacy by forcing the French government, which could not have stopped them if they had wanted, to acquiesce in their presence by stating that it was a temporary measure. The worry in 1941 was that the Japanese would move into the south of Indochina. Such a step would have brought the Japanese much closer to the Dutch East Indies, the most important source of oil and bauxite in East Asia, as well as to Malaya and the Philippines, the British and American colonies that barred their way to those natural resources.

The dialogue between Leahy, Welles, and Roosevelt about French Indochina started in February 1941, when Chauvel brought confidential French diplomatic cables into the American embassy and read them aloud to Leahy. The Japanese military in French Indochina had decided to strike south instead of north, and in the "near future" would move to take over the rest of the country.[44] Chauvel argued that the move was part of a coordinated effort with Germany to distract the United States from intervening in Europe. Leahy agreed that the Germans and Japanese were acting in cahoots in the Pacific and in a report he sent to the State Department (Welles) after talking with Chauvel claimed that the Japanese "have reached some agreement with the Germans designed to keep us occupied in the Far East . . ."[45]

Chauvel's report and Leahy's estimation were mostly accurate, as both Adolf Hitler and his farcical foreign minister, Joachim von Ribbentrop, had urged the Japanese to direct their efforts southward and pledged them German support in case the United States opted for war.[46] Chauvel kept feeding Leahy similar intelligence. In April 1941, he told Leahy, again exploiting confidential information straight from French foreign ministry sources, that the Japanese now had an extra incentive to attack Indochina and Singapore.[47]

What Roosevelt was hearing from Leahy was that any attempt by the Japanese to move into southern Vietnam was not just a Japanese issue, it was part of a greater Axis plan of attack. From that point on, Roosevelt started viewing the French Empire as an integrated whole for American policy and seeing any Japanese move toward Indochina as the equivalent of a German move toward North Africa. Leahy was told this explicitly in May 1941 (which was a particularly fraught period because of increased collaboration negotiations between Darlan and the Germans), and he told Pétain that the United States stood ready to take action against "any nation, including the Axis powers" that made a move to take over any part of the French Empire.[48] Leahy was careful in his diary not to say exactly how threatening the language was, but he did record that the tone was so harsh that a shaken Pétain would not reply until Darlan came back from a meeting with the Germans.

When, therefore, the crisis over Indochina blew up in July, much of the thinking that Roosevelt had done on the subject had come through the lens of Leahy, Welles, and Vichy. This period represented their three-headed combination at its most effective. Regular communication flowed between Welles and Leahy as they dealt with the details of American-French relations. Welles would then go to Roosevelt for discussions and guidance and feed this back to Leahy. Direct communications between Leahy and Roosevelt was usually reserved for courier-borne letters. Leahy would send about one per month to the president. Detailed and gossipy, his letters provide some of the best descriptions of the situation at the time. Roosevelt's direct letters to Leahy were less frequent, one every few months, and were written more to provide emotional support to his friend than to pass along any specific information. On the other hand, working through Welles, the two men could interact surprisingly quickly. If Leahy sent a message to Welles, he could be sure that it would be communicated rapidly to Roosevelt and the president was willing to act on Leahy's recommendations. In April 1941, Leahy wired from France to recommend that Roosevelt should freeze German and Italian assets in the United States, an action the president ordered a few weeks later.[49] In early 1942, after reviewing a report from Leahy that said that the Vichy government would not resist if the Germans moved into French North Africa, Roosevelt quickly passed along this view to Winston Churchill.[50] On the other hand, if Roosevelt wanted something important from Leahy, he would tell Welles and news would quickly reach Vichy. When the Pétain government began its show trials of Third Republic political leaders such as Paul Reynaud, Édouard Daladier, and Leon Blum, Roosevelt went through Welles to tell Leahy to demand an official transcript from the French government.[51]

The interactions of the three were vital in the eventual decision to embargo oil to Japan. On July 16, 1941, during a meeting with Darlan and Pétain, Leahy was told that the French expected the Japanese to occupy southern Vietnam in the coming days.[52] It seemed that everything he had been told since February was about to come true. Within two days the news had been reported back to the State Department. Leahy described the Japanese move not as a unilateral act but as part of a coordinated Japanese-German move to distract the United States. Smelling a Darlan-shaped rat, Leahy was dismissive when the French admiral tried to argue that the Japanese were not acting with German approval.

> Darlan suggested that Germany probably does not look with much favor on the acquisition of the Dutch Islands by Japan and that a consultation between French and German authorities might be used to delay a decision. He expressed a fear that Japan may move against Indochina within a week whether the French Government agrees or not. He did not mention what seems to be an obvious advantage to Germany in getting the United States involved in the Pacific if we should object to a Japanese move southward.[53]

When Leahy's alarming report was received in Washington, it made a stir. The admiral was quickly cabled back with a verbal message (almost certainly from Roosevelt) that he was to give word to Pétain and Darlan about American opposition to such a move.[54] Leahy told the French leadership that if they did not oppose the Japanese move they would lose Indochina regardless—because if the United States went to war in the Pacific the last thing they would do was hand back the French Empire afterward.[55] Darlan then tried to convince Leahy that the Germans were not backing the Japanese move, but the ambassador thought it was all lies. By this time Leahy had given up hope that Vichy would do anything to help. Both Leahy and Welles believed that the French, who when dealing with the United States and the United Kingdom were endlessly sensitive about their imperial prerogatives, were being shockingly supine with the Japanese. It seemed particularly odd to them that at the exact moment when the French were endlessly complaining over British encroachments in Syria and even threatening to go to war against the United Kingdom, that Vichy would casually hand over control of Indochina without the slightest protest if, as Leahy was being told, the Germans did not want the Japanese to do this. It just didn't make any sense to either man. When, therefore, the Japanese did move into southern Indochina in late July and Vichy sanctioned the move, it seemed to both Leahy and Welles (and one assumes Roosevelt) that it was part of a coordinated Axis plot. Welles remarked that the Japanese were being allowed in by the French with "hardly a protest," while Leahy claimed that it was "spineless" and a further indication that the Axis was trying to befuddle the United States.[56] Welles and Roosevelt both seemed worried that it could be a stepping-stone for Japan to aid Germany in its fight against Russia by thereupon attacking the Soviet Union.[57] Furthermore, Leahy warned Roosevelt that if nothing were done in response, it would be an open invitation to the Germans to believe that they could seize French North Africa. As he wrote to the president in one of his personal letters: "Now that Vichy has without objection handed Indochina over to Japan it will be difficult to refuse Germany a present of French Africa when a new demand backed by threats is made."[58]

The fact that two of the three people whom Roosevelt trusted most on foreign-policy issues at the time (the other was Harry Hopkins, but he was in the United Kingdom and the Soviet Union in the summer of 1941) were telling him that this was a move that needed a tough response helps explain just why Roosevelt took the hard line with the Japanese that he did. When Roosevelt explained his response to the Japanese move to his cabinet, Secretary Ickes described the American action as being necessitated by the "craven" cooperation of Vichy with the Axis.[59] In the end, therefore, it makes no sense to see Roosevelt's decision to take strong action against Japan over Indochina as some impromptu or impulsive move. It was a considered response to what was believed to be a coordinated Axis attempt to change the course of the global war. In that way, Leahy in Vichy made a material difference in pushing the United States down the road to Pearl Harbor. It is impossible to see any other American ambassador making such an impression on the president.

CHAPTER 12

Dark Days

Dear Bill:

I have written you very seldom of late because I have been more or less laid up with a low-grade infection, probably intestinal flu, since the first of May. The result is that my actual output of mail is about cut in half.

You have certainly been going through a life that has aspects akin to punching bags, roller coasters, mules, pirates, and general hell during these past months.

I think both you and I have given up making prophecies as to what will happen in and to France tomorrow or the next day.

I feel as if every time we get some real collaboration for the good of the French (especially for the children) started, Darlan and some others say or do some stupid or not wholly above-board thing which results in complete stoppage of all we would like to do.

Now comes the Russian diversion. If it is more than just that it will mean the liberation of Europe from Nazi domination—and at the same time I do not think we need worry about any possibility of Russian domination. I do wish there were a nice central place in the ocean to which you and I could fly in a few hours and spend a few days together. I think of you both often.

> My affectionate regards,
> As Ever,
> Franklin D. Roosevelt[1]

When the president wrote this letter in late June 1941, he was well aware that Bill Leahy was under great pressure. The previous two months had seen not only the confrontation over French Indochina but a growing crisis regarding the depth of Vichy's collaboration with the Nazis. In May, the Darlan government had commenced negotiations with the Nazis that opened up the possibility of France becoming a German ally. Leahy, whose first priority as America's ambassador was to limit French collaboration, began to feel the squeeze. Tokens of friendship such as Roosevelt's thoughtful note were crucial in helping him cope with the stress.

Despite the strain, Leahy remained convinced that the Germans would eventually lose the war. At dinner one night, he lectured the visiting Japanese ambassador to Spain against believing in Germany's final victory.[2] Yet repeated German conquests on the battlefield must have made his confidence seem unreal to Vichy leaders. In the Balkans, Greece, and North Africa, the British Army seemed powerless to stop German advances. Admiral Darlan was as convinced of Germany's inevitable triumph as Leahy was of Britain's. Despite Leahy's warnings against allowing the Axis greater access to the French Empire, he expected his words of caution had little impact. "I received . . . a definite impression that following British defeats in Libya, Yugoslavia, and Greece," he wrote, "the Marshal [Pétain] and his Government are moving rapidly toward 'collaboration' with Germany and that there is now likely to be no effective objection made by France to any demands that may be received from Germany."[3]

Indeed, Germany's successes were a key reason that Darlan, then at the height of his power, made his Laval-like gambit.[4] He hoped to make France a more reliable actor in German eyes and to secure concessions, most important the return of the hundreds of thousands of French soldiers still being kept as prisoners of war under the armistice terms.[5] In Darlan's eyes, collaboration was a policy that was beginning to look more attractive.[6]

Leahy first heard rumors in April that Darlan was thinking of cozying up to the Nazis. In May, he was given credible reports that the Germans would be allowed extensive access to French North Africa.[7] At the time there was a constant stream of sources from within the French government telling Leahy that Vichy would soon allow German troops into the French Empire or were to pass over to the Germans supplies such as fuel from French stockpiles. Leahy turned to media pressure to let Darlan and Pétain know he was aware of what they were doing. *New York Times* reporter G. H. Archambault penned a front-page story on May 14 that highlighted the warning Leahy had given Pétain about more collaboration.[8] Roosevelt also let Leahy know that he had passed to Cordell Hull the admiral's information that the French would soon sign a deal with the Germans for greater collaboration.[9] On May 16, in response to Leahy's making public his warning, the Vichy government issued a public statement that any deal it struck with the Nazis would not see France go to war with Britain.[10] Despite the smoke screen, Darlan and Pétain continued playing their dangerous game.

On May 28, it even seemed, briefly, that Darlan had concluded his pact with the devil. He signed the Protocols of Paris, which went far beyond the terms of the 1940 armistice in allowing the Germans to make use of the French Empire in their war against the United Kingdom. Three specific concessions were agreed to: the Germans were allowed to use Dakar (in present-day Senegal) as a U-boat base to attack British trade; they could use the Tunisian port of Bizerte to supply Rommel's Afrika Korps, which was fighting the British in Libya and Egypt; and they could make use of French bases in Syria to attack British oil interests in present-day Iraq as part of the nationalist uprising led by Rashid Ali.[11] In return, French payments to the Nazi state were reduced and some highly skilled French prisoners were released from German prisoner-of-war camps. Darlan had allowed his pathological hatred of the British and his cringeworthy respect of the Germans to take a series of dangerous steps down the road to making Vichy France a German ally.

When the protocols were announced, they were met by fierce American opposition. Roosevelt had Cordell Hull (who had been kept out of the loop in the discussions between himself and Leahy) issue the most forthright American statement condemning the agreement.[12] However, it was not the American response that neutered the Paris

Protocols. It was the overall weakness of the French position. Darlan's Syria gambit was quickly foiled when the British worked with Charles de Gaulle's Free French to invade the colony and replace the pro-Vichy forces then in power.[13] With Syria taken out of the equation, much of the German interest in the protocols evaporated.[14] The Germans had no wish to make concessions to Vichy if they had little to gain. So, instead of allowing France to become an ally, the Germans preferred to continue using the powers of the victor over the vanquished and backed away from Darlan.[15]

There were some elements within Vichy that seemed to react immediately to the strong American condemnation of the protocols. Some have argued that Gen. Maxime Weygand, who was playing a careful game of cozying up to American diplomats while still solidly supporting Pétain, played an important role in keeping the protocols from being ratified.[16] The fact that the United States made its displeasure so clear certainly affected the pro-Vichy French press, which started accusing the Americans in general, and Leahy in particular, of being a constant block to the brave new world of Franco-German cooperation. The New York Times picked up on this theme, publishing a story that included a quote from the strongly collaborationist French journal L'Oeuvre: "Each time that, for more or less avowable reasons, the brake has been applied to the development of Franco-German collaboration there reappears the disquieting figure of Admiral William D. Leahy, Ambassador of President Roosevelt, of Churchill and of Stalin, all at once."[17]

This struggle over Vichy collaboration marked an important transition in Leahy's expectation for a constructive relationship between France and the United States. Though he had always been skeptical that Pétain would do much to oppose the Germans, Leahy grew to believe that the marshal, for all his protestations, was a deceiver and a much stronger advocate of collaboration than he let on.[18]

A few weeks later, his fears about Pétain's true intentions received a boost. On August 12, while Leahy was attending the opera with the cream of Vichy society, Marshal Pétain's speech announcing the outlawing of parties and the de facto suspension of the French Assembly was broadcast over the theater's sound system. It marked the formal beginning of a Pétainist dictatorship and represented the extinguishing of Leahy's last bit of hope in the old marshal. A few days later he unburdened himself in one of his personal letters to Roosevelt: "It is discouraging, from the point of view of those of us who are confirmed believers in representative government, to see France completely in the hands of a dictator."[19]

Leahy was so worn-out by the dispute that he finally took Roosevelt's concern to heart, and he and Louise set off on a holiday to Switzerland, driving through beautiful mountain valleys and along the lakes of a country still at peace. In the absence of rationing they ate their fill, excited to indulge in steaks that could be found nowhere in France. The contrast between a defeated and depressed France and the calm prosperity of Switzerland put Leahy in a reflective mood. In Geneva, he visited the headquarters of the defunct League of Nations, now being used as a children's center.[20] For Leahy, who believed that the intentions behind the league were laudable, if its failure was to be expected, it was a "sad awakening from the dream of Woodrow Wilson and his collaborators." Despite his sorrow, his trip represented one of the final moments in which he felt relaxed during his last nine months in Vichy. The coming months would be some of the worst of his life, and culminate in a life-changing catastrophe.

Leahy had so little faith left in Vichy that he started speaking positively about French Communists, writing that they were "the only organized self-styled political party and the only group with sufficient courage to act against the invaders."[21] His sympathy for the Communists was also motivated by the fallout from Operation Barbarossa, the German invasion of the Soviet Union on June 22. When the German Army surprised Stalin and the Red Army by pouring across the border, it marked the beginning of the largest and most horrific land war in human history. Millions of German troops and thousands of German tanks in four massed spearheads smashed through Soviet lines, killing, capturing, and laying waste to everything in their path. As the German

Army marched, black-booted, seemingly unstoppable, it seemed to many in Europe that the entire continent would be theirs by Christmas. William Leahy thought otherwise.

From the moment the Germans launched Barbarossa in 1941, Leahy believed that they had started a fight they could never win. He knew that conquering such a vast and unpredictable land would be beyond German capabilities, and he also knew Franklin Roosevelt well enough to know that the American president would do everything in his power to stop them. The day after the invasion commenced, Leahy met with the Soviet ambassador to Vichy and, even without official guidance from Washington, told the Soviet diplomat that he believed the US government would have "full sympathy" for the Soviet Union in its struggle with Nazi Germany.[22]

News of great German victories trickled into Vichy, but also whispers of heavy German losses. Leahy believed he could tell the truth by how he was treated by pro-Germans in the government: the friendlier they were toward him, the more he suspected the war in the east was going badly for the Reich.

As Leahy realized, the invasion also played into the hands of the collaborationists by strengthening their personal and political stake in a German victory. Barbarossa unleashed a type of exterminatory warfare that had so far only been hinted at in Europe. Atrocities and mass killings had, of course, plagued Germany's invasion of Poland, but the Nazis' incursion into the Soviet Union unleashed even more grotesque behavior, and the rate and extremity of the bloodshed spiraled upward. It became more and more apparent that the postwar world would have to go decisively one way or the other, and the losers would be faced with a particularly bleak, maybe even nonexistent future.

For Darlan, the immediate reaction to Barbarossa was to collaborate even more, regardless of the failure of the Protocols of Paris.[23] In July the Vichy government allowed for the establishment of a French volunteer force to fight with the Germans against the Soviets, with whom, legally, Vichy France was still at peace.[24] Also, mostly under Darlan's direction, France handed over 1,700 vehicles and 3,600 tons of fuel to Germany.[25] Finally, Darlan attempted to please the Germans (and satisfy a personal prejudice) by instituting internal crackdowns on Communists and Jews. Leahy remarked in his diary that the Jews were now scapegoats for everything going wrong in France.[26]

Indeed, the Pétainist regime's anti-Semitic laws discriminated against Jews in everyday life in France, representing a first step in the Vichy government's cooperation with the Holocaust.[27] Leahy was aware that the new laws represented something ominous, but as the American ambassador, he felt there was little he could do to intervene.[28] He had seemed to accept certain common prejudices about Jews in his own life, but never seemed to think much beyond this. In Vichy, his basic prejudice seemed unchanged, but at the same time he believed that some Jewish figures were among the strongest fighters against Nazi power. He took pleasure in being attacked by the most virulent anti-Semitic press in France, and even sent one of the articles to "Pa" Watson in case the president wanted to read it.[29]

Leahy tended to view the plight of Jews in Vichy as an issue that required him to be personally detached. Roosevelt had not mentioned the Jewish question to him during their original meeting, in his letter of instruction, or in any of the communications sent to Leahy in France. On the other hand, Leahy was told repeatedly that he was to do everything possible to win over the confidence of Pétain. What he did was take the omissions and commissions and judge that he should not make an issue of Vichy's anti-Semitic policies. He could compliment Jewish resistance and commiserate about Jewish suffering, but he would only complain about the discrimination against them quietly and irregularly. History must also assume that is exactly what Franklin Roosevelt wanted him to do.

One issue that did cause Leahy to act was the fate of Maxime Weygand. A French hero of World War I, Weygand had been brought back into military service after the German breakthrough of May 1940, and conducted the defense of France during its remaining weeks of independence. This he did with skill and some élan. The French Army fought with considerably more determination under Weygand when their situation was hopeless than they had when the Germans first attacked. After the armistice, Pétain made Weygand his defense minister, but then sent him to North Africa to oversee the French colonies, entrusting him with the most important job outside of France itself. Weygand played a subtle game, manipulating American sentiment brilliantly. Roosevelt referred to Weygand as "our friend," and in the State Department his fate was accorded huge importance.[30] Unlike other major Vichy figures, Weygand stated clearly to the Americans, including Leahy, that he wanted Germany to lose the war and, echoing what Marshal Pétain said earlier, that the United States was France's greatest hope for the future. He even talked about doing everything possible to help the United States if and when America joined the war. Because of this stance, he convinced the Americans to send him a significant amount of aid for North Africa, which bolstered French control.

Leahy remarked that in giving Weygand so much aid in North Africa, they had made it possible for him to block the approval of the Paris Protocols.[31] Yet Weygand had no intention of ever betraying Pétain. He spoke of the older man in terms of greatest respect and saw his role as one to support Pétain at almost any cost. As such he was, perhaps unconsciously, one of the great success stories of the Vichy government in 1941. He kept French North Africa wedded to Vichy France while gaining material aid from the Americans to keep it stable.

Unaware of his duplicity, Leahy and Roosevelt also esteemed Weygand because the French marshal was so hated by the Germans, who began pressuring Pétain to sack Weygand and replace him with somebody more malleable. Leahy did everything possible to protect Weygand, once again turning to the *New York Times* to leak news that if Weygand were sacked, Leahy would be recalled to Washington.[32] Working with Sumner Welles, Leahy called on Pétain on the same day that the undersecretary of state called on the Vichy ambassador to Washington, both demanding clarity about Weygand's status and the future of French North Africa.[33] If not given such assurances, both threatened to end all American aid to France and the French Empire. Yet the ultimatums fell short. Pétain, regrettably as he told the admiral, eventually had to sack Weygand, claiming that if he did not, the

Germans would take over unoccupied France. It was an example of the limits of Leahy's ability to influence Vichy policy. For Leahy, it was another sign that Pétain lacked the courage or even desire to take any step that could possibly irritate the Germans.[34] The marshal, he vented to Roosevelt, had the backbone of a jellyfish.[35]

Leahy regretted Weygand's dismissal because he viewed him as one of the few French actors who could help the United States win the war. This was not the case with Charles de Gaulle. The leader of the Free French movement was well known to Leahy. In March 1941 Pétain ranted about de Gaulle to Leahy, saying that the British had told him that de Gaulle was no supporter of their war effort and the marshal therefore wondered why they did not "eliminate" him.[36] Leahy's lack of support for de Gaulle and Gaullists during his time at Vichy has led to some fierce criticisms.[37] This is rather odd. Leahy, perceptively, judged that the Gaullists had more support in France than was apparent on the surface, and told Roosevelt as much after Pétain's rant.[38] However, he also correctly judged that de Gaulle's support was not strong enough at the time to affect Vichy policy. Moreover, as senior politicians in Vichy believed that they were operating under a death sentence issued by the Gaullists, it would have been disastrous for Leahy to have argued for de Gaulle to become the official voice of France.[39] Finally, if Leahy had somehow thrown his support behind de Gaulle, it would have destroyed his relationship with Pétain, the nurturing of which was the most important task he was given by President Roosevelt.

Thus, Weygand became the great American hope, which is why Roosevelt and Leahy valued him as they did and reacted with such anger when, on November 18, he was removed as Vichy's commander in North Africa. Before Weygand's sacking could lead to a final break between the United States and Vichy, however, it was overshadowed by something infinitely more dramatic. On December 7, 1941, the Japanese bombarded the US Pacific Fleet in Pearl Harbor, Hawaii.

Using six aircraft carriers and the finest trained naval aviators in the world, the Japanese Navy caught the US Pacific Fleet unawares early on that Sunday morning. Launching waves of torpedo and dive-bombing attacks, they laid waste to many of Leahy's prized battleships.

All eight of the Pacific Fleet's dreadnoughts were hit, four of which were either sunk outright or put out of commission for years. Crucially, however, the Japanese revealed how little they understood the great transformation that was about to hit naval warfare. They left almost entirely unscathed all the fuel and repair facilities in the great base. Moreover, they made no attempt to find and sink the US aircraft carriers, a number of which had recently been dispatched from Pearl Harbor.

Though Leahy sat halfway around the world from the mayhem that engulfed the fleet he had done more than anyone else to create, the attack came as no shock to him. In late 1941, as American-Japanese relations were deteriorating and war looked distinctly possible, H. Freeman Matthews asked Leahy what the Japanese might do; Leahy replied, "I would not be surprised if they attacked Pearl Harbor."[40]

In Vichy, Leahy first heard about the attack while listening to an evening radio show that was interrupted for a special announcement. His first thoughts were for his fellow sailors and the reputation of the American Fleet. But soon more immediate concerns came to light. It was feared that the Germans might use the attack to order their supporters in Vichy to seize the US embassy. Escape routes had to be worked out for the American diplomats—Leahy preferred one that headed directly down to the Mediterranean coast instead of trying to make for Spain—and plans to destroy all confidential material were reexamined.[41]

When Leahy heard President Roosevelt, over a surprisingly clear radio broadcast, describe December 7 as "a day which will live in infamy," he was energized, believing it represented an important marker on the road to victory: "It made a dramatic picture of the most powerful nation of the world embarking on an all out war to destroy the bandit nation of the Orient. The war formally declared today will in my certain opinion result in the destruction of Japan as a first class sea power regardless of how much time and treasure are required to accomplish that."[42]

Perversely, the attack on Pearl Harbor, followed by the German declaration of war on the United States, allowed Leahy a sense of hope for the first time in months. With America in the war, he could now talk to the Vichy government as a combatant, with the immense military resources of the United States backing up his every statement. He swung into action and started browbeating Vichy officials. The day after the attack, Leahy asked for, and received, a statement from Pétain that the French government would stay neutral. This was all window dressing for what happened a few days later.

On the evening of December 11, Leahy was ushered in for another meeting with Pétain and Darlan. It had recently been announced that Germany and Italy had also declared war on the United States, so that the world now was involved in one giant interconnected cataclysm. The atmosphere in the room was noticeably different from that at any other time in the past year. Leahy no longer had to threaten based on possibilities. Now he looked both Frenchmen in the eye and told them coldly that the United States would look on any aid given to the Axis as a hostile act and that Vichy would suffer. The United States would seize any part of the French Empire it wanted, or attack any French military force it thought a threat. Once again, he stated clearly that the Axis would be destroyed.

One can imagine the fear that gripped Darlan and Pétain as the American ambassador spoke. They still were living under a constant threat of German aggression, but they understood that with the United States fully engaged, the war, and Germany, could turn apocalyptic. Desperately trying to find common ground with Leahy, Darlan pronounced how wonderful it would be if the United States destroyed Japan, and attempted to row back from the past nine months of ever-growing collaboration, claiming that for three days he had thought of nothing but how to prevent a break between Vichy and the United States. For his part, Pétain spoke of this being "one of the great and terrible moments of history."[43] Considering his message delivered, Leahy left the meeting in a good mood and headed off for a dinner with diplomats friendly to the United States. Pétain and Darlan, one assumes, had a less relaxing evening.

The entry of the United States into the war also precipitated an event that made a lasting impression in Leahy's vision of Charles de Gaulle. On Christmas Day, Gaullist forces seized the small French-controlled islands of Saint-Pierre and Miquelon off the east coast of Canada. This move, done without US knowledge, struck Leahy as typical Gaullist grandstanding and made his relations with Darlan and Pétain even trickier.[44] It confirmed in Leahy's mind that de Gaulle was more concerned with restoring French pride and establishing his dominance in French politics than in winning the war as quickly as practicable with as few American casualties as possible. This was also the conclusion that Roosevelt and Welles came to at the same time. They could see no gain out of the move except for the personal glory of de Gaulle, and were more than aware of the problems it caused for Leahy.[45]

Leahy had had enough of quarrelsome Frenchmen. With America now in the war, he hoped he would be summoned back to Washington to take the promised post by Roosevelt's side. He even took it upon himself to start acting like Roosevelt's senior military adviser, sending the president a letter listing the officers whom he thought should have the most important naval commands. Leahy told Roosevelt that Ernest King, Chester Nimitz, and his old friend Thomas Hart were the best men to lead the fleet through this crisis. It is impossible to say how much this one letter mattered to the president, but not long after receiving it, he gave them the three most important commands available at the time. Roosevelt named Ernest King his chief of naval operations and CINCUS, while Nimitz became commander in chief of the Pacific Fleet. Hart was sent to take control in the most difficult area of operations in early 1942, becoming the overall Allied commander of naval forces in the Southwest Pacific.

The call for Leahy to return to Washington did not come as quickly as the admiral hoped. Both Roosevelt and the British government believed that Leahy needed to stay in place as a carrot dangled in front of Vichy to help Pétain resist the huge pressure coming from the Germans. A frustrated ambassador sent pleas to both Sumner Welles and Roosevelt to arrange his recall. One letter, sent on February 20, claimed that his recall was now necessary because the Vichy government was a lost cause.[46] "While one should have great sympathy for the Marshal in his almost impossible position," he wrote, "and a real affection for the unorganized, inarticulate, depressed people of France, it would appear that the time has passed when this war for the preservation of our civilization permits of giving further consideration to the pride or sensibilities of defeated France."[47]

Roosevelt commiserated, but still felt it was too soon to break completely with Vichy. He wrote back only two days later saying that Leahy would have to wait for "weeks" because the military situation was so uncertain that he did not want to do anything that would force Vichy to become a German ally.[48] Leahy thus had to keep doing his assigned job. At least he could now be ruthless. In early January the pro-German French press started complaining that Leahy was intervening too obviously in the Vichy decision-making process.[49] They had a point. Leahy was so relentless with Darlan that the French admiral eventually cracked. In early March 1942, he sent Leahy an emotional letter complaining that the tone of warnings that Leahy was giving him were so harsh that he was treating the French government with "scorn."[50] Leahy, who detested impulsive writing, waited a day to respond and treated Darlan's outburst with contempt. He claimed that the one thing he had learned from the whole experience was never to send a letter when angry.

Leahy's contempt was also combined with incredulity at Darlan's behavior. Leahy believed any rational French actor should now want to back away from political power. He viewed the different players who were scheming to hold on to authority as deluded, scrambling to get the best deck chairs on the *Titanic*. To Leahy, a sensible Darlan would have jumped at this opportunity to escape from the odor of collaboration, as one that was going to end up on the wrong side of history. Yet, Darlan did the opposite, and as the tide turned inexorably against him, he begged, pleaded, and plotted to stay in power. The problem Darlan had was that the United States entering the war had increased Laval's political leverage significantly, as the Germans lost any incentive to stay out of French internal affairs and wanted as pro-Axis a government as possible. The early months of 1942 saw a constant drip-drip of stories that Laval was going to be brought back by Pétain to try to appease the Germans. Even in April, after Laval had been named prime minister by Pétain, Darlan was begging for more time. One of Leahy's final reflections about the

French admiral was that if the true level of his collaboration became known, he would lose his head when the war was over.[51]

The one man Leahy knew would lose his head was Laval himself, and it was a fittingly bizarre ending to Leahy's ambassadorship that his penultimate formal meeting was with the great collaborator. Laval's appointment was in many ways a gift to Leahy, the final straw that led to his recall to Washington. However, Leahy still did not want to meet with him, detesting everything for which Laval stood. Yet the Frenchman was insistent that they meet, to the degree that he paid an official visit to the American embassy for the pleasure of Leahy's company. Exactly what Laval wanted to accomplish is unclear, as he spent most of his time trying to convince Leahy that a German victory was inevitable. Laval portrayed himself as a patriot. Leahy thought he was a crook, writing in his diary:

> M. Laval in a very frank discussion of the present and future policy of his Government gave the impression of being fanatically devoted to the interests of France with a conviction that they are bound irrevocably together with the interests of Germany.
>
> The impression is necessarily qualified by persistent reports to the effect that he has always in the past and does now use his political office to advance his personal private fortune. It is a fact that starting with nothing he has advanced himself from the position of a delivery boy for a provincial town grocery to a very rich man and a power in French political life.
>
> He is a small man, swarthy complexioned, careless in his personal appearance, and with a pleasing manner of speech.
>
> As a result of this very frank discussion of the present situation and future prospects I am convinced that M. Laval is fully committed and may be expected to go as far as he can in an effort to collaborate with Germany and to assist in the defeat of what he termed Soviet-British Bolshevism.

Leahy then concluded in classic deadpan:

> He definitely is not on our side in the war effort.[52]

Leahy's bitter tone was not just due to the bizarre logic of French politicians. He was dealing with the greatest personal crisis of his life—the death of his wife. Louise had not only been a huge support during their entire married life, she had been particularly important in keeping him on an even keel in Vichy. In his diary, Leahy revealed almost nothing about her health until things became serious; it seemed that even in such a private outlet, he could not bear to address what was happening. On her birthday, February 15, he noted simply that no celebration was possible. On February 21, due to a doctor's warning, Louise was not allowed to attend a formal luncheon. Still, he did his best to look after her in the midst of the great diplomatic crisis. March 21 was an unseasonably warm late-winter's day in central France, so Leahy bundled Louise into the ambassador's car and took her for a drive into the countryside. They passed through the lovely medieval village of Ris, enjoying their last happy journey together. A few days later Louise's condition worsened and her Vichy doctors advised an operation for an "abdominal" problem, which probably meant a hysterectomy. She was thought to be in so much danger that she could not risk the journey back to the United States.[53] The strain was so great that Leahy began suffering from nightmares.[54] Following the operation she stabilized a bit, but on April 21, just as Louise seemed well enough that they could start planning the journey back to America, she suffered an embolism and died quickly and, it seems, peacefully.

Leahy was devastated. "Her death is a crushing emotional shock to me that is beyond understanding of anyone who has not had an identical experience," he wrote. "It has left me not only crushed with sorrow, but permanently less than half efficient for any work the future may have in store for me and completely uninterested in the remaining future."[55]

Leahy brooded for weeks, his grief exacerbated by the gruesome spectacle of having to travel with her coffin back to the United States. As he departed Europe for the comfort of America, he may have pondered his life spent in uniform, with Louise at his side, now all of it seemingly at an end. Had he chosen to retire now, no one could have failed to understand, and had he retired, he would have enjoyed a brilliant, if soon forgotten, career. But William Leahy would cope with his wife's passing the only way he knew how—by devoting himself fully to his job, his nation, and his president. After some forty-five years in the US Navy, he had not yet seen the years that would shape one of the most significant careers in American strategic history. Leahy's future would not be uninteresting.

CHAPTER 13

Chief of Staff to the Commander in Chief

On June 1, 1942, William Leahy finally arrived into New York Harbor on the Swedish-registered SS *Drottningholm*, marking the end of the most horrible journey of his life. A month earlier, he had departed Vichy with Louise's body, heading for home. When he reached Lisbon, the crisis of war made it difficult for him to secure transportation, and for three weeks he was stuck in Portugal, watching over his wife's corpse, heartbroken yet desperate to get back to Washington.

In New York, he was greeted by a group of family and old friends.[1] To some he seemed depressed and diminished, Louise's death having clearly taken its toll. Yet rather than linger, he headed straight for Penn Station, where he boarded the first train to the capital. When he arrived, he was quickly ushered in to see Cordell Hull and Sumner Welles, who were full of praise for his performance in Vichy. But Leahy was anxious for a new task; he wanted to see Roosevelt. Unfortunately, the president was out of town and would not be back until June 5.

While waiting, Leahy organized Louise's funeral in their longtime church, St. Thomas, and then saw her buried in Arlington National Cemetery. Her loss was a pain he felt deeply for the rest of his life. He never contemplated remarriage and, to keep a connection with her, soon rejoined the vestry at St. Thomas. He held this position for much of the war, sometimes spending hours discussing policy on relatively insignificant church matters not long after working on issues of the gravest international importance. Incidentally, Roosevelt was also a parishioner at St. Thomas, possibly a factor in Leahy's decision to return to an active role in the Episcopalian Church. Years later, following the president's death, Leahy would reflect, "Roosevelt was the same kind of Christian that I tried to be."

Roosevelt called for Leahy as soon as he returned to the Oval Office. The admiral's diary describes a banal meeting, with Roosevelt telling him to have a rest and to return the following week to "discuss several tasks that he wants me to undertake."[2] Yet the president had grander expectations for his old friend. The war that lay ahead was unlike any faced by previous presidents. America was forced to confront two massive, highly organized, and technologically advanced enemies in Germany and Japan. The response from the US Armed Forces would be, by necessity, far-reaching and complex, and the diplomatic challenges would be complicated and numerous. Any president relies on a wide range of advisers, but in grappling with such an enormous problem as a world war, Roosevelt knew he needed a single person to rely on, a man he trusted implicitly, to assist in overseeing all matters military and diplomatic. A new role had been shaping in Roosevelt's head for several years, that of a chief of staff, and one name always came to mind for that position: William Leahy.

The job was to have two main roles. The first was to preside over the Joint Chiefs of Staff, representing the president to the military and in return communicating strategic questions from the military back to its commander in chief. This would make Leahy the highest-ranking officer in the US Armed Forces throughout the war; the president made clear that Leahy was to be senior to George Marshall and Ernest King.[3] He was using the phrase "chief of staff" in the army manner, which implied power in the chain of command, and not the navy one, which was for an executive officer. Leahy, to be sure this was understood, explicitly informed Marshall that they were using army nomenclature.[4] Certain army officers, if not Marshall, grasped this immediately. Gen. Walter Bedell Smith, who would serve as one of Eisenhower's closest aides in the war, remarked that Leahy "will almost certainly become a super-Chief of Staff" for Roosevelt.[5]

The second role Roosevelt had in mind was more intimate. The chief of staff was to be Roosevelt's most senior military adviser, a regular presence in his professional and personal life. He and Leahy would meet daily to discuss both the crucial issues of the moment and the larger strategic questions for the future.[6] One of the first instructions outlining the role was an executive order that Leahy was to be made the recipient of all the military reports coming into the White House. He was to be sent complete information on every army and navy operation, both current and projected, and the most sensitive intelligence reports. Combined, he was to have all the information that Marshall and King only had separately, plus more from other sources.

George Marshall, who served as chief of staff of the army, believed that his own sway was to thank for Leahy's new role.[7] Soon after the president had broached the subject with Leahy, Marshall told Leahy that it was he who had suggested to Roosevelt that Leahy be appointed as the president's chief of staff to coordinate the functioning of the armed services.[8] In fact, Marshall's influence was minimal at best. Roosevelt had planned on Leahy's appointment since 1939 and had discussed it with the admiral over the years. Though Marshall almost certainly did not see it, he was a Roosevelt outsider, and Leahy a true insider. The admiral had known Roosevelt for decades. The two men had worked closely together and had socialized; Leahy had long been a familiar face to the president's family. Having spent almost no personal time with Roosevelt, Marshall did not understand the president's thinking, nor did he fathom the power of the position Roosevelt and Leahy were constructing. Assuming that the role of chief of staff was mostly to coordinate discussion amongst the armed forces, he failed to fully grasp that its defining element was to act as Roosevelt's senior strategic adviser. Ernest King, an aggressive and somewhat paranoid man, did realize that it would lessen his and Marshall's influence with the White House, and opposed the appointment. Roosevelt rejected King's pugnaciousness, telling him that Leahy would make a "very good" chief of staff.[9] King, however, was wise to be skeptical.

Leahy's new official title was Chief of Staff to the Commander in Chief, Army and Navy of the United States.[10] For most people, he was simply Roosevelt's chief of staff, there being no civilian equivalent at the time. On July 6, the president formally offered him the post, and Leahy accepted.[11] At a press conference announcing the new role, Roosevelt publicly downplayed its importance, worried that critics would think he was ceding too much presidential authority.[12] Asked what Leahy's role would be, Roosevelt lied, saying the admiral would mostly do the president's legwork—summarizing reports and the like.[13] Roosevelt could do this knowing that Leahy would not take the slight personally.

Leahy was more than willing to play along with Roosevelt's fiction. He wanted as little publicity as possible and rarely discussed his role in policy-making. He declined any detailed interviews when appointed; indeed, he refused almost all interviews during the war. Naturally, a flurry of speculation arose in the press. "Leahy's Role in the War: Real Importance of the Admiral's Task as Aide to the President May Appear Later," read a *New York Times* headline.[14] Famed columnist Arthur Krock, confused by just what Leahy was supposed to do, implied that the position of chief of staff would be too weak, especially for those who wanted the president to appoint one military man as overall commander of American forces.[15] It took months before the press caught on to Leahy's real power. In late September his face adorned the cover of *Life* magazine, along with a story entitled: "Admiral Leahy: The President Calls Him a Legman but He Plays a Powerful Part in Running the War."[16] The *Washington Post* editorialized in October about how influential he truly was.[17] Leahy refused to comment, and so, little that was concrete could be written about his growing influence—which suited him just fine.[18]

If the public was misled about Leahy's role, to those in the White House it was clear that the admiral was no mere legman. In fact, he was the president's gatekeeper to the war, charged with providing the commander in chief with a full picture of the conflict each morning.[19] Arriving at the executive mansion around eight thirty a.m., Leahy would spend about an hour sifting through telegrams and intelligence reports before Roosevelt, a late riser, was ready for him. Often the admiral would encounter the president, escorted in his wheelchair by his valet, en route to the meeting. "With his long cigarette holder clamped in his mouth at a jaunty angle, his Navy boat cape—a gift from Mrs. Roosevelt—thrown about his shoulders, he rode his wheel chair proudly erect, more like the winner of a Roman chariot race than a confirmed cripple," recalled Adm. Wilson Brown, who witnessed such encounters.[20] Leahy had to hurry to keep up. The briefings typically took place in the White House Map Room, Roosevelt's highly exclusive chamber devoted to the most up-to-date wartime information. Surrounded by large maps, Leahy would outline the war's most recent developments, briefing the president on highly sensitive information. Roosevelt, at ease with his trusted confidant, would muse aloud on the war and international politics, using the admiral as a sounding board.

Roosevelt had assembled his Map Room after seeing Churchill's mobile equivalent, which the British prime minister had brought to Washington in December 1941. Installed just next to the Oval Office, the room's walls were blanketed with outsized maps detailing all the world's combat theaters. Lines of advance and retreat were marked and remarked in grease pencil. Pins were added to show individual units or large warships; a particularly large pin denoted a vessel with one of the president's sons on board. The duty officers' desks were huddled in the middle of the room and the maps kept at a low height to allow for Roosevelt to be wheeled from wall to wall to examine detail. At times, Leahy himself would push the president's wheelchair.

Aside from Roosevelt, only two individuals were allowed unrestricted access to the Map Room: Harry Hopkins and William Leahy.[21] Everyone else, including George Marshall, Ernest King, Cordell Hull, and Henry Stimson, had to be either accompanied by one of these two men or be given special permission to be allowed inside.* Leahy enjoyed being part of the Map Room setup. Not long after his first visit there, he told the room's controlling officer, Captain John L. McCrea, that there was more information in the room than anywhere else in Washington.[22] He was right. The Map Room housed the only complete

---

* Doris Kearns Goodwin, in her history of the Roosevelts during the war, completely misses Leahy's involvement with the Map Room, stating blithely that Marshall and King had unrestricted access. They certainly did not. Doris Kearns Goodwin, *No Ordinary Time: Franklin and Eleanor Roosevelt—The Home Front in World War II* (New York: Simon & Schuster, 1994), 311.

set of the president's highly confidential correspondence with world leaders such as Churchill, Stalin, and Chiang Kai-shek.

Leahy's first week as chief of staff attested to the centrality and confidentiality of his new role. On July 24, he met privately with the president to discuss the overriding question of the moment: whether the United States should invade North Africa in 1942, as Leahy favored, or build up forces in the United Kingdom in anticipation of an invasion of France, as favored by Marshall, King, and Henry "Hap" Arnold, the chief of the army air forces. Roosevelt also asked Leahy to take a confidential message from Marshall and King, who were in London, to Secretary of War Stimson. The next day, Leahy met with FDR, Stimson, Arnold, and Lt. Gen. Joseph McNarney, Marshall's deputy, to discuss the plans for an invasion of North Africa. Later, Leahy met with Crown Princess Martha of Norway, a mistress of Franklin Roosevelt (naturally, the admiral said nothing about the relationship), and also the French ambassador.

On July 27, Leahy met with the two most senior British military officers in Washington, DC, Field Marshal Sir John Dill and Adm. Andrew Cunningham, to discuss a range of issues, including the possible invasion of North Africa. He then lunched with Secretary of the Interior Harold Ickes and discussed war production. The following day, he met with Roosevelt, King, Marshall, and Hopkins to analyze the results of the latter three's trip to Britain. Afterward, Roosevelt asked Leahy to relay another confidential message, this time to the State Department. In the afternoon Leahy, for the first time, presided over a meeting of the Joint Chiefs of Staff. On July 29, two senior Chinese generals called on Leahy to plead for more supplies for their forces fighting the Japanese. That evening Leahy dined with Secretary of the Navy Frank Knox and Roosevelt's spy chief and head of the Office of Strategic Services, William Donovan. On July 30, Leahy presided over the first meeting of the Combined Chiefs of Staff, the military board overseeing the Western Allies, to help push forward plans for the invasion of North Africa. Later that evening, he was called in by the president to meet with him and Arnold to discuss an urgent British request for more aircraft in Egypt to help contain the advance of Erwin Rommel's Afrika Korps.

It was a whirlwind first week. In seven days, Leahy met with every major figure in the American strategic policy-making structure and many of the most important men representing America's allies. Assuming Leahy had five or six daily briefings with Roosevelt in that week, he would have met with the president at least ten times.[23] All of this occurred during one of the more fraught moments of the war, when Roosevelt's time was at a premium. The establishment of such an extraordinary position marks an important development in the history of American government. Leahy and Roosevelt were in the process of creating what we now know of as the role of national security adviser.

Before Leahy, there was no person in the White House whose job it was to sit and talk strategy with the president. Presidents often had unofficial advisers, such as Col. Edward House (who was, in fact, not a colonel, nor had even served in the military) for Woodrow Wilson and, at times, Harry Hopkins for FDR. Yet it was unprecedented for a serving military officer to be assigned as daily adviser to the president. Moreover, even though Leahy was a military officer, he was used by Roosevelt in many roles that we normally would think of as civilian. He became one of Roosevelt's most trusted means of connecting with the State Department. Not only did he transmit confidential messages, Leahy quickly reestablished his close professional relationship with Sumner Welles. The two men would meet to work on a number of tricky questions, including the status of American diplomats in neutral Europe and then the establishment of a ruling agency in North Africa after Operation Torch.[24]

All of these roles, and the need to make himself available to meet with Roosevelt at any time of the day or night, was so intense that Leahy soon ended up moving from Georgetown, where he was staying with his son's in-laws, to the Hay-Adams Hotel next to the White House. He resided there for months until the small Florida Avenue town house that he had bought with Louise was vacated by the tenant who had rented it when the Leahys went to France. Proximity to the White House was important for him—it is impossible to know how many times Leahy met with Roosevelt during the war. While the admiral shows up in Roosevelt's appointment diary on 166 different days, this figure would have represented a small fraction of the meetings they held. As Leahy was a member of the White House staff, his talks with the president, including most of his morning briefings, were not normally recorded. It would not be possible to list all their meetings, as at times they spent entire weeks together, talking all day. Meetings occurred in the White House; on board ships, planes, and trains; in North America, Europe, Africa, and Asia. In the end, the two men had thousands of encounters, which all together would have lasted for many thousands of hours.

Six weeks after taking office, Leahy was invited by the president for a weekend at Shangri-La, the presidential retreat in Maryland's countryside now known as Camp David.[25] Joined by Harry Hopkins and Assistant Secretary of the Navy James Forrestal, the group whiled away the evening discussing American strategy. Leahy spent the night, leaving only the following day. Such closeness to the president revealed a fundamental difference between Leahy and any other military figure.

With the two men spending so much time together, it was unsurprising that Leahy began to interact more and more with others close to the president. A few days after the overnight trip to Shangri-La, Leahy was invited to dine en famille with the president and Eleanor Roosevelt.[26] From that point on he ate regularly with the first couple.[27] Leahy's relationship with Eleanor was never as close as that with the president—not necessarily a bad thing in FDR's eyes. Roosevelt's own relationship with his wife was complex. The couple had flirted with divorce after his sexual indiscretions became known to Eleanor in 1918, and the marriage had grown increasingly distant as time passed. For the sake of his political standing as much as anything else, they stayed legally bound. In the White House, Eleanor behaved more as a policy advocate than a spouse. When the two got together—a relatively rare occurrence—she usually pressed Franklin on political issues, almost always arguing for more radical positions on the New Deal or foreign policy. As FDR aged and grew increasingly weary, he often found spending time with the energetic and principled Eleanor to be precisely what he did not want to do.[28] He was more relaxed in the company of his mistresses and was more than happy to have Leahy along with him at those times. Eleanor never realized that Leahy spent time around Franklin and his lovers and never hesitated to approach the admiral with policy questions. On September 7, 1942, for instance, she called to get Leahy's opinions about the practicality of the United States taking in a thousand children, most of them Jewish, being held in French prisons.[29] Leahy was supportive.

During Leahy's early months as chief of staff, only one man surpassed him for influence with the president, and that was Harry Hopkins. A dynamic, enigmatic figure, Hopkins inspired either affection or deep loathing in those with whom he worked. He was a creature of Roosevelt's New Deal, which he had used to reach the top of the US government. Born and raised in Iowa, after graduation from Grinnell College he set out to do good. He moved to New York, where he took different jobs trying to alleviate the poverty of the city's most disadvantaged. After the Great Depression hit, the governor of New York at the time, Franklin Roosevelt, appointed Hopkins to coordinate the state's relief efforts. When Roosevelt became president a few years later, he brought Hopkins with him to Washington. Hopkins rose meteorically up the federal government's ranks, running many of the most famous New Deal programs, including the Federal Emergency Relief Administration and the Works Progress Administration. Roosevelt came to see Hopkins as a true devotee. He also increasingly enjoyed Hopkins's company.

Hopelessly disorganized, the often sick, chain-smoking, skinny-to-the-point-of-emaciated Hopkins could seem desperately unwell to those meeting him for the first time. When sober he could be opaque and reserved, but when he drank heavily, he could come across as shockingly crude. Many of those who spent time with Hopkins, including Leahy and Winston Churchill, concluded that he had a penetrating mind, strong convictions, and the ability to cut right to the heart of an issue. Hopkins could put his finger on exactly the question that needed to be answered at any point in time. He also had a feline understanding of Roosevelt's wishes, which he combined with his own ideological similarities with the president to nurture their intimate relationship. More than Leahy, Hopkins shared many of Roosevelt's basic political and international ideas. Hopkins favored the more radical New Deal programs espoused by the president and was willing to fight for them. In 1940 and 1941, it was Hopkins whom Roosevelt trusted more than anyone else with the creation and implementation of US foreign policy, often bypassing the State Department entirely, with the exception of Sumner Welles.

Their closeness was remarkable. Hopkins's special status was recognized when Roosevelt convinced him to move into the White House to be available constantly for advice and support. As the president came to rely on Hopkins more and more, the man became more concerned with protecting his special position in Roosevelt's court. In doing so, he worked against anyone else gaining too much authority. He could be ruthless, using both derision and gossip to undermine anyone who appeared to be a threat to his supremacy. Harold Ickes, William Bullitt, and Bernard Baruch, to name just a few, all believed that Hopkins manipulated the president to exclude them from policy-making.[30] When Leahy appeared in Roosevelt's daily life, Hopkins was inclined to be suspicious. The two men had hardly interacted at all before this. Leahy had happily used some of Hopkins's WPA largesse when he was governor of Puerto Rico, but otherwise they had operated in different circles. Thrust together in the Roosevelt White House as the president's two closest advisers, a worried Hopkins convinced FDR to channel all political correspondence from heads of state through him, thus cutting Leahy out of the loop if Hopkins so desired.[31]

It was the one clear setback that Leahy would experience during his time as Roosevelt's chief of staff, but it was not to last. The two men, who seemed to be polar opposites to those on the outside, grew to respect and, possibly, trust each other. They even shared some important characteristics: both were Midwesterners from non-wealthy backgrounds; both preferred government service over making money (though Hopkins was careful to marry into a great deal of cash); and both were political animals. Most decisively, both men were devoted to Franklin Roosevelt, making a productive relationship between them a necessity, particularly once Hopkins discovered that he couldn't drive a wedge between the president and his chief of staff.

The more Hopkins and Leahy worked together, the greater their mutual respect grew. So comfortable was Roosevelt with the two that he regularly had them around for evening chats that could stretch on until well after midnight.[32] He also started inviting them both for holidays or trips to Hyde Park. Roosevelt preferred to draft foreign policy documents with Hopkins and Leahy. The admiral later admitted that Roosevelt would often rewrite State Department policy papers without informing the diplomatic service, saying the president "would get Harry or me to help him."[33]

Following a renovation of the East Wing of the White House, both Leahy and Hopkins received prized offices, allowing them to be available to the president at odd times and with little notice.* Each office had its own bathroom—quite an extravagant feature for the time—so that its occupier could freshen up in case of unexpected meetings with the president. Roosevelt was usually careful to look out for their prerogatives.[34] The occupants of the East Wing and their staffs considered themselves to be living in a rarefied world; when FDR was out of town they were allowed use of the presidential swimming pool and movie theater.[35]

Leahy played an unusually close role in Roosevelt's life, but Roosevelt also had an enormous impact on Leahy's. Roosevelt took a man instinctively more conservative, isolationist, and cynical, and by the force of his personality made him more liberal, international, and, dare it be said, hopeful. Serving Roosevelt gave Leahy, working now well past the navy's age of retirement, a newfound energy. Settled in as chief of staff, he had quickly integrated himself into the president's daily life. Now Leahy was prepared to use his position to impose his own strategic stamp on the US military. As the military chiefs of staff would soon learn, Leahy had a particular vision of how the war should be fought, and he was determined to get his way.

---

* There were three main offices in the new East Wing. James Byrnes received the third.

CHAPTER 14

Chairman of the Joint Chiefs of Staff

The Joint Chiefs of Staff, a small group of senior officers who helped plan and control strategic operations across the armed services of the United States, was ordered into existence by Franklin Roosevelt in January 1942.[1] In April, he named the Joint Chiefs as the official American representatives on the Combined Chiefs of Staff, a joint body of American and British officers established to coordinate military action during the war.[2] With two strokes of his pen, Roosevelt had created an institution that many Americans had dreaded. They feared that a unified armed forces general staff, which smacked of European militarism, would lead to too much power for the army and navy. If the critics had seen the Joint Chiefs of Staff operate for the first six months of its existence, however, they would have wondered why they had ever been worried.

Originally, there were three chiefs: Gen. George Marshall, chief of staff of the army; Adm. Ernest King, chief of naval operations and commander in chief of the US Fleet; and Gen. Hap Arnold, chief of staff of the US Army Air Force. All three were type A personalities who had fought their way to the top of their profession. Together as a corporate body, they were dysfunctional. The two soldiers and one sailor had fundamentally incompatible views of grand strategy. Marshall wanted to concentrate on the war against Germany and prepare for a cross-channel invasion of France at the earliest possible moment. King wanted a free hand to devote as many resources as possible to the war against Japan. Arnold, meanwhile, prioritized the development of a strategic bombing force to lay waste to the economic infrastructures of Germany and Japan. The result was a slow-motion car crash as Roosevelt had to constantly referee disputes, particularly between Marshall and King. As someone who naturally avoided conflict, the president found this exhausting and irritating.

The crisis in the Joint Chiefs compounded an unexpected crisis in the war. While no one thought that World War II would be easy, the first six months for the United States were far worse than expected. Both the Russians and the British failed to stop German advances on the Eastern Front and North Africa. In the Atlantic, German U-boats exacted a terrifying toll on American trade, decimating shipping up and down the East Coast and well into the Gulf of Mexico. These losses of fuel and bauxite ate into the ability of the United States to produce all the matériel it needed to fight the war. In the Pacific, matters were even worse. During the first six months after Pearl Harbor, the Japanese ran wild. Showing themselves to be a far more formidable adversary than almost anyone imagined, the Japanese pushed the Americans, British, and Dutch out of thousands of square miles of territory and ocean. They seized the Philippines, all of French Indochina, and modern-day Malaysia, Indonesia, Thailand, and Burma. In doing so, Japan established control over a vast empire of natural resources, which, if allowed to function as a unit, could support an even more powerful war machine. By the summer of 1942, defeating the Axis looked to be a far more difficult task.

Had the dysfunctionality within the American Joint Chiefs continued, it could have made things even worse. Only the Joint Chiefs of Staff, working with the president, could answer the fundamental questions of American grand strategy: What kind of armed forces should the United States construct? Should those armed forces primarily be used first in a war against Germany? Should France be invaded in 1942, 1943, or 1944? Should the United States concentrate on one, two, or even three drives against Japan? Should the US Armed Forces have one supreme commander in each area, or should it divide command when needed?

Perhaps the only question that Marshall, King, and Arnold agreed on was their strong opposition to an invasion of French North Africa, (Morocco and Algeria), an operation that was first given the code name Gymnast but is much better known by its later moniker, Torch.[3] The operation seemed to them a dangerous waste of resources and a diversion away from fighting the wars that they wanted. The problem was that Franklin Roosevelt saw in Torch the perfect solution to his strategic dilemma. Worried by the losses suffered in the Atlantic and the Pacific, Roosevelt did not want to rush into a risky invasion of France before he believed American forces were ready. On the other hand, he wanted to give US troops combat experience in a theater that could be controlled through American air-sea dominance. North Africa fit the president's bill nicely.

As Roosevelt started looking more and more positively on Torch, Marshall, King, and Arnold decided they needed to help him see sense. On July 10, the three sent a memorandum to Roosevelt arguing against an invasion of North Africa and asking the president to focus on Operation Bolero—the buildup of forces in Britain in anticipation of a landing in France.[4] Marshall was particularly violent in his opposition to Torch. He wrote a number of papers opposing the plan, also enlisting the secretary of war, Henry Stimson, to lobby Roosevelt against the attack.[5] Marshall eventually became so worked up that he made a stupid and, as it turned out, empty threat to abandon his Europe or Germany-First policy if the North African invasion were approved.[6]

The Joint Chiefs may have been against him on this issue, but Franklin Roosevelt had one strong ally among senior American officers in his fight for Torch: his old friend and strategic confidant, William Leahy. Back in May 1941, surveying the world war from his perch in Vichy, the admiral recognized that if the United States seized French North Africa, a "vulnerable point" in Germany's position and something that could be achieved through US sea power, it would help turn the course of the war. He believed that 250,000 men, backed up by US air and sea forces, could seize Morocco and Algeria before the Germans would have time to ship enough forces across the Mediterranean to stop them, imprisoning the Nazis in Europe and shortening the war "by half." He was impatient to strike. "Some day, to win the war superior pressure must be applied at a weak point in the German military campaign," he wrote in his diary. "Today the vulnerable spot is North Africa."[7]

By the time Leahy returned to Washington in June 1942, more than a year later, he had even more reasons to support Torch.[8] Seizing North Africa, he believed, would help protect vulnerable Allied shipping in the Atlantic, depriving the Germans of possible new air and sea bases while at the same time decimating German and Italian shipping in the Mediterranean, putting a permanent block on their expansion.

As the new position of chief of staff was being shaped, Roosevelt and Leahy spent much of their time discussing Torch.[9] Marshall and King were in London in the middle of July, leaving the two friends to plan alone. Only Arnold was still in Washington, and he and Henry Stimson met once with Roosevelt and Leahy to discuss the operation, which both Arnold and Stimson opposed. It made no difference. The president was determined to press ahead with Torch, and Leahy was determined to see the president's, and his own, wishes enacted.

On July 28, 1942, the Joint Chiefs met for the first time since Leahy had been named Roosevelt's chief of staff.* It was clear that things had changed at the top of the American military hierarchy. There were now four people around the rectangular table in the Public Health Services Building on Constitution Avenue (which was dubbed the Combined Chiefs of Staff Building at this point in the war). Leahy took the chair and was the first person to speak. Torch quickly dominated. Ernest King attacked the operation, saying that he feared it would result in a military disaster such as the British had experienced at Gallipoli. He also argued that it would make the buildup of US forces in the United Kingdom impossible.[10] Leahy listened to King and decided to fall back on subtlety. He did not criticize King's position directly but argued that a North Africa invasion could help preparations for an eventual invasion of Europe by getting more troops in the theater quickly.

Two days later, there was a meeting of the Combined Chiefs of

---

* The regular meetings of the JCS were scheduled for midday on Wednesdays, and often began with a simple lunch. At important times they could meet far more often. Though Leahy, Marshall, King, and Arnold were the most powerful men around the table, other senior officers attended as aides and members of the JCS staff.

Staff.[11] Now the American chiefs were together with the senior representatives of the British Armed Forces based in Washington, including Field Marshal Sir John Dill and Adm. Sir Andrew Cunningham. Once again, Leahy took the chair. This time, however, he would not be so subtle. His first interjection was to tell the other chiefs that Torch was going to proceed. Indeed, he called for operational planning to be sped up so that the operation could be launched as soon as possible.

George Marshall, who had been quiet on the subject on July 28, could not comprehend what was happening. After Leahy said that planning for Torch should be accelerated, Marshall acted like he could still stop the operation. He went into a long monologue on the drawbacks of Torch, concluding, bizarrely, that if it was approved it would leave the British Isles open to a possible seaborne Nazi invasion.[12] Leahy, who understood amphibious operations more than Marshall, would have realized that argument was nonsense. The British representatives, who supported the launch of Torch, made no mention of a possible German invasion. As Marshall would not budge, however, Leahy ended the meeting playing his strongest card. He told the chiefs that he would report their difference of opinion back to Roosevelt.[13] However, he made it clear that the operation would go ahead, that the chiefs would have one more week to get on board, and by then a date must be chosen for the operation. George Marshall had been swatted aside.

Though Marshall and King remained strongly opposed to Torch, they had no recourse but to proceed with an operation they loathed. The story of this decision is the perfect example of the other role that Roosevelt had laid out for Leahy: "presiding" over the Joint Chiefs of Staff. This role metamorphosed into the more well-known position: chairman of the Joint Chiefs of Staff. From this perch, Leahy shaped American grand strategy in World War II more than anyone but the president (and, at times, even more than Roosevelt himself). It gave him his most immediate control over the allocation of American forces in the field. Leahy did not believe that the chiefs should interfere much, if at all, in tactical operations. Instead, he believed that they should decide overall theater priorities for personnel and equipment, and then allow the commanders in the field to get on with the job.[14]

President Roosevelt was determined that Leahy be recognized as the senior member of the Joint Chiefs. Once Leahy was appointed, the president began to severely limit the amount of time he spent with the other chiefs, both personally and in correspondence. His communications were usually relayed through Leahy, or sometimes Hopkins (and occasionally both men as their relationship strengthened).[15] Anyone who wants to see the dramatic distance that appeared between Roosevelt and Marshall and King need only look at Roosevelt's papers.[16] The president regularly exchanged correspondence with the heads of the army and navy until September 1942, after which letters between them vanish almost completely. Indeed, no records of direct communications between Roosevelt and Marshall exist between early September 1942 and May 1944. Correspondence with King ceases completely in August 1942.

When it came to basic information on the state of American forces in the field, Roosevelt immediately shifted to having it channeled through his chief of staff. In September 1942, he ordered King and Marshall to provide him with daily updates through Leahy of the matériel available to American forces fighting in the South Pacific.[17] Roosevelt also used Leahy to canvass the chiefs on geopolitical issues and report back, including sensitive topics such as the amount of force the United States should deploy to China.[18] At other times, Roosevelt issued quite peremptory orders for Leahy to have the other Joint Chiefs fulfill.[19] Of course, this was another one of the aces up Leahy's sleeve. The other chiefs, as they saw the president far less often, could never be entirely sure when Leahy was asking for information whether it was for himself or for the president. On the other hand, it meant that the other chiefs often had to go groveling to Leahy to get decisions from the president.[20]

Leahy was not chairman of the Joint Chiefs of Staff as the position is understood today. He was much more powerful. He usually referred to himself as the "senior" member whose role it was to "preside" over the others, as this was the formulation that he and Roosevelt first devised. His superiority came because of his position as the president's representative, and in his mind, as well as in the minds of others in the White House, this made him the most important chief.[21] As the president's representative, he was free from any civilian authority except for

Roosevelt. When the position of chairman of the Joint Chiefs was finally authorized by Congress in the National Defense Act of 1947, it was placed under the Secretary of Defense.[22] In fact, Leahy eventually decided that the two-headed post that he and Roosevelt constructed was so powerful that it needed to be cut down to size.

He was right to be concerned. From Leahy's perspective, civilian input into the American strategic decision-making process, with the exception of Hopkins, was worryingly nonexistent. Vice President Henry Wallace and Secretary of State Cordell Hull had little understanding and no influence over strategic policy. Wallace, a committed left-wing New Dealer, was, like most vice presidents, chosen for political reasons, and he devoted himself overwhelmingly to domestic concerns. His most important foreign-policy statements usually involved the need for a strong US-Soviet relationship, to the point that Leahy had little confidence in his instincts. Cordell Hull, meanwhile, played the role of world statesman, but when important decisions were made he was rarely in the room. If Wallace's and Hull's lack of influence was no shock, what was surprising was how unimportant the civilian heads of the army and navy were when the crucial decisions were made. Secretary of War Henry Stimson and Secretary of the Navy Frank Knox were kept at arm's length from the cozy clique of Roosevelt, Leahy, and Hopkins, and even from Marshall, Arnold, and King.

Stimson and Knox came relatively late into Roosevelt's orbit, both being appointed in 1940. Politically their value stemmed from the fact that they were internationalists who supported massive aid for Great Britain in its struggle against Nazi Germany. As Republicans, they allowed Roosevelt to appear bipartisan in the run-up to the presidential election of 1940. However, like Hull, they were denied the most important confidential information: neither was allowed open access to the White House Map Room, and neither was regularly included in the grand strategic conferences of the war. Roosevelt certainly did not confide in either, and, considering their senior position, met with each infrequently and in groups—hardly ever alone.

Stimson lacked influence partly because of Leahy's antipathy for him. The secretary of war was one of those characters in history that looked and acted like he should be a powerful statesman but usually bungled the opportunity. Impeccably bred and with a dignified, silver-fox hairstyle, Stimson was a Republican Party grandee from a wealthy New York family. Leahy lost respect for him when Stimson served as secretary of state for the hated Herbert Hoover. For Leahy, Stimson represented everything that was wrong in American foreign policy-making. He talked loudly but carried a puny stick. He regularly condemned Japanese policy but refused to do anything tangible to back up his statements.[23] When he joined the Roosevelt administration in 1940, Stimson was seventy-three years old, though in quite good health, and from the beginning Roosevelt treated him with his special blend of respect and neglect. Stimson was included in the American delegation to the Arcadia Conference in Washington, DC, in December 1941, but thereafter was usually excluded from the most important meetings of World War II. It is notable how infrequently Roosevelt met with Stimson once Leahy had established his position in the White House. Between January 1, 1943, and Roosevelt's death in April 1945, approximately twenty-eight months, Stimson appears in Roosevelt's meeting diary only thirty-eight times. About half of these meetings involved other people (including Leahy much of the time), and many of the private meetings ran for only five to ten minutes.[24]

Knox was even less influential. Before becoming secretary of the navy in 1940, he had barely spoken a word to Roosevelt. He was a progressive Republican who made his name as the owner and editor of the *Chicago Daily News*.[25] When World War II broke out in Europe, Knox became one of the most outspoken advocates of aid to the Allies. His passion to support the British appealed to the president, but Leahy considered him ineffectual. Moreover, as the war went on, Knox's health deteriorated and he lost almost all the influence he had over the fleet. In 1944 Leahy remarked that King dominated the navy because Knox was too weak.[26] Like Stimson's, Knox's meetings with Roosevelt were kept to a minimum.

With Stimson and Knox out of the loop, there was no one to limit Leahy's power except Roosevelt. More than aware of that fact, Leahy was careful not to be seen using his position as chairman of the Joint

Chiefs to dictate policy. Instead, he saw his role as facilitating productive discussion and directing the Joint Chiefs' bureaucracy. He would have been a failure if Marshall, King, or Arnold had felt that their views were not respected—even when their views were overruled. Moreover, it would have been unnecessary and counterproductive for Leahy to fight with the other chiefs. To get his way, Leahy did not have to convince Marshall, King, or Arnold—he had to convince Franklin Roosevelt. That was the reason for his periodic reluctance to express strong views during meetings of the Joint Chiefs. This has led to an erroneous assumption that Leahy was an impartial chairman.[27] He was often extremely partial, but he rarely had to, or wanted to, proclaim his partiality.

His actions as chairman of the Joint Chiefs say a great deal about his nature in general. Observers often remarked on the way he controlled discussions with a few, occasionally self-effacing, words. Officers who served on the staff of Ernest King, who had some difficult moments with Leahy during the war, admired Leahy's ability to handle their irascible boss. Adm. James Fife, one of the navy's leading submariners, served as a senior aide to King, often sitting in on the meetings of the Joint Chiefs. He quickly came to see Leahy as a "wonderful operator" who "never wasted a single word at any time."[28] Adm. Richard "Close In" Conolly, who also served on King's staff, commented on Leahy's subtlety, remembering that Leahy talked rarely at the meetings, opting to guide the discussion with gentle nudges only to "quash the arguments if they weren't leading in the proper direction."[29]

From 1943 until 1945 Adm. Robert Dennison, then a captain, served on the Joint Chiefs of Staff's joint planning staff. He marveled at how Leahy controlled the other chiefs.

> He didn't really use any pressure, but his technique was most interesting. I attended a good many meetings and one of the things he used to do—Marshall, for example, would start discussing some plan of his, something he thought we ought to be doing next and Leahy would say, "Well, George, I'm just a simple sailor. Would you please back up and start from the beginning and make it simple, just tell me step one, two, and three, and so on." Well, Marshall or

Arnold or whoever it was, kept falling for this thing and explained to this simple old sailor. And as they did it—which is what Leahy knew damned well would happen—and went through these various steps, they themselves would find out the weakness or misconception or that there was something wrong with it. So he [Leahy] didn't have to start out by saying "This is a stupid idea and it won't work."[30]

The relationship between Leahy and Marshall is one of the most fascinating and important in US strategic history—to say nothing of the fact that it is often completely misunderstood. Their interactions would not only be crucial during World War II, they would help shape US policy at the start of the Cold War. Within the White House it was realized that Leahy was appointed to be senior to Marshall, though it did take a while for the general to realize that himself.[31]

Marshall certainly had a sense of his own grandeur and believed that others should as well. He had a need to seem to be in control, an august, formal, and upright figure. Where Leahy was caustic and clubbable, and used his political skills to get his way, Marshall relied on an impression of austere formality. It was one of the reasons the general's relationship with Roosevelt was weak. Roosevelt usually opted for an air of faux friendship with people with whom he worked, treating them to their faces as trusted friends and opting to call them by their first names (he always called Leahy "Bill"). When the president called Marshall "George," the general made his disapproval known. It was a tactical mistake by Marshall, as Roosevelt never seemed particularly comfortable in his presence and, once Leahy returned from France, seems to have hardly spent any time privately with the general. When Roosevelt died, Marshall went to the burial at Hyde Park and remarked that it was the first time he had ever been invited to Roosevelt's family home.[32]

Despite the popular perception of Marshall as the Joint Chiefs of Staff's dominant figure, the other chiefs never hesitated to challenge him and never deferred to his demands.[33] Even Arnold, technically Marshall's subordinate in the army chain of command and a close friend, was willing to fight his superior to protect his beloved air force. Yet historians are not alone in overestimating Marshall's power—Marshall himself boasted of his own influence. In a memo to the director of the War Department's Information Bureau, he acknowledged Leahy's position as the senior member but crowed, "Confidentially, of course, I have built him up to a certain extent in his position."[34]

Marshall's unnecessary and insecure puffery masked a growing realization about just how powerful Leahy was becoming. By the time Marshall wrote this, he had already been bested by Leahy on the issue of Torch and would soon be outmaneuvered on the issue of American construction priorities. By November 1942, Marshall was worried enough about Leahy's influence that he tried to go around the admiral and use Harry Hopkins to get to Roosevelt. Marshall and Hopkins had developed a close relationship in the 1930s, and Hopkins's support was one of the reasons Marshall became the army chief of staff. In this instance, he wanted Hopkins to convince Roosevelt to appoint a separate secretary to attend cabinet meetings, so that information from them could be transmitted to himself directly without Leahy as a buffer. As he admitted to Hopkins, "I am getting into very delicate ground here.... I should take this up directly with Admiral Leahy, and I will talk to him about it, but frankly, I know you are more familiar with these matters than he has yet had time to become."[35] Hopkins had better judgment than to press the issue, and Marshall's gambit went nowhere.

On the other hand, Leahy understood Marshall's need to be seen as a great man and was happy to play along with the public persona the general cultivated. In his memoirs, Leahy walked a fine line using stereotypical words about Marshall's greatness while also admitting that the two had some distinctly different policy views: "In the postwar period, General Marshall and I disagreed sharply on some aspects of our foreign policy. However, as a soldier he was in my opinion one of the best, and his drive, courage, and imagination transformed America's great citizen army into the most magnificent fighting force ever assembled."[36]

A close parsing of this phrase shows Leahy's doubts. As he admitted, he had a different geopolitical vision from Marshall and considered Marshall to have US priorities upside down during the Cold War. In his stress on Marshall as a soldier, with his focus on army building (as opposed to employment), Leahy once again was careful to limit his praise to Marshall's more bureaucratic skills as opposed to his strategic vision. These doubts about Marshall's outlook were in addition to Leahy's skepticism about Marshall as a negotiator. Maybe the most important thing to realize about their relationship was that Leahy was not in the least bit intimidated by Marshall. Leahy almost always took a hard line when he disagreed with Marshall, and as long as Franklin Roosevelt lived, the admiral emerged triumphant.

Leahy's relationship with King was no closer, even though the two naval officers had crossed paths many times over the preceding decades. King graduated from Annapolis four years after Leahy and was a very different personality. More of a loner, King rose to the top by being fiercely independent and driven. He was also a heavy drinker and a serial philanderer. Not surprisingly, King was not an easy person to like, and Leahy certainly did not include him among his close naval friends. Yet in the 1930s they worked well together as bureau chiefs, and through this, Leahy developed a high opinion of King as a leader.[37] When the war broke out, he had recommended King to Roosevelt as one of the best officers in the navy.

King was less positive about Leahy.[38] A controlled personality, Leahy was politically sensitive and often preferred to operate indirectly, all reasons Roosevelt liked him so much. King was openly aggressive and assertive, a proverbial "bull in the china shop." He was uncomfortable with Leahy's political manners. Yet their differences in character could sometimes make them an effective team, as Leahy learned to take advantage of King's wrath. King's temper was legendary; his daughter said that he was the most even-tempered man in the fleet—he was always in a rage. He was used to getting his way through intimidation and fear. His natural aggression in Joint Chiefs meetings allowed Leahy to sit back and act as the reasonable, impartial chairman, even when what he wanted was to enact a policy quite close to King's. As Leahy admitted to a close aide, King "certainly lives up to his reputation of being a tough you know what, and in dealing with the British, he sometimes shocks me. But, thank goodness he does, because he takes care of it for both of us."[39]

Leahy's relationship with Arnold was the least complicated. He respected Arnold, seemed to like him personally, and interfered relatively little in the specifics of his strategic plans as air chief. In truth, the admiral's interest in the specifics of strategic bombing was not profound. While he believed airpower would be decisive in winning the war, he didn't believe that strategic bombing was on its own a key factor. He was doubtful of accuracy claims, believing that the technology available at the time was not as exact as the proponents of airpower attested. Yet Leahy never really quarreled with Arnold, trusting the general to deploy his forces in the best way possible.

Despite his differences with each of the Joint Chiefs, Leahy worked well with Marshall, King, and Arnold, and that was one of the reasons that the body functioned so much more effectively after his appointment than before. He imposed order because, as the president's representative, he was the most important member. Indeed, he was the most powerful chairman of the Joint Chiefs of Staff in American history, with or without congressional authorization. Over the coming years, Leahy would refine the post and make it more influential. It became another source of intelligence, plugging him in even more directly with army and navy commanders below Marshall and King. It allowed him even more access to the State Department as he became the main conduit between it and the Joint Chiefs. Finally, it allowed him some real bureaucratic power. Not long after taking his post, Leahy, as senior member, became the signatory of all official orders. This seemingly small move eventually became a power that Leahy used during the war and afterward to get his way.

Yet what is most remarkable about Leahy's tenure as chairman of the Joint Chiefs of Staff was that it was only his *second* most powerful position.

CHAPTER 15

The Grandest Level of Strategy

H istorians relish rehashing the great strategic decisions that supposedly determined the outcome of World War II: Britain's resolve to fight on after the fall of France, Hitler's decision to invade the Ukraine instead of aiming for Moscow, Japan's doomed attack on Midway Island. Such choices add an air of suspense to the war, but they also miss the point about how modern war is won or lost. Decisions on *when, where,* and even *if* can only be made after the careful determination of an even more important series of strategic choices. These choices, which represent the highest level of grand strategy, are about *what* kind of armed forces should be constructed. Every power in World War II had to assess what weaponry they needed to build their armies and navies, and, moreover, how to balance the need for military manpower with the necessity for industrial workers to assemble war machinery. Never do these decisions receive the intense focus reserved for the use of military force, but they are determinative.

Finding the shape of America's military was a tumultuous and at times bitter process. It witnessed the intersection of political, military, economic, and social interests and involved questions of how the American population, both male and female, should be mobilized, to what degree civil liberties should be curtailed, how billions of dollars should be spent, and, ultimately, where and how many Americans would die on the battlefield. Leahy was the only individual who played both a decisive role in these decisions and then helped determine the subsequent strategic choices of when and where American forces would be used.

In January 1942, nearly a month after Pearl Harbor had thrust the nation into war, President Roosevelt in his State of the Union Address called for an immense industrial yield, proclaiming that American output in 1942 and 1943 combined would include 185,000 aircraft, 125,000 tanks, 55,000 antiaircraft guns, and 16 million tons of merchant shipping.[1] At the same time, the army planned a fighting force of extraordinary size, a formidable 215 divisions, 61 of which were to be heavily armored.[2] It was a fantastical plan, yet one far beyond the nation's productive and personnel resources.

By the summer of 1942, the United States was suffering through a personnel and production crisis, and it was clear that American industry could build nothing like as much equipment as planners had assumed. Complicating matters, the armed services demanded more and more bodies to fill their ranks, a direct contradiction with the need to keep skilled industrial workers at their jobs. Industrial production was coming up short. Donald Nelson, chairman of Roosevelt's War Production Board, reported to the president in August that American production was set to come in far below expectations, with aircraft falling short by at least one-third.[3] The shortfall set in motion America's most important strategic debate of the war.

A test of whether any individual has power within a governmental structure is whether he or she can determine policy. Can they shape the decision-making process so that choices are made following their ideas as opposed to that of others? By this standard, when it came to the shape and size of America's armed forces, William Leahy was far more powerful than all the other chiefs, indeed anyone else in the American decision-making structure other than Franklin Roosevelt. To understand how Leahy exercised his influence, it is best to start with his overall strategic ideas of how the United States should fight the war.

After a career spent in the naval service, and with his added diplomatic experience, Leahy returned from France with an innate bias about how the United States should engage and defeat the Axis. It was based on the overwhelming application of air- and sea power to first halt the Axis advance and then wear down their ability to resist. Like Alfred Thayer Mahan, Leahy conceived of war as a struggle over lines of trade and communication. The Allies needed to cut off the Germans and the Japanese from their different sources of production, weaken their economic fundamentals, and, if necessary, invade only once the result was beyond question. Leahy had no stomach for massive land battles, which, he believed, would inevitably lead to high and unnecessary casualties. Therefore, he saw no need for the United States to prioritize production for a large army. In his mind, mass armies belonged to the past, and America needed to win an air-sea war based on machinery over human sacrifice.

In this, he was joined by Franklin Roosevelt, probably one reason why the president determined early on that Leahy would be his point man in the military in determining the answers to these questions. It is worth noting that Roosevelt first started taking a hard line against a large army not long after Leahy became his chief of staff.[4] Both agreed that the army's future size needed to be reduced to keep production high.[5] Both also believed the war would be won through the control of supply and movement. Yet surprisingly for a man so enamored of sea power, Roosevelt pushed for the production of aircraft over everything else, including ships. Having been captivated by the impact of airpower as the war had developed, he decided that the United States needed to seize air superiority to defeat Germany and Japan, and called for the production of a whopping 131,000 aircraft in 1943, 100,000 of which would be combat planes. It was a remarkable figure, imaginable only if all other construction projects were cut drastically, and it caused an intense political and strategic struggle among the top war planners.

George Marshall, with the army's needs at the forefront of his mind, had completely different priorities from the president's. Focused on an army-centric, Germany-first strategy that called for a cross-Channel invasion as early as possible, he wanted a formidable land army with millions of soldiers supported with phalanxes of tanks. If Marshall were to get his way, air and sea production would have to bear the brunt of the cuts everyone knew were coming. At the same time, he would need to keep Hap Arnold and the US Army Air Force on his side; if he called for cuts to aircraft production that were too steep, the mercurial Arnold might rebel. Not to mention that the president himself prized air production over all else. Taking a middle line, the army argued for a balance between aircraft and ground equipment.[6] The navy, it seemed, would be left to deal with an ever-dwindling slice of the budget.

The Joint Chiefs first debated the production crisis on October 20. George Marshall and the army's supply chief, Lt. Gen. Brehon Somervell, attacked Roosevelt's aircraft-focused plan and called for a united military front to force the president into line.[7] In essence, they wanted the Joint Chiefs to undermine the president and take the authority to give direct instructions to the War Production Board about what the United States should construct for its armed services. Admiral King was more circumspect, speaking up for a new balanced program; Leahy, as chairman, was restrained. In the meeting, he called for joint staff planners to come up with a new construction plan by November 10, which could then be presented to the president.

Marshall was determined to get his way. Attempting to circumvent Leahy to put pressure on the president, Marshall and other senior army officers submitted to Harry Hopkins in October a plan calling for 7.5 million soldiers in uniform by the end of 1943. Though it fell short of early 1942 expectations, they were still asking for a very large ground force, allowing the army to mobilize 111 divisions and 224 air force combat groups.[8] This move to cut out the president's chief of staff showed just how weak Marshall was in Roosevelt's power structure. Rather than embracing Marshall's ideas, Hopkins went to the president and warned him against the military's machinations. He said that the "Army and Navy" (he didn't use the phrase "Joint Chiefs of Staff," thereby leaving Leahy out of the charge) were trying to trick FDR into accepting a reduced aircraft construction plan.[9]

If Leahy had seemed noncommittal about production during the Joint Chiefs meeting of October 20, it was because he was spending much of his private time with the president on this very issue and had no need to engage in debates with his fellow chiefs. In fact, Roosevelt spoke far more to Leahy than to the other chiefs during the production controversy.[10] Between October and December, the height of the dispute, the two men dissected the issue in their daily morning briefings and at least seventeen extra meetings, often involving only themselves and at times Harry Hopkins.[11] In terms of the president's time, the other chiefs were peripheral. Ernest King lunched with Roosevelt on October 7 and Hap Arnold had a half-hour meeting with him on October 8; incredibly, George Marshall had not a single minute alone with Roosevelt during this crucial period of the war.

Leahy was quickly revealing himself to be the glue holding together the president's war effort, and he used his access to Roosevelt to destroy Marshall's plans.[12] On October 23, Leahy met with Roosevelt, Donald Nelson, and the heads of the different American industrial-production agencies, and the president gave approval to increase the production of escort vessels for the ongoing sea war—money directed not toward Marshall's army but to the navy.[13] On October 26, Leahy spoke with Secretary of the Interior Ickes about the balance between civilian and military production. Later that day, Leahy and Ernest King met with Roosevelt and, in a sign of how important the war against Japan was at the time, convinced the president to order twenty additional ships to the Pacific.[14]

At such an early stage of the war, Leahy knew that preserving America's workforce was of paramount importance. Chairing a meeting of the Joint Chiefs, he listened as the civilian heads of different regulatory agencies—including the War Production Board, the War Manpower Commission, and the Office of Economic Stabilization—addressed the mounting industrial crisis. Leahy realized that he would need to take the lead and block the formation of a large army to make sure that production was available for air and sea needs. "It appears clear from statements made by the informed officials," he wrote, "that with ten million men in the Armed Services . . . great difficulty will be encountered in providing sufficient material for the war effort and for civilian use."[15]

Having made his choice, Leahy focused on deciding exactly what the United States would build with its industrial workforce. While the nation's eyes were locked on the invasion of North Africa, Leahy was determined not to lose sight of the Pacific. Epic clashes such as the Battle of the Coral Sea and the Battle of Midway had convinced him, the longtime advocate for the battleship, that now the aircraft carrier was the weapon that would defeat Japan, and he wanted to make sure that enough of them were built that victory in the Pacific theater could happen as quickly as possible. Thus, aircraft-carrier production could not be held back by the overwhelming focus on aircraft—even if that meant changing the president's stated priority list.

On November 10, less than forty-eight hours after American troops landed in Morocco, Leahy chaired a meeting of the Joint Chiefs. Marshall and King, preoccupied by the invasion, were represented by subordinates. When Hap Arnold spoke in favor of Roosevelt's aircraft plan—which had been reduced to a final target of 107,000 planes, 82,000 of which were combat—Leahy openly differentiated himself from the president. The building of aircraft carriers was so important, in his opinion, that they trumped FDR's plan for a focus on aircraft alone.[16] He instructed the joint army and navy planners to go prepare a new priority list to be given to the president.

When the planners reported back a few days later, Leahy's influence was evident. The list now had three specific first-class priorities: Roosevelt's 107,000 aircraft plan, a new destroyer escort plan, and Leahy's carriers.[17] Yet Leahy was hardly trying to circumvent the president. On November 20, he sent to Roosevelt a formal memo arguing that while he accepted the president's plan for 107,000 aircraft in 1943, it shouldn't preclude other areas. Conflating his own preference with that of the Joint Chiefs as a whole, he wrote, "There is no item which the Chiefs of Staff consider to be more important than aircraft carriers and escort vessels."[18]

Over the next few days Leahy worked directly with Roosevelt and Donald Nelson, head of the War Production Board, to finalize the new priority list. From his point of view, the other Joint Chiefs were not helpful, and he bypassed them almost entirely. "I am convinced that

Mr. Nelson is making every effort to meet the military and naval needs," he wrote, "and I get very little useful assistance from the Navy Department or the Army Air Force."[19]

A few days later, Leahy sent Nelson a letter specifically laying out the new production priorities, combining Roosevelt's desire for aircraft with his own preference for more carriers. Leahy told Nelson that the 1943 target production of aircraft was to be FDR's preferred figure of 107,000. At the same time, aircraft-carrier construction was to be prioritized so that 13 aircraft carriers (larger than escort class) would be completed in the calendar year 1943.[20]

Leahy's success was unprecedented. He achieved his vision, even more so than Roosevelt. In 1943, even after great industrial exertion, the United States manufactured fewer than 85,000 aircraft, only 53,000 of which were combat planes. Yet American shipyards finished 15 aircraft carriers of either the *Essex* or *Independence* class, two more than Leahy originally envisaged.[21] These carriers became the backbone of the fast-carrier strike force that dominated the war against Japan in 1944. The army, meanwhile, suffered the brunt of the cuts. It was now planned that the United States would build almost 50 percent fewer tanks by the end of 1943, with cuts in artillery production of 33 percent and small arms of 13 percent.[22] The meaning of these cuts would be clear soon: the United States would not be able to invade France in 1943, as George Marshall wanted, but would have to wait until 1944, Leahy's preferred target year. It was as decisive a triumph as Leahy could have imagined.

Leahy had won the debate over production priorities, but he still had to make sure that the armed forces did not recruit so much manpower that it would compromise the reaching of his targets.[23] If early military manpower demands were met, the United States would have more than 11.5 million men in uniform by early 1944.[24] By late 1942, the army was still hoping for a force of more than 8.2 million by the end of 1943, which would then grow more in 1944.[25] Leahy thought such plans not only excessive but dangerous, leading to the military gaining too much authority in civilian affairs. Army plans, he claimed, would have "wrecked" the labor market.[26] How he blocked these plans showed just how subtly Leahy could manipulate his different positions to ensure the outcome that he and the president wanted.

The first step was to keep the workers who were so valuable to America's war effort from being driven out of their jobs. The staff planners on the Joint Chiefs, for instance, advocated that the working week for factory workers in vital industries be increased by almost a third, to fifty-four hours. This would, it was argued, allow the United States to have a better chance to meet its production targets while freeing up more men to fight.[27] This politically naïve plan would have been social dynamite, and Leahy was determined to squash it. He had the reference to a fifty-four-hour week deleted from the joint staff planners' report that had been prepared for the Joint Chiefs.[28] At a December 1 meeting of the Joint Chiefs, he stated that the military should not try to dictate personnel policy to the civilian administration. To Leahy any such move was a dangerous example of the military expanding its powers.

Having kept the military from advocating such a self-destructive policy, Leahy was left with the conundrum that he was presiding over a committee whose members mostly supported the maximum increase possible in the size of the armed forces. Marshall and King continued to push ahead with their earlier recruitment plans.[29] Yet Leahy did not feel he could, or should, oppose them directly during Joint Chiefs meetings. Instead, he used his time with the president to subvert their wishes. He allowed Marshall to argue for as large an army as possible and sent that forward as the formal recommendation of the Joint Chiefs. Yet in private moments with the president, as he later admitted, Leahy spoke against such a plan.[30] Leahy was perfectly aware that he and Roosevelt agreed on this question and was confident of getting the right result.[31]

He knew exactly what he was doing. The president continued to turn to Leahy over Marshall, King, or Arnold when it came to matters of personnel policy. In early 1943, Roosevelt appointed a committee of five trusted individuals to analyze the politically sensitive question of personnel controls and domestic legislation.[32] Leahy was the only military man on the committee, the rest being civilian heavyweights: Harry Hopkins, James Byrnes, Bernard Baruch, and Samuel Rosenman.[33] Together they had to recommend policy on the kind of issues that military leaders normally avoided—such as the rise in wages and prices, and to what degree controls should be put in place for both or either.[34] The overarching question was whether the United States should opt for draconian labor laws. These laws would have allowed the federal government to force any individual it wanted into war work, which would have freed up more existing industrial workers for the army and navy. But it would have been politically controversial and unprecedented within the history of American civil liberties. Marshall and the army were supportive. Leahy helped spike their hopes. In personnel committee meetings, Leahy sided with those who argued against strict labor laws. He was, for instance, strongly opposed to any plan that would see the federal government conscript labor. Eventually, the committee, with Leahy's wholehearted approval, decided against recommending coercive laws. It was an example of his behind-the-scenes operation. He used the trust of the president, plus the myriad different positions in which he had been placed, to guarantee that the United States followed his strategic ideas.

The United States, in the end, fought precisely the war that William Leahy wanted it to fight. It was an air-sea machinery-based war, with a remarkably small land army, all things considered. The army's eventual strength of 7.7 million at the high point of the war was still much smaller than they had expected to have by the end of 1943 and was more than 2 million men smaller than Marshall wanted it to be in 1942.[35] This restriction in army manpower led to what is known as the "90-division gamble."[36] This small-army gamble, in which Marshall had called for 215 divisions at the start of the war—coming on the heels of the decision to focus on aircraft and aircraft-carrier construction—represented the most important strategic decision that the US government would make during World War II. This decision pre-answered most of the American strategic debates that would occur in the coming years. It decided the outcome of more battles and campaigns than the actions of famous battlefield commanders, whom we like to think of as the individuals who determine the outcomes of wars.

William Leahy had produced a tour de force on how to exercise power in Washington.

CHAPTER 16

From Casablanca to Trident

A few minutes after ten on a cold, clear January night, an automobile quietly pulled up next to a railway siding near the federal government's Bureau of Engraving and Printing. Waiting in the frozen darkness was a five-car train, its markings obscured by black paint. One car stood out—armor-plated, it had thick, bulletproof glass windows that could withstand a close-range burst of machine-gun fire. A small party emerged from the automobile, including one man who was lifted into a wheelchair. Once the party was safely aboard the armored car, the train began to clank slowly north.[1] Any bystander who had recognized the man in the wheelchair would have assumed that Franklin Delano Roosevelt was on his way to Hyde Park for a well-earned rest.

Several miles outside of Washington, the train abruptly changed course, swinging south. The president was heading not to the Hudson Valley but to Miami, Florida, and, eventually, Morocco, though not even his White House staff knew of the plan. In North Africa, US forces had taken over most of French Morocco and Algeria following the successful Torch landings in November 1942. A thousand miles to the east, the British 8th Army, led by Gen. Bernard Montgomery, had defeated Erwin Rommel's Afrika Korps during the Battle of El Alamein. In Russia, the Nazis had been halted at the Volga River, with the German 6th Army entombed in the frozen hell of Stalingrad. Now, with the German military machine stopped in its tracks, Franklin Roosevelt was on his way to see Winston Churchill to plan for final victory in World War II. The question was not if Germany would be defeated but how.

Every aspect of the trip was historic: Roosevelt was to be the first president to leave the country during wartime, the first to fly across the Atlantic, and the first to visit Africa while in office. Joining him were his doctor, Adm. Ross McIntire; his aide, Capt. John L. McCrea; Harry Hopkins; and William Leahy.* Yet those not aboard his train were as revealing as those who were. George Marshall, Ernest King, and Hap Arnold traveled separately to Casablanca. Journeys with the president were social affairs, when he would bond with those at this side over cigarettes and cocktails, gossiping and talking through politics and strategy. But his chiefs had been excluded, a separation that spoke of their secondary position in his life.

What's more, the three cabinet members supposedly most involved in making American foreign and strategic policy—the secretary of state, the secretary of war, and the secretary of the navy—were nowhere to be found. Not only were Cordell Hull, Henry Stimson, and Frank Knox forbidden from attending the conference, they were not even allowed to partake in the most important planning meetings and were kept from seeing many of the key agreements for months afterward. So determined was Roosevelt to emasculate his senior cabinet colleagues that he asked Churchill not to include Hull's counterpart, Foreign Secretary Anthony Eden, in the British delegation.[2]

Upon reaching Miami, Roosevelt's party switched to a flying boat for a series of hops through the Caribbean to Brazil, and then across the Atlantic to Africa.[3] Their first landing was Port of Spain, Trinidad, where the party disembarked for an evening's rest. Leahy, running a high fever, was examined by McIntire. Diagnosed with a serious case of bronchitis, the admiral was ordered to remain in Trinidad until he had recovered.[4] The president's most trusted adviser had no choice but to miss the Casablanca Conference.

---

* Roosevelt's favorite secretary, Grace Tully, was also there, though she would leave the party in Florida.

When Roosevelt was told that Leahy could not continue, his mood soured. "This is not civilized," he moaned in a letter to a confidante, Margaret Suckley. "[Leahy] hated to stay but was a good soldier & will go to the Naval Hospital & get good care—I hope he won't get pneumonia—I shall miss him as he is such an old friend & a wise counsellor."[5] Yet, while Roosevelt thought Leahy was disappointed to be left behind, Harry Hopkins suspected that the admiral was secretly relieved. "I felt that he never had his heart in this trip and was going only because the President wanted him to," Hopkins wrote. "He doesn't seem unhappy at the idea of remaining in Trinidad till we get back."[6] Hopkins may very well have been correct about Leahy's reluctance to attend the conference, for Casablanca held the risk of a disastrous performance by the American delegation. Faced with the responsibility of planning the war's next steps with their British allies, Roosevelt's chiefs could not even agree on a basic strategy.

The run-up to Casablanca showed that William Leahy had developed a profound strategic difference with George Marshall, one he had kept partly under wraps. While Marshall, eager to defeat Hitler, pressed for a Germany-first approach, Leahy wanted to fight a more balanced war. Not that the admiral took the Nazis lightly; indeed, he believed Germany represented a greater threat to America than did Japan, and that Nazism needed to be crushed. Yet he opposed a Germany-first strategy for two important reasons.

The first was unnecessary casualties. Too aggressive an approach to Germany could very well lead to an attack too soon, before the United States was prepared. Only a month before departing for Casablanca, during a meeting with the president and his Joint Chiefs, Marshall had pushed for a cross-Channel invasion of France in 1943. Roosevelt was seemingly supportive of a heavy focus on Germany yet fended off his army chief's proposal with his typically light touch. But a few days before leaving, Marshall tried again, calling for an invasion of the Brittany peninsula. Heavy casualties could be expected, he admitted, but callously remarked, according to the meeting's minutes, "we could replace troops."[7] Leahy was undoubtedly appalled. For him, the operation was simply too risky. Until the Allies had secured complete air and sea control in the Atlantic and over any landing beaches in France—something that did not look possible in 1943—an invasion had too high a chance of "failure or great loss of life."[8]

Leahy and the president had spent much of their time discussing military strategy in the run-up to Casablanca, and he understood Roosevelt's thinking on the subject.[9] The two shared a similar outlook, and it is doubtful that the admiral had to do much lobbying against an early cross-Channel invasion. Indeed, there is no strong evidence that Roosevelt supported such an operation. In January Roosevelt even blocked Marshall's idea, refusing to authorize any assault on Brittany. Instead, he argued for more delay, asking "if it wouldn't be possible for us to build up a large force in England, and leave the actual decision in abeyance for a month or two." Leahy leapt in with support, saying the president's suggestion "had considerable merit" and that the United States should delay making any decision until the situation was clearer.[10] The closeness between Roosevelt and Leahy had quickly steered the debate away from what could have resulted in a catastrophic decision; the president and the admiral wielded power, not Marshall. At no time was there ever to be an official American policy to argue for a cross-Channel invasion in 1943. As events would show, it was always Marshall and the army driving this position, with little support from other quarters.[11]

The second reason Leahy opposed a Germany-first strategy was that it would hinder the fight against Japan. Though the US government had declared after Pearl Harbor that war against Germany would be its highest priority, in 1942 it did the exact opposite.[12] As the Japanese expanded their power rapidly across the southern and western Pacific, the United States spent the first twelve months of the war sending equipment to stem the Japanese tide—significantly more than was used to fight the Germans.[13] This imbalance was exacerbated by the enervating struggle for control of Guadalcanal, a six-month battle that caused unprecedented sea and air losses on both sides. In August 1942, US Marines surprised Japanese forces on the island, seizing an airstrip they had just completed. The next few months would witness one of the greatest attritional struggles of the war. The Japanese, determined to retake the airfield, which the Americans renamed Henderson Field, committed some of their best naval and army forces to the fight. They inflicted the greatest-ever defeat at sea on the US Navy, the Battle of Savo Island, and the Marines protecting Henderson Field were constantly besieged. Roosevelt was so worried about the island that he often ordered new production to be sent there instead of diverting it to North Africa or Europe. By the end of 1942, the United States had a clear majority of air assets and an overwhelming majority of its sea power in the Pacific.

In December, when the situation on Guadalcanal had stabilized and the Americans were working on taking the entire island, Roosevelt told the Joint Chiefs that from now on only 20 to 35 percent of American forces should be sent to the Pacific, with the remainder deployed against Germany. This put Leahy in a bind. A Germany-first strategy, he felt, would stunt America's progress in the war with Japan. He believed Japan would eventually lose that war, but he worried that if the Japanese were ignored for two or three years while Germany was defeated, they would turn the Pacific into a giant island-to-island death trap that would consume American lives. In addition, the extra time it would take to defeat Japan could lead to a catastrophic collapse in China.

In his diary, Leahy worried that the strategic importance of the war against Japan was not understood—in particular that the British were so obsessed with Europe that they would hinder his policy goals. "I have an idea that Great Britain will not give any useful assistance to a Burma expedition at the present time," he wrote, "and it is my opinion that from the long distance American view point of essentials in our war effort, the opening of the Burma Road and the support of China should have a very high priority."[14] A few weeks later, as the fighting around and on Guadalcanal was reaching a crescendo, he went even further, claiming that, far from focusing on Germany, the US war effort "should now be concentrated against Japan."[15] He also argued that commitments to Great Britain and Russia might make this impossible—tying his skepticism about an early invasion of France into his larger geopolitical outlook.

Leahy's doubts about British intentions were not driven by a dislike of the British, a common prejudice among US naval officers of his generation; rather, they had everything to do with his conception of American national interest. Leahy was an anti-imperialist with isolationist proclivities. He wanted to fight the war to win it as quickly as possible, with as few American casualties as possible, and he wanted to ensure that the United States was in the best strategic position as possible at the war's conclusion. He had no interest in fighting to preserve the British Empire and was determined that when the interests of the two nations clashed, he would do everything possible to make sure the American position triumphed.

Heading to Casablanca, Leahy was thus at complete strategic odds with George Marshall about both Europe and the Pacific, and this would have led to unbearable tension in the American delegation. Missing out on the conference lanced that particular boil. Yet losing Leahy was also a disaster for the Americans. The admiral was, more than anyone else, the force that bound the president and the Joint Chiefs together, working as a team. Without him, the American leadership immediately reverted to the dysfunctionality of its early months. At Casablanca, Roosevelt, Marshall, Arnold, and King all had different agendas that either ignored, or even undermined, the positions of the others.

After a tortuous series of flights across the Caribbean, to Brazil, over the Atlantic to West Africa, and then north to Morocco—McIntire, who worried about Roosevelt's high blood pressure and weakening heart, ordered the plane, where possible, to cruise at no higher than 9,000 feet—the president's contingent arrived in Casablanca on January 14. They were led to the suburb of Anfa, an old Phoenician settlement far from the city center, and housed in a modern hotel complex that resembled a California bungalow, ringed with barbed wire and hastily constructed fortifications. Waiting for the Americans was the British delegation. Well drilled, well rested after a much shorter flight, and ready to fight for what they wanted, the British, from Churchill on down, had arrived with a more coherent war strategy than the Americans. They were committed to Germany-first and wanted to make as little effort as possible in the Pacific until the Nazis had been defeated. Their view of how to defeat Germany, however, was very different. Unlike Marshall, the British did not want to invade France in 1943, and probably not in 1944 either. Churchill, a World War I combat veteran, was haunted by images of British youth being mowed down by ruthless, gray-faced Germans as they slogged across the fields of northwest Europe. As the British prime minister well knew, the United Kingdom was suffering from a personnel crisis far more acute than that in the United States. The British population, the smallest of the Great Powers, had been fully mobilized since 1940, and there was no way to increase the size of the British Armed Forces without reducing the productive workforce. Keeping British casualties down was therefore a political and economic imperative. The fight over this issue promised to be bitter.

Instead of invading France, Churchill wanted to fight the Germans in the Mediterranean, leaving the Russians to deal with the bulk of the German Army. He favored operations against Italy, Greece, or Yugoslavia, which he optimistically—and nonsensically—called the "soft underbelly" of Europe. Fighting in such areas, he believed, would not only save British manpower, it would secure the eastern Mediterranean, an area considered vital to the maintenance of the British Empire. In Churchill's mind the United Kingdom was fighting World War II to protect the existence of the empire, not to see its "liquidation."[16]

Dealing with such British unanimity, the American delegation at Casablanca broke into pieces, unable to mount effective counterarguments without Leahy. The first gathering of the Leahy-less Combined Chiefs was held on January 14 and showed just how poorly Marshall and King operated together.[17] Marshall opened by stating the president's policy that the Allies should devote 30 percent of their effort to the war against Japan and 70 percent against Germany (without letting the British know that this was Roosevelt's figure and not his own). King added that the United States at present was sending only 15 percent of its available forces to fight Japan, a remarkably deceptive statement; the reality was that it had more than half in the Pacific. His deception revealed his true intention: to get tacit approval to devote as many resources as he could to the Pacific war. King had tipped off the British that he, at least, had no interest in invading France in 1943 if it undermined the war against Japan. The American chiefs were obviously divided.

In response, the British chiefs offered their own perspective. The chief of the imperial general staff, Field Marshal Sir Alan Brooke (later Lord Alanbrooke); the First Sea Lord, Adm. Sir Dudley Pound; and the chief of the air staff, Air Marshal Sir Charles Portal, all spoke at length, but together they outlined their coherent vision of a war in the Mediterranean or, in the case of Portal, in the skies over Germany.

Out of his depth, Marshall showed that the debate was already lost. Instead of taking the British head-on, he said meekly that he was "concerned" that operations in the Mediterranean would not be worth the effort. When it came to invading France, all he could muster was a statement that he was "inclined to look favorably" on operations that would be launched from the United Kingdom.[18] He got the limpest of support from King, who only really came alive when he discussed the importance of the war against Japan. Two days later, King finally said that an invasion of Brest "needed careful consideration," but that was about the extent of his support for European operations.[19] Arnold, meanwhile, mostly stayed out of the invasion discussions, focused instead on the launching of a strategic air campaign against Germany— on which he was much closer to Portal than Marshall and King. By the end of the conference, the war in Europe was agreed very much along British lines, with an invasion of Sicily given precedence in 1943 and any invasion of France shelved for at least a year. The Mediterranean would become the main theater of Anglo-American effort for 1943.

To be fair to Marshall, his lack of success was partly due to the president basically hanging his army chief of staff out to dry. At Casablanca, Roosevelt seemed uninterested in a 1943 invasion of France. When he sat down with Churchill and the Allied Combined Chiefs, or just Hopkins, Marshall, King, and Arnold, it was to receive briefings about the state of the war, not to construct a united war-fighting strategy. Roosevelt was much more excited by being an international statesman than an Allied warlord. He spent much of his time on French affairs, trying to curb the influence of Charles de Gaulle and the Free French in favor of Gen. Henri Giraud. His one great contribution to the conference came as a surprise to almost everyone else: the doctrine of Axis Unconditional Surrender. This controversial demand, which made it clear to the Germans, Italians, and Japanese that there would be no negotiated peace, only total defeat, had been discussed before Casablanca but was not on the American agenda going into the talks.[20] Yet Roosevelt became attracted to the idea and had it added to the final communiqués. To some it was a blunder that stiffened German and Japanese resistance and turned the war into a fight to the death.

On January 24 the Casablanca Conference concluded, but not until the twenty-eighth did Leahy receive an update of the summit when Marshall and King, again traveling apart from Roosevelt, touched down in Trinidad. Not long after the two had departed, Roosevelt arrived with Hopkins to pick up his convalescing chief of staff. They lingered on the island for a day as the president recovered from the exhaustion of travel, showing off the gifts he had received from the sultan of Morocco, including a gold mounted sheik's knife.[21] On January 30—the president's sixty-first birthday—Leahy, Roosevelt, and Hopkins boarded a flight back to the United States. The three men, the apex of America's strategic power, drank Champagne, ate cake, and admired the view as the plane passed over Haiti. Marshall, out of touch with the president, remained blissfully unaware of Roosevelt's stopover in Trinidad, as well as his impromptu celebration.

When Leahy learned of the decisions made at Casablanca, he was underwhelmed. Faced with the opportunity to outline the quickest and most humane path to end the fighting, the American delegation had been outfoxed by the British. The United States was now committed to a Mediterranean strategy about which Leahy had mixed feelings, while at the same time, they had received no guarantees from the British that they would help open a route into China or even a British commitment to invade France in 1944. Back in Washington, Leahy thoroughly analyzed the conference with the president, Marshall, and King, later venting in his diary that "little of value to ending the war" had been accomplished.[22] The president, likewise, was unimpressed with the chaotic American performance at Casablanca. Roosevelt was embarrassed by how little he, the other chiefs, and Hopkins had accomplished, believing that their only clear success was the announcement of the unconditional surrender policy.[23]

Though Casablanca had mostly been a disappointment, the failure highlighted two important points. For Leahy, the Casablanca agreements solved the problem of his doubts over Marshall's European strategy. With a cross-Channel invasion in 1943 out of the question, Leahy could now make common cause with Marshall in pushing for D-Day in 1944. Overall, the American Joint Chiefs had far fewer grand strategic differences after Casablanca than before. Furthermore, it was a stark reminder that Roosevelt, Marshall, King, Arnold, and Hopkins, left to their own devices, were a mess. They needed the kind of subtle organization and direction that only Leahy could provide—and Leahy and Roosevelt were determined they get that guidance for the rest of the war. The president looked at the results of Casablanca and practically the first thing he did after returning to Washington was to issue an order that gave Leahy greater access to information than any other person in the US government. On February 11, 1943, the president issued a written order for Leahy that "the Map Room was to make a copy of each incoming dispatch for the President from any of the heads of Government with whom he corresponds. This copy is to be available at all times in the Map Room for your perusal."[24]

Franklin Roosevelt was making William Leahy his go-to figure, for the precise reason that the president understood that he needed Leahy to organize American grand strategy. From now on, because of Leahy's unlimited access to Roosevelt's correspondence, along with the military intelligence he received through the Joint Chiefs and his direct connections to high-ranking members of the State Department, the admiral would have a more complete picture of the American war effort (and international geopolitics) than any other person in the American government, including the president. It was what made him the second most powerful man in the world—for as long as Franklin Roosevelt lived.

Roosevelt's order was also a sign that Hopkins's plan to limit Leahy's influence had failed; indeed, it showed that Leahy was replacing Hopkins as the president's most trusted adviser. This passing of the torch happened for a number of reasons, including Hopkins's declining health, new bride, and chaotic way of transacting business. In July 1942 Hopkins married Louise Macy, who was flirtatious, sixteen years younger, and very rich.[25] At first, Macy moved into the White House to live with Hopkins but, not surprisingly, wanted to spend time alone with her new husband. She chafed at all the demands Roosevelt placed on their lives and began to resent the lack of independence. Macy made her feelings known, belittling life in the White House in a way that the suspicious Roosevelt thought insulted both himself and Eleanor.[26] Franklin Roosevelt was a jealous man, and as he understood that Hopkins was no longer just his creature, his feelings toward his erstwhile favorite began to cool.

To make matters even more grim, Hopkins was dying. His stomach cancer, first diagnosed in 1937, had led to three-quarters of the organ being removed. For a while, after receiving plasma injections, he functioned at a surprisingly high level. Being so central in Roosevelt's life provided him the adrenaline needed to cope. By 1943, however, he began to noticeably weaken, his weight dropped alarmingly, and he started suffering from malnutrition.[27] The fact that he continued to smoke and drink hardly helped.

Hopkins's declining health accentuated one of his real shortcomings as a presidential aide: his predilection for keeping things "fluid," which masked his organizational chaos.[28] He was known to walk out of the Map Room with the most confidential documents stuffed carelessly into his pockets.[29] In comparison to Hopkins's ramshackle appearance and habits, Leahy stood out to the president as paragon of controlled competence. The widowed admiral had no other loyalties, never lost papers, and was punctilious in bringing issues to Roosevelt's attention and then reporting the president's decisions to the rest of the government. Leahy was always at the White House at the allotted time and was rarely sick. His physical appearance was always tidy, and he made sure that his uniforms were crisp and clean. He even worked hard not to gain weight, which was not always easy, as he enjoyed socializing and good food and certainly did not deprive himself of alcohol. One of the ways that he controlled his weight was to limit what he ate for lunch. He was known to dine only on graham crackers and a glass of milk.[30]

Considering all this, it is not surprising that Roosevelt started shifting responsibility for many tasks from Hopkins to Leahy—not just strategic but also political. Leahy's contacts with the State Department became even more regular. In the run-up to Trident—the next strategic meeting with America's British allies—Leahy worked with Sumner Welles to articulate American policy toward France and, more important, the treatment of territories that the United States had occupied. The two men basically decided that the United States, in the short term, should maintain control over different occupied territories to increase American leverage in the upcoming strategy conferences.[31] Leahy sent a telegram to General Eisenhower making this clear.

The admiral became, in the words of one perceptive observer, the "immediate court of appeal" for all American strategic plans.[32] Leahy became so powerful as chairman of the Joint Chiefs of Staff that he squashed a suggestion that the Joint Chiefs be formalized with a written charter. [33] He did not want any possible limitations on his interactions with the president. As he told Marshall and King, this "body now appears to function in a reasonable satisfactory manner . . . [I]f there is a question as to authority of the Joint Chiefs of Staff, they now have access to the President and can seek guidance on any matter they desire."[34]

Five days after Roosevelt issued his order giving Leahy complete access to his correspondence, the admiral set to work preparing for Trident. On February 16, the Joint Chiefs, having previously analyzed the meager results from Casablanca, started discussing what they wanted to achieve with the Brits. When it came to the war in Europe, there was now unanimity that France should be invaded in 1944. Leahy was convinced that by that year the Germans would have no reasonable possibility of stopping the invasion and that it was a political imperative both domestically in the United States and internationally to keep the Soviet Union in the war.

While Leahy was committed to invading France in 1944, he stood opposed to making the Mediterranean a permanent area of Anglo-American effort. Leahy did not want the United States to fight a war in the Mediterranean to protect the British Empire, and to forestall this he wanted American involvement in the region in 1943 to be limited to one island assault.[35] As early as February 1943, he was even voicing doubts about the need for an invasion of Sicily, worried as he was by unnecessary American casualties.[36] As it turned out, his support for Torch was not a sign of a commitment to a Mediterranean strategy—in many ways it was a repudiation of one.[37] He supported an invasion of North Africa as part of his worldwide maritime strategy and to get US troops acclimated to battle in an area where he thought casualties would be low. He saw no benefit whatsoever in expanding the land war either onto the Italian mainland or into the eastern Mediterranean. To Leahy such operations would not shorten the war by a day and might even lengthen it by dispersing Allied force in to the areas the seizure of which would make no difference in compelling Germany to surrender.

Leahy now had a clearer idea of how he wanted to proceed in Europe, but he remained, as always, determined to make the Pacific a major priority. He was especially concerned that the Japanese not conquer more of China. To ensure this, he needed from the British a commitment to help open a land route into China through Burma, an operation code-named Anakim. Leahy was convinced that if more aid did not get through to America's Chinese allies, the Nationalist regime might fall. So devoted was he to Anakim that he spent a great deal of his time on it in the months leading up to Trident. Sumner Welles saw how committed Leahy was to Chinese questions and started feeding the admiral as much information from the State Department as he could.[38] At the end of February Leahy met with Madame Chiang Kai-shek, the glamorous, intelligent, and powerful wife of the Chinese Nationalist leader, to express his commitment to China.[39] Furthermore, he met with two senior Chinese diplomats to discuss his hopes for Anakim. Wellington Koo and T. V. Soong were both in Washington to argue China's case for more support in the war against Japan, and in Leahy they found the most sympathetic of ears.[40] The admiral and Koo had first become friendly in Vichy, where their ambassadorships coincided. Leahy thought Koo "highly attractive and very intelligent."[41] He was also fond of Soong, heir to one of China's great industrial families and a leading politician in Nationalist Chinese circles, now serving as the Chinese foreign minister. Leahy and Soong closely coordinated their efforts to apply pressure on the British to proceed with Anakim. In early May, the admiral brought Soong to a meeting of the Joint Chiefs so that he could explain Chinese policies and desires to Marshall and King.[42] Leahy even set up a special meeting between Soong and Roosevelt to reassure the Chinese diplomat about the president's commitment to China. After the meeting Soong sent Leahy an effusive report, saying that the president was fully behind Anakim and had promised to press the British about it. Soong ended the letter with a tribute to all that Leahy had done for US-Chinese relations.[43] It was a tribute the admiral richly deserved. Leahy even changed official American strategic language when it came to the importance of China. During Casablanca, with Leahy absent, the US delegation had signed up for a clear Germany-first policy that called for only enough force to be sent to the Pacific to maintain "pressure" against Japan.[44] In the documents prepared by the Joint Chiefs of Staff under Leahy's direction before Trident, the word "unremitting" was suddenly placed before "pressure." He also made sure that Anakim was one of the top two American priorities. It was usually listed second, just behind the commitment to a cross-Channel attack in 1944.

Leahy made sure that Roosevelt strongly supported his hard line with the British over Pacific strategy and the need for Anakim. Yet the operation presented a major strategic problem. If a land route were to be opened into China to allow supplies to reach the Nationalists, the British would have to take a lead by attacking out of India and into Japanese-controlled Burma. When it came to the war in the Pacific, the British were determined to do as little as possible until Germany had been defeated. They saw no reason to deploy their own equipment and lose valuable manpower making a risky offensive into Burma. British officials were far more skeptical than Leahy and Roosevelt about the future importance of China and saw little need to fight the war with that in mind. The lack of interest that the British had in China was made clear in their preparations for Trident. Churchill seems almost boastful in his memoirs about his intention going into the meeting to try to block American plans for an attack into Burma.[45] He listed supporting the Chinese war effort as only the sixth highest strategic priority for the United Kingdom—which even then was probably an overstatement made to appease American concerns.[46]

The reality of British reluctance to exert force in the Pacific was one that Leahy understood, and as he told the president, if the British did not play ball, the United States should feel itself free to ignore Germany-first. "If Anakim proves impossible," he wrote in a memo to Roosevelt, "due to lack of British support or other reasons, and no adequate alternative can be agreed upon, the United States will expand and intensify its operations in the Pacific, in order to counteract the advantage which Japan gains by Allied failure to support China."[47]

On May 8, at a meeting of the Joint Chiefs, Leahy presented all the different strategy papers that had been prepared for the upcoming conference, then scripted how Trident would begin, saying that the US delegation would start by laying out its global strategy.[48] Leahy was justifiably proud of the wide strategic scope and clarity laid out in these documents.[49] He particularly commended a report entitled "Conduct of the War 1943–1944."[50] This paper, along with a memorandum Leahy sent to Roosevelt entitled "Recommended Line of Action at the Upcoming Conference," provided the blueprint that the United States would follow exactly during Trident.[51]

The conference opened four days later in an unseasonably hot and humid Washington, DC. The heaviness in the air was appropriate. Although victory was heralded from every newspaper, with the German and Italian forces in North Africa surrendering on May 13, it quickly became clear that the Americans and British were not going to easily surmount their strategic differences. During the first meeting, Churchill, with typical eloquence, made a passionate case for a Mediterranean strategy. Yet he provided no commitment to a cross-Channel invasion in 1944 and, Leahy wryly observed, talked about a full effort in the war against Japan—once Germany had surrendered, of course.[52] Roosevelt replied briefly, demanding a cross-Channel invasion in 1944 and an immediate effort to keep China in the war.

This fundamental disagreement set the tone of what would be, for most men in attendance, an exhausting two weeks. One exception was Leahy: he oozed confidence during Trident. When the Combined Chiefs first met alone, Leahy took the chair and gave a clear exposition of American strategic aims, the longest oration he would make during the entire conference. He called for an invasion of France in 1944 and a major commitment to help China in 1943, complete with his emphasis on wanting "unremitting" pressure placed on Japan.[53] His gauntlet thrown, he sat back and allowed others to do most of the talking. Over the coming days he would let both British and American delegates go on at length, listening intently and judging. When he interjected, which he did with increasing regularity, it was always to provide a staccato statement that steered the conversation away from what he considered unnecessary diversions and back to the fundamental issues of grand strategy. He was relentless, willing to put both the British and George Marshall in their places. During the first meeting, after Alanbrooke and Marshall had gone on at great length about the war in Europe, Leahy gently chided them on their myopia, saying that "the Pacific could not be neglected; it was too vital to the United States," and that immediate action was needed to "maintain China in the war."[54] A little while later, when the conversation once again bogged down over how much commitment the Allies should make to Mediterranean operations in 1943, Leahy asked pointedly how they all thought the Soviets would react if it looked like the cross-Channel invasion was being shelved in favor of operations in Italy.[55]

The next day the chiefs started again with a long statement by Alanbrooke about British strategy and the need for the Mediterranean to be the lead theater of operations in 1943 and beyond. He even accused the Americans of going back on their Casablanca pledges by not showing enough commitment to operations in that region. As soon as Alanbrooke was done, Leahy contradicted him outright, saying that nothing the Americans were arguing for contravened Casablanca, that France needed to be invaded in 1944 and that the Pacific remained a major area of strategic investment regardless of the Germany-first policy.[56] Indeed, Leahy seemed to take a little pleasure in tormenting Alanbrooke, asking the British general point-blank if he honestly believed that an attack in the Mediterranean could strike a serious blow to Nazi power.

For Leahy, China was not to be abandoned, and his temper was put to the test when the British wheeled out Field Marshal Archibald Wavell. A repeated failure consistently promoted throughout his career as a way of moving him on, Wavell had been beaten soundly by Rommel in the Desert War of 1941 and deposited into India, where he was promoted to field marshal and put in command of the British Army. He was brought to Trident to explain the difficulties of a land offensive into Burma, which he did in great detail.[57] Leahy's response revealed a barely concealed contempt: What, he asked Wavell, did he plan to do, then, to help the Chinese?[58] After Wavell blathered on again about all the problems involved in getting aid to China, Leahy dismissed his arguments by saying that, regardless of the tactical challenges, it remained "essential" for the Allies to find a way to aid the Chinese.

Leahy's impatience with Wavell and Alanbrooke stemmed from his conviction that both were typical soldiers, with a primitive, land-based understanding of war, out of their depth in grasping the fundamentals of modern industrial/technological warfare. Leahy was becoming convinced that it was the application of Anglo-American air- and sea power that would determine the course of the war—and that air- and sea power were the most effective ways to materially damage the Germans and Japanese. He thought generals such as Alanbrooke, who obsessed only over engaging German divisions, to be fighting more Napoleonic wars than modern ones.

Leahy's persistence was one of the reasons that nerves frayed during the conference. Alanbrooke seemed close to exhaustion. His diary entries covering these days are a litany of gloom; after the war he confessed that the pressure he endured led him into a "deep depression."[59] In need of a break to regain their energy and calm their nerves, the Combined Chiefs traveled to Colonial Williamsburg, the eighteenth-century capital of Virginia, where they toured the historical pastiche—restored at great expense by John D. Rockefeller—and larked in a swimming pool like young boys. It barely helped.

When the chiefs returned to Washington, their profound differences surfaced once again. Trying to find some way to wiggle out of a commitment to Anakim, Alanbrooke delivered a long and deliberately obtuse interjection on Pacific strategy.[60] Disastrously, his case was supported by the untrusted Wavell. Leahy listened to their rambling presentations, which involved no effort to open a road into China to get support to the Nationalists fighting Japan, and said that would not be enough. He wanted a British commitment to a ground offensive in Burma to open the road, and would accept nothing less.[61]

When it seemed no settlement was possible, Leahy placed a proverbial gun to the British head and dared Alanbrooke to pull the trigger. The admiral proposed that under the circumstances the American and British chiefs should submit separate reports to Roosevelt and Churchill.[62] Presumably, the countries could then go their own way and fight the war as each saw fit. It was a catastrophic turn for the British; already strapped of manpower and supplies, going it alone would basically deprive them of any influence over American strategy. There was an immediate call for a closed session of the Combined Chiefs that afternoon, a talk so sensitive that no minutes were kept. When the doors finally reopened, the British had made the major concession of agreeing to Anakim in 1943—though only when the monsoon season was over.

The concession made, work began on the final report, which was delivered to Roosevelt and Churchill on May 24.[63] Even then, negotiations were not finished. Though the Combined Chiefs had accepted the basic American strategy, Churchill made one final attempt to seize back the initiative. He asked for a delay and made an impassioned plea for his views. It failed: Roosevelt was not to be moved. Unlike at Casablanca, the president was a rock of support for his American chiefs during Trident. Leahy fondly remembered FDR's faith in him for the rest of his life.

The final Trident communiqué contained commitments to the two operations Leahy most supported. In Europe, there would be a buildup to launch a cross-Channel invasion in the spring of 1944, with a target date of May 1; Mediterranean operations in 1943 could be attempted only if they did not interfere with these preparations. In the Pacific, the Allies would exert "unremitting" pressure against Japan. This included a clear commitment to a ground attack into Burma in 1943, the objective of which was to open a land route to get supplies into China.

Leahy's satisfaction was obvious. The agreements represented a vindication of his personal strategic preferences. What's more, the twelve days of intense discussions seemed to energize him. Whereas Alanbrooke was drained and irritable, Leahy was full of gusto and infused with an energy that belied his years.* Not only did he chair every meeting of the Combined Chiefs and attend many sit-downs with Roosevelt and Churchill, he met regularly with State Department officials and foreign diplomats. He attended dinners thrown by the Czech embassy, a reception in the Chinese embassy, and had many meetings with important figures such as T. V. Soong, financier Nelson Rockefeller, and the Australian foreign minister, H. V. Evatt. He even kept up a steady social calendar. Indeed, the social high point of the two weeks was more revealing of his unique status than any political meeting. At a dinner party thrown by one of Franklin Roosevelt's relations, the admiral was seated beside the guest of honor, Roosevelt's mistress du jour, Princess Martha of Norway. He had a wonderful time.[64]

The American delegation owed its success at Trident to a large degree to Leahy's preparation and coordination of US efforts. Of course, securing a British commitment to operations such as Anakim and a cross-Channel invasion were not enough. There was still the question of forcing them to deliver. As the next six months and three more conferences would show, these issues were far from settled. In the end, while Leahy's vision was more successful than not, a tortured road needed to be walked.

---

* Leahy, at sixty-eight, was the oldest member of the Combined Chiefs, and considerably older than Roosevelt or Hopkins. The only participant at the conference older than Leahy was Winston Churchill, by six months.

CHAPTER 17

Difficult Friends

B y the summer of 1943, the Germans and Japanese had been forced onto the defensive nearly everywhere. Leahy, never particularly graceful with the English language, thought Winston Churchill summed up the situation best when he described the season as being bathed in the "mellow light of victory."[1] In Europe, American ground troops faced battles of only limited importance; an invasion of Sicily was scheduled for July, but little effort was to be expended in the Mediterranean afterward—or so the admiral hoped. In the east, the Germans were preparing for their final great offensive against Russia, an immense yet ultimately doomed attack on the Kursk salient. Indeed, it looked as if the Soviets would do the heavy lifting in the war against Germany that summer, leaving the western Allies on the sidelines. In the Pacific, fighting had quieted since February, when the Japanese finally admitted defeat and pulled out of Guadalcanal. Now the main striking forces of the Japanese and American navies were keeping their distance, licking their wounds and preparing for the next clash.

In Leahy's eyes, something profound, if less obvious, was developing. In May, the German U-boat threat in the Atlantic had been broken for good, allowing for the practically uninterrupted flow of supplies to Europe. On the other side of the globe, the Japanese were losing control of more and more of the vast Pacific, experiencing their first difficulties with shipping resources around their far-flung empire. At last, the Allies were gaining a stranglehold on the world's oceans, and to Leahy this control of the sea was the vital first step toward victory. Moreover, coordinated, strategic airpower was about to be deployed in the skies over Germany for the first time, bringing the war home to the German population and productive machinery. Though Leahy was no expert in strategic bombing, and was opposed to the indiscriminate targeting of civilians, he believed that bombing could put the Germans under enormous strain. Finally, US war production, which in 1942 had come in far below expectations, was now ramping up. Everything from aircraft to tanks to Leahy's beloved aircraft carriers was starting to appear in ominously large numbers for the Axis powers. This equipment could now be deployed in relative safety to most places across the globe, while the Germans and Japanese were losing the ability to deploy their war equipment without significant losses. Just as the admiral had long theorized, air- and sea power were steadily choking the life out of Nazi Germany and Imperial Japan.

For Leahy, it was a summer of fighting fires and holding hands. Having secured everything he wanted at Trident, he was determined to see the British live up to their promises. This would not be simple. Despite their earlier agreement, Churchill and his commanders were not going to give up their fight against an invasion of France in 1944, and they would continue to delay an operation into Burma for as long as possible. The British were going to be a problem, but they were not the most irritating ally Leahy first had to confront; that honor went to a tall, oddly shaped, dogged, and disconcerting Frenchman.

William Leahy hated Charles de Gaulle. He had first soured on the general near the end of his ambassadorship in Vichy, when the Free French leader authorized the seizing of Saint-Pierre and Miquelon. This move, which occurred right after Pearl Harbor had been attacked, and which had not been approved in Washington or London, made Leahy's job in Vichy more difficult while making no discernible difference in the course of the war. After Leahy's return to Washington, matters only grew worse. During Torch, de Gaulle's antics confirmed that he was more interested in personal vindication and restoring the glory of France than in achieving the quickest possible Allied victory with the fewest casualties. When news of the landings was announced, de Gaulle, instead of being elated at an Allied success, went off in a huff at what he believed was a personal insult at not being involved. Distrustful of the general, Leahy used his influence to keep de Gaulle from having any say in the newly occupied territories of North Africa.

Leahy's personal antipathy toward de Gaulle also helps explain why Roosevelt was so rough on the French general in 1942 and 1943.[2] The president regularly tried to marginalize or even humiliate the French leader, starting with completely excluding him from any knowledge of Torch.[3] Yet Roosevelt's extreme suspicion of de Gaulle has been poorly explained by historians. One of the main reasons for the strength of the president's actions toward de Gaulle was that he and Leahy became a strongly self-reinforcing team.[4]

Indeed, the admiral's distrust of the French general was soon to boil over into an obsessive, irrepressible loathing. When American soldiers landed in North Africa, Adm. François Darlan, Leahy's old foil from Vichy, happened to be in Algiers. Faced with a large army on his doorstep, Darlan decided to save his skin and throw in with the United States, making a deal with Eisenhower to order French forces to stop fighting. Self-interest was a main motivation, yet Leahy was also convinced that Darlan's actions saved American lives.[5] He even thought it required real bravery by Darlan to break with Marshal Pétain, to whom most French military officers remained loyal. Leahy certainly did not trust Darlan any more than he did while in Vichy, but he did appreciate that Darlan had taken a step that would benefit Americans in contrast to the constantly prickly and grandstanding de Gaulle.

When Darlan was murdered on Christmas Eve 1942, shot by a young Gaullist sympathizer who had been trained by British intelligence, Leahy suspected that de Gaulle had played a role in authorizing the assassination. He went to see Roosevelt on Christmas Day, and they decided that Gen. Henri Giraud was to be put in charge of all civil and military affairs in US-controlled North Africa, while de Gaulle, who was about to visit America, was to be isolated from power as much as possible.[6] Thereafter, hating and distrusting de Gaulle became almost a religion for Leahy.[7] He was overheard to say that it would be better for the Allied war effort if de Gaulle were sent up in an airplane with one wing.[8] It is not clear if he was joking.

The assassination of Darlan represented the beginning of a long struggle between Leahy and Roosevelt on the one hand, and the British, the State Department, and de Gaulle himself on the other, for control of French forces in North Africa. The problem Roosevelt and Leahy had was that in backing Giraud, they were supporting a weak reed. Tall and erect, this French general appeared every inch the powerful leader, but his dignified bearing masked his limited abilities. Giraud had been captured by the Germans in 1940 and was catapulted to celebrity in April 1942 when he escaped from his prison camp and made his way over the Swiss mountains before reaching Vichy France. When his escape became known, Heinrich Himmler ordered his assassination, and Giraud was smuggled to safety with Allied help. Once out of France, he became an enthusiastic supporter of Torch, even asking to be named its supreme commander.[9] When it was made clear that this would not happen, he knuckled down and was an obedient soldier, promising to publicly support American forces and do his best to bring the French Army around. The pledge alone made him far preferable to de Gaulle. Leahy was rather unimpressed with Giraud at first but decided to back him anyway.[10]

Leahy did everything possible to help Giraud.[11] De Gaulle, however, was determined to come out on top.[12] Unfortunately for Leahy, de Gaulle was a far greater personality and politician than the hapless Giraud. Even though de Gaulle was forbidden from going to North Africa for much of the first half of 1943, he maneuvered brilliantly to sideline Giraud. In May, the two were named joint presidents of the newly formed Comité français de libération nationale (CFLN), which was supposed to unite all effective French factions in one political entity. It ended up being the most unequal of coalitions.

Leahy did not understand that at first. In June he schemed with Harry Hopkins to make sure that de Gaulle gained no command authority over any French forces fighting with the Allies in North Africa.[13] In July, Leahy was Giraud's chief sponsor when the French general visited Washington. Leahy, representing Roosevelt, met Giraud when he flew in on July 7 and spent much of the next three days escorting him around the capital, introducing him to powerful political figures and discussing strategic plans.[14] He still thought Giraud had a reasonable chance of asserting his authority in North Africa, but he would soon be sadly disabused. As the summer went on, it became clear that no matter how much Leahy worked against it, de Gaulle would triumph over Giraud and take sole control of the CFLN. It would take far longer, however, for Leahy to reconcile himself to such a development.

While Leahy's efforts to sideline de Gaulle were beginning to unravel in the summer of 1943, his attempts to keep the British government committed to the Trident agreements were also coming under strain. Operation Husky, the Allied invasion of Sicily, blew away the domestic supports propping up the regime of Benito Mussolini, Italy's Fascist dictator. When US, British, and Canadian forces went ashore on July 9, it was obvious that the island would be conquered relatively quickly. Though the Germans and some Italian forces fought well, all they could hope to do was slow the Allied advance. After a few weeks of intense combat, the Axis troops had been pushed back into a small pocket in northeast Sicily, centered on the forbidding slopes of Mount Etna. Soon, they would be pulled back entirely to the Italian mainland, which would itself be invaded.

Seeing the powerlessness of Axis forces in the face of a full Anglo-American amphibious assault, the Fascist Party quickly tossed Mussolini aside, replacing him with a military government that immediately sent out peace feelers to the Allies, making it clear that they would like to switch sides. The prospect of Italy being offered up to the Allies was so enticing that it caused even some Americans to reconsider their attachment to an invasion of France as the quickest way to drive Germany out of the war. George Marshall, for a moment, changed his tune about the value of fighting in the Mediterranean. On July 26, the Joint Chiefs held a meeting to discuss strategy in light of what seemed to be the imminent Italian collapse. Marshall spoke about the need to get troops onto the Italian mainland as soon as possible.[15] Leahy was more circumspect and refused to say whether he thought the potential collapse of Italy was a game-changer. He did admit that Roosevelt now believed that there was a real chance that Allied strategy would have to be significantly revised.[16]

The possible Italian collapse supercharged what was originally shaping up to be a low-key grand-strategy summit, code-named Quadrant, scheduled for August in Quebec. Roosevelt had first suggested to Churchill that they meet in Canada to find a way to coordinate action with Joseph Stalin.[17] Yet with Italy teetering, the strategic debate between making a greater effort in the Mediterranean or sticking to the plan to invade France the following spring reappeared.

Before Roosevelt could tackle the issue at Quadrant, he needed a vacation. On July 30, he and a small party boarded the *Ferdinand Magellan* and headed north, the beginning of a month in which Leahy and Roosevelt would be together for all but five days. After a stopover in Hyde Park, FDR's train continued north, crossing the Canadian border into Ontario, eventually reaching Georgian Bay on Lake Huron. There the train, now up to a total of ten cars, was turned into a lakeside hotel.[18] The party happily camped, venturing out daily onto the lake to fish from whaleboats. Sunburns did little to dampen the happy mood. Reeling in smallmouth bass and walleyed pike, the revelers turned the excursions into daily competitions, with everyone throwing money into a pool for the person who caught the most fish. Either Roosevelt or Leahy won every day. Leahy seemed pleased when Harry Hopkins joined the party on August 4, as he was an atrocious fisherman whose presence only added to the pot. Evenings were spent around a campfire, with cookouts, cocktails, and lots of talk. Despite the late nights, Leahy still had a job to do, and each evening he would quietly slip away to attend to the president's confidential correspondence, determining what Roosevelt needed to see and drafting replies for him to approve. It required a great deal of effort to be both friend and chief of staff to Franklin Roosevelt. Leahy inevitably grumbled about the late nights, though he never let the president know.[19]

Refreshed, Roosevelt and Leahy returned to Washington to prepare for Quadrant. A holiday in the sun had done little to quiet the admiral's doubts about operations in Italy, and once back he again became perhaps the strongest American critic of a Mediterranean strategy. When the Joint Chiefs assembled on August 9, he called for the insertion of a statement in the American preparatory documents that the invasion of France would always have "overriding" priority over Mediterranean operations when it came to the allocation of vital equipment.[20] He was not alone. The next day, in a meeting between the chiefs and the president, it was clear that American support for a greater effort in Italy had waned. This practical American unanimity on the Mediterranean was a relief, but the issue he was most forceful about was one that had been temporarily overlooked during the Italian kerfuffle: getting the British to follow through on their commitment to Anakim.[21] Leahy was looking for more than words. He wanted a firm date by which the operation would be launched and a concrete list of the forces to be employed.[22]

His impatience on the question revealed that he continued to doubt that the British were committed to the Pacific war. As he had in 1942, Leahy started from the basis that America must plan to fight Japan without the British playing a meaningful role.[23] Churchill had promised at Trident that the British would launch the attack from India into Burma at the end of the monsoon season, which typically occurred in October. That date was now approaching, and there was little sign that a major operation was in the offing. Whether the British were willing to follow through would have important consequences on the upcoming Quebec Conference and Leahy's plans on how America should fight the global war.

On August 11 Roosevelt headed to Hyde Park to meet with Churchill—for once without Leahy, the one and only time during America's war that the admiral did not travel with the president to a grand strategy conference. It was thought prudent to send the chiefs to Quebec first to see if they could work out some of their differences, so Churchill and Roosevelt decided to spend a few days in the president's home. Two days later, Leahy flew from Washington with George Marshall in an army plane bound for Quebec City. When they arrived, a heavy, dark mist hung over the city; landing the plane was thought too dangerous, and the flight was diverted to Montreal. When Leahy and Marshall finally reached Quebec City by car, they found the British chiefs waiting in the Château Frontenac, a grand, castle-like hotel that dominated the city's skyline from a bluff that reached out magnificently above the St. Lawrence River. There the chiefs would spend the next three days by themselves, fighting, predictably, about the value of an Italian campaign, an invasion of France, and the course of the Pacific war.

It was clear that the British still hoped to entice the Americans into forgetting about D-Day by having them commit to ever more expansive Mediterranean operations. Alanbrooke began the proceedings by arguing that the impending Italian collapse offered the Allies a unique chance to strike a great blow against the Germans, and that this should now be the focus of their efforts. Yet Leahy had no desire to take part in a rehash of old arguments, and on the discussion of Europe he was usually enigmatically quiet, willing to let Marshall do the talking. He spoke occasionally, for the most part only to draw a line under an issue—and in the process to emphasize that he was the senior member of the American chiefs.[24] When a difficult problem arose he made clear to the British chiefs that he was more than happy to wait until Roosevelt arrived before deciding how to proceed.[25]

When talk turned to the Pacific, however, Leahy came alive, ready to duel. When Admiral King called for more resources to be diverted to the fight against Japan, Leahy jumped in, saying that he believed the British, as a good ally, should launch Anakim—but if they did not, the United States would have a plan in place to shift forces from Europe into the Pacific *before* the Germans were defeated. It was as clear a threat as he would ever make on the subject, and he gave it more force later when he asked the British to commit formally to a date for launching Anakim.[26]

Leahy's harping on the British setting a firm date for Anakim (and Overlord) was aimed at undermining the main tactic that the British were using to delay or even avoid both operations. Alanbrooke liked to argue that such operations should not have hard dates, but should only be launched when the conditions were judged appropriate, such as when it was clear that the Allies could land in France without the risk of large casualties or could surge into Burma once they judged that they had enough force on hand to make the offensive a foregone conclusion. Leahy, who wanted an overwhelming victory as much as Alanbrooke, believed that they needed to set a date to start both operations so that they could focus on accumulating the forces needed to make them happen. Alanbrooke became so frustrated with Leahy, and the rest of the American delegation's request for dates by when operations would be launched, that he accused them of trying to run the war through a series of "lawyer's agreements, which, when once signed, can never be departed from."[27]

The arrival of Roosevelt and Churchill in Quebec, early in the evening of August 17, brought issues to a head. Now agreements would have to be reached. For Leahy, the president's arrival only served to add more responsibilities to his already full workload. In Quebec the president, along with Eleanor Roosevelt, were housed in a suite at the governor-general's summer residence in the Old Citadel. Only one other person could be housed with the president, and Roosevelt selected Leahy. So the admiral checked out of the Château Frontenac and settled into a room next to the president's.[28] Alone with Roosevelt, Leahy took over the management of the president's professional life. He was put in charge of a mobile version of the White House Map Room, which was set up near their accommodation and controlled the flow of all information to and from Roosevelt.[29] Roosevelt also trusted Leahy to handle many responsibilities such as sensitive press relations, keeping his press secretary in the dark on most issues.[30]

Two days after their arrival, Roosevelt and Churchill met for a formal conference with the chiefs. When Italian mainland operations were discussed, the president made it clear that he did not want a full-scale effort made to take the whole peninsula. Instead, he called for an increase in the number of troops shipped to the United Kingdom to prepare for D-Day.[31] As for the Pacific, Roosevelt, using a slightly bizarre analogy of the Japanese Empire being a large slice of pie, argued for an invasion of Burma to open a road into China. It was everything for which Leahy could have hoped.

The last few days of Quadrant were in some ways the most predictable of any of the grand strategic conferences of the war. The issues were well-known and the arguments unsurprising.[32] In the end the agreements reached reflected the relative balance in raw power between the United States and the United Kingdom. No matter how much they argued against it, the British were forced to continue with the commitment that they had made at Trident that Operation Overlord would be launched around May 1, 1944.[33] Nothing done in the Mediterranean in the meantime would be allowed to disrupt these plans for the invasion of France. When it came to the launching of Anakim, the British seemingly had one success, in that they delayed the launch date of the operation from October 1943 until February 1944. However, the price that they had to pay for that was considerable; they were basically separated out completely from having any influence over US actions in the Pacific, in the process undermining the whole notion of Germany-first. The final joint statement agreed to at Quadrant allowed the United States, for the first time, to determine for itself the amount of force it wanted to expend in the Pacific (from the east), while the British could determine for themselves the amount of force that they would use against Burma (from the west): "The principle has been accepted that the forces to carry out operations from the East, including the Southwest Pacific, shall be provided by the United States, and for operations from the West by Great Britain."[34] During Trident there had been specific mentions of how much force would be sent to the different theaters. Now they were being decoupled and the United States given carte blanche. This freeing of US power explains why Leahy was happy with the overall decisions reached, even if he felt stymied by the British reluctance to attack into Burma. If the British continued to drag their heels on Anakim, the United States could on its own send to the Pacific whatever it thought necessary to defeat Japan. It was a policy Leahy had been arguing for since September 1942.

It also helps explain Leahy's jaunty mood at the end of Quadrant. He summed it up as a "very busy, pleasant ten-day trip."[35] Except for the local water, which he thought gave him indigestion, he seemed to enjoy every part of the summit, including the long dinner parties in the evenings. Both Alanbrooke and Churchill, on the other hand, found Quebec to be a nasty combination of exhausting and depressing. Alanbrooke complained in a series of bleak diary entries about the Americans, whom he blamed for being unable to recognize his own strategic genius. By the end of the conference he had reached the end of his tether: "The conference is finished and I am feeling the inevitable flatness and depression which swamps me after a spell of continuous work, and of battling against difficulties, differences of opinion, stubbornness, stupidity, pettiness, and pig-headedness."[36]

And one does feel a little sorry for Alanbrooke. Eight months earlier, at Casablanca, the British had outmaneuvered the Americans into agreeing to make the Mediterranean the major theater of war for at least 1943 and perhaps longer, while making no clear commitment to invading France, and reaffirming Germany-first at the same time. Now, within six months, the British had been forced twice to agree to invade France in May 1944, to accept that the Mediterranean was, and would continue to be, a secondary theater, while at the same time progressively losing any influence over how much force America could send to the Pacific. The one clear British victory, the delaying of Anakim, had in many ways subverted their overall purposes in the war. Though the British would continue to fight for what they wanted, in the end the Quadrant decisions pointed the way to how the war would be brought to its conclusion. The whole process had also reconfirmed Leahy's centrality to the making of grand strategy. Now he could go and have another break with his good friend Franklin Roosevelt and actually relax. He would need it. As both Roosevelt and Leahy knew, Joseph Stalin was lurking.

CHAPTER 18

Top Dog

A fter Quebec, Roosevelt needed a rest. While Hopkins, Marshall, King, and Arnold returned to Washington, the president headed directly to Hyde Park, taking along only his secretary, his press secretary, and Leahy.[1] For three days Roosevelt and Leahy relaxed, chatting in the president's new study, and taking country drives together, which resulted in visits to some of Roosevelt's distant cousins. When the party finally returned to the White House on August 30, the president and his closest adviser had been together almost every day for an entire month. During that time they had decided on grand strategy and participated in one of the most important conferences in World War II, doing more to direct the course of the war than any other top officials.

The personal time that Roosevelt and Leahy spent together was indicative of how the admiral had supplanted Harry Hopkins in the president's affections, both personally and professionally. Leahy was vital to a functional White House, and a visit to his office on September 23 showed that Hopkins understood this new reality. Hopkins came by to tell Leahy a story as lurid as one could have imagined in the 1940s: rumor had it that Under Secretary of State Sumner Welles, another Roosevelt insider, had been implicated in a drunken homosexual scandal. Hopkins felt he needed to get Leahy onside before convincing the president to act.

Though Hopkins did not realize this, Leahy had almost certainly learned of the story many months earlier, but perhaps understanding Roosevelt's fondness for his old friend, he had never mentioned it to the president. The incident in question had taken place in September 1940. Welles's cool demeanor was a mask to cover his homosexuality. Knowing that even hints about his desires could destroy his reputation, the thrice-married Welles's life was built around the outward show of being heterosexual. Over time his repressed needs drove him to binge drink, during which time his self-control could evaporate and his urges emerge. Aboard an overnight train, a well-lubricated and emotionally liberated Sumner Welles propositioned a number of African American railway porters in his Pullman car, reportedly only stopping after all had refused.[2]

At the time, the story was reported to Roosevelt, who asked the FBI to investigate. When they concluded that Welles had in fact propositioned the porters, the president sat on the information, hoping the incident would melt away. For a while it seemed that it would, and Welles remained Roosevelt's favored contact in the State Department. Yet Welles had enemies who were jealous of his access and influence. Cordell Hull was the greatest of these. Hull's jealousy came from personal frustration at being increasingly marginalized during the war while Welles, his nominal subordinate, was far more involved in policymaking. The secretary of state started putting pressure on Welles to resign, though he never pressed Roosevelt as directly on the matter.

In his efforts to get rid of Welles, Hull was supported by the aggressive and self-destructive William Bullitt. Bullitt's jealousy toward Welles was simple: he wanted Welles's job. Having already served in two major ambassadorial roles, Bullitt was convinced that he had the ability and experience, to say nothing of the intelligence, needed to steer American foreign policy in such a crucial time. What he did not have was the faith of Franklin Roosevelt. After Bullitt returned home from his controversial ambassadorship to France in 1940, the president kept the wealthy, ambitious Pennsylvanian at arm's length. He would send Bullitt on diplomatic missions, but he resisted giving him a permanent post. With his signature charm, Roosevelt would regularly dazzle

Bullitt with promises of important jobs in the future, but nothing specific ever materialized. It was a superb example of Roosevelt's mask of bonhomie being used to thwart a man's ambition.

Eventually the nasty triangular relationship of personality and interest reached a crescendo. To put it simply, Hull and Bullitt set out to destroy Sumner Welles.[3] The two first heard news of Welles's drunken night on the train sometime in 1942 and started spreading the story around Washington, hoping that it would make it into the press.[4] They claimed that incident made Welles such a security risk that he needed to be removed from the State Department. Hull clearly discussed the "scandalous rumor" about Welles with the *New York Times* journalist Arthur Krock.[5] No newspaper was willing to print the story, yet whispers around Washington grew louder. In their nasty quest, Hull and Bullitt were able to take advantage of Welles's personality. His aloofness meant that he had few supporters other than the president. His aristocratic nature, which made Roosevelt comfortable, led him to be detached from others. The way that Roosevelt favored him also led to lower morale in the State Department, where he had few colleagues willing to fight on his behalf.[6]

At first, Roosevelt did everything in his power to protect Welles. As assistant secretary of the navy, Roosevelt had called for strict punishment of naval personnel who were found to have engaged in homosexual activity, even authorizing a sting operation to catch homosexual sailors in the act.[7] In the intervening years, he became aware of the role of physical desire in his own life as he engaged in numerous affairs with women who were not his wife. By the 1940s he was more than willing to overlook the sexual activity of those he valued. He even believed that making allowances for sexual urges was the proper, Christian thing to do.[8]

But by September 1943, even Roosevelt was losing the ability to protect Welles. The story was thought to be on the verge of breaking nationally. (It would, though not for many years, eventually being published in a gossip magazine in the 1950s.) As such, Roosevelt either had to face a complete break with Hull or reluctantly accept Welles's resignation. That he eventually did the latter was something that Roosevelt never forgot, nor forgave. He had already marginalized Hull by this point, so there was little else he could do to the secretary of state but ignore him more obviously. Roosevelt's open wrath was unleashed on Bullitt. In this case the mask that characterized most of the president's interactions dropped. The sense of loss was so raw that Roosevelt's darker side came out.

He belittled Hull as "an old fool" and accused Bullitt of leaking the story to "that bitch friend of yours," Cissy Patterson, publisher of the *Washington Times-Herald*.[9] A few nights after Welles resigned, an emotional Roosevelt held a small dinner party for six people, all of whom he could trust. Among those attending were his mistress, Princess Martha of Norway, Margaret Suckley, and Leahy.[10] He went through the whole episode in detail, clearly viewing Welles's actions as a drunken mistake. However, Roosevelt was still incandescent at the behavior of Bullitt, and it was evident to those around the table that he never again wanted to speak to the former ambassador.

This sting in the tail for Bullitt would last for as long as Roosevelt lived. The president set out to destroy him by sabotaging Bullitt's political career. With no government job on offer from the White House, Bullitt decided to run for mayor of Philadelphia. Roosevelt told the leaders of the Democratic Party in Pennsylvania to "cut his [Bullitt's] throat."[11] Bullitt lost. With no political future as long as Roosevelt was president, in 1944 he signed up to fight with the French Army; sadly, from Roosevelt's perspective, he emerged unscathed.

This spectacular falling-out between Roosevelt and Bullitt put Leahy in an awkward position. Until the moment he resigned, Welles worked closely with Leahy, the two almost always bypassing Hull and going directly to Roosevelt on important questions.[12] If anything, their relationship in 1943 seemed stronger. Not long after returning with the president after Casablanca, Leahy met twice with Welles for detailed surveys of US foreign policy, including relations with Vichy France, American policy toward newly occupied foreign lands, and the effectiveness of US propaganda.[13] On the other hand, though Leahy liked Welles personally, there was no indication that Leahy advised Roosevelt to keep the undersecretary of state.

Bullitt, on the other hand, had gone to great lengths to cultivate

Leahy and turn him against Welles. In March 1943 he invited Leahy to lunch à deux at his large house on Kalorama Street to discuss how he could fix a "completely disorganized and inefficient" State Department.[14] Leahy would have listened to Bullitt's ideas with interest, as he usually did, but also with a note of caution. He obviously enjoyed Bullitt's conversation, but also thought the man was in need of greater self-control. As he later said, Bullitt "usually has interesting ideas about how to solve a problem, and some of them sound excellent."[15]

Leahy greeted Welles's resignation cautiously, commenting only that his departure would at least lead to greater harmony within the State Department, as Hull and he had worked so poorly together.[16] There is no indication that Leahy ever passed moral judgment on Welles's behavior. Certainly, if Welles's crisis had been heterosexual in nature, it is unlikely that Leahy would have cared—at the time, Leahy was abetting Roosevelt in a string of affairs with several different women. On the whole, the admiral seemed rather forgiving of people's personal tastes. Yet the fact that Welles's scandal involved interracial homosexuality might have made a difference for the conventional Leahy. While he liked one openly gay person, Bernard Baruch's lesbian daughter, Belle, he might have seen Welles's homosexuality as a serious security risk. Following his resignation, Welles seems to have mostly disappeared from Leahy's life. Leahy agreed with Hopkins that it would be unwise for the president to send Welles to Russia on a special mission—something Roosevelt considered to demonstrate that he still cared for his friend.[17] In fact, Hopkins phoned Leahy before going to Roosevelt, to make sure that the admiral would support him in this move to block any Welles mission.[18] Their lobbying probably kept the mission from occurring. Leahy certainly never condemned Welles, but neither did he seek him out.

With Welles out of his administration, Roosevelt became even more reliant on Leahy. Certainly, Hopkins was not up to the task. In October 1943, his malnutrition and anemia were found to be so serious that he was once again put on regular plasma transfusions.[19] His growing weakness was accentuated a few weeks later when his wife finally convinced Hopkins to move into a family home in Georgetown. This physical distance increased the growing emotional chasm between Hopkins and Roosevelt. Leahy even admitted in his memoirs that Hopkins moving out of the White House had led to some strains with the president.[20]

Working together over the past few years, Leahy had grown genuinely fond of Hopkins, despite the latter's leftist leanings. "Sure, he's a pinkie, but he's frank about it," the admiral said, as recalled by the young Map Room staffer George Elsey.* "He's for the proletariat and the underdog. I didn't like him before I started to work with him, but I do now. By God, he delivers the goods. He puts his shoulder to the wheel and works."[21] It was high praise coming from a reserved military man like Leahy. Like himself, Hopkins was committed to winning the war because it was a moral fight that had to be won. Both men were focused on helping the president do this regardless of personal advantage. Even more admirable, Hopkins shrugged off the high salary his skills could have commanded in private enterprise and chose instead to serve his country. "He's always been associated with the down-and-outers," continued Leahy. "He doesn't care about money." The admiral clearly saw something of himself in the idealistic, determined Harry Hopkins.

By contrast, Leahy was becoming even more damning about Cordell Hull. The secretary of state came off in Leahy's eyes as supercilious and vain, refusing a state visit to Africa for fear of illness and griping constantly about the press.[22] The admiral recorded in his diary:

> At ten A.M. called by appointment with Mr. Hull . . . who spoke at length about the press attacks by some newspapers on the State Department's foreign policy, which attacks he said are made for the purpose of aiding the opposition political party in the United States. He is particularly incensed at Mr. Drew Pearson whose articles which have wide distribution have been seriously critical of Mr. Hull's Department. I received an impression that Mr. Hull is actuated in his attitude towards Mr. Pearson by personal irritation

---

* Elsey worked in the White House for almost a decade, first as a Map Room aide, but then later rose to be an adviser to President Truman. Leahy liked the younger Elsey very much and was unusually open in his presence.

William Daniel Leahy as a young cadet at the US Naval Academy at Annapolis, circa 1896.

A mustachioed Cadet Leahy on the USS *Oregon* during the Battle of Santiago, July 1898. Leahy stands next to Captain Charles E. Clark, whom he considered an exemplary commander.

Leahy with fellow cadet Cyrus Miller on the *Oregon*.

Leahy with his wife, Louise, and their only child, William H. Leahy, on Mare Island, California, in 1905.

Leahy (*back row, second from right*) with the officers of the USS *California*. From the very start he was driven to succeed, as the determination on his face attests.

In 1911, Leahy was chosen to serve as an aide to President William Howard Taft, an early indication of the lieutenant commander's political skills.

Leahy was successful at cultivating senior officers in the fleet. Two of his greatest patrons were Albert Niblack (*left*), who became his brother-in-law, and H. T. Mayo (*right, center*), who was responsible for bringing Leahy to Washington for the assignment that would change his life.

America's first all-big-gun battleship, the USS *South Carolina*. The advent of such dreadnoughts made gunnery skills crucial, and Leahy capitalized by becoming a leader of the gunnery school, which dominated much of the US Navy until World War II.

Assistant Secretary of the Navy Franklin Roosevelt (*in top hat*) attends the launch of the battleship USS *Tennessee* at the Brooklyn Navy Yard in 1919. Physically dynamic and vigorous, Roosevelt impressed Leahy immediately as the best kind of political leader. LIBRARY OF CONGRESS

Rear Admiral Leahy sits for a portrait in full uniform in 1929. A confident and successful officer, Leahy would soon be tested by the Great Depression, which would wipe out his savings and leave him with a large debt.

Vice Admiral Leahy (*front row, center*), commander of the battle force, poses with his battleship captains in 1935. If war had broken out at this time, he would have called the shots in any great sea battle.

Admiral W. H. Standley, the departing chief of naval operations, welcomes Leahy as his successor in 1936. Though they attempted to appear friendly before the cameras, the two men had waged one of the nastiest feuds in the history of the US Navy.

Above and below: President Roosevelt often invited Leahy along on vacations and official trips, enjoying the admiral's counsel and camaraderie. Here they relax together on the USS *Houston* during a fishing trip, before observing a fleet exercise in the Caribbean.

Leahy with Louise in Puerto Rico. In 1939, President Roosevelt appointed the retiring admiral as governor of the island territory. He proved surprisingly effective, overseeing clean elections and securing a large amount of New Deal funding for the island.

In 1941, Leahy was appointed ambassador to Vichy France following that nation's capitulation to Germany. Here, he makes his formal goodbye to Marshal Pétain in April 1942, having been recalled to Washington. Louise had died just days earlier; the immense strain can be seen on Leahy's face.

Soon after his return to Washington, Leahy was appointed by Roosevelt to a unique new role, officially titled as Chief of Staff to the Commander in Chief, Army and Navy of the United States. It was a job in which he would wield considerable power over the shaping of World War II.

Above and below: During a flight back from Trinidad following the Casablanca Conference, President Roosevelt, Admiral Leahy, and Harry Hopkins—the apex of America's strategic power—celebrated FDR's birthday with cake and Champagne.

A weak and emaciated Harry Hopkins smiles for the camera, in a photograph discovered in Leahy's private collection. When Leahy assumed the role of chief of staff, Hopkins attempted to limit his influence; but when that failed, he worked well with the admiral.

A seat in Roosevelt's cabinet did not guarantee influence. Secretary of the Navy Frank Knox (*right*) and Secretary of War Henry Stimson (*left*) were rarely consulted by the president and were usually excluded from the most important strategy meetings. Roosevelt trusted Under Secretary of State Sumner Welles (*center*).

One of Leahy's many duties during the war was serving as the chairman of both the Joint Chiefs of Staff (*above*) and the Combined Chiefs of Staff (*below*). He refereed disputes between Ernest King, George Marshall, and Henry "Hap" Arnold on the Joint Chiefs, while at the same time enforcing Roosevelt's wishes. On the Combined Chiefs, he often dueled with Field Marshal Sir Alan Brooke (*right side, third from top*) over differences concerning European and Pacific strategy.

American and British officials gather together at the Quebec Conference in September 1944. *Front row, from left*: Marshall, Leahy, Roosevelt, Winston Churchill, Brooke, and Field Marshal Sir John Dill. *Back row*: Major General Sir Leslie Hollis, Sir Hastings Ismay, King, Air Marshal Sir Charles Portal, Arnold, and Admiral Sir Andrew Cunningham.

In July 1944, Roosevelt journeyed to Hawaii to confer with General Douglas MacArthur (*left*) and Admiral Chester Nimitz (*center*) at Pearl Harbor. He insisted on bringing Admiral Leahy to advise him on Pacific strategy, keeping the other Joint Chiefs—Marshall, King, and Arnold—away from the meeting.

On the USS *Quincy*, en route to the Yalta Conference, Leahy dines with Roosevelt and friends for what would be the president's final birthday celebration. To the right of Leahy is Roosevelt's daughter, Anna.

Roosevelt, Marshall, Leahy, and King meet at Malta during the Yalta trip. Photographs showing senior military officials smoking cigarettes were typically kept from the public. This photo was never released during the war.

Leahy and Roosevelt meet with Saudi ruler King Abdulaziz Al Saud, better known as Ibn Saud. Their discussion further reinforced Leahy's opinion that the United States should stay out of the Middle East.

Along with Secretary of State James Byrnes (*far left*), Leahy played a pivotal role in preparing President Harry Truman (*center*) to meet Joseph Stalin (*far right*) at the Potsdam Conference in 1945.

In late 1945, in the wake of victory in World War II, Admiral Leahy was adopted as a member of the Sioux tribe in South Dakota. Seven years earlier, he had been adopted by the Chippewas in his native Wisconsin. He took great pride in both of these honors.

At Leahy's suggestion, President Truman visited Key West, Florida, in 1946, and was immediately taken with the warm climate and relaxing sea breezes. The admiral accompanied him often. Here, the two friends weigh a catch of fish during a competition. Truman seems to be searching Leahy's face for signs of approval, while the crusty old sailor appears more interested in assuring the fish are weighed correctly.

While Truman and Leahy did not always see eye to eye on questions of foreign policy, the new president grew to value his chief of staff's discretion and loyalty. In 1946, Truman awarded Leahy with his second of three Distinguished Service Medals.

Fleet Admiral Leahy in one of his final formal portraits. The president's decisions to involve the United States in the Eastern Mediterranean and the Middle East seemed to accelerate the admiral's aging.

In 1952, Leahy (*second from left*), then retired, attended the fifty-fifth reunion of his Annapolis class. He was joined by his lifelong friend, Admiral Thomas Hart (*fourth from left*).

which is probably exactly what Mr. Pearson wants to accomplish.... I do not understand why he should permit the articles of opposition columnists to get under his skin.[23]

Hull's incompetence led to his marginalization within the Roosevelt administration. When he needed important information from the White House, such as on US policy in the eastern Mediterranean, he usually had to go through Leahy to get it.[24] He often found himself shut out. In August 1943 Hull heard a rumor that the United States was about to formally recognize de Gaulle's Comité français de libération nationale as the legitimate government of France. Desperate to confirm the report, he called Leahy's office, only to be told the admiral was fishing with Roosevelt in Canada and wasn't to be disturbed.[25]

While Leahy was dismissive of Hull, he was building strong links with rising personalities in the strategic decision-making structure, including Averell Harriman and James Forrestal. Harriman became the new US ambassador to the Soviet Union just as the Welles crisis was unfolding. Another wealthy, ambitious financier who moved into diplomacy, the savvy Harriman had begun cultivating Leahy in 1942, when he started dropping by the admiral's office for policy discussions not long after Leahy became chief of staff.[26] In September 1943, once he heard that he would be named the ambassador in Moscow, Harriman came by for another chat. He wanted to get Leahy's approval for his proposed plan of action in Moscow and in exchange asked the admiral to supply him with information that would allow Harriman to "acquire credit for giving such information in exchange before the Soviets get it from other sources."[27] The gambit worked. Leahy liked Harriman. They held similar beliefs on the best way to deal with the Soviets, and the admiral was willing to share important information with the new ambassador.[28] Though it was never stated, there was certainly an unspoken agreement by which Harriman supplied Leahy with important information in return. For the next two and a half years, while Harriman served as ambassador, he stopped by Leahy's office whenever he was in Washington.[29]

Leahy's relationship with Forrestal was even closer. The assistant secretary of the navy was rising in Roosevelt's estimation, seen as someone with much greater drive and intelligence than Secretary Knox.[30] Another man of great wealth, Forrestal had served as one of America's first naval aviators during World War I before making his fortune on Wall Street. A devout Roman Catholic of Irish background, Forrestal was also a committed New York Democrat, a sure way to get noticed by Franklin Roosevelt. In 1940 the president appointed Forrestal to be the navy's assistant secretary. With the ineffective Knox above him, the workaholic and driven Forrestal became increasingly powerful in the Navy Department. Indeed, Forrestal often bypassed Knox (and at times even Ernest King) on sensitive issues and went right to Leahy. In September 1943 Forrestal wanted to rethink the entire naval building program. Most delicately, Forrestal wanted to cancel two of the super-heavy 45,000-ton battleships then under construction, which he knew were particular favorites of King's. To get action he went through Leahy to the president, leaving both Knox and King out of the loop.[31] Roosevelt, in his response, was more than willing to keep working directly with just Forrestal and Leahy. King remained completely unaware of the Leahy-Forrestal axis. In late October he claimed confidently in a meeting of the Joint Chiefs that only low-level members of the Navy Department could have possibly suggested canceling the 45,000-ton beasts.[32]

These kinds of relationships not only gave Leahy greater influence across the policy-making sphere; they were a key reason that Roosevelt was willing to delegate power through Leahy. The admiral had his own connections and could get things done. There was simply no one else in Roosevelt's life who bridged the personal and professional so completely. He was, undoubtedly, top dog.

CHAPTER 19

Cairo and Tehran

On September 8, 1943, a telegram arrived in the Map Room of the White House for which Franklin Roosevelt had been waiting expectantly. Joseph Stalin was finally agreeing to meet the president in person.[1] For months Roosevelt had been trying to charm Stalin into coming to a summit with him and Winston Churchill. He believed that it was vital to develop a personal relationship with the Soviet leader, both to see the war to its earliest possible conclusion and, even more important, to establish the basis for a lasting peace afterward. The president had sent telegrams and dispatched American diplomats to convince Stalin to meet, but to no avail.

With war raging on Soviet soil, Stalin, always suspicious, had long judged it too risky to leave Moscow. In late July, after the failure of the German Army to break through Soviet lines and the Allied invasion of Sicily, Hitler had called a halt to German assaults on the Kursk salient, the largest tank battle of the war. Throughout August, Soviet forces began pushing the Germans back methodically, recapturing the cities of Kharkov and Orel. Now set on retaking Kiev, the capital of the Ukraine, the road to Berlin was visible.

At last, Stalin decided the time was right to come face-to-face with Roosevelt—on his own terms, of course. When the president suggested meeting in Alaska or North Africa, Stalin, afraid of flying and still wary about being out of his country for too long, objected. He offered to travel only as far as Iran, a short train ride over the border from the Soviet Union. Roosevelt protested that such a long journey could lead to a constitutional crisis in America, where the president had to be available to sign or veto laws within ten days of their passage. Stalin refused to budge. If the meeting were held anywhere more distant, he replied, he would send his foreign secretary, Vyacheslav Molotov, in his place. Faced with such obstinacy, Roosevelt gave in.

The prospect of a summit with Stalin was simply too tantalizing for the president. It also caused a flurry of discussion in the White House as American-Soviet relations now became the main topic of conversation. Roosevelt approached the question with fuzzy optimism.* He wanted a postwar arrangement based on a close relationship of what he called the Four Policemen: the United States, the Soviet Union, Great Britain, and China. What's more, he wanted to establish a new United Nations organization to foster international cooperation. By employing his personal charm and charisma, he believed he could convince Stalin to work with him on these objectives. A non-ideological soul, Roosevelt believed that the Soviet Communist dictatorship was metamorphosing into something more benign, an authoritarian form of social democracy.[2] Though he realized there would be problems when it came to the future issues—such as the fate of eastern Europe once it had been occupied by the Red Army—he considered such boils lanceable. Harry Hopkins shared his hopes.

William Leahy was different. At times he could be swept up by the president's vision and speak of a future, cooperative peace based on American-Soviet amity. That he did so at all demonstrated how powerful an influence Franklin Roosevelt was over him, because it ran against every fiber of his being. At heart, Leahy did not trust the Soviets. When his innate skepticism emerged, he admitted to friends that he was unsure exactly how Roosevelt could accomplish what he wanted with Stalin. Sensing at times that Roosevelt had crossed the line into self-deception,

---

* Leahy, who had more exposure to Roosevelt's postwar ideas than almost anyone else, was not sure how the president planned to square the circle of maintaining friendly relations with the Soviets and yet at the same time resist the spread of a Communist dictatorship into eastern Europe while also getting a United Nations established. He implied that Roosevelt assumed that his personal abilities would help keep relations on an even keel and contain any crises.

Leahy would talk about the president's internationalist "globaloney," or "all that pinko yakety-yak."[3]

Despite his suspicions, Leahy was not a simplistic, hard-line anti-Communist. He approached American-Soviet relations from a balance-of-power perspective.[4] He had little faith that America and Russia would be great friends after the war, yet he had no interest in fostering conflict between the two nations. Instead, he counseled skeptical restraint, understanding what the Soviet Union was and realizing that the United States would have to accept a great many of Stalin's demands. Leahy came to the conclusion early on, for instance, that the United States had to reconcile itself to the Soviets ruling eastern Europe in almost any way they saw fit. On September 22, 1943, after a long discussion with Hopkins, the admiral admitted in his diary that it was "inconceivable to me that Stalin will submit to the re-establishment of sovereignty in Poland, Latvia, Lithuania and Estonia, and it appears certain that the Soviet Government with its superior military power . . . can force acceptance of its desires upon America and Great Britain."[5]

In early October Leahy sat down with Roosevelt and Hull in the president's office to discuss the secretary of state's upcoming visit to Moscow to help coordinate the plans for the great summit.[6] The president was at his optimistic best, speaking about the chances of reaching an amicable agreement with the Soviets over the division of Germany and of convincing Stalin to accept China as an equal in the Great Power game of world politics. Leahy listened attentively but was unconvinced. Until the war was over, the United States would hear warm words from the Russians, but once Germany was conquered, he believed, Stalin would let Roosevelt know exactly what he wanted—and by that time there would be little the United States could do but accept the great bulk of his demands.

Leahy's sense of resignation marked him out as perhaps the least enthusiastic senior American policy maker about the plan for another set of grand strategic summits. If he had only a flickering faith in Soviet friendship, he was also growing exasperated by the constant British attempts to wriggle out of their commitments made at Trident and Quebec. Leahy's support for an invasion of France in the spring of 1944 had, if anything, strengthened. He had received intelligence that Stalin might very well cut a deal with Hitler if the cross-Channel invasion were delayed. Moreover, the Italian situation, which seemed so promising after the landings in Sicily, had been bogged down quickly. Far from being a pushover, the Germans were able to rush enough force into Italy to hold on to the vast majority of the Italian peninsula with only a modest amount of support from their Italian allies. In September, when American troops went ashore at Salerno in southern Italy, the Germans were waiting, and it looked for a while that the Americans might be pushed back into the sea. Fighting all the way up the hilly, narrow Italian boot threatened to be a bloody and time-consuming mess. Leahy turned his attention to Overlord, content to leave the Italian campaign behind.[7]

Churchill had other ideas. In October 1943 he hit upon the notion of embroiling the Allies in an operation to liberate the Greek island of Rhodes, situated in the easternmost part of the Aegean Sea. Italian forces garrisoned there had ended up in a shooting war with German troops who had been sent to keep watch on their supposed allies. Churchill, in an effort to help the Italians, argued for a major Allied amphibious operation to seize the island.

Leahy smelled a rat. He believed that the move was a diversion from the war against Germany, which, if approved, would lead to a wide-scale expansion of the war into the Middle East. To him, the Middle East was an area of British interest, not American, and he wanted the United States to stay out.[8] When Churchill asked the Americans for valuable landing craft to attack Rhodes, Leahy blocked the request from his position on the Joint Chiefs, refusing to give Eisenhower permission to release the vessels.[9] The next day, Leahy had Marshall and King come to his office to write a response to Churchill, only to receive another request before their first rebuff had been sent out.[10] The frustrated admiral just wanted to get on with what he believed had been agreed to twice: invade France, help China, and continue to fight the Japanese.

From such a vantage point, little was to be gained from another meeting with the British. Yet with the date in Tehran set, the British pressed their American "cousins" for a bilateral conference before embarking for Iran. Reluctantly, Roosevelt agreed to a rendezvous in Cairo. With little doubt that a Mediterranean offensive remained at the top of Churchill's wish list, Roosevelt, in an effort to prevent excessive bickering over what the Americans considered to be a dead issue, turned the tables and invited Chiang Kai-shek.[11] It was hoped that the Chinese leader's presence would pressure the British to do more in the Pacific while reducing the time to fight over European strategy. To further limit discussions, the conference was confined to a period between November 22 and 27.

Fed up with grueling transoceanic flights, Roosevelt commandeered America's newest and most powerful battleship, the USS *Iowa*, for the voyage. Stretching the length of three football fields and displacing more than 45,000 tons at standard weight, the *Iowa* itself was a testament to the combined vision of Leahy and Roosevelt, having been constructed thanks to their efforts to modernize the navy in 1938. The massive ship offered the president as much protection as any world leader could have desired. Cocooned by steel plates more than a foot in depth, she was armed with nine 16-inch guns, and her sides bristled with antiaircraft weapons. She could steam at over 33 knots, making her practically invulnerable to submarine attack. For even greater security, the ship was to be constantly screened by three different teams of three destroyers as the convoy zigzagged across the Atlantic to confuse any German U-boats they might encounter.

On Friday, November 12, the American delegation boarded the *Iowa* at its anchor off Cherry Point, Virginia. Being the superstitious old sailor that he was, Roosevelt ordered the vessel to stay in port until just after midnight, as Fridays were considered bad-luck days to begin sea voyages. A few minutes after twelve, as the calendar flipped to Saturday, the great battleship crept quietly out into the Chesapeake Bay. Once again, Leahy was at sea.

Having had little time to prepare for Cairo and Tehran, much work had to be done in transit. For the first time, all of America's strategic leaders—FDR, Leahy, Hopkins, Marshall, King, and Arnold—traveled together, allowing Leahy to preside over the Joint Chiefs every day during the crossing.* The president, in poor health, joined their sessions only twice, preferring to pass on his strategic input through his chief of staff. When he did attend, he inevitably sided with Leahy during disputes. When Marshall backed a British plan for the immediate appointment of an Allied Supreme Commander in the Mediterranean and Middle East, Leahy countered that any appointment must wait until a Supreme Commander had been selected for the invasion of France.[12] He believed that naming a separate Mediterranean commander prematurely would allow the British to expand operations into the Aegean and the Middle East. Roosevelt backed his friend, voicing skepticism about the Mediterranean and putting off any such move.

As Leahy worked diligently to prepare for the upcoming summits, the president spent much of his time resting on the *Iowa*'s decks, taking in the sea air. To keep him amused, the task force laid on some maneuvers. During one exercise, Roosevelt, with Leahy by his side, watched while the *Iowa*'s guns fired skyward at balloons standing in as enemy aircraft. At once, the guns swung low and began firing furiously into the water. A voice over the loudspeaker yelled, "This is not a drill!"[13]

Surging through the seawater, coming straight for the president's ship, was an American torpedo. The immense battleship rapidly pivoted, taking evasive action. For what seemed hours—but was just a few minutes—the *Iowa*'s guns blasted into the sea, trying to detonate the torpedo before it had a chance to change the course of history. Eventually, an explosion was heard a few thousand yards from where Roosevelt sat, watching intently. As he soon learned, an escorting destroyer, the USS *William D. Porter*, had accidentally discharged a live torpedo right at the American strategic leadership. Ernest King was livid and not a little embarrassed to have seen one of his prized vessels take aim at the president in front of the leadership of the US Army. He ordered the arrest of the destroyer's entire crew, the first and only time that has happened in American history. In the end, Roosevelt counseled forgiveness, and after a detailed inquiry no one was severely punished.

---

* Even though they all traveled together, Roosevelt refused to have his meals with Marshall and King. They ate in a general officers' mess on board, while Roosevelt ate with Leahy, Hopkins, and his personal staff.

The president's party docked in North Africa on November 20, still facing two flights and a stopover in Tunis before reaching Cairo. They clambered aboard a waiting C-54 transport, which featured only two sleeping berths for the long ride. Roosevelt took one, and the other was offered to Hopkins, who was noticeably ill. Leahy, robust as always, was forced to sleep in his seat.

When the team arrived in Cairo on November 22, Roosevelt was escorted to his quarters at the American ambassador's compound, taking with him only Hopkins and Leahy. The two men accompanied him that evening to an intimate dinner with Churchill. Leahy's presence represented a notable distinction between himself and the other American chiefs. Over the coming two weeks, Leahy would not only represent the president in military discussions, he would take part in many important political talks as well.

The formal gathering of British and American war chiefs was held at Cairo's Mena House Hotel, situated almost directly beneath the Great Pyramid at Giza. As expected, the British were determined to make the Mediterranean the conference's top priority; just as Roosevelt intended, Chiang Kai-shek forced the Pacific war as the dominating issue. Indeed, the first full day was devoted entirely to the war against Japan. Chiang said little, but it was clear that the Chinese wanted both a commitment on Burma and a radical increase in the amount of aid that they were receiving.[14] Undeterred, the British made yet another attempt to delay or cancel outright any assault into Burma. In particular, they opposed having to launch an attack on the Andaman Islands, which the Chinese and Americans argued was an unavoidable precursor to any attack into Burma. For Leahy, the issue went beyond a simple argument over strategy—the United States and the United Kingdom viewed the world differently, he opined. "The British obviously did not have the same deep interest in China that we had," he later wrote. "They seemed to overlook the fact that the defeat of Japan would cost many more ships, lives, not to mention dollars, if Chiang's ill-equipped, ill-fed armies were not kept in the field."[15] Roosevelt remained aggressive on the issue, but the British continued to balk.[16]

Only periodically were the British able to turn the discussions to the Mediterranean. On November 24, Leahy listened as Churchill gave a long exposition on the importance of the Mediterranean theater, a poor, disjointed lecture, in the admiral's view.[17] When Churchill finally finished, Roosevelt thanked him for his ideas and then bogged down the discussion on details. No decision on the Mediterranean could be made, Roosevelt argued, until Stalin and the Soviets had been consulted. All present knew full well that the Russians would accept nothing less than an invasion of France. The next morning was devoted to the Pacific, but when the British again demanded to revisit the Mediterranean question, it was decided to hold an off-the-record meeting of the chiefs. With note-takers absent, the British made an explicit argument against Operation Overlord. The Americans were unmoved. According to Leahy, they would accept no changes to Overlord, and the meeting accomplished nothing.[18]

Leahy's tactics with his British counterparts showed his growing frustration. As the conference was in British-controlled territory, Leahy deferred to Alanbrooke, who did a great deal of the chairing. Instead, the admiral listened and often made his interjections with pointed questions deliberately aimed to unsettle those with whom he disagreed. On November 24, Ambassador Averell Harriman briefed the chiefs on the positions that he expected the Soviets would take at Tehran. To silence any doubts about Soviet support of an invasion of France, Leahy asked Harriman the Soviet stance on Overlord; Harriman answered that Stalin was going to "demand" the operation.[19] Even this did not settle the matter, for on November 26 the British tried again. Gen. Henry Maitland "Jumbo" Wilson, the commander of British forces in the Middle East, was brought forth to tell the American chiefs how crucial it was to get Turkey into the war on the Allied side and to expand the war into Greece and the Balkans through a series of amphibious assaults.[20] After hearing these grandiose plans, Leahy asked if the Turks would be capable of launching, or even taking part in, amphibious operations. The amiable Briton had to admit that they could not, but he helpfully added that with a huge amount of support from the western Allies they might be able to launch some limited operations. Leahy's point had been made.

Matters of grand strategy were set aside for the evening of Thursday, November 25, when Marshall, King, and Arnold sat down with their British counterparts for a Thanksgiving meal. It was the second most important dinner party in Cairo that night. Roosevelt was also hosting Churchill for turkey and pumpkin pie on the banks of the Nile, with the pyramids as a backdrop. Leahy was the only war chief invited.

The meetings the next day accomplished little but to accentuate Anglo-American differences. Overall, achievements at Cairo were meager, so limited in fact that Roosevelt and Churchill agreed to reconvene for a few days after meeting Stalin. So, a little more than twenty-four hours after the Thanksgiving festivities ended, the delegates packed up their belongings and boarded a fleet of aircraft for the journey to Tehran. During the flight, the excitement palpably, if quietly, built. As Leahy looked out the window of the C-54 as it passed over the cradle of much of human history, appearing to him a blasted and desolate wasteland, he was looking forward to the next few days. He was eager to meet Stalin and take the measure of the man. This would happen on a more intimate level than he could have expected.

For the duration of the conference, Roosevelt was slated to be housed in the American legation in Tehran. Yet, not long after arriving, he was informed by the Soviets of rumors of assassins targeting the president. As a precaution, of course, Marshal Stalin offered to put Roosevelt up in the enormous fortified Soviet compound a few miles away. Both the president and his chief of staff had serious doubts that any such plot existed, but Roosevelt was so keen to impress Stalin with his friendliness that he eventually accepted the offer.[21] Roosevelt was allowed to bring only two people with him to live in the Soviet fortress and, naturally, took Leahy and Hopkins.

The next day a convoy of official vehicles covered by a large military force was assembled at the American legation. They rolled through the main gates onto the streets of Tehran, driving to the Soviet compound by the most obvious route. A few minutes later, a lone vehicle with Roosevelt, Leahy, and Hopkins left the American legation by another exit and drove at breakneck speed through the unpatrolled side streets of the congested city. Even though this lone vehicle took a longer and counterintuitive route, it reached its destination before the larger convoy. Once inside the Soviet world, Roosevelt, Leahy, and Hopkins were prisoners of Joseph Stalin. They were housed comfortably together in what had until recently been an unused building—Leahy claimed it still could have used an extra cleaning—and provided everything they needed for their stay. Every person they encountered, from butlers to secretaries, were in fact trained NKVD operators, each of whom carried at least one concealed weapon, their pistols often visibly bulging from their clothing. The three Americans were given formal passes, with only their names written in English, which they were to keep at hand at all times and to present if challenged. Never before had an American president been so completely under the thumb of a foreign power. That Roosevelt put himself so willingly into Stalin's clutches was a sign of just how invested he was in the meeting.

The president would not have to wait long to meet Stalin. A few minutes after settling into his new accommodations, Roosevelt was called to a private chat with the Soviet leader.[22] For the next hour, the two men analyzed the state of the war and bonded by denigrating the French. Roosevelt went to extraordinary lengths to charm Stalin, agreeing with almost everything he said. At one point he even claimed that British rule in India needed to be completely overhauled and replaced by something closer to a Soviet system.

Leahy did not see Stalin up close until the first plenary meeting was held that afternoon. The dictator was often a shock to those seeing him in person for the first time. Soviet press photographs were airbrushed and manipulated to make him appear taller and more handsome. In truth, he stood only five feet five inches, with terribly pockmarked skin and a withered arm that he tried to hide in well-tailored uniforms. His hands and face were stained from the tobacco he smoked constantly by cigarette or pipe. Yet if Stalin's appearance was underwhelming, he quickly displayed his mettle through keen and ruthless political skills. Roosevelt opened the meeting by outlining the war in the Pacific and in Europe. He ended by discussing operations in the Mediterranean, basically asking Stalin to comment on their usefulness from the Soviet perspective. Stalin, after summarizing the fighting on the eastern front (which was surprisingly pessimistic, considering the Soviet advances of the previous months), was more than happy to build on Roosevelt's opening. Politely but firmly, he disparaged the importance of the Italian campaign to defeat Hitler and argued for an overwhelming invasion of France to take the war to the heart of Germany. Churchill, unsettled, went to great lengths to talk up the war in the Mediterranean. Stalin again calmly but clearly insisted the focus had to be Overlord and "question[ed] the wisdom" of any other operation, be it in Italy, southern France, or even the Balkans, unless it clearly assisted an invasion of northern France.[23]

Leahy found himself more impressed with Stalin than perhaps he wanted to be—an impression he would keep for the rest of his life. In his diary he described the man as "soft-spoken and inflexible in his purpose."[24] Later he would remember Stalin speaking "quietly," "briefly," "bluntly," all words of praise from the to-the-point Leahy.[25] He preferred Stalin's direct, matter-of-fact style—the admiral never fully embraced Churchill's poetic eloquence—and believed that the dictator had a relentless focus on the Soviet Union's national interests.

At Tehran, Leahy used Stalin's directness, as well as the similarity in American and Russian strategic outlook, in his continuing efforts to keep the British from avoiding D-Day. On November 29 the Combined Chiefs met with a Soviet military delegation to discuss the establishment of a western front. Alanbrooke argued that Allied operations in the Mediterranean were tying down upward of fifty German divisions in Italy and the Balkans.[26] The Soviets seemed unconvinced. Leahy was mostly quiet, interjecting only to ask chiefs to explain things in more detail to their Soviet counterparts.

The next day the American and British chiefs met alone. Alanbrooke again argued for a greater effort in Italy and the Balkans. He wanted to send more landing craft to Eisenhower to help him in those endeavors, perfectly aware that this could delay Overlord. An impatient Leahy replied immediately, saying that the Soviets wanted Overlord in May, the Americans wanted Overlord in May, and that they must agree on a date. "If this matter were settled," he declared, "everything would be settled." For the next hour Alanbrooke, battling for all the British chiefs, tried to do everything possible to delay D-Day. He was not against the invasion of France, he claimed; he just did not want to see it launched until the Germans were weaker; in the meantime, it would be far better to use landing craft in the Mediterranean or even, remarkably, in the Pacific. Finally, Leahy's patience was at an end. Turning to the British field marshal, he pointedly asked "whether he believed that the conditions laid down for Overlord would ever arise unless the Germans had collapsed beforehand."[27]

Leahy was intent to quash any more British attempts to delay Overlord, and if he had to rely on Stalin's clear demands to do so, then so be it. His last word on the subject was that only a small delay, to June 1, would be acceptable to the Russians.[28] A few hours after Leahy sniped at Alanbrooke, the British delegation caved to the relentless American and Soviet pressure, agreeing, once again, to support a cross-Channel attack in spring 1944.[29]

While Leahy enjoyed Stalin's directness when it came to Overlord, it quickly became apparent that it was a double-edged sword, at least for Roosevelt. As part of Stalin's support for Overlord was an insistence that Roosevelt do something that the president had been mulling for months, but to which he had been unwilling to commit himself. It was the selection of a supreme commander to launch Overlord. It had been the worst-kept secret in Washington that Roosevelt was going to send George Marshall to Europe to lead the invasion of France.[30] Marshall desperately wanted the job and had already started preparing his belongings for the move.[31] In exchange, it was assumed that Eisenhower would be brought back to Washington to replace Marshall as the army's chief of staff. Roosevelt had discussed the decision with Leahy a number of times and continued to prevaricate. One of the problems with such a move was that the Joint Chiefs were functioning well by the end of 1943. Leahy, Marshall, King, and Arnold, for all the times they did disagree, had grown comfortable with one another and felt they worked well as a team. King was particularly vociferous about this.[32] Roosevelt, ever tiring, grew increasingly reluctant to rock the boat.

Churchill had no interest in speeding up the process of supreme-commander selection; indeed, Roosevelt's indecision served his purpose of continuing to make the Mediterranean the theater of most activity. Stalin, however, understood that serious planning for Overlord could not commence until the operation had a commander, and he was more than willing to confront Roosevelt. On November 29, Stalin asked point-blank who would command the invasion. Roosevelt squirmed, surprised at Stalin's directness, and replied meekly that he had not yet decided. This was not good enough for Stalin. He shot back that, in that case, "nothing will come out of these operations."[33] Roosevelt tried to calm the waters by claiming all the important positions below the supreme commander had been filled, but that only made things worse. Stalin refused to accept such reasoning, saying that "there must be one person in charge." Roosevelt would have to decide soon.

While Stalin discomfited Roosevelt on the question of supreme commander, Leahy was most edgy when it came to the discussions of the postwar world. He felt uneasy when Roosevelt's idealism clashed with Stalin's earthier views. At both the plenary sessions and their private meetings, Roosevelt spent a good deal of time outlining his ideas of the United Nations to Stalin and Churchill, in the hope that he could interest them in investing in the new institution.[34] Stalin did not seem to understand how much the UN meant to Roosevelt. He replied to one of the president's hopeful presentations with a classic Great Power rebuff: "If Russia, Great Britain and the United States wish to keep the world at peace they have the military and economic power to do so, and they do not need the assistance of a lot of small powerless nations to help them."[35] In this area, Leahy felt Churchill was much closer to Stalin than to Roosevelt.

Stalin was also far less interested in the future of China. Roosevelt tried to get Stalin to accept the idea of China being one of the "Four Policemen" that would keep the peace when the war was over. Stalin replied that he considered China too weak for such a role.[36] However, the most worrisome fault lines started emerging over the treatment of individual European countries. It was the first time the Big Three shared ideas on the shape of the world that they were about to win. This involved both the vanquished and the liberated. Everyone around the table agreed that Germany's war potential should be destroyed as completely as possible, but little specific was agreed on about how to divide the country.[37]

The future of Poland caused Stalin to show his teeth. During the final plenary meeting of the Big Three, Roosevelt, preparing to leave and in good spirits, said that he hoped that the Polish government-in-exile would be allowed to open negotiations with the Soviet government on how to handle the eventual liberation. Instantly, Stalin cut off the president. The Polish government-in-exile, made up of elements that had fled the Nazis in 1939, was to him a Capitalist anathema that should never return. He told the president that the Polish government-in-exile was working with the Nazis and was killing the true partisans fighting for Polish liberation. Leahy's fears were being realized. Ultimately, the Soviet Union would do whatever it wanted in eastern Europe, regardless of Franklin Roosevelt's charm.[38]

As the Tehran Conference came to a close, Leahy found himself conflicted. All of his doubts emerged during the final conference banquet, on November 30. For most, it was a triumphant celebration. It was also Churchill's birthday, which added an extra festive touch to the proceedings. Churchill sat between Roosevelt and Stalin as the Russians led the party through a lengthy series of toasts. Roosevelt praised Churchill, Churchill praised Stalin—even prophesying that he would go down in history as "Stalin the Great"—while Stalin praised the Russian people, who he said were willing to die by their millions to guarantee victory.

While everyone else was celebrating, something was gnawing away at William Leahy. Seated as the most senior American military officer, only two chairs to Roosevelt's right, he looked on as the party became more unwound and emotional. He felt that the Soviet hosts were pressing too much alcohol on their guests in a deliberate attempt to get them drunk—not an imperceptive guess, as Stalin liked to watch those around him get inebriated to test their true emotions. All this Tehran bonhomie, Leahy felt, was a mass delusion; the United States and the Soviet Union were never going to be the close friends after the war that everyone around the table said that they would be. The Soviet Union was still a totalitarian country, and Stalin was still a brutal dictator, and toasts and goodwill would not change that. "Stalin is quick in repartee and sinister in appearance," he recorded in his diary that night.[39]

The next day, as Leahy was preparing to depart Tehran, he fell into a conversation with Harry Hopkins and Charles Bohlen. Bohlen, who like Leahy felt that Poland was getting a raw deal, complained that Roosevelt's performance would do nothing to keep the Polish people from being subjugated by the Soviets after the war. Leahy listened sympathetically, then turned and with what one imagines a sad glint in his eye said to the much more pro-Soviet Hopkins, "Well, Harry, all I can say is, nice friends we have now."[40]

Leahy's mood cannot have been helped by the fact that American and British delegates had to fly back to Cairo for the most pointless summit of the war. Having forced British acquiescence to D-Day once again, the Americans were not going to change their mind. Yet for four days Churchill pleaded, wheedled, joked, and even threatened to get the Americans to reconsider and make the Mediterranean the main theater of operations. Churchill even engineered the appearance of a delegation from the Turkish government led by President Mustafa İsmet İnönü. Using promises of aid and threats of being left behind, Churchill tried to convince the Turks to join the Allies. In a manner Leahy found impressive, İnönü refused to give in.[41] Leahy did not want to see the Turks bullied into joining the war, both for their own sake and that of the Allies.[42]

He just wanted to get home. On December 3, Alanbrooke called for the adoption of an ambitious agenda that would have the chiefs basically going over the entire war and rehashing many of the questions they had been discussing for a year. Leahy agreed, but reminded him that the Americans were leaving after December 6 and there was nothing the British could do to stop their departure.[43] On December 4 Churchill suggested that the chiefs stay for a "few days" extra to go through strategy. Leahy, contradicting Churchill in front of the chiefs, adamantly refused.[44] The Americans were leaving on December 7, and Churchill would have to accept that.

Leahy's desire to end the second Cairo Conference quickly may have stemmed from his first unambiguous strategic setback of the war. Having been compelled to support D-Day, the British would give no ground on Burma. Churchill was immovable on the question of assaulting the Andaman Islands, and in this case the British were willing to hoist the Americans on their own petard. They said that to prepare for the assault on France they needed all the landing craft that they possessed in Europe and would allocate none to the war against Japan. Having put such pressure on the British to attack France, Roosevelt had no choice but to accept this fait accompli and agreed to the postponement of the Burma operation.[45] Leahy believed in his gut that this was the wrong choice and would be seen by the Chinese as a form of abandonment. He did admit that by this time the Burma campaign was more a political necessity than a military one, more important to make sure that China stayed in the war than to defeat Japan.[46] Yet there was nothing he could do to force the issue.

That left only one major decision to make, and it would be Roosevelt's verdict alone: the supreme commander for D-Day. By the end of the Cairo Conference, Roosevelt had to act. He opted for no change and kept Marshall as the head of the army, letting Ike have the glory of commanding D-Day. He told the disappointed Marshall, who betrayed no emotion, on December 5. Leahy had no idea which way Roosevelt was leaning, and the president did not let him know the ultimate decision until December 7, when the two men were sitting side by side flying away from Cairo.[47] Leahy was pleased, as it meant that the now smooth-running Joint Chiefs would remain unchanged. Roosevelt seemed motivated by the desire to avoid any unnecessary disruption. He had told Marshall that he felt "sick" at the prospect of losing him. This was as much a comment on Marshall's weakness as Marshall's strength. For the past year and a half, ever since Leahy returned from France and assumed the mantle of chief of staff, Roosevelt had regularly overruled Marshall on questions of grand strategy. Regardless of the number of times he'd been slighted, Marshall would move forward and discharge his duty diligently.

After two weeks of high-stakes diplomacy, Roosevelt was exhausted. Another series of grueling flights took him across the Mediterranean, complete with a stopover to visit American forces on Sicily. He, Leahy, and Hopkins did not reach the *Iowa* until the evening of December 9. The president dined with his two closest advisers, then went right to bed. For the next week, as the *Iowa* zigzagged its way back across the Atlantic, Roosevelt either stayed in bed or lounged on the deck. No meetings were held, and no decisions reached.

It was an indication of what was in store for Leahy in 1944.

CHAPTER 20

Acting President

Bill, I'm going to promote you to a higher rank."[1] In early January 1944, an increasingly gaunt and weak Franklin Roosevelt turned to William Leahy in the White House and told his friend that he wanted to make him the only serving five-star military officer in America.[2] He said nothing about promoting Marshall, King, or Arnold, but Leahy was adamant that the other Joint Chiefs be advanced as well, and the president relented. Leahy quickly moved to put Roosevelt's plan into operation, meeting with his old friend Carl Vinson, still chairman of the House Naval Affairs Committee, to start the process.[3] The promotion plan entered the congressional pipeline, and it took most of the year to work itself out.

Roosevelt's decision to promote Leahy happened when the admiral was at the height of his power. He was firmly entrenched in the White House as Roosevelt's most important strategic adviser and more than comfortable as chairman of the Joint Chiefs. He had grafted his strategic vision of how the war would be won in both Europe and the Pacific on the American war effort. France would be invaded in the spring, the Italian campaign returned to its secondary status, and the war in the Pacific, for all the fine words about Germany-first, would receive a huge amount of American effort. From Leahy's point of view, the war was progressing well; he hoped Germany might be beaten by the end of 1944 and thought the Japanese would be forced to capitulate by the end of 1945.[4] Leahy's biggest worry was not the war—it was Roosevelt's health. The president had returned from Cairo and Tehran in a state of utter exhaustion. Though the two men continued with their daily briefings when the president was well enough to be in the White House, the start times were pushed later and later into the morning as Roosevelt slept more.

In his memoir, Leahy trod a fine line when discussing the decline in Roosevelt's condition. "The terrific burden of being in effect Commander-in-Chief of the greatest war yet recorded in global history began to tell on Franklin Roosevelt in 1944," he wrote. "He required more rest and it took him longer to shake off the effects of a simple cold or of the bronchitis to which he was vulnerable."[5] In truth, Roosevelt was dying. His heart was deteriorating and his arteries were narrowing; his blood pressure could soar to critical levels, putting him at constant risk of heart failure or stroke. His appearance could shock those who had not seen him for a while. He steadily lost weight, his cheeks hollowing and his skin taking on a grayish hue. His hands shook, and he often slumped back in his wheelchair, seemingly exhausted or disinterested. He was barely able to work. He took two weeks completely off in January, and more than a week each in February and March, spending much of the time in Hyde Park. The American people, however, were deceived. The president's personal physician, Adm. Ross McIntire, later destroyed some of Roosevelt's medical files to keep the truth from emerging.[6] The doctor stated that Roosevelt, who was only sixty-two years old, was in fine condition for a man of his age.

Leahy knew this was not true, though he never said it out loud. Both at the time and later, he was torn between writing about what he was seeing in his friend and his desire to protect first the man and then the legacy of Franklin Roosevelt. Personally, he worried constantly about Roosevelt's health. One of the reasons Leahy was so important at the time was that he was covering for the president, who skipped whole workdays or -weeks. When these absences were mentioned, Leahy usually described the president's health issues through their outward explanations such as bronchitis or influenza, never admitting the deeper underlying health concerns, such as hypertension or heart failure.

To complicate matters, Harry Hopkins's health was even worse.[7]

On New Year's Day Hopkins collapsed, and three days later he checked himself into the hospital for emergency medical care. His weight had dropped to 126 pounds, and the malnutrition brought on by his surgically reduced stomach had left him perilously weak. It began a months-long process of Hopkins shuttling in and out of treatment, often at the Mayo Clinic, undergoing operations and being kept away from Roosevelt. This physical separation accentuated the already growing emotional distance between him and the president.

These twin developments meant that Leahy controlled much of American strategic and foreign policy between January 1944 and Roosevelt's death. The president, understanding how much he had grown to rely on the admiral, started involving Leahy even more in both his political and private life.[8] At the same time, Leahy became more forward with his own policy preferences. It was a noticeable shift, as if he was aware that his influence was growing.

When it came to the day-to-day operations, Leahy started acting even more ruthlessly as a gatekeeper protecting the president. A range of people, from the other Joint Chiefs to industrialists to representatives of Allied nations and even major American political figures, had to go through Leahy to get issues brought to the president's attention. Moreover, Leahy often became the voice of the president. Many, maybe even most, of the telegrams that were sent out under Roosevelt's name to Churchill and Stalin were drafted by Leahy in 1944, one of the reasons that Roosevelt's messages at this time were particularly dull.

Leahy also became the court of appeals who could decide even the most sensitive policy questions in Roosevelt's stead. On January 22, when Roosevelt was in Hyde Park, Assistant Secretary of War John McCloy came to Leahy to get approval for General Eisenhower to turn over the civil administration of areas of liberated France to the Gaullist CFLN after D-Day.[9] Though it must have pained Leahy to say so, he replied that if it was all right with the State Department, it was all right with him. On February 4, Leahy drafted and sent to Churchill a formal telegram urging the British to turn over some captured Italian naval assets to the Soviets.[10] Leahy was determined to see the British live up to their end of the agreements. On February 23, the day after Roosevelt had left on another rest trip to Hyde Park, Leahy worked with the new undersecretary of state, Edward Stettinius Jr., Sumner Welles's replacement, to clarify US policy toward oil-producing regions of the Middle East. In March, much of Leahy's time was spent on different economic issues. For instance, the Electric Boat Company of Groton, Connecticut, the largest American submarine manufacturer, went to Leahy to try to protect the draft deferments of three hundred of its specialists.[11] In March, just after Roosevelt had returned from another Hyde Park stay, Leahy lunched with Secretary of the Treasury Henry Morgenthau to discuss when the United States should offer a new wartime loan to its allies—the beginning of regular lunch meetings between the two.[12] Even William Bullitt took advantage of Leahy's immense influence to try to regain entry to Roosevelt's court. In March, he invited Leahy to dinner, during which he begged the admiral to intercede on his behalf with the president.[13] Leahy's influence stretched only so far; there was to be no rehabilitation with Bullitt.

No matter how much work Leahy handled in order to allow the president to recuperate, however, Roosevelt's health did not improve. Leahy admitted in late March that even after another week of total rest, the president's "bronchitis" remained persistent. It was therefore decided that Roosevelt needed a long break, somewhere warm and completely isolated from the stresses of the Oval Office. On April 8, the president's train once again pulled out of Washington late at night and headed south.

Roosevelt was aiming for Hobcaw Barony, a remote estate in South Carolina owned by Bernard Baruch. There is something touching, if melancholy, about Leahy and Roosevelt during this holiday. For the next month, Leahy had to be both the president's close friend and his sole link to serious war work.[14] Hobcaw, made up of approximately 20,000 acres of pine forests, streams, and swamps, was far removed from Washington and a perfect place for Roosevelt's "recuperative vacation."[15] Except for the incessant bugs, which seemed to particularly irritate the admiral, it was an oasis of quiet and privacy.[16] Baruch's daughter Belle, who resided on a neighboring estate, was a tall lesbian who lived openly with a number of lovers—or, as Leahy quaintly termed them, her "women friends."[17] The admiral found Belle to be educated and entertaining, and he marveled in his diary that she had been the only one to shoot an alligator during an afternoon's hunt.[18] A bond of friendship formed, and they stayed in touch beyond the president's visit. Belle would even visit the admiral when she passed through Washington.[19]

Leahy did everything possible to protect Roosevelt while at Hobcaw. To those in the know, he was practically running the war. William Rigdon, who tracked all the in- and outgoing information from the White House Map Room, noted how Leahy was in control.

> My Hobcaw log, and all other logs, show that Admiral Leahy was always close to the President. He was not only the President's chief planning officer, head of the Joint Chiefs of Staff, and the highest ranking American officer on military duty—he held "five-star" commission number one—but he was also the President's confidant and adviser on matters other than the military. FDR trusted him completely.[20]

The routine at Hobcaw showed how weak Roosevelt had become and how much he had grown to rely on Leahy. After an early breakfast, Leahy would review all the top secret dispatches sent to the president. He would answer some on his own, disregard others, and decide which few were so important that they needed to be discussed personally with Roosevelt. The president rose late—his plan during the trip was to sleep twelve hours a day—and was unable to work until noon, at which point they went through the messages Leahy had selected. For about an hour they would make decisions and plan responses before Roosevelt's workday was done and lunch was served.[21]

The early afternoon saw the president resting for a few more hours, until approximately four o'clock, when his party usually went for an excursion. Car rides and alligator hunts were options, but mostly they chose fishing trips along the snakelike system of creeks and inlets that carved up the marshland or led out into the Atlantic Ocean. The fishing was terrible, mostly slow trolling as the president let his line dangle limply in the water. Leahy usually sat next to Roosevelt, at the president's insistence.[22] Once back, they would enjoy an early dinner, sometimes with jokes at the expense of Pa Watson, followed by a movie or a game of cards. Roosevelt typically retired to bed not long after dinner was over.

Slowly, Roosevelt's health began to improve, albeit marginally, but more than a week after they arrived, Leahy wrote to his aide, Comm. J. V. Smith, that he still had no idea when the party would return to Washington.[23] On April 28, Secretary of the Navy Frank Knox died suddenly of a heart attack. The president, deciding that he wasn't strong enough to attend the funeral, sent Pa Watson in his place. He kept Leahy beside him.

Official visitors were kept to an absolute minimum, as Roosevelt wanted only trusted friends around him. Perhaps Roosevelt's favorite visitor was the woman who had once nearly ended his marriage. Lucy Mercer had been serving as the social secretary to Eleanor Roosevelt when she embarked on an affair with her boss's husband sometime in 1916. When Eleanor discovered the relationship in 1918, Franklin almost left his wife, but he was forcefully persuaded by his mother to stay married and avoid scandal. But if Franklin Roosevelt was capable of truly loving a woman, that woman was Lucy Mercer. He continued to have contact with her for decades, and during World War II began to spend time with her when he and Eleanor were apart.[24]

When it came to Lucy Mercer, Leahy was at his most discreet. During the president's stay in Hobcaw, Mercer lodged in a nearby house and visited Roosevelt frequently.[25] Elliott Roosevelt, the president's son, claimed she came by almost daily.[26] Eleanor, on the other hand, was allowed to visit only once.[27] As Leahy was in near constant presence with the president, he would have regularly dined and chatted with Mercer, yet never mentioned it in his diary or to interviewers.

Another favored visitor to Hobcaw was Margaret Suckley, an old confidante and distant cousin of Roosevelt's. She arrived in May and found him still "thin & drawn & not a bit well."[28] "Everyone conspires to keep the atmosphere light," she wrote.[29] Suckley found that Roosevelt, having sensed that his doctors were not being honest with him, was now better informed about the seriousness of his medical condition.[30]As a man possessing but a faint echo of religious belief, a man who loved life and power but was also a realist, Roosevelt must have been aware at times that his health was failing. At others, he undoubtedly tried to forget this reality and press on with the presidency. This acceptance of these contradictory impulses helps explain his behavior during the last year of his life, at moments living in denial and at others more realistic about how much longer he had left.

Leahy, who had long since grown comfortable with Suckley, confided in her that, to protect the president's health, he had been rigorously controlling the information shown to FDR and described his dilemma, inadvertently admitting to the immense power he was wielding. Leahy confessed that every morning he had to sort through a pile of the president's confidential correspondence, "analyze it, pass judgement, and make a recommendation to the Pres. Half the time it is almost a question of 'tossing a coin' to decide one way or the other."[31]

On May 6 the president finally returned to the White House, his health only marginally better than when he had left nearly a month prior. Leahy wrote optimistically to an aide that "the Boss is in good shape at the end of his vacation."[32] Admiral McIntire reported to Leahy that the president had returned to his "normal condition" of health.[33] Yet McIntire knew just how weak Roosevelt was; "normal" was hardly a ringing endorsement.

Back in Washington, Leahy returned to his duties with gusto. On his first two days back, he chaired a meeting of the Joint Chiefs, met with Constantine Brown for the latest Washington gossip, and conferred or dined with a wide variety of influential men in the administration, including Edward Stettinius, Averell Harriman, James Forrestal, Undersecretary of War Robert Patterson, and Ernest King. For good measure, he also hosted the naval representatives of the Dutch and Free French governments.[34]

Roosevelt's return to Washington marked the start of one of the most intensely political periods in Leahy's life. With the presidential election fast approaching, and the war effort ongoing, the spring and summer of 1944 offered constant opportunities to dabble in the political and public side of Roosevelt's existence. A few days after returning from Hobcaw, for instance, Roosevelt turned once again to Leahy. "Bill, I just hate to run again for election," he confided. "Perhaps the war will by that time have progressed to a point that will make it unnecessary for me to be a candidate."[35] Yet when Roosevelt announced a few weeks later that he would stand, Leahy was not surprised.

On the day after Roosevelt's announcement, Harry Hopkins, who had just returned to work from another long break in the Mayo Clinic, stopped by Leahy's office so that the two men could discuss politics. The most important issue was the vice presidency. The serving vice president, Henry Wallace, was on the far left of the Democratic Party and was no favorite of Leahy's. Roosevelt eventually decided to replace Wallace with someone with greater ability to appeal to centrists. Hopkins felt that he could use Leahy to influence the president and pushed Jimmy Byrnes's candidacy.[36] Leahy also thought Byrnes was the best person to be vice president. For the past two years Leahy had worked closely with him on issues of US war production and manpower policy. Byrnes, a powerful South Carolina senator, had been appointed by Roosevelt to the Supreme Court in 1941. Not long after the war started, Roosevelt asked Byrnes to leave the court and serve as the head of the Office of War Mobilization, an organization set up to cope with the shortfalls in US war production experienced early in the conflict. This Byrnes did with some panache and, like Leahy and Hopkins, received one of the coveted three prime offices in the new East Wing of the White House. During the war, Byrnes impressed Leahy with his drive to the degree that Leahy began subtly lobbying Roosevelt to add the South Carolinian to the Democratic ticket in 1944.[37] Roosevelt, however, had started souring on Byrnes the more he worked closely with him. The president, recognizing a streak of extreme self-importance in Byrnes, felt the man was too full of himself. Roosevelt in the end opted for Sen. Harry Truman to complete the Democratic ticket. Later, Leahy would give thanks for Roosevelt's decision.

The fact that Harry Hopkins now needed Leahy's support on issues like Roosevelt's VP had, perhaps strangely, led to the relationship between the two arriving at its most trusting point. When Hopkins was well enough to work, he and Leahy would draft important telegrams together, particularly ones of a sensitive political nature.[38] At other times they worked together to control the Joint Chiefs. Once, when Hopkins felt Ernest King, the committed Anglophobe, had given a deliberately antagonistic order to the American naval commander in the Mediterranean to forbid the use of American equipment in a British-led operation, he hurried to Leahy to get the order countermanded. After the two chatted, Leahy agreed with Hopkins and advised the chief of naval operations that it would be sensible if he backed down—which King dutifully did.[39] Even vital questions such as aid to the Soviet Union, which were extremely important to Hopkins and which he had tried to dominate earlier in the war, now often were referred to Leahy in the hope that the admiral would get the preferred decision from the president.[40]

With so much power in his hands, the praise Leahy received went up a notch. He received unsolicited and even cringe-worthy messages from some of the most important people in the United States who wanted to take advantage of the admiral's influence with Roosevelt. Maybe the most remarkable example of this was a letter from Bernard Baruch sent not long after Roosevelt and Leahy had left Hobcaw. The wealthy financier felt he needed to let Leahy know how wonderful he was—"You are just tops. You are a good sailor, a fine statesman, and a splendid friend."[41] Of course, Baruch's acclaim was in the hope that Leahy would find a position for him in Roosevelt's government.

Leahy undoubtedly enjoyed such lavish praise, so much so that he kept a copy of the letter in his diary. Regardless, he was one of the least self-interested people among the powerful names of American history. He never used his post for financial gain and had little in the way of possessions or property. He was normally scrupulous about not using his influence to benefit himself or his family. In early 1944, one of his brothers asked if Leahy could prevent the transfer of his son who was in the navy and based in Chicago, but who had recently been ordered to Newport—and presumably from there into action.[42] Leahy refused. Only one example can be found of Leahy asking for a favor for a family member. In late 1944, he wrote to David Sarnoff, the boss of RCA and NBC and one of the most influential media figures in America.[43] He asked

Sarnoff as a "personal request" to employ his niece, Caroline Leahy, in NBC's new television division. Sarnoff, who knew exactly with whom he was dealing, immediately sent back a handwritten note saying that he would be delighted to help Caroline in any way that he could.[44]

Another way that Leahy's increased authority can be seen after Hobcaw is in his direct dealing with cabinet members. One of the first things Leahy advised Roosevelt to do when they returned from South Carolina was to appoint James Forrestal the new secretary of the navy.[45] Leahy had excellent relations with Forrestal and believed that they could work closely together. Roosevelt quickly made the appointment. In addition, Leahy's lunches with Morgenthau became even more regular, as he used the treasury secretary to keep tabs on issues that mattered to him.[46] One of these was the future of the Lend-Lease Agreement, which Roosevelt first announced in 1940 as a way of getting aid to Britain after the fall of France, and had been used to provide both Britain and the Soviet Union with massive amounts of economic and military support. Leahy, with his isolationist proclivities, wanted to make sure that lend-lease would end when the war was over. On learning that Roosevelt was going to appoint Morgenthau the chairman of a committee to oversee the future of lend-lease, Leahy scheduled a lunch with the treasury secretary to get a full update on his plans.[47]

As he was building his connection with Morgenthau, Leahy's already strong links with the State Department became even more intimate. Part of that was institutional and part personal. In late 1943, after Sumner Welles's forced resignation, the State Department started addressing formal inquiries for the Joint Chiefs of Staff directly to Leahy, and the responses they received were scrutinized and signed by the admiral as well.[48] In 1944, H. Freeman Matthews, Leahy's old Vichy subordinate, became the deputy director for the Office of European Affairs, working with the admiral to improve the flow of crucial documents between the military and the diplomats.[49] Matthews would call Leahy if he needed special information, or to get the Joint Chiefs' approval for different State Department directives.[50] On the other hand, Cordell Hull's declining health meant that he became an even more peripheral figure to Leahy's life. In the summer of 1944, Hull was such an outsider that he was often left to communicate with Roosevelt through Leahy, and even then he could not be sure to get an answer.[51] By November, he was in such poor condition that he had to resign.

Leahy's interactions with the State Department revealed another one of his personal positions that might come as a surprise—his desire to make sure that civilian agencies were not overshadowed by the military. Clearly the amount of power he had accumulated made him uneasy. Far from trying to keep the State Department at bay and concentrate more authority in his hands, he became worried that American diplomats were being kept in the dark about White House plans. It was why he became the driving force behind the appointment of a special State Department liaison with whom he would meet daily. The diplomat chosen for the job was Charles "Chip" Bohlen, whom Leahy had first encountered in 1943 and had grown to trust.

Before his appointment, Bohlen had fallen for the widespread caricature of Leahy as a crusty hard-liner.[52] He expected to find Leahy, who was supposedly "not known for his kindness towards diplomats," to be hostile.[53] He was surprised to discover that the admiral was "forthcoming and receptive," and they ended up having "many interesting discussions about the future of the world, particularly Europe and France." Eventually they developed a pattern of humorous banter that had them almost playing caricatures of themselves. Leahy in his "snapping-turtle manner" would make some crack about de Gaulle, while Bohlen would reply by pointing out France's important geopolitical position, which he admitted Leahy "knew better than I did." Leahy would then "grudgingly admit" that, de Gaulle notwithstanding, the United States had to maintain good relations with France.[54]

To George Elsey, Leahy's relations with Bohlen and the State Department revealed a great deal about the admiral's true nature. Instead of being "an anti–State Department man, as some people assumed," Leahy was "the one man around the White House who kept constantly saying, 'But the State Department ought to be consulted.'" It was Leahy who insisted that the State Department be brought into a closer relationship with the White House. Elsey was so impressed by Leahy's determination to respect civilian power that he became increasingly frustrated by those who ignorantly pigeonholed the admiral. When asked whether Leahy tried to increase the power of the military, he answered, "Not at all." Admiral Leahy was "the one strong man in the White House during the war who was trying to keep political and foreign policy matters in some sort of perspective with President Roosevelt."[55]

Leahy was so central to Roosevelt's professional life that the president was reluctant to let the admiral leave his side. One of the few times Leahy and Roosevelt were separated in the spring and summer of 1944 was part of a big ruse. The great event looming after the president returned from Hobcaw was the long-awaited invasion of France. From late 1943 through the spring of 1944, American, British, and Canadian forces had been congregating in southern England, feverishly training for the upcoming assault. The Allies, as Leahy had planned, now had complete air and sea control in the English Channel and could proceed confident in their ability to get these troops to France without much German interference. Everything was now set to kick off in early June, as soon as General Eisenhower gave the order.

Leahy, able to only wait and watch, was used to trying to lull the Germans into thinking the invasion was not imminent. On June 4, he made a rare and very public trip to Iowa to deliver the commencement address at Cornell College. When, on June 6, American troops splashed ashore in Normandy, the chairman of the Joint Chiefs of Staff was touring Hampton, Iowa, the town of his birth, before members of the press.

That evening, Leahy quietly boarded an overnight train to Washington. Roosevelt, who had also prominently left town before D-Day, hurried back to the White House, and the two were soon reunited. Together they followed events intently as Allied forces dueled with the Germans across Normandy's patchwork terrain. The next few weeks would be trying. While the Germans had no prospect of throwing their attackers into the sea, their resistance was much stiffer than the Allies had expected. Only in late July would the German lines in Normandy crack open, allowing the Anglo-American armies to pour on through and liberate almost all of France.

Almost immediately after the invasion was launched, Marshall,

King, and Arnold were sent to the United Kingdom to witness operations in person. Yet Roosevelt wanted Leahy to remain by his side in Washington.[56] Their daily meetings continued throughout the month.[57] Perhaps the most remarkable thing about this period was not that Leahy was playing such an important part in Roosevelt's life, or that he was wielding so much power, but that he was doing it relatively anonymously. Press coverage of his role, with a few notable exceptions such as the D-Day trip to Iowa, were rare. He remained a shadowy figure in the national picture, always there, supporting the president, but rarely commented upon. He continued to eschew the press, refusing interviews.[58] Leahy's success at keeping such a low profile was both cagey and occasionally humorous. Even some of Roosevelt's closest relations had no idea who he was. During one of Leahy's many visits to Hyde Park in the summer of 1944, Mrs. Kermit Roosevelt, a daughter-in-law of Theodore Roosevelt who was also staying with the president, came downstairs one morning for breakfast and fell into conversation with "an elderly gentleman in civilian clothes who looked vaguely familiar." Thinking the man was some poseur, she asked in patronizing tones, "Do you live here?" "No, Mrs. Roosevelt," William Leahy replied, "I am the chief of staff to the President."[59]

He might as well have said: *No, Mrs. Roosevelt, I am the acting president of the United States.*

CHAPTER 21

Leahy's War

I n September 1944, as Douglas MacArthur was preparing to launch an invasion of the Philippine island of Leyte, Leahy sat down to compose a memo about the next steps to take once the island had been seized.* Two options were being debated by the Joint Chiefs: allowing MacArthur to expand his attacks in the Philippines—MacArthur's and Marshall's preference—or leaving the Philippines behind to strike the Japanese-held island of Formosa, King's preference.

Leahy's thinking on the matter was decidedly different from everyone else's. He was convinced that as soon as the Philippines were secure, Japan was doomed. Without those vital naval and air bases, Japan would lose all ability to transport supplies and raw materials around its far-flung empire. Most consequentially, their ships and aircraft would be starved of oil. With its war machine left sputtering, even Japan's fanatical leadership would have to eventually admit defeat. For the United States to launch another major amphibious assault after securing the Philippines, particularly assaults on large islands, seemed to Leahy to be strategically unnecessary, politically dangerous, and ethically dubious. Forcing an engagement with the one large military force the Japanese had left, their army, might even be counterproductive. Assaults on Formosa or even Japan itself would cost too much blood and

---

* This memorandum is included in its entirety in Appendix A.

treasure while making not the slightest difference in the outcome of the war.

With the desire to limit fighting as much as possible, Leahy eventually opted to support MacArthur's attack into Luzon after Leyte—indeed, he would prove instrumental in getting the plan approved—but only to complete the Allied reclaiming of the Philippines and try to limit other operations. Once it was taken, Leahy believed the United States would have no need to launch any more amphibious assaults closer to Japan. Instead, he pointed to "our overwhelming air and sea supremacy" as the key to victory. "My conclusion," Leahy wrote, "is that America's least expensive course of action is to continue and intensify the air and sea blockade, with an intensified air bombardment of Japan's war industry, and at the same time reoccupy the Philippines."[1] By halting Japanese mobility on the seas and destroying her transportation and factories ashore, American lives would be saved and the war would be won.

"It seems necessary that the Joint Chiefs of Staff should obtain a decision on the highest political level as to whether we should take a shorter course toward the already certain defeat of Japan at greater cost in life and material, or a longer course at much less cost," he concluded.[2] On September 5, he read the memo aloud to the Joint Chiefs, then had it placed, verbatim, into the minutes.[3] It was the work of a strategist at the height of his powers, its clarity and force a testament to Leahy's vision.

Indeed, over the previous two years Leahy had done more than any other American to determine the strategic choices of the United States. So effectively had he wielded power in the White House, among the Joint Chiefs, and during the grand strategic conferences, that America had fought Leahy's war more than anyone else's, including George Marshall's. In fact, examining the issues that the two men fought over during Leahy's first year in office, it's obvious who was more powerful. Leahy won every major argument.

Date/Issue	Leahy Position	Marshall Position	Roosevelt Choice
July 1942: Should the US invade North Africa?	Yes, had even devised a similar plan in 1941.	Consistently fought against the idea.	Leahy Position
October–December 1942: What military equipment should receive priority for US construction?	Air- and sea power should dominate. Wants large aircraft program as long as aircraft-carrier construction is protected.	Resisted cuts to land-army construction, fights against aircraft getting absolute priority.	Leahy Position
September 1942–early 1943: What is the right size of the US Armed Forces, and how will this affect labor policy?	Must keep war production high and happy to limit armed forces size. Don't bring in coercive labor laws.	Wants large army as highest priority, willing to countenance large extension to working week.	Leahy Position
November 1942–January 1943: Should the US government press for a cross-Channel invasion in Europe in 1943?	No, too risky and could lead to very high casualties. Wait until 1944, when air and sea control is guaranteed.	Yes, willing to undertake risky invasion and suffer high casualties.	Leahy Position
1942–1943: Should the US fight a Germany-first war or a balanced war between Europe and Asia/Pacific?	Balanced war. Cannot let the Japanese get entrenched in the Pacific; need to show support for China.	Consistently Germany-first. The war against Japan can wait until Germans defeated.	Leahy Position

Having determined what the US Armed Forces would be, and where they would fight, Leahy's next challenge was to subvert the policy of Germany-first so that the United States sent the forces he thought necessary to fight the Pacific war. In this he walked in lockstep with Ernest King. At Trident and Quebec and in Washington he argued strenuously for making the war against Japan a major priority, eventually neutering Germany-first to such a degree that it became meaningless. His efforts provided backing for the rather schizophrenic war that the United States fought in 1943 and early 1944. In 1942, as mentioned earlier, there was no considered plan for the allocation of US forces, so that, when made available, men and equipment were sent much of the time on an ad hoc basis to any area of the world that was considered most important. If anything, it meant that the United States fought a Japan-first war for much of the time, especially as the struggle over Guadalcanal intensified.

In 1943 and early 1944, however, the United States fought two very different wars.[4] The US Army and Army Air Force sent approximately two-thirds, and sometimes more, of their equipment and manpower to fight the Germans. In doing this they were following the wishes of Franklin Roosevelt as expressed in December 1942, and the stated policy of the US government. The navy, by contrast, sent approximately 90 percent of its forces to the Pacific to fight Japan, including the vast majority of its major warships, almost all of its air force, and almost every member of the Marine Corps. Overall, this divided war meant that at no time did America fight a Germany-first war. Instead, from 1943 until Germany's surrender in 1945, the United States divided its striking power approximately equally between Europe and the Pacific.

The only way to understand the disconnect between Roosevelt's stated policy and the reality of the two wars is that Leahy allowed for it to happen, whether by misleading the president, which is doubtful, or by Roosevelt's tacit consent. As the Joint Chiefs were the military body responsible for the allocation of US equipment as part of the global war, they were the officials who sanctioned the war being fought in this way. Marshall and Arnold were allowed to deploy the army and air force to Europe, and King was given a free hand to send the fleet to the Pacific. They could all operate with Leahy as their chairman, knowing that Roosevelt had no objection to what they were doing.

This evenly split American war deployment made a massive difference to the war against Japan. Far from being an insignificant industrial power, as many Eurocentric historians of the war imply, Japan built an impressive amount of advanced air and sea equipment between 1942 and 1944. In relative terms, Japan should be seen as the economic equivalent of the Soviet Union, only with the ability to manufacture technologically more advanced equipment.[5] Had America allowed the

Japanese time to consolidate their enormous gains of early 1942 and firmly establish a defensive perimeter around the western Pacific, the fight across the ocean would have been far bloodier than it turned out to be—even with US victory all but assured.

Because so much force was sent to fight the Japanese, the Joint Chiefs could, and did, start disagreeing about the best way forward in the Pacific. The parameters of this debate were to a large extent determined by the choices that Leahy had earlier shaped. His maneuverings, including protecting aircraft-carrier construction, prioritizing air-sea production instead of land munitions, and making sure that the United States sent far more war matériel to the Pacific than it admitted publicly, meant that starting in mid-1943 American commanders could conceive of the kind of far-ranging air-sea battles that heralded a new era in warfare. The US Navy was able to deploy large carrier battle groups—integrated naval task forces based upon large fleet carriers protected and constantly resupplied by phalanxes of support vessels—which allowed many hundreds of aircraft to be continually launched against Japanese targets far removed from any fixed American bases. Beginning with the assaults on the Gilbert and Marshall Islands, most famously Tarawa (November 1943) and Kwajalein (January 1944), the United States was able to bring the war more directly to the Japanese and start crippling Japan as a functioning power.

Until 1944 much of Leahy's time was spent acting as a referee between the army and the navy about the command in the Pacific. In March 1942, the Joint Chiefs had divided the Pacific somewhat uneasily between the two famous officers who would dominate the war against Japan. Gen. Douglas MacArthur was given command in the Southwest Pacific Area (SWPA), leading from Australia up through New Guinea to the Philippines. Adm. Chester Nimitz was made the commander in chief of the Pacific Operating Area (CinCPOA), and specifically assigned the Central Pacific as his personal responsibility. A constant tension arose between MacArthur and Nimitz over the amount of naval power that was to be given to the former to help in his movements up through the Southwest Pacific. Admiral King, who kept quite a tight leash on navy allocations, often starved MacArthur of naval airpower and usually made him get by with a mixed force of smaller naval vessels such as cruisers and destroyers.

In March and April 1943 the Joint Chiefs had to devise a workable command arrangement for the Pacific. The catalyst was a growing dispute over command between MacArthur and one of the most colorful, if not the most diplomatic, naval officers of the war, Adm. William "Bull" Halsey. In a sign that Leahy was far from being a navy partisan, he supported MacArthur being allowed to exercise control over all the naval forces in his area.[6] In exchange, Leahy made sure that Nimitz had a free hand in the Central Pacific to head out and destroy the Japanese Navy.[7] In early 1944 there was another bitter fight, which Leahy thought particularly silly, over whether MacArthur or Nimitz would control the recently captured naval base at Manus Island, north of Papua, New Guinea.[8] In the end a reasonable compromise was reached, with MacArthur being given command of the base on the condition that all navy vessels, including those not under his command, could use the facility when needed.

When it came to the specifics of Pacific strategy in early 1944, the debate was between an American Army–supported offensive directed toward the Philippines, which would then open an access of advance along the Chinese coast, or a navy-supported drive through the Central Pacific aimed at the great Japanese naval base at Truk Atoll or the Mariana Islands, even closer to Japan. For the Joint Chiefs this debate came to a head during a special meeting on March 11.[9] It marked one of the first times that Leahy started throwing his weight around on the specifics of the Pacific war. Nimitz spoke for the Central Pacific command, while Gen. Richard Sutherland represented MacArthur. Sutherland argued against any Mariana operation, stating that putting too much emphasis on the Central Pacific would tie down American resources for all of 1944.[10] Nimitz spoke mostly about the need to neutralize Truk. Leahy was relatively quiet in this meeting, but it was clear from one of his few interventions what he believed the United States should do. After hearing a discussion about how the Japanese could reinforce Truk from the Marianas, he retorted that the Marianas were the key, not Truk. The

Marianas had to be taken as they were on "a direct line with Japan" and could best be supplied by American air- and sea power.[11]

Leahy's prioritizing of the Marianas makes perfect sense considering his growing confidence in the air-sea war. He knew the Marianas well, having first visited them in 1899. These islands, most famously Saipan, Tinian, and Guam, provided the Japanese with crucial bases from which to protect the movement of raw materials from the Dutch East Indies to Japan. If the United States could seize them, they could go a long way to breaking the Japanese economy by starving it of resources. When the Joint Chiefs meeting broke up, Leahy headed to the White House with King and Nimitz for a discussion with Roosevelt on Pacific strategy.[12] The four men analyzed the subject for hours.[13] The following day, the Joint Chiefs of Staff issued an updated directive for operations in the Pacific in 1944.[14] It called for exactly what Leahy wanted: the seizure of the Marianas as soon as possible.

When the subsequent attack, known by its code name, Operation Forager, was launched in June 1944, the navy brought a massive force to the Marianas at precisely the same time that Normandy was being invaded in Europe. It helps show how hollow Germany-first was as a policy. By almost any measure, the navy deployed at least ten times as many combat vessels to take the Marianas as they did during the D-Day landings, and they brought along an entire air force as well.[15]* Leahy followed the attack on the Marianas with great interest. An early report about a Japanese attack on US warships supporting the landings on Saipan illustrated the importance of America's naval airpower. In a clash known as the Great Marianas Turkey Shoot, Japan lost approximately 500 aircraft in combat with US naval planes. Leahy wrote that it provided a "full justification" of the navy's construction of a separate air arm before the war.[16] He also wrote confidently that with the destruction of Japanese naval airpower, the fate of the Marianas was sealed.

Though the Japanese Army would resist bitterly, Leahy was right. Saipan, Tinian, and Guam all inevitably fell to American forces over the

---

* As part of Operation Forager, the US Navy deployed 15 aircraft carriers, 7 battleships, 20 cruisers, and 67 destroyers. To support the D-Day landings on Normandy, Operation Neptune, the navy deployed no aircraft carriers, 3 older battleships, 3 cruisers, and 34 destroyers.

coming few weeks. The capture of the Marianas was the decisive blow to Japan's ability to resist and marked the moment when the war went into an unstoppable tailspin for the Japanese. Now there were two major options on the table for the United States: head to the Philippines as MacArthur desperately wanted, or attack Formosa as King counseled. Both operations promised to be difficult and bloody—attacking large landmasses in which entire Japanese armies could be based. It was when faced with the prospect of taking either that Leahy first started arguing that the United States rely on an air-sea power blockade to compel Japanese surrender and avoid operations such as the invasion of Japan, which would cost too many American lives.

On July 10, a special meeting of the Joint Chiefs convened to hear new planning staff ideas for bringing the Pacific war to a close. Leahy listened but was unimpressed. "These plans contemplate an invasion of the Japanese Islands with which I am not in full agreement, but which assumption appears necessary to the preparation of alternative plans," he noted in his diary.[17] His opposition to an invasion of Japan was long-standing.[18] He still believed that the Pacific war was more about the future of China than anything else and recoiled at the notion of sacrificing large numbers of American soldiers and sailors in what he considered an unnecessary operation. In reaction to this briefing, Leahy admitted that he would not try to block an invasion of Japan right away. Instead, he would continue to emphasize how bloody an invasion would be and propose alternatives. In other words, he would not stop the planning for these attacks; he would just do his damnedest to make sure that the plans were never realized: "It was my opinion, and I urged it strongly on the Joint Chiefs, that no major land invasion of the Japanese mainland was necessary to win the war. The JCS did order the preparation of plans for an invasion, but *the invasion itself was never authorized*."[19] It was a risky strategy but was the only one open to him as everyone else, except Roosevelt, was operating on the assumption that an invasion would occur.

The summer dispute over whether to attack the Philippines or Formosa was overlaid with domestic politics. Rumors swirled that MacArthur, were he not allowed to retake the Philippines, might permit his name to go forward for the Republican nomination for president in

November. With the election looming, Roosevelt, sensing an opportunity to be seen as a forceful commander in chief, took the dramatic and unnecessary step of summoning MacArthur and Nimitz to meet with him in Pearl Harbor. The two officers could have been represented by surrogates, but the trip allowed the president numerous photo opportunities. Roosevelt wanted to keep Marshall and King at arm's length. They, along with Arnold, were not informed about the upcoming meeting.[20] The only officer he wanted and needed at his side was Leahy.

On July 13, Roosevelt and Leahy departed Washington, and for the first time Harry Hopkins was also left behind on an important trip. Considering that the purpose of the voyage was political, his absence was particularly surprising. Instead, the president included Samuel Rosenman, another trusted adviser and speechwriter and a friend of Leahy's (with whom Leahy would collaborate closely in the next two years). Traveling in the *Ferdinand Magellan*, the party's first stop was Hyde Park, where Roosevelt showed Leahy the progress on his library and took him for a drive around the countryside. After a few days the presidential train rolled into Chicago, the site of the Democratic National Convention. Roosevelt met with high-powered Democratic leaders before informing his staff that he had decided on Harry Truman as his choice for the vice presidency. Soon thereafter, Roosevelt formally accepted the Democratic nomination to run again in 1944.

A few days later the presidential party reached California, where the military laid on a large amphibious assault for Roosevelt's inspection, involving 10,000 men staging a mock invasion just north of San Diego. Leahy found the chaos of the port at war both impressive and overwhelming, describing the scene as a crowded mess with "motor traffic beyond belief."[21]

At San Diego the party boarded the heavy cruiser USS *Baltimore* for the journey to Hawaii. Roosevelt and Leahy stayed in adjacent cabins, and in the evenings the two friends would watch films in the admiral's quarters. Days were spent on deck as the president discussed the war with his most trusted adviser and prepared to meet with the mercurial MacArthur. On July 26, thirteen days after leaving Washington, Roosevelt and Leahy sailed into Pearl Harbor.

Seeing MacArthur again brought out mixed emotions in Leahy. They had been friendly since meeting on the West Coast as young officers, both embarking on stellar, yet different, careers.[22] Though they had not crossed paths for many years, Leahy became familiar with the MacArthur family, mostly through the general's nephew, Douglas MacArthur II, a foreign service officer who had worked for him in Vichy. General MacArthur was a publicity seeker of the highest order, always in the press either self-glorifying or complaining about being neglected. Leahy, who disliked grandstanding as a rule, heard reports from officers he trusted, such as Nimitz and Halsey, that MacArthur was an egomaniac suffering from delusions of grandeur.[23] Leahy, as desperate as anyone for Roosevelt to be reelected, was worried that MacArthur might try for the Oval Office himself, and he monitored his statements on political matters.[24]

When the general arrived to see Roosevelt, he sported his trademark brown leather jacket, which, along with a corncob pipe and aviator sunglasses, were part of his carefully cultivated public persona. Dashing and distinctive his look may have been, but it was certainly not regulation dress. "Douglas," intoned Leahy, taking him down a peg, "why don't you wear the right kind of clothes when you come up here and see us?"[25] MacArthur, unaccustomed to being teased or questioned about his obedience to regulations, sheepishly claimed it was cold on the plane. Leahy had made his point: MacArthur was not the most senior man in the room.

The meeting that followed was one of the oddest affairs of World War II. Sitting before a large map of the Pacific, Roosevelt and Leahy awkwardly posed for photographs with Nimitz and MacArthur. When matters turned to the war, Nimitz discussed a possible assault on Formosa, Admiral King's preferred target, but also spoke in favor of an attack on Mindanao, the southernmost major island in the Philippines. MacArthur, hearing the name of the island nation he loved, spoke up on behalf of liberating all the Filipino people who had been abandoned to the Japanese and who had suffered grievously under their rule, infusing his emphatic performance with political sophistication. The general implied that any attack on the Philippines would be victorious in a relatively short time, and with considerably fewer casualties than the United States would suffer on Formosa. MacArthur claimed all he needed were some extra landing craft; he already had enough in the way of troops and airpower to retake the entire archipelago.

For Leahy, MacArthur's confidence was the final piece of the puzzle. The admiral knew that the Philippines' size and location were ideal for the United States to coordinate its air, sea, and land forces most easily to defeat Japan.[26] Yet he had worried that the United States could get bogged down slogging its way through the archipelago's many islands.[27] Now MacArthur's assurance of success convinced Leahy that there was a way forward that would not require an invasion of Japan—or of Formosa, for that matter.[28] Seizing the Philippines would allow American air- and sea power to blockade Japan fully, preempting any further attacks closer to the home islands, and hastening an end to the fighting.

Leahy therefore strongly encouraged action on the matter and was pleased when Roosevelt decided that MacArthur would be allowed to invade the Philippines, at least the island of Leyte, in the coming months. In his diary, the admiral admitted that the operation would assist him in "preventing an unnecessary invasion of Japan which the planning staffs of the Joint Staff and the War Department advocate regardless of the loss of life that would result."[29] Leahy was willing to use his authority to thwart any invasion of Japan—and he was willing to take on the entire US government to do so.

With the Pacific war's next grand act decided on, Roosevelt and Leahy boarded the *Baltimore* for the return journey to the continental United States. To give the ailing president more time to rest, the ship cruised north toward the dramatic coastline of Alaska. Along the way, Leahy took up his fishing rod again, partly to amuse Roosevelt.[30] Once in Alaskan waters, heavy fog set in. The president's party was transferred to a destroyer for the inland route back to the naval base at Bremerton, Washington. The limited visibility forced the destroyer to cruise slowly. The presidential party finally reached port on August 12, two weeks after departing Pearl Harbor.

A cross-country train returned the president to the White House on August 17. Leahy had spent thirty-four consecutive days with Roosevelt, morning, noon, and night. Despite Roosevelt's long rest, the president seemed unengaged and listless. It was left to Leahy to brief

Marshall, King, and Arnold on the decisions over Pacific strategy.[31] Indeed, Roosevelt had hardly any time for the other Joint Chiefs; between his return to Washington and the end of the year he had one private meeting with Marshall, and none with King or Arnold.[32]

One man who now recognized that Leahy was far more important than the other chiefs, and adjusted accordingly, was Douglas MacArthur. After witnessing Leahy's rapport with Roosevelt up close, the general began to approach the admiral directly with crucial requests rather than going through Marshall. For instance, not long after the decision had been made to attack the Philippines, MacArthur worried that, after capturing Leyte, he would be forbidden to proceed to Luzon. Bypassing Marshall, he made his case directly to Leahy.[33] Liberating Luzon, he claimed, was the only way to prevent the civilian disaster that was sure to happen if the island were left in Japanese hands. Afterward, MacArthur told James Forrestal, who was visiting the Pacific theater, that he felt he had Leahy's support for the Luzon operation, which meant that the attack would go forward.[34]

It was a sign that MacArthur had grasped the real power structure in Washington, and he was right to do so. Leahy was working so closely with Roosevelt that his personal identity seemed almost joined to the president's. For instance, in his diary his final summation of the trip to Pearl Harbor was written as if the trip had been for his benefit and not just Roosevelt's: "The journey, long in miles and full of interest, gave to the President and to me personal contact with the controlling commanders of our war effort in the Pacific, and provided us with information upon which to base decisions on future strategy and action in that area."[35] His words seemed to place him at the same level as the commander in chief. As uncharacteristic as it was, it was the truth. He was the United States' most important grand strategist, and America was now fighting Bill Leahy's war.

CHAPTER 22

Atomic Bombs and Elections

When the presidential train finally pulled into the siding by the Bureau of Engraving and Printing on August 17, Washington, DC, was bathed in the sedating light of victory. Nazi Germany seemed on the verge of a final collapse. When German defenses around Normandy had crumbled in late July, the Wehrmacht had been sent into a headlong retreat. Paris was on the verge of liberation, and soon the German Army would be back to almost the 1939 border of the Reich. On the eastern front, conditions seemed even worse for the Germans. The Red Army had launched a massive offensive, code-named Operation Bagration, which overwhelmed German troops. The Soviets surrounded and captured masses of German soldiers, more than had surrendered during any previous battle of the war. When the dust settled, approximately 400,000 Germans had been made prisoners and the Red Army had reached the outskirts of Warsaw. Many in Germany understood that Hitler had brought the country to an irretrievable disaster, and in late July a coup had been launched against the regime, including Claus von Stauffenberg's assassination attempt on the German dictator. Though Hitler escaped with minor injuries, it seemed that the Nazi state might not survive to Christmas.

Washington, for the first time since Pearl Harbor, seemed a city at peace. While Congress was still formally in session (it would remain so for almost the entire war), with the 1944 elections looming, many politicians had left town to visit their home states. Others were away escaping the heat and humidity of the capital in August. The quiescent mood suited the president, who spent much of his time having long lunches under the magnolia tree in the White House garden or dozing through tea breaks on the sun porch. Leahy, however, was not allowed a break. He had to both prepare for an upcoming conference with the British in Quebec, Octagon, and catch up with what had been going on in the world while he and the president had been coasting slowly across the country.

Roosevelt continued handing Leahy control over the most delicate issues. In August 1944, one of the more tragic events of a very tragic war commenced when the Polish population of Warsaw began an uprising against their German occupiers. The Red Army, which was only miles away, refused to help, happy to let the Poles and Germans kill each other so that they could sweep up the mess afterward.

When Roosevelt returned to Washington, he was besieged by the Polish ambassador and foreign secretary, who were frantic to get aid to their fellow citizens. With the election approaching, it was both a strategic and political question for Roosevelt, who was worried about the state of Polish-American opinion. Knowing he could trust the admiral, he told the Polish diplomats that they were to use Leahy as the best conduit to himself.[1] It was a bittersweet obligation for the admiral. He wanted to get aid to the Poles, but he had already accepted that the Soviets were going to dominate that area, and believed that nothing worthwhile would be achieved there without Stalin's support—which would never be forthcoming. Leahy listened to the Poles with great sympathy, keeping the president from having to do so, but he also was aware that little could be done to help their brave fighters. As he later admitted, "The Russians had other plans for Poland."[2]

In comparison, the preparations for Octagon were one of Leahy's easier tasks. With the war in Europe going so well, and the United States doing the lion's share of the fighting in the Pacific, the most contentious issue facing the Combined Chiefs was to what degree the Americans would let the British play a significant role in the final attacks against Japan. The British had offered to send a large Royal Navy carrier task force to join the American Pacific Fleet once Germany had been defeated. Admiral King, though, not wanting the Royal Navy to claim any credit for the eventual victory, argued against accepting the offer. Beyond this, there were some Anglo-American disagreements over the future of Germany and the continuation of lend-lease, but the chiefs themselves could be assured of a relatively smooth ride. When, on the evening of September 9, Leahy and Roosevelt headed back to the Bureau of Engraving and Printing with the rest of the president's personal staff, Leahy was thinking he could look forward to some stress-free days.

As the president's team clambered aboard the train they knew so well, however, there was one glaring omission. Harry Hopkins was nowhere to be found. Though Hopkins's health had temporarily stabilized and he was back in Washington (he'd met with Roosevelt earlier that day) and desperate to come to Canada, Roosevelt snubbed his former favorite.[3] He no longer saw Hopkins as vital to the smooth running of his team and no longer valued Hopkins's companionship. He started turning his back on or ignoring his former favorite so obviously that Secretary of the Treasury Henry Morgenthau, for one, was disconcerted.[4]

By this time in the war, Leahy alone was indispensable, as the British were now coming to understand. When the American delegation arrived in Quebec City, Leahy and Roosevelt were separated from the rest and brought, once again, to the governor-general's residence in the citadel, where they were housed next door to each other for the duration of the talks. Everyone else was placed in Château Frontenac. As Churchill was also housed in the Citadel, and Hopkins was in purgatory, the prime minister could finally see Leahy in the right light. Almost immediately after their arrival, the two men were chatting in the citadel, when Churchill asked Leahy about the British offer to send a fleet to the Pacific. Leahy, confidently answering on behalf of the American government, said the British naval force would be more than welcome.[5] The prime minister was impressed.

For the rest of the Quebec talks, which lasted from September 12 to 16, Leahy was as good as his word. The chiefs delved into the question of the British offer most deeply on September 14. Leahy maintained that the question was not whether the British would be allowed to send a large naval force to the Pacific, it was simply where that force would be deployed. King, still grumbling, tried to find a way to block British participation and argued that any decision on the use of the British Fleet would later have to be referred to the president for a final approval. Leahy slapped King down in front of the British, saying that if the chief of naval operations still "saw any objections," it was up to him to bring them up to the president now.[6] Leahy's strong support was one of the reasons that the British did eventually dispatch their own carrier battle group to the Pacific in 1945.[7] This force, the British Pacific Fleet, acquitted itself with great distinction during the fighting off Okinawa.[8]

One issue that became more heated than expected at the talks was the fate of Germany, and Leahy's role in this revealed him at his most subtle—or devious, depending on your point of view. Another member of Roosevelt's court who had become more influential with the decline of Hopkins was Morgenthau. It was in 1944 that the treasury secretary started pushing the famous plan that now bears his name. Under the Morgenthau Plan, the defeated Germany was to be emasculated, stripped of almost all of its industry, its population made reliant on soup kitchens provided by their conquerors, and the entire country forcibly transformed into a giant farm that could never again threaten its neighbors.

By the time of Octagon, Roosevelt had been persuaded by Morgenthau to support such a punitive peace and it soon took over much of the secret negotiations during the talks, very much against Leahy's instincts. Unfortunately for him, of all the American chiefs, Leahy was the only one to get embroiled in the discussions. He was the only chief who attended a small dinner party with Roosevelt, Churchill, and Morgenthau on September 13 when the issue was first debated. It was a combative evening. Morgenthau pushed hard for his plan, and Roosevelt provided him surprisingly strong backing. The president claimed that the industrious Germans could quickly transform even an innocuous-looking furniture factory into an arsenal of war. Churchill was torn. He hated to disagree so openly with Roosevelt, but he saw real peril in the creation of a weak, useless Germany in the center of Europe, especially with the enormous Red Army that would assuredly be stationed nearby.

The British had always traded well with the Germans, and the war had so dislocated the British economy that they looked on resumption of trade with their erstwhile enemy as something that could help their own recovery from the war.

Churchill stood up to Roosevelt and Morgenthau that night, deploying all his eloquence, sarcasm, and irascibility. Leahy sat silently—as he almost always did when he disagreed with the president—radiating waves of discomfort. Though he believed the Nazis deserved punishment, Leahy did not want to decimate the German state or people. After the meal, Morgenthau described the exchanges to Harry Dexter White, the Treasury Department official who would later be accused of spying for the Soviet Union.[9] Though quiet, Morgenthau said Leahy seemed ill at ease, and the treasury secretary wondered if Leahy was instinctively closer to Churchill on the question than to the president.[10]

Churchill and Roosevelt returned to the issue throughout the next two days, and the prime minister eventually initialed a document that seemed to give assent to the plan. Leahy was there, lurking in the background, playing a duplicitous game. While the admiral did not sit in on all the meetings when Roosevelt and Churchill discussed the plan, he talked it over with the president a number of times. He made it seem to Roosevelt that he was more supportive of the plan than he really was. When, on September 15, Morgenthau asked the president about the negotiations, Roosevelt replied by telling a rather surprised treasury secretary that "Leahy had been favorable to my [Morgenthau's] plan."[11]

Acutely aware of Roosevelt's moods, Leahy was keeping his powder dry. He remained opposed to the plan but knew this was not the right time to try to change the president's mind. When talking with Morgenthau, however, Leahy let slip how little he wanted to do with the plan. One of the real sticking points at Octagon was the different zones to be allocated to the British and Americans, as it would be up to the occupying powers to strip their zones of industry. During the talks it was agreed that the British would occupy the Ruhr and Saarland, areas where there were high concentrations of German industry. Leahy admitted that he was more than happy with such an arrangement, as that meant the British would have to do the real dirty work in Germany.[12]

Winston Churchill seemed to sense a greater kinship with Leahy as the talks developed. Clementine Churchill, his wife, who shared a number of meals with the admiral during the summit, wrote to her daughter speculating that Leahy had replaced Hopkins as Roosevelt's favored adviser.[13] Soon Churchill himself would approach Leahy about opening up a personal and private channel to the admiral. It happened after the end of an extraordinary few days right after Octagon.

As soon as festivities in Canada were over on September 16, Roosevelt, Leahy, and the president's staff piled once again onto the presidential train. When they arrived outside Hyde Park early on the morning of the next day, only Leahy, Roosevelt, and two trusted secretaries disembarked. What followed was the most sensitive Anglo-American meeting of the entire war. Roosevelt was so worried about information leaking about the talks he was about to have that he excluded the State Department completely and his meeting diary was left entirely blank.[14] Roosevelt and Churchill were going to discuss the most awesome weapon in human history, the atomic bomb.

On the morning of September 18, Winston Churchill's train pulled into Hyde Park. He was followed a few hours later by an odd duo: the former British king Edward VIII—now known as the duke of Windsor since his abdication of the throne to marry his American love, Wallis Simpson—and Harry Hopkins. The duke was there to pay his respects, and Leahy was impressed by the man's vigor, having expected to find a weak and roguish voluptuary. Of course, Leahy's instinctive republicanism soon emerged. He found it ludicrous that Churchill, "one of the two most powerful men of his age," had to bow obsequiously to a supercilious and failed ex-monarch.[15] After a few pleasantries, the duke was sent packing. Hopkins was allowed to stay. He had been invited up so that he could see Churchill, though he was not entirely rehabilitated in the president's eyes, as the next few days would show.

To outsiders it would have seemed that the leaders of two of the world's most powerful countries were taking a few days of much-deserved R & R. For much of the time the party went on country rides, in between a series of meals at sites dotted around the estate, where they pontificated on whatever took their fancy. On the nineteenth, during a lunch at Eleanor Roosevelt's preferred cottage, Val-Kill, the First Lady and the prime minister engaged in a spirited debate over the future of international politics. Roosevelt, a natural "uplifter," argued that increasing living standards around the world was the key to maintaining peace, while a curmudgeonly Churchill claimed that only a rock-solid Anglo-American alliance could keep darker forces at bay. Leahy was riveted, instinctively sympathetic to Churchill's balance-of-power understanding of world politics but impressed with the First Lady's determination.

A few hours later, after dinner back in the main house, while the other guests scattered to relax, read, or chat, Franklin Roosevelt, Winston Churchill, and William Leahy retreated into the president's study to talk.[16] It was the first time the president and the prime minister had a frank and detailed exchange on atomic weapons and power development, and Leahy was the only other person in the room.

Leahy's description of these historic talks revealed nothing but his personal disquiet. Ever careful, he only referred to the atomic project in his diary by its code name, Tube Alloys.

> Six to eight pm. Conferred with the Prime Minister and the President on a number of political matters.
>
> An oral agreement was made that the United States and Great Britain would continue to collaborate after the war on the development of the highly secret project known as Tube Alloys. *PS. code word for a new weapon project in which I have no confidence.*[17]

Leahy hated everything to do with the atom bomb. He hoped it would never be built, and, God forbid if it were, he prayed that the United States would never use it first.[18] The bomb had been in development for three years now, under the auspices of the Manhattan Project. Roosevelt had originally approved a massive investment in atomic research because he had been assured by Albert Einstein and others that the Nazis were working to build an atomic bomb of their own. By late

1944, however, the German attempt had floundered, whereas the Manhattan Project, after the expenditure of billions of dollars, was on the verge of producing a workable weapon.*

The atom bomb is probably the best example of an issue over which Leahy had enormous influence during his career, but in which his role is almost entirely misunderstood or mischaracterized.[19] For example, in the 1950s, George Marshall sat for a series of interviews with his biographer, Forrest Pogue, in which the general puffed himself up hugely, making it seem as if he had been in control of US atomic policy during the war. He stated twice that Leahy did not know of the atom bomb project until just before its testing in July 1945, more than half a year after Leahy discussed the bomb privately with Roosevelt and Churchill.[20]

Leahy in his memoir mentions it being a factor in his thinking by the summer of 1944, though he would have known about the weapon from the moment he became Roosevelt's chief of staff.[21] He was one of the few people with whom Roosevelt felt he could discuss the project in detail.[22] From the moment Leahy found out about the weapon, he was appalled both ethically and strategically. He viewed it as even more horrible than biological and chemical weapons, both of which he always argued the United States should never use first.[23] Only two months before these Hyde Park meetings, for instance, as Leahy and Roosevelt were traveling to Pearl Harbor, there was a "spirited" discussion with Roosevelt and some other advisers about a new biological weapon that could threaten Japan with domestic collapse by destroying Japan's rice crop.[24] Leahy took the lead, arguing against this horrible new weapon, looking Roosevelt straight in the eye and saying, "Mr. President, this would violate every Christian ethic I have ever heard of and all of the known laws of war. It would be an attack on the noncombatant population of the enemy. The reaction can be foretold—if we use it, the enemy will use it."[25]

He would fight against the use of atomic weapons with even greater

* The Manhattan Project is sometimes assumed to be the most expensive American weapons program of the war. This is not true. The development of the very-long-range B-29 bomber cost a billion or so more.

force. Of all the American strategic leaders, military or civilian, Leahy was the one most opposed to the use of such weapons and the one most opposed to the use of any indiscriminate weapons against civilian targets.[26] Unfortunately, there is often a focus on the times that Leahy argued that the bomb would never work, in a way that makes him sound like some fussy old Luddite. Leahy's claim that the bomb would never work, which he made a number of times, was in fact not a prediction but an intense form of wish fulfillment. He was always painfully aware that the bomb might work, but he was desperately hoping that it would not. He admitted this to someone he trusted very much, H. Freeman Matthews. Leahy mentioned the existence of the bomb to Matthews before it was tested (a rare act of confidence) and admitted that he as much hoped the bomb would not work as expected it not to, saying, "I don't think this thing is going to work, this bomb. But . . . if it does, it's going to have terrible, terrible consequences for the future."[27] What stood out in Matthews's mind was the intensity of Leahy's hatred of the atomic bomb, which he saw as something truly awful, a "terrible thing for the world."[28]

We can only imagine exactly what Leahy would have said in the room with Roosevelt and Churchill on September 19, though it would have been entirely negative. It is worth noting that as Roosevelt came to rely more and more on Leahy, his pronouncements about the atomic bomb became far more negative. During this meeting, the president seemed reluctant to discuss the bomb as a weapon, preferring to talk about the peaceful use of atomic energy after the war. The British aide-mémoire written after this meeting made it clear that Roosevelt was uncomfortable with the idea of crossing the atomic threshold. The president said that when "a 'bomb' is finally available, it might perhaps, after mature consideration, be used against the Japanese."[29]

The next day the house party broke up. Churchill, having seen Leahy and Roosevelt work so closely at both Quebec and Hyde Park, made his move. As the prime minister was getting ready to board his train to New York, he pulled Leahy aside and asked the admiral if he could "write me from time to time personal letters in regard to problems that may arise."[30]

Leahy's reaction to Churchill's offer of a more intimate connection revealed just why the admiral had risen so high. Instead of being flattered that one of the most famous and powerful men of his time wanted to open a private communications channel, Leahy blanched. He made it clear that he would look on surreptitious messages from Churchill less than kindly. If anything, this rebuff made Churchill even more interested in finding out more about Leahy, as the coming years would attest.

Leahy's loyalty, first, last, and always, would be to Franklin Delano Roosevelt, which the president understood. For the next two days the president kept the admiral close. After almost everyone else left Hyde Park early on September 19, the president and his chief of staff spent another day and a half relaxing at the estate. The president could not bring himself to head back to Washington, and work, until almost midnight on September 20, when he, Leahy, and his daughter, Anna, traveled back to Washington together.

Once back in Washington, Leahy became both hyper-politicized and, at the same time, more openly cocky than he had ever been before. One development that came out of Hyde Park was that Leahy was now Roosevelt's preferred contact for atomic discussions with the British—and the president wanted to make sure that Leahy had as much information as possible about the state of the Manhattan Project. On their first full day back in the White House, Roosevelt and Leahy were briefed by Vannevar Bush, head of the US Office of Scientific Research and Development, about recent atomic developments.[31] On October 2, to make sure that Leahy had as complete a picture as possible, the head of the Manhattan Project, Col. Leslie Groves, came by the admiral's office for another private briefing about the bomb's development. Both meetings served only to depress the admiral, who continued hoping that the project would fail.

While Leahy gained little pleasure from his growing importance in Roosevelt's atomic policy–making life, he was if anything more assertive than usual when it came to issues in which he truly believed, as both Morgenthau and Marshall discovered in October. Leahy's disputes with Marshall were about American policy over China, something that would divide the two for the rest of their lives.

During 1944 the situation in China began to deteriorate alarmingly. It was the one area of the world where Axis forces were successfully on the offensive as the Japanese Army extended its control over Northern and Central China and the regime of Chiang Kai-shek seemed powerless to stop them. Meanwhile, the senior American commander in the area, the aptly nicknamed "Vinegar Joe" Stilwell, began to fulminate. The acerbic Stilwell had been in his post, perhaps the trickiest position in the entire US Army, since 1942, increasingly falling out with the Nationalists and the senior US Army Air Force commander in China, Gen. Claire Chennault. In 1944 Stilwell came to believe that he alone could stabilize the situation and lobbied to be given command over almost the entire Chinese Army. By now he despised Chiang Kai-shek and other Nationalists as corrupt, incompetent thieves and started publicly referring to the Chinese leader as "Peanut."

George Marshall was a rock of support for Stilwell throughout his command, always pressing the president to increase Stilwell's authority. Having handed Stilwell this poisoned chalice, Marshall believed he had a personal obligation to defend Stilwell's interests. Leahy was more circumscribed. He was sympathetic to Stilwell at first, but also felt that the US-Chinese relationship was always more important than any individual.

The Chinese Nationalists always saw Leahy as a fair dealer in the administration, and as their relations with Stilwell festered, they turned to the admiral to try to get Stilwell replaced. In July 1944 Chiang Kai-shek sent a confidential message directly to Leahy asking him to intercede with Roosevelt against Stilwell.[32] Leahy was not willing to go that far, but in an attempt to placate the Nationalists, he pushed Roosevelt to send a close associate, Patrick Hurley, a Leahy friend and former secretary of war under Herbert Hoover, to China to improve relations.[33] In sending Hurley, Leahy also opened up another confidential means of communicating with the Chinese.

By the time Leahy returned to Washington from Hyde Park in late September, the situation had become worse, and the admiral turned decisively against Stilwell. Leahy heard that Stilwell was publicly insulting Chiang Kai-shek, which to him was a sign that Stilwell was not up to the job. To Leahy, the military must always remain subordinate and show respect to civilian authorities, and if Stilwell did not have enough self-control to keep from mocking his superiors in public, he could not be trusted with such an important command.

In just a few days, Leahy ruthlessly destroyed Stilwell's position. On October 14, Hurley reported to Leahy that Stilwell was no longer acceptable to the Chinese and needed to be replaced.[34] Leahy reacted immediately, sending an order to Lt. Gen. Joseph McNarney, Marshall's deputy, to prepare a list of possible replacements. Yet Marshall remained committed to his fellow general. He threw a tantrum and seemed willing to force a rupture in US-Chinese relations to protect Stilwell. Marshall wrote to Roosevelt—in a letter that had to be passed on by Leahy—saying that if Stilwell were relieved the United States should send no replacement, and let the Japanese have their way with the Nationalists.[35] In defending Stilwell, Marshall had the strong support of Secretary of War Stimson.[36] To Leahy, this was all madness, and childish madness at that. If the Chinese government, a valued US ally and a power that would be ever more important in the postwar world, formally demanded Stilwell's removal, he had to go.

It was decided that Marshall would come and make his case with the president on October 16, though Leahy, naturally, would be in the room with him. What followed was a textbook example of the Roosevelt-Leahy-Marshall relationship during the war. The meeting started at just after noon, not long after Roosevelt first appeared on that Monday morning and right after the president and Leahy would have had their daily briefing on the state of the war. One of the reasons the president was up so late, especially by his standards, was that the night before he had held a small dinner party for only ten people in the White House, one of whom was Leahy, and stayed up until almost midnight.

As the three men gathered in the Oval Office, the president probably sitting in his wheelchair behind his desk, with the admiral and general standing respectfully before him, Marshall would have been given the floor, as he had only fifteen minutes to make his case. Marshall pressed Roosevelt "strongly" to keep Stilwell in his post, arguing that the general was the only American officer who stood "any chance of correcting the existing bad military situation in China."[37] And then Marshall, politely but firmly, was led away. At that point, Leahy might not even have had to say anything else. He had already made his case to Roosevelt that Stilwell had to go as soon as possible—that the general had "failed completely" to respect the authority of the Chinese in their own country.

Roosevelt, faced with diametrically opposing positions, one from the stiff if compliant Marshall, and the other from the trusted and invaluable Leahy, made up his mind immediately. Stilwell was out. He was relieved of his command before the end of the month.

If Leahy could afford to crush Marshall's hopes so openly, he had to be more careful with Morgenthau. Leahy returned from Quebec determined not to give in on the Morgenthau Plan. He was aided immeasurably when details of the plan were leaked to the press, and Roosevelt started receiving strong criticism for supporting such a harsh peace. The British also made it clear that no matter what document Churchill initialed at Octagon, they were still not happy. Behind the scenes, Leahy lobbied the president to repudiate the plan. Roosevelt, realizing that he had signed up for something far more controversial than expected, started backing away from its harsher provisions.* He even started disavowing Morgenthau himself, believing that the secretary of the treasury had led him down the garden path. Roosevelt told Stimson that Morgenthau had pulled "a boner."[38] By October 19, with the president in retreat, Leahy was willing to tease the chastened Morgenthau. During what was an otherwise pleasant and productive lunch, Leahy shocked Morgenthau by telling him straight that he had been working to change the president's mind since Quebec, saying, "You will never get your plan through."[39]

Leahy's role in Roosevelt's retreat from the Morgenthau Plan helps encapsulate the mystery of much of his influence. Was he single-handedly responsible for changing the president's mind? Almost certainly not. Roosevelt would have taken many things into consideration—the political implications of bad press with the election looming, continued

---

* The Morgenthau Plan would eventually be killed off in its entirety by President Truman, much to Leahy's approval.

British resistance, the strong opposition of others in his administration, including Hull and Stimson, as well as the views of the trusted Leahy. However, Leahy's influence is the one factor never mentioned in the history books, whereas Stimson, bizarrely, is often portrayed as the key force pushing the president to back down. Between the return from Quebec and Leahy's lunch with Morgenthau on October 19, Roosevelt had only one meeting with Stimson, on October 3. The secretary of war was a minor player in the president's world.

The best sign that Leahy was instrumental in changing Roosevelt's position was that the admiral did everything later in life to cover his own tracks. In his memoir he pretended that the Morgenthau Plan never existed and claimed, entirely disingenuously, that he never participated in any political discussions at Quebec. Moreover, he tried to expunge from the official histories the idea that Roosevelt had ever supported the Morgenthau Plan. In 1956, when he was asked to read and comment on a draft of Maurice Matloff's official history of the grand strategy of the war, Leahy lied twice, saying that he never recalled discussing the Morgenthau Plan at Quebec and that, furthermore, he never remembered Roosevelt supporting the plan at any time.[40] Having been able to swing the president around to his way of thinking, Leahy had no need to have his success recorded in history. He was happy enough to have won.

Leahy's ability to tweak Morgenthau about his opposition to the plan was more than a power play; it was an indication that, from a holistic point of view, the two men were getting along quite well. Indeed, a week later they had another lunch that Leahy termed a "grand affair," after which they joked about how they were both being spied on by the Russians.[41] They were bound by one thing more than anything else: the reelection of Franklin Roosevelt. The presidential election of 1944 was the tensest of Roosevelt's four, and Leahy and Morgenthau were both wrapped up in it in their different ways. Though the president seemed to be in the lead throughout, the Republican challenger, Gov. Thomas Dewey of New York, ran an effective campaign, and as the vote approached it looked like the result would be uncomfortably close.

During their lunch on October 19, Leahy and Morgenthau talked politics a great deal and the admiral made it clear, notwithstanding his supposedly nonpolitical stance, that he would do what he needed to help the president win. Dewey was attacking Roosevelt for sending Americans into combat without all the necessary supplies. It was a rather bizarre charge, as American troops were the most lavishly supplied of all the nations' combatants, but it seemed to be having some impact. Morgenthau and Leahy discussed how best to blunt these attacks, with the admiral telling the treasury secretary he was "wholly in sympathy" with Morgenthau's political plans and more than willing to "back him up" if he went public.[42]

The election began taking over more and more of Leahy's life. The final 1944 trip that Leahy took with Roosevelt had the admiral act as political and military adviser wrapped up as one. With the vote approaching, Roosevelt wanted Leahy at his side during political tours. Yet the president's declining health meant that he was rarely strong enough to campaign, limiting his activity to the final three weekends before the vote.[43] The longest of these efforts was a tour of New England in early November, and Leahy was an eager participant in the process. He traveled with Roosevelt to speeches in Bridgeport, Connecticut; Springfield, Massachusetts; and then Boston. Leahy was exhilarated by the rapturous reception that Roosevelt received—particularly from the 40,000 people who crammed into Boston's Fenway Park. On the other hand, Leahy had mixed opinions of the celebrities he encountered. He enjoyed Frank Sinatra's rendition of "America" but disliked having Orson Welles accompany the party to a number of campaign stops. He decided that Welles was a phony.[44]

When the campaigning was over, Leahy, with a select group of family and friends, went with Roosevelt to Hyde Park to await the result. On the day of the vote, the admiral became tense. He sat next to Roosevelt for most of the afternoon as the party discussed politics.[45] When standing, he guzzled coffee and paced nervously around the house waiting for news. When the vote tallies finally started coming in, Leahy hovered by the ticker tape so that he could be the first to grab the results and rush over to Roosevelt for analysis.[46] The two whipped each other up into a bit of a lather that night, and neither could sleep. Leahy blamed his inability to rest on all the coffee, but the truth was that there was no way he could have rested until Roosevelt's reelection had been guaranteed. The tension of that night lived with Leahy for the rest of his life. He told Harry Truman years later that he was still up at four a.m., waiting, as Roosevelt said, "for the son of a bitch [Dewey] to concede."[47] In the end, Leahy was the last person in the house to go to bed, but when he did, he was able to sleep the sleep of the victor. Roosevelt had won more comfortably than expected, capturing 36 states and 432 electoral votes to Dewey's 12 states and 99 electoral votes.

When it was clear that not only had Roosevelt been reelected but that the Democrats had kept their hold on both houses of Congress, Leahy was delighted, describing it as an "overwhelming victory."[48] He was right to be pleased. It meant that he would remain embedded in the heart of American power—as long, of course, as Franklin Roosevelt lived.

CHAPTER 23

Yalta and Death

ranklin Roosevelt's fourth inaugural was a ruse. Previous inaugurals had involved enormous crowds of spectators, noisy parades, soaring rhetoric, and celebrations across Washington, DC. But on January 20, 1945, a gray midwinter day, wartime austerity was used as an excuse for the truncated service needed to hide the president's weakness from the American people. At noon, after a private church service in the White House, the president was wheeled out to the South Portico to be sworn in. Those who saw him up close were struck by how thin he had become. The new vice president, Harry Truman, who had little personal experience with Roosevelt before being elected and would have little after, remembered Eleanor Roosevelt saying not long before this, "I can't get him to eat. He just won't eat."[1]

Milling around the snow-flecked White House grounds was a tiny, invitation-only crowd of fewer than 5,000.[2] They watched as the president was quickly sworn into office and then began his final inaugural address. His body weaker than ever, standing in his heavy, painful metal braces was a massive exertion for Roosevelt. He could only muster a slow monotone, and it took him more than five minutes to complete the speech's twenty-two forgettable sentences.[3] Its rhetorical high point might have been "We have learned that we need to live as men, not as ostriches." The president then retreated into the White House for lunch. The short ceremony had taken its toll. After the meal,

Roosevelt disappeared into his bedroom, not to emerge for almost four hours.

William Leahy watched this charade as one of the honored guests on the South Portico, accompanied by his granddaughter. Though the gathering of Roosevelt's inner circle exchanged glances and concerned nods, all directed to the president's condition, Leahy tried to pretend everything was fine. Putting as positive a spin as possible on what he had witnessed, Leahy claimed to be unaware "of any marked deterioration" in the president's health.[4]

The inauguration occurred after another long period during which Roosevelt did almost no work. He was basically on an extended holiday from November 21 until New Year's Eve, spending just over a week in Washington as he shuttled back and forth from Hyde Park to his winter White House in Warm Springs, Georgia. In one way, it was good that the president had been able to rest. In two days he would leave on the most famous and controversial international journey of his career, to the small Russian Black Sea resort town of Yalta. He would need whatever energy he had left to negotiate with Joseph Stalin.

There is a fine line between self-confidence and insufferability, and after the election, with Roosevelt relying so vitally on him, Leahy tested that standard. His unique access to Roosevelt, his ability to be the voice of the president to the rest of government, allowed him to dabble in areas that were far outside the remit of a military chief of staff. He could see the president every day, sometimes more than once, while senior cabinet members such as Morgenthau had to beg to get ten minutes with Roosevelt.[5] When he wanted, Leahy was the most powerful man in Washington, as his constant interference in the debate over lend-lease revealed.

Lend-lease, the plan by which the United States provided billions of dollars of military equipment and raw materials to its allies, primarily the Soviet Union and Great Britain, had been an outstanding success. Before America entered the fighting, it had helped the British tie down much of the German military machine, and after Pearl Harbor was attacked it helped knit the Allies together into a far more powerful fighting force. Leahy wanted the program wound up as soon as the war was over. This was his personal position, and not that of the president, who was vague on the subject. No matter how often he worked with the internationalist Roosevelt, Leahy had an instinctive isolationism in his worldview that emerged most strongly during this debate. One of the reasons Leahy was so keen to have his regular lunches with Morgenthau was that they allowed him to interfere with lend-lease.

The future of the plan was an obsession of the British government. During the war, the economy of the United Kingdom, partly because of lend-lease, had become dangerously contorted. The British had stopped almost all their overseas trade and devoted themselves to war production. The United States had benefited by replacing the British in many of the world's markets. To keep support flowing to the British economy and to help prepare for the postwar world, Churchill dispatched the famous economist John Maynard Keynes to America in September 1944 to discuss the future economic relationship between the two countries.

The problem that Keynes, Morgenthau, and everyone else had was in getting Roosevelt to commit to a specific policy, and this is where Leahy stepped in with a typical example of his conniving self-deprecation tactics to impose his will. The issue dominated Washington for the second half of November. On the seventeenth, Keynes and the British delegation pressed their case for a large infusion of dollars into the British (and world) system to pave the way for economic recovery after the war.[6] Keynes was looking for a lend-lease allocation of $6.75 billion in 1945, considerably more than Britain needed to fight the war. There was a great deal of sympathy in the American government for the United Kingdom's position, and people such as Hopkins, Morgenthau, Assistant Secretary of State Dean Acheson, and soon-to-be secretary of state Stettinius were inclined to be generous. Yet they could do nothing without knowing the president's ideas, and to do that they had to go through Leahy.

To get Leahy onside, Morgenthau organized a special briefing for the admiral. On November 18, precisely at eleven a.m., a high-powered delegation from the State, Treasury, War, and Navy Departments, including Dean Acheson, Robert Patterson, Robert Lovett, and Harry Dexter White, trooped obediently into Leahy's office. Leahy looked at this group of savvy, self-confident operators, and outmaneuvered them all. He began by playing the well-worn simple-sailor card, claiming he "didn't know much about lend-lease and, in any case, didn't know what he had to do with the matter."[7] Having disarmed the group, Leahy slipped seamlessly into the role of chairman, listened to the discussions, and then began to guide the decision-making. What he was most concerned with was blocking the transformation of lend-lease into a postwar reconstruction program, which was precisely what Keynes wanted. Leahy wanted no commitments that would outlast the war, believing that American negotiators seemed to be doing just that. He asked "why any commitment had to be made to the British and why there would have to be any agreement between the President and the Prime Minister. . . . The program, in other words, constitutes a sort of moral commitment and would doubtless be used so by the British."[8] Soon all the other powerful people in the room were singing his tune. Acheson, who was initially sympathetic to the British plan, agreed that no long-term agreement should be concluded and the group assented.

On November 21, Leahy and Morgenthau sat down with Roosevelt at the White House to discuss the way forward. In this more private setting, Leahy dropped his humble persona and laid down a clear policy line that he wanted Roosevelt to follow, including the making of no commitments that would outlast the war and a 1945 lend-lease allocation of only $5.3 billion for the British.[9] Roosevelt was so pleased with Leahy's clarity that he asked the admiral to serve on a small committee to decide the American government's stance. When alone, the two friends joked about how it was working out, with Leahy saying, "Mr. President, I know almost nothing about lend-lease, and I don't want to go to jail when they begin, after the war is over, to investigate what has been done with this money." Roosevelt replied with a smile, "If you go to jail, I'll be going along with you."[10]

Morgenthau took this lesson to heart. The following day he met with the American lend-lease negotiating committee and was explicit that the US government would make no commitments that would outlast the war.[11] Keynes, a crafty negotiator, sensed that something was different. In the coming week instead of dealing with the Americans en bloc, he decided to shuttle between those he considered most sympathetic. He talked to Hopkins, Stettinius, and Acheson individually and got them to approve a statement that he planned to make on November 29, which made it sound like longer-term commitments were being made. When Morgenthau got wind of what Keynes was up to, the first thing he did was call Leahy and let him know of the plot. A furious admiral sputtered down the phone line to Morgenthau that he would go immediately to see Roosevelt and that he "didn't care a damn" if the British lost all lend-lease support due to Keynes's maneuvering.[12]

The stage was now set for a meeting of the Roosevelt administration's big beasts. In the late afternoon of November 27, Morgenthau, Leahy, Hopkins, Acheson, and Leo Crowley (the head of the Foreign Economic Administration, which oversaw lend-lease) gathered in Morgenthau's office.[13] Stettinius, who was preparing for his new position as secretary of state, took part by telephone. Leahy spoke right at the beginning—as the voice of President Roosevelt. He said he had just talked to the president, and that Roosevelt, to make the American position clear, wanted an American statement released before Keynes said anything. Hopkins was rattled. Still unsure of his standing with Roosevelt, he trashed Keynes and repudiated his statement, claiming the Briton was either a liar or a fool: "I don't care what Keynes said. The question is, did I say to him this was approved. The answer is no!" Hopkins was so worried that he atypically wrapped himself in the flag, yelling, "I don't like foreigners. If it is the word of a foreigner against mine . . ."[14] before Morgenthau stepped in to calm things.

The rest of the meeting went according to the script of Leahy and Morgenthau, and it was agreed that the United States, through Crowley, would release a statement before Keynes spoke. In a final touch, Leahy, with Hopkins, as "two of the President's closest advisers," were asked to read and comment on a final draft of the statement. When he was given the text, Leahy wanted it toughened it up considerably, to the point that it would have been almost insulting to the British.[15] He excised paragraphs he thought irrelevant and removed anything that smacked of a long-term commitment. Morgenthau included almost all of Leahy's changes but in one instance kept the word "will" in the document when Leahy wanted it to say "would" (which Leahy viewed as less of a commitment on the part of the United States). This small omission of Morgenthau's worried the secretary of the treasury so much, he felt compelled to call Leahy to explain. Morgenthau, a wealthy, successful businessman with one of the most senior positions in the Roosevelt administration, was scared of Leahy.

(M) Look, Admiral we've taken most of your suggestions; we haven't taken them all.

(L) Uh huh.

(M) But that's give and take.

(L) Well it was only my effort to help Mr. Secretary.

(M) Yeah, I know.

(L) That was all.

(M) But I want to personally call you.

(L) Fine.

(M) And tell you it was a great help and comfort to have you advising me.

(L) Well, that's very kind of you to say that. Of course I want to do everything I can with my limited knowledge of the subject.

(M) Well, your knowledge wasn't so limited. But anyway, I just want to thank you and say we went just as far as we could to meet your suggestions . . . Admiral, I've worked with you so long, I know—in the first place, you took a lot of trouble to write me those suggestions. And I'm just calling you up to let you know I appreciate it.[16]

In the end, not only did the American statement get issued, Leahy got his way almost entirely on the amount of lend-lease aid Britain was due in 1945. The British were offered only $5.5 billion, with a very Leahy-like proviso that as soon as Germany surrendered (which looked to be soon), Britain's lend-lease allowance would be slashed by 43 percent.[17]

One of the reasons Leahy was so free to throw his weight around over lend-lease was that, from a strategic point of view, there was relatively little for the Joint Chiefs to do in late 1944 and early 1945. There was a brief flurry of activity when the Germans launched their final offensive, the attack into the Ardennes known as the Battle of the Bulge. Yet those in Washington could do little but watch. Militarily, the biggest development for Leahy occurred on December 15, when his promotion became official and he was made the first five-star military officer in American history. Leahy was raised to the rank of fleet admiral that day, with George Marshall made a general of the army the following day. All members of the American military would thus be forced to salute Leahy first for the rest of the admiral's life. He would remain the highest-ranking officer in American history until George Washington was posthumously given his sixth star in 1976.*

However, not everything was celebrations, promotions, and political victories. Perhaps Leahy's most important task was one he looked forward to least, the upcoming summit with Stalin and Churchill. Once again, there remained the question of venue if the Soviet dictator was to be involved. Stalin continued to refuse to travel far and demanded that the president make another grueling trip, this time to the Soviet Union itself. "The Boss thinks he ought to meet those savages again," Leahy complained, "but it seems that Uncle Joe, as they call him, says that the meeting will have to be in Russia. My old bones dread the idea of Moscow in winter, and that awful cold won't do the President any good either."[18] Eyes turned to the Black Sea coast, one of the most temperate parts of the Soviet Union. It was eventually decided that the leaders and their staffs would gather in Yalta, a resort town on the southernmost tip of the Crimean Peninsula, where the imperial tsars had built a series of extravagant palaces. The conference was given the code name Argonaut, which Leahy thought a little frilly.

The last trip the president and his chief of staff would take started on January 22. After an overnight train trip to Newport, Virginia, they boarded the cruiser USS *Quincy* for the journey across the Atlantic into the Mediterranean. The other Joint Chiefs and Harry Hopkins were not in the party and made their way across the Atlantic in aircraft.[19]

---

* There are two other cases where officers could be said to have reached a higher rank. Adm. George Dewey, after the Spanish-American War, was raised to the rank of admiral of the navies, which was never used again. After World War I, Gen. John J. Pershing was raised to the rank of general of the armies but wore only four stars on his uniform.

That being said, the president traveled with a relatively large group, a sign, perhaps, that he knew he needed more help at the upcoming conference. James Byrnes, for one, was part of the delegation, as was Edward J. Flynn, the former boss of Tammany Hall and Democratic Party chairman, who had been a New York political associate of Roosevelt's for decades and with whom Leahy had worked for Roosevelt's reelection in 1940. Roosevelt's daughter, Anna, at this point known by her married name, Boettiger, also accompanied the president, in the process breaking American regulations against having women aboard warships. Because of this, Leahy, for the first time, did not occupy the cabin directly next to Roosevelt's. That was reserved for Anna. Instead, Leahy shared a two-room setup with Byrnes.

When Roosevelt's sixty-third birthday was celebrated on board with a small dinner, Leahy sat next to Anna, who was her father's favorite child.[20] The admiral's close friendship with his friend's daughter was important in keeping Roosevelt functional. The two tried to convince the president to cut down on his drinking and to go to bed as early as possible—with only partial success.[21] Anna enjoyed teasing the admiral in front of her father. Later on, back from Yalta, Roosevelt would laughingly describe how Leahy became increasingly worried by the number of toasts Anna was tossing back during one of the official banquets. Anna was egging Leahy on, and it wasn't until afterward that she confessed that her glass was being filled only with ginger ale.[22]

Anna's presence on the *Quincy* did not keep Roosevelt and Leahy from privately discussing sensitive issues. The most politically charged was the fate of Henry Wallace, Roosevelt's former vice president who was dumped in favor of Harry Truman. In an attempt to soothe Wallace's hurt feelings, Roosevelt had announced his intention to appoint him the next secretary of commerce. Instantly, a large number of Republicans and conservative Democrats threatened to oppose the nomination. Wallace's backers, led by Eleanor Roosevelt and Henry Morgenthau, bombarded the president on the *Quincy* with telegrams pleading with him to support his new choice.[23] Even though Leahy had no love for the left-wing Wallace, he counseled Roosevelt to stick to his decision. He thought it would look weak to act like he had made a mistake and advised the president that he "should permit his nomination to follow constitutional procedure and should accept the decision of the Congress."[24] Roosevelt did, and Wallace was eventually confirmed.

When the *Quincy* entered the Mediterranean, the war situation was so placid that the president sailed directly to the island of Malta. There, FDR and Leahy met up with Stettinius, Marshall, and King, and a short time later they were joined by Winston Churchill, who was accompanied by his daughter Sarah. There followed two days of talks between the British and American delegations, with Leahy usually being the only military man included in the smaller family meals held afterward with Roosevelt, Churchill, and their daughters. Waiting for them at Malta was Harry Hopkins. In a desperate attempt to remain at the center of power, Hopkins had dragged himself to the talks, but he was weak and no longer fully trusted by Roosevelt. He could barely eat and seemed to live on paregoric, an opium-based anti-diarrheal painkiller, which sapped his strength.[25]

Leahy and Roosevelt left for the Crimea on February 2, flying in the new presidential plane christened the *Sacred Cow*. The most luxurious aircraft in the world, this specially modified Douglas VC-54C Skymaster had bulletproof windows, a presidential desk, a refrigerator, and even an elevator so that Roosevelt could be whisked up and down with ease. Leahy loved it. Due to Roosevelt's dangerously high blood pressure, the plane remained at a low altitude during the flight, but upon landing, things changed. The official airfield for the conference was ninety miles from Yalta, and Leahy and Roosevelt were forced to endure a long series of mountain roads to reach the Livadia Palace, where they were to be housed. This enormous white wedding cake of a building had more than one hundred rooms and had been built by Tsar Nicolas II, who used it for summer holidays. It had been looted by the Germans but had been put in a serviceable condition by a Soviet team working around the clock. The president was given a large suite, formerly used by the tsar, while Leahy was given a room nearby that had been used by the famous seducer and mesmerist Rasputin.[26] The notion of the old admiral staying in Rasputin's "tower" caused Roosevelt and Anna to giggle.

Though the Soviets had poured resources into the palace's restoration—supposedly they had assigned an army of Romanian prisoners to labor on the job—it was still a long way from reaching the levels of comfort and efficiency to which the president and chief of staff had grown accustomed. The grand bedrooms were infested with bedbugs, Leahy's most of all, and all the beds were eventually blasted with heavy doses of DDT.[27] Even so, the next morning Leahy found a particularly large insect on his pillow. Mosquitoes were also a problem, and Leahy continued to believe he was a particular target for their attentions. When he sat for long periods, during meetings or the interminable dinners, he would be covered in bites. He thought the food too rich for his tastes, and he believed the alcoholic evenings were excessive. To delight their American guests, the Russians, particularly at the start of the talks, provided mountains of caviar for breakfast. While this might have pleased sophisticated State Department palates, Leahy wanted something simpler. One morning, according to Anna Roosevelt, the admiral went to great lengths to try to communicate with a non-English-speaking waiter that all he wanted for breakfast was one egg, a piece of toast, and coffee. After they gesticulated wildly to each other, the waiter indicated that he understood, only to show up a few minutes later with a tray laden with caviar, ham, smoked fish, and vodka. Leahy snapped, bellowing, "For God's sake send me someone who speaks English and get this fellow and his wares out of here!"[28]

Leahy's irritability stretched to more than just the food. He found the overall arrangements for the talks chaotic and unstructured. Yet the biggest reason for his irritability was that he was tired and overworked. Even though there was an unprecedentedly large American delegation at Yalta, Roosevelt believed that Leahy was the only man he could completely trust. Before the talks started, he surprised the admiral by saying, "Bill, I wish you would attend all these political meetings in order that we may have someone in whom I have full confidence who will remember everything that we have done."[29] It was a remarkable thing to ask. As the senior American military man, Leahy would have been expected to devote himself to the meetings of the Combined Chiefs of Staff. Roosevelt, however, now told Leahy he wanted him at the more numerous plenary meetings involving himself, Churchill, and Stalin.

Leahy took the request to heart. His diary entries on Yalta are some of the most detailed of his career as he tried to record as much of the discussion and agreements as possible.[30] Hopkins, in comparison, was a peripheral figure. Though invited to the plenary meetings as an American delegate, he missed many, having to spend entire days in bed. Moreover, his personal relationship with Roosevelt was now distant. He was rarely invited to dine with the president, and the two communicated infrequently. After the conference, Hopkins rushed back to America, saying that he was dying and needed to get to the Mayo Clinic as soon as possible.[31] Roosevelt made no efforts to try to have him stay. Their final words were a curt good-bye.

Leahy suspected that Roosevelt knew that he himself was dying, and this was why he had asked the admiral to act as a witness to what he had agreed to at Yalta.[32] There is probably some truth in this. Roosevelt's health at Yalta varied significantly by the day, even by the moment. Leahy liked to describe the president as performing well, achieving most of his important goals, but much of the time he was overcome by exhaustion, his heart beating irregularly and his skin turning from a bright pink to a waxy gray.[33] In the darker moments, Roosevelt would have looked to his legacy and seen Leahy as the one person at Yalta he could trust to protect it.

Acting as the president's eyes and ears like never before, Leahy experienced Yalta as a deluge of meetings. The conference stretched on for eight days, from February 4 to 11, with the admiral often having to shuttle back and forth between the plenary meetings, gatherings of the Joint Chiefs and the Combined Chiefs, and, in one instance, a meeting alone with the Soviet military command. In the evenings, he had to write his notes or attend official dinners, often not reaching his bed until after midnight. Roosevelt deferred almost everything to Leahy, even allowing the admiral to chair meetings that the president had with the American chiefs. Military talks were by far the easiest, the issues mostly technical, involving the best way to coordinate Allied military operations with the war against Germany coming to an end. Leahy realized that meetings with Soviet military authorities were of only limited value, as only Stalin could make the real decisions.

If the military meetings were not particularly heated, the plenary meetings more than made up for that. These were the moments when Roosevelt, Stalin, and Churchill sat around a table with their highest-ranking political aides determining the fate of the world. Leahy was listed third in the American delegation, after only Roosevelt and the secretary of state.

Leahy's behavior during the plenary meetings was enigmatically consistent. He said not a single word on the record. Instead, he observed everything with his owl-like visage, absorbing all that he could and writing it down afterward to remember. He was able to watch Stalin at close quarters once again and remained impressed with the ruthlessness and skill with which the Soviet dictator pressed his case. In response, Stalin came to understand that Leahy, this silent, watchful figure whom Roosevelt obviously valued, played a pivotal role in the president's life. On February 8, at a formal dinner Stalin hosted in honor of Roosevelt, the Soviet dictator directed Vyacheslav Molotov, whom the Americans considered the second most important person in the Soviet delegation and Stalin's most likely successor, to make the formal toast in Leahy's honor. It was a signal that Stalin recognized the admiral as the second most important person in the American delegation. Both Stalin and Molotov came to touch glasses with the admiral.[34]

The story of Yalta, from Leahy's perspective and that of Roosevelt, was not one of drama or controversy loved by historians. Rather, it was a story of a grinding series of negotiations during which the United States achieved some real successes but had to make some serious concessions. Yalta is the most controversial of the grand strategic conferences, with partisans on different sides either attacking the conference as a craven sell-out by the Americans to Soviet barbarism or praising Roosevelt for making needed concessions to keep the wartime alliance together. The argument mostly surrounds the discussions on eastern Europe and whether Roosevelt agreed to sanction Soviet domination of the region, most controversially Poland.

From the point of view of those there, this issue was but one of many that were faced. To begin with, the fate of Germany dominated the discussions. There were some disagreements about whether it should be stated clearly that Germany was to be "dismembered" and the amount and type of reparations that should be paid to the Soviet Union. Leahy felt the Soviets were being a little too grasping but did nothing to reduce their demands. He said when the discussions were over that "if those Krauts get even an inkling of what's in store for them, they won't stop fighting until they're all dead."[35] There was a definite difference of opinion as to whether France was to be given an occupation zone in Germany. The Soviets saw no reason to treat the French as a Great Power and made it clear that if the French were given a part of Germany to occupy, it would come out of the British and American zones. Churchill and Roosevelt, however, wanted to rehabilitate the French and argued for their inclusion. Leahy had some sympathy for the Russian position and joked that he would be more than happy to give the French the entire American zone.[36] Though an attempt at humor, it revealed his hope that the United States would not be transformed into the world's policeman at the end of the war. Leahy wanted American troops out of Europe.

There were also some differences of opinion about the United Nations, which Leahy knew mattered a great deal to Roosevelt, but about which he believed Stalin and Churchill were still far less enthusiastic. For Leahy, the decisive agreement was the confirmation that the Great Powers would have a veto on what became the UN's Security Council. He was surprisingly depressed at this, revealing how Roosevelt had shaped his outlook. The admiral was convinced that if the Great Powers had vetoes, it would make the UN too weak.[37] On the other hand, Leahy also felt that the Soviets were more helpful on China than they needed to be. They promised to support the Nationalist regime of Chiang Kai-shek after the war. Around this time, Leahy, for once, lost patience with the Nationalists and was overheard saying that, considering their ineffectiveness, the United States should cooperate more closely with the Soviet Union.[38] He was therefore pleased when Stalin promised to try to work with the Nationalists, telling Averell Harriman that "this makes the trip worthwhile."[39]

Yet, Leahy was also deeply troubled about two issues: Soviet participation in the war against Japan and the fate of Poland. Previously, Roosevelt had asked the Soviets to commit to joining the Pacific war once the Germans were defeated, and by this point the Soviets were happy to do so. They did not want to be left behind in what would be an easy victory with its consequent spoils. Leahy, however, now saw no reason to get the Soviets involved. He told the president, "The Japs are already licked. We don't have to land in Japan, we don't have to do anything more to them."[40]

Leahy was still confident that American air- and sea power had already decided the war in the Pacific without the need for an invasion of Japan. He had even won Roosevelt around to his way of thinking. On February 8, when the president outlined his vision of the Pacific war during a one-on-one meeting with Stalin, he told the Soviet leader that he "hoped that it would not be necessary actually to invade the Japanese islands and would do so only if absolutely necessary. The Japanese had 4,000,000 men in their army and he hoped by intensive bombing to be able to destroy Japan and its army and thus save American lives."[41]

If anything, Roosevelt's talk about the ability to end the war without an invasion alarmed Stalin, and the Soviets went to great lengths to assure the Americans that they could join the Pacific war within two months of Germany's surrender. As Roosevelt had been asking the Soviets to do this for years, and the US Army still seemed determined to get the Soviets to join, all he could do was accept the offer.[42] Leahy agreed, through the most gritted of teeth.

All these other issues were eventually overshadowed by the decisions over Poland. The Polish question first erupted on February 6 and lingered like a bad smell over the American delegation for the rest of the talks. The Soviets were in complete charge of Poland and were putting trusted Communists in control on the ground, leaving the Americans floundering about how to respond. The Soviets were imposing a new "Lublin" government made up of Polish Communists who would do what they were told. Stalin was also re-creating a new Poland far to the west of the 1939 border, keeping all the territory he had seized in his cynical deal with Hitler and giving the new state German lands in East

Prussia and Silesia in return. In doing so, they were disestablishing the old Polish government, which had fled after the Nazi attack in 1939, and which had been a loyal ally of the United Kingdom and United States during the war.

When faced with this new reality, Roosevelt quickly capitulated in all but one area. He told Stalin he "was not so concerned with frontiers" and "not so concerned on the question of the continuity of the government." In a particularly damaging slight to his erstwhile Polish allies, the president claimed that there "really hasn't been any Polish government since 1939."[43] He was trying to wow Stalin with reasonableness. In exchange for accepting the Soviets' rewriting of the Polish question, the president wanted one thing. He wanted the Lublin government enlarged to include some democratic elements.

To try to coax Stalin to compromise, the president deployed much of his remaining strength. He sent a private letter to the Soviet dictator pleading his case, claiming that if he did not, Roosevelt could suffer politically back home.[44] In the plenary sessions and in private he tried to convince Stalin of the need to expand the Polish government. However, even with the strong support of Winston Churchill, he achieved little. Stalin did agree to a statement that the Lublin government would be "broadened" to include some democratic elements. Yet there was nothing definite about this government, including any prewar Polish elements, and moreover the meaning of the word "democratic" was left vague.

Leahy knew that this agreement was a fig leaf for a clear US defeat, though it was one he was expecting, and as such he tried to have it both ways. In his diary he pulled no punches, saying that the Yalta agreements left the Soviet Union the "dominant power in Europe," which held out the prospect of future conflicts.[45] With more right-wing acquaintances, he went even further, supposedly railing against the US delegation at Yalta, made up of "pinkos and do-gooders" who were too willing to accept Soviet demands.[46] After seeing the final text on Poland, Leahy told Constantine Brown that he said to Roosevelt, "Why look here Mr. President! This damn thing is so elastic you can stretch it from here to the moon. The Bolshies can interpret it any way they want to."[47] An exhausted Roosevelt replied, "I know it Bill, but I'm too tired to fight any more."

Despite his exasperation, for the rest of his career Leahy publicly acted as an advocate of the Yalta agreements, warts and all.[48] This conflict of mind can be seen in his memoirs, when he edited his exchange with Roosevelt to make it far more benign: "Mr. President, this is so elastic that the Russians can stretch it all the way from Yalta to Washington without technically breaking it." The president replied, "I know, Bill—I know it, but it's the best I can do for Poland at this time."[49]* Leahy argued that the United States needed to stand by what it had signed and believed those who wanted to repudiate Yalta were being needlessly aggressive.

When Leahy left the Crimea on February 12, he was more exhausted and conflicted than at the end of any of the other grand strategic conferences. Things did not improve during the car trip back over the mountains to the airfield. His car filled up with gasoline fumes, so it was decided to rip out the windows and proceed completely unprotected along what Leahy considered both the most beautiful and most dangerous roads he had ever traveled. When he arrived at the presidential plane, Leahy told Roosevelt the trip was like riding in a "recently emptied gasoline drum."[50]

Leahy and Roosevelt were not, however, heading directly to Washington. An interlude had been arranged in the Mediterranean that represented an important moment in reinforcing Leahy's perception of US policy toward the Middle East. After leaving the Crimea, the president's plane flew to Egypt, where Roosevelt and Leahy reboarded the *Quincy*. Over the next few days the president would meet with some of the key leaders in the region, including Prince Farouk of Egypt, the Ethiopian emperor Haile Selassie, and the Saudi ruler King Abdulaziz Al Saud, better known as Ibn Saud. Once again Leahy was in control of events in Roosevelt's professional life and gave such preemptory orders to the State Department that Stettinius, for one, was shocked.[51]

The talks with Ibn Saud marked the moment when Middle Eastern politics became a major issue for Leahy. The most difficult question was

---

* The recollection to Brown is probably the more accurate. In his memoirs, Leahy was still trying to maintain the fiction that Roosevelt was operating as normal, and he would have wanted to edit out any mention of the president being "too tired."

whether the United States was going to support the immigration into Palestine of the remnant of Europe's Jewish population that had survived the Holocaust. It was not until February 1944 that Leahy first mentioned the possibility of the Holocaust in his diary. He had a meeting with John Pehle, assistant secretary of the treasury and later head of the US government's War Refugee Board, who had been sent by Morgenthau to brief him about attempts to rescue Jews "from their present predicament in Germany and German-Occupied Europe."[52] On July 8, 1944, Leahy met once again with Pehle, who told him that German agents in Cairo had offered to swap Germans in their custody (Leahy did not write "Jews") in exchange for American supplies of trucks and food. Pehle also said that there were reports that the Germans were systematically killing the Jews of Hungary by the "thousands."[53]

Leahy was strongly opposed to using the Holocaust to change the situation in the Middle East. In this, he was far more pessimistic than Franklin Roosevelt, who went into the meeting with Ibn Saud hopeful that a solution to the problem of Jewish immigration could be found. Roosevelt's talks with Ibn Saud were some of the more colorful of his presidency. The Arab ruler was making his first trip ever outside of his own country. He brought along forty-eight retainers and had to be transported on a US destroyer, USS *Murphy*, through the Suez Canal to meet with Roosevelt. The Arab delegation was particularly puzzled by the African American mess boys they met on the ship, assuming they too were Arab and becoming confused when they could not converse in their supposed native tongue.[54]

The president did his best to ingratiate himself with his guest. The chain-smoking Roosevelt refused to smoke in front of the fundamentalist Arab chief. Instead, after a round of talks he would be wheeled into the ship's elevator and the car stopped between floors so that he could smoke in peace. Roosevelt was hoping he could charm Ibn Saud into approving the emigration of more European Jews into Palestine, but the Saudi king, with all courtesy, refused to bend.[55] When the president asked Ibn Saud what should happen to Europe's Jewish population after the war, the Arab ruler replied promptly, "Give them and their descendants the choicest lands and homes of the Germans who had oppressed them."[56] Leahy's sympathies were with Ibn Saud.[57] He described the Saudi king as behaving with "great dignity and courtesy" and, unlike many others in Washington, was convinced that Arabs would wage war for decades if Jewish immigration into Palestine was encouraged.[58]

After these talks, the presidential party headed back in the *Quincy* to the United States. It was a journey of sadness. As the American delegation was leaving Yalta, Pa Watson suffered a massive stroke. The president's longtime, much-loved aide was brought aboard the *Quincy*, where he lingered, incapacitated, before dying a few days later.[59] Something inside Roosevelt gave up at that moment. For the return journey he did little but sit on deck, smoking silently, staring out at the immensity of the ocean.

When the American delegation returned to Washington, Roosevelt showed no improvement. Over the few days, he and Leahy had their regular meetings and Leahy attended the Roosevelts' fortieth wedding anniversary dinner on March 17, one of only eighteen guests invited.[60] Yet for most of the final six weeks of his life, Roosevelt did little.[61] At the rare moments when he said something of substance, he took positions close to Leahy's, including on the atom bomb. One of his last acts as president was to hand Stimson in March 1945 a memorandum that argued that the bomb would prove to be a great waste of money.[62] The admiral would have been proud.

After the anniversary dinner, Roosevelt left for a week in Hyde Park, and when that didn't help him feel any better, he decided to head down to Warm Springs, Georgia, for another three-week break. It was while the president passed through Washington on March 29 that the two old friends spoke their final words. Leahy joked with Roosevelt, saying that he could get more work done when the president was away. Roosevelt managed a little humor in response while at the same time acknowledging Leahy's special role in his life: "That's all right, Bill. Have a good time while I'm gone because when I come back I'm going to unload a lot of stuff on you and then you'll have to work very hard."[63] He was then wheeled away.

On April 12, Roosevelt died.

Leahy heard about the president's death from the radio as he was relaxing at home after work.[64] He hurried back to the White House to see what he could do, arriving not long after Harry Truman. When Leahy appeared, he was allowed upstairs to grieve with Eleanor Roosevelt.[65]* It was the start of three of the most difficult days of Leahy's life, certainly the worst since Louise's death. He had to bring the new president up to speed on the state of the war, about which Truman was shockingly uninformed, while at the same time mourning the loss of his friend. When Roosevelt's body reached Union Station on the morning of April 14, Leahy was there, and he accompanied the coffin and the Roosevelt family during the solemn procession along Pennsylvania Avenue back to the White House. The body was carried in a caisson that had been covered in black cloth and was borne along by six white horses and a select honor guard. They passed surging crowds numbering in the hundreds of thousands, many sobbing and some hysterical. Then, silence reigned. Only those considered particularly close to Roosevelt were allowed to watch as the body was brought through the doors of the White House and laid in state in the grand East Room, which had been bedecked in floral tributes from the very grand to the simple. The flowers covered every open space, reaching up almost to the ceiling. There followed a dignified late-afternoon funeral, conducted in the Episcopalian rite, open to two hundred people, including leading foreign representatives, Leahy, and the Roosevelt family.

Leahy had to greet many of the dignitaries as they arrived, including the British foreign secretary, Anthony Eden, and most incongruously Princess Martha, who represented Norway. Harry Hopkins also flew in from the Mayo Clinic, where he was under intensive care, adding an even more somber note to the proceedings. Hopkins looked like he might not survive the day. At ten that evening, Roosevelt's body left the White House for the last time, heading back to Union Station for the train trip to its final resting place in Hyde Park. There, the following morning, the body was interred in the rose garden of the Roosevelt

---

* Leahy and Henry Morgenthau were the only non-family members allowed to mourn with the First Lady that night, as they were considered particularly close to the president.

family home as planes flew over paying their respects and the mourners sang "Now the Laborer's Task Is Done."

By the end of the funeral Leahy, who had been living on adrenaline for three days, was on the verge of a nervous breakdown. Not long after boarding the special government train, which had been sent to take VIPs back to Washington, Leahy was joined in his carriage by Secretary of Labor Frances Perkins, the first woman ever to serve in a US cabinet, and someone who had also known Roosevelt for decades. Leahy went to pieces, as Perkins later recalled:

> I had a long talk with Admiral Leahy on the way down. I've known him pretty well. He was very, very sad and very depressed, and he said to me this, which I've often thought of since: "This is the most terrible thing that could have happened from the point of view of the peace of the world, and I don't see the end yet." Then he said, "If only he could have been spared just one year more, I would have given anything. I think we might ride over a very serious problem. If he could have been spared even six months—eight months—but a year . . . If we could have had a year, many things that are going to trouble us I think would not have troubled us."

Leahy continued unburdening himself to Perkins. He spoke of Yalta, how Roosevelt had tried to work with Stalin, going out of his way "to make friends with people who were not ordinarily conceived of as too friendly." He marveled at the president's ability to lift others "above the level of their ordinary attitudes, so that in a kind of atmosphere of happiness and good will, they had perhaps gone further than they knew." With Roosevelt gone, Leahy worried that the whole system he had constructed might fall apart. He looked at Perkins with terrible sadness written across his face and said all might have been well if Roosevelt could have lived a little longer, even only "one year more."[66]

Leahy, not surprisingly, never admitted to such weakness. In his diary there is no mention of his talk with Perkins, just an admission that he experienced "sad memories" on the train.[67] Perkins's description of Leahy's reactions seems the more accurate. Roosevelt's death would have been less of a surprise to Leahy than almost anyone else. Even though he knew Roosevelt was a very sick man, he was overwhelmed on both a personal and political level. He had lost a close friend, someone he'd spent more time with than any other over the previous three years, someone who had nurtured and pushed his career to unparalleled heights, and—though he might have struggled to use the word himself—someone he loved. The emotional tribute Leahy penned for Roosevelt in his diary was longer than that which he wrote for Louise, and in some ways even more maudlin.

This world tragedy deprives the Nation of its leader at a time when the war to preserve civilization is approaching its end with accelerated speed, and when a vital need for the competent leadership in the making and preservation of world peace is at least seriously prejudiced by the passing of Franklin Roosevelt who was a world figure of heroic proportions. His death is also a personal bereavement to me in the loss of a devoted friend whom I have known and admired for thirty-six years,* since we first worked together in the First World War....

The Captain of the Team is gone.[68]

---

* Leahy was so distraught that he got the years wrong. He first met Roosevelt in 1913 in the Navy Department, so their friendship started thirty-two years earlier, not thirty-six, as he wrote in his diary.

CHAPTER 24

Truman

During the afternoon of April 12, 1945, Vice President Harry Truman was going about his business in the Capitol Building. After presiding over the Senate, he ambled over to the House of Representatives to shoot the breeze with the Speaker, Sam Rayburn. A senator from 1935 to 1945, Truman was at home in the halls of Congress. He was a practical, politically sensitive man, skilled at cutting deals. He also liked people, chatting with them, drinking with them, singing with them, and most of all playing poker with them.

When he reached the Speaker's office, Rayburn unexpectedly told Truman that he had Stephen Early, the White House press secretary, on the line. He handed the phone over and Truman was told, "Please come right over . . . and come through the main Pennsylvania Avenue entrance."[1] Truman had no idea of the enormity of what he was about to learn. Roosevelt rarely summoned his vice president for meetings and had never shared confidences with him. Now Truman was being called in at short notice for what he thought was a private tête-à-tête. He was so excited that he practically ran to the government-chauffeured car that was always waiting for him, moving so quickly that he left his Secret Service escort behind.

Once he arrived at the White House, he sensed that things were different. He was directed to the elevator and sent up to the second floor, where the Roosevelts had their private quarters. There he was shown to the First Lady's study, where Eleanor Roosevelt, dignified as always, was waiting. When he walked through the door, she moved closer to him, placed her arms gently around his shoulders, and said quietly: "Harry, the President is dead."

Truman did not understand what he was being told. He looked at Eleanor and offered his condolences. "Is there anything that I can do for you?" She replied perfectly, "Is there anything we can do for you. For you are the one in trouble now."[2] Realizing his predicament, tears welled up in Truman's eyes. They both stood there for a few minutes, silent, unsure of what to do next.

World War II would stop for no one. Truman had reached the White House around five thirty p.m. An hour and a half later, all the cabinet members who were in Washington, plus Speaker Rayburn and Supreme Court chief justice Harlan Stone, had assembled with him. Truman had also sent cars to collect his wife, Bess, and their teenage daughter, Margaret. This large group decamped to the Cabinet Room, crowding into the relatively small space dominated by its large oval table surrounded by heavy leather chairs. There was a brief flurry of activity when it was realized that no one had a Bible, so the White House was scoured until one was found. Finally, confident of God's blessing, the most important ceremony in the United States commenced. At 7:09 p.m., Justice Stone administered the oath of office to Truman, who stood terrier-like, muscles taut, staring straight ahead, his eyes prominently framed by his favored large oval glasses.[3] Now the thirty-second president of the United States of America, Truman bent down and kissed the Bible. Soon all his energy drained away and, exhausted, he made excuses and went to bed.

While Truman was being sworn in, Leahy hovered quietly in the background. Truman acknowledged Leahy's presence, but the two did not speak that night. It was not until the next day that they started to feel each other out. When Leahy showed up for the usual morning briefing, it was clear that the new president was very different from the old. As Roosevelt had become weaker, the start time for the morning briefings was pushed later and later, until, by the final weeks, the meetings could start as late as noon. The early-rising, energetic Truman, by contrast, was ready to go. Leahy, who had internalized Roosevelt's clock and was an emotional mess trying to cope with his friend's death, was unprepared at the scheduled start time. He had to frantically get things ready when summoned to meet with the president and was unusually flustered when he arrived at the Oval Office. Truman, on the other hand, was tense. Their first encounter was witnessed by Adm. Wilson Brown, Roosevelt's naval aide, who came in with Leahy.

> He [Truman] was alone in the presidential office, seated behind the large desk still covered with F.D.R.'s trinkets and gadgets—looking rather small in contrast to the larger figure of his predecessor. His expression of alert expectancy, so cleverly hit upon by some cartoonists, made me feel at once that he would note accurately all I had to say and how I said it. We moved up to his desk, and Leahy, standing as we had been brought up to do when making reports to seniors, and always did with F.D.R., began to give a general outline of what war problems the Joint Staff were working on. The President interrupted at once, "For God's sake sit down! You make me nervous! Come around here in the light where I can get a good look at you." And when we had pulled up chairs he examined each one of us in turn, just as some doctors do, without the least trace of self-consciousness about the fact that we were also examining him.[4]

The briefing itself was routine. At eleven a.m., however, the president had to steel himself for something more intimidating—the first meeting of his strategic leadership team. The Joint Chiefs along with Stimson and Forrestal were escorted into Truman's office to provide the president with an overview of the war. As he sat surrounded by figures who had reached almost mythical status during the last three years, Truman lost confidence. After relatively short briefings by his chiefs, the president forced the pace, trying to end the meeting as quickly as possible. He babbled, telling the chiefs what a splendid job they were doing and how he would be happy if things carried on exactly as they had under Roosevelt. He then adjourned the meeting, and everyone filed out.

Leahy lingered. The two needed to discuss how, or even whether, Truman wanted him to continue in office. The admiral was in emotional turmoil. Reflexively, he started talking about Roosevelt, how much FDR had meant to him and how depressed he was at his death.[5] It made an enormous impression on the new president. He saw Leahy as a man who loved Roosevelt and served him with devotion, and who was willing to resign immediately so that Truman could appoint someone whom he trusted. Truman decided on the spot that he wanted Leahy to stay, at least until the war was over. He would later recount in his memoirs:

> Leahy had occupied a unique position in the White House under President Roosevelt. He was a man of wide experience and was well known for his directness of expression and independence of judgement. Direct in his manner and blunt expression, he typified the Navy at its best, and Roosevelt had appointed him to act in a highly confidential role as chief of staff to the Commander in Chief. Prior to World War II there had been no such position in our government, but in Leahy's hands it soon proved to be immensely useful.

When Truman asked Leahy to stay on, the admiral replied, "Are you sure you want me, Mr. President? I always say what's on my mind." Truman said that was exactly what he wanted, as long as Leahy understood that if the president did not take his advice, he would be expected to follow orders to the letter. Leahy, with a twinkle in his eye, told Truman, "You have my pledge. You can count on me."[6]

Though Truman and Leahy agreed things would operate as they had before, that was impossible. A friendship of thirty-two years could not be replicated in a few days or even years. Leahy also had to get over his initial doubts about Truman's fitness for office; before he became president, Truman had appeared to Leahy as a second-rater. Their first significant interaction was in 1939, when Truman called Leahy and, in the act of a bush-league politician, tried to wheedle a promotion for a friend in the naval reserve.[7] When Roosevelt chose Truman to be his vice president in 1944, Leahy was underwhelmed, saying he had no significant "international experience."[8] Truman also did not initially distinguish himself in Leahy's eyes by bringing some ineffectual old-time cronies into the White House.[9]

Leahy's opinion about Truman's lack of international experience is one with which the new president would have heartily agreed. That being said, Truman was better prepared to be president than it is sometimes claimed. His career had shown that behind the friendly exterior lurked a man of great ambition and drive. He was born in 1884 with nothing close to a silver spoon in his mouth. The son of a Missouri farmer, Truman spent his youth similarly to Leahy. The family, not wealthy, moved a few times as the father tried to establish himself in different towns. Truman was educated in different public schools in the Kansas City area, distinguishing himself in none. He wanted to attend West Point or Annapolis but could not get an appointment to either. He compensated by joining the Missouri National Guard in 1911. He thrived as an artilleryman, and this led to a profound difference from Leahy and Roosevelt. Truman was an army man to his bones and had a distinguished World War I record. Sent to France not too long after the US entry in the war, Truman was made captain of the 129th Artillery and saw action in some of the most famous American battles on the western front. After the war, he remained in the reserves, eventually rising to the rank of colonel.

It was when he returned from the war that he entered politics. When a small men's department store that he co-owned went bankrupt, Truman, who had no college education, ran for the position of judge in Jackson County, just outside of Kansas City. He won, though this opened up one of the more controversial aspects of his political career. He received strong support from the powerful Democratic Party boss in Kansas City, the famously corrupt Thomas Pendergast.[10] Pendergast's organization fixed elections, took and gave bribes, and used violence to get its way, and now Truman was viewed as part of its machine. Pendergast lived like a king, dominating Kansas City until he was finally jailed in 1939 for tax evasion. The boss was directly responsible for the event that catapulted Truman onto the national stage, his election to the US Senate in 1934.

Truman's time in the Senate showed how he could evolve. Derisively known as the senator from Pendergast when first elected, he seemed a typical hack. With Pendergast's fall and the coming of the war, however, Truman became a political force in his own right. During the war he became famous as chairman of the Truman Committee, a special Senate body established to investigate fraud and inefficiency in war production. He showed steely resolve and political savvy, gaining national notoriety.

When Roosevelt tapped him on the shoulder, however, it was not because he saw Truman as someone who could run the US government with him. He saw an effective politician who could help him be re-elected by appealing to more centrist Southern and Midwestern Democrats and someone who would do what he was told. Roosevelt did not have to worry about Truman trying to be a co-president, a major concern with James Byrnes. Once elected, Roosevelt saw Truman rarely and did not involve him in high policy discussions. Leahy followed Roosevelt's lead and kept the new vice president at arm's length.

The distance between Leahy and Truman would have to be rectified quickly. The first four months of the Truman presidency saw the surrender of Germany, the Potsdam Conference, the debate over whether to invade or drop the atom bomb on Japan, and the eventual Japanese capitulation. There were also relationships to establish and foreign leaders to meet. To some members of the White House staff, it was fascinating how Leahy quickly built a powerful role in the new administration. For instance, Leahy was immediately allowed to continue doing one of his most sensitive jobs, the drafting of confidential telegrams to Churchill and Stalin.[11] He also was willing to control the information he sent to the new president, if it suited his policy purposes. A few weeks after Truman took over, Leahy sat on a request from Churchill to Truman for aid to help the British stabilize the situation in Syria, an area out of which Leahy was desperate to keep America, claiming it was "a damned British plot, I'll have no part of it."[12] When Leahy eventually did bring the message to Truman, he persuaded the president to take the position he wanted.

George Elsey described Leahy metamorphosing rapidly into a Harry Hopkins–like figure for the new president. He noticed how Truman kept Leahy close at hand to discuss important international and strategic questions.[13] For those who first came to the White House with Truman, the process was even more surprising. Truman's administrative staff at first did not know who Leahy was, even leaving him off the list of those people who were given a copy of the president's daily schedule.[14] That mistake was quickly rectified. Matthew Connelly started working with Truman as a Senate staffer in 1941; in 1945, he moved with Truman to the vice president's office, and when Truman became president, Connelly went with him to the White House as the president's appointment secretary. Having no previous experience of Leahy, he was impressed by how quickly the admiral built up a powerful position through the control of the most confidential information.

> Leahy was a very capable naval officer. He was also a very intelligent fellow and he had been there under Roosevelt...[H]e had two offices, one in the White House and one in the Pentagon. He would report to the President on military and military secret problems, which I had nothing to do with and wanted nothing to do with because if there was any leak, I would not have a finger point to me. So all top secret information regarding military matters was brought to the President every morning after the staff meeting by Admiral Leahy.[15]

Truman impressed Leahy from the beginning far more than expected. The morning briefings between the two continued punctually and even more frequently than they had with Roosevelt, for the simple reason that Truman was healthy and did not spend so many weeks away from the White House. Moreover, the new president was a hard worker and made sure to read all the confidential material Leahy prepared for him. Roosevelt, in the last few years, avoided immersing himself in policy details.

Their personal interactions also went smoothly, even if there were noticeable differences from the Roosevelt years. Truman and Leahy were far more formal. Truman never called Leahy "Bill," preferring to address him as "Admiral." He eventually started bringing Leahy with him on holidays and having him around for evening dinners or poker games, but at first their relationship was professional, not social.

This highlighted the great policy change that happened from the moment Truman became president. In the last two years of Roosevelt's life, Leahy's position was unique for being both bureaucratically central to the making of policy and a close personal friend. Under Truman, Leahy's special position was diminished, and he moved from being *primus inter pares* to one of a handful of influential policy makers. There were other important rivals for Truman's favor, and Leahy for the first time in years found himself losing important policy fights.

Perhaps most notable was the increase in influence of Byrnes and Marshall. Truman had come to know James Byrnes in the Senate and had a slight inferiority complex toward the South Carolinian. He knew that many Democrats believed Byrnes would have been the better choice for vice president and was determined to keep him happy. From the moment he became president, Truman made Byrnes a trusted adviser, naming him the presidential representative on the Interim Committee, which debated the use of the atomic bomb. When Secretary of State Stettinius resigned because of ill health in June 1945, Truman quickly appointed Byrnes as his replacement.

George Marshall, likewise, was listened to with far greater seriousness. Truman, the army man, practically worshipped the general. Where Roosevelt felt uncomfortable around Marshall and often overruled him, Truman was far more solicitous. After the war, he gave him three of the most important positions he could think of: special emissary to China, secretary of state, and then secretary of defense.

Finally, other people in the administration, such as Henry Stimson, who seemed to hold important posts but whom Roosevelt had marginalized or ignored, were, at first, treated as serious policy makers by the new president. They started showing up far more at White House meetings, and their outlooks were taken into consideration as decisions were reached.

Leahy was no longer top dog, just one of many big ones.

Both the continuities and differences in Leahy's positions can be seen in policy choices made as the war against the Germans and Japanese moved to their gory endings. If there was one area where Leahy retained a great deal of authority, it was in helping shape Truman's reactions toward America's European allies, the Soviet Union, the United Kingdom, and France. One of the issues that the two men had to work on immediately was the future of US-Soviet relations. A few days after Roosevelt's death, President Truman called a meeting of his war cabinet to discuss the Polish situation. Truman believed that the Soviet Union was breaking the Yalta agreements, and in this he was supported by James Forrestal. Stimson and Marshall, on the other hand, as they were never included in Roosevelt's inner circle, admitted that they had little idea of what had been specifically meant by the Yalta agreements. It was left to Leahy to step up and explain to the group the reality of Yalta. He wanted the government to walk a fine line—saying that they expected the Russians to take some steps to honor their pledge at Yalta to broaden the Lublin government with democratic elements, but at the same time to understand that the Soviets were going to control Poland for now and the Americans were going to have to accept that.[16]

Two weeks later the redoubtable and brutal Soviet foreign secretary, Vyacheslav Molotov, arrived in Washington to meet with the new president. Leahy knew Molotov as a shrewd negotiator and believed that he was even more of a hard-liner than Stalin. The new president asked the admiral to hold his hand during both the preparations to meet with Molotov and the meeting itself. The main issue for discussion was, inevitably, Poland.[17]

When Molotov was shown into Truman's office, the president laid out the policy that Leahy had prepared for him. Leahy was there, standing behind the president, offering constant support. For Molotov, it was disconcerting. He had been used to the wily charms of Franklin Roosevelt, and now he was faced by the directness of Middle America. Truman told Molotov, in undiplomatic language, that the US government believed that the Soviets were violating the Yalta accords over Poland and wanted them to do something to broaden the base of the Lublin government.[18] Molotov, according to the president, was shocked, saying, "I have never been talked to like that in my life." The president snapped back, "Carry out your agreements and you won't get talked to like that."[19] No matter how much Leahy missed Franklin Roosevelt, he loved Truman's directness—even if he still understood that Poland would not be free anytime soon.

> The President's attitude was more than pleasing to me, and I believe it will have a beneficial effect on the Soviet attitude toward the rest of the world. They have always known that we have the power, and now they should know that we have the determination to insist upon the declared right of all people to choose their own form of government.
>
> I personally do not believe it is possible to exclude dominant Soviet influence from Poland but that it is possible to give to the government of Poland an external appearance of independence.[20]

Truman was also willing to defer to Leahy when it came to many questions of Anglo-American and Franco-American relations. As the new president came to office Nazi Germany was on the verge of surrender. A week after the meeting with Molotov, Adolf Hitler shot himself in the ruins of Berlin. The next few days were dominated by the planning for the inevitable German surrender. Leahy shuttled back and forth between the Oval Office, the Map Room, and his own office, checking up on news and keeping the president up-to-date on the latest developments. Everything came together on May 7—the day after Leahy's seventieth birthday—which Leahy termed a "day not to be forgotten."[21] It began at 1:20 a.m., when Leahy was first informed from the War Department that General Eisenhower had cabled to say that the German high command had signed the surrender terms, which meant that the Wehrmacht was to stop all combat on May 8. He rushed to inform Truman, and then cabled Stalin and Churchill. Stalin, however, refused to respond. Truman did not want to formally announce the end of the war until the Soviet leadership had acknowledged the impending surrender. Events started spiraling out of control when the news was broadcast on German radio and crowds in London started celebrating wildly.

Leahy had to rush to the Pentagon, where there was the most

secure telephone line in the world. For the next few hours he was in constant contact with Churchill, the two engaging in an increasingly tense exchange about whether the surrender could be announced. Leahy kept saying that the American position was that they needed to wait until "Uncle Joe" acknowledged the surrender, while Churchill was desperate to formally acknowledge what the crowds outside his office were already celebrating. Only at 4:20 p.m. Washington time, when Moscow radio announced that the Soviets had formally accepted the German surrender, could the official announcement be sent out.

At the moment of victory, Leahy felt deflated. His thoughts turned to Franklin Roosevelt; he wanted only to be able to share this moment with the man he believed had done more than anyone else to make it happen. His melancholy was amplified when he received a sweet handwritten letter from Eleanor Roosevelt saying how much Franklin would have wanted to be alive to witness this moment with him.[22] As he looked upon the crowds in Washington, which were cheering, screaming, kissing, and exploding with sound and release, Leahy felt alienation.[23]

Leahy was also at the center of Franco-American relations during the first few months of the Truman administration, though not always in ways he liked. One moment, which exposed him to public comment, was his peculiar interjection into the trial of the disgraced French marshal Philippe Pétain. After Leahy had left Vichy in 1942, Marshal Pétain played an objectionable and pathetic role for the remainder of the war. Mostly a figurehead, he remained the face of an increasingly brutal regime. After D-Day he was forced to move to Germany, returning to France only in April 1945, when he was promptly arrested and put on trial for treason.

Leahy thought this trial vindictive and unnecessary. He certainly did not condone Pétain's behavior but also thought it pointless and dishonorable to threaten the eighty-nine-year-old with execution. The marshal wrote to Leahy asking him to come to France to testify on his behalf. Leahy was never going to do that, and instead chose to release a public letter. What Leahy wrote was portrayed by many as a defense of the old marshal. It was not. Actually, Leahy was very critical of Pétain, even if he did believe the marshal was motivated by a desire to protect the French people.

During that period [January 1941–April 1942] you did on occasion, at my request, take action that was in opposition to the desires of the Axis and favorable to the Allied cause. . . .

However, I must, in all honesty, repeat my opinion expressed to you at the time that positive refusal to make concessions to Axis demands, while it might have brought immediately increased hardships to your people, it would, in the long view, have been advantageous to France.[24]

What seemed to bother Leahy most in this matter, and others, was the whole idea of victor's justice. When it came to trying both the German and Japanese leadership, a group of men who had condoned horrible atrocities, Leahy believed that their guilt should not lead the Allies to take steps that would dishonor the Allied victory. In particular, he believed that the charge of waging aggressive war should not be a crime, as it would be used in the future to execute the leadership of any losing side.[25]

Leahy saw the Gaullists acting in an even more extreme fashion, as they had not even won the war but were nevertheless taking a victor's justice. One of the reasons Leahy started trusting Truman more at this time was that he was able to convince the new president to take a hard line with de Gaulle. After the surrender of Germany, de Gaulle refused to order French troops, which had been fighting on the Franco-Italian border, to withdraw into France.[26] It seemed to Leahy that the Gaullists were planning to annex these Italian border territories. Leahy also had been given reports that French forces had threatened to take "forcible action" against American troops in the area that were trying to prevent such a takeover. It was just one more example of why he detested de Gaulle, and he stoked Truman's anger.[27] Leahy recorded in his diary:

When I reported the incident to him [Truman] he said quickly, "The French are using our guns, are they not?"

I replied, "Yes, sir."

He then said, "All right, we will at once stop shipping guns, ammunition and equipment to de Gaulle.[28]

For Leahy, it represented a rare victory over de Gaulle, as reports soon came in that the president's threat had led to the French backing down—or, as Leahy termed it, de Gaulle "had begun to show signs of coming to his senses."

While the end of the war in Europe showed how much influence Leahy maintained, the debates over how the war in the Pacific should end revealed how significantly the policy-making environment had changed against him. There were two linked questions to be faced once Truman became president: whether the United States should plan on invading the main Japanese islands, and whether, if it proved operable, the United States should use the atomic bomb.

The change from Roosevelt to Truman altered the terms of debate for both questions. While Roosevelt was increasingly reluctant to discuss or even contemplate the usage of atomic weaponry, Harry Truman was excited, one might say entranced, by its possibilities. The overwhelming power of the bomb made a great impression on Truman, sometimes energizing him. The bomb's power also appealed to him strategically on a greater level than it did to Roosevelt. Truman voiced few doubts about using it and seemed almost giddy when it worked.

Truman's more positive vision of the atomic bomb made Leahy's job of trying to persuade the president not to use it practically impossible—though he did try. Leahy was one of only two people in the room when Truman was given his first detailed briefing about the atomic bomb, the other being Vannevar Bush, the director of the US Government's Office of Scientific Research and Development.* After the president had been let in on the biggest secret in the world, Leahy started in immediately with his negativity, once again mixing up his hopes with his expectations: "This is the biggest fool thing we have ever done . . . The bomb will never go off and I speak as an expert on explosives."[29]

It was the first of many examples of Leahy trying to sour Truman on the bomb. Yet it quickly became apparent that there were many

---

* Truman was told that the United States was developing "the greatest project in the history of the world" by Stimson a few hours before this meeting but given no details about the atomic bomb. It was only when the new president sat down with Bush and Leahy that he was given a full briefing.

more advisers in Truman's court, such as Byrnes and Marshall, who favored using the bomb. It was extremely important, then, that when Truman set up the Interim Committee in May 1945 to discuss what to do with the bomb, he made Stimson the chairman and Byrnes his personal representative.[30] Leahy was not a member, a decision that would have been inconceivable had Roosevelt been alive.

The Interim Committee, under Stimson's weak chairmanship, moved inevitably to support the use of the atomic bomb against Japan, if it was shown to be workable. By the June 1 meeting, at which George Marshall was a special invitee, Byrnes felt confident enough to claim that the committee supported the idea "that the bomb should be used against Japan as soon as possible, that it be used on a war plant surrounded by workers' homes; and that it be used without prior warning."[31] Had Leahy been at the meeting he would have fought against each of those statements. He did not want the bomb to be dropped, but he would have been particularly appalled by the wide basis of support for using it without warning on a civilian target. He had pressed Byrnes personally on these points, but from outside the committee structure. When Byrnes and Leahy first met on May 20 to discuss the atom bomb, Leahy was his normal skeptical self.[32] However, Byrnes was more than happy to override the admiral, and they did not discuss the issue again until June 4, when Byrnes stopped by Leahy's house to let him know the state of play.[33] Once again Leahy attacked the whole concept of using the bomb, while Byrnes defended it. Not being on the committee, there was little Leahy could do.

Leahy may have been on the outside looking in for much of the work being done on atomic weapons, but this was not the case when it came to the invasion of Japan. Leahy remained convinced that his strategic vision of not invading Japan was still ethically and politically the best way forward. If anything, his conviction on this point had strengthened. If he didn't want to spend many American resources occupying Japan, then he certainly didn't want to spend much American blood invading it. Leahy worked methodically to try to undermine the case for any invasion, starting with that of the southern island of Kyushu. When meeting with Marshall and King during Yalta, Leahy made it clear that he wanted the army to undertake only operations in the Pacific that were necessary to win the war, and which were based on limiting American casualties as much as possible.[34] During the next few months, as the United States attacked Iwo Jima and Okinawa, Leahy was appalled at the mounting American casualty toll. On both islands the Japanese changed tactics to fight grinding, attritional, defensive battles. Earlier in the war, Japanese defenders showed a mixture of extreme bravery and foolishness, often launching attacks against their American enemies that led to them being slaughtered in large numbers. By 1945, the Japanese were done with that and now dug themselves deep into caves and prepared defensive positions, forcing the American marines and soldiers to come to them. This exacted a terrifying toll. At Iwo Jima, which the United States attacked in February, American casualties, for the first time in the war, exceeded those of the Japanese.* Okinawa, which was attacked in April, ended up being the bloodiest battle the Americans would fight in the entire war. Almost 50,000 Americans were made casualties on this small island, more than 12,000 of whom died. Leahy paid close attention to American losses in both campaigns and could see any invasion of Japan turning into a super-Okinawa, littered with American corpses.

Leahy considered the saving of lives as one of the guiding principles of his strategic decisions and believed all other commanders should think likewise.[35] To him, the army seemed bizarrely bent on unnecessary human destruction. Marshall by mid-1944 seemed to accept that the United States would have to invade the Japanese heartland.[36] He started refocusing the US Army on that task as the war against the Germans wound down, and, more troublingly, began to willfully put as optimistic a spin as possible on the costs of any such invasion. MacArthur started pushing for an invasion long before the fighting on the Philippines was over. In April 1945, he pressed for an invasion of Kyushu, which he naturally would lead, as a preliminary to the main assault on Honshu.[37] It was part of a regular army argument that Kyushu would not be well defended, whereas not to invade would prolong the war

---

* In the battle for Iwo Jima almost 7,000 Americans were killed and approximately 20,000 were wounded. The Japanese garrison of approximately 20,000 was wiped out almost entirely.

"indefinitely." With the Soviet Union about to get into the war against Japan, MacArthur argued, this might not be in America's interest.

The stage was therefore set for the most unequal fight Leahy would wage during the entirety of World War II. He was determined to stop both the atomic bomb from being dropped and Japan from being invaded. He was also bound to lose.

CHAPTER 25

The End of the War

At 3:30 in the afternoon of Monday, June 18, 1945, the grand strategic leadership team of the United States assembled in the White House to discuss death: the potential destruction of many tens of thousands of Americans and hundreds of thousands, if not millions, of Japanese.[1] President Truman called the meeting in response to a memorandum that William Leahy had written four days earlier.[2] As Leahy, Marshall, King, Stimson, Forrestal, Assistant Secretary of War John McCloy, and Gen. Ira Eaker (representing Hap Arnold, who had suffered another heart attack) filed into the Oval Office, they were preparing to discuss Operation Olympic, the plan to invade Kyushu, the southernmost of Japan's home islands.[3] There was a remarkable sense of unanimity amongst the participants. All but one strongly supported Olympic and pressed the president to approve the operation. Leahy was the exception.

As everyone settled in, Truman took the chair, depriving Leahy of one of his previous positional advantages. The president began the discussion by turning to the greatest supporter of the Kyushu invasion, George Marshall. Marshall's performance during this meeting did him little credit. He began by arguing that Japan's situation was analogous to that of Germany before the Normandy invasion; in other words, there would still need to be an invasion before it was brought to its knees. In truth Japan was much closer to defeat. Marshall then plunged in with a drastically one-sided argument in favor of Olympic. When it came to expected American casualties, the crux of the argument, Marshall claimed that the best comparison was MacArthur's campaign in the Philippines, during which one American was lost for every five Japanese soldiers. This was a much more favorable ratio for the Americans than the costly battles of Iwo Jima and Okinawa, during which the ratios were given as 1.25 and 2 Japanese casualties to every American, respectively. Marshall provided no reason why the Philippines was a better model than Iwo Jima or Okinawa and refused to state exactly how many American casualties this 5-to-1 ratio would cause. It reflected a tendency that he had already shown to accept high US casualties in operations that he supported. King spoke next and sided with the general. Leahy, increasingly agitated with the optimistic spin of the other chiefs, snapped. He was convinced that any invasion would be much bloodier, and he wanted everyone in the room to face that reality. He "pointed out that the troops on Okinawa had lost 35 percent in casualties. If this percentage were applied to the number of troops to be employed in Kyushu, he thought from the similarity of the fighting to be expected that this would give a good estimate of the casualties to be expected. He was interested therefore in finding out how many troops are to be used in Kyushu."[4]

Marshall and King did their best to talk around Leahy's point. King replied that Kyushu would be easier to take than Okinawa because the larger island would offer significantly more room to maneuver, but then he admitted that the casualty rate on Kyushu would probably fall halfway between the Philippines and Okinawa. Marshall spoke next and had to admit that 766,000 Americans would be involved in the assault on Kyushu. He then went on to claim that Kyushu was being defended by only 350,000 Japanese troops, and that it would be almost impossible for this number to be increased. Both of these statements were soon proven false, and one can only hope that Marshall was simply a fool and not deliberately lying.[5]

Some have assumed that Leahy was arguing for a 35 percent expected casualty rate out of the 190,000 combat troops involved (with a casualty figure of 60,000).[6] This is on the very low side. Though he didn't offer a final casualty figure himself, Leahy had brought the discussion to the point that American casualties should not be seen as simply a percentage of American troops involved; they should be seen in light of the number of Japanese troops committed. In that case, he was imagining the possibility of 100,000 or more American casualties. This was clear to both Marshall and King, who, after Leahy spoke, continued to try to paint a rosy picture about any invasion, claiming that the Japanese would be unable to provide any reinforcement to their troops.

Leahy refused to back down. He brought up the fact that, far from being a large landmass that would allow for maneuverability, Kyushu was crisscrossed by high mountain ranges. This was an obvious attempt to make another parallel to Okinawa, the taking of which had been hindered by a series of steep ridges on the south of the island from which the Japanese had extracted their pound of flesh. At this point the rest of the participants, who had been silent while the chiefs clashed, all piled in to support the invasion, including Eaker, Stimson, and Forrestal. Being opposed by everyone else in the room still did not make Leahy back down. He made one final bid to thwart the invasion. What about, he proposed, modifying the "unconditional surrender" formula to make it possible for the Japanese to capitulate but save a little face or at least weaken their resistance and preserve American lives? It was Leahy at his straightforward best. According to the minutes:

> Admiral Leahy said that he could not agree with those who said to him that unless we obtain the unconditional surrender of the Japanese that we will have lost the war. He feared no menace from Japan in the foreseeable future, even if we were unsuccessful in forcing unconditional surrender. What he did fear was that our insistence on unconditional surrender would result only in making the Japanese desperate and thereby increase our casualty lists. He did not think this was at all necessary.[7]

Leahy's arguments failed to alter the course, however, and Truman gave the go-ahead to continue the planning of Olympic. Yet the admiral's undermining of Marshall's rosy casualty forecasts had dented Truman's confidence in the operation. The president spoke dejectedly afterward about how any invasion of Japan could turn into one giant Okinawa from the bottom of Kyushu to the top of Hokkaido.[8] And Leahy was not done fighting.[9] He used his daily access to Truman to lobby continually against the attack, hammering home the number of expected American casualties.[10] He brought to Truman's attention the increasing number of Japanese troops on Kyushu and the toll they could be expected to take. There were many more Japanese troops on Kyushu than Marshall had claimed, and the Japanese were still able to significantly augment this force. By the end of July, US signals intelligence reported that not only did the Japanese have at least half a million troops deployed on Kyushu, they were continuing to reinforce their armies with many more.[11] Intelligence also revealed that most Japanese troops were being deployed in southern Kyushu, precisely where the Americans were planning to land. They would have extracted a horrible toll. Eventually Truman started walking back his commitment to Olympic.[12]

In a sign of his determination to use all the levers of power at his disposal, Leahy told the other Joint Chiefs that he would approve the invasion on their behalf only if he had an explicit order from Truman to do so.[13] It was the most important sign of how his role as the senior member or chairman of the Joint Chiefs had evolved since he first appeared in 1942. By 1945, his signature is what made a Joint Chiefs of Staff order official. The other chiefs could issue orders only if Leahy was not available, and even when they did, Leahy could countermand them if he felt they were in error. Leahy was now threatening to use this power to stop any invasion. It was a power play, and one that might very well have worked if the atom bomb had not exploded. Truman hated giving explicit orders at this time, preferring delegation and consensual decision-making. Leahy was gambling, with real strength, that Truman would not order his chief of staff and the chairman of the Joint Chiefs of Staff to start an invasion over his stated objections.

The irony for Leahy was that the atomic bomb, the usage of which he opposed with the same conviction that he held against the invasion of Kyushu, ended up trumping his attempts to thwart Olympic. The first successful atomic test, in July, opened to Truman the prospect of avoiding a Japanese invasion and still achieving a quick victory. News of the test reached Truman and Leahy when they were in Potsdam, Germany, for the final grand strategic conference of the war. Fittingly code-named Terminal, the Potsdam Conference was Truman's first chance to meet with Stalin and involved discussion of both the postwar European settlement and the best way to bring the war against Japan to a close. Leahy, Truman, and Byrnes were the three dominant members of the US delegation.[14] It was Leahy who advised Truman in early May 1945 that he should meet with Stalin and Churchill as soon as possible to try to nip in the bud what seemed to him to be a deteriorating relationship.[15] The admiral was troubled by Stalin's lack of trust as the war in Europe ended. The Soviet dictator even convinced himself at one point that the United States and Great Britain were trying to arrange a separate peace with Nazi Germany. There was also the question of eastern Europe, a problem that was stretching far beyond Poland. Yugoslav forces, led by the Socialist Josip Broz Tito, who had been well supplied by the Allies during the war, had started expanding outside of their country as Nazi rule collapsed. They seemed set on annexing parts of northeastern Italy, including the city of Trieste. Leahy could see this spiraling into a direct East-West conflict.

As both Leahy and Byrnes had been at Yalta, they were the natural people to prepare Truman to meet with Stalin. The president told his wife, Bess, that he would have to "rely" upon them.[16] Amazingly, Harry Hopkins, who seemed close to death after Yalta, had improved enough that it was decided to send him to meet Stalin to prepare the way for the larger summit.[17] The admiral was, as ever, worried about Hopkins's health and ability to keep things orderly. He wanted to make sure that Harry did not "give away the store," and so, along with Marshall and King, briefed Hopkins on the state of play on May 23.[18]

When the White House party left for Potsdam on July 6, it seemed like a rerun of a well-rehearsed show. As with FDR, the president's inner circle boarded the presidential train at the special siding by the Bureau of Engraving and Printing. After reaching the great naval base at Norfolk, Virginia, they transferred to the cruiser USS *Augusta*, which had been used to take Roosevelt to the famous Nova Scotia Conference with Churchill in 1941. Leahy was given the cabin next to the president's and spent much of his time prepping Truman for the upcoming talks.

However much things felt the same, everything was different. The president demanded his breakfast at seven a.m., which Leahy found refreshing but which was less pleasing to other members of Truman's staff. Where Roosevelt spent much of his time relaxing on deck, enjoying the sea air, the new president gamboled around the ship like a tourist. He inspected the *Augusta* from stem to stern, walking and speaking in his snappy, fast-paced manner. He revealed a boyish fascination with the different technologies available on a modern warship, particularly those related to gunnery. He made sure to eat one meal in each of the different messes and spent a lot of time with the enlisted sailors. The president even changed the nighttime entertainment. While Roosevelt preferred a film in his room after his evening meal, the music-mad Truman added concerts to the mix, and during dinner ordered the *Augusta*'s band to play lustily. The president remembered these concerts warmly, Leahy less so.[19] "Truman's fondness for music was evidenced in the concerts we had at dinner every night," he later wrote. "I enjoyed them when I had nothing else to do, which wasn't very often."[20] In many ways, Germany being out of the war was a drawback to Leahy. "There was no danger of being shot at now, so the President could have all the music he wanted."

At least with the Germans out of the war, the *Augusta*, its lights ablaze, could sail straight for Europe, so the trip was relatively short. On July 15, the presidential party cruised into the port of Antwerp, where they transferred to a motor caravan, which drove through the Belgian countryside to Brussels. From his car window, Leahy saw few signs of war, just placid scenes of fat cows grazing in green fields, as if the world had always been at peace. In Brussels, the party shifted to the president's plane for a two-stage flight to Berlin. Things quickly changed. As the plane passed over Germany, Leahy looked down on scenes of devastation. Having been laid to waste by the Anglo-American strategic bombing campaign, German cities were burnt-out shells. Kassel, for one, did not seem to have a single undamaged building. When the party eventually landed in Berlin they found a city that looked wrecked beyond repair. Dead bodies floated in flooded underground stations. Masses of refugees poured into the city, while others fled outward. Hunger, depression, and ruin were everywhere. Throughout his long military career Leahy had never seen destruction on an industrial scale. Though he had been briefed on the plans to bomb German cities, he had always thought that the attacks, at least from the American air forces, were targeted at German industry and Germany's ability to wage war. What he now saw was a cataclysm. He blamed the Nazis.

> Germany which today is wrecked and enslaved had, before the Nazi regime, every prospect of a prosperous happy future in concert with the other civilized nations. Hitler's Nazi philosophy is the single cause of the disaster that has come upon the German people.[21]

Once in Berlin, the party made its way south to Potsdam, made famous as the home of the pleasure palaces of Frederick the Great. In the eighteenth and nineteenth centuries it had grown into a handsome city full of noble residences for the German aristocracy. The Soviets, living up to the reputation that they had established at Yalta, had in a short time returned some of the finest residences into the proper condition for a meeting of such importance. Truman, Leahy, and Byrnes were driven to a large house in Babelsberg near the Cecilienhof, the main venue for the talks. The house was a rococo mansion that had belonged to a famous German movie producer; Leahy was told that the mogul and all his staff had been packed off to a Russian labor camp. The house had the touch of Nazi Hollywood about it, with an ornate ballroom complete with gold trimmings, and a beautiful, well-tended garden that stretched down to a lake. It was quickly dubbed the Little White House, no one caring that it was painted yellow and red.

Leahy was given a two-room suite near the president and, all things considered, Truman, Leahy, and Byrnes made it a happy home. The ease of the interactions between the three dominant Americans made a great impression on Emilio Collado, who was one of the State Department officials accompanying the president. One Saturday afternoon he stopped by the Little White House to get a memorandum signed by Truman. He later recalled:

There was a big ballroom and it was like ballrooms, empty. Little gilt chairs around the edge; it was quite a handsome big room looking out on this lake, with a raised platform and a grand piano on it. Seated at the grand piano was an alert small man in shirt sleeves with a drink on the corner of the piano. Standing alongside him was a naval gentleman with no coat on, just the uniform pants. The third gentleman was the Secretary of State. He said, "What have you got there?"

I said, "Well this is the letter to the Prime Minister."

He said, "Have you got it cleared by everybody?"

I said, "We finished clearing it with the Admiral just before lunch" and the Admiral looked up and said, "Yeah, I agreed to it." The President looked up from the piano and asked for a fountain pen. I produced one and he signed the memorandum. I then turned around (when you're ahead you leave) and he started to play the piano and they were singing as I left. I thought it was nice, these three people sitting there playing . . . They weren't drunk or anything like that; they each had a drink. I have often thought of that picture: the five-star admiral, the Secretary of State, and the President together on a Saturday afternoon, having a little music.[22]

The only moment Leahy seemed discomfited was when two small ivory statues were stolen from his bedroom. As the house was in the Soviet occupation zone, a strict order had been issued that no one was to "liberate" any souvenirs. Leahy was so incensed at the theft that he oversaw an investigation to find the guilty party.[23] The lucky criminal eluded detection.

Another picture of the relaxed relationship between Leahy and

Truman at Potsdam was given by Robert Murphy, a diplomatic adviser on General Eisenhower's staff. Murphy had been invited to the talks and encountered Leahy and the president at the airport in Berlin. Murphy was elated when Leahy told him to come for a meeting as soon as possible. The admiral had warmed a great deal to Truman, telling Murphy, "The new President is alright. He couldn't be any more different from Roosevelt, but he has all the necessary qualities to make a good President and Commander in Chief."[24]

Leahy also gossiped to Murphy about the fall of Henry Morgenthau. The treasury secretary had hoped to stay on under Truman and even made a play to increase his authority.[25] He went to Truman and threatened to resign if he were not brought to Potsdam. The new president, who had no preexisting relationship with Morgenthau, thought little of the man's outlook, particularly about Germany. Truman had heard about the Morgenthau Plan and hated it. When Morgenthau offered to resign, the president, much to Morgenthau's surprise, quickly accepted and ushered him out the door.[26]

Leahy's relaxed air at Potsdam was also due to the widespread recognition of his importance. He was the most experienced member of the American team, comfortable attending both the political and military staff talks. The Soviets showed him particular distinction. During the American banquet on July 19, Molotov was selected to give the Soviet toast to Leahy, describing the admiral as the "permanent member of all international conferences."[27]

Leahy was at ease around Stalin. The Soviet dictator first appeared in Potsdam a day later than expected, because, Truman said, he had suffered a minor heart attack. Once Stalin arrived, he went right to the Little White House to meet the new president. In an oddly disorganized affair, Truman unexpectedly invited the Soviet dictator to stay for lunch. Stalin was reluctant, but with the American president pressing him, he relented. During the meal, which Leahy attended, Stalin deliberately misled Truman about Hitler's fate, telling him that he believed that the German dictator had escaped from Berlin and was still hiding somewhere.[28] The Russian dictator also did his best to put the American president at ease, complimenting the quality of the Californian wine he was offered. Truman made sure to send him a case as a memento.

Stalin's negotiating prowess continued to impress Leahy, who believed that the man drove a hard but not unreasonable bargain. Yet he seemed more convinced than ever about the inherent brutality of the Soviet regime. While driving back to the Little White House one day, Truman and Leahy's car was stopped by a Soviet lieutenant. The young officer did not recognize its famous passengers and started to inspect the vehicle. His mistake had to be corrected by more senior officers, who harangued the younger man. Leahy leaned over and whispered to Truman, "I'll bet that Lieutenant is shot in the morning."[29] In a more serious moment, Leahy let slip just how brutal he expected the Soviets to be. During one of the main plenary sessions there was a discussion about the large parts of eastern Germany to be given to the new Polish state. Stalin said that the transfer would pose little problem because all the Germans had left. Leahy turned to Truman and whispered that indeed the Germans were gone, as the Bolsheviks "have killed them all."[30]

The meetings and ceremonies of Potsdam offered an opportunity for Leahy to grow closer to the man whose invitation for correspondence he had snubbed the year before. Winston Churchill shared with Leahy a hatred of long concerts. The music battle of Potsdam, as it came to be known, was started unwittingly by President Truman during the official American banquet on July 19. As the highlight of the evening's entertainment, Truman had asked a young pianist named Eugene List, a US Army enlistee, to perform after dinner. Truman and Stalin were so taken by List's playing that they continually asked for encores, and the music poured forth, much to Leahy's and Churchill's growing annoyance, until one a.m. Not to be outdone by the American president, Stalin ordered four musicians from Moscow flown in for the Soviet banquet two days later and kept them playing until after one thirty a.m.[31] Leahy and Churchill, irritated and unamused, took solace in their shared exasperation, sticking to the back of the room and visibly showing their boredom. Churchill got his revenge two days later during the British dinner when he ordered an entire military band to play until two a.m.[32]

Several days later, Leahy was shocked when he received news that the hero of the British Empire had been thrown out of office. Like almost all Americans, Leahy had assumed that Winston Churchill would be rewarded for his war leadership, but the British people, more interested in their own economic and social condition, had, in a landslide, opted for the Labour Party, which was promising a national health service and more state housing. After shepherding Britain through the most desperate days of the nation's long history, Churchill and his Conservative Party were out of power.

Leahy heard the news while in London. Hardly immune from enjoying the perks of office, on July 25 he had flown from Berlin to the United Kingdom ostensibly to confer with the US ambassador, John Winant. In truth, he was far more interested in visiting old friends. As he was about to board his flight back to Germany the next day, he received a telephone call telling him that Churchill was out. He felt the loss surprisingly deeply: "This . . . is in my opinion a world tragedy. I do not know how the Allies can succeed without the spark of genius in his qualities of leadership."[33] His mood did not improve when he saw the new prime minister, Clement Attlee, in action. Leahy considered Attlee a second-rate politician. Attlee sensed Leahy's skepticism, though assumed, wrongly, that it was because the admiral believed Britain did not matter much in world politics.[34]

The negotiations at Potsdam placed far more emphasis on Leahy's political role than his military position. Now that Germany had surrendered, military matters were less important, and those conferences were left to Marshall and King. The ultimate task ahead was for the victors to determine the shape of the postwar world. The Americans chosen to attend these crucial meetings with President Truman were Secretary of State Byrnes and Fleet Admiral Leahy. Also included was Joseph Davies, the former ambassador to the Soviet Union and a special adviser to the president.

Sitting with the Allied leaders and their advisers at a large round conference table, Leahy enjoyed watching Truman's directness with the Soviet leadership, feeling responsible for molding the president's outlook.[35] After Truman had chaired the first plenary session, Leahy lauded his boss, saying he'd "never seen an abler job."[36] Truman lapped up the praise, boasting about it in a letter to Bess. Yet when it came to actual agreements, Potsdam was a disappointment. Discussions about Poland and eastern Europe, about the division of Germany and the reparations that the Soviets were entitled to from the defeated Nazi state, led to only the bare bones of agreements. When an issue proved too difficult to solve, it was handed over for further discussion at the upcoming foreign secretaries' conference, which was scheduled to start in London not long afterward. In the end, even though Leahy tried to argue that Potsdam had accomplished some good, results were few. For Leahy, the most important development was that Truman had behaved well in front of Stalin. He believed the American president had been firm when necessary, had given way when there was no realistic alternative, and now had a better idea with whom he was dealing.

Leahy's misgivings about the Soviet desire to join the war against Japan did not weaken during the Potsdam Conference, and indeed intensified after July 16, when reports were delivered to Truman that the atomic bomb had been successfully tested in the New Mexico desert. Leahy knew that the United States could not keep the Soviet Union from the joining the Pacific war, but he did keep Truman from issuing a public statement saying that America wanted the Soviets to fight Japan, for which Stalin had asked. [37]

Leahy's position on the Soviet entry into the war, combined with his skepticism about the atomic bomb, does shed some light on one of the most contentious issues surrounding the decision to attack Hiroshima and Nagasaki. Many of those who criticize the decision argue that it was done more to intimidate the Soviet Union than drive Japan to surrender. Leahy's outlook shows how relatively unimportant this consideration was. He was more than willing to allow the Soviets to attack into Northern China if it meant that the atomic bomb did not have to be dropped. At no point did he seem to consider or mention that anyone else around Truman was motivated by the need to intimidate the Soviets. The real split was between the mass of those around Truman who wanted to drop the bomb to end the war and those like Leahy who had ethical doubts about its usage. The president was clearly more influenced by the former.

Truman's private papers include some handwritten notes he made in Potsdam.[38] They reveal that prior to the testing of the bomb in New Mexico, the president considered the atomic option as a way to guarantee an end to the war against Japan, and not as a weapon with troubling ethical considerations:

P.M. [Churchill] and I ate alone. Discussed Manhattan (if it is a success). Decided to tell Stalin about it. Stalin had told the P.M. of telegram from Jap Emperor asking for peace. Stalin also read his answer to me. It was satisfactory. Believe Japs will fold up before Russia comes in.

I am sure they will when Manhattan appears over their homeland.[39]

After he received word of the bomb's success, Truman's language changed, and he sounded more like Leahy:

We have discovered the most terrible bomb in the history of the world. It may be the fore prophesied in the Euphrates Valley Era, after Noah and his fabulous Ark. . . . An experiment in the New Mexican desert was startling—to put it mildly. Thirteen pounds of the explosive caused the complete disintegration of a steel tower 60 feet high, created a crater 6 feet deep and 1200 feet in diameter, knocked over a steel tower ½ mile away and knocked men down 10,000 yards away. The explosion was visible for more than 200 miles and audible for 40 miles and more.

The weapon is to be used against Japan between now and August 10th. I have told the Sec. of War Mr. Stimson to use it so that military objectives and soldiers and sailors are the target and not women and children. Even if the Japs are savages, ruthless, merciless and fanatic, we as the leader of the world for the common welfare cannot drop this terrible bomb on the old Capitol or the new.[40]

His words reveal how much Leahy had influenced Truman's emotional reckoning with the destructive power of the bomb, though without shaping his intentions. The president said that the bomb would not target women and children, but he did nothing to ensure this. In fact, he handed over the choice of targets to the War Department and the USAAF, which paid no attention to this desire. Hiroshima and Nagasaki were chosen because they were considered militarily important targets, despite the hundreds of thousands of civilians who lived in both cities.[41]

On August 6, while Truman and Leahy were sailing back to the United States aboard the *Augusta*, the president was handed a message reporting the bombing of Hiroshima. Truman rejoiced. Speaking to a cheering group of staffers and sailors onboard, he claimed that this was "the greatest thing in history."[42] While Truman celebrated, Leahy withdrew into himself. When he heard about the level of destruction that the bomb had caused, his mood darkened more. In his diary he wrote:

> The press this morning reports that the atomic bomb, dropped on Hiroshima the day before yesterday, destroyed more than half the city and brought from the Japanese Government charges against us of cruelty and barbarism in that the attack was effective principally against non-combatants, women and children. Although Hiroshima was a naval base it is probable that the destruction of civilian life was terrific.
>
> Some of our scientists today say that the area attacked will be uninhabitable for many years because the bomb explosion has made the ground radioactive and destructive of animal life.
>
> The lethal possibilities of such atomic action in the future is frightening, and while we are the first to have it in our possession, there is a certainty that it will in the future be developed by potential enemies and that it will probably be used against us.[43]

This last sentence is important: Leahy believed that in using the atomic bomb first, the United States had not only acted unethically, it had opened itself up to the possibility of being attacked by such weapons. One reason he had fought against the use of the bomb was that he wanted the United States to demonstrate to the world that even though it had a monopoly on these terrible weapons, it would never use them first. Now that it had, and in a first strike on a civilian target no less, it seemed to him that other powers would feel less constrained about using them against America.

The Japanese asked for terms on August 10, when Leahy, Truman and Byrnes were back in Washington. The reactions of Leahy and Byrnes show how differently they viewed the end of the war. When the Japanese first explored surrender, they said they were willing to accept the Allied terms specified at Potsdam. Leahy wanted to accept the Japanese offer immediately. Byrnes, however, wanted the Japanese to be humiliated by being forced to publicly acknowledge the principle of unconditional surrender. It was a stance that caused Leahy to lose faith in Byrnes's judgment. Throughout the day, in the White House and during a meeting of the Joint Chiefs, Leahy argued for an immediate acceptance of the Japanese offer.[44] By the evening, Truman agreed with the admiral and a message was drafted for Churchill and Stalin saying that the Japanese offer to agree to the Potsdam statements, once confirmed, would be accepted as the equivalent of unconditional surrender.

By August 14, both Allies had acknowledged the US statement and the Japanese had reconfirmed their acceptance of the Potsdam accords. At seven p.m. that evening, Truman called Leahy on the phone and told him that he was going to announce the surrender and that he wanted Leahy to join him in the Oval Office for the historic moment. When the announcement was made, the only men sitting next to the president were Cordell Hull, James Byrnes, and William Leahy. In photographs of the event, Byrnes looks pleased, Hull tired, and Leahy nonplussed.

Leahy believed the war's end should be marked quietly. As the streets of Washington once again erupted with the din of victory, he once again felt detached from his fellow citizens. He acknowledged that "the proletariat considers noise appropriate and the greatest number of people in Democracies must have their way," but he just wanted to get home and reflect.[45] He missed Franklin Roosevelt greatly.

Leahy's dark mood was worsened by the weapon used to end the war. To those closest to him, including his secretary, Dorothy Ringquist, the use of the atomic bomb so distressed Leahy that it affected him physically, representing the moment when his usually robust health finally began to deteriorate. "Dorothy, we will regret this day," he told her. "The United States will suffer, for war is not to be waged to wipe out women and children."[46]

CHAPTER 26

Two Speeches

During the last few months of 1945, the baubles of victory arrived in waves for the men who had directed the US armed services in World War II. Almost every day a new honor was bestowed on Leahy, Marshall, King, and Arnold, from the small and sentimental to the grand. In early September, Leahy visited South Dakota, where he was adopted into the Rosebud Tribe of the Sioux Indians.[1] For a moment, the septuagenarian was transformed into a young boy, performing a Native American dance so energetically that a *New York Times* reporter was taken aback.[2]

America's allies and other foreign powers also got in on the act. Leahy received a decoration from the Polish government-in-exile, a bittersweet award, as he had long accepted that the Soviets were going to rule Poland. The Saudi government, perhaps understanding Leahy's sympathy for their position, sent him a number of gifts, including a sword.[3] A week before joining the Sioux, Leahy had been forced to endure another Washington visit by Charles de Gaulle.[4] He presented Leahy, Marshall, King, and Arnold the Grand Cross of the Legion of Honor, the highest award bestowed by the French state.[5] This brought out mixed emotions, as Leahy still suspected that de Gaulle was liquidating his rivals. On November 21, the British made America's Joint Chiefs Knights of the Grand Cross of the Order of the Bath, the United Kingdom's highest award that can be given to military officers of another state. The ceremony was held in the British embassy in Washington and, in a twee touch, was followed by a tea party.[6] Though Leahy might have been loath to admit it, he enjoyed himself, even bringing along his granddaughter, Louisita.[7]

The different sides of Leahy's nature were stimulated by these honors. The macho Bill Leahy liked to subvert the whole process. He was known to say, when hearing a particularly poetic tribute, that it "would be nice if set to music."[8] Yet he also seemed increasingly invested in the awards, scrutinizing the different portraits and busts that were commissioned of him. In September, he was brought in to see a formal bronze bust of himself being sculpted by Felix de Weldon, one of the most successful World War II memorialists. (His most famous work is the US Marine Corps War Memorial, commemorating the flag-raising on Iwo Jima, in Arlington, Virginia.) The sculptor had enjoyed carving Leahy, finding him unexpectedly approachable.[9] Leahy believed de Weldon did a weak job in capturing his likeness, considering it unsatisfactory except when seen in profile.[10]

On the day that Leahy was made a British knight it was also announced that Marshall and King would be retiring as the chiefs of staff for the army and navy. As Arnold had already been put on light duty because of his failing heart, it marked the end for the team that had guided American grand strategy in World War II. With the war over, Leahy assumed that he too would be moving on. He was being wooed by Trans World Airlines (TWA), owned by America's first billionaire, Howard Hughes. Throughout the fall of 1945, Leahy met with TWA officials who wanted him to serve as a roving ambassador for the airline.[11] It was a canny move, as Leahy had already done a good deal to establish US airline policy during the war. The salary on offer was very large and would have provided Leahy for the first time in his life with a considerable cushion of wealth. Harry Truman had other ideas.

By November 23, 1945, the president had decided that he wanted Leahy to remain by his side for as long as the admiral was physically capable of working. After Truman and Leahy discussed the implications of Marshall's departure, the president told his chief of staff that he wanted him to continue serving "as long as I feel able to do so."[12] It was a remarkable request for the president to make of the old admiral, though one that was most welcome. For all his flirtations with TWA, more than anything else, Leahy wanted to remain at the center of power.

During the six months between Roosevelt's death and Truman's request, the admiral had impressed the new president with many of the same attributes that had appealed to FDR. Truman instinctively understood Leahy's worldview, seeing the admiral as "shrewdly on the conservative side."[13] He also understood that Leahy was fiercely loyal to the office of the presidency, was discreet, was not out for any personal gain (beyond the exercise of power), and could be relied upon to enforce Truman's wishes even if the president overruled him. In a town like Washington, it was a rare combination.

Truman also felt that he needed Leahy's experience to help him navigate in an uncertain world. The end of World War II posed new challenges for the United States, the most pressing being its future relationship with the Soviet Union. The Soviets were in the process of imposing their will on the lands they had occupied in 1944 and 1945, keeping a massive Soviet Army deployed from the Baltic to the Balkans to maintain their authority. There was no catastrophic event at this time, just a continued process of force whereby the Soviets ensured that Communist regimes were in place everywhere on their border, regardless of whether that country had been a friend or foe of Germany in the war. Poland was joined by Romania, Bulgaria, Hungary, and Czechoslovakia. Most people around the president recognized that the United States and the Soviet Union were not natural allies. Beyond that, there was a huge range of opinions between those who believed that the wartime cooperation could continue in the postwar world and those who believed that the inherent oppositional forces between capitalism and communism were going to lead to an increasingly hostile relationship—perhaps even war.

Other conundrums awaited US policy makers. The era of European imperial rule was ending. Having been economically and in some cases emotionally exhausted by the two world wars, the United Kingdom, France, Holland, Belgium, and Portugal were turning inward. Their rule was being challenged by increasingly assertive independence movements across the globe. If there was one region where the decline of European influence presented the greatest challenge to the United States, it was the Middle East. Modern-day Israel, Egypt, Syria, Lebanon, Jordan, and Iraq were either under the direct or indirect control of Britain or France, and that control was weakening. The United States was left wondering whether it should try to exercise authority to compensate.

There was also China. Though Japanese troops were being withdrawn from throughout the many thousands of square miles of that country, it was not clear who would control the lands they left. It was widely assumed that the Chinese Nationalists would eventually emerge as the dominant force in China, yet much of the country was in chaos and the Chinese Communist Party led by Mao Tse-tung was showing considerable power in parts of the north and southeast.*

Leahy spent much of late 1945 pondering these issues, and began trying to articulate the fundamental principles he believed should underlie US actions. His views on America's place in the world were those of an instinctive isolationist who understood that the war had made isolationism impossible, his ideas flavored by three years of exposure to Franklin Delano Roosevelt. As he surveyed the world, Leahy acknowledged that most of his immediate hopes had been realized. Nazism had been crushed and Japan vanquished, leaving the United States the dominant power in the Pacific and Europe, for the moment stable. The American position in the Western Hemisphere had never been stronger, with South and Central America very much under the US umbrella.

When it came to US-Soviet relations, Leahy was a skeptic, with unorthodox tendencies. He never believed that the wartime alliance was anything more than a temporary arrangement. When serving Franklin Roosevelt, Leahy could sometimes talk himself into a more hopeful view. Now he began arguing, in saltier language, that communism was antithetical to the American way of life. Yet he did not foresee or desire a war with the Soviet Union, and he wanted an understanding with the

---

* It is more common today to write Mao Zedong instead of Mao Tse-tung. As I used the anglicized spelling of Chiang Kai-shek instead of Jiang Jieshi, for consistency I have used the same form for Mao.

Soviets, which meant that they were not to be challenged directly in eastern Europe.

Leahy also believed that where the United States was dominant, it should do everything possible to foster democratic states, with free markets supporting a New Deal–like state sector. He was happy to see the end of the imperial era and believed that the United States could play a positive (non-militarized) role in moving formally colonized nations toward independence. He recoiled at the notion of large numbers of American troops being based around the world, and he certainly didn't want the United States to intervene militarily in other peoples' conflicts.

Leahy had time to think about these issues because his new routine with President Truman functioned so efficiently. With the war over, the once constant flow of telegrams between London, Moscow, and Washington had ebbed to a peacetime pace, and since the appointment of James Byrnes as secretary of state, Truman allowed the State Department more autonomy.[14] Truman no longer needed Leahy to act as his constant buffer with the armed forces, and the Joint Chiefs were no longer needed to maintain continual watch over the largest war effort in human history. The civilian heads of the navy and army, James Forrestal and Robert Patterson, were more forceful than their predecessors. With less work on the admiral's docket, the president started using Leahy as a national security adviser more than anything else.

Preparing for and conducting the morning presidential briefings became the focus of Leahy's day. The admiral would reach the White House between eight and eight thirty a.m., where, well-known to everyone, he could slip in quietly. He would visit the Map Room and his office in the East Wing, collecting the different classified reports and messages that had been put aside for his scrutiny. Leahy would spend the next hour drinking coffee and reading the reports, deciding which ones were important enough to bring to Truman's attention. He would then stroll to the Oval Office, making sure to be ready to start the briefings with the punctual president at 9:45.

The meeting that followed was the single most important daily discussion in the United States. The door to the president's office was firmly shut, and no one else, except sometimes another intelligence officer, was allowed in. This made what happened in the meetings a source of mystery. Leahy was comfortable in, and even somewhat territorial about, the Oval Office. One soft leather armchair next to the president's desk, which the admiral found particularly comfortable, became known as Leahy's chair to other White House staffers, who made sure to leave it free when he was around. Leahy preferred sitting to the president's left, and the two men would have been close enough to pass documents back and forth as they discussed the world situation.

When Leahy and Roosevelt had met, FDR had done most of the talking. Now Truman would often ask Leahy to explain issues and outline options. Leahy took to the new role and for the first time in his career thought more and more about the articulation of foreign policy. He came to believe that the United States, and the world, would benefit from a clear statement of American principles. This led to one of the most important—and least recognized—parts of his career, his powerful influence over early Cold War rhetoric. He did this through shaping the two most important speeches of the postwar period, Harry Truman's Navy Day address given in New York City on October 27, 1945, and Winston Churchill's world-famous "Iron Curtain" speech (properly called the "Sinews of Peace") delivered just over four months later.

The best way to understand Leahy's role is to start, oddly enough, with his social calendar. Some misinformation that Leahy did not mind spreading was that he disliked socializing. It has been said that he was so determined to avoid going out that he told his staff to RSVP positively to many invitations but then he simply would not show up. Supposedly, he preferred retreating in the evenings to his small town house to read. Leahy did always keep a few books on his nightstand, favoring Perry Mason mysteries and historical narratives, both fiction and nonfiction.[15] But he remained a social animal, and in late 1945 he chose to head out most evenings, perhaps because his less exhausting work schedule helped enable a burst of socializing. For the first time since returning from Vichy France, Leahy was forced to confront the reality of being an old widower who had never had time to properly mourn.

While Leahy was happy to remain married to Louise's memory, he still sought out the opposite sex for companionship. He liked what he considered vivacious and well-behaved "ladies." He often became fond of different nurses who had treated him or other family members over the years and would have them over for dinner—though in his diary he was usually careful to point out that there was an escort.[16]

He became particularly close with his longtime secretary, Dorothy Ringquist. On trips, Leahy often made a point of picking up gifts for her, and she was known to send him treats such as candy when he was traveling. He often shared with her his hopes and fears regarding important issues. This was a considerable show of confidence and trust from a person who was notoriously careful with secrets. After the war, on days when he had no social events, he would invite her back to his house for lunch. He instructed his orderly to make sure that there was a bottle of sherry, Ringquist's favorite tipple, on hand for her visits. The orderly often forgot, and she was forced to drink bourbon, Leahy's preferred drink. It happened so regularly that she developed a fondness for the whiskey.

The social events that Leahy most enjoyed were small dinner parties of Washington, DC, power brokers. Leahy was a prized guest, and regularly dined out with those who had, or wanted to have, influence over the new Truman administration. On October 7, he went to the apartment of Samuel Rosenman and his wife, Dorothy. Leahy had worked with Rosenman, another adviser to Roosevelt and Truman, since 1943, and considered him one of the most trustworthy people he had ever met.[17] They shared a growing skepticism about the performance of James Byrnes and wanted to have Truman be more assertive in running US foreign policy.[18]

A few days later, Leahy was invited to dine with his old friend William Bullitt, who had returned to Washington in August after his purgatorial stint in the French Army. Bullitt still wanted to be a player in the State Department and hoped that with Roosevelt's death he might finally be rehabilitated. During the meal, Bullitt made a suggestion that sent Leahy's mind racing and demonstrated his power in Washington. Bullitt recommended that President Truman make a general statement on US foreign policy along the lines of Woodrow Wilson's famous

Fourteen Points. Within two weeks, Leahy took Bullitt's suggestion and turned it into the most important speech that Harry Truman would give in the first two years of his presidency.

Leahy decided immediately that Truman's upcoming Navy Day speech in New York City would be the perfect opportunity for such a statement. The speech had been scheduled for a while, but Leahy now became the driving force in shaping it in a new and dramatic way. In Truman's memoirs, the president provides no detail of why the decision was made to frame the speech as a series of points, simply saying he decided to do so just before it was given.[19] Yet Leahy's diary tells a different story. After his dinner with Bullitt, Leahy spent much of the next ten days crafting the address as a series of points. To do this he turned to Samuel Rosenman, calling him in for long meetings on October 22 and 25. They were the only meetings that he recorded on those days, demonstrating how personal the process had become. Eventually, Leahy and Rosenman boiled down the fundamental goals of US foreign policy into twelve points.[20]*

The final text of the speech is the best summary of Leahy's outlook as it had evolved to that time and was both a statement about the coming Cold War and an attempt to keep alive the legacy of Franklin Roosevelt. The first three points were clear calls for the United States to distinguish its behavior from that of the Soviet Union in eastern Europe. The United States stood against all territorial expansion and aggression against other states, it stood for the return of sovereignty for those who had lost their independence, and it opposed changes in national territories unless they were ratified by the peoples involved. The fourth point, for balance, was a statement of American support for decolonization, saying that people not only in Europe but Asia, Africa, and the Western Hemisphere should have self-government.

Having tweaked the nose of America's imperialist allies, the fifth and sixth points returned to the general idea of tension with the Soviets, offering one olive branch but also one contrast. The US promised to stand by its wartime allies, including the Soviet Union, though at the same time attacked the Soviets' attempts to dominate in eastern

---

* The twelve points are included verbatim in Appendix B.

Europe by saying America would not recognize any government "imposed" upon a nation by a foreign power. Point six was a verbatim restatement of the stance Leahy had been taking on Poland since 1943:

> We shall refuse to recognize any government imposed upon any nation by the force of any foreign power. In some cases it may be impossible to prevent forceful imposition of such a government. But the United States will not recognize any such government.

Points seven and eight were more traditional American concerns as the United States once again pledged to respect freedom of the seas and equal access to trade. Points nine through twelve were homages to Franklin Roosevelt. Point nine was a restatement of Roosevelt's "good neighbor" policy toward Latin and Central America. Point ten was a call for international economic cooperation to improve the life of the poor and repressed. Point eleven was a commitment on the part of the United States to stand for freedom of expression and belief. Point twelve was a statement of commitment to the United Nations.

The Navy Day address can also be recognized as Leahy's handiwork because of its negative discussion about the atom bomb. Atomic weapons took up more of the text than any other single issue. They were the focus of eight paragraphs, and the president, who had celebrated the bomb in August, now spoke Leahy-like rhetoric about its terrible consequences.[21] The speech also called for atomic weapons to be made illegal: "The highest hope of the American people is that world cooperation for peace will soon reach such a state of perfection that atomic methods of destruction can be definitely and effectively outlawed forever."[22] Ever so subtly, Leahy was taking control over US atomic policy from those who had argued for dropping the bomb on Hiroshima and Nagasaki.

On October 26, Truman and Leahy left for New York City, traveling in a presidential train packed with thirty-five reporters, making this the best-covered speech Truman had ever given. After a night spent sleeping on the train, the presidential motorcade first headed to Brooklyn for the commissioning ceremony of the new 45,000-ton super–

aircraft carrier USS *Franklin D. Roosevelt*. After a short address, the president returned to Manhattan, where the motorcade headed up Broadway through the "Canyon of Heroes" before enormous cheering crowds of onlookers. Riding in the open-top car with Truman and New York mayor Fiorello La Guardia, Leahy was overwhelmed. "I never before saw so many people in one day," he wrote. "All were noisily enthusiastic; making a triumphal procession such as no Roman Emperor could have dreamed of in Rome's Golden Era."[23] He was a little bewildered, and the intense emotions of the day struck him as alien: "Mob psychology is something about which I have no knowledge, and whatever it was that impelled millions of people to stand for hours on the cold streets and break into hysterical applause when the President passed, is completely beyond my understanding."[24]

Newspapers estimated that more than 5 million people saw President Truman's car making its way uptown, though they also guessed that the crowds were slightly smaller than those who had greeted General Eisenhower in June.[25] Yet Truman's day had something Eisenhower's didn't. After reaching Central Park, the president was driven to the Sheep Meadow, where more than a million people were waiting to hear him speak. It was here that he delivered the speech written for him by Leahy and Rosenman. Afterward, another parade plodded through Manhattan's Upper West Side to the Seventy-Ninth Street Boat Basin, where Truman and Leahy were put on a navy cutter and sailed out to the great battleship USS *Missouri* for lunch. In the afternoon, the two were transferred to the destroyer USS *Renshaw*, and the president was sailed past miles of the most famous American naval vessels from the war. Truman reviewed battleships, cruisers, aircraft carriers, destroyers, and even submarines, each of which fired a crisp twenty-one-gun salute. The display was capped off by an overflight of a thousand naval aircraft. Truman described it as the "happiest day of my life."[26]

Leahy, for all his forced disapproval, was gratified. He believed that the speech had made a statement that would garner worldwide attention. He crowed that this "statement of the foreign policy of the United States based on righteousness and justice . . . will attract microscopic attention by the Governments in Europe and Asia, and which may succeed in forcing our diplomatic appeasers to pay closer attention to the vital interests of America."[27]

Once back in Washington, Leahy made sure that the speech's importance was recognized throughout the American government. Its points were circulated with emphasis to the Joint Chiefs and the State Department. It was even codified in State Department policy. By December 1, a secret pamphlet had been drafted, entitled "Tentative Foreign Policy of the United States of America."[28] It was a direct restatement of the twelve Navy Day points. A few weeks later the "tentative" was gone and the State Department released a public paper simply entitled "Foreign Policy of the United States," quoting the points verbatim.[29]

There was an immediate understanding in both the United States and around the world that the Navy Day address represented an important change. Almost every major paper in the country wrote an editorial on the address; the *New York Times* said the most important aspect of the speech was its timing, delivered as relations with the Soviet Union were beginning to fray.[30] Major Democratic politicians in Congress, including those who had been critical of Truman's foreign policy, such as Sens. Burton Wheeler and Alben Barkley, rose as one to praise the speech's vision.[31] Republicans, meanwhile, grumbled.

Among America's allies the speech's importance was widely recognized. British and French newspapers generally approved of the principles spelled out by Truman but were critical of the president's decision not to discuss sharing the atomic bomb.[32] Elsewhere the speech went over well. It was praised from sources as disparate as the Spanish Francoist press to Jawaharlal Nehru, leader of the Congress Party of India.[33]

The person most affected by the speech was Winston Churchill. The former British prime minister, still adjusting to life out of power, was growing increasingly worried. His nightmare scenario was that the United States might withdraw from Europe, forcing a weakened Britain to lead western Europe in the face of the growing menace of the Soviet Union. When, on November 7, Churchill was given a copy of the Navy Day address, his heart leapt. He strode immediately into the House of Commons to praise the new tone coming out of Washington. Churchill described the speech as a "momentous declaration to

the world" and took instant steps to take advantage of the crucial opening Leahy had given him.[34] The next day Churchill accepted a long-
standing invitation from Truman to make a foreign-policy address at
Westminster College in the president's home state of Missouri.[35] Leahy's Navy Day principles had laid the groundwork for what would become one of the hallmarks of Churchill's oratory, the famed "Iron
Curtain" speech. It was just the beginning. By the time Churchill rose
to speak in Missouri on March 5, 1946, he had spent more time discussing his speech with Leahy than any other American, and he had edited
the speech to suit Leahy's tastes.

Leahy's role in the crafting of Churchill's address started early. The
admiral was instrumental in arranging many of the most sensitive issues surrounding the speech, such as Churchill's travel plans and the
handling of delicate press inquiries.[36] On January 7, 1946, Churchill departed England for America, setting out across the Atlantic aboard the
great Art Deco cruise liner RMS *Queen Elizabeth*.[37] When he arrived,
he headed directly to Miami, where he hoped to enjoy the warmth and
recover from a serious bronchial condition.

The coming weeks would see a further confirmation in both Churchill's and Leahy's minds about the need for a clear statement. On February 9, Joseph Stalin delivered his most important address of the early
Cold War. While "campaigning" for reelection to the Soviet legislature
(the Communist Party received 99.2 percent of the votes in the end),
Stalin made a speech blaming World War II entirely on a crisis in capitalism, making clear that, regardless of his alliance with the Americans
and Britons during the war, he considered communism and capitalism
to be incompatible systems.[38]

The day after Stalin spoke, Churchill flew up to Washington to
discuss his own speech, determined to spend only a day in the capital
before returning to the Florida sun. He would meet with only two
Americans, Harry Truman and William Leahy. When Churchill landed
on the afternoon of February 10, the two men there to meet him were
Lord Halifax and Admiral Leahy. The three headed back to the British
embassy to help Churchill prepare to discuss the speech with Truman.
After dinner, Leahy escorted Churchill to the Oval Office, where he and

Truman spent the next hour and a half going through the text. Then Truman headed off to bed, and Leahy took Churchill back to the British embassy, where the two old warriors spent the next few hours dissecting the speech further. Leahy knew very well how important the address was, describing its subject as the "necessity for full military collaboration between Great Britain and the U.S. in order to preserve peace in the world."[39] Leahy also understood that the speech would be a shot across the Soviets' bow. The two kept talking until midnight.

Nearly two weeks later, a document appeared that has become talismanic in the origins of the Cold War: George Kennan's "Long Telegram."[40] On February 22, Kennan, the chargé d'affaires in the US embassy in Moscow, sent the State Department a paper arguing for a toughening of US policy toward the Soviet Union. This paper is usually seen as laying down the intellectual foundations of the policy of containment, the policy shift marking the beginning of the Cold War. Containment meant that the United States should no longer look on the Soviet Union as an ally but instead look on it as a potential foe and resist any further attempts by the Soviets to expand their sphere of influence. Today, the State Department claims that Kennan "formulated" the containment policy, adding, even more grandly, that Kennan's ideas "became the basis of the Truman Administration's foreign policy."[41] It is as if Kennan's thoughts were so profound that they created a miasma that slowly engulfed the Washington elite.[42]

It is a bizarre view, as there is no evidence that President Truman ever read, or was even interested in, the Long Telegram. Leahy was aware of the document but paid it scant attention, not even mentioning Kennan's existence in his diary until 1947.[43] Leahy said that according to the people he trusted in the State Department, Kennan was "the best that they've got, and that's not saying a hell of a lot."[44] In truth, Kennan was a marginal figure in White House thinking.[45] By the time the Long Telegram appeared, the move toward containment, due to Leahy's efforts starting with the Navy Day and "Iron Curtain" addresses, was already well under way.

On March 3, Churchill returned to Washington and called on Leahy, determined that the two together analyze every word of the speech.[46]*

* This is the story in the Prologue.

For the next three days the two worked closely together, either alone or in groups, until Churchill took the stage in Fulton, Missouri.

The two-day trip to Fulton was made in the presidential train, with Leahy and Churchill both housed in the president's carriage. Part of the trip was a geopolitical seminar. They discussed relations with the Soviet Union, and Leahy told Churchill how the United States was starting to toughen up. Churchill later told Clement Attlee how both Leahy and Truman told him that the United States was using the pretext of the death of the Turkish ambassador to dispatch a powerful naval force, including two *Iowa*-class battleships and two aircraft carriers, to the Dardanelles.[47]

Traveling with Harry Truman was a world away from the sleepy trips with Franklin Roosevelt: Truman's train was like a political rally and party bus rolled into one. Leahy found himself in company with the president's old political cronies, a boisterous group who liked having a good time. Alcoholic beverages flowed freely, stopping only during meals, an oddity that Churchill found particularly vexing.[48] The men also indulged in one of Truman's great passions, poker, involving lots of strange rules and wild cards. Leahy, a keen card player who was unafraid to gamble, adapted to the new, noisier environment. He became a regular poker player with the president and started developing friendships with those around Truman.

When the party reached Fulton, Leahy took his customary back seat. Churchill delivered his soaring oration while Truman sat on the stage behind him, beaming with approval. Leahy was just as happy as the president and praised the speech lavishly. He claimed that it should "go down in history as one of the most powerful influences in bringing about close British-American collaboration to preserve world peace."[49] He also enjoyed twisting the knife: "It will produce a sharply unfavorable reaction in Soviet-Russia, and highly unfavorable comment from vocal communists, 'fellow-travelers' and 'pinkies' in the United States."

Leahy's pleasure partly stemmed from his own deep if hidden involvement. One major problem with understanding this is that Leahy lied in his own diary, writing on March 3 that during the meeting in the British embassy when he went through the speech with Churchill that he "could find no fault" in the address.[50] It was typical Leahy deception. Leahy's fingerprints can be seen throughout the text. Twice near the beginning, Churchill refers to the geopolitical ideas that he had been discussing with "American military men" or his "American military colleagues."[51] Leahy was the only US military officer with whom Churchill discussed the speech.

Churchill also took positions identical to those that Leahy had argued for during the preceding few months. He argued that if it were to defend free nations, the United Nations needed to be given real force, in a direct echo of the Navy Day address. Churchill also repeated Leahy's exact position on atomic weapons—namely, that their control should not be given to an international body. Moreover, Churchill put stress on the coordination of US and UK air-sea power.[52] Finally, the ideas that Churchill ascribed to American "military" men mirrored what Leahy was saying about relations with the Soviets. It was not a blanket condemnation of the Soviet Union. Churchill, like Leahy, was not calling for aggression against the Soviet Union.[53] The entire thrust of the speech was that a new accommodation with the Soviets needed to be pursued, but one based on reality, not the hopeful notions of the wartime alliance.

It might be argued that this is all inference, as Churchill claimed afterward that the speech was all his work.[54] In this case, it is Churchill who lied. He even went out of his way privately to thank Leahy for shaping the speech. The two men's relationship continued to deepen after Fulton, to the point that they regularly exchanged cards and letters. In a letter Churchill sent to Leahy in 1948, on a completely unrelated matter, he added (in ink), "Your advice about the Fulton draft proved sound."[55]

CHAPTER 27

Personal Snooper

y January 1946, the bond between Harry Truman and William Leahy strengthened to the point of friendship. It was not nearly as intense or emotionally reliant as the admiral's relationship with Franklin Roosevelt, but it was real. Truman had begun to routinely include Leahy in his leisurely outings with friends, and two weeks into the new year, the president reiterated his desire that Leahy remain his chief of staff "indefinitely."[1]

Yet one doubt about Truman still lingered in Leahy's mind. At times, the president could act in ways the admiral considered undignified, even silly.[2] On January 24, Truman hosted an Oval Office ceremony to award Samuel Rosenman a medal of merit. Afterward, the White House staff decamped for lunch in the president's study. During the meal, Truman stood, beaming with pride, and produced a flowing false mustache, a black cloak, and a wooden dagger. He thrust these props on a startled William Leahy. Then the president brought out a large black hat and another cloak and dagger, which were given to Adm. Sidney Souers, who was serving as the deputy director of naval intelligence.[3] Suitably pleased with himself, the president read aloud an announcement—perfectly calibrated for a local Moose Lodge gathering.

To My Brethren and Fellow Dog House Denizens:

By virtue of the authority vested in me as Top Dog, I require and charge that Front Admiral William D. Leahy and Rear Admiral Sidney W. Souers, receive and accept the vestments and appurtenances of their respective positions, namely as Personal Snooper and Director of Centralized Snooping. In accepting these symbols of trust and confidence, I charge each of you not only to seek to better our foreign relations through more intensive snooping but also to keep me informed constantly of the movements and actions of the other, for without such coordination there can be no order and no era of mutual trust.[4]

One can imagine Leahy in that moment, wearing the false mustache, the ridiculous black cape draped around his shoulders, clutching the childish wooden dagger, fondly remembering the patrician dignity of Franklin Roosevelt. Though the ceremony itself was juvenile, Truman was marking something quite serious. He was naming Leahy his personal representative to, and Souers as the first director of, the newly formed Central Intelligence Group, the founding organization of what would become the CIA.*

Leahy was an obvious choice for Truman, as the admiral had been the president's original purveyor of intelligence since he had assumed office. During the final months of his administration, Truman recounted to a group of CIA officers how the agency was born, saying, "I had a conversation with Admiral Leahy, and suggested to him that there should be a Central Intelligence Agency, for the benefit of the whole government as well as for the benefit of the President, so he could be informed. And the Admiral and I proceeded to try and work out a program. It has worked very successfully."[5]

Leahy's influence over the early CIA was pervasive, from determining its structure to selecting its leadership. He was responsible for the selection of its first three directors, Souers, Gen. Hoyt Vandenberg, and Adm. Roscoe Hillenkoetter, the first and last of whom had served under

---

* From here on I will refer just to the CIA for the sake of clarity.

Leahy in Vichy France, and he did his best to guide its operations. One of the earliest officers assigned to the Central Intelligence Group was Adm. Arthur McCollum, a naval intelligence specialist who described Leahy as the "father-confessor" of the early CIA, admitting that Leahy, more than Souers, controlled events. "The moving force behind it was Admiral Leahy," McCollum recalled, "who was still acting as Chief of Staff to the President and was very much interested in a thorough-going intelligence organization being set-up and functioning. As I mentioned before, the general feeling in Washington, and I don't know why, was that the OSS had outlived its usefulness."[6]

McCollum's ignorance about the circumstances behind the elimination of the OSS—the Office of Strategic Services, America's wartime intelligence service—was another example of Leahy's discretion. The admiral was more responsible than anyone else for the downfall of the OSS, run by its famous director William "Wild Bill" Donovan. Leahy's hostility had everything to do with his views of what an intelligence agency should do and what it should avoid. In his view, the purpose of an intelligence service was to provide information to allow the political and military leadership to plan wisely in its quest to keep the country safe. He was skeptical of the value of covert operations or interfering in the actions of other states. In his experience, covert operations were expensive and rarely productive.

His time in Vichy only confirmed these prejudices. The intelligence collected from a wide range of sources within the Pétain government had been helpful, yet he saw little merit in the different schemes proposed by the OSS. In 1944, when asked to vet an internal State Department report on US-Vichy relations between 1940 and 1942, Leahy thought the report accurate except for its "undue stress" on the OSS's "subversive activities."[7]

Leahy was particularly damning of the OSS during the war. Donovan either met with Leahy or sent representatives to him on a regular basis, trying to demonstrate what a useful job his spooks were doing. Leahy was unmoved. In January 1944, he recorded, "Brigadier Magruder and Colonel Buxton of the O.S.S. called to acquaint me with some information collected by secret agents in Europe, all of which is interesting and most of which is of doubtful authenticity."[8]

Leahy's doubts drove him to limit OSS influence, cutting the organization entirely out of the loop at important times. In March 1944, he forbade the OSS from playing any role in the peace negotiations that were going on with eastern European governments desperately trying to abandon their Nazi allies.[9] A few months later, on behalf of the Joint Chiefs of Staff, Leahy used his influence with Roosevelt to keep the OSS from developing its own industrial espionage arm.[10] Roosevelt, at the same time, started using Leahy and the Joint Chiefs for many major intelligence jobs. In March 1944, in a personal letter to Leahy, Roosevelt handed over all power to control US cryptanalysis operations—code breaking—to the chiefs.[11] One of the last memoranda the president would ever send Leahy was a request for the admiral's views on the future setup of the American intelligence service.[12]

Part of the problem for Leahy was Donovan himself, about whom he harbored personal doubts. In Wild Bill, Leahy saw a self-important fantasist. Right before the Torch landings, Donovan had assured him that if the OSS were given $2 million, it would be able to convince fourteen French divisions to come over to the American side.[13] By March 1945, Leahy was writing about Donovan as if he were a charlatan: "Received information today . . . that General Donovan of OSS recently told the Polish Ambassador in Washington that he should not worry about the Russians in Poland because we will straighten out all of the problem at the San Francisco Conference next month."[14] Considering the reality of Poland's fate, Leahy must have thought Donovan had lost his senses.

Some savvier members of the OSS realized Leahy's power and attempted to cultivate the admiral. Allen Dulles, an OSS officer who would later be instrumental in pushing the CIA down the road of covert operations, began lobbying Leahy in September 1944 to be kept as part of any new intelligence agency, coming by the admiral's office to plead his case.[15] This did not keep Dulles from later incurring Leahy's wrath. When he heard that Dulles was leading the OSS's attempts to make contacts within the Japanese government and start negotiations to end the Pacific war, Leahy slapped him down.[16]

The changeover to the Truman administration made Leahy even

more aggressive in his attacks on Donovan, as Truman, unlike Roosevelt, had no preexisting relationship with Wild Bill. In August 1945, Leahy ridiculed Donovan's attempts to insert the OSS into Korean politics.[17] Donovan tried to get Truman to recognize a provisional Korean government led by Mr. Kim Ku, whom Wild Bill was supporting. Leahy, witheringly, wrote a letter to Truman telling him to stay away from Ku and advising the president to send Donovan an official note saying it was not "proper for any agents of Donovan's office to transmit to the President messages from officials of self-styled governments that are not recognized by the Government of the United States."[18]

Leahy's mockery helps explain why Truman, from the beginning of his presidency, was so negative about both Donovan and the OSS.[19] With the war ending, different plans were being discussed for the new American intelligence service. Donovan proposed an agency just like the OSS, with a director who reported directly to the president and which had no oversight from the rest of the Cabinet or Congress, the perfect setup for the self-styled, swashbuckling rule breaker, but Truman killed it instantly. On September 20, 1945, the president terminated the OSS with an executive order and cut Donovan out of his professional life.[20]

Two options for replacing the service were being discussed, respective plans from the Joint Chiefs of Staff and the State Department.[21] The plan from the Joint Chiefs of Staff was William Leahy's. Shortly before Truman killed off the OSS, Leahy wrote to the president, Forrestal, and Stimson, enclosing a detailed Joint Chiefs memo on a new intelligence bureau.[22] It attacked Donovan's plan as one that would lead to a CIA able to operate outside of the law with little oversight. Leahy knew that Donovan's plan was dead in the water, as, in a particularly sensitive touch, he put forward the Joint Chiefs' plan as one that should be followed upon the "liquidation" of the OSS.[23]

Leahy's plan called for a controlled intelligence service with strong oversight. The new agency would be overseen by what he called the National Intelligence Authority (NIA), composed of the secretaries of state, war, and the navy, with a Joint Chiefs representative—in other words, Leahy himself. The NIA would establish and oversee the

Central Intelligence Agency, where their different resources would be pooled. The president would select the director of the CIA, who could be either a military officer or a civilian and who would be in charge of the day-to-day operations. The director would sit on the NIA, but only as a non-voting member.

The director's initial responsibility would be to come up with an efficient way to coordinate information collection and distribution from the existing sources within the US government, chiefly the intelligence divisions of the Navy, War, and State Departments and the remnants of the OSS. The NIA would have oversight of any such plans. As it was, there were to be strict limits on what the director could suggest. The CIA could under no circumstances ask for any law-enforcement or police powers. Covert operations, if they were to happen at all, were a tiny part of the new CIA's remit.

The State Department, in response, wanted to house any new intelligence agency in Foggy Bottom. It would become the controlling agency, and the preexisting Navy and War Department intelligence bureaus would be compelled to hand over their information to them.[24] This plan would have made the secretary of state considerably more powerful than any other cabinet officer, almost a co-president, having concentrated in his or her hands both the diplomatic and intelligence resources of the American government.[25] Byrnes loved the plan. Leahy killed it.

In fact, Leahy was determined that neither Byrnes nor the State Department be given control of America's intelligence apparatus, for the simple fact that he had doubts about the ability of both to be an effective guardian of America's secrets. These doubts emerged because of Leahy's unparalleled access to highly confidential information. By late 1945 Leahy had received reports from a range of credible sources that the Soviet Union had placed a large number of agents inside the US government. The first of these reports occurred in May 1945, when Julius Holmes, assistant secretary of state for administrative affairs, made a special appointment to speak with the admiral.[26] He informed Leahy that personnel in both the State Department and the Naval Intelligence branch had recently been caught spying for the Soviets, and Leahy quickly passed that information to Truman.

In the coming months things would get much worse. The two most important developments were the cases of Igor Gouzenko and Elizabeth Bentley. A young cipher clerk in the Soviet embassy in Ottawa, Gouzenko defected to Canada in September 1945.[27] He told stories of many Soviet spies in both the Canadian and American governments. Canadian prime minister Mackenzie King, a favorite of Leahy's, personally handed a dossier of Gouzenko's information to Truman on September 30.[28] On November 7, Elizabeth Bentley, an American Communist who had become a Soviet agent acting both as an informant and as a courier for information from other Soviet agents in the US government, turned herself in to the FBI. The day after her surrender, J. Edgar Hoover sent a handwritten letter to President Truman saying that there was a new source of information about Soviet penetration of the US government, and a month later the FBI sent a detailed report on the subject to the White House.

Much of the historical discussion of the Gouzenko and Bentley cases has focused on whether they provided clear evidence for the guilt of two accused Soviet agents from within the American government, Harry Dexter White and Alger Hiss. For Leahy, the point was not guilt or innocence but the fact that the US government had been infiltrated by a significant number of Communist spies. At the end of November 1945, in a rather jarring diary entry about Byrnes, Leahy wrote of his worries that the secretary of state was being influenced by "communistically-inclined" advisers.[29]

Weeks later, when Leahy surveyed the world at the start of the new year, he showed similar concern. He believed there was little chance for war in the coming year, placing his hopes on the new United Nations and the possibility it would outlaw the use of atomic weapons. Yet he feared that the State Department was sowing the seeds of a future conflict. He accused it of adopting a "policy of appeasement of the Soviet Government that is reminiscent of Mr. Chamberlain at Munich," and admitted that he started "the new year in the bad graces of the State Department which does not come out into the open with its opposition."[30]

"Bad graces" was an understatement. A few days prior, Leahy's anger at the secretary of state had finally boiled over, and he exploded at the man—in front of President Truman, no less. For months, Leahy had been losing faith in James Byrnes, finding his enormous ego off-putting, especially when compared to what he considered the secretary's lack of meaningful achievements.[31] Byrnes, in return, was jealous of Leahy's power, boasting after his appointment that he would take the admiral down a peg, that he would make Leahy stop acting like he was secretary of state.[32]

Things between the two men deteriorated markedly during the last few months of 1945. Byrnes spent much of the fall of 1945 in London and Moscow, as part of the foreign secretaries' conferences held to settle outstanding issues left over from Potsdam.[33] He often refused to provide important updates to the White House, surprising seasoned diplomats with his amateurishness.[34] Leahy believed that Byrnes's performance showed he was not up to the job. At first Byrnes was unnecessarily aggressive, and Vyacheslav Molotov, the Soviet foreign secretary, threatened to walk out of the negotiations. Over a secure teletype line, Byrnes had to turn to Leahy, pleading with him to telegram the Soviets asking them to stay.[35] Leahy, who could not reach Truman, acted decisively and sent a soothing message to the Russians, which kept Molotov from leaving.

After this blunder, Leahy believed that Byrnes overcompensated, agreeing to meaningless declarations with the Soviets in an effort to keep them happy.[36] In December, when Byrnes paid a visit to Washington, he made things worse in Leahy's eyes by arguing that the Chinese Nationalists should be forced into a coalition with the Communists.[37] Leahy concluded that Byrnes, who had been dripping with braggadocio six months earlier, had been seduced by "pink" elements in the State Department. Truman privately told the admiral that he was also surprised by Byrnes's weakness on China.[38] Whereas Byrnes was still putting a positive spin on things, Leahy—or the "tough old Admiral," as Truman called him at the time—was pushing the president down a more skeptical path.[39]

Leahy's temper finally flared aboard the president's yacht, the USS *Williamsburg*, during a holiday cruise on the Potomac. When Truman learned that Byrnes was planning to deliver a radio address to the country outlining his great achievements with the Russians—and did not intend to clear his speech with the White House—the president ordered the secretary to report to the *Williamsburg* at once. Both Truman and Leahy believed Byrnes's claims of success were nonsense, considering what few agreements the secretary had reached to be unnecessarily supine.

What happened when Byrnes arrived on board ship is the subject of some disagreement. Byrnes claimed that Truman expressed "wholehearted approval" of his work, while Leahy voiced only moderate disappointment with the agreements on Romania and Bulgaria.[40] Truman claimed that he ripped into Byrnes, putting the arrogant secretary in his place.[41] Yet witnesses reported that it was William Leahy who humiliated Byrnes.[42] Truman's press secretary, Matthew Connelly, recalled that "when Byrnes arrived we were having dinner and Admiral Leahy sat directly across from Byrnes at the dinner table, then Leahy took him apart to a fare-the-well [*sic*]. He never let him off the hook."[43] John Snyder, who would later become treasury secretary, and Harry Vaughan, Truman's close friend, both remembered Leahy being the aggressor, with Vaughan reflecting that the admiral gave Byrnes "a hell of a chewing out."[44]

In Leahy's diary, he described criticizing the Moscow agreements Byrnes had negotiated, saying that both he and Truman believed that they were in opposition to the president's own statements (and that meant Leahy's Navy Day address). Leahy "repeatedly" asked the secretary of state "for information as to what benefits accrue to the United States and was unable to get a satisfactory reply."[45]

Leahy was the only person in the United States, other than Truman himself, who could have ripped into Byrnes and emerged with an enhanced reputation. His aggression in defense of presidential supremacy, but also in defense of his own foreign-policy vision, cemented the personal bond between himself and Truman. It helps explain why Truman decided to concentrate so much power in Leahy's hands when it came to the establishment of America's new intelligence service. He even used him as the highest-ranking intelligence courier in the history of the United States.

In February 1946, the president sent Leahy to Canada for what was officially to be a routine diplomatic mission in which the admiral would represent Truman at the retirement dinner of the governor-general to Canada, the Earl of Athlone.[46] In reality, the president had sent his chief of staff to collect the most up-to-date information from Prime Minister Mackenzie King regarding the Gouzenko case. What he learned made a huge impression on the admiral. He was shocked by how much intelligence the Soviets had been able to extract from their Canadian sources, including details about the Manhattan Project.[47]

Meanwhile, the new National Intelligence Authority had started operating. Truman had formally approved a structure for the NIA and the CIA along the exact lines laid out in Leahy's plan, with one change. Instead of there being a specific Joint Chiefs representative on the NIA, the president decided that he wanted a personal representative, and he chose Leahy. That meant that when the NIA met, Leahy spoke for Truman, which allowed him to control much of the CIA's development until the middle of 1947.

The board's first meeting, on February 5, focused on how the CIA would operate under the NIA.[48] Byrnes, chairing the meeting, demanded the right to summarize the NIA's decisions to the president. It was a clear power grab from the secretary of state, and Leahy, already accustomed to humiliating James Byrnes, let him know that this would not happen. Even in the sanitized minutes of the meeting, Leahy clearly slapped Byrnes down.

> SECRETARY BYRNES stressed the fact that it was his function to furnish the President with information on which to base his conclusions.
>
> ADMIRAL LEAHY expressed his understanding that the President wanted the information from all three departments (State, War and Navy) summarized in order to keep him currently informed. Admiral Leahy pointed out that Secretary Byrnes presents the viewpoint of the Department of State while the President would like to receive significant information available in all three department[s] in a single summary.[49]

Unsurprisingly, Leahy ended up being one of two people who supplied Truman with information on the NIA and the CIA. The other was the director of the CIA himself, and this did represent a change in Truman and Leahy's morning routine. Now the director could join the president and the admiral for at least part of every morning briefing, passing on the CIA's newest intelligence summary.

All of this is indicative that William Leahy had reached a new and unexpected high point in his career. Instead of being eased into an honorable and lucrative retirement at the end of the war, he had carved out a central if different role in the new administration. His relationship with Truman, which he knew to be the bedrock of his influence, had strengthened since April 1945, as he had shown himself to be committed to the person and the office. He had used that influence to rhetorically shape the coming Cold War through both the Navy Day address and the soon-to-be-delivered "Iron Curtain" speech. He had triumphed over William Donovan and James Byrnes in the struggle to establish a new intelligence structure for the United States, and he had transformed himself into the most important conduit of intelligence information within the White House. The real question was not how powerful Leahy was; it was for how long his influence would last.

CHAPTER 28

Priorities

In early 1946, a raft of newspaper columns appeared by some of the most influential reporters of the day discussing the enormous influence of Adm. William Leahy. He was described as a mysterious, Machiavellian figure, pushing President Truman to take a harder line on communism while at the same time laying waste to his own enemies—most prominently the secretary of state, James Byrnes. Republican-supporting columnist Drew Pearson claimed that Leahy had much more influence over Truman than did Byrnes, and that the admiral was driving the president to launch a preventative war against the Soviet Union.[1]

Pearson's latter point was nonsense; Leahy was not advocating for war. Yet the speed with which news of his split with Byrnes had made it out into the public was unsettling, especially for a man who avoided publicity. He believed that the person responsible for the stories was Byrnes himself, who cultivated the press as assiduously as any figure in Washington. In an attempt to squash the rumors, Leahy spoke on the record to the *New York Herald Tribune*: "If you want to write the truth . . . you can say that Admiral Leahy has never made any attacks on Mr. Secretary Byrnes, that he considers Mr. Secretary Byrnes a very good friend."[2] When the stories did not stop, a frustrated Leahy went to the State Department and warned Byrnes to back off.

Yet there was a great deal of truth to the reports. Leahy had indeed

fallen out with Byrnes, and was thinking about advising Truman to select a new secretary of state. And he was trying to play a major role in
pushing US foreign policy in a personal direction. The problem was
that the newspaper pieces were in many ways too accurate. As the
greatest behind-the-scenes political operator in America, he knew that
becoming well-known could weaken his power in the White House.
Simply put, he didn't want people to know his methods of operation.

A number of different policy disputes in areas beyond Soviet relations had begun to dominate Leahy's time: US policy on China, the role
of atomic weapons in US strategy, the reorganization of America's strategic structures (both the creation of the CIA and the new Department
of Defense), and the US position in the Middle East. The most frustrat-
ing were the first and last.

In 1946, US-Chinese relations reached a point of confrontation. Far
from simplifying matters, the end of World War II had made things
more difficult, as huge parts of China once occupied by the Japanese
were now up for grabs. While Chiang Kai-shek and the Nationalists asserted some authority in the middle of the country, the Communists,
led by Mao Tse-tung, established a strong base in the north and had real
force in the south. Civil war was in the air.

Most of those around Truman, including Byrnes, George Marshall,
and Secretary of War Robert Patterson, were determined to push the
Chinese Nationalists and Communists into a coalition government.
They had concluded that Chiang Kai-shek and his Nationalist Party
were corrupt and incompetent.[3] In December 1945, the president had
sent Marshall to China as his personal emissary, his assignment being
to bring the two sides together.[4]

Marshall's mission turned out to be a disaster.[5] To get the Nationalists in line, he threatened to withhold US aid unless they promised to
work with the Communists. When this failed, in late July 1946 he delivered on his ultimatum and placed the Nationalists under an arms embargo.[6] In August, Marshall reported to the president that the United
States should abandon the Nationalists if they continued to resist.[7] His
embargo would last for almost a year.

Yet the general had underestimated Communist strength. The

Nationalists desperately needed aid precisely when Marshall turned off the taps. Despite his claims, US support to the Chinese in 1945 and 1946 had been quite limited, while the Communists received significant military aid from the Soviet Union, as well as Japanese equipment abandoned at the end of the war. Rather than pushing the two sides toward a coalition government, Marshall had weakened the Nationalists at precisely the moment Leahy wanted them to be strengthened, thereby opening up the possibility of the Communists seizing national power.

From Washington, Leahy watched Marshall's stumbles with a combination of dread and disbelief. Before departing for China, Marshall had told Leahy that he was going to "tell Chiang that he had to get on with the Communists or without help from us," a position the general repeated when he returned to Washington. Leahy later quipped, "I thought he was wrong then, both times."[8] Leahy had no confidence that a Communist-Nationalist coalition would bring stability, calling the idea foolish in 1945. His views of communism convinced him that Mao's ultimate goal would always be the seizure of complete control. As such, Leahy believed that the only alternative open to the US government, as unpalatable as it might be, was to provide as much support for the Nationalists as possible, giving them the best chance to triumph in a straight fight.[9]

Leahy's sympathy for the Nationalists remained well-known in Washington. He was briefed regularly by the Chinese ambassador, Wei Tao-ming, who complained that his nation was being bullied by General Marshall into a coalition when what they really wanted was to fight communism.[10] Chiang Kai-shek reached out to the admiral personally in April, sending the Chinese military attaché, Gen. Shang Zhen, to ask for advice on how to deal with Marshall.[11] Yet Leahy was hamstrung. His only lever of power to help the Nationalists was to persuade President Truman that he should repudiate Marshall. Leahy tried a number of times and always failed. Leahy claimed that Truman was sympathetic to his position, but Marshall and the State Department remained unmovable. "The President is all right," Leahy told a colleague, "he's behind Chiang. But those 'pinkies' in the State Department can't be trusted."[12] Leahy's faith in Truman was misplaced. When the two discussed the issue privately, the president seemed supportive of the Nationalists, but he would never undermine Marshall.

While pushing for a greater American commitment to China, Leahy continued his bitter opposition to US involvement in the Middle East. Truman was under strong political pressure to support the continuing immigration of European Jews to Palestine. Leahy was convinced that Jewish emigration would only unsettle the region, leading to decades of conflict with the Arab population, which would be a huge drain on American time and resources. He was increasingly bewildered by the cavalier way in which some discussed the impact of this immigration. During a car ride with the president and Judge Joseph Hutcheson Jr., a leading board member of the Anglo-American committee set up to study the question of Jewish immigration, Leahy listened as Hutcheson spoke optimistically about the resettlement of an additional 100,000 Jewish refugees into Palestine, believing it could be achieved quickly and calmly. Leahy considered him delusional: "I fear that he has underestimated the importance of the King of Arabia and of the Moslem reaction to this proposed solution to the problem."[13] The admiral would do everything possible to keep the United States from formally supporting such emigration, even using the Joint Chiefs to argue that the United States could not afford a military commitment to the region.[14]

Another source of conflict for Leahy was the evolving shape of America's national-security state. The key question that emerged in the spring of 1946 was Adm. Sidney Souers's successor as director of the CIA. It was thought prudent that the next head come from the army, and Dwight Eisenhower, serving as the army's chief of staff, suggested a second-rate staff officer, Gen. Charles Bonesteel. At sixty-one years old, Bonesteel had enjoyed an unremarkable career and was set to retire in the not-too-distant future.[15] In suggesting Bonesteel, Eisenhower was trying to hide Leahy's preferred candidate, Gen. Hoyt Vandenberg.

Vandenberg, at forty-seven, was the rising star of the US Army Air Force. With a stellar service record from the war, he had worked in military intelligence since 1945 and was considered next in line as the army air force chief of staff. He was exactly the kind of officer Leahy thought should run the CIA: forceful, competent, and technologically conversant. Eisenhower, wanting Vandenberg to take over the army air force, was determined to block his appointment to the CIA. On April 26, Leahy personally asked Eisenhower to release Vandenberg.[16] Ike said he would think it over, but the next day he went behind the admiral's back to convince President Truman to appoint Bonesteel. Leahy fought back, writing to the president on May 9 that Vandenberg was the only man for the job.[17] Truman reacted immediately, and Vandenberg took office as CIA director in early June. One of his first meetings in his new post was with Leahy.[18]

Leahy repaid Vandenberg by being a strong supporter of the new director's plans to give the agency some teeth. As the originator of the plan that brought the CIA into existence, Leahy often took it upon himself to explain to the other NIA board members how the agency was supposed to operate. He wanted Vandenberg to have the power to set up his own show administratively, and he wanted to make sure that Vandenberg had a large enough budget to provide the president with meaningful intelligence.[19] Yet he wanted it understood that the NIA was the enabling and supervisory body for the CIA, and that the new agency could not undertake OSS-style operations without NIA approval. He emphasized that point in the second meeting of the NIA after Vandenberg took over.

> Admiral Leahy stated that the President authorized him to make it clear that the President considered the responsible agency in the present arrangement to be the NIA. The President stated that the Director of Central Intelligence is not responsible further than to carry out the directives of the NIA. Admiral Leahy said that there were some indications that the Director of Central Intelligence with the Intelligence Advisory Board, might tend to assume greater control over intelligence activities than was intended.[20]

Later, when he thought Vandenberg was going too far in requesting funds, Leahy told him to economize.[21] It was Leahy who understood that the NIA had two purposes for the new CIA. One was to be a shield to allow the new group to get off the ground and make sure it had enough support to do its job. The other was to monitor the CIA, to keep it from evolving into the wasteful and counterproductive organization that the OSS had become. He was also determined to make sure that the CIA did not spy on American citizens. In August 1946, FBI director J. Edgar Hoover wrote to Leahy saying he was worried that the CIA would become involved in domestic intelligence.[22] Leahy told him not to worry, offering to explain things in greater detail if Hoover was still concerned.[23]

Leahy may have been pleased with the new CIA, but he was far less content with the ongoing dispute over the future of the armed services. The watchword of the day in 1946 was "unification." What this meant was not entirely clear, but it usually entailed a single US Department of Defense, with one cabinet-level defense secretary, which would incorporate the departments for the army and navy. In most scenarios, the air force would then be spun out of the army, and the three services would become equals. The idea of a unified department had been around for a while, but no concrete steps had been taken to push the process along. President Roosevelt had been mostly uninterested in the subject, but Truman was supportive, which caused headaches for Leahy. For most naval officers, unification was a code word for the subordination of the fleet to the army and the air force, and they were determined to fight the process.

This unification dispute was the nastiest inter-service feud in American history. It saw the army and navy lobby backers in the White House, Congress, and the media with increasing frenzy. Emotions were so raw that the smallest things could cause a dramatic reaction. When Vannevar Bush was tapped by Truman to put together a Joint Research and Development Committee to see how the services could better coordinate their scientific efforts, he wanted to name the esteemed scientist Dr. Lloyd Berkner as his deputy. Air Force general Carl "Tooey" Spaatz and Secretary of War Robert Patterson, himself a former soldier, both panicked because Berkner had served in the naval reserve. They each tried to blackball the appointment.[24]

Leahy was skeptical of unification in general, worried about two possible developments. The first was that the navy would lose the Marine Corps, as all ground-combat units would be given to the army. The second was that the navy would be forced to yield all non-carrier aircraft to the air force. These were not groundless concerns, as Eisenhower called for exactly such an arrangement in a letter to Leahy and the other chiefs in April 1946.[25]

Yet with Truman increasingly committed to a single Defense Department, Leahy repressed his doubts. When Sam Rosenman sent him a statement in support of unification, Leahy showed his loyalty to the president, saying that while he was still personally opposed to the policy, he would do his best to make it work, even editing Rosenman's statement to make it more effective.[26] Leahy was true to his word on this, within limits. He became the most cooperative senior American naval officer when it came to unification. Many of his fellow admirals fought to the end against the process, but Leahy chose to maintain the president's trust on the issue. He even represented Truman at many of the meetings during which the difficult questions were thrashed out.[27]

The discussions about unification reveal one important element in Leahy's outlook: his strong desire to get rid of his own job. Believing in the limitation of military power, he argued against formalizing his position as chief of staff and chairman of the Joint Chiefs.[28] In his view, no one person should wield as much power as he had in the war, calling it "extremely bad and dangerous."[29] As discussions heated up, his opposition to his own post hardened.[30] In a White House meeting on unification involving the president, Leahy spoke forcefully against continuing his role, saying, according to the minutes, "that had he wanted to secure power for himself during the war he could have arrogated a great deal to himself." Truman was convinced, and Leahy's opposition had made sure, that there would never be another figure such as him in American history.[31]

Meanwhile, he remained determined to prevent the United States from ever launching an atomic first strike again, working to change Truman's mind about the ethical value of the atomic bomb. Truman's evident excitement about the Hiroshima and Nagasaki bombs made this a difficult task, but over the coming years the president would change his tone and outlook completely and practically rule out the United States ever again launching an atomic first strike. The only senior adviser continually pushing him down this path was William Leahy.

In October 1945, Leahy, from his position as chairman of the Joint Chiefs, argued for a commission to study the fallout from America's use the atomic bomb. Not wanting a whitewash, he called for an equal number of civilian and military members for any commission.[32] The next day, Leahy drew up a memorandum for the president in which he urged Truman to make a public declaration that the United States would use atomic weapons in the future only if it had preapproval by the United Nations.[33] A few weeks later, in November, a British-Canadian delegation led by Clement Attlee visited Washington to confer with President Truman on various issues, the most important of them being the future of atomic weapons. Leahy argued that the moment was right to try to outlaw atomic weapons. The British, supported by James Byrnes, were opposed. The British and Canadian governments were determined to allow Britain to develop its own atomic bomb first. Leahy was aware of the powerful forces arrayed against him, but noted that Truman was starting to change sides: "The President has repeatedly expressed to me his desire to obtain by agreement with other nations an effective prohibition of the use of atomic bombs, but he yields to pressure by Mr. Attlee and Mr. Byrnes to approach the problem with a joint-Anglo-British announcement of many words and little force."[34]

The Navy Day address had dwelled on the transformative impact of the atomic bomb, and now Leahy made sure that Truman's next major foreign-policy address also contained a strong anti-atomic element. The president's Army Day address, given in Chicago in April 1946, was also written by Leahy and Rosenman.[35] In it, Truman talked about the need for universal military training for American youth.[36] This was not conscription but a call to have American youth prepared to fight in the future if the need arose. This might seem a militarist call, and certainly it was not pacifistic, but it was anti-atomic. The strongest reason Leahy had for supporting universal training was that it meant, in the case of war, the United States would not have to employ atomic weapons because its armed forces were too small.

Even after no progress was made with the British and Byrnes in November, the president and his chief of staff kept encouraging the secretary of state to push for an international prohibition on atomic weapons. In January, Truman, almost certainly following Leahy's lead, asked Byrnes to push for such an agreement while the secretary was in London, where the Big Three and others maintained a semipermanent headquarters for their foreign secretaries. Byrnes balked, claiming that any move in that direction would fail because of British objections.[37]

The American military's desire to make atomic weapons a viable first-strike option gave Leahy a sense of urgency in his desire to see the bomb outlawed. Gen. Leslie Groves, the head of the Manhattan Project, argued that as atomic bombs were offensive weapons, the United States had to be prepared to use them in a first strike. The nation should be ready and willing to drop large numbers of atomic bombs on civilian targets at the start of the next war, he asserted. Groves wanted a war of extermination, arguing, "If used in sufficient numbers, it [the atomic bomb] can completely destroy the densely populated centers of any nation on earth."[38]

Such arguments drove Leahy mad, and he decided that military men such as Groves had to be prevented from having control over the use of atomic weapons. Leahy was able to use his influence on the NIA to monitor what was happening with the Manhattan Project, and Groves. Leahy called for the transfer of all atomic intelligence to the NIA, thus weakening Groves's control of information through the Manhattan Project and the new Atomic Energy Commission.[39] It was then Leahy's job to go back from the NIA to Truman to make sure that this happened.

Leahy regularly rebuked American officers who he believed were irresponsibly discussing atomic weapons. In July 1946, he reprimanded Gen. Curtis LeMay and Adm. William Blandy for being quoted in the press about how and why atomic bombs could be used in the future.[40] Leahy wanted to keep all discussion about the question forbidden until the Joint Chiefs of Staff, which he controlled, had been able to study all available reports.[41]

It was preparation for what would be one of the last successful fights that Leahy would ever wage. But first, a crisis in American-Soviet relations was about to change world history.

CHAPTER 29

Cold War

At noon on March 12, 1947, President Truman rose to address a joint session of Congress, and the cavernous chamber of the House of Representatives, which had been seething with energy, became deathly quiet. Over the next half hour, the president announced, in the bluntest language, that the United States would deploy its vast power across the globe to contain communism. Truman made common cause with the world's "free peoples," promising $400 million in military and civilian aid for Turkey and Greece and demanding Congress authorize the deployment of American military personnel in the region. Though the Soviet Union was never mentioned by name, there was no doubt who the enemy was. The wartime alliance was over. The Cold War had begun.

As the address was delivered, William Leahy, resplendent in full fleet admiral's uniform, was seated on the floor of Congress, just ten feet to the president's right. An insider among insiders, he had been driven to Congress with Truman, and after the speech the two would board a plane together and head to Key West, Florida, for a week's vacation. To many around Washington, the speech represented a vindication of Leahy's vision, the natural extension of the line he had been pushing since the end of the war. The *New York Times* claimed that Leahy had done all the behind-the-scenes work "formulating" the new "Truman Doctrine."[1]

They were wrong. The Truman Doctrine, and the decision to intervene militarily in Greece and Turkey, were to Leahy mistakes, possibly historic ones, that could turn the United States into the world's policeman and in the process see America meddling around the globe in areas in which it had no concern. The speech that Truman delivered represented a defeat for Leahy's vision, and in many ways marked the beginning of a steep decline in his ability to influence the president and American foreign policy.

A few months earlier he had been in control of much of the White House's thinking on the Soviet Union. Truman, in fact, viewed him as one of the few people he could trust for honest advice. In May 1946 Leahy paid a visit to England, ostensibly for a holiday, but it was more a political/ diplomatic mission to collect information on the state of the Western alliance. In London, he met with the heads of the army, navy, and Royal Air Force, as well as the top men of the British government, including Prime Minister Clement Attlee and Foreign Secretary Ernest Bevin.

Leahy was interested in finding out their views on relations between the Soviets and the West and the state of British defense planning. In Bevin, the American admiral found a kindred spirit on foreign policy. A large and brawny man now softening around the middle, Bevin had emerged from deep working-class roots to become foreign secretary in 1945. He understood the imperial age was doomed and spoke about the coming independence for India and Egypt. Bevin wanted the United Kingdom to play a leading role with the United States in restricting, but not fighting, the Soviet Union. Deeply skeptical of Soviet intentions, he told Leahy that he believed that the Soviets were a long way from being able to wage war against the West. When Leahy returned to Washington, he told James Forrestal that Bevin was a man to be respected and cultivated.[2]

Even Leahy's socializing in London had a diplomatic purpose. He visited Buckingham Palace for a chat with King George and was once again struck by the monarch's well-mannered superciliousness.[3] At least they were able to reminisce about Franklin Roosevelt, which made the time pass pleasantly enough. For Leahy the most meaningful social event was a small dinner party thrown in his honor by Winston Churchill.

It was held in Churchill's town house, recently purchased on one of London's finest streets, Hyde Park Gate. It was an intimate affair, the only other people in attendance being Churchill's wife, Clementine, their daughter Mary, and her companion for the evening, a son of Lord Cholmondeley, unremarkable to Leahy except for the fact that his last name was pronounced "Chumley."[4]

As the meal was served, Leahy studied Churchill with his measured eye. He was alarmed that the former prime minister's health had not improved since he delivered the "Iron Curtain" speech. Gripped by vertigo, Churchill swayed when standing, looking as if he could topple over at any minute. He worked himself up into a lather, enraged at the anti-imperial policies of the Labour government. Convinced that only white Britons could rule India, he prophesied that, if given independence, India would descend into chaos and be taken over by a nationalist demagogue who would undo all the great things that the British had done. He argued that Ireland should be reincorporated into the British Empire, a notion that Leahy found ridiculous.

The two old warhorses found common ground over US-Soviet relations. They patted each other on the back about the toughening rhetoric emanating from Washington, as well as plans for a stronger American military. Yet, when the meal ended, Leahy was more depressed than anything else. He had had a splendid time but was convinced that because of Churchill's imperialist "dreams" and "inability to readjust himself to changed world conditions," the former prime minister's political career might be at an end.[5]

Once back in Washington, Leahy briefed the president about his trip. The president was clearly confused. Having hinted openly about changes in the US-Soviet relationship, he was unsure how far to push his new line. He decided that he needed one document combining the ideas of the top people in his administration, and charged Clark Clifford with the task of compiling a report. One month after Leahy returned from Britain, Clifford stopped by Leahy's office with George Elsey to ask the admiral to participate.*

* The memorandum that they wrote is often referred to as the Clifford Report, though Elsey claimed to have done most of the work.

Clark Clifford was the young man in a hurry of the Truman administration. A St. Louis lawyer before the war, he was immersed in the
Missouri Democratic machine, which brought him to Truman's attention. A naval officer during the war, Clifford was named Truman's naval aide in 1945 and quickly impressed and ingratiated himself with the
president. There was a whiff of Harry Hopkins about Clifford. Instinctively political, he moved from naval aide to special counselor to the
president, a position that allowed him to dabble in almost every element of Truman's life. He would eventually become one of the great
power brokers of the Democratic Party and Lyndon Johnson's last secretary of defense during the Vietnam War.

The aging, grumpy Leahy and younger, forward-planning Clifford
were the stylistic bookends of the Truman White House. This led to some
competitiveness in their interactions. When Clifford first approached
Leahy about help with his report, the admiral was a little miffed, his pride
hurt that Truman had not asked him to do the job.[6] After his brief let-
down, Leahy jumped in behind the project and, in a sign that his opinion
still carried weight, had more influence over its final shape than any other
policy maker. The wily admiral schooled Clifford on how to keep the military from dominating the final product. As Clifford later recalled:

> I showed Leahy a draft of a letter to the Joint Chiefs of Staff asking
> for their views on how to deal with the Soviet Union. Leahy, expe-
> rienced in the ways of the military, insisted on restricting the re-
> quest to "military policy" only, so that the Chiefs could not, in his
> words, "stretch it into an excuse to render a political opinion." I
> was struck by Leahy's loyalty to the interests of the President
> rather than the uniformed services, and the careful way he tried to
> prevent the President from getting undesirable pressure from the
> military outside their proper area of responsibility. It was a lesson
> I would remember when I dealt with the military as Secretary of
> Defense under Lyndon Johnson.[7]

Outwardly Leahy remained his normal cantankerous self. When
discussing the report with Elsey, he suggested it be short and sweet,

joking that it "ought to come out and say that the Russians are sons of bitches!"[8] However, in print, Leahy was surprisingly restrained. He eventually fed three different reports to Clifford and Elsey: one a personal statement of his own views, one a CIA report on Soviet capabilities, and the last a memorandum from the Joint Chiefs of Staff.[9] The tone of each was remarkably cautious and non-threatening, especially when compared to the more bellicose ones produced elsewhere. The Joint Chiefs report was, as Leahy had intended, devoted strictly to military policy.[10] There was no talk of a rollback of Soviet influence. The United States was to keep its defenses strong, should look to keep areas not under Soviet domination out of Communist control, and, in a particularly Leahy-like nod, should strengthen its intelligence-gathering capacity. The CIA report, which he would not have written but which he vetted, was also not alarmist. Its second point was that the Soviet Union was still so relatively weak that it would need to avoid a conflict with the United States for an indefinite period.[11] By comparison, the War Department's response, written by Robert Patterson, began with a discussion of Soviet expansion in the Middle East, arguing that the United States needed to be ready to intervene there quickly.[12] The secretary of war also called for a large military buildup, with a focus on long-range strategic airpower, one assumes atomically armed.

The paper that Leahy wrote with his own ideas is one of the most revealing documents he ever produced.[13]* Reading it, one can see him at his desk, pince-nez perched low on his crooked nose, birdlike, holding pencil and paper, organizing his thoughts. Leahy liked to write documents out in longhand on eight-by-ten-inch pads, in his large, legible, slightly oval handwriting, before sending them to a trusted secretary to be typed. He often refused to dictate his thoughts, worried that he might reveal something too sensitive. He wrote in the bullet-point style that came naturally, and used the macho slang of his spoken vocabulary. He wrote of "commy" influence, "Red" propaganda, and "suckers" for the Communist message.

The salty language and machine-gun writing style could not hide

---

* The paper in its entirety is reproduced in Appendix C.

Leahy's thoughtful ideas. The first three pages were reflective, practically intellectual, as he outlined his vision of Soviet behavior. He did accept, as Stalin had said publicly in February 1946, that capitalism and communism were fundamentally incompatible. He was convinced that the chance of there being any permanent friendship between the United States and the Soviet Union was unlikely. Yet he was convinced that the Soviets neither wanted nor would be able to fight a war against the United States for many years. Leahy wrote that not only was the Soviet Union "weaker than the United Western Powers," Soviet communism had major systemic handicaps. While the Communist Party was adept at crushing opposition and ruling dictatorially, it was "no longer a source of emotional inspiration to the people."

Because he was so convinced of the Soviet Union's weakness, Leahy did not want the United States to do anything stupid and make things worse. He called for America to study communism "patiently and objectively" and to fight it with education and propaganda, not bombs and bullets. In the same way that Leahy had wanted the United States to make a positive statement to the world by not using the atomic bomb when it had the chance, he now wanted America to show the world that it was greater than the Soviet Union by not overreacting. His last point was a plea from the heart. Leahy called for the United States to maintain its "own principles with courage and self-confidence. Our greatest danger is that of becoming like those with whom we are coping."[14]

It was a more subtle policy than was offered by anyone else close to the president. Communism was an enemy, but it was not yet a threat.

The final report produced by Elsey and Clifford in September was a combination of Leahy's softer tone and the harsher views of others. It made a huge impression on Truman, who considered its conclusion so "hot" that he refused to circulate the document and kept it locked in the White House.[15] It was the real precursor document to the policy of containment, and the section on policy recommendations was almost identical to the Truman Doctrine as announced in 1947.[16] It was also the high point of Leahy's influence over the road into the Cold War. When the decision was made six months later to move the United States into a more aggressive posture against the Soviet Union, Leahy would be in a much weaker position.

This was not immediately apparent. Indeed, the two major cabinet changes that were made between the Clifford Report and the crisis over Greece and Turkey in February 1947 seemed to show Leahy up to his old tricks, wielding a backstairs knife as skillfully as always. The first was the firing of Henry Wallace, the secretary of commerce, whom Leahy despised. He considered Wallace to be as pink as smoked salmon and as naïve as Eleanor Roosevelt. In July 1946, Wallace wrote to Truman arguing that the United States should slash its defense budget and share the secret of atomic weapons with the Soviets.[17] Leahy viewed him as an appeaser. Wallace, meanwhile, made the classic mistake of underestimating Leahy. When Wallace tried to describe him years later, it was clear he did not understand the admiral at all, remarking, "I looked upon him as rather a stiff and unaware kind of person without much ability to look beneath the surface."[18]

Leahy repaid Wallace's underestimation with ruthless political maneuvering. Things came to a head on September 12. During a trip to Europe, Wallace gave a public speech that called for America to moderate its increasingly harsh stance toward the Soviet Union, implying that there was a moral equivalence between the Soviets and the United Kingdom. It instantly became a major talking point in European capitals. Wallace claimed, correctly, that the speech had been approved by the president and asked for vindication. Truman, sheepishly, admitted that Wallace had shown him a draft before leaving, but that he had not looked at it closely.[19]

When news of the speech reached Washington on September 18, Leahy pounced. Not caring that the president had approved the text, Leahy went immediately to Truman and demanded that Wallace be fired because the secretary was now completely out of step with the administration.[20] That night Leahy had dinner with Forrestal, Patterson, and William Bullitt and continued the attack. He believed that Wallace's speech could weaken Western resolve, and the evening became an intense discussion between the president's chief of staff, the secretary of war, and the secretary of the navy about what to do. Two days later Wallace was out and it was the arguments that Leahy made to Truman on September 18 that were used to publicly explain the reason for Wallace's firing.[21] Averell Harriman, a Leahy favorite, was quickly appointed in Wallace's place.

The next major change was the resignation of James Byrnes. Though the relationship between the president and the secretary of state seemed also to stabilize through 1946, Truman and Leahy both knew Byrnes was a dead man walking.[22] The only question was one of timing. Truman had already identified George Marshall as the ideal replacement, but the general was in China and would not be back until early 1947. It does seem, therefore, that what Truman and Leahy did was mark time. They got along as well as possible with Byrnes, waiting for a time to make a change. In December, Byrnes concluded a meaningless set of agreements with the Soviets and, flush with success, offered his resignation. The president accepted with pleasure. Marshall was immediately appointed in his place.

The press speculated about Leahy's role in Byrnes's departure. The *United States News*, which ran a major profile of Leahy, assumed that Byrnes's resignation was a sign that the admiral was in control of US foreign policy: "So Admiral Leahy's ideas now predominate. He has attained a position of a well-established, highly-considered elder statesman, toward which he has moved steadily and naturally for many years. His influence obviously is to be great for some time to come."[23]

The reverse was true. While tension between Truman and Byrnes had given Leahy more influence behind the scenes, as he was able to team up with the president against the secretary of state, George Marshall had reappeared, severely reducing Leahy's influence. Truman remained in awe of the general, and bent over backwards to please him, especially early in his time as secretary of state. Leahy, of course, was not in awe of Marshall. He would have preferred Forrestal to replace Byrnes, but Truman was going to have Marshall come hell or high water.

With Marshall in place, the Cold War could truly be launched. The general was more Eurocentric than Leahy, and instinctively more inclined to intervene when the moment appeared, as it did almost immediately. Everything kicked off on February 27, 1947. Two weeks later the world had changed, and a message from Ernest Bevin's Foreign Office in London was the catalyst.

The British had informed Marshall on February 21 that they could no longer afford to aid Greece and Turkey. Both countries were thought at risk of Communist takeover, the Greeks from a Soviet-backed Communist insurgency and the Turks from Soviet military encirclement. Moreover, British troops would be pulling out of Greece soon. Truman, Marshall, and Undersecretary of State Dean Acheson, another policy maker whom Truman was growing to trust, started a mind-meld and judged that if Greece fell to communism (which they believed likely without American aid), it would be the first domino of many. The result would be that the eastern Mediterranean and then much of the Middle East could become Communist in short order.[24]

This alarmist view—as it turned out the Soviets were not supporting the Communist insurgency in Greece in any meaningful way—quickly became the dominant narrative, and it was decided that Congress needed to be brought on board to support a massive infusion of aid into Greece and Turkey. On February 27, Truman hosted a high-powered congressional delegation, including Arthur Vandenberg, chairman of the Senate Foreign Relations Committee, and Joseph Martin, the Speaker of the House, and scared them witless. Marshall and Acheson wove a story of a huge Soviet plot to take over both Greece and Turkey. Marshall was underwhelming (at least, according to Acheson), and it was left to the undersecretary to save the day by playing the apocalypse card.[25] "We have arrived at a situation which has not been paralleled since ancient history," Acheson warned. "Not since Athens and Sparta, not since Rome and Carthage, have we had such a polarization of power."[26] Furthermore, Acheson argued, Greece was on the verge of falling to the Communists, which would represent a direct threat to the security of the United States.

Leahy listened to these extreme arguments with a great deal of skepticism. He did not believe either that Greece or Turkey were in such peril and, even if they were, was convinced that these were not areas of US national interest, the fate of which should turn America into the world's guardian. He silently fumed, listening to all these breathless arguments about the importance of Greece and the need for massive American aid, when at the same time Marshall and the State Department were saying and doing the exact opposite when it came to China.[27] Yet there was nothing Leahy could do. Everyone else in the administration who mattered, including Truman, Marshall, Patterson, and Forrestal, thought otherwise.

In his diary, he erupted, at Marshall, at the State Department, and at the road that America was about to take. "I personally feel that there will be a violent reaction by our people against entangling political involvement in Europe in violation of a traditional American policy," he wrote. "I am unable to understand General Marshall's apparent willingness to become involved in saving the Greek and Turkish Governments."[28]

Right after this meeting, Truman and Leahy departed to Mexico for an official visit.[29] Flying down on the president's plane, for four days they were indulged by their Mexican hosts. Leahy loved Mexico City, finding it similar to Paris, yet the issue of Greece and Turkey, which would have to be decided as soon as they returned to Washington, must have been ever-present in his mind. He was tight-lipped about his conversations with Truman during the trip, but the president must have made clear to the admiral that he was going to press ahead with aid for Greece and Turkey.

As soon as Truman and Leahy returned from Mexico, a cabinet meeting was called so that the president could have unanimous backing for the momentous change he was about to implement. It was the most difficult meeting Leahy had attended since his return from Vichy France, maybe the most humiliating one he endured in his entire career. In his diary, he tried to control his emotions and described the decision to aid Greece as a strategic necessity, though he did think that there would be a large number of Americans who would be shocked by the change in policy and the new international commitment that the United States was making.[30]

The meeting was a humiliation for Leahy.[31] He spoke twice, the first time just after Truman had gone out of his way to slight the policy Leahy believed in more than almost any other. When Julius Krug, the secretary of the interior, made the obvious point that in stopping aid to

Chiang Kai-shek and the Chinese Nationalists, the government was doing the exact opposite of what it said it needed to do with Greece and Turkey, Truman responded with a blast at the Chinese, saying, "Chiang Kai-shek will not fight it out. Communists will fight it out—they are fanatical. It would be pouring sand in a rat hole under present situation."[32]

After hearing his hopes for China dashed in front of the entire cabinet, Leahy meekly said that Marshall also believed the time was not right to aid the Nationalists, but that conditions might change in the future. He made the final interjection of the meeting, saying that the American people needed to be told exactly what was happening:

> Leahy: Agreed with the decision. It will work toward a major war—or a bobtail flush will cause the Russians to capitulate. Unless we have a govt in Greece with which we can work. The people of the U.S. should be brought in and told—it is Communism or free enterprise.[33]

After the meeting, Leahy did everything possible to help the president prepare for his coming address to the American people. On March 10, he sat in on another meeting between Truman and various congressional leaders. Though Leahy tried to be sympathetic to Truman in his diary, it was clear that his heart was not behind the new policy.

> It is my personal opinion that while action to retard the spread of the philosophy of Communism is urgent and necessary to the preservation of political freedom, the proposed support of Greece is a reversal of the traditional American policy to avoid involvement in the political difficulties of European States.
>
> The conference today and the President's address to Congress may be of supreme importance to widely dispersed freedom loving peoples of the world, and they may be a milestone on the way to another world war.[34]

With the Cold War setting in, Leahy was one of the most skeptical people in Washington. He was worried that America, under a president he respected greatly, was reacting with unnecessary aggression over

Greece and Turkey and was betraying the country's ideals at the same time.[35] He was not convinced that the country was under the kind of threat that the State Department or the president claimed, and was worried that in taking this action, the United States might make things worse. After the decision had been made to send aid for Greece and Turkey, the Joint Chiefs under Leahy's supervision produced a memorandum on the military situation in the region.[36] In Greece, circumstances were portrayed as surprisingly positive. All the fighting was in the north of the country, Greek government forces were on the offensive and gaining ground, and their morale was on the rise. In Turkey, while the army needed new equipment, its discipline and morale were excellent and loyalty to the government was unimpeachable. If the Soviets invaded, it was claimed that the Turkish Army on its own could hold out for three to four months.

Leahy could not even hide his doubts about the Truman Doctrine from the press. As part of the great push to get congressional and popular support for aid to Greece and Turkey, both Marshall and Leahy were wheeled out to give confidential briefings to important reporters, including *New York Times* columnist Arthur Krock.[37] Marshall spoke at length about the seriousness of the situation and the need to pour money into Greece. Leahy was terse, dispirited, even contradictory:

He [Leahy] contributed only three bits of information: Truman was extremely dubious about the Greek-Turkish program, and Marshall sold him on it. . . .

Among other things the Admiral said were: that he didn't think we would have trouble with the Russians for five years and didn't think we'd have trouble with them then . . . he didn't like the Truman Doctrine; that, nevertheless, he thought it was important to keep Greece and Turkey from going down the drain; that Turkey could hold out against the Russians for three months (the army puts it at two weeks or 50 days at the most), that even if the war and navy budgets were cut as proposed in Congress, they could probably get along all right; that this had always happened in the past and would probably happen again.[38]

Krock was struck by the toll the pressure was taking on the admiral. When he had last seen Leahy months earlier, the admiral seemed his usual ageless self. Now he was an old man, unhappy, more taciturn, and more uncertain. Krock made a note that Leahy was "aging fast."[39]

Leahy's failure to keep America from going fully down the Cold War rabbit hole bothered him for the rest of his life. He hated the fact that the United States was now a global enforcer. Not long after the Truman Doctrine was announced, he let rip, complaining that Truman's statement to support the world's "free peoples" in their struggles was a historic error that "will be accepted by many peoples as a stated policy of interference with their internal affairs. It is a direct reversal of American policy."[40] He even complained, rather pathetically, that Truman only included that line because Leahy never saw the final draft of the speech. Otherwise, Leahy told himself, he could have "detected this error."

It was a pipe dream. There was nothing Leahy could have done to stop the president. Marshall, Acheson, Forrestal, Patterson, and practically everyone else around Truman would have steamrollered the old admiral. The policy that Leahy wanted the United States to follow was too nuanced for the others. He wanted the United States to toughen up against the Russians, to realize that communism was inimical to Capitalist America. He also believed that the United States should foster democratic principles around the world, especially in the light of the collapse of the European empires that he saw happening all around. But he did not want the United States to become overly militarized and overextended, involving itself in making and unmaking governments and throwing its weight around in areas not directly connected to American security. To William Leahy, that was the easy and wrongheaded choice of the powerful.

CHAPTER 30

Key West

F
ewer than two hours after President Truman started speaking to
Congress on March 12, 1947, he was airborne, having taken off on a
five-hour flight to Florida. The strain of the previous three weeks
had exacted a toll, and Truman's doctor ordered him to take an immediate rest. After landing at Boca Chica Airfield, the president and his
party of seven trusted companions, including Admiral Leahy, Clark
Clifford, Harry Vaughan, and William Hassett, Truman's secretary,
were quickly whisked to the submarine base at the US Naval Station on
nearby Key West.[1]

The William Leahy who clambered down the gangway of the president's plane into the soothing warmth of southern Florida was noticeably changed, both physically and emotionally, from five years at the
center of power. To many of Truman's young staffers, he seemed im-
possibly old. They nicknamed him the "sea dog," and he looked the
part. His hair, which had been thinning for decades, was almost gone
from the crown of his head. Where it had been gray, it was now increasingly white. His eyebrows had grown bushier and could stand out
alarmingly. The wrinkles on his face had deepened and lengthened,
and the previously small jowls hung down lower, accentuating his overall chelonian appearance. Though he still stood erect, his belly peeked
out over his belt. In casual clothes, he would hike his trousers up high
to cover the bulge.

It was because of Leahy that the president's party was in Florida in the first place. In November 1946, on Leahy's recommendation, Truman had visited Key West—and fallen in love. A small naval base on the southernmost tip of Florida, Key West had everything Truman needed to recharge. The clear blue water was warm enough to swim in year-round, the sea breezes soothing, and the modest but comfortable accommodations exactly to the president's taste. Truman could unwind, play poker, have a drink, and sing in comfort and privacy. He would visit eleven times before leaving office, bringing Leahy with him every time the admiral was healthy enough to come.

It was an indication of how their relationship was evolving. As Truman diverged from the admiral on policy recommendations, he integrated him more and more into his personal space. At holidays, not just to Key West but also Camp David, Leahy was now an automatic companion. The president also brought the admiral on overseas trips and in one case sent Leahy to be his official representative. It was almost that by making him more of a friend, he was providing compensation as Leahy's direct influence began weakening. Leahy, whose life could have been much lonelier, was gratified. Sometimes women showed interest in him, including some who sent him proposals by mail. One particular suitor was a California widow almost twenty-five years younger, who mailed in a picture of herself for his approval and began her letter, "All work and no play makes Johnny a dull boy—You must not let that happen to Willie Leahy!"[2] While the admiral was happy to remain devoted to his late wife's memory, he still needed human companionship, and being part of the president's lively social circle mattered a great deal.

In Key West, Truman and those closest to him would stay in the commandant's house, quickly dubbed the Winter White House. Built in a style best termed Militaro-Caribbean, it was shaded by palm trees and only a few yards from the sea. The president stayed alone in the best bedroom—he banned women, including his wife, from his holidays in all but exceptional circumstances—and since there were only four other bedrooms, everyone had to have a roommate, except Leahy. The admiral was given a private room next to the president, which turned

Clifford green with envy. The younger man was so irritated that for a while he avoided coming to Key West when Leahy was there.[3]

This one tiff aside, Key West was a place to escape. Mornings were mostly spent on base. Breakfast was between seven and eight, and Leahy and Truman were among the first to rise. Conversations around the table were at times serious, as the president and his chief of staff re-created their White House roles, with Leahy briefing Truman about overnight events. At other times, they talked sports or the weather, and even bickered. Truman respected Leahy, but sometimes he enjoyed taking the older man down a peg or two. Now at seventy-one years of age, Leahy could come off as grumpy and imperious, and one morning Truman finally called him on it. It had been understood that when Leahy ordered prunes for breakfast, he was to get exactly three. On this morning, a bowl with three prunes was dutifully placed in front of him. Leahy impatiently motioned the waiter to come back. Perhaps the prunes were too big, or he decided he didn't want them after all, but regardless, Truman stared the admiral down, taunting him: "Don't you say a word to that boy—I heard you tell him three, you eat them."[4] Leahy shut up and ate his fruit.

The prune incident was not representative of the general atmosphere at Key West. The younger members of the White House staff were fond of Leahy. Louis Renfrow, who became one of Truman's aides during this time, recalled, "Admiral Leahy was one of the finest men, and probably the most serious individual you've ever met, and yet he had no feeling about trying to impose his importance on anyone."[5] Philleo Nash, another Truman aide, did not get to know Leahy until their paths crossed at Key West. They bonded over a shared Wisconsin heritage, and Nash quickly discovered that spending time with the old admiral was one of the best things about being there. He considered Leahy to be one of the finest people he had ever met, describing him as "very, very charming."[6]

Days at Key West were typically passed sedately, with the president wandering the base, chatting with sailors. Many mornings involved a trip to the enlisted men's beach. Truman's party would don their swimming trunks for a quick dip, sometimes followed by volleyball matches or beach football. But much of the time was spent loafing and sunbathing. Leahy, conscious of his dignity, often avoided swimwear.

After lunch, the party would sometimes go fishing, the waters around Key West being some of the finest deep-water fishing grounds in the world. Truman was not nearly as passionate about the sport as Roosevelt, and the trips were spent in idle relaxation. "Adm. Leahy and I went fishing yesterday—unannounced," Truman wrote to his wife, Bess. "They do it differently here. We sat on the back end of a crash boat in two easy chairs and had a navy captain bait our hook and take the fish off. It was a trolling job entirely. I caught three and the Adm. three.... They were nice fish but I don't know why we caught them except that this is Friday and we can furnish some of our Catholic friends something they can eat today."[7]

Truman enjoyed inspecting the base's naval vessels, and often invited Leahy along, giving him the prized seat next to him in the car. On one inspection tour, Truman's devilish nature came out and he took pleasure in tormenting the old admiral. A captured German Type XXI U-boat, the most advanced submarine of the day, was brought into the base. When a ride in the boat was mentioned, Leahy shuddered, muttering under his breath, "Count me out, I'm not the least bit interested in it."[8] Though he recognized the military value of submarines, he considered them "dirty things," and throughout his career had avoided serving on them.[9] Truman saw an opportunity to correct this shortcoming. He immediately scheduled a visit, listing Leahy as an official member of his party.[10] Once the president's crew had clambered inside the U-boat, Truman, much to the evident worry of his security team and an increasingly alarmed Leahy, ordered the sub to dive. Soon they were 450 feet below sea level, and the air became stale and dank. The admiral was miserable. Once safely ashore, he kept his discomfort to himself and spoke only of his admiration for German technology.[11]

Perhaps Truman's favorite activity at Key West was gambling. Poker games went on morning, afternoon, or evening, whenever Truman felt the urge—although all mention of poker was censored in the president's activity logs.[12] Leahy knew how to handle himself at a poker table, and Truman learned quickly to respect his prowess, writing to his wife that he had lost $3 one evening while the admiral had won more than $40, commenting that Leahy was "a tough player as you'd imagine."[13]

To Leahy, poker was a man's game to be taken seriously. Truman was known to throw pots so that less wealthy staff members would not lose too much. Roger Tubby served as White House assistant press secretary after Leahy retired, though he was at Key West for one of Leahy's last visits. He witnessed the two men in action:

> I had one disastrous evening at the poker table . . . in no time at all I was really in the hole. I think the President realized that I was rather unhappy. I had four children at home. I remember one particular hand where it was straight poker, and so I thought, "Now I know what I've got." I came up with a pretty good hand. And so I stayed in, and several others stayed in, and the pot got bigger and bigger. Then people began to drop out, and ultimately it was just the President and myself, and he threw in. I think it was Admiral Leahy [who] said, "Wait a minute, Boss. You can't do that." He was very improper—the whole thing was very improper. He picked up the President's hand and looked at it and he said, "Why, you ain't even got a pair of deuces." Well, it was simply the President staking me, getting me out of the hole.[14]

While they gambled, the men smoked and drank. The logs of the Key West trips were replete with small cocktail parties. The president was even known to start his day with a shot of bourbon. By this stage in life Leahy was a daily drinker, favoring bourbon and water or martinis. Typically he had at least one at lunch or dinner, and sometimes a cocktail or two in between. He preferred his drinks stiff. At a party thrown by Harry Vaughan, a watered-down punch was served, causing Leahy to quip to Truman that he would need to fix himself a real drink when he went home.[15]

His lunchtime drinking was so regular that Albert Murray, the famous painter commissioned to do a portrait of Leahy, dreaded their afternoon sessions. The admiral, in full dress uniform, weighed down by heavy aiguillettes, would stroll in after a few martinis, settle into his portrait chair, and promptly fall asleep. It happened so often that Murray developed a routine to rouse him so that he could paint. "I would drop a brush on the floor, and it would wake him up. I would turn my back to him and his mouth would fall open, and he would drool all over his uniform and the aiguillettes and everything else. I would take forever to pick the brush up and when I would finally get up he would be finishing mopping himself off with his handkerchief and making the remark, 'Gee, I must have dozed off for a moment.'"[16]

As much as he drank, he smoked even more. Still a chain-smoker into his seventies, his cigarettes were always close at hand. During the war, photographs of senior military figures smoking were often suppressed so as not to offend the more delicate elements of the American public. Yet many of Leahy's wartime pictures usually featured an ashtray in easy reach. After the war, Leahy ceased to care, even allowing *Collier's* to print a photo of him with a lit cigarette clenched visibly between his fingers. William Hassett teased him about it, writing, "The bold photograph with the conspicuous cigarette alarms me. . . . Shame on you not even to conceal your wickedness."[17] In April 1947, after a massage—another Leahy indulgence—the admiral fainted. His doctor told him to cut back on the cigarettes and coffee. He might as well have told him to stop breathing.

Leahy's growing inability to care about such things was a sign of his growing grandiosity. He was lathered in praise. Two- and three-star admirals and generals, normally not the most emotional bunch, would send him the most cloying notes.[18] In 1947, he met with Lt. Gen. Albert Wedemeyer to discuss the man's mission to China. Leahy had always liked Wedemeyer, a self-confident operator, and had been instrumental in having him named as Joseph Stilwell's replacement in 1944. Wedemeyer outdid himself after the meeting in letting Leahy know how wonderful he was, writing, "I enjoyed so much our brief visit at the Army-Navy Club the other day. Every time I talk to you, for several days thereafter I have a feeling of happiness and contentment in the knowledge that a man of your fine character is so close to the throne. You epitomize to me the highest traditions of an American official, military or civil, and I hope that your health will maintain so that you can contribute to stability in our country."[19]

Such praise, heaped on top of the many honors he received, certainly seemed to free Leahy to tease whomever he wanted (with the exception of the president). One of his favorite targets was Dwight Eisenhower. Ike was chief of staff for the army from 1945 to 1948, thus serving on the Joint Chiefs under Leahy's chairmanship. The two never got along particularly well. Eisenhower wanted a more active Joint Chiefs, while Leahy wanted to keep the group from becoming a peacetime general staff. Leahy also distrusted Eisenhower's political ambitions, which were an open secret in Washington. During meetings of the chiefs, Leahy would needle Ike by calling him "Mr. President," causing sniggering around the table. Eisenhower, flustered, would be forced to deny the undeniable and claim he had no White House ambitions. Chester Nimitz was still laughing about it years later.[20]

After a long career, Leahy's habits and attitudes seemed ingrained. In early November 1946, not long before Truman's first visit to Key West, the president asked Leahy to go to Chile to represent the United States at the inauguration of the new president, Gabriel González Videla.[21] Though Videla was Leahy's friend from Vichy, where he had grown fond of the young Chilean on the diplomatic circuit, Leahy remained Leahy, as Spruille Braden, the State Department official assigned to help him prepare for the visit, discovered. When Braden looked at Leahy, he saw an old, unthinking American racist. He later recalled that Leahy "insisted on referring to the Chileans as 'those spicks,' although he was going down on this mission of friendship."[22]

Despite his callousness, Leahy enjoyed his visit. He was flown down to Panama, where he boarded the great battleship USS *Wisconsin* for the cruise to Valparaiso. A large overflight of aircraft marked his arrival, and when his task force reached Chilean waters, he was greeted by an eighteen-gun salute, one more than he believed he was entitled to. Once on land, he had a number of confidential meetings with President Videla, speaking a combination of French and English, a pattern they had established in Vichy. They discussed both foreign and domestic policy, and Leahy, again revealing how the New Deal had penetrated his thinking, applauded Videla's plan to break the power of old economic monopolies, describing him as a Chilean equivalent of an American Democrat. On the cruise home, the old admiral had to be transferred from the *Wisconsin* to a destroyer by highline, suspended over the sea in a small steel crate, which swayed from side to side as he was being transported.[23] He might have preferred a submarine dive.

Back in Washington, Leahy did his best to improve US-Chilean relations.[24] He continued to be in regular contact with Videla, helping the Chilean president even after he had added Communist members to his government.[25] Leahy returned to South America a few months later, this time accompanying President Truman to Brazil in late August 1947 to attend the closing of the Inter-American Conference, which was being held in Rio de Janeiro, and then the formal celebrations of Brazil's Independence Day. Rather than flying home, the president elected to sail back aboard the great battleship USS *Missouri*. It was the first time Truman had ever crossed the equator while at sea, which meant, according to naval custom, the president's initiation into the court of Neptune. Nearly half a century had passed since Leahy had experienced his own initiation as a young sailor back in 1898. He took part in the silly ceremony, playing the role of Number One Shellback, standing next to the sailor performing Neptune as the president participated with gusto.[26] Truman was spared any indignity, but was asked to provide each member of Neptune's court with an autographed picture.

A few days after arriving in Washington, a small ceremony was held in the Oval Office in which the CIA's first director, Sidney Souers, was sworn as the executive secretary of the new National Security Council. At the same time, Admiral Roscoe Hillenkoetter, who had served under Leahy in Vichy, was sworn in as the new head of Central Intelligence. On the surface, Leahy's influence still looked immense, as both men had been handpicked by him. Yet the ceremony marked the beginning of the end.

CHAPTER 31

On the Outside

The swearing-in of Admirals Souers and Hillenkoetter was the result of the recently enacted National Defense Act of 1947. Passed by Congress that July, it was a halfway house on the way to the creation of a united Department of Defense. It combined the old Navy and War Departments into one National Military Authority with three branches for the fleet, the army, and the newly independent air force. While it did establish a new post for a Secretary of Defense—which went to James Forrestal—the services retained a great deal of their autonomy and still had their own secretaries.

The only decisive thing the bill achieved was to decrease the authority of William Leahy. His position of chief of staff to the president was not sanctioned, mostly because he had fought against its inclusion. Because there was no mention of the chief of staff, Leahy was not given a place on the National Security Council, the new bureaucracy charged with guiding American strategic policy. Chaired by the president, it included the secretaries of defense and state; the secretaries of the army, navy, and air force; and the chairman of the National Security Resources Board. The director of the Central Intelligence Agency was put on the National Security Council, but as a non-voting member. The new committee was given the responsibilities of the abolished National Intelligence Agency. At the stroke of the president's pen, Leahy's influence over the CIA had evaporated.

At the same time that Leahy was losing a post, a successor was being groomed to take over his most important role.[1] By creating an executive secretary of the National Security Council, the National Defense Act also set the stage for the first sanctioned national security adviser. Admiral Souers, whom Truman appointed, was set to take over the president's morning briefing from Leahy when the older admiral retired.* With his authority weakening, Leahy was left trying to influence policy indirectly. From the summer of 1947 to 1948, that was Leahy's life, sometimes involved in policy, sometimes not.

Leahy had selected Admiral Hillenkoetter, an ally, to be in charge of the CIA, but now he could no longer control the agency's purpose and operations. When the CIA was founded, covert operations were a negligible part of its remit, as Leahy intended. The original charter drawn up for Truman's signature did not mention covert operations.[2] Leahy understood that covert operations would be something the CIA would do, yet he wanted to keep them, and the CIA as a whole, under control.[3] Without the guidance of William Leahy, the National Security Council began to reimagine the CIA as a far more meddlesome agency.

As his influence continued to wane, Leahy grew ever more distressed about what the United States was on the verge of doing in the Middle East, and not doing in China. Throughout 1947, Truman continued to support Marshall's embargo on aid to the Nationalists in the secretary of state's quixotic quest to force a coalition with the Communists. The result was a continuing deterioration in the Nationalists' position. The Chinese Communists, flooded with aid from the Soviet Union, extended their control over large parts of northern and central China.[4]

Leahy was briefly cheered that summer when Truman chose Albert Wedemeyer as a new special representative to China.[5] Marshall had blocked Wedemeyer's appointment as ambassador to China the previous year because he believed the man might offend Communist sensibilities.[6] Truman, perhaps understanding that abandoning the Nationalists

---

* In 1949, Souers took over Leahy's role in the morning briefing and has been referred to as the first national security adviser in American history. He was the second, as all he was doing was re-creating the role that Leahy had filled since 1942.

was not an altogether sensible policy, decided to let Wedemeyer have a shot.

When Wedemeyer got to China, he found the situation far worse than expected.[7] A fanatical anti-Communist, he felt that US diplomats were undermining Chiang Kai-shek. When he returned to Washington in October, Wedemeyer went right to Leahy and said that without a complete change in American policy, including "munitions, spare parts, ammunition," and economic funds to stabilize the economy, the Nationalists would soon be defeated.[8] He begged Leahy to advise Truman to replace the American ambassador to China, John Leighton Stuart, a former missionary who was an enthusiastic supporter of forcing a Communist-Nationalist coalition.

Had Roosevelt been alive, Stuart would have been out within the week. Now Leahy hit a brick wall. Stuart, protected by Marshall, remained in office for twenty-one more months, until the moment of Mao Tse-tung's final triumph. Leahy could also not help the Nationalists by getting rid of the arms embargo, though he did try, pressing everyone he could, including Forrestal and Truman, but the president would not budge.[9] By early 1948, Leahy's need to show that the US government had set itself up for failure in China became obsessive. He prepared a fifteen-page timeline on developments in China between 1943 and the end of 1947.[10] It was a chronology of State Department errors and a primal scream of frustration.

It was not until early 1948 that Truman and Marshall seemed to comprehend the disaster that they had helped precipitate. It finally dawned on them that the Nationalists were about to be defeated, and much sooner than expected.[11] The embargo was revealed to be what it had been all along, something that punished the Nationalists and rewarded the Communists.[12] There was also a realization that the administration would suffer politically if it were to be seen to have done nothing as China went red, which set off a last-minute scramble to support the Nationalists.[13] In April, Congress authorized $338 million in military and economic aid for China, with the president given an additional $125 million to dispense if he thought it necessary.[14] The simple fact that the amount given was identical to the money allocated to

Greece and Turkey revealed once again to Leahy how the administration had its priorities upside down.

For as the United States was watching China fall, the administration seemed to Leahy to be moving decisively into the Middle East and eastern Mediterranean. Jewish immigration, which Truman supported, led first to tension and then bloody confrontation in Palestine. The British, who had a mandate still in operation from the League of Nations, were keen to wash their hands of the crisis. One idea was to partition Palestine into Jewish and Arab sections. When this occurred in late 1947, US policy makers debated whether America should recognize, and thereby legitimize, the move.[15] Leahy was convinced that the partition might lead to decades of war, which would "dwarf" the present local dispute.[16] In October 1947, from his position as chairman of the Joint Chiefs, he argued that the United States should avoid any interference in the growing conflict between Jews and Muslims. If America became the guarantor of partition, he insisted, it would "prejudice United States strategic interests in the Near and Middle East and that United States influence in the area would be curtailed to that which could be maintained by military force."[17] Leahy understood that the Middle East's oil reserves would make it increasingly important for the United States and the world, but felt that the region's stability could best be guaranteed by preventing it from becoming an area of direct US-Soviet competition.[18]

Leahy's stances on China and the Middle East, both of which conflicted with President Truman's positions, contributed to his loss of influence. The president, knowing what he would hear from the admiral, and perhaps unwilling to listen, turned to him for advice less often. Leahy still briefed Truman every day and chaired the Joint Chiefs, but otherwise he had much less to do. Others still consulted him, but less frequently, and more and more often decisions were reached without his input.

With less to keep him occupied, Leahy spent more time with his family and his past. On December 30, 1947, DC society descended on the Washington Club for the coming-out party of Louise Beale Leahy.[19] Louisita, now nineteen, was a sophomore at Hollins College in Virginia.

Her devoted grandfather arrived to a reception of seven hundred guests, many of whom were faces from his own past. Though he never would have said it, the fact that he was the senior military officer and a major personality in the capital made the party a big event, and many in attendance had come to pay respect to him as much as to his granddaughter.

During a stopover in Puerto Rico while on a weeklong presidential tour of the Caribbean in February 1948, Leahy returned to La Fortaleza, the mansion in which he had lived with Louise after President Roosevelt had appointed him governor of the island in 1940. Looking out over the beautiful gardens, his thoughts turned to his late wife, and waves of emotion came over him as he remembered one of the happiest years of his life. That night, a formal reception was held in the president's honor, and as Truman regaled the crowd of five hundred with an impromptu performance of "The Merry Widow's Waltz," Leahy caught up with as many old friends as he could find. The president's party departed the next day, headed to the US Virgin Islands, but Leahy was determined to get back to Puerto Rico as soon as possible.[20]

The next month, the admiral returned to the Caribbean for a conference in Key West, Florida, to help referee an ongoing crisis set off by the ambiguities of the National Defense Act. The different services, especially the navy and air force, continued to operate as independently as possible, and Secretary of Defense Forrestal, who had been appointed to the new cabinet position in order to allay some of the navy's concerns, became frustrated by the overlapping areas of authority between himself and the service secretaries. Leahy was particularly unhappy, believing that air force general Carl Spaatz, army general Omar Bradley, and chief of naval operations Adm. Louis Denfeld were too prejudiced by their selfish service interests and missed the big picture.[21] Eventually it was decided to sit the key people down and force a solution.

Leahy knew that President Truman wanted an agreement, and if one were not forthcoming, he would force one on the services. Just as when Roosevelt was alive—but rarely now—at Key West Leahy would become the voice of the president.[22] The debate revolved around which of the navy's capabilities the fleet could keep, and four days before the conference Leahy wrote some preparatory notes.[23] He wanted the navy to retain the Marine Corps and both its carrier and ground-based air capabilities, but he expected sacrifices. He wanted the air force to become the dominant player in strategic bombing and he wanted the marines to be more proactive in training with the army on amphibious operations.

Leahy's sketch was replicated almost identically in the final Key West decisions.[24] Indeed, the agreement laid out much of the framework for the defense structure under which America operates to this day. The Marine Corps was left within the navy, with a peacetime strength of no more than four divisions (far larger than it had ever been in peacetime). Its operational plans were supposed to be limited to two division missions so that it would not become a rival army, though even this was open to interpretation. Perhaps even more important, the navy was allowed to fly aircraft from land if they were part of naval responsibilities, including antisubmarine operations. The air force was given control of strategic bombing operations and tactical airpower in support of ground troops. The fleet could attempt some strategic air operations as long as they could be justified as part of its sea control responsibilities. Forrestal, who chaired the discussions and subsequent follow-up talks, saw Leahy as his greatest support in reaching a deal.[25]

With Key West out of the way, Leahy was soon finally able to return to Puerto Rico. In April, the president sent him down to negotiate a relatively small matter, the transfer of different properties from the federal government to the island territory. After three days of talks, Leahy, using the flimsiest excuses, stayed for another week, catching up with good friends. Outside of his Annapolis classmates, it was the largest group of close friends he ever made at one time in his life.

Leahy probably wished that he had never left Puerto Rico. In May 1948, the Middle East once again flared into action as David Ben-Gurion, the head of the World Zionist Organization, declared independence for a separate state of Israel. Leahy, naturally, wanted the United States not to recognize the new state. He was joined by George Marshall, who also worried about the impact of recognition on US relations with Arab countries. If Clark Clifford's memoirs are to be believed, Clifford convinced Truman to take the dramatic step of extending "de facto" recognition to Israel. It occurred after Clifford and Marshall each made presentations to Truman in the oval office—the president evidently finding Clifford more persuasive than Marshall.[26] There is no sign that Leahy was in the room.[27] One assumes that by this point Truman knew exactly where the admiral stood on the question.

For Leahy, it was another crushing defeat. On May 14, the day Truman publicly announced recognition, Leahy prophesied that the United States would soon find itself enmeshed in an unending religious war. "The Palestine situation at the present time, in my opinion, points directly toward a civil war between the Jews and the Moslems in Palestine and possibly in the Moslem inhabited areas of the Middle East," he wrote. "It appears certain that recent developments have been disadvantageous to the interests of the United States and may drag the United States into a war between the two religious groups."[28]

Leahy's relative weakness would have been a huge shock to many Americans, where the perception persisted that he was a Machiavellian power broker, pushing militarism and interventionism on an impressionable Truman. Not long before he made his first trip to Puerto Rico, Leahy was publicly attacked by, of all people, Albert Einstein. The world-famous scientist was the coauthor of a public report released by the National Council Against Conscription entitled "The Militarization of America."[29] Along with a cohort of worthies from academia, the clergy, and commerce, Einstein attacked Leahy as the textbook example of the growth of military power under the Truman administration. From the Boy Scouts upward, they argued, America was being manipulated into preparing for war, including the possible use of atomic weapons. The report caused a minor sensation, with some newspapers picking up on the criticism of Leahy. The *Washington Post* weighed in, attacking Leahy's influence over government policy and calling for his position as chief of staff to the commander in chief to be abolished.[30]

Leahy did his best to act unruffled, telling the president "that being attacked in the public press on a problem of National Defense by such a thoroughly established American as the German Jew Einstein, who acquired citizenship in 1940, or by his pink associates, is a high compliment indeed."[31] But the criticism hurt, especially at precisely the time when Leahy, contrary to Einstein's assertion, was struggling to prevent the United States from adopting an atomic weapon first-strike policy. As relations with the Soviets deteriorated, the idea of atomic war had moved from the hypothetical to the alarmingly real, and US officials had begun discussing the use of atomic weapons against the Russians. Leahy used whatever bureaucratic influence he had left to block a first-strike policy, and it represented one of his few successes in the postwar era.

For the first time, Leahy tried to define what a weapon of mass destruction was, and when or how such terrible weapons could ever be used. He circulated a paper to the Joint Chiefs with the most detailed definition yet given. Arguing that the very survival of humanity was at stake, Leahy believed that the country needed to define what was meant by "weapons of mass destruction," and then do its best to limit their usage. In Leahy's eyes, WMDs were practically any destructive force not capable of being delivered on a target with precision, a particularly all-encompassing proviso that would severely limit the use of military power:

Major Weapons Adaptable to Mass Destruction Are as Follows:
All atomic explosives.
All lethal chemical weapons.
All biological weapons
All missiles carrying heavy explosives or incendiary charges that are not so
   designed as to be capable of precision attack on military objectives.[32]

Leahy's definition is more stringent than the official American definition of WMDs in use today.[33] In this way, he represented something that we see now as very modern. He stood for tight, internationally based controls and norms on the use of any weapons that could be targeted on civilians, with the strongest possible limitations on nuclear, biological, and chemical armaments.

Leahy was just getting started. In July 1947, during a meeting of the Joint Chiefs with Marshall and Forrestal, the use of atomic weapons was analyzed.[34] Eisenhower, Nimitz, and Marshall—or, as Leahy termed them, the army and navy, despite the fact that Marshall was now secretary of state—spoke in favor of the use of atom bombs against the Soviet Union in case of war, which would be a first strike, as the Soviets had not yet exploded their own weapon.[35] Leahy opposed them, saying that "atomic bombs should not be employed by the United States in war, except in direct retaliation for their use by an enemy." Soon, Leahy would be at odds with the air force. In November 1947, the air force proposed a war plan based on the immediate and massive use of atomic weapons in case of a Soviet attack into western Europe.[36] The admiral was not to be moved, and answered that it was his hope that atomic bombs would not be used by the United States in any way, as America should never "inaugurate such a barbarous attack on non-combatants."

In March 1948, the air force upped the ante and proposed JCS-1854, a plan that in Leahy's eyes endorsed a first-strike atomic policy. Using one of the levers of power he had left, his ability to block a move as chairman of the Joint Chiefs, Leahy refused to send the plan forward. He wrote to the chiefs that because JCS-1854 was "based on an assumption that atomic weapons are necessary" and that the chiefs had not been given "authority" to use atomic weapons, that he was "unable to approve" the plan.[37] A few weeks later, the air force returned with a new idea, the Halfmoon Joint Emergency War Plan, which was built around a massive atomic first strike. In the first days of war, the United States would have dropped fifty atomic bombs on the twenty largest Soviet cities, killing many millions of Soviet civilians.

When Leahy first read Halfmoon, he moved decisively to have it denuclearized. On May 12, during a meeting of the chiefs, he demanded a war plan based entirely on conventional weapons, claiming that it was a presidential order.[38] The next day he sent Halfmoon back to the air force, saying that it must be reworked in a way "that does not necessitate the use of atomic bombs for its implementation, and in the consideration of a possibility that atomic bombs may not be available because of their having been outlawed or otherwise prohibited." He then added, in a nice touch, "I am unable to approve JCS-1854/44."[39]

The military establishment flailed around in reaction to Leahy's obstinacy. On May 19, the secretary of the army, Kenneth Royall, wrote to the National Security Council calling for an entirely new discussion on the use of atomic weapons, in light of the ethical criticisms that were being made against them, complaining, "I understand that in some quarters the desirability of the United States initiating atomic warfare has been questioned, particularly on the grounds of morality."[40]

Royall's "some quarters" could only be William Leahy.

It is one of the last, and finest, examples of how William Leahy's policy role has been missed. When Halfmoon is discussed, usually two things are stated: that the plan was approved by the Joint Chiefs on May 19 (and this was approval for an atomic plan) or that Truman was the reason there was a conventional alternative to a first use of atomic weapons in Halfmoon.[41] The reality was different. Halfmoon was only approved by the Joint Chiefs after Leahy vetoed the initial version that was overly reliant on atomic weapons, and after he had it replaced with a conventional alternative. Leahy, after three years of lobbying against a first-strike policy, had succeeded in swaying President Truman.

A little over a month later, Leahy's commitment to a prohibition against an atomic first-strike policy was tested like never before, when the United States and the Soviet Union almost went to war.

CHAPTER 32

Fading Away

At the end of World War II, the Allies had divided Germany into four zones of occupation, controlled respectively by France, Great Britain, the United States, and the Soviet Union. Berlin, the nation's capital, located within the Soviet zone, was itself divided among the four powers. By 1948, this arrangement had become a relic, left over from when the Soviets were still allied with their wartime partners. To have any chance of installing an effective Communist state in East Germany, as the Soviet portion of the country was known, the Soviets knew that they had to isolate West Berlin. On June 24, reacting to the American and British decision to limit their access to the resources of West Germany, a clear violation of the alliance agreements, the Soviets started ringing the city in the ugly barbed wire and concrete barriers that would eventually become the Berlin Wall. At the same time, they blockaded all road and rail access into Berlin from the west. The Berlin Crisis had begun, and a new world war seemed frighteningly possible.

The Soviets calculated, not without reason, that a city that could not be supplied by truck or train would have to be abandoned—and at first many American policy makers agreed with them. Faced with the Soviet move, splits emerged within the Truman administration between hard-liners who contemplated military action and those who counseled restraint. Leahy, himself a relic, was the softest of the soft.

His hope throughout the crisis was that the Americans and British would hold Berlin peacefully. He believed that a world war over Berlin would be pointless and preferred withdrawal instead of shooting.* This led him to be an instant and forceful advocate of the establishment of an air bridge to supply Berlin.

For a brief moment, it was almost like the clock had been turned back. The president quickly took the admiral into his confidence, and the two men worked in harmony to implement a peaceful American response. Most important for Leahy, Truman allowed him to represent the administration's positions on Berlin to the armed services, the cabinet, and even the British. It meant that for once he attended a meeting of the National Security Council.[1]

It was on the Joint Chiefs of Staff, however, that Leahy played his most forceful role, dialing down the possibility of a military confrontation between West and East. Leahy stood in sharp contrast to a large number of others in the military/intelligence state. Truman's air force aide, Col. R. B. Landry, wrote to Leahy calling for a special war room to be set up in the White House, as he was convinced that war would break out in a few months at the latest.[2] The CIA was all over the place, with some reports claiming that there was no way that the Soviets could ever back down over Berlin, and that war was inevitable.[3] The British were also aggressive, calling for the shooting down of Russian barrage balloons over Berlin.[4]

Leahy threw cold water on all the fire he could find, making sure that the West opted to supply Berlin by air. On June 30, six days after the beginning of the crisis, the American chiefs sat down with representatives of the British chiefs to discuss a united Anglo-American response.[5] When Leahy looked around the table it must have seemed a familiar yet surreal sight. On the American side, the roles of Marshall, King, and Arnold were being played by Omar Bradley, Louis Denfeld, and the new head of the air force, Hoyt Vandenberg, who had left his role in Central Intelligence the previous year. Confident, even a little

---

* Leahy was more worried about the impact on West Germany if Berlin were lost than the direct result of losing the city itself. Even then, he was convinced that a war over Berlin would have been an extreme overreaction.

smug, Leahy believed that neither his American nor his British colleagues had any idea how difficult it was to control grand strategy on this
level. "It does not appear to me," he wrote in his diary, "that they have
any conception of details of the war work demanded of the Joint Staff."[6]

As if presiding over a meeting of the Combined Chiefs back during
the war, Leahy took the chair and guided the conversation. He was assertive when he needed to be, letting the other chiefs know what the
eventual outcome would be, but at the same time allowing everyone to
voice their opinions. He began the meeting by introducing a paper submitted by the British representatives and asking for their comments.
He then, as if Roosevelt were alive, turned himself into the voice of the
president, to let the different officers know exactly what the US government would and would not do. "Admiral Leahy said that the President
felt it very necessary for us to remain in Berlin," read the meeting's
minutes. "He stated that the balloon problem appeared to be exagger-
ated and that there was no evidence from what he had been able to determine that the Russians would attempt to block the passage of our
planes in the air corridors.[7]

As his energy and confidence rose, Leahy spoke with force while
always counseling caution. When it was suggested that the Allies send
an armed land convoy toward Berlin, he stomped on the idea, speaking
"at some length" on how the Americans and British together still lacked
"sufficient strength to fight convoys through."[8] It was the kind of plan
he detested, one that was provocative but risky and would only succeed
if the Soviets caved completely. He could not see how it would be worth
the risk.

For the rest of the year, Leahy continued to play the long game over
Berlin. When it was shown that an airlift could deliver enough supplies
to support the people of West Berlin, and that the Soviets were not dead
set on World War III, he felt vindicated. By October, when the air force's
commander in charge of the airlift, Gen. Lucius Clay, gave a briefing to
Truman, Leahy, Patterson, and Forrestal, Leahy was already looking
ahead to a years-long process of rebuilding the West German economy.[9]

The crisis over Berlin crystallized Leahy's fears about a future
atomic war, and if anything he became more obstreperous than he had

been only weeks earlier when he first blocked Halfmoon. He realized that the Soviets would soon have atomic weapons—one analysis he read guessed by 1953 at the latest, perhaps even by 1950.[10] In some minds, the Soviets should be threatened with an atomic strike now, before they had the ability to strike back. Leahy was appalled. In July 1948, at the height of the Berlin Crisis, Forrestal met with Bradley and Marshall, asking for clear instructions on the use of atomic weapons. Bradley, speaking for the army, said that a war plan existed that called for the use of atomic weapons, but that he could not get it approved by the Joint Chiefs of Staff as "Admiral Leahy had expressed a wish for a plan at the present time on the assumption that such a weapon [atomic bombs] would not be available or at least not used."[11]

Leahy's final act in the atomic tug-of-war was his stubborn opposition to NSC-30, a paper from the National Security Council in which the army and air force advocated for instructions on when they could use atomic weapons.[12] It was another attempt by the air force to gain acceptance for a war plan based on an overwhelming atomic first strike. When the Joint Chiefs met on October 4 to discuss the matter, Leahy did not bother to hide his disapproval, saying, "I personally cannot approve the use of atomic bombs by America except in retaliation."[13]

Faced with Leahy's implacable hostility, there was nothing that could be done. Only two clauses of NSC-30 were ever formally approved: the ones that guaranteed that the president and the president alone would have final say on the use of atomic weapons. The National Security Council later admitted that NSC-30 was more a repudiation of a first-strike policy than anything else.[14]

Perhaps the greatest sign of Leahy's tenacity on the question of atomic bombs was the way in which American policy became much more aggressive after he retired. Only a few days after he left the Joint Chiefs in 1949, the air force gained approval of its "Trojan" war plan against the Soviet Union, which called for the dropping of 133 atomic bombs, including eight on Moscow and seven on Leningrad.[15] The famous doctrines that we associate with the early Cold War—the *Dr. Strangelove*-like "Massive Retaliation" or "Mutually Assured Destruction"—were all creations of the early 1950s, once Leahy's brake had been lifted.

Before that, for Leahy's ethical reasons as much as anything else, the United States was steered into a non-first-use policy.

This one success cannot obscure what was Leahy's least happy period in the White House. While he got along well with Truman, their views on strategic policy (except for atomic weapons) had diverged alarmingly. Truman admitted as much in September, telling Leahy that they no longer saw "eye to eye" on many issues. Leahy watched with a barely suppressed, righteous anger as the Chinese Nationalist regime collapsed and Mao Tse-tung's Communists methodically took over most of China's large cities.[16] For the admiral, this was the greatest American foreign policy tragedy of his career. When his friend Wellington Koo, now the Chinese ambassador in Washington, came to Leahy to plead for increased and expedited aid, the admiral looked across the table with sympathy and frustration, but could offer little assistance. He would continue to do everything he could for the Nationalists, but as he suspected, their peril was beyond anything he could hope to help.

At the same time, Leahy watched helplessly while the CIA transformed into a force committed to widespread covert operations. The driver for this was Allen Dulles, who had once come to Leahy begging to be allowed to stay in the new intelligence setup. In June 1948, Dulles began pushing for an interventionist "Special Services Unit."[17] The National Security Council eventually approved Dulles's vision, without Truman or Leahy in the room.[18]

Dulles would go on to help shape the interventionist CIA that became famous during the Cold War. Right after Leahy retired in 1949, a committee Dulles chaired drafted a report about the future of the agency, spinning a false narrative about the great accomplishments of the OSS during World War II and arguing that the CIA needed to be far more aggressive when it came to covert operations.[19] The one holdout against this brave new world was Leahy's appointment, Roscoe Hillenkoetter, but he would soon be replaced by Walter Bedell Smith, and Dulles's changes would be implemented. Dulles would eventually write Leahy out of the history of the early CIA.[20]

The Truman administration was passing him by. Now seventy-three, the admiral was tired and haggard; even worse, his kidneys had begun to malfunction.[21] He hardly presented a young, dynamic face to the country, and this mattered as Harry Truman was in the midst of one of the closest and hard-fought presidential campaigns in American history. The 1948 election, the first without Franklin Roosevelt in twenty years, seemed balanced on a knife's edge as the voters were showing signs that they were tired of the Democrats. The Republicans had captured the House of Representatives two years prior and had once again turned to Thomas E. Dewey, Roosevelt's opponent in 1944. The Truman campaign countered by trying to energize its liberal base, not a constituency enamored of the old admiral. There were even signs that Leahy had become an electoral liability. After the attack by Albert Einstein, a steady stream of articles criticized Leahy's behind-the-scenes power, portraying him as an out-of-touch fossil in love with military action. On September 20, Leahy's sometime co-conspirator Constantine Brown published a column saying that Leahy would be forced out as soon as the election was over:

> President Truman is being urged by some of his most intimate political advisers to retire Fleet Admiral William D. Leahy, his chief of staff. Among those urging such action are Secretary of Defense Forrestal and the President's principal political advisers in the White House—Clark Clifford and David K. Niles.
>
> Secretary Forrestal considers Admiral Leahy an "interference" in the Joint Chiefs of Staff, where he represents the President. The White House advisers regard him as a political liability in the present campaign, in which they believe Mr. Truman must make a strong bid for a liberal vote. Mr. Clifford and Mr. Niles consider Admiral Leahy an "old-fashioned reactionary."[22]

Leahy had received no advance warning of the piece and was devastated.[23] He immediately wrote to the president asking to be relieved of his duties. Truman, who was campaigning and almost certainly had nothing to do with the article, acted immediately to reassure him. He wrote a letter to Leahy by longhand and had it sent Air Mail special delivery from Bakersfield, California, in between campaign stops. It was one of the kindest notes he ever wrote.[24]

> Dear Admiral,
>
> I am writing this on the train going 90mi. an hour. I hope you will be able to read it.
>
> I received your letter enclosing an article by Constantine Brown. I wish I could get my hands on him and on the fellow who gave him the false information on which he based his piece.
>
> I want you in the White House. I have the utmost confidence in you. You tell me what you think. While you and I don't see eye to eye on some things, we are always frank with each other.
>
> Don't pay any attention to any lying stories the gossipers write. It's part of the political farce as it's played in this country. The opposition try to hurt me by hurting my friends.
>
> Please don't let it bother you. When I have something to say to you, I'll say it to you.
>
> You are my friend and I am yours, come hell or high water.

When Truman did not hear back from Leahy for four days, he grew worried. He sent another letter just to be sure that the admiral had received the first note.[25] Meanwhile, he harshly rebuked Clark Clifford, who wrote Leahy a groveling letter denying any involvement with Brown's piece, even claiming the idea of Leahy leaving the White House had never crossed his mind.[26] Clifford then sent Brown a letter saying that his article was a "wicked and malicious lie."[27] Yet the story had to emerge from somewhere, and Clifford as a source makes by far the most sense. His letters to Leahy and Brown are so over-the-top, they hint at a guilty conscience. On September 29, Clifford's name again appeared in an article attacking Leahy, this time written by Drew Pearson, who claimed to have been given a verbatim quote from Truman about the need to get rid of Leahy: "He's [Leahy] gotten too reactionary. . . . He and George Marshall are hardly on speaking terms. Everything Marshall proposes, Leahy tears to pieces. Clark Clifford tells me the public reaction to him is bad."[28]

Leahy had to have realized that his time in the White House was nearing its end; yet despite the political attacks, he remained devoted to the president. When Truman, much to the surprise of many, won a convincing victory on November 5 and the Democrats regained control of Congress, the admiral was pleased, writing in his diary, "The astonishingly favorable result was accomplished by Harry Truman with his own efforts, by his complete conviction of the righteousness of his cause, and without assistance from any other person. His party gained control of the legislative branch of our government and he therefore has now a freedom of action that has not been in the President's hand for a long time."[29]

A day after Truman returned to Washington in triumph, he invited Leahy and other close advisers and staff members down to Key West for a two-week holiday. Once again, the admiral accompanied the president on the car ride to the airport and down to Florida. When the two men attended a Baptist service, Truman made sure that his old chief of staff was seated on his right. But Leahy rarely took part in volleyball games or fishing trips, nor did he revel in the stream of politicians and cabinet members who came to pay homage to the victor. Instead, he spent his time working on his own personal papers, likely preparing his memoirs.

Leahy was growing weaker, and emotionally preparing himself to go. Only a few days after returning to Washington, Truman invited Leahy to come with him to Philadelphia for the Army-Navy football game.[30] Aboard the train, headed north, Leahy privately asked Truman to relieve him as chief of staff sometime in January 1949. Truman responded with a question: Would Leahy consider taking an ambassadorship in Europe?

The offer was Truman's attempt to raise Leahy's spirits, for the admiral's confidants knew that he believed he would not live long after retirement. A young military aide to the White House, Lou Renfrow, recalled the admiral stopping by his office to gift him an autographed picture shortly before stepping down. "Lou, this retirement business is bad because after you retire, then you don't live very long," Leahy told him. "You just kind of fade away."[31]

Renfrow was so moved that he told the president of Leahy's prediction. Truman immediately took steps to lift the admiral's spirits. According to Renfrow, during their next briefing, Truman came up with a plan to keep Leahy feeling useful.

"Bill, you're the only one who went to all these conferences with Roosevelt: Yalta, Casablanca, Canada, the ocean and everyplace else. You're the only one that went to all of them. I want you to sit down and from your memoranda and from your memory, write everything you remember about every one of these conferences. I'm going to give you an office in the Pentagon; I'm going to give you enough staff to do it, and you can take your time, but I want that report."

"Why," the Admiral said, "Mr. President, that'll take me two or three years."

He said, "I don't give a damn how long it takes you. Bill, I want you to do that. That's important, because I want it on the record."*

It would not be so simple. In December, a series of medical tests revealed that Leahy was suffering from a partial blockage of the kidneys.[32] An operation, which would keep him incapacitated for three weeks, was scheduled for early January. In the meantime, he tried to enjoy his last days in office. Much of his professional time was spent accompanying Truman to official events, such as the Gridiron Club and various diplomatic receptions. He received a note from Douglas MacArthur congratulating him on all that he had accomplished and urging him to stay on as chief of staff if he still could. Christmas was spent with his son and his family.[33] Professionally very few people were still consulting him. On December 21 the Dutch naval attaché called to explain Dutch policy in its growing war to hold on to its Pacific empire in modern-day Indonesia. Leahy, anti-imperialist as always, believed that the Dutch were right to be worried that their time there was at an end.

---

* Renfrow was not in the room, so we cannot be sure the exchange is verbatim. It would have been unusual for Truman to address Leahy as "Bill," but perhaps near the end they were more informal than they had been earlier.

The last official meeting Leahy recorded was on December 28, 1948. His friend the Chilean president, Gabriel Videla, sent the Chilean ambassador in Washington to warn him that the Argentinians were fomenting revolution.[34] But of course there was little Leahy could do to help. One of the most successful and influential careers in the history of American government was at an end.

CHAPTER 33

The Forgotten Man

Almost a decade after William Leahy left the White House, a reporter from the *Norfolk Virginian-Pilot* paid a visit to the old admiral. "On the 17th floor of towering Bethesda Naval Hospital an 83-year-old gentleman sits alone," the reporter later wrote. "He wears a checkered bathrobe and smokes placidly in a cushioned wheelchair in his two-room corner suite. There is neither radio nor television to disturb the silence. . . . He is the only patient on the floor."[1] Leahy had grown weaker over the years, his skin more wrinkled. Wrestling with immobility due to a broken hip, his weight had dropped, hollowing out his frame.

Yet his blue eyes remained penetrating, his memory unusually sharp. When discussion inevitably turned to World War II, the admiral recalled Stalin as "a great leader for the Russians" who "succeeded in getting a great deal of assistance from the Americans." Churchill was "a great friend," and Leahy mentioned that they still exchanged Christmas cards. When the reporter brought up de Gaulle, the admiral, largely isolated now, with few visitors and little contact with the world outside the hospital, was stunned to learn that the general had, three months earlier, become the premier of France. His hackles up, Leahy dismissed de Gaulle as an egoist and violent nationalist, croaking, "He thirsted for power!"

When he was asked about Franklin Delano Roosevelt, he grew

silent for a moment, gathering his thoughts, and then launched into a lucid monologue about the president's greatness, praising Roosevelt's qualities as a war leader, his ability to listen to argument, and his instinctive ability to make the right decision. As the reporter later wrote:

> At their daily sessions the President sometimes brought up matters that they had not discussed in years. Then he asked the Admiral's opinion.
>
> If it did not jibe with what Admiral Leahy had said in the past, the President would look puzzled and say, "Bill, that's not what you told me a year ago."
>
> "Well my President, if I told you something a year ago—that was wrong, because what I'm telling you now is right."
>
> Then they would both smile; it was a long-standing personal joke.[2]

That Leahy would still be alive ten years after leaving the White House had been inconceivable to him in 1949. An adverse reaction to the penicillin administered as part of his kidney operation had almost killed him, and kept him hospitalized for more than three weeks. Stuck in bed, he missed Truman's inauguration, but the president visited him in the hospital and presented him with a gold-plated .38 caliber Colt revolver that he knew Leahy admired. No longer having the cantankerous admiral around seemed to make Truman miss him more than he expected. He did everything possible to help Leahy recover, and when he was better, Truman ordered him to Key West until he could come down and join him.

In Key West, following doctor's orders, Leahy sunbathed daily, swam, and took his vitamins. He also had daily injections, though he was never quite sure what was in them. The rest did him good, and he completed a draft of his memoirs. By the time the president arrived in March, Leahy seemed healthier. He returned to Washington with Truman and for a few days appeared in his new office in the Pentagon. He met with James Forrestal and was given a gift by the Joint Chiefs of Staff, a silver cigarette case with their signatures engraved on it. On

March 25, President Truman presented him with his third Distinguished Service Medal.

Then Leahy's health quickly spiraled again. By late May, he was found to have two blockages of the urethra and had to be rushed in for another operation. Too weak to work, he did little else that summer but convalesce. By September he was showing signs of improvement, able to keep a watchful eye on the big story of the day, the revolt of the admirals.

In October 1949, navy fears about the course of service unification boiled over. In a public testimony before Congress, Adm. Louis Denfeld, chief of naval operations, repudiated administration policy.[3] When Leahy heard about the revolt, he was torn. While he instinctively sided with his beloved navy, he loathed anything that smacked of insubordination and disloyalty to the president. Publicly, he was mute. When approached by a reporter, he said nothing.[4] His absence from office probably contributed to the revolt, as he was not available to be an intermediary between the fleet and the president. Now, even in his weakened state, he began to pass on some of Truman's thoughts on the matter to the navy.[5]

For the rest of the year his health fluctuated, and he was confined to the hospital for long periods, poring over the proofs of his memoirs, which arrived in November, finding the chore unspeakably tedious. In early 1950, he was laid low by excruciating headaches and was so weakened that he had to decline an invitation from the president to come to Key West. Then something unexpected happened. In springtime he stabilized and strengthened. Though hardly robust, he was well enough to travel, see friends, work a little, and, most important, enjoy life. He joked about his improvement, saying, "I feel fairly well for a cripple."[6] It set the stage for almost five years of relatively good health, and he made the most of it. He had been so devoted to work during World War II and the difficult years that followed that he had neglected to spend time with his son and his granddaughter. Now, his health seemingly renewed, family became his main preoccupation. Father and son grew close, and William Jr. made a point of bringing Leahy to dinner in his family's home in Chevy Chase, Maryland. In June 1950, the newly married Louisita gave birth to Leahy's first great-grandchild, a girl named Elizabeth. Louise and her husband, John Cusworth Walker, would eventually have seven children, three of whom were born while Leahy was healthy.

He was, of course, an adoring great-grandfather, but he missed his late wife enormously. He made a point of going to Arlington National Cemetery on their anniversary to leave flowers on Louise's grave, and to see the patch of ground next to her in which he would be laid to rest. At least once, he discussed the possibility of seeing her in another life. He certainly made no effort to meet another companion. One close friend, former classmate Louis Powell, cheekily asked whether the admiral was stepping out with someone new. Leahy answered back playfully, but it was clear the memories of Louise were enough: "Replying to your questions, I have not yet acquired a mink coat or even anybody upon whom one could be appropriately draped."[7]

Leahy also spent time connecting with his second family, his friends from the navy, particularly his classmates from Annapolis. He loved attending navy reunions, and exchanged letters with former colleagues such as Powell, Thomas Hart, and others. He often discussed his own health, making fun of the indignities of old age. As he joked with Hart: "A long time ago I gave up horse riding. Not so long ago, warped vision put a stop to any shooting in which I used to be generally accepted as pretty good. It might be possible now for me to shoot at an elephant, but there is no assurance that I could hit one from a safe distance."[8]

He received letters from sailors who had served under his command, and always wrote back. In 1951 he heard from a former enlisted man from the *New Mexico*, the battleship Leahy had commanded twenty-five years prior. Leahy replied enthusiastically with as much information about different crewmates as he could provide. "It is more than a pleasure to receive your letter that resurrected vivid memories of this wonder ship New Mexico at the time when we were shipmates. Every incident to which you refer is treasured in my memory."[9]

His memoir was published in March 1950. He hated writing, and it showed: he produced the least entertaining memoir of any of the major Allied military or political figures of World War II. The work emerged almost straight from his diary, and he removed nearly every personal touch, rendering the text unemotional and detached. Even the title he chose, *I Was There*, was observational, not active. When his publishers saw the first draft, they were disappointed. To enliven the leaden prose, they asked him to include as many amusing anecdotes as he could, but Leahy would not budge, saying, "I don't want any funny stories in the book."[10] He was true to his word.

When *I Was There* was released, it was greeted with a collective yawn. The *Washington Post* tried to be kind about its plodding pace and lack of personality, though ended up making him seem creepy more than anything else: "Admiral Leahy was always something of a puzzle to the public in his White House days. To those who didn't know him, there was something sinister about his owlish profile and his always solemn manner. He usually looked in his photographs as if he were forever smelling bad fish."[11] The *New York Times* just made him sound dull: "William D. Leahy, as he emerges from his own pages, seems to be an able, conscientious, industrious, tactful, honorable man without much sense of humor."[12] The book did not sell well, and when Leahy approached a publisher a few years later with a proposal for a book about his time in Puerto Rico entitled *A Sailor's Adventure in Politics*, he was turned down quickly.[13]

If Leahy was disappointed with the mediocre reviews of *I Was There*, his formal nature prevented him from saying so. That was not the case when it came to a far more serious event a few months later, the outbreak of the Korean War. When Soviet-backed troops from North Korea launched their surprise offensive against the South in June 1950, one of the first things President Truman did was bring Leahy in for a confidential briefing by Omar Bradley. This was followed a few days later by a private meeting between Leahy and Truman so that the president could ask his advice. Leahy was confused by the president's need for his views, though gratified. "A reason for the President's sending for me and giving me all the information in his possession in regard to the situation is not apparent to me," he wrote. "He seemed to wish to talk to somebody in whom he had confidence, or perhaps he just wished to be polite to his one-time chief of staff."[14]

Leahy had a better understanding of the course of the war than Truman did. The president was surprisingly upbeat, thinking that American and Korean forces could hold off the Communists. Yet Leahy warned that US forces were inadequate and would be driven back into a pocket near the south coast of Korea.[15] This is precisely what happened. Leahy understood that the only way to hold Korea would be to mobilize a significant army. He suggested ten divisions, two of which should be from the Marine Corps. As history would show, he was spot on the mark.[16]

While Leahy enjoyed being involved in the discussions, it served to reopen the one great wound that would never heal: China. When first told about the North Korean attack, he knew what was to blame. "I personally do not expect a war with Russia in the immediate future," he wrote, "but it does seem very likely that our failure to assist the Chinese Government during the past three years will eventually bring the United States into a war with the Soviet Republics."[17] Part of Leahy did not see the reason to fight for Korea. When he had run the Joint Chiefs of Staff and was asked to give his strategic opinion on Korea's value, he replied that, in and of itself, the peninsula was unimportant. He believed it was only vital if the United States were going to maintain a connection to China, and with China already "lost," Korea had little strategic value left. As he confided to Powell, "Of course a real war is possible, but I do not think it is likely now or in the near future. I have personally had enough wars to last me a long time."[18]

His bitterness about China was as enduring as his devotion to Franklin Roosevelt. When Truman named George Marshall as secretary of defense a few months into the war, Leahy said that he thought the general would be a good choice "except for his attitude toward China, with which I have been in complete disagreement."[19]

Leahy's appearance and advice about Korea made an impression on the president, and he seriously considered finding a job for the old man, discussing with Dean Acheson the possibility of Leahy becoming the next American ambassador to the Hague.[20] Truman also explored the appointment of Leahy as Marshall's replacement as the head of the American Red Cross.[21] In September, he arranged for Leahy and Marshall to discuss the mechanics of a handover, but the admiral's doctors rejected the idea, saying the travel and speechmaking would be too much for him.

This might have been a mistake. While Leahy was hardly springy, he was surprisingly active. For New Year's 1951, he joined Truman on a cruise aboard the *Williamsburg*, where they might have reminisced about the thrashing Leahy gave James Byrnes six years earlier. In March, he returned to Key West with Truman, and for the rest of the president's time in office he accompanied him on every vacation he had in Florida. Strong enough to take part in swimming and fishing excursions, he even re-created part of his role as chief of staff, sorting through the confidential correspondence sent to the president in Key West and briefing him on international developments.

He also made regular trips to Wisconsin, delighting in the memories of his youth. In the summer of 1950 he paid a two-week visit, taking in the Fourth of July parade in Ashland, touring his old high school, and hosting a dinner for all the "old-timers" he could find. He even did something that he had once vowed he would never do: he went to Wausau to visit the graves of his parents and his brother. He had been away for so long that the local cemetery was now many times bigger, and he was unable to locate their headstones. Or that, at least, was what he claimed—perhaps the pilgrimage was simply too much for his emotions to bear.[22]

Leahy's Wisconsin roots made him a target of influence with the state's most notorious son, Sen. Joseph McCarthy. Embroiled in his campaign to smear his enemies as Communist spies, the senator employed Leahy's criticisms of George Marshall's inability to understand the value of China as part of his attacks against the general. When he first made his main speech about Marshall from the Senate floor, he sent Leahy a copy of the address, with an ingratiating cover note.[23] Believing McCarthy was dead wrong when it came to criticisms of Marshall's patriotism, he kept the senator at arm's length.[24] The only time he recorded meeting McCarthy was in August 1952, when they were both in the hospital at the same time and the senator, who was up for reelection, stopped by Leahy's bed uninvited.[25]

One reason why Leahy would have nothing to do with McCarthy was the man's criticisms of Harry Truman. The president remained warm toward the admiral in retirement, and Leahy responded with increased loyalty. This was most seen in the famous confrontation between Truman and Douglas MacArthur, which resulted in the general's dismissal in 1951. Leahy viewed the firing of MacArthur as an act of "high courage" on Truman's part.[26] For Leahy, the fact that the president had determined that this was in the national interest was enough, and he believed Americans should accept the decision. This was even as he had some sympathy with MacArthur's strategic vision. Yet Leahy could not understand why so many Americans, including some members of Congress, lavished praise on the general. He found their adulation of a military officer dismissed by his commander in chief to be "strange."[27] To Leahy, civilian control of the military was, as always, sacrosanct.

His loyalty to the memory of Franklin Roosevelt was even stronger, and when healthy he played an active role in the Franklin Roosevelt Memorial Foundation, being reelected to its board as late as 1954. His ideas on the purpose of the foundation were strongly progressive, advocating for the study of social problems in the United States.[28] He thought the foundation should help improve the lives of the disadvantaged and foster international cooperation. Even in death, Roosevelt could push Leahy down surprising paths.

He could become sentimental when remembering Roosevelt. In 1953, William Hassett sent him the text of a speech he had given on the eighth anniversary of Roosevelt's passing. Leahy's response showed how much he missed FDR.

> While you and I treasure in our memories an understanding appreciation of the courage, decision and devotion to the cause of Americanism that Franklin Roosevelt taught by example to everybody, it is hoped that in spite of the passage of the years your splendid and beautifully expressed address of appreciation will be read

by a host of his countrymen who did not have our advantage of personal association, and for whom he gave the best years of his life and finally his life itself.[29]

What particularly irritated Leahy was the charge, which became common in the late 1940s and 1950s, that Roosevelt was either too weak or too foolish in his dealings with Joseph Stalin at the Yalta Conference in 1945. After retiring, Leahy reacted aggressively, even with friends, when they made similar charges. When Patrick Hurley publicly attacked Roosevelt for his performance at Yalta, Leahy defended his late friend with passion: "I don't believe, from my daily contacts with Franklin Roosevelt, that he believed he ever made any mistake at Yalta. . . . I don't believe Hurley deliberately publishes falsehoods about these matters, but I do think he is all mixed up."[30] The last article that would ever be published under Leahy's name was a detailed defense of Roosevelt at Yalta.[31]

Another development which reemphasized Roosevelt's greatness to Leahy was Dwight Eisenhower becoming president. When Truman decided that he would not run for president in 1952, it lessened Leahy's interest in the contest. He could muster little enthusiasm for Adlai Stevenson, and even though he had worked closely with Eisenhower for years, he was not convinced of the latter's skills. After Eisenhower was elected, he would occasionally invite the admiral in for meetings, but it was more out of a sense of decorum than anything else. Leahy told friends that Eisenhower could not compare to FDR as commander in chief.[32]

The election of Dwight Eisenhower to the presidency marked the definite end of any residual influence that Leahy had over US policy. Right after the election, he was brought to the White House to help sort through President Truman's secret correspondence, the filing of which was still being done to Leahy's specifications.[33] It was a somber moment, standing in the storied mansion surrounded by the secret and confidential letters and memoranda that had been the source of much of his power, knowing that in two months both of the administrations he had served would be consigned to history. His talks with Truman were tinged with sentimentality. He was asked to make a gift of an object that could be put in the museum that Truman was planning for his hometown of Independence, Missouri. The choice Leahy made was enigmatic. He returned the gold-plated revolver that Truman had given him in the hospital in 1949. It was as if he were saying that it was from the president that all of his influence had come, and to understand Truman's importance in his life, he needed to return to the president a gift he had been given.

Leahy disconnected from international politics, and his remaining years were passed in relative quiet. He enjoyed visits from old friends, such as Anna Roosevelt and Constantine Brown, and sometimes with important senators or congressmen who came to pay respects. He kept in touch with members of the Roosevelt and Truman White House staffs, such as William Hassett and George Elsey. In 1957 he broke his hip in a fall. After a stay in the hospital, he made his final major trip, a journey to Pearl Harbor, in the hope that the warm weather and sunshine would aid his recovery. When back in Washington, he spent most of his time in his suite of rooms atop the Bethesda Naval Hospital. People would occasionally write to him expressing their concern, but would receive replies from his secretary, Dorothy Ringquist, on his behalf. Aside from his son and grandchildren, visitors became an increasing rarity. Yet when news got around that Leahy might not last long, one person made a special visit to say good-bye. On May 3, 1959, Harry Truman came to pay his last respects.[34] It is unlikely that Leahy could have carried on much of a conversation at this point, but were he conscious, he would have been touched.

On July 20, 1959, William Leahy died. The cause of his passing was officially described as a "cerebral vascular accident."[35] After a lifetime of national service, adventure, political maneuvering, and shaping world history, they could just as well have written "old age."

Epilogue

Fleet Admiral William Daniel Leahy's death was announced by the US Navy. On July 22 at noon, his casket was moved into the Bethlehem Chapel of the Episcopal Cathedral in Washington, DC, and for the next twenty-four hours his body lay surrounded by a naval honor guard before being brought into the nave for the funeral. His eleven honorary pallbearers consisted of his old friend Bill Hassett and ten naval officers who included his few remaining living friends from the Annapolis class of 1897. After the service, a motor procession brought the admiral to his final resting place in Arlington Cemetery. A nineteen-gun salute was fired, and then Leahy was laid beside his wife, Louise, where she had awaited him for seventeen years. Neither Dwight Eisenhower, Harry Truman, nor George Marshall were in attendance.

Newspapers marked his passing, but the articles were perfunctory and often mistaken. The *New York Times* noted how he had all but disappeared from the public mind, having lived as a "recluse" for the past few years.[1] The *Washington Post* missed his importance entirely, writing, "Yet despite his inner position, his contribution to evolving defense concepts probably was not profound."[2]

When George Marshall died three months later, the reaction could not have been more different. President Eisenhower issued a public proclamation announcing Marshall's passing and extolling his greatness. He ordered that the national flag be flown at half-mast on all US government buildings, military facilities, and warships, both at home and abroad, and to be kept that way until after the funeral. Both

Truman and Eisenhower attended the funeral, and Truman described Marshall as "the greatest general since Robert E. Lee . . . the greatest administrator since Thomas Jefferson. He was the man of honor, the man of truth, the man of greatest ability. He was the greatest of the great in our time."[3] The general's death was soon followed by a hagiographic biography, the foundation of Marshall scholarships, a Marshall library, Marshall public schools, Marshall awards—a whole industry to perpetuate his memory. To this day, historians claim, with scant evidence, that he determined US strategy in World War II.

Admiral Leahy has largely disappeared from the national mind. Despite the enormous power he wielded during World War II, a war the United States fought to his strategic ideas more than any other and a conflict that still shapes America's identity, there are today no William D. Leahy foundations, public schools, statues, or libraries. As his greatest service was in the White House, the US Navy has remembered him more shoddily than they should. In 1962, a new guided missile cruiser, the USS *Leahy* (DLG-16), was named for him. It was the best ship of its class, and would serve with distinction into the 1990s, but it was hardly a vessel worthy of the highest-ranking sailor in American history. A simple marker, in a small park in Ashland, Wisconsin, sandwiched between Lake Superior and a highway, serves as one of America's few tributes to the man who, more than any other, helped America triumph in World War II. Leahy would have preferred it that way.

Acknowledgments

A number of those who know me well have remarked on how quickly I was able to research and write this book after the publication of *How the War Was Won*. This was due to the extraordinary support I received from many quarters, without which this book would still be many years from completion. More than any other person or institution, the appearance of Mathilde Von Bulow in my life provided the emotional and intellectual sustenance needed to produce this work. She was able to learn more about William Leahy than she ever imagined possible, and in return provided me with contentment, support, and love. I definitely got the better end of that deal. This book would never have been written without her, and to her it is dedicated.

I would also like to thank my immediate family, as always. In this case I must start with my sister Sarah, who has read more of the manuscript of this book, in different forms, than anyone else. Her advice was invaluable, and she demonstrated an amazingly perceptive knack for pointing out areas in need of improvement. You the reader owe her thanks you can never know. I would also like to apologize to her husband, Sam, for taking up so much of her time!

The remaining members of my family all helped with their constant support and cheer. My father became almost as interested in Leahy as I, and my mother was always there with a kind word and an uplifting remark. My brother, Bill, is my best friend, my sister Elizabeth one of the foundations of my life, and her husband, Jamie, and their three sons, Andrew, Sam, and Ben, help keep me grounded. I must also thank my aunt Anne for providing me wonderful breaks in Hingham. Finally I would like to thank Steve and Lori. It was during our trip to the Highlands, during a discussion over tea at Inverlochy Castle, that the decision was made to press ahead with this project.

Acknowledgments

There are also two superb professionals from the publishing world whom I must mention. My agent, Alexa Stark, showed an awareness that someone as relatively unknown as William Leahy could be the subject of a book worthy of representing. My editor at Penguin Random House, Brent Howard, did more to shape the final structure of this book than anyone else. His demanding and discerning eye has taught me a great deal about writing. Thanks to both.

I need also to express my heartfelt thanks to two great institutions: the University of St. Andrews and the National Endowment for the Humanities. As this book was being written I was honored beyond measure when St. Andrews appointed me to its new chair in strategic studies. The university and the School of International Relations, where I now happily reside, is unstinting in its support of my research and has provided the perfect home to see this volume through to completion.

The National Endowment for the Humanities, in awarding me one of its Public Scholar Fellowships, provided the final impetus to complete this work. As it provided me with an entire year's research leave, I was able to throw myself completely into the task of writing. Without this award not only would the volume have taken far longer; it would have been much less coherent.

Other institutions also provided valuable support. The Naval Historical and Heritage Command in Washington awarded me a Hopper Research Fellowship, which allowed me a crucial month of work in their most excellent archive and library (of which Leahy would be proud). The Harry Truman Library also helped fund a trip to Independence to look at their excellent collection, without which no Leahy biography would be complete. The University of Glasgow, which was my home for almost twenty years, also provided crucial support during the early stages of this project.

There are so many friends, colleagues, and students who have contributed to keeping me going through all this that I could never mention all of them. However, I would like to pay special tributes to Cian, Hew, Gary and Joan, Guy, Helen, Kathy, Marina, Matthew, May (and Ed), Peter, Simon, Simon, Stuart, Tim, Tony, and Will. You all helped greatly both as friends and as scholars.

Finally, I need to thank William Leahy, for being both so elusive and so fascinating at the same time.

APPENDIX A

TOP SECRET   **September 5, 1944**

Discussion of Pacific Strategy, Joint Chiefs of Staff

In endeavoring to reach a decision on the correct procedure in our post Leyte operations against Japan, I have after much thought arrived at the following estimate of the situation as it appears to me at the present time.

The sole purpose of any operations to be undertaken by our forces available, or that can be made available in the Western Pacific, is the defeat of Japan.

We now have in the Western Pacific *overwhelming superiority in sea and air forces.*

We have in prospect no effective bases for the fleet nearer to Japan than the one in Leyte which may be assumed in view of our almost certain success of the projected Leyte operation.

The nearest satisfactory fleet base is Pearl Harbor, approximately distant 3100 miles from Japan or from Formosa.

Our nearest supply base is San Francisco, distant 4500 miles, with a subsidiary well stocked base for supplies and replacement in Oahu, distant 3100 miles.

The Japanese Army at the present time dispersed in widely separated theaters of operations is markedly superior to American ground forces that are in the Western Pacific or that can be made available there in any foreseeable time.

Any increase in American ground forces in the Western Pacific must obtain its supplies and reinforcements from San Francisco via Oahu.

There are at present time 19 Divisions in Japan proper, about 750,000 Japanese troops in Manchuria that can, with some difficulty because of surface and submarine attack, be moved back to Japan in the event of an attack on their homeland. The total force of the Japanese Army is estimated at 78 divisions, a large part of which can not be returned to Japan because of *American superiority in the air and on the sea.*

It is unreasonable to expect that we can in the foreseeable future have available in the Western Pacific any other local superiority in ground forces unless the Soviet Armies join with us or unless and until Chinese Armies are organized in great numbers, armed, equipped and trained in modern methods of warfare.

There appear to be under consideration only three courses of military action by American ground troops against Japan after Leyte:

From North to South—

1. Occupation of the Philippines including Luzon.

---

* This memorandum shows Leahy at the height of his influence. The constant references to the first person and the final appeal to Roosevelt reveal him to be more than willing to fight to get his way. The stress on air-sea power to defeat Japan instead of a land invasion is to be found throughout. The air-sea mentions are in italics for emphasis. The copy of this memorandum is in the Leahy NHHC Mss.

2. Occupation of Southwestern Formosa and Amoy.

3. Occupation of the Southern end of Kyusho [*sic*].

Of these three, occupation of the Philippines can be accomplished with the forces available.

Occupation of Southwestern Formosa and Amoy will require Army and Marine forces totalling 500,000 men. Service troops to the number of about 100,000 are not now available for this operation, but probably can be made available.

Occupation of Southern Kyusho will eventually require about the same force as the Formosa-Amoy operation. It has the advantage of promising less enemy resistance to the first landing—and the disadvantage of being close to the Japanese Fleet based in the Inland Sea, and the shore based air forces in Japan proper, both of which may be expected to make serious difficulties for the landing of troops after the first wave.

Success by the American Forces in any one of these three operations will make serious difficulties for Japan by curtailing shipping to the East Indies and to the mainland of Asia.

It is not reasonable to assume that complete success in any one of them will cause a collapse of the Japanese war effort.

It would appear that a collapse of Japan can be brought about only by the destruction of the Japanese Army in Japan, or by a destruction of Japan's will to fight *by an effective sea and air blockade and bombardment.*

Judging by past experience with small contingents of the Japanese Army, it does not appear to me possible at the present time to provide from our distant bases and land a sufficient American Army in Japan to destroy the Japanese Army.

A whole-hearted participation by the Soviet Government might make a destruction of the Japanese Army possible.

The Chiefs of Staff are in possession of all available information as to the prospects of assistance from Russia, and as to the time when it may possibly be forthcoming.

It appears evident that of these three operations seizure of the Philippines would be less costly in life and resources and not more costly in time than either of the other two.

Seizure of Formosa-Amoy would be expensive in men and resources. Its success would place us in an excellent position to interfere with Japanese commerce and to make bombing attacks on Japanese industry.

Seizure of Southern Kyusho would probably require the same expenditure of men and resources as the Formosa operation, even if the Japanese Fleet could be neutralized by the American Fleet so far from its base. It is entirely possible that a desperate inferior naval force operating from a near-by base could seriously interfere with a landing on Kyusho.

A successful and sustained occupation of the Philippines, of Formosa, or of Kyusho will succeed in shortening the war with Japan.

The last two, at any rate, hold some risk of failure with a certainty of high cost in life; while a strangulation of Japan *by effective sea and air blockade* will probably require a longer time to bring the war to an end, but with less cost to us in life and material because of *overwhelming sea and air supremacy.*

We hear objections made to any course of action that would fail to keep employed against the enemy all of our forces available in the Pacific Area.

I think that principle was sound in the European war where constant attrition of the enemy and an early decision were necessary.

I do not think the principle is sound in the Japanese war because Japan is willing to lose many more men than we can send to that area in any reasonable time if ever, and because efforts to arrive at an early decision may not be justified by the cost in American lives involved therein.

My conclusion is that America's least expensive course of action is to *continue and intensify the air and sea blockade,* with an intensified air bombardment of Japan's war industry, and at the same time to reoccupy the Philippines.*

My second choice would be the Formosa-Amoy campaign.

My third choice would be Kyusho.

It does not appear to me that under existing conditions wisdom points at the present

* It is important to see here that Leahy is still looking at strategic bombing as a means of attacking Japanese industry and not as a means of attacking Japanese civilians

time to a necessity of accepting the great expenditure of life and treasure involved in a ground forces attack on the numerically superior Japanese Army.

It seems necessary that the Joint Chiefs of Staff should obtain a decision on the highest political level as to whether we should take a shorter course toward the already certain defeat of Japan at greater cost in life and material, or a longer course at a much less cost.*

WDL

* This is Leahy's direct warning to the other chiefs that he will go to Roosevelt to get a final decision.

APPENDIX B

1. No territorial expansion or selfish advantage. No plans for aggression against any other state, large or small. No objective which need clash with the peaceful aims of any other nation.

2. The eventual return of sovereign rights and self-government to all peoples who have been deprived of them by force.

3. No territorial changes in any friendly part of the world unless they accord with the freely expressed wishes of the people concerned.

4. All peoples who are prepared for self-government should be permitted to choose their own form of government by their freely expressed choice, without interference from any foreign source. That is true in Europe, in Asia, in Africa, as well as in the Western Hemisphere.

5. By the combined and cooperative action of our war allies, help the defeated enemy states establish peaceful democratic governments of their own free choice. And try to attain a world in which nazism, fascism, and military aggression cannot exist.

6. Refuse to recognize any government imposed upon any nation by the force of any foreign power.

7. All nations should have the freedom of the seas and equal rights to the navigation of boundary rivers and waterways and of rivers and waterways which pass through more than one country.

8. All states which are accepted in the society of nations should have access on equal terms to the trade and the raw materials of the world.

9. The sovereign states of the Western Hemisphere, without interference from outside the Western Hemisphere, must work together as good neighbors in the solution of their common problems.

10. Full economic collaboration between all nations, great and small, is essential to the improvement of living conditions all over the world, and to the establishment of freedom from fear and freedom from want.

11. Continue to strive to promote freedom of expression and freedom of religion throughout the peace-loving areas of the world.

12. The preservation of peace between nations requires a United Nations Organization composed of all the peace-loving nations of the world who are willing to jointly use force, if necessary, to insure peace.

APPENDIX C

UNDATED (1946) LEAHY NOTES ON RELATIONS
WITH THE USSR,* WRITTEN IN PREPARATION
FOR THE CLIFFORD/ELSEY MEMORANDUM

I. Russian Postwar Outlook (Acc. to official propaganda machine).
1) USSR is encircled by capitalism—there can be no permanent coexistence with capitalism.
2) Cap. World is inherently plagued by internal conflicts, U.S. vs. G.B. is greatest.
3) These conflicts generate wars:
a) Bet. cap. States, or:
b) Against socialist (communist) world. In endeavoring avoid (a), capitalists seek (b).
4) Conflict with USSR—while disastrous to those attempting it—would delay Soviet progress and hence must be forestalled.
5) War—or other conflict—bet. Cap. States holds possibility of danger to USSR, but holds great hopes of Soviet advancement provided USSR remains strong militarily and retains present ideals and leadership.
6) Cap. world is not all bad since it contains
a) Some wholly "enlightened" (i.e. commy) elements
b) Others (called progressive or democratic) whose reactions and activities are favorable to USSR
7) Most dangerous of Bourgeois—capitalists are moderate socialist or social-democratic leaders (called by Lenin fake friends of the people) because they use socialist devices to serve capitalist interests.

II. From above, Soviets deduce:
1) All possible must be done to increase relative strength of USSR and reduce capitalists.
2) Must direct efforts towards exploitation of differences between cap. powers. If war results, internal upheavals and revolutions should be promoted.
3) "Democrat-Progressive" elements in Cap. countries should be used to influence Govt's., on lines agreeable to USSR.
4) Wage relentless battle against socialist and social democratic leaders.

III. Analysis of Party Line:
1) Does not represent feelings of Russian people who are friendly, desire peace and prosperity.
2) Assumptions in I. are mostly false because:
a) Peaceful coexistence of soc. & cap. countries arise not from capitalism per se but from advanced industrialism and urbanism—troubles hitherto not found in USSR because of her backwardness.
b) The worker can and does benefit from the cap. system more than from commy.

* These are almost certainly Leahy's notes for Clifford, as they are the only other document in Leahy's folder about the Clifford Memorandum other than Truman's letter asking for the report and the report itself.

3) Russians were suckers for Marxism because:
   a) Only in a land which had never had friendly neighbors could the doctrine thrive.
   b) It justified their sense of insecurity, fear of outside world, dictatorship, and sacrifices.
   c) As result, today they can't get along without it—it is "the fig leaf of their moral and intellectual respectability."
4) There is great question if anyone in USSR—Stalin included—receives a true picture of the outside world. In secretive atmosphere pervading Soviet Govt., possibilities for distorting truth are infinite. The Russians do not believe in the existence of objective truth and hence believe all statements to be cloak for some ulterior motive.

IV. Practical implementation of Soviet program—conducted on 2 levels—officially in name of Govt and by subterranean methods, for which Govt. disclaims responsibility. Movements in internal politics made on official plane will normally be instituted only after their success has been assured by subterranean activities.
   1) Internal policy will be devoted to increasing mil. & industrial strength of USSR, shows to impress foreigners, secretiveness re true state of internal affairs.
   2) Wherever it looks promising, Soviet influence will be expanded—i.e. Iran, Turkey, Korea, Manchuria.
   3) UNO will get Russian participation and support only so long as they see in it an arena where their expansionist aims can be pursued. They do not view UNO as the mechanism for a stable world society, and if they think their desires can be better served by other methods, will not hesitate to abandon it.
   4) Contests of cap. nations with backward or dependent peoples will be weakened by Soviet on theory creation of political vacuum favors commy penetration. Therefore, they wish to participate in trusteeship agreements in order to complicate situation for cap. powers and weaken their influence.
   5) Russians will energetically strive to strengthen relations with countries wherein they sense opposition to the Western powers—i.e. Argentina, Germany, Middle East.
   6) International economic policy is not clear, but trade will probably be confined to their own security zone unless large long-term credits are given them.
   7) Cultural relations will be confined to closely supervised official visits with much vodka and speeches and no permanent effects.

V. Implementation of policy on unofficial plane:
   1) Strengthen inner core of Comintern in all countries.
   2) Emphasize difference between elite (above) and rank and file of communist party which will be thrust forward as bona fide partisans of political tendencies approved by Soviet.
   3) Encourage communist penetration in labor unions, youth movements, religious & racial societies, publishing groups etc.
   4) Penetrate international organizations in order to sidetrack Western Govts. and build up international lobby favorable to Soviet interests.
   5) Boost Russian Orthodox Church and its affiliates
   6) Encourage the Pan-Slav movement.
   7) Utilize policies and propaganda machines of governments favorable to USSR such as Bulgaria, Yugoslavia, CCP.

VI. U.S. faces problem of coping with a political force fanatically committed to the belief that there can be no permanent peace between us and that Soviet security requires the disruption of our society and destruction of our way of life. This force is backed by 180 million people with world's richest territory. It has also a world wide underground skilfully and capably managed. Finally, Soviet Govt., is seemingly impervious to facts and to the truth, selecting only such items as suit its fancy.

There are, however, certain rays of hope:

1) Soviet does not, like Germany, work by fixed plans, nor take unnecessary risks. While impervious to reason, it is highly sensitive to force. It can and does withdraw readily when strong resistance—backed by force—is encountered.

2) The USSR is still weaker than the United Western Powers.
3) The success of Soviet internal policy is not yet proved. Can they withstand a transfer of power from one group to another? The communist party is still a highly successful dictatorial political machine, but is no longer a source of emotional inspiration to the people.
4) All Red propaganda is basically destructive and is therefore easy to combat by any intelligent and constructive program.

VII. Possible methods of combatting Russia:
1) Recognize the character of the opposition and study it patiently and objectively.
2) Educate our own public to Russian realities, not alone by the press, but by government. This should be done at once, regardless of any fears as to the effect of such a policy on U.S.-Russian relations. We can't lose anything anyway—our stake in Russia is very small.
3) Our own society must be made healthy. Communism is a malignant parasite which feeds on diseased tissue.
4) Take the lead in showing other nations the kind of world we want to live in—if we don't, Russia will.
5) Maintain our own principles with courage and self-confidence. Our greatest danger is that of becoming like those with whom we are coping.

Select Bibliography

William Leahy Papers

One of the interesting elements of doing research on Leahy was that his personal papers are spread around different archives. In the end notes I use the following notations to list them.

Leahy Diary: William D. Leahy Papers, Library of Congress Manuscript Division, Washington, DC. The diary is noted two ways. Through 1934 it is noted by volume and page number, as Leahy recorded events very unevenly. Sometimes whole years would be covered in a page or two, with no reference to specific dates. From 1934 onward, the diary is noted by date. When quoted in the text, the diary is included in its actual language, complete with grammatical and spelling mistakes.

Leahy LC: William D. Leahy Papers, Library of Congress Manuscript Division, Washington, DC. There is a small collection of different Leahy papers here, other than the Diary.

Leahy NHHC: William D. Leahy Papers, Operational Archives Branch, Naval History and Heritage Command, Washington, DC. These papers are made up of two distinct possessions. There are hard copies of Leahy's official papers, many from his time as chief of staff to the commander in chief. There are also microfilm copies of Leahy's more personal papers, the hard copies of which are housed in the Wisconsin Historical Society, Madison.

Leahy JCS: Records of the Chairman of the Joints Chief of Staff: Chairman's File: Admiral Leahy 1942–1948: US National Archives and Records Association (NARA), College Park, Maryland, RG 218. An underutilized source base, not just about Leahy but for understanding the US military in World War II. These are Leahy's files as chairman on the Joint Chiefs and show his central role in controlling the flow of information from the top of the US military to the White House.

US Government Papers

(US)

Annual Reports: Commander of the Battle Force (US National Archives and Records Association [NARA], National Archives Building, Washington, DC).

Central Intelligence Agency Records (US National Archives and Records Association [NARA], College Park, MD), RG 263.

General Board Papers, Subject Files, Navy Department (US National Archives and Records Association [NARA], National Archives Building, Washington, DC).

Foreign Relations of the United States (FRUS). An invaluable collection of US government records, which includes the official transcripts from all the grand strategy conferences. They can be accessed online at: https://uwdc.library.wisc.edu/collections/frus/.

War Department Historical File, Hereafter WD Historical (US National Archives and Records Association [NARA], College Park, MD).
Joint Chiefs of Staff, Minutes of Meetings 1942–1945: Hereafter JCS Minutes.
Combined Chiefs of Staff, Minutes of Meetings, 1942–1945. Hereafter CCS.

(UK)

Cabinet Office Papers (Cab), National Archives, Kew Gardens, UK.

Personal Papers

Dean Acheson Mss., Harry S. Truman Presidential Library, Independence, MO.
Henry A. Arnold Mss., Library of Congress Manuscript Division, Washington, DC.
Bernard Baruch Mss., Princeton University, Seeley G. Mudd Manuscript Library, Princeton, NJ.
Vannevar Bush Mss., Library of Congress Manuscript Division, Washington, DC.
Winston Churchill Mss., Churchill College, Cambridge, UK, and Online.
Clark Clifford Mss., Harry S. Truman Presidential Library, Independence, MO.
Sir Andrew Cunningham Mss., British Library, London, UK.
George Elsey Mss. (Elsey Mss), Harry S. Truman Presidential Library, Independence, MO.
James Forrestal Mss., Princeton University, Seeley G. Mudd Manuscript Library, Princeton, NJ.
Anna Roosevelt Halsted Mss., Franklin and Eleanor Roosevelt Presidential Library, Hyde Park, NY.
Arthur Harris Mss., RAF Museum Archives, London.
Harry Hopkins Mss., Franklin and Eleanor Roosevelt Presidential Library, Hyde Park, NY.
Ernest King Mss., Library of Congress Manuscript Division, Washington, DC.
Arthur Krock Mss., Princeton University, Seeley G. Mudd Manuscript Library, Princeton, NJ.
George Marshall Mss., George C. Marshall Foundation, Virginia Military Institute, Lexington, VA.
H. Freeman Matthews Mss., Princeton University, Seeley G. Mudd Manuscript Library, Princeton, NJ.
Henry Morgenthau Mss., Franklin and Eleanor Roosevelt Presidential Library, Hyde Park, NY.
Robert Patterson Mss., Library of Congress Manuscript Division, Washington, DC.
Sir Charles Portal Mss., Christ Church Library, Oxford.
Eleanor Roosevelt Mss., Franklin and Eleanor Roosevelt Presidential Library, Hyde Park, NY.
Franklin Roosevelt Mss., Franklin and Eleanor Roosevelt Presidential Library, Hyde Park, NY. (A large selection of these, including the president's most confidential files from the war, are now online through: http://www.fdrlibrary.marist.edu/archives/collections /franklin/?p=collections/findingaid&id=502.)
John C. Slessor Mss., National Archives, UK (part of Air Ministry Archives).
Carl Spaatz Mss., Library of Congress Manuscript Division, Washington, DC.
Harry Truman Presidential Papers, Harry S. Truman Presidential Library, Independence, MO.

Oral Histories

Columbia Oral: These are transcripts of interviews held at the Library of Columbia University, New York, NY. Some are available online, but others must be consulted in the archive itself: http://library.columbia.edu/locations/ccoh.html.
NHHC Oral: These are transcripts from the Library of the Operational Archives Branch, Naval History and Heritage Command, Washington, DC. These are transcripts of interviews with a large number of US Navy officers.
Truman Oral: Harry Truman Presidential Library, Independence MO, NARA. These are transcripts of interviews done with a wide range of personalities with experience of the Truman administration. They are all accessible online at: https://www.trumanlibrary .org/oralhist/oral_his.htm.

Selected Books and Articles

Books

Acheson, Dean. *Present at the Creation: My Years at the State Department.* New York: W. W. Norton, 1969.

Adams, Henry A. *Witness to Power: The Life of Fleet Admiral William D. Leahy.* Annapolis: Naval Institute Press, 1985.

Adelman, Jonathan R. *Hitler and His Allies in World War II.* New York: Routledge, 2007.

Albion, Robert G. *Makers of Naval Policy, 1798–1947.* Annapolis: Naval Institute Press, 1980.

Alperovitz, Gar. *Atomic Diplomacy: Hiroshima and Potsdam, The Use of the Atomic Bomb and American Confrontation with Soviet Power.* New York: Pluto Press, 1994.

Asbell, Bernard, ed. *Mother and Daughter: The Letters of Eleanor and Anna Roosevelt.* New York: Coward, McCann & Geoghegan, 1982.

Ayers, Eben A., and Robert H. Ferrell. *Truman in the White House: The Diary of Eben A. Ayers.* Columbia, MO: University of Missouri Press, 1991.

Baer, George. *One Hundred Years of Seapower.* Palo Alto: Stanford University Press, 1998.

Barlow, Jeffrey G. *Revolt of the Admirals: The Fight for Naval Aviation, 1945–1950.* Washington, DC: Department of the Navy, 1994.

Barnhart, Michael A. *Japan Prepares for Total War: The Search for Economic Security, 1919–1941.* Ithaca: Cornell University Press, 1987.

Baruch, Bernard. *The Public Years.* London: Holt, Rinehart and Winston, 1960.

Beruff, Jorge Rodríguez. *Strategy as Politics: Puerto Rico on the Eve of the Second World War.* San Juan: Universidad de Puerto Rico Press, 2007.

—— and Jose L. Bolivar Fresneda, eds. *Islands at War: Puerto Rico in the Crucible of the Second World War.* Jackson, MS: University Press of Mississippi, 2015.

Bishop, Jim. *FDR's Last Year: April 1944–April 1945.* New York: Pocket Books, 1975.

Bland, Larry, ed. *The Papers of George Catlett Marshall,* volume 3. Baltimore: Johns Hopkins University Press, 1991.

Bogle, Lori Lyn, ed. *The Cold War,* volume 2. New York: Routledge, 2001.

Bohlen Charles. *Witness to History: 1929–1969.* New York: Norton, 1973.

Bostdorff, Denise M. *Proclaiming the Truman Doctrine: The Cold War Call to Arms.* College Station: Texas A&M University Press, 2008.

Bradford, James, ed. *Makers of the American Naval Tradition, 1880–1930.* Annapolis: Naval Institute Press, 1990.

Brooks, John. *Dreadnought Gunnery and the Battle of Jutland: The Question of Fire Control.* London: Routledge, 2005.

Brown, Constantine. *The Coming of the Whirlwind, 1914–1952.* Chicago: Henry Regnery Co., 1964.

Buell, Thomas. *Master of Sea Power: A Biography of Fleet Admiral Ernest J. King.* Annapolis: Naval Institute Press, 1995.

Building the Navy's Bases in World War II: History of the Bureau of Yards and Docks and the Civil Engineer Corps, 1940–1946. Washington, DC: Government Printing Office, 1947.

Bullitt, Orville, ed. *For the President Personal and Secret: Correspondence Between Franklin D. Roosevelt and William C. Bullitt.* Boston: Houghton Mifflin, 1972.

Burns, James MacGregor. *Roosevelt: The Soldier of Freedom.* New York: Harcourt Brace, 1970.

Byrnes, James. *Speaking Frankly.* New York: Harper Brothers, 1947.

Campbell, Thomas M., and George C. Herring, eds. *The Diaries of Edward R. Stettinius, Jr., 1943–1946.* New York: New Viewpoints, 1975.

Chappell, John D. *Before the Bomb: How America Approached the End of the Pacific War.* Lexington: University of Kentucky Press, 1997.

Chisholm, Donald. *Waiting for Dead Men's Shoes, Origins and Development of the US Navy's Personnel System, 1793–1941.* Palo Alto: Stanford University Press, 2001.

Churchill, Paul Addison. *The Unexpected Hero.* Oxford, UK: Oxford University Press, 2005.

Churchill, Winston. *The Second World War,* volume 4. New York: Houghton Mifflin, 1953.

Clifford, Clark. *Counsel to the President: A Memoir.* New York: Random House, 1991.

Coletta, Paolo E. *American Secretaries of the Navy,* volume 2. Annapolis: Naval Institute Press, 1980.

Condit, Kenneth. *The Joint Chiefs of Staff and National Policy,* volume 2, 1947–1949. Washington, DC: Joint History Office, 1996.

Cook, James F. *Carl Vinson: Patriarch of the Armed Forces*. Macon, GA: Mercer University Press, 1984.

Costigliola, Frank. *Roosevelt's Lost Alliances: How Personal Politics Shaped the Cold War*. Princeton: Princeton University Press, 2012.

Cross, Graham. *The Diplomatic Education of Franklin D. Roosevelt, 1882–1933*. London: Palgrave, 2012.

Dallek, Robert. *Franklin Roosevelt and American Foreign Policy, 1932–1945*. New York: Oxford University Press, 1995.

Danchev, Alex. *Establishing the Anglo-American Alliance: The Second World War Diaries of Brigadier Vivian Dykes*. London: Brasseys, 1990.

——and Daniel Todman, eds. *War Diaries, 1939–1945: Field Marshal Lord Alanbrooke*. London: Phoenix Press, 2002.

Daniels, Jonathan. *The Man from Independence*. London: Victor Gollancz, 1951.

Dilks, David. *Churchill and Company: Allies and Rivals in War and Peace*. London: I. B. Tauris, 2012.

Donovan, Robert J. *Conflict and Crisis: The Presidency of Harry Truman, 1945–1948*. Columbia: University of Missouri Press, 1996.

Ehrman, John. *Grand Strategy*, volume 4. London: HMSO, 1956.

Einolf, Christopher J. *America in the Philippines, 1899–1902: The First Torture Scandal*. New York: Palgrave, 2014.

Elsey, George M. *An Unplanned Life: A Memoir by George McKee Elsey*. Columbia: University of Missouri Press, 2005.

Ferrell, Robert H. *The Dying President: Franklin D. Roosevelt, 1944–1945*. Columbia: University of Missouri Press, 1998.

——. *Harry S. Truman and the Cold War Revisionists*. Columbia: University of Missouri Press, 2006.

——. *Truman and Pendergast*. Columbia: University of Missouri Press, 1999.

——, ed. *Off the Record: The Private Papers of Harry S. Truman*. Columbia: University of Missouri Press, 1997.

Freidel, Frank. *Franklin D. Roosevelt: A Rendezvous with Destiny*. Boston: Little, Brown 1990.

Frank, Richard B. *Downfall: The End of the Imperial Japanese Empire*. New York: Penguin, 2001.

Freud, Sigmund, and William Bullitt. *Thomas Woodrow Wilson: A Psychological Study*. Boston: Houghton Mifflin, 1967.

Gaddis, John Lewis. *The United States and the Origins of the Cold War, 1941–1947*. New York: Columbia University Press, 2000.

——, et al., eds. *Cold War Statesmen Confront the Bomb: Nuclear Diplomacy Since 1945*. Oxford, UK: Oxford University Press, 1999.

Geisst, Charles R. *Encyclopedia of American Business History*. New York: Facts on File, 2006.

Gellman, Irwin F. *Secret Affairs: Franklin Roosevelt, Cordell Hull and Sumner Welles*. Baltimore: Johns Hopkins Press, 1995.

Germany and the Second World War, volume 6. Oxford, UK: Oxford University Press, 2001.

Giangreco, D. M. *Hell to Pay: Operation Downfall and the Invasion of Japan*. Annapolis: Naval Institute Press, 2009.

Gilbert, Martin. *"Never Despair": Winston S. Churchill, 1945–1965*. London: Heinemann, 1988.

Goldstein, Erik, and John Maurer, eds. *The Washington Conference, 1921–22: Naval Rivalry, East Asian Stability and the Road to Pearl Harbor*. London: Routledge, 1994.

Goodwin, Doris Kearns. *No Ordinary Time: Franklin and Eleanor Roosevelt—The Home Front in World War II*. New York: Simon & Schuster, 1994.

Harper, John Lamberton. *The Cold War*. Oxford, UK: Oxford University Press, 2011.

Hart, Justin. *Empire of Ideas: The Origins of Public Diplomacy and the Transformation of US Foreign Policy*. Oxford, UK: Oxford University Press, 2013.

Hass, Lawrence J. *Harry and Arthur: Truman, Vandenberg and the Partnership That Created the Free World*. Lincoln, NE: Potomac Books, 2016.

Hall, Christopher. *Britain, America and Arms Control, 1921–1937*. New York: Palgrave, 1987.

Harriman, W. Averell, and Elie Abel. *Special Envoy to Churchill and Stalin*. New York: Random House, 1975.

Hearn, Chester G. *Carriers in Combat: The Air War at Sea*. London: Stackpole, 2005.

Heinrichs, Waldo. *The Threshold of War: Franklin D. Roosevelt and American Entry into World War II*. Oxford, UK: Oxford University Press, 1988.

Heiss, Mary Ann, and Michael Hogan, eds. *Origins of the National Security State and the Legacy of Harry S. Truman*. Kirksville, MO: Truman State University Press, 2015.

Herken, Gregg. *The Winning Weapon, The Atomic Bomb in the Cold War, 1945–1950*. Princeton, Princeton University Press, 1988.

Hone, Thomas C., Norman Friedman, and Marj D. Mandeles. *American and British Aircraft Carrier Development, 1919–1941*. Annapolis: Naval Institute Press, 1999.

——and Trent Hone. *Battle Line: The United States Navy, 1919–1939*. Annapolis: Naval Institute Press, 2006.

Howard, Michael. *Grand Strategy*, volume 4. London: HMSO, 1972.

Hull, Cordell. *The Memoirs of Cordell Hull*, volume 1. New York: Macmillan, 1948.

Husain, Aiyaz. *Mapping the End of Empire: American and British Visions of the Post-War World*. Cambridge, UK: Cambridge University Press, 2014.

Irwin, Manley. *Silent Strategists: Harding, Denby and the US Navy's Trans-Pacific Offensive, World War II*. Lanham, MD: University Press of America, 2013.

Jackson, Julian. *De Gaulle*. London: Haus Publishing, 2003.

——. *France, the Dark Years, 1940–1944*. Oxford, UK: Oxford University Press, 2001.

Jeans, Roger B. *The Marshall Mission to China, 1945–1947: The Letters and Diary of Colonel John Hart Caughey*. Plymouth, UK: Rowman and Littlefield, 2011.

Jordan, Jonathan W. *American Warlords: How Roosevelt's High Command Led America to Victory in World War II*. New York: Dutton Caliber, 2015.

Karsten, Peter. *The Naval Aristocracy: The Golden Age of Annapolis and the Emergence of Modern American Navalism*. New York: The Free Press, 1972.

Kimball, Warren. *The Juggler: Franklin Roosevelt as Statesman*. Princeton: Princeton University Press, 1991.

King, Ernest, and Walter Muir Whitehill. *Fleet Admiral King: A Naval Record*. New York: Norton, 1952.

Knox, Dudley W. *A History of the United States Navy*. New York: G. P. Putnam & Sons, 1936.

Kuehn, John T. *Agents of Innovation: The General Board and the Design of the Fleet That Defeated the Japanese Navy*. Annapolis: Naval Institute Press, 2008.

Lacey, Michael James, ed. *The Truman Presidency*. Cambridge, UK: Cambridge University Press, 1991.

Larrabee, Eric. *Commander in Chief: Franklin Roosevelt, His Lieutenants, and Their War*. New York: HarperCollins, 1987.

Lash, Joseph P. *Eleanor and Franklin, The Story of their Relationship, Based on Eleanor Roosevelt's Private Papers*. New York: New American Library, 1971.

Laub, Thomas. *After the Fall: German Policy in Occupied France, 1940–1944*. Oxford, UK: Oxford University Press, 2010.

Leahy, William. *I Was There*. New York: McGraw-Hill, 1950.

Leffler, Melvyn. *A Preponderance of Power: National Security, the Truman Administration and the Cold War*. Stanford: Stanford University Press, 1992.

Leffler, Melvyn, and Odd Arne Westad. *The Cambridge History of the Cold War*, volume 1. Cambridge, UK: Cambridge University Press, 2010.

Leighton, Richard, and Robert Coakley. *Global Logistics and Strategy, 1940–1943*. Washington, DC: Government Printing Office, 1955.

Levin, Linda L. *The Making of FDR: The Story of Stephen T. Early, America's First Modern Press Secretary*. New York: Prometheus Books, 2008.

Lisio, Donald J. *British Naval Supremacy and Anglo-American Antagonisms, 1914–1930*. Cambridge, UK: Cambridge University Press, 2014.

Logevall, Frederick. *Embers of War: The Fall of an Empire and the Making of America's Vietnam*. New York: Random House, 2012.

Love, Robert William Jr., ed. *The Chiefs of Naval Operations*. Annapolis: Naval Institute Press, 1980.

Marrus, Michael R., and Robert O. Paxton. *Vichy France and the Jews*. Stanford: Stanford University Press, 1995.

Matloff, Maurice. *The 90 Division Gamble*. Washington DC: Center for Military History, 1990.

Maurer, John, and Christopher Bell, eds. *At the Crossroads Between Peace and War: The London Naval Conference of 1930*. Annapolis: Naval Institute Press, 2014.

Mayers, David. *FDR's Ambassadors and the Diplomacy of Crisis: From the Rise of Hitler to the End of World War II*. Cambridge, UK: Cambridge University Press, 2013.

McCullough, David. *Truman.* New York: Simon & Schuster, 1992.

McMahon, Robert J. *Dean Acheson and the Creation of the American World Order.* Dulles, VA: Potomac Books, 2009.

Meid, Pat. *US Marine Operations in Korea, 1950–1953: Vol. V, Operation in West Korea.* Washington, DC: Historical Division USMC, 1973.

Messer, Robert L. *The End of the Alliance: James F. Byrnes, Roosevelt, Truman and the Origins of the Cold War.* Chapel Hill: University of North Carolina Press, 1982.

Miller, Edward. *Bankrupting the Enemy: The US Financial Siege of Japan Before Pearl Harbor.* Annapolis: Naval Institute Press, 2007.

——. *War Plan Orange: The US Strategy to Defeat Japan, 1897–1945.* Annapolis: Naval Institute Press, 1991.

Miller, Merle. *Plain Speaking: An Oral Biography of Harry S. Truman.* New York: Berkley Publishing, 1973.

Miller, Roger G. *Billy Mitchell: Stormy Petrel of the Air.* Washington, DC: Office Air Force History, 2004.

Mills, Walter., ed. *The Forrestal Diaries: The Inner History of the Cold War.* London: Cassel & Co., 1952.

Miscamble, Wilson D. *The Most Controversial Decision: Truman, the Atomic Bombs, and the Defeat of Japan.* Cambridge, UK: Cambridge University Press, 2011.

Mitter, Rana. *Forgotten Ally: China's World War II, 1937–1945.* New York: Penguin, 2014.

Muller, James W. *Churchill's "Iron Curtain" Speech Fifty Years Later.* Columbia: University of Missouri Press, 1999.

Murphy, Robert. *Diplomat Among Warriors: The Unique World of a Foreign Service Expert.* New York: Doubleday, 1964.

Musicant, Ivan. *Empire by Default: The Spanish-American War and the Dawn of the American Century.* New York: Henry Holt, 1998.

O'Brien, Phillips P. *British and American Naval Power: Politics and Policies, 1900–1936.* Westport, CT: Praeger, 1998.

——. *How the War Was Won: Air-Sea Power and Allied Victory in World War II.* Cambridge, UK: Cambridge University Press, 2015.

O'Connell, Robert L. *Sacred Vessels: The Cult of the Battleship and the Rise of the US Navy.* Oxford, UK: Oxford University Press, 1991.

Offner, Arnold A. *Another Such Victory: President Truman and the Cold War, 1945–1953.* Palo Alto: Stanford University Press, 2002.

Organizational Development of the Joint Chiefs of Staff, 1942–2013. Washington, DC: Joint History Office, Office of the Chairman of the Joint Chiefs of Staff. April, 2013.

O'Sullivan, Christopher D. *FDR and the End of Empire: The Origins of American Power in the Middle East.* New York: Palgrave, 2012.

——. *Sumner Welles: Post-War Planning and the Quest for a New World Order, 1937–1943.* New York: Columbia University Press, 2009.

Parrish, Thomas. *Roosevelt and Marshall: Partners in Politics and War.* New York: William Morrow, 1989.

Paxton, Robert. *Vichy France: Old Guard and New Order, 1940–1944.* New York: Knopf, 1972.

Persico, Joseph. *Franklin and Lucy: Mrs. Rutherford and the Other Remarkable Women in Roosevelt's Life.* New York: Random House, 2009.

Pogue, Forrest. *George C. Marshall: Organizer of Victory, 1943–1945.* New York: Viking, 1973.

Potter, E. B. *The Naval Academy: Illustrated History of the United States Navy.* New York: Galahad Books, 1971.

Rearden, Steven. *A Council of War: A History of the Joint Chiefs of Staff, 1942–1991.* Washington, DC: Joint History Office, 2012.

Rigdon, William. *White House Sailor.* Garden City, NY: Doubleday, 1962.

Roll, David L. *The Hopkins Touch: Harry Hopkins and the Forging of the Alliance to Defeat Hitler.* Oxford, UK: Oxford University Press, 2013.

Rooney, David. *Stilwell the Patriot: Vinegar Joe, the Brits and Chiang Kai-shek.* London: Greenhill Books, 2005.

Roosevelt, Eleanor. *This I Remember.* New York: Harper Brothers, 1949.

Roosevelt, Elliott, ed. *F.D.R.: His Personal Letters.* New York: Duell, Sloan and Pearce, 1970.

—— and James Brough. *Rendezvous with Destiny: The Roosevelts of the White House.* London: W. H. Allen, 1977.

Rosenman, Samuel. *Working with Roosevelt*. New York: Harper and Brothers, 1952.

Roskill, Stephen. *The War at Sea, volume 3: The Offensive*. London: Naval and Military Press, 2009.

Reynolds, David. *From World War to Cold War: Churchill, Roosevelt and the International History of the 1940s*. Oxford, UK: Oxford University Press, 2006.

Schlesinger, Arthur M. *The Coming of the New Deal, 1933–1935: The Age of Roosevelt*. Boston, Houghton Mifflin, 2003.

Schmitt. Waldo L. *Decapod and other Crustacea Collected on the Presidential Cruise of 1938*, volume 3531. Washington, DC: Smithsonian Institution, 1939.

Schnabel, James F. *History of the Joint Chiefs of Staff, volume 1: The Joint Chiefs of Staff and National Policy, 1945–1947*. Washington, DC: Government Printing Office, 1996.

Schneller, Robert J. Jr., *Breaking the Color Barrier: The US Naval Academy's First Black Midshipmen and the Struggle for Racial Equality*. New York: NYU Press, 2007.

Schwarz, Jordan A. *The Speculator: Bernard M. Baruch in Washington, 1917–1965*. Chapel Hill: University of North Carolina Press, 1981.

Sherwood, Robert. *Roosevelt and Hopkins: An Intimate History*. New York: Harper, 1948.

———. *The White House Papers of Harry L. Hopkins*, volume 2. London: Eyre and Spottiswoode, 1949.

Smith, Kathryn. *The Gatekeeper: Missy LeHand, FDR and the Untold Story of a Partnership That Defined a Presidency*. New York: Touchstone, 2016.

Smith, R. Elberton. *The Army and Economic Mobilization*. Washington, DC: Government Printing Office, 1959.

Spalding, Elizabeth. *The First Cold Warrior: Harry Truman, Containment and the Remaking of Liberal Internationalism*. Lexington: University Press of Kentucky, 2006.

Steely, Skipper. *Pearl Harbor Countdown: James O. Richardson*. Gretna, LA: Pelican Publishing, 2008.

Stoler, Mark A. *Allies and Adversaries: The Joint Chiefs of Staff, The Grand Alliance and US Strategy in World War II*. Chapel Hill: University of North Carolina Press, 2000.

———. *Allies in War: Britain and America Against the Axis Powers, 1940–1945*. London: Hodder Arnold, 2005.

Sumida, Jon Tetsuro. *In Defence of Naval Supremacy: Finance, Technology and British Naval Policy, 1889–1914*. London: Routledge, 1993.

Taylor, Jay. *The Generalissimo: Chiang Kai-shek and the Struggle for Modern China*. Cambridge, MA: Harvard University Press, 2009.

Thomas, Martin. *The French Empire at War, 1949–1945*. Manchester, UK: Manchester University Press, 1998.

Truman, Harry S. *Memoirs: Volume I, Years of Decision*. Garden City, NY: Doubleday, 1955.

———. *Memoirs: Volume II, Years of Trial and Hope*. Garden City, NY: Doubleday, 1955.

Tsou, Tang. *America's Failure in China, 1941–1950*. Chicago: University Chicago Press, 1963.

Walker, Hugh Dyson. *East Asia: A New History*. Bloomington, IN: Author House, 2012.

Ward, Geoffrey. *Closest Companion: The Unknown Story of the Intimate Friendship Between Franklin Roosevelt and Margaret Suckley*. Boston: Houghton Mifflin, 1995.

Wedemeyer, Albert. *Wedemeyer Reports*. New York: Henry Holt, 1958.

Weintraub, Stanley. *15 Stars: Eisenhower, MacArthur, Marshall: Three Generals Who Saved the American Century*. New York: Free Press, 2007.

———. *Final Victory: FDR's Extraordinary World War II Presidential Campaign*. Philadelphia: Da Capo Press, 2012.

Welles, Benjamin. *Sumner Welles: FDR's Global Strategist*. New York: St Martin Press, 1997.

Welles, Sumner. *Naboth's Vineyard: The Dominican Republic, 1844–1924*. New York: Payson and Clarke, 1928.

———. *Seven Decisions That Changed History*. New York: Harper, 1951.

———. *The Time for Decision*. London: Hamish Hamilton, 1944.

Williams, Francis. *A Prime Minister Remembers: The War and Post-War Memoirs of the Rt Hon Earl Attlee*. London: William Heinemann, 1961.

Winik, Jay. *FDR and the Year That Changed History*. New York: Simon & Schuster, 2015.

Woods, Randall B., and Howard Jones. *Dawning of the Cold War: The United States Quest for Order*. Athens: University of Georgia Press, 1991.

Wright, Monte, and Lawrence Paszek, eds., *Soldiers and Statesmen: Proceedings of the 4th Military History Symposium United States Air Force Academy*. Washington, DC: Office of Air Force History, 1973.

Articles

Anderson Jr., Irvine H. "The 1941 De Facto Embargo on Oil to Japan: A Bureaucratic Reflex." *Pacific Historical Review* 44, no. 2 (May 1975).

Borowski, Harry. "A Narrow Victory: The Berlin Blockade and the American Military Response." *Air University Review* (July–August 1981).

Brown, Wilson. "Aide to Four Presidents." *American Heritage* 6, no. 2 (1955).

Chao, Hsiang-ke, and Lin Hsiao-ting. "Beyond the Carrot and the Stick: The Political Economy of US Military Aid to China, 1945–1951." *Journal of Modern Chinese History* 5, no. 2 (2011).

Craig, Bruce. "A Matter of Espionage, Alger Hiss, Harry Dexter White and Igor Gouzenko, the Canadian Connection Reassessed." *Intelligence and National Security* 15, no. 2 (2000).

Faerstein, Eduardo, and Warren Winkelstein. "William Gorgas, Yellow Fever Meets Its Nemesis." *Epidemiology* 22, no. 6 (November 2011).

Funk, Arthur L. "Eisenhower, Giraud and the Command of 'Torch.'" *Military Affairs* 35, no. 3 (October 1971).

Giangreco, D. M. "Casualty Projections for the US Invasions of Japan, 1945–1946: Planning and Policy Implications." *Journal of Military History* 61 (July 1997).

Halsted, James A. "Severe Malnutrition in a Public Servant of the World War II Era: The Medical History of Harry Hopkins." *Transactions of the American Clinical and Climatological Association* 86 (1975).

Melka, Robert L. "Darlan Between Britain and Germany, 1940–41." *Journal of Contemporary History* 8, no. 2 (1973).

Muir, Malcolm, Jr. "American Warship Construction for Stalin's Navy Prior to World War II: A Study of Paralysis of Power." *Diplomatic History* 5, no. 4 (1981).

Okumiya, Masatake. "How the Panay Was Sunk." *Proceedings* 79, no. 6 (June 1953).

Rofe, J. Simon. "'Under the Influence of Mahan': Theodore and Franklin Roosevelt and Their Understanding of American National Interest." *Diplomacy and Statecraft* 19, no. 4.

Roosevelt, Franklin D. "Our Foreign Policy: A Democratic View." *Foreign Affairs* 6, no. 4 (July 1928).

Reichardt, Tony. "The First Presidential Flight." *Air and Space Magazine*, January 18, 2013.

Reynolds, David. "Wheelchair Diplomacy: FDR and American Foreign Policy, 1933–1945." *Diplomatic History* 39, no. 3 (June 2015).

Rosenberg, David Alan. "American Atomic Strategy and the Hydrogen Bomb Decision." *Journal of American History* 66, no. 1 (June 1979).

Shields, J. G. "Charlemagne's Crusaders: French Collaboration in Arms, 1941–1945." *French Cultural Studies* 18, no. 1 (Feb. 1, 2007).

Stoler, Mark. "George C. Marshall and the 'Europe-First' Strategy, 1939–1951: A Study in Diplomatic as Well as Military History." Marshall Foundation Online: http://marshall foundation.org/marshall/wp-content/uploads/sites/22/2014/04/EDStoler.pdf.

———. "The Pacific-First Alternative in American World War II Strategy." *International History Review* 2, no. 3 (July 1980).

Varley, Karine. "Vichy and the Complexities of Collaborating with Fascist Italy: French Policy and Perceptions Between June 1940 and March 1942." *Modern and Contemporary France* 21, no. 3 (2013).

Notes

Prologue

1. Leahy Diary, March 3, 1946.
2. For a transcript of the Sinews of Power speech, see: https://www.nationalchurchill museum.org/sinews-of-peace-iron-curtain-speech.html.

Chapter 1: THE EDUCATION OF A NAVAL OFFICER

1. If one takes into account inflation, $113,903 in 1960 would be worth $916,357 today. See http://www.saving.org/inflation/inflation.php?amount=100,000&year=1960.
2. The Leahy boys other than William were John, Arthur, Stephen, Robert, and Earl. The daughter was named Margaret.
3. In 2010, the population of Ashland was only 8,210. http://www.coawi.org/about -ashland/community-profile/.
4. NHHC Oral, Albert K. Murray Interview, 123.
5. The *Constellation* can still be visited today in Baltimore Harbor. It is sometimes mistakenly said that this *Constellation* is the same one that was laid down in the early nineteenth century, which became one of the two most famous ships in the early navy of the United States. That is not true, though this vessel was built using some of the timbers from the older, more famous vessel. http://www.historicships.org/constella tion.html.
6. Peter Karsten, *The Naval Aristocracy: The Golden Age of Annapolis and the Emergence of Modern American Navalism* (New York: The Free Press, 1972), 39–43.
7. Capt. W. D. Puleston, *Annapolis, Gangway to the Quarterdeck* (New York: D. Appleton Co, 1942), 115.
8. Leahy Diary, 1: 274.
9. Robert J. Schneller Jr., *Breaking the Color Barrier: The US Naval Academy's First Black Midshipmen and the Struggle for Racial Equality* (New York: NYU Press, 2007).
10. Naval Academy Public Affairs, "Naval Academy Class of '78 Shines with Four 4-Stars," January 15, 2016, http://www.navy.mil/submit/display.asp?story_id=92723. The other classes were 1927, 1933, 1973, and 1978.
11. Leahy Diary, see text of broadcast of *Who's Who* about Leahy in February 1943. The text is in the diary between June 30, 1943, and July 1, 1943.
12. Columbia Oral: Thomas Hart Interview, 1: 44.
13. Ibid., 54–55.
14. Leahy Diary, 1: 1.
15. Ibid., 1: 7.
16. Ivan Musicant, *Empire by Default: The Spanish-American War and the Dawn of the American Century* (New York: Henry Holt, 1998), 330, 334–35.
17. Leahy Diary, 1: 33–34.
18. Ibid., 44.

19. E.B. Potter, *The Naval Academy: Illustrated History of the United States Navy* (New York: Galahad Books, 1971), 128–29.
20. Leahy NHHC, "Notes on Activities of the Battleship *Oregon* in the War with Spain 1898," undated manuscript.
21. Leahy Diary, 1: 53.
22. Henry A. Adams, *Witness to Power: The Life of Fleet Admiral William D. Leahy* (Annapolis: Naval Institute Press, 1985), 18.
23. Leahy Diary, 1: 62.
24. Ibid., 63.
25. Ibid., 72–73.
26. Ibid., 87.
27. Leahy NHHC, Leahy to "George" (seems to be serving as US Naval Attaché in China), July 24, 1925.
28. Leahy Diary, 1: 79.
29. Ibid., 82.
30. Ibid., 84.
31. Dudley W. Knox, *A History of the United States Navy* (New York: GP Putnam & Sons, 1936), 368–69.
32. Leahy Diary, 1: 95–97.
33. Leahy NHHC, "President Roosevelt's Ear at Vichy," August 28, 1941.
34. Leahy Diary, 1: 99.
35. Christopher J. Einolf, *America in the Philippines, 1899–1902: The First Torture Scandal* (New York: Palgrave, 2014), 62–77.
36. Adams, *Witness to Power*, 45.
37. Leahy Diary, 1: 95.
38. Ibid., 105–7.
39. Ibid., 111.
40. Ibid., 133.
41. Ibid., 125.
42. Ibid., 105.
43. Barlin was made a bishop in 1900, and as this party was for the highest ranks of Filipino society, it would make sense that he was there and would be the center of attention.
44. Leahy Diary, 1: 118.
45. Ibid.
46. Ibid.
47. Ibid., 117.

CHAPTER 2: BUILDING A CAREER AND FAMILY

1. Leahy Diary, 1: 119.
2. Ibid., 236.
3. Leahy's relationship with his father was likely uneasy. Michael Leahy's relative lack of success probably did not impress his driven son, and it is worth noting that the most common thing William mentions about Michael is his wish for him to stay in Wisconsin and attend law school. Leahy made no secret of his desire to leave home, thereby disappointing his father.
4. Henry A. Adams, *Witness to Power: The Life of Fleet Admiral William D. Leahy* (Annapolis: Naval Institute Press, 1985), 19.
5. Niblack's papers are kept in the Indiana Historical Archive, which has a short biography of him: http://www.indianahistory.org/our-collections/collection-guides/admiral-albert-p-niblack-collection-1843–1929.pdf (accessed February 2016).
6. He arrived in March 1903, according to his diary.
7. *San Francisco Call*, "Gives Dinner at a Club to His Fiancee," February 4, 1904.
8. Leahy Diary, 1: 121.
9. Columbia Oral, Thomas Hart Interview, 1: 54.
10. Leahy Diary, 1: 54.
11. *San Francisco Call*, "The Smart Set," December 2, 1910, 8.
12. Leahy NHHC, Leahy to Mary Niblack, August 14, 1948.
13. For Leahy's description of the earthquake and subsequent fire, see Leahy Diary, 1: 154–59.

14. Leahy Diary, 1: 160.
15. Ibid.,129.
16. Ibid.,130.
17. Eduardo Faerstein and Warren Winkelstein, "William Gorgas, Yellow Fever Meets Its Nemesis," *Epidemiology* 22:6, 872.
18. The *California* would later be rechristened the USS *San Diego*. The ship was sunk by a German mine in World War I, the largest American warship lost in that conflict.
19. James Bradford, "Henry T. Mayo, Last of the Independent Naval Diplomats," in James Bradford, ed., *Makers of the American Naval Tradition, 1880–1930* (Annapolis: Naval Institute Press, 1990), 258–67.
20. *New York Times*, June 9, 1915, 22.
21. Bradford, "Henry T. Mayo," 253–81.
22. The usually reserved Leahy was particularly fulsome in his praise for Mayo when the latter gave up command of the *California*. See Leahy Diary, 1: 182.
23. Adams, *Witness to Power*, 27.
24. A great deal has been written about gunnery developments before World War I, usually about the Royal Navy. The decisions that the Royal Navy made about gunnery are often seen as key to the positives and negatives of their performance in the war. Two books with quite different opinions are: Jon Tetsuro Sumida, *In Defence of Naval Supremacy: Finance, Technology and British Naval Policy, 1889–1914* (London: Routledge 1993); and John Brooks, *Dreadnought Gunnery and the Battle of Jutland: The Question of Fire Control* (London: Routledge, 2005).
25. Leahy Diary, 1: 186.
26. Ibid., 168.
27. Ibid., 198.
28. Ibid., 173.
29. Ibid., 196.
30. Ibid., 178–80.
31. For a description of the entire intervention, see ibid., 199–203.
32. Ibid., 199.
33. Ibid., 200.
34. Ibid., 201.
35. Ibid., 208.
36. Leahy NHHC, Leahy to Southerland, September 19, 1912.
37. Leahy Diary: Southerland to Gill, September 20, 1912.
38. Leahy Diary, 1: 185.
39. Ibid., 209.

CHAPTER 3: ENTER FRANKLIN ROOSEVELT

1. Robert Dallek, *Franklin Roosevelt and American Foreign Policy, 1932–1945* (New York: Oxford University Press, 1995), 7–10.
2. Graham Cross, *The Diplomatic Education of Franklin D. Roosevelt, 1882–1933* (London: Palgrave, 2012), 33–34. Accessible online at http://www.palgraveconnect.com.ez proxy.lib.gla.ac.uk/pc/doifinder/10.1057/9781137014542.0016 (Accessed: December 11, 2015).
3. J. Simon Rofe, "'Under the Influence of Mahan': Theodore and Franklin Roosevelt and Their Understanding of American National Interest," *Diplomacy and Statecraft* 19:4, 732–45. Accessed online: http://www.tandfonline.com/doi/abs/10.1080/0959229080 2564536#.Vsw_v_mLSUk.
4. Eric Larrabbee, *Commander in Chief: Franklin Delano Roosevelt, His Lieutenants and Their War* (New York: Simon & Schuster, 1988), 634.
5. William Leahy, *I Was There* (New York: McGraw Hill, 1950), 3.
6. Ibid.
7. Henry A. Adams, *Witness to Power: The Life of Fleet Admiral William D. Leahy* (Annapolis: Naval Institute Press, 1985), 31–32.
8. Ibid.
9. Columbia Oral, Thomas Hart Interview, 1: 54
10. *Washington Times*, "Mrs. Daniels Guest at Luncheon Today," February 19, 1917, 7.
11. *Washington Times*, "Daniels Calls on Mrs. Eopolucci," April 10, 1917, 4.
12. Leahy Diary, 1: 211.

13. Ibid.
14. Ibid.
15. Leahy NHHC, Caperton to Secretary of the Navy, July 18, 1916.
16. Leahy NHHC, Leahy to Caperton, September 1, 1916.
17. Adams, *Witness to Power*, 32.
18. Joseph P. Lash, *Eleanor and Franklin: The Story of Their Relationship, Based on Eleanor Roosevelt's Private Papers* (New York: New American Library, 1971), 199.
19. Leahy NHHC, Leahy to Caperton, September 1, 1916.
20. Leahy went into great detail about the hunt for the *Nordskov* in his diary; it certainly seems the most exciting part of his World War I service. See: Leahy Diary, 1: 218–20.
21. Hanson Baldwin, "Two New Pilots Help Steer Our Navy Program," *New York Times*, March 28, 1937.
22. The post of Chief of Naval Operations was created in 1915. At this point it operated more as a first among equals with the various bureau chiefs. Thomas C. Hone and Trent Hone, *Battle Line: The United States Navy, 1919–1939* (Annapolis: Naval Institute Press, 2006), 127.
23. Leahy Diary, 1: 225.
24. Leahy Diary; see text of Broadcast of *Who's Who* about Leahy in February 1943. The text is in the diary between June 30, 1943, and July 1, 1943.
25. Leahy Diary, 1: 226.
26. Ibid., 232–33.

CHAPTER 4: THE ROARING TWENTIES

1. One of the best physical descriptions of Leahy was written not long after he became chief of staff to Franklin Roosevelt, "Sailor, Diplomat, Strategist," *New York Times*, November 29, 1942.
2. Frank Kluckhohn, "To the Navy He's Just Bill," *New York Times*, August 2, 1942.
3. Leahy NHHC, "Interesting Incident of Service in Turkish Waters . . ." Leahy also described the incident in his diary: Leahy Diary, 1: 257.
4. Columbia Oral, Admiral Harold Train, 214.
5. Leahy Diary, 1: 234.
6. For descriptions of the details of the 1916 naval act, see: Phillips P. O'Brien, *British and American Naval Power: Politics and Policies, 1900–1936* (Westport, CT: Praeger, 1998), 116–20. For another mention, see: Donald J. Lisio, *British Naval Supremacy and Anglo-American Antagonisms, 1914–1930* (Cambridge, UK: Cambridge University Press, 2014), 7–8.
7. Leahy Diary, 1: 234.
8. Ibid., 235.
9. Ibid., 242.
10. Ibid., 247.
11. Ibid.
12. Ibid., 248.
13. Constantine Brown, *The Coming of the Whirlwind, 1914–1952* (Chicago: Henry Regnery Co., 1964), 133–34.
14. Leahy Diary, 1: 249, 251.
15. Leahy NHHC, Leahy to Niblack, July 3, 1921.
16. Leahy wrote a detailed description of his sightseeing in Istanbul: Leahy Diary, 1: 244–47.
17. Ibid., 245.
18. Leahy NHHC, "Interesting Incident."
19. Ibid.
20. Leahy Diary, 1: 243.
21. William Braisted, "Mark Lambert Bristol, Naval Diplomat Extraordinary of the Battleship Age," in James Bradford, ed., *Makers of the American Naval Tradition, 1880–1930* (Annapolis: Naval Institute Press, 1990), 340–48.
22. Leahy Diary, 1: 243.
23. Ibid., 250.
24. Leahy NHHC, Leahy to Niblack, July 3, 1921.
25. Leahy NHHC, Memorandum for Chief of Naval Operations, undated but written as Leahy was leaving Constantinople.

26. A great deal has been written about the Washington Conference specifically, and naval arms control in the interwar period more generally. One of the best books include: Christopher Hall, *Britain, America and Arms Control, 1921–1937* (New York: St. Martin's Press, 1987).

27. For an excellent collection of articles on the Washington Conference see: Erik Goldstein and John Maurer (eds.), *The Washington Conference, 1921–22: Naval Rivalry, East Asian Stability and the Road to Pearl Harbor* (London: Routledge, 1994).

28. Leahy Diary, 1: 287.

29. Ibid., 183. Leahy spelled Curtiss's last name as "Curtis."

30. In his letters to Niblack in the mid-1920s, Leahy regularly grumbled about naval aviators. See: Leahy NHHC, Leahy to Niblack, December 14, 1925, and January 23, 1926.

31. Roger G. Miller, *Billy Mitchell, Stormy Petrel of the Air* (Washington, DC: Office Air Force History, 2004). See pages 27–33 for a description of some of Mitchell's most famous tests, including the 1921 attacks on the *Ostfriedland*, a captured German World War I battleship. Available online at: http://www.afhso.af.mil/shared/media/afhistory /Billy_Mitchell_Stormy_Petrel.pdf.

32. Leahy Diary, 1: 288.

33. Ibid., 134.

34. Ibid., 282.

35. "Watchdog in the White House," *Collier's,* 9 October 1948, 77.

36. Leahy Diary, 1: 271.

37. Ibid., 272–3.

38. Leahy NHHC, Leahy to Niblack, September 26, 1922.

39. Leahy Diary, 1: 293.

40. Ibid., 244.

41. Ibid., 275.

42. Ibid., 263.

43. Leahy NHHC, Leahy to Niblack, September 18, 1925.

44. Leahy Diary, 1: 296.

45. Ibid.

46. Ibid., 308.

47. Leahy NHHC, Leahy to Niblack, December 14, 1925.

48. Leahy Diary, 1: 312.

49. Leahy NHHC, Leahy to Reece, November 23, 1951.

50. Leahy NHHC, Reece to Leahy, November 9, 1951.

51. Leahy Diary, 1: 311.

52. In his diary the name of the bank is written as "Calusa," though the town in California is today called Colusa.

53. Leahy wrote two letters to Niblack in 1925–1926 in which he gave a glimpse of his concerns over the state of his investments. In both it's clear that he was a little confused by the business decisions being made by the bank and worried about the value of the land in California. However, even though he expressed these doubts, he also seemed reluctant to sell either. See Leahy NHHC, Leahy to Niblack, December 14, 1925, and January 23, 1926.

CHAPTER 5: DEPRESSION

1. Leahy Diary, 2: 312.

2. Robert G. Albion, *Makers of Naval Policy, 1798–1947* (Annapolis: Naval Institute Press, 1980), 245.

3. For an excellent overview of the 1930 London Conference see: John Maurer and Christopher Bell (eds.), *At the Crossroads Between Peace and War: The London Naval Conference of 1930* (Annapolis: Naval Institute Press, 2014).

4. In the end, Hoover was able to reduce the budget for FY 1931–32 to less than $360 million. There is a helpful web page with all annual USN budgets, maintained by the Naval Historical and Heritage Command: https://www.history.navy.mil/research /library/online-reading-room/title-list-alphabetically/b/budget-of-the-us-navy-1794-to -2004.html.

5. Albion, *Makers of Naval Policy,* 246.

6. Phillips P. O'Brien, *British and American Naval Power: Politics and Policies* (Westport, CT: Praeger, 1998), 218.

7. Leahy Diary, 1: 311.
8. Ibid., 312.
9. Leahy's dislike of Herbert Hoover was so intense that his view of the president was probably unfair. Modern scholarship argues that Hoover did try to take some actions to ameliorate the impact of the Great Depression, but his efforts were not publicized, as he did not want to add to the air of crisis. That being said, Hoover did not attempt anything along the lines of Roosevelt's New Deal.
10. Leahy Diary, 2: 10–11.
11. See: Craig L. Symonds, "William Veazie Pratt," in Robert William Love Jr. (ed.), *The Chiefs of Naval Operations* (Annapolis: Naval Institute Press, 1980). There was a great deal of animosity in the fleet toward Pratt because of his perceived policy of favoring too small of a fleet (see pages 76–78). In many ways, however, this was a result of shooting the messenger, as the political situation at the time meant that the USN was going to receive little in the way of extra naval building. See O'Brien, *British and American Naval Power*, 210–16.
12. Leahy Diary, 1: 314.
13. Leahy NHHC, Leahy to Schofield, April 27, 1931.
14. Ibid.
15. Leahy NHHC, Leahy to Watkins, June 6, 1931.
16. Leahy Diary, 2: 31.
17. Ibid., 12.
18. Leahy Diary, handwritten section at start, entitled "To William Harrington Leahy."
19. Ibid., 314–15.
20. "Watchdog in the White House," *Collier's,* October 9, 1948, 77.
21. Leahy Diary, "To William Harrington Leahy." This was written while Leahy was commander of the destroyers of the US Fleet (1931–32).
22. Leahy NHHC, Leahy to Clark, April 14, 1933.
23. "Navy Is Stressing Anti-Aircraft Fire," *New York Times*, December 13, 1929.
24. US General Board Minutes, NARA, February 3, 1931, 13.
25. Norman Friedman, *Naval Anti-Aircraft Guns and Gunnery* (Barnsley, UK: Seaforth, 2013), 110.
26. US General Board Minutes, NARA, May 1, 1931, 19.
27. Leahy NHHC, Leahy to Craven, October 14, 1932. Also see: Leahy Diary, 2: 15.
28. Leahy Diary, 2: 39.
29. Ibid., 14.
30. Ibid., 23.
31. Ibid., 24.
32. Ibid.
33. Ibid., 27.
34. Ibid.
35. "*Saratoga* Grounded, Then Freed in 4 Hours," *New York Times,* August 19, 1932, 3.
36. Leahy Diary, 2: 33.
37. "Captain Steele to Retire," *New York Times*, December 29, 1932, 3.
38. Franklin D. Roosevelt, "Our Foreign Policy, A Democratic View," *Foreign Affairs* 6, no. 4 (July 1928), 573–86. If Roosevelt did support the process, it should be noted that he was very critical of the Republicans for not building the navy up to treaty limits.
39. Leahy Diary, 2: 34.
40. Ibid., 28.
41. Ibid., 32.
42. Ibid., 34.
43. Ibid., 39.
44. Leahy Diary, August 12, 1941. On this day Leahy paid $1,000 to help settle the final part of his debt.
45. Columbia Oral, Thomas Hart, 1: 54.
46. Leahy Diary, 2: 41.
47. Ibid., 44.
48. Ibid., 71.

Chapter 6: NEARING THE TOP

1. Robert G. Albion, *Makers of Naval Policy, 1798–1947* (Annapolis: Naval Institute Press, 1980), 252.

2. Arthur M. Schlesinger, *The Coming of the New Deal: 1933–1935, The Age of Roosevelt* (Boston: Houghton Mifflin, 2003), 287–88.
3. George Baer, *One Hundred Years of Seapower* (Palo Alto: Stanford University Press, 1998), 58.
4. For a good background discussion of the creation of the CNO position, and the strengths and weaknesses of the position, see: Robert W. Love Jr., ed., *The Chiefs of Naval Operations* (Annapolis: Naval Institute Press, 1980), xii–xxii.
5. Leahy Diary, June 15, 1933.
6. Ibid., February 24, 1933.
7. Ibid., February 22, 1936. See also: Henry A. Adams, *Witness to Power: The Life of Fleet Admiral William D. Leahy* (Annapolis: Naval Institute Press, 1985), 71.
8. Columbia Oral: Thomas Hart Interview, 1: 43–44.
9. Leahy NHHC, October 17, 1934, telephone conversation between Ruggles and Leahy.
10. NHHC Oral, John Hyland Interview, 25.
11. Baer, *One Hundred Years of Seapower*, 129–31.
12. Albion, *Makers of Naval Policy*, 253–54.
13. Phillips P. O'Brien, *British and American Naval Power: Politics and Policies, 1900–1936* (Westport, CT: Praeger, 1998). Appendix II has a list of all ships laid down by type from 1930–39.
14. Ibid., 212.
15. Leahy Diary, January 31, 1934.
16. Adams, *Witness to Power*, 73.
17. Leahy Diary, May 24, 1934.
18. Ibid., June 19, 1934.
19. *New York Times*, June 9, 1915, 22.
20. Donald Chisholm, *Waiting for Dead Men's Shoes: Origins and Development of the US Navy's Personnel System, 1793–1941* (Palo Alto: Stanford University Press, 2001), 686–88.
21. Leahy Diary, March 15, 1935.
22. Leahy NHHC, Vinson to Swanson, June 19, 1935.
23. Ibid., Swanson to Vinson, June 21, 1935.
24. John Walter, "William Harrison Standley," in Love, *The Chiefs of Naval Operations*, 92. Also see: Adams, *Witness to Power*, 71–72.
25. Love, *The Chiefs of Naval Operations*, 92.
26. Ibid., 94.
27. For a mention of Leahy's good relationship with Swanson while at the Bureau of Navigation, see: Chisholm, *Waiting for Dead Men's Shoes*, 681. Also see: Leahy Diary, June 15, 1933.
28. Leahy Diary, December 20, 1933.
29. The hierarchy in the Navy Department went: secretary of the navy, chief of naval operations, assistant secretary of the navy, and then chief of the bureau of navigation.
30. Leahy Diary, December 15, 1934.
31. *Annual Report Commander of the Battle Force*, July 1, 1935–June 24, 1936. This is Leahy's first full report and has a list of all the ships made available to the battle force.
32. Leahy Diary, January 10, 1935.
33. Ibid., February 12, 1935. Also see: Roosevelt to Leahy, March 14, 1935, included after March 15, 1935, diary entry.
34. Ibid., July 13, 1935.
35. Ibid.
36. "President as 'Foe' Sees Navy Fight," *New York Times*, October 3, 1935, 14.
37. Leahy Diary, October 4, 1935.
38. Ibid., December 31, 1935.
39. Ibid., September 14, 1936.
40. Ibid., January 16, 1936.
41. NHHC Oral, Donald J. MacDonald Interview, 23–24.
42. Truman Oral, William Rigdon Interview, July 16, 1970, Truman Library Online. https://www.trumanlibrary.org/oralhist/rigdon.htm.
43. *Annual Report Commander of the Battle Force*, July 1, 1935–June 24, 1936, 1.
44. Ibid., 5–6.
45. Ibid., 4.
46. Leahy Diary, April 25, 1936.
47. Ibid., September 26, 1935.

48. *Annual Report Commander of the Battle Force*, July 1, 1935–June 24, 1936, 16.
49. Ibid.
50. Ibid., 11.
51. Robert L. O'Connell, *Sacred Vessels: The Cult of the Battleship and the Rise of the US Navy* (Oxford, UK: Oxford University Press, 1991), 308.
52. Chester G. Hearn, *Carriers in Combat: The Air War at Sea* (London: Stackpole, 2005), 34.
53. Leahy Diary, November 19, 1936.
54. Ibid., October 5, 1936.
55. Ibid., May 26, 1937; July 14–16, 1937; October 27, 1937.
56. Ibid., November 4, 1936.
57. Leahy was obviously pleased when Roosevelt's Supreme Court plan failed. See: Leahy Diary, July 22, 1937.
58. "Leahy Will Direct Naval Operations," *New York Times*, November 11, 1936, 53.

CHAPTER 7: RISING IN ROOSEVELT'S COURT

1. Leahy Diary, January 5, 1937.
2. Ibid., May 21, 1937.
3. "Sumner Welles, 69, Diplomat Is Dead," *New York Times*, September 25, 1961, 1.
4. Sumner Welles, *Naboth's Vineyard: The Dominican Republic, 1844–1924* (New York: Payson and Clarke, 1928).
5. Sumner Welles, *Seven Decisions that Changed History* (New York: Harper, 1951), 86.
6. Charles Bohlen, *Witness to History: 1929–1969* (New York: Norton, 1973), 129.
7. Harold Ickes, for instance, was very critical of Roosevelt's reliance on Welles: *The Secret Diary of Harold L. Ickes* (London: Weidenfeld and Nicolson, 1955), 2: 340, 505.
8. Leahy Diary, February 10, 1938.
9. Ibid., December 24, 1937.
10. Ibid., January 27, 1937.
11. Ibid., April 20, 1937.
12. Ibid., June 26, 1937
13. "Leahy Regrets Calling Soviet Citizens Slaves," *Washington Post,* July 1, 1937, 7.
14. Leahy Diary, January 25, 1937.
15. Malcolm Muir Jr., "American Warship Construction for Stalin's Navy Prior to World War II: A Study of Paralysis of Power," *Diplomatic History* 5, no. 4 (1981), 337–52.
16. Leahy Diary, April 15, 1937.
17. Ibid., January 25, 1937
18. Ibid., March 3, 1937.
19. Ibid., June 30, 1939.
20. FDR PSF, Leahy to Roosevelt, March 17, 1938. Document can be accessed online at: http://www.fdrlibrary.marist.edu/_resources/images/psf/psfa0096.pdf.
21. Leahy Diary, April 15, 1937.
22. Franklin Roosevelt's daily White House meeting diary can be accessed online at: http://www.fdrlibrary.marist.edu/daybyday/. This allows the user to do a word search in a specific date range. A search for "Craig" during Leahy's time as CNO will reveal that the general is listed in the diary only thirteen times; however, one of these was a different person with the last name Craig. http://www.fdrlibrary.marist.edu/daybyday/search /? str=Craig& start_ date =1937–01– 01& end_ date= 1939–08– 31& type= daylog& search _submit=&submitted=t .
23. These were thirty-eight meetings with Woodring and four with Swanson.
24. Leahy Diary, July 27, 1937, January 29, 1938. These two meetings went on for approximately 2.5 hours each.
25. FDR Mss., PSF, Navy File 1936–1937, FDR to "Mac," December 22, 1937.
26. Leahy Diary, May 21, 1937.
27. Ibid., August 20, 1937
28. Ickes, *Secret Diary*, 2: 180, 192.
29. Ibid., 192–93.
30. Rana Mitter, *Forgotten Ally: China's World War II, 1937–1945* (New York: Penguin, 2014), 98–101, 189.
31. Ickes, *Secret Diary*, 2: 198–99.
32. Leahy Diary, September 1, 1937.
33. FDR Mss., PSF, Navy File 1936–1937, Leahy to FDR, August 23, 1937.

34. Columbia Oral, Robert Carney Interview, 2: 216.
35. Leahy Diary, January 9, 1937.
36. NHHC Oral, Bernard Austin Interview, 57–58.
37. Ibid.

Chapter 8: Leahy's Navy

1. Leahy Diary, September 21, 1937.
2. Ibid., December 12, 1937.
3. Masatake Okumiya, "How the Panay Was Sunk," *Proceedings* 79, no. 6 (June 1953), 587–603.
4. Robert Dallek, *Franklin D. Roosevelt and American Foreign Policy, 1932–1945* (Oxford, UK: Oxford University Press, 1979), 33.
5. Charles Bohlen, *Witness to History: 1929–1969* (New York: Norton, 1973), 128–29.
6. Leahy Diary, December 13, 1937.
7. Ibid.
8. Constantine Brown, *The Coming of the Whirlwind, 1914–1952* (Chicago: Henry Regnery Co., 1964), 254.
9. Leahy Diary, December 14, 1937. There was only one other person in the room: Admiral Hepburn.
10. Ibid., November 26, 1937.
11. Christopher Hall, *Britain, America and Arms Control, 1921–1937* (London: Palgrave, 1987), 143–70, for a discussion of how the system ended.
12. Leahy Diary, July 10, 1937.
13. For a general discussion of the Big Gun, some of which discusses Leahy, see: Thomas C. Hone and Trent Hone, *Battle Line: The United States Navy, 1919–1939* (Annapolis: Naval Institute Press, 2006), 174–77; Robert L. O'Connell, *Sacred Vessels: The Cult of the Battleship and the Rise of the US Navy* (Oxford, UK: Oxford University Press, 1991), 304–8; Edward Miller, *War Plan Orange: The US Strategy to Defeat Japan, 1897–1945* (Annapolis: Naval Institute Press, 1991), 217; Thomas C. Hone, Norman Friedman, and Marj D. Mandeles, *American and British Aircraft Carrier Development, 1919–1941* (Annapolis: Naval Institute Press, 1999), 52.
14. FDR Mss., Official File, Navy Department, Leahy to FDR, December 15, 1937.
15. James F. Cook, *Carl Vinson: Patriarch of the Armed Forces* (Macon, GA: Mercer University Press, 1984), 129.
16. Leahy Diary, January 5, 1938.
17. Ibid., January 6, 1938.
18. Ibid., January 13, 1938.
19. Ibid., January 29, 1938
20. Ickes, *Secret Diary*, 296.
21. Cook, *Carl Vinson*, 130–35. See also: Leahy Diary, May 18, 1938.
22. Leahy Diary, June 15, 1938.
23. Ibid., June 16, 1938.
24. General Board Subject File (GBSF) NARA, 420–22, Ten-Year Shipbuilding Program. July 25, 1938.
25. Hone, Friedman, and Mandeles, *American and British Aircraft Carrier Development*, 196.
26. John T. Kuehn, *Agents of Innovation: The General Board and the Design of the Fleet That Defeated the Japanese Navy* (Annapolis: Naval Institute Press, 2008), 141–42.
27. Columbia Oral, Emory Scott Land Interview, 129. Leahy was very interested in making sure that the fleet was well supplied with high-speed tankers. See Leahy Diary, January 3, 1938.
28. Brown, *Whirlwind*, 253.
29. Miller, *War Plan Orange*, 221–22.
30. Brown, *Whirlwind*, 253.
31. "Leahy Insists on Navy Able to Crush Any Foe," *Washington Post*, April 6, 1938, X2.
32. See Leahy Diary, January 6, 1939; January 17, 1939; January 30, 1939; March 6, 1939. The issue created a bit of a political firestorm, with Roosevelt backing Leahy's arguments on Guam, but in the end Congress demurred. See: *New York Times*, January 19, 1939, "President Backs Fortifying Guam"; January 26, 1939, "War Base on Guam Is Upheld by Leahy"; March 8, 1939, "Barkley Outlines the Foreign Policy of the Administration."
33. Leahy Diary, January 6, 1939.
34. Miller, *War Plan Orange*, 242.

35. FDR Mss., PSF, Navy File 1936–1937, FDR to Leahy, August 22, 1937.
36. Ibid., PSF, Navy File 1936–1937, Leahy to FDR, August 23, 1937.
37. Ibid., PSF, Navy File 1936–1937, Leahy to FDR, September 24, 1937.
38. Ibid., PSF, Navy File 1936–1937, Leahy to FDR, October 11, 1937.
39. Ibid., PSF, Navy File March–December 1938, Leahy to FDR, March 24, 1938.
40. Leahy Diary, 2: 14.
41. Ibid., March 27, 1935.
42. Ibid., March 12, 1938.
43. Ibid., March 17, 1939.
44. Ibid., January 30, 1935; March 16, 1939.
45. Ibid., September 17, 1938.
46. Ibid., July 21, 1938.

CHAPTER 9: THE FIRST RETIREMENT

1. Leahy Diary, March 6, 1939.
2. Ibid., October 23, 1938.
3. FDR PSF, Leahy to FDR, March 17, 1938. Accessible online at: http://www.fdrlibrary
.marist.edu/_resources/images/psf/psfa0096.pdf.
4. Leahy Diary, December 1, 1938.
5. The Hepburn Report was a congressionally mandated report on the need to expand
American naval power and installations. It was filed on December 27, 1938, and called
for the spending of $326 million on different naval projects. http://www.ibiblio.org
/pha/USN/77–2s202.html.
6. Leahy Diary, March 11, 1939.
7. Ibid., May 15, 1937.
8. Jessie Arn Ardt, "Gray Ladies Regret Mrs. Leahy's Departure," *Washington Post*, August 6, 1939, S6.
9. Leahy Diary, August 14, 1938.
10. Felix Belair, "Roosevelt Leads War Game Survey," *New York Times*, February 27, 1939.
11. Leahy Diary, March 1, 1939.
12. Ibid., March 16, 1939.
13. Harold Ickes, *The Secret Diary of Harold L. Ickes,* vol. 3 (London: Weidenfeld and Nicolson, 1955), 598.
14. Leahy Diary, April 12, 1939.
15. Ibid., April 14, 1939. For a copy of Roosevelt's letter to Hitler and Mussolini, see: http://
www.presidency.ucsb.edu/ws/?pid=15741.
16. Manley Irwin, *Silent Strategists: Harding, Denby and the US Navy's Trans-Pacific Offensive, World War II* (Lanham, MD: University Press of America, 2013), 112.
17. Leahy Diary, July 7, 1939.
18. General Board Papers, Subject Files, Navy Department, NARA. CNO to All Bureaus,
May 27, 1939.
19. Henry A. Adams, *Witness to Power: The Life of Fleet Admiral William D. Leahy* (Annapolis: Naval Institute Press, 1985), 117.
20. Leahy Diary, August 30, 1939.

CHAPTER 10: GOVERNOR OF PUERTO RICO

1. The Coalición came about through a deal between two main political parties and supported US statehood for the island. Jorge Rodríguez Beruff, *Strategy as Politics: Puerto Rico on the Eve of the Second World War* (San Juan: Universidad de Puerto Rico Press, 2007), x–xi.
2. Ibid., 209–11.
3. Ibid., 261.
4. Leahy Mss., NHHC, "Unofficial Personal Notes on the Policy of the United States . . ."
Leahy Memorandum (undated), 1. Leahy says that in strategic terms Roosevelt sent him
to Puerto Rico to make sure that a naval air base was built up as quickly as possible.
5. Leahy Mss., NHHC (microfilm), "Sailors Adventure in Politics, Puerto Rico, 1939–1940," 14.
6. Ibid.

7. Harold Ickes, *The Secret Diary of Harold L. Ickes* (London: Weidenfeld and Nicolson, 1955), 3: 42.
8. Ibid., 2: 641.
9. Beruff, *Strategy as Politics*. Page 238 has a useful chart with all of Leahy's different positions. Beruff refers to Leahy as being as close to a US "proconsul" as there ever was in Puerto Rican history.
10. "Leahy Gets a Third Post," *New York Times,* October 24, 1939, 10.
11. José L. Bolívar Fresneda, "The War Economy in Puerto Rico, 1939–1945," in: Jorge Rodríguez Beruff and José L. Bolívar Fresneda, eds., *Islands at War: Puerto Rico in the Crucible of the Second World War* (Jackson: University Press of Mississippi, 2015), 113.
12. *New York Times*, October 2, 1939.
13. Leahy kept a number of newspaper clippings and testimonies from his time in Puerto Rico. One of the most interesting is a typed-up copy of an article that spells out the progressive, New Deal–like policies he helped implement.
14. Leahy Diary, January 12, 1940.
15. "President Favors an Insular 'RFC,'" *New York Times*, January 31, 1940, 7.
16. Leahy Diary, October 7, 1940.
17. "Leahy on Way Here," *New York Times*, December 31, 1939, 6.
18. "Puerto Rico Bid to Stokowski," *New York Times*, December 29, 1939, 10.
19. Leahy Diary, July 26, 1940; August 3, 1940.
20. Ibid., October 14, 1940.
21. Ibid., October 6, 1940.
22. "Luis Munoz Marin Is Dead at 82," *New York Times*, May 1, 1980, A1.
23. Beruff, *Strategy as Politics*, 217–18.
24. Leahy Diary, November 9, 1940.
25. Beruff, *Strategy as Politics*, 272–73.
26. Ibid., 261–90. This whole chapter details the deterioration in Leahy's relationship with the Coalición and the 1940 election,
27. Ibid., 278–79.
28. Ibid., 188.
29. Ickes, *Secret Diary*, 3: 348–49.
30. Leahy Diary, November 1, 1940.
31. Beruff, *Strategy as Politics,* 289–90.
32. Ickes, *Secret Diary*, 3: 389.
33. Leahy Diary, April 19, 1937.
34. Ibid., May 21, 1937.
35. Ibid., July 28, 1940.
36. For a record of the six meetings between Leahy and Roosevelt see: http://www.fdrli brary.marist.edu/daybyday/search/?str=Leahy&start_date=1939-09-01&end_date=1940 -11-01&type=daylog&search_submit=&submitted=t.
37. This was a meeting on May 3, 1940, which went from 8:30 p.m. to 8:45 p.m. See: http:// www.fdrlibrary.marist.edu/daybyday/daylog/may-3rd-1940/.
38. Leahy Mss., NHHC (microfilm), "Sailors Adventure in Politics, Puerto Rico, 1939–1940," 8.
39. *Building the Navy's Bases in World War II: History of the Bureau of Yards and Docks and the Civil Engineer Corps, 1940–1946* (Washington, DC: Government Printing Office, 1947), 5. Accessed online at: https://www.ibiblio.org/hyperwar/USN/Building_Bases /bases-18.html.
40. Beruff, *Strategy as Politics*, 359.
41. Leahy Diary, May 8, 1940.
42. Beruff, *Strategy as Politics*, 359–62, has a description of the work undertaken in 1940.
43. "Puerto Rico to Be Our Gibraltar in the Caribbean, Says Leahy," *New York Times*, May 25, 1940, 6.
44. "Puerto Rico Hails Vieques Base Plan," *New York Times*, February 16, 1941, 20.
45. For a description of the facilities, see: *Building the Navy's Bases in World War II*, 8–9.
46. Skipper Steely, *Pearl Harbor Countdown: James O. Richardson* (Gretna, LA: Pelican Publishing, 2008), 110.
47. "Admiral Leahy Arrives from Puerto Rico, Sees Battleship Still Backbone of Defense," *New York Times*, May 22, 1940, 14.

48. Robert G. Albion, *Makers of Naval Policy, 1798–1947* (Annapolis: Naval Institute Press, 1980), 565–66.
49. William Leahy, *I Was There* (New York: McGraw-Hill, 1950), 287.
50. Steely, *Pearl Harbor Countdown*, 357.
51. Ibid., 92.
52. Ibid., 353–55.

CHAPTER 11: AMBASSADOR TO VICHY FRANCE

1. William Leahy, *I Was There* (New York: McGraw-Hill, 1950), 6.
2. Leahy Diary, President of USA to Governor of Puerto Rico, November 17, 1940.
3. Ibid., November 18, 1940.
4. "Puerto Rico Bids Leahy Farewell," *New York Times*, November 29, 1940, 10.
5. Harold Ickes, *The Secret Diary of Harold L. Ickes* (London: Weidenfeld and Nicolson, 1955), 3: 376–77.
6. Sigmund Freud and William Bullitt, *Thomas Woodrow Wilson: A Psychological Study* (Boston: Houghton Mifflin, 1967), 47–55.
7. For a description of the LeHand-Bullitt relationship, see: Kathryn Smith, *The Gatekeeper: Missy LeHand, FDR and the Untold Story of a Partnership That Defined a Presidency* (New York: Touchstone, 2016), 141–49.
8. FDR PSF, Bullitt to State Department, June 11 and 12, 1940.
9. FDR PSF, FDR to Bullitt, June 9, 1940. Accessible online at: http://www.fdrlibrary.marist.edu/_resources/images/psf/psfa0306.pdf. There was some effort after the war by Bullitt's defenders to say that FDR had preapproved this plan and that Hull was the person most unhappy with the decision. However, in Roosevelt's papers it's clearly the president who suggests to the secretary of state that a telegram be sent to Bullitt to move with the French government to Bordeaux. For a defense of Bullitt, see: Orville Bullitt, ed., *For the President Personal and Secret: Correspondence Between Franklin D. Roosevelt and William C. Bullitt* (Boston: Houghton Mifflin, 1972), 474–75.
10. Ickes, *Secret Diary*, 3: 344.
11. Sumner Welles, *Seven Decisions that Changed History* (New York: Harper, 1951), 55.
12. Ibid., 55–56. See also, Sumner Welles, *The Time for Decision* (London: Hamish Hamilton, 1944), 126–27.
13. Leahy Diary, December 2, 1940.
14. Leahy, *I Was There*, 9.
15. There is a copy of the letter in the Leahy diary, right at the start of the 1941 year book.
16. Leahy NHHC, "Unofficial Personal Notes on the Policy of the United States . . ." Leahy Memorandum (undated), 2.
17. Ickes, *Secret Diary*, 3: 367.
18. Both Leahy and Welles made the point that Roosevelt was focused on the French Fleet at this time, believing that sea power remained the determining factor in the war.
19. Ickes, *Secret Diary*, 3: 482 (cabinet meeting took place on April 20, 1941).
20. Ibid., 521 (cabinet meeting on May 25, 1941).
21. An English-language copy of the Franco-German armistice can be read at the invaluable Avalon Project website. The main section having to do with the disposition of the French Navy is Article VIII. http://avalon.law.yale.edu/wwii/frgearm.asp (accessed July 2015).
22. Welles, *Seven Major Decisions*, 47.
23. There is an excellent memorandum on the role that food supplies could play in American diplomacy with Vichy at the time that was handled by FDR and Welles (and, one assumes, Leahy). See: FDR PSF, Welles Memorandum, February 8, 1941.
24. Leahy Diary, February 25, 1941. Leahy misspells Archambault's name in *I Was There* as Archembault, 11.
25. "Leahy Tells Vichy Britain Will Win," *New York Times*, January 29, 1941, 7.
26. Elsey Mss., Box 103, There are some undated handwritten pages by Leahy here that describe the trip to Vichy.
27. Julian Jackson, *France: The Dark Years, 1940–1944* (Oxford, UK: Oxford University Press, 2001), 177.
28. Leahy Diary, February 2, 1941.
29. Leahy to FDR, January 25, 1941, copy kept in Leahy Diary.

30. Leahy Diary, February 24, 1941.
31. The fact that he was short and a navy man probably mattered more, but his moments of anger were definitely remarked upon.
32. Leahy Diary, February 24, 1941.
33. Peter Jackson and Simon Kitson, "The Paradoxes of Vichy Foreign Policy," in Jonathan R. Adelman, *Hitler and His Allies in World War II* (New York: Routledge, 2007), 110.
34. Leahy, *I Was There*, 48.
35. *Foreign Relations of the United States* (FRUS) 1941, Europe, vol. 2. In April 1941 there was a flurry of correspondence about the *Dunkerque*. Though it's not clear how influential Leahy was in Vichy decision-making, he did put real pressure on the French government not to move the *Dunkerque*. In the end, it wasn't brought back to France until after the United States joined the war and greater German pressure was placed on Vichy. This FRUS volume can be accessed online at: http://digital.library.wisc.edu/1711 .dl/FRUS.FRUS1941v02.
36. Henry A. Adams, *Witness to Power: The Life of Fleet Admiral William D. Leahy* (Annapolis: Naval Institute Press, 1985), 143–48.
37. MacArthur was the person who briefed Leahy on protocol issues and prepared him for his initial meetings with Pétain. Leahy NHHC, MacArthur to Ambassador, January 7, 1941.
38. He outlined these different groups in a summary evaluation of personalities given in his diary at the start of the volume for 1942.
39. In Leahy's diary for 1942, there is a section included after the index and before the daily entries in which Leahy writes a description of different personalities in the Vichy administration. The description of Couve de Murville, which makes clear his importance, is on 12–13.
40. Ibid., 7.
41. FDR Mss., Confidential file, Box 20, Leahy to State Department, June 13, 1941.
42. Frederick Logevall, *Embers of War: The Fall of an Empire and the Making of America's Vietnam* (New York: Random House, 2012), 31.
43. See: Michael A. Barnhart, *Japan Prepares for Total War: The Search for Economic Security, 1919–1941* (Ithaca, NY: Cornell University Press, 1987); Edward Miller, *Bankrupting the Enemy: The US Financial Siege of Japan Before Pearl Harbor* (Annapolis: Naval Institute Press, 2007), 203–4; Irvine H. Anderson Jr., "The 1941 De Facto Embargo on Oil to Japan: A Bureaucratic Reflex," *Pacific Historical Review* 44, no. 2 (May 1975), 227–29. Waldo Heinrichs portrays FDR as more forceful, but still tentative when it came to the final decision to embargo oil. Waldo Heinrichs, *The Threshold of War: Franklin D. Roosevelt and American Entry into World War II* (Oxford, UK: Oxford University Press, 1988), 145.
44. FDR Mss., Confidential file, Box 20, Leahy to State Department, February 8, 1941.
45. Ibid. At the time Vichy and Nazi Germany were discussing improved relations at Wiesbaden.
46. *Germany and the Second World War* (Oxford, UK: Oxford University Press, 2001), 6: 229–30.
47. FDR Mss., Confidential file, Box 20, Leahy to State Department, April 16, 1941.
48. Leahy Diary, May 13, 1941.
49. Ickes, *Secret Diary*, 3: 492.
50. FDR Mss., FDR to Churchill, telegram, January 29, 1942.
51. Robert Sherwood, *The White House Papers of Harry L. Hopkins* (London: Eyre and Spottiswoode, 1949), 2: 505.
52. Leahy Diary, July 16, 1941.
53. Ibid., July 19, 1941.
54. Ibid. Leahy writes of receiving a verbal message from "Washington" that he was to pass on. Considering the rapid turnaround from his message on July 16, it makes the most sense that Welles went right to Roosevelt and received a response, which he passed back to Leahy.
55. Leahy, *I Was There*, 47.
56. Ibid.; Welles, *Seven Decisions*, 66.
57. Heinrichs, *The Threshold of War*, 141.
58. Leahy to FDR, July 28, 1941. A copy of the letter is kept in the Leahy Diary.
59. Ickes, *Secret Diary*, 3: 591–92.

CHAPTER 12: DARK DAYS

1. Leahy Diary, June 26, 1941. There is a copy of the letter from FDR kept here.
2. Ibid., April 17, 1941.
3. Ibid., May 13, 1941.
4. Robert L. Melka, "Darlan Between Britain and Germany, 1940–41," *Journal of Contemporary History* 8, no. 2 (1973), 69–72.
5. Robert Paxton, *Vichy France: Old Guard and New Order, 1940–1944* (New York: Knopf, 1972), 111.
6. J. G. Shields, "Charlemagne's Crusaders: French Collaboration in Arms, 1941–1945," *French Cultural Studies* 18, no. 1 (2007), 92.
7. H. Freeman Matthews Mss., *Memoirs of a Passing Era*, unpublished manuscript, 481.
8. G. H. Archambault, "Leahy Sees Petain Who Gets Nazi Bid," *New York Times*, May 14, 1941, 1.
9. FDR Mss., Confidential file, FDR to Leahy, May 13, 1941.
10. G. H. Archambault, "Vichy Surprised at Roosevelt View," *New York Times*, May 17, 1941, 1.
11. Paxton, *Vichy France*, 117.
12. "Hull Sees Vichy Doing Job for Hitler in Syria," *New York Times*, June 14–15, 1941, E3.
13. Martin Thomas, *The French Empire at War, 1949–1945* (Manchester, UK: Manchester University Press, 1998), 101–7.
14. Paxton, *Vichy France*, 123–24.
15. Karine Varley, "Vichy and the Complexities of Collaborating with Fascist Italy: French Policy and Perceptions Between June 1940 and March 1942," *Modern and Contemporary France* 21, no. 3 (2013), 323.
16. Thomas Laub, *After the Fall: German Policy in Occupied France, 1940–1944* (Oxford, UK: Oxford University Press, 2010), see chapter 2.
17. "Paris Press Assails Leahy," *New York Times*, August 5, 1941, 4.
18. William Leahy, *I Was There* (New York: McGraw-Hill, 1950), 44.
19. Leahy Diary, August 26, 1941.
20. Ibid., August 22, 1941. Leahy and Louise crossed over into Switzerland on August 18 and stayed until August 23.
21. Ibid., August 26, 1941.
22. Ibid., June 23, 1941.
23. Peter Jackson and Simon Kitson, "The Paradoxes of Vichy Foreign Policy, 1940–42," in Jonathan Adelman, *Hitler and His Allies in World War II* (London: Routledge, 2007), 107.
24. Shields, "Charlemagne's Crusaders," 884. It is worth noting that the original recruitment for the LVF was only a few thousand.
25. Julian Jackson, *France: The Dark Years, 1940–1944* (Oxford, UK: Oxford University Press, 2001), 183.
26. Leahy Diary, September 20, 1941. See also: Ibid., 181.
27. Michael R. Marrus and Robert O. Paxton, *Vichy France and the Jews* (Stanford: Stanford University Press, 1995), 123–25.
28. Leahy, *I Was There*, 53.
29. Leahy Diary, August 5, 1941.
30. Cordell Hull, *The Memoirs of Cordell Hull* (New York: Macmillan, 1948), 1: 1038.
31. Leahy Diary, August 26, 1941.
32. "See US-Vichy Break," *New York Times*, November 22, 1941, 3. Also see: Robert Murphy, *Diplomat Among Warriors: The Unique World of a Foreign Service Expert* (New York: Doubleday, 1964), 125.
33. Bertram Hulen, "US Aid to French Expected to Stop," *New York Times*, November 20, 1941, 2.
34. Leahy Diary, November 25, 1941.
35. Ibid., November 22, 1942.
36. Pétain railed against de Gaulle in a meeting on March 18, 1941. The best description of this is not in the diary per se but in a letter that Leahy sent to FDR on March 19, 1941, a copy of which is kept in the diary.
37. David Reynolds, "Wheelchair Diplomacy: FDR and American Foreign Policy, 1933–1945," *Diplomatic History*, 568. Advance access publication, accessed online (July 2015) http://dh.oxfordjournals.org/ at University of Glasgow on July 24, 2015.
38. Leahy Diary, March 21, 1941, letter in diary.

39. Ibid., July 28, 1941. It is in this letter that Leahy said de Gaulle's support in France was not strong enough to make a difference and that Pétain's cabinet ministers believed that the Gaullists had pronounced a death sentence on them.
40. Matthews, *Memoirs of a Passing Era*, 486.
41. Leahy, *I Was There*, 62–63.
42. Leahy Diary, December 8, 1941.
43. Ibid., December 11, 1941.
44. Leahy, *I Was There*, 75. Also see: David Mayers, *FDR's Ambassadors and the Diplomacy of Crisis, from the Rise of Hitler to the End of World War II* (Cambridge, UK: Cambridge University Press, 2013), 148–49.
45. Benjamin Welles, *Sumner Welles: FDR's Global Strategist* (New York: St. Martin Press, 1997), 287–88.
46. Leahy Diary, February 20, 1942.
47. FDR Mss., PSF, 1942 France, Leahy to FDR, February 20, 1942. Accessed online at: http://www.fdrlibrary.marist.edu/_resources/images/psf/psfa0292.pdf.
48. Leahy Diary, February 22, 1942.
49. G. H. Archambault, "Paris Press Hits at Petain and US," *New York Times*, January 4, 1942, 1.
50. Leahy Diary, March 8, 1942.
51. Ibid., April 27, 1942.
52. Ibid., April 27, 1941.
53. Adams, *Witness to Power*, 175.
54. Leahy Diary, April 9, 1945.
55. Ibid., April 21, 1942.

CHAPTER 13: CHIEF OF STAFF TO THE COMMANDER IN CHIEF

1. Leahy Diary, June 1, 1942.
2. Ibid., June 5, 1942.
3. Leahy NHHC, "Unofficial Personal Notes on the Policy of the United States," undated, 5.
4. William Leahy, *I Was There* (New York: McGraw-Hill, 1950), 97.
5. Alex Danchev, *Establishing the Anglo-American Alliance: The Second World War Diaries of Brigadier Vivian Dykes* (London: Brasseys, 1990), 154.
6. Leahy Mss., NHHC Microfilm, Leahy to Rosenman, June 19, 1947.
7. Probably the most extreme example of Leahy's appointment being ascribed to Marshall is Thomas Parrish, *Roosevelt and Marshall: Partners in Politics and War* (New York: William Morrow, 1989), 250–51. See also: Jonathan W. Jordan, *American Warlords: How Roosevelt's High Command Led America to Victory in World War II* (New York: Dutton Caliber, 2015), 195; and Forest Pogue, *George C. Marshall: Organizer of Victory, 1943–1945* (New York: Viking, 1973), 7–8.
8. Leahy Diary, June 6, 1942.
9. Ernest King Mss., Library of Congress Manuscript Division, Washington, DC, Box 35, "Questions for Fleet Admiral King," June 22, 1948. This was a series of questions sent to King by the naval historian Richard G. Albion, which King answered in writing.
10. We can say that this is the exact title because it was how the position was recorded in the presentation of the Gold Star to Leahy after the war, in lieu of him already having received one Distinguished Service Medal previously. See: Leahy NHHC, Presidential Presentation, February 5, 1946.
11. Leahy Diary, July 6, 1942.
12. There were a number of other quizzical editorials published in reaction to the new appointment. See: "Admiral Leahy," *Washington Post*, July 23, 1942, 14.
13. Frank Kluckhohn, "Leahy Will Do Detail Work to Help President Plan War," *New York Times*, July 22, 1942, 1.
14. Frank Kluckhohn, "Leahy's Role in the War," *New York Times*, July 26, 1942, E5.
15. Arthur Krock, "In the Nation, Admiral Leahy's New Role," *New York Times*, July 23, 1942, 18.
16. *Life*, September 28, 1942.
17. "Leahy's Appointment," *Washington Post*, October 2, 1942, 10.
18. George Elsey, *An Unplanned Life: A Memoir by George McKee Elsey* (Columbia: University of Missouri Press, 2005), 75.

19. Leahy NHHC, Leahy to Rosenman, June 19, 1947. See appended description of Leahy's position.
20. Wilson Brown, "Aide to Four Presidents," *American Heritage* 6, no. 2 (1955). Accessible online at: http://www.americanheritage.com/content/aide-four-presidents?page=show.
21. William Rigdon, *White House Sailor* (Garden City, NY: Doubleday, 1962), 7–8. Rigdon also pointed out that the duty officers were given access, but they had no role in policy and just oversaw operations in the Map Room.
22. FDR Oral, John McCrea Interview, March 19, 1973, 6. https://fdrlibrary.org/documents /356632/390886/mccrea+maproom.pdf/e10e4efe-e2cf-4b81-a5b4-06dc2eac74a7.
23. This is based on the assumption that the two men had six daily briefing sessions as opposed to the four separate meetings mentioned in the diary.
24. Leahy Diary, November 5 and December 9, 1942.
25. Ibid., September 12, 1942.
26. Ibid., September 16, 1942.
27. He was invited for another small dinner with Franklin, Eleanor, and Harry Hopkins and his new wife on December 1. See Leahy Diary, December 1, 1942.
28. Bernard Asbell, ed., *Mother and Daughter, The Letters of Eleanor and Anna Roosevelt* (New York: Coward, McCann & Geoghegan, 1982), 177.
29. Leahy Diary, September 7, 1942.
30. Harold Ickes, *The Secret Diary of Harold L. Ickes* (London: Weidenfeld and Nicolson, 1955), 2: 479–80; 615–16; Bernard Baruch, *The Public Years* (London: Holt, Rinehart and Winston, 1960), 293.
31. Elsey, *An Unplanned Life*, 25.
32. Leahy Diary, December 1, 1942.
33. Jonathan Daniels, *The Man from Independence* (London: Victor Gollancz, 1951), 259.
34. Thomas M. Campbell and George C. Herring, eds., *The Diaries of Edward R. Stettinius, Jr., 1943–1946* (New York: New Viewpoints, 1975), 185.
35. NHHC Oral, J. V. Smith Interview, 148.

CHAPTER 14: CHAIRMAN OF THE JOINT CHIEFS OF STAFF

1. The Joint Chiefs were first created by Roosevelt as the American military officers who served on the Combined Chiefs. They started fulfilling this function in January 1942 and met for the first time alone as the US joint chiefs in February 1942. See: Joint History Office, Office of the Chairman of the Joint Chiefs of Staff, *Organizational Development of the Joint Chiefs of Staff, 1942–2013*, 1–3. Accessible online at: http://www.dtic .mil/doctrine/doctrine/history/councilofwar.pdf.
2. Leahy Mss., NHHC, Marshall to King, May 19, 1944, see attached memo.
3. Eric Larrabee, *Commander in Chief: Franklin Roosevelt, His Lieutenants, and Their War* (New York: HarperCollins, 1987), 133.
4. War Department, Special Staff, NARA, Marshall, King and Arnold to FDR, July 10, 1942.
5. FDR Mss., Marshall Safe File, Stimson to FDR, July 1942.
6. The Marshall Foundation has an excellent paper online by the historian Mark Stoler on Marshall's ideas on the Second Front Policy, which mentions his strong opposition to the invasion of North Africa. See: Mark Stoler, "George C. Marshall and the 'Europe-First' Strategy, 1939–1951: A Study in Diplomatic as Well as Military History," 9, http://mar shallfoundation.org/marshall/wp-content/uploads/sites/22/2014/04/EDStoler.pdf
7. Leahy Diary, May 22, 1941.
8. William Leahy, *I Was There* (New York: McGraw-Hill, 1950), 111.
9. From just Leahy's diaries we know of eight meetings in July with FDR before the meeting of the JCS (July 6, 7, 16, 22, 24, 25, 27, 28), and there would have been morning briefings starting on July 24. There were also phone calls and some shorter meetings that were not recorded. Torch was the main subject of their discussions on July 22 and 24, and one assumes that it was discussed in the other meetings as well.
10. JCS, 26th Meeting, July 28, 1942, 1.
11. CCS 34th Meeting, July 30, 1942.
12. Ibid., 2.
13. Ibid.

14. This comes from the draft of a short piece Leahy wrote for the Army-Navy journal and which is in his papers in the NHHC. See "Joint Chiefs of Staff: The American High Command," September 17, 1945. ". . . the American High Command, charged by the President with the formulation of strategy, supervision of troop deployment and equipment, and general direction of all operations against the enemy . . . the designation of objectives to be taken and the basic orders for the employment of armies, navies and air forces. Theater commands were established and theater commanders were clothed with full authority over all the army, navy and air forces assigned to them for operations. Functioning as a General Staff responsible to the Commander in Chief, and acting with his approval, the Joint Chiefs assembled the forces, named the strategic objectives and designated the commanders to carry out the broad missions."

15. Leahy JCS, Deane to Marshall and King, September 26, 1942. Also see: James F. Schnabel, *History of the Joint Chiefs of Staff*, volume 1: *The Joint Chiefs of Staff and National Policy 1945–1947* (Washington, DC: Government Printing Office, 1996), 3.

16. The Franklin Roosevelt Papers have been digitized and are online through this portal: http://www.fdrlibrary.marist.edu/archives/collections/franklin/?p=collections/find ingaid&id=502. The Marshall and King files are in the President's Secretary Files (PSF). FDR, PSF Safe File. To access the King file, see: http://www.fdrlibrary.marist.edu/_re sources/images/psf/psfa0039.pdf. To access the Marshall file see: http://www.fdrlibrary .marist.edu/_resources/images/psf/psfa0044.pdf.

17. Leahy NHHC, Leahy to Marshall and King, September 13, 1942.

18. Leahy JCS, FDR to Leahy, August 24, 1942.

19. Leahy NHHC, Early to Leahy, June 8, 1944.

20. Ibid., Smith to Leahy, May 4, 1944.

21. Ibid., "Unofficial Personal Notes on the Policy of the United States As It Appeared to Me at Times During World War II." Typed Leahy notes, 5. Also see: George Elsey, *An Unplanned Life: A Memoir by George McKee Elsey* (Columbia: University of Missouri Press, 2005), 24.

22. *Organizational Development of the Joint Chiefs of Staff, 1942–2013* (Washington, DC: Joint History Office, Office of the Chairman of the Joint Chiefs of Staff), April 2013, 22.

23. Leahy Diary, 2, 32.

24. FDR Mss, Online, Daily Calendar, accessible at: http://www.fdrlibrary.marist.edu /daybyday/search/?str=stimson&start_date=1943–01–01&end_date=1945–04–20&type =daylog&search_submit=&submitted=t&s_page=1. I did a word search for Stimson in Roosevelt's online appointments diary starting on January 1, 1943, until Roosevelt's death on April 12, 1945. This search actually brings up thirty-nine results, but one of those days doesn't actually have a meeting with Stimson recorded (February 3, 1943), so thirty-eight meetings seems to be the right figure. Stimson did have some private lunches with FDR, but the other private meetings could be very short. At least three were only five minutes long.

25. Paolo E. Coletta, *American Secretaries of the Navy* (Annapolis: Naval Institute Press, 1980), 2: 678.

26. Leahy Diary, January 15, 1944.

27. Leahy's role as chairman has rarely been treated well, and usually he is described blandly as a detached or impartial head. See: Edward S. Miller, *War Plan Orange: The US Strategy to Defeat Japan, 1897–1945* (Annapolis: Naval Institute Press, 1991), 326. See also: Steven Rearden, *Council of War: A History of the Joint Chiefs of Staff, 1942–1991* (Washington, DC: Joint History Office, 1991), 7; and James MacGregor Burns, *Roosevelt: The Soldier of Freedom* (New York: Harcourt Brace, 1970), 452.

28. Columbia Oral, Fife Interview, 388–89.

29. Columbia Oral, Connelly Interview, 375.

30. NHHC Oral, Dennison Interview, 69–70.

31. Elsey, *An Unplanned Life*, 24.

32. Forest Pogue, "The Wartime Chiefs of Staff and the President," in Monte Wright and Lawrence Paszek, *Soldiers and Statesmen* (Washington, DC: Office of Air Force History, 1973), 24.

33. Stanley Weintraub, *15 Stars: Eisenhower, MacArthur, Marshall—Three Generals Who Saved the American Century* (New York: Free Press, 2007), 195. Without referring to a single Leahy-based source, the author states that Marshall was first among equals and was the de facto leader of the Joint Chiefs of Staff.

34. Larry Bland, ed. *The Papers of George Catlett Marshall* (Baltimore: Johns Hopkins Press, 1991), 3: 338.
35. Bland, *The Papers of George Catlett Marshall*, 3: 424.
36. Leahy, *I Was There*, 104.
37. See: Thomas Buell, *Master of Seapower: A Biography of Fleet Admiral Ernest J. King* (Annapolis: Naval Institute Press, 1995), 100.
38. King Mss., Box 35, King to Dobbyns, June 22, 1951. Also see: Buell, *Master of Seapower*, 185.
39. NHHC Oral, J. V. Smith Interview, 139.

CHAPTER 15: THE GRANDEST LEVEL OF STRATEGY

1. FDR State of the Union Address, January 6, 1942, available online at: http://www.pres idency.ucsb.edu/ws/?pid=16253.
2. Richard Leighton and Robert Coakley, *Global Logistics and Strategy, 1940–1943* (Washington, DC: Government Printing Office, 1955), 131.
3. Phillips Payson O'Brien, *How the War Was Won: Air-Sea Power and Allied Victory in World War II* (Cambridge, UK: Cambridge University Press, 2015), 49–52.
4. Leighton and Coakley, *Global Logistics and Strategy*, 605.
5. Leahy Diary, October 1, 1942.
6. In an attempt to get Hopkins onside, the army in the form of Lt. Gen. Brehon Somerville, who was in charge of army supply, sent him on October 17 a ten-page memo on the production situation. This memorandum is the best example of army thinking at the time; it called for the balanced air-ground construction plan and wanted to make sure that the army could reach its hoped-for level of 7.5 million troops by the end of 1943. Hopkins Mss., 125, Somerville to Hopkins, October 17, 1942.
7. JCS 38th Meeting, October 20, 1942, 1–3.
8. Marshall memorandum for Leahy, King, and Arnold, August 24, 1942, in Marshall Papers, accessed online through Marshall Foundation, http://marshallfoundation .or/library/digital-archive/memorandum-for-admiral-w-d-leahy-admiral-e-j-king-and -lieutenant-general-h-h-arnold/. Marshall followed up this memorandum with a private letter to King two days later asking for the navy's support for his mobilization figures.
9. Hopkins Mss., 125, Hopkins memo for FDR, October 20, 1942.
10. FDR Mss., Online, PSF Leahy Navy File, FDR to Leahy and Hopkins, November 20, 1942.
11. Ibid., Daily Calendar, accessible at: http://www.fdrlibrary.marist.edu/daybyday/. If you search "Leahy" between October 1 and December 15, you will see meetings on: October 1, 3, 5, 13, 15, 17, 19, 22, 23, 26; November 9, 11, 16, 25; and December 10, 12, 14.
12. William Leahy, *I Was There* (New York: McGraw-Hill, 1950), 129.
13. Leahy Diary, October 23, 1942.
14. Ibid., October 26, 1942.
15. Ibid., November 3, 1942.
16. JCS Minutes, November 10, 1942, 1.
17. Arnold Mss., reel 198, Somervell et al memo for JCS, recommended priorities for 1943.
18. Ibid., Leahy to FDR, November 20, 1942.
19. Leahy Diary, November 23, 1942.
20. Leahy JCS, Leahy to Donald Nelson, November 26, 1942.
21. US Navy at War, Official Report. Appendix B. Available at: http://www.ibiblio.org/hy perwar/USN/USNatWar/USN-King-B.html.
22. FDR Mss., PSF 172–2, War Progress Report, November 27, 1942, 4.
23. Leahy, *I Was There*, 129.
24. Leahy Mss., NHHC, Memorandum for Admiral Leahy, "Manpower Requirements for the Armed Forces," September 23, 1942.
25. Maurice Matloff, *The 90 Division Gamble* (Washington, DC: Center for Military History, 1990). There is an online version of this accessible at: https://history.army.mil /books/70–7_15.htm.
26. Leahy, *I Was There*, 129–30.
27. JCS Minutes, November 24, 1942, 3.

28. Ibid.
29. JCS Minutes, February 16, 1943, 7.
30. Leahy, *I Was There*, 129–30.
31. Leahy Diary, October 1, 1942.
32. Jordan A. Schwarz, *The Speculator: Bernard M. Baruch in Washington, 1917–1965* (Chapel Hill: University of North Carolina Press, 1981), 449.
33. Samuel Rosenman, *Working with Roosevelt* (New York: Harper and Brothers, 1952), 386–87.
34. Leahy Diary, February 4, 1943.
35. R. Elberton Smith, *The Army and Economic Mobilization* (Washington, DC: Government Printing Office, 1959), 178–79.
36. Matloff, 90 division gamble, http://www.history.army.mil/books/70–7_15.htm.

CHAPTER 16: FROM CASABLANCA TO TRIDENT

1. Leahy Diary, January 9, 1943.
2. David Roll, *The Hopkins Touch: Harry Hopkins and the Forging of the Alliance to Defeat Hitler* (Oxford, UK: Oxford University Press, 2013), 247.
3. Tony Reichardt, "The First Presidential Flight," *Air and Space Magazine*, January 18, 2013. Accessed online at: http://www.airspacemag.com/daily-planet/the-first-presidential -flight-2901615/?no-ist.
4. Leahy Diary, January 12–13, 1943. Leahy said that his temperature reached 101.4 degrees.
5. Geoffrey Ward, ed., *Closest Companion: The Unknown Story of the Intimate Friendship Between Franklin Roosevelt and Margaret Suckley* (Boston: Houghton Mifflin, 1995), 197.
6. Robert Sherwood, *The White House Papers of Harry L. Hopkins* (London: Eyre and Spottiswoode, 1949), 2: 668.
7. JCS Minutes, January 7, 1943, 4.
8. NHHC Oral, J. V. Smith Interview, 119.
9. Leahy Diary, August 25, 1942.
10. JCS Minutes, January 7, 1943, 6.
11. Albert Wedemeyer, *Wedemeyer Reports* (New York: Henry Holt, 1958), 185–86. After the January 7 meeting, Marshall told his staff that FDR had supported Bolero, which wasn't the case. However, even Marshall did not say it with a great deal of conviction.
12. Mark Stoler, "The Pacific-First Alternative in American World War II Strategy," *International History Review* 2, no. 3 (July 1980), 432–52.
13. O'Brien, *How the War Was Won*, 203–5.
14. Leahy Diary, September 9, 1942.
15. Ibid., September 20, 1942.
16. On November 10, 1942, Churchill made his most famous speech on the subject, which has come to be known as the "End of the Beginning" address. In it he said he had not become prime minister "in order to preside over the liquidation of the British Empire." For online excerpts of the speech see: http://www.churchill-society-london.org.uk /EndoBegn.html.
17. CCS Minutes, January 14, 1943, 10:30 a.m. This transcript of this meeting can be found in *Foreign Relations of the United States. The Conferences at Washington, 1941–1942 and Casablanca 1943* (Washington, DC: Government Printing Office, 1941–1943), 545. Online access to be found at: http://digital.library.wisc.edu/1711.dl/FRUS.FRUS194143.
18. CCS Minutes, January 14, 1943, 10:30 a.m.
19. CCS Minutes, January 16, 1943, 10:30 a.m., 587. See http://digicoll.library.wisc.edu /cgi-bin/FRUS/FRUS-idx?type=turn&entity=FRUS.FRUS194143.p0673&id=FRUS.FRUS 194143&isize=M.
20. Elsey Mss., Box 4, Memorandum for the President, July 26, 1949. Elsey wrote this paper for President Truman to give him an idea of how the unconditional surrender policy appeared and was developed. It is clear that Leahy had no idea it was going to be proposed by FDR at Casablanca.
21. Leahy Diary, January 29, 1943.
22. Ibid., February 2, 1943.
23. Leahy Mss., NHHC, "Unofficial Personal Notes on the Policy of the United States As It Appeared to Me at Times During the War," 8.

24. Leahy Mss., NHHC, Mott to Leahy, February 12, 1943.
25. Roll, *The Hopkins Touch*, 206–7.
26. Frank Costigliola, *Roosevelt's Lost Alliances: How Personal Politics Shaped the Cold War* (Princeton: Princeton University Press, 2012), 84.
27. James A. Halsted, "Severe Malnutrition in a Public Servant of the World War II Era: The Medical History of Harry Hopkins," *Transactions of the American Clinical and Climatological Association* 86 (1975), 23–32.
28. John C. Slessor Mss., National Archives UK, Air 75/52, Undated Slessor Memorandum.
29. NHHC Oral, JV Smith Interview, 123; George Elsey, *An Unplanned Life: A Memoir by George McKee Elsey* (Columbia: University of Missouri Press, 2005), 32.
30. Leahy Diary, see text of Broadcast of *Who's Who* about Leahy in February 1943. The text is in the diary between June 30, 1943, and July 1, 1943.
31. Leahy Diary, February 6 and 10, 1943.
32. Arthur Harris Mss., 35, 40, Thornton to Harris, March 15, 1943.
33. JCS 62nd Meeting, February 16, 1943. The meeting the week before had focused on what had been achieved (or not) at Casablanca.
34. JCS 72nd Meeting, April 6, 1943, 4.
35. JCS 69th Meeting, March 23, 1943, 2.
36. JCS, 62nd Meeting, supplementary minutes, 2.
37. Michael Howard, *Grand Strategy*, Vol. 4 (London: HMSO, 1972), 4: 423.
38. Leahy JCS, Welles to Leahy, May 17, 1943.
39. Leahy Diary, February 21 and 23, 1943.
40. Leahy Diary, May 5, 1943.
41. Leahy Diary, April 16, 1942.
42. JCS 77th Meeting, May 4, 1943, supplementary minutes.
43. Leahy JCS, NARA, RG 218, Soong to Leahy, May 18, 1943.
44. CCS, Draft Memoranda, "Conduct of War in 1943," January 18, 1943. Accessed online at: http://digital.library.wisc.edu/1711.dl/FRUS.FRUS194143.
45. Winston Churchill, *The Second World War* (New York: Houghton Mifflin, 1953), 4: 702.
46. Meeting in the White House, May 12, 1943, 2:30 p.m. This statement seemed very much a sop to American concerns as the British confidential position heading into Trident was to work to block Anakim in 1943. Cabinet Papers UK (Cab) 121/153. Aide-mémoire for opening conversations, May 8, 1943.
47. FDR Mss., PSF 2, Memorandum, Leahy to FDR, May 8, 1943, 2 (pages are unnumbered; it's on the second page).
48. JCS, 78th Meeting, May 8, 1943, 5. There is actually a detailed memo from May 4, laying out the structure for the Trident meetings. Leahy Mss., NHHC, LCS memo for Leahy, Marshall, King, and Arnold, May 4, 1943.
49. JCS, 78th Meeting, May 8, 1943, 1.
50. Ibid., 8.
51. FDR Mss., PSF 2, Memorandum, Leahy to FDR, May 8, 1943; JCS paper, "Conduct of the War in 1943," May 8, 1943.
52. Leahy Diary, May 12, 1943.
53. CCS, 83rd Meeting, May 13, 1943, 1–2, 12, Annex A.
54. Ibid., 8.
55. Ibid., 9.
56. CCS, 84th Meeting, May 14, 1943, 2.
57. Ibid., 8–11; CCS 90th meeting, May 20, 1943, 2–3.
58. CCS, 84th Meeting, May 14, 1943, 8–11.
59. Alex Danchev and Daniel Todman, eds., *War Diaries 1939–1945: Field Marshal Lord Alanbrooke* (London: Phoenix Press, 2002), 406.
60. CCS, 90th Meeting, May 20, 1943, 2–3.
61. Ibid., 4, 6–7.
62. Danchev and Todman, *War Diaries*, 407.
63. Final Report of the CCS, 25 May 1943. Accessed through FRUS online at: http://digicoll.library.wisc.edu/cgi-bin/FRUS/FRUS-idx?type=turn&entity=FRUS.FRUS1943.p0466&id=FRUS.FRUS1943&isize=M.
64. Leahy Diary, May 18, 1943.

Notes

CHAPTER 17: DIFFICULT FRIENDS

1. William Leahy, *I Was There* (New York: McGraw-Hill, 1950), 165.
2. There are whole books on the subject of FDR's policy in World War II that discuss de Gaulle in detail but do not contain a single mention of Leahy. See: Christopher D. O'Sullivan, *FDR and the End of Empire: The Origins of American Power in the Middle East* (New York: Palgrave, 2012).
3. For example, see: Robert Sherwood, *Roosevelt and Hopkins: An Intimate History* (New York: Harper, 1948), 629; and Warren Kimball, *The Juggler: Franklin Roosevelt as Statesman* (Princeton: Princeton University Press, 1991), 67.
4. Truman Oral, H. Freeman Matthews Interview, June 7, 1973, 3. See online at www.trumanlibrary.org/oralhist/matthewh.htm.
5. Leahy Diary, November 8, 1942.
6. Leahy, *I Was There*, 142.
7. Charles Bohlen, *Witness to History: 1929–1969* (New York: Norton, 1973), 206.
8. George Elsey, *An Unplanned Life: A Memoir by George McKee Elsey* (Columbia: University of Missouri Press, 2005), 28.
9. Arthur L. Funk, "Eisenhower, Giraud and the Command of 'Torch,'" *Military Affairs* 35, no. 3 (October 1971), 103.
10. Leahy, *I Was There*, 116.
11. Leahy believed that Giraud's idea that French troops could play a major role in an attack on Italy, and that Italy could be conquered by a few hundred thousand troops, was very naïve. Leahy Diary, July 9, 1943.
12. Julian Jackson, *De Gaulle* (London: Haus Publishing, 2003), 24.
13. Leahy Diary, June 17 and 19, 1943.
14. Ibid., July 7–9, 1943. Also see: Leahy NHHC, Leahy to Dobyns, October 25, 1950.
15. JCS, Special Meeting, July 26, 1943, 1–2.
16. Ibid., 2.
17. FRUS, *Conferences at Washington and Quebec, 1943* (Washington, DC: GPO, 1943), 391. Accessible online at: http://digicoll.library.wisc.edu/cgi-bin/FRUS/FRUS-idx?type=turn&entity=FRUS.FRUS1943.p0505&id=FRUS.FRUS1943&isize=M.
18. For a description of the holiday, see: Leahy, *I Was There*, 174; and William Rigdon, *White House Sailor* (Garden City, NY: Doubleday, 1962), 28–34.
19. Rigdon, *White House Sailor,* 34–35.
20. JCS, 102nd Meeting, August 9, Supplementary Minutes, 2.
21. JCS, 103rd Meeting, August 10, 4.
22. JCS, Meeting with Roosevelt and Stimson, August 9, 1943, 4.
23. JCS, 102nd Meeting, August 9, 1943, 1.
24. CCS Meeting, August 16, 1943, 2:30 p.m., 873. Accessible online at: http://digicoll.library.wisc.edu/cgi-bin/FRUS/FRUS-idx?type=turn&entity=FRUS.FRUS1943.p0984&id=FRUS.FRUS1943&isize=M.
25. CCS Meeting, August 15, 1943, 2:30 p.m., 863. Accessible online at: http://digicoll.library.wisc.edu/cgi-bin/FRUS/FRUS-idx?type=turn&entity=FRUS.FRUS1943.p0976&id=FRUS.FRUS1943&isize=M.
26. CCS Meeting, August 17, 1943, 2:30 p.m., 877. Accessible online at: http://digicoll.library.wisc.edu/cgi-bin/FRUS/FRUS-idx?type=turn&entity=FRUS.FRUS1943.p0991&id=FRUS.FRUS1943&isize=M.
27. Danchev and Todman, *War Diaries*, August 24, 1943, 447.
28. FRUS, President's Log, 286–87, http://images.library.wisc.edu/FRUS/EFacs/1944/reference/frus.frus1944.i0011.pdf.
29. Elsey, *An Unplanned Life*, 38.
30. Linda L. Levin, *The Making of FDR: The Story of Stephen T. Early, America's First Modern Press Secretary* (New York: Prometheus Books, 2008), 345–46.
31. Meeting of Roosevelt and Churchill with CCS, August 19, 1943, 5:30 p.m., 896. Accessible online at: http://digicoll.library.wisc.edu/cgi-bin/FRUS/FRUS-idx?type=turn&entity=FRUS.FRUS1943.p1010&id=FRUS.FRUS1943&isize=M.
32. CCS Meeting with Roosevelt and Churchill, August 23, 1943, 2:30 pm. Starting on 942. Accessible online at: http://digicoll.library.wisc.edu/cgi-bin/FRUS/FRUS-idx?type=turn&entity=FRUS.FRUS1943.p1055&id=FRUS.FRUS1943&isize=M.
33. "Report of the Conclusions Reached by the Combined Chiefs of Staff," August 24, 1943, 1121–32. Accessible online at: http://digicoll.library.wisc.edu/cgi-bin/FRUS/FRUS-idx?type=turn&entity=FRUS.FRUS1943.p1235&id=FRUS.FRUS1943&isize=M.

34. Ibid., 1126.
35. Leahy Diary, August 24, 1943.
36. Danchev and Todman, *War Diaries*, 447.

CHAPTER 18: **TOP DOG**

1. Leahy Diary, August 26, 1943.
2. Irwin F. Gellman, *Secret Affairs: Franklin Roosevelt, Cordell Hull and Sumner Welles* (Baltimore: Johns Hopkins University Press, 1995), 235–37.
3. There are a number of different descriptions of how Hull and Bullitt colluded to bring down Welles. One of the best is: Christopher O'Sullivan, *Sumner Welles: Post-War Planning and the Quest for a New World Order, 1937–1943* (New York: Columbia University Press, 2009), chapter 8. There is an online accessible copy of this book at: http://www.gutenberg-e.org/osc01/frames/fosc08.html.
4. Gellman, *Secret Affairs*, 237, 302–4.
5. Arthur Krock Mss., Princeton University, Book 1, Memoranda, 143.
6. Charles Bohlen, *Witness to History: 1929–1969* (New York: Norton, 1973), 129.
7. Graham Cross, *The Diplomatic Education of Franklin D. Roosevelt, 1882–1933* (London: Palgrave, 2012), 98–99.
8. Benjamin Welles, *Sumner Welles: FDR's Global Strategist* 342–(New York: St. Martin's Press, 1997), 45.
9. Ibid., 345
10. Ward, *Closest Companion*, 243. "At dinner, I sat opposite the P. [resident] with Adm. Leahy on my right, & Major Hammond on my left. The princesses on each side of the P. It was very nice—everyone could put in a word, & the P was 'himself'—No one to act up to!"
11. Welles, *Sumner Welles: FDR's Global Strategist*, 354.
12. One of the issues that brought Welles and Leahy together was their shared interest in China. In 1943, they regularly discussed Chinese issues and brought them directly to Roosevelt. See Leahy JCS, NARA RG 218, Welles to Leahy, May 17, 1943.
13. Leahy Diary, February 6 and 10, 1943.
14. Ibid., March 4, 1943.
15. William Leahy, *I Was There* (New York: McGraw-Hill, 1950), 123.
16. Leahy Diary, September 26, 1943.
17. Ibid., September 17 and 22, 1943.
18. Leahy, *I Was There*, 184.
19. James A. Halsted, "Severe Malnutrition in a Public Servant of the World War II Era: The Medical History of Harry Hopkins," *Transactions of the American Clinical and Climatological Association* 86 (1975), 27.
20. Leahy, *I Was There*, 138.
21. George McKee Elsey, *An Unplanned Life: A Memoir by George McKee Elsey* (Columbia: University of Missouri Press, 2005), 41.
22. Leahy Diary, October 31, 1943; December 23, 1943.
23. Ibid., September 24, 1942.
24. Cordell Hull, *The Memoirs of Cordell Hull* (New York: Macmillan, 1948), 1368.
25. Welles, *Sumner Welles: FDR's Global Strategist*, 297.
26. Leahy Diary, November 12, 1942.
27. Ibid., September 27, 1943.
28. Leahy, *I Was There*, 186.
29. Leahy Diary, April 20, 1945; May 11, 1945; February 21, 1946.
30. While Forrestal was becoming more important, one should be careful not to overstate his role at this time. Between 1943 and Roosevelt's death, he met with the president thirteen times, according to Roosevelt's diary. See: http://www.fdrlibrary.marist.edu/daybyday/search/?str=Forrestal&start_date=1943-01-01&end_date=1945-04-20&type=daylog&search_submit=&submitted=t&s_page=1.
31. Leahy JCS, Forrestal Memo for FDR, September 21, 1943.
32. JCS, 120th Meeting, October 26, 1943, 1.

CHAPTER 19: CAIRO AND TEHRAN

1. Stalin to Roosevelt, September 8, 1943, FRUS online, http:// digicoll.library.wisc.edu / cgi-bin/FRUS/FRUS-idx?type=turn&entity=FRUS.FRUS1943CairoTehran.p0115&id=FRUS.FRUS1943CairoTehran&isize=M.
2. FDR, PSF 62, FDR to Knox, May 4, 1942.
3. George Elsey, *An Unplanned Life: A Memoir by George McKee Elsey* (Columbia: University of Missouri Press, 2005), 42; Constantine Brown, *The Coming of the Whirlwind, 1914–1952* (Chicago: Henry Regnery Co., 1964), 306.
4. NHHC Oral, J. V. Smith Interview, 126.
5. Leahy Diary, September 22, 1943.
6. Ibid., October 5, 1943.
7. JCS, 119th Meeting, Supplementary Minutes, 6. Here Leahy is being very skeptical about the US Army proposing a strategy change making the Italian campaign more central.
8. Leahy JCS, RG 218, draft letter, Leahy to Berle, October 20, 1943.
9. JCS, 117th Meeting, Supplementary Minutes, 2–3.
10. Leahy Diary, October 7–8, 1943.
11. John Ehrman, *Grand Strategy* (London: HMSO, 1956), 4: 158.
12. JCS Meeting of FDR with JCS, November 19, 1943, 3–5.
13. William Leahy, *I Was There* (New York: McGraw-Hill, 1950), 196.
14. Alex Danchev and Daniel Todman, eds., *War Diaries 1939–1945: Field Marshal Lord Alanbrooke* (London: Phoenix Press, 2002), 477.
15. Leahy, *I Was There*, 202.
16. King Mss., LC, Box 35, "Mr. Roosevelt vs. Chiang Kai-shek," 6. King gives a detailed description of how forceful FDR was on the issue of getting aid to China at Cairo.
17. Meeting of Roosevelt, Churchill, and the Chiefs of Staff, November 24, 1943, 11 a.m. Accessible online at: http:// digicoll.library.wisc.edu/cgi-bin/FRUS/FRUS-idx?type=turn&entity=FRUS.FRUS1943CairoTehran.p0429&id=FRUS.FRUS1943CairoTehran&isize=M.
18. Leahy, *I Was There*, 201.
19. JCS Meeting, November 24, 1943, 9:30 a.m. Accessible online at: http://images.library.wisc.edu/FRUS/EFacs/1943CairoTehran/reference/frus.frus1943cairotehran.i0011.pdf.
20. CCS Meeting, November 26, 1943, 2:30 p.m. Accessible online at: http://images.library.wisc.edu/FRUS/EFacs/1943CairoTehran/reference/frus.frus1943cairotehran.i0011.pdf.
21. Leahy Diary, December 8, 1943. In this entry Leahy jokes that he assumed those who planned the assassination were quickly liquidated by the Russians when they weren't needed.
22. Roosevelt-Stalin Meeting, November 28, 1943, 3 p.m. See transcript: http://digicoll.library.wisc.edu/cgi-bin/FRUS/FRUS-idx?type=article&did=FRUS.FRUS1943CairoTehran.i0012&id=FRUS.FRUS1943CairoTehran&isize=M.
23. Meeting of Roosevelt, Churchill, Stalin, and staff, November 28, 1943, 4 p.m. Accessible online at:http://digicoll.library.wisc.edu/cgi-bin/FRUS/FRUS-idx?type=article&did=FRUS.FRUS1943CairoTehran.i0012&id=FRUS.FRUS1943CairoTehran&isize=M.
24. Leahy Diary, November 29, 1942.
25. Leahy NHHC, "Unofficial Personal Notes . . . ," 13–16.
26. CCS Meeting, November 29, 1943, 10:30 a.m. Accessible online at: http://digicoll.library.wisc.edu/cgi-bin/FRUS/FRUS-idx?type=article&did=FRUS.FRUS1943CairoTehran.i0012&id=FRUS.FRUS1943CairoTehran&isize=M.
27. Ibid.
28. Leahy Diary, November 30, 1943.
29. The British were convinced that not only did Marshall want to be supreme commander, he would definitely get the job. Sir Charles Portal Mss., Christ Church Library, Oxford, Leigh-Mallory to Portal, November 1, 1943.
30. Robert Sherwood, *Roosevelt and Hopkins: An Intimate History* (New York: Harper, 1948), 758.
31. Ernest King and Walter Muir Whitehill, *Fleet Admiral King: A Naval Record* (New York: Norton, 1952), 317.
32. Second Plenary Meeting, Tehran Conference, November 29, 1943, 4 p.m. There are two copies of minutes from this meeting, one kept by the American diplomat Charles Bohlen

and the other by the JCS. They agree on all major points though occasionally phrase things differently. For copies of both minutes see: http://digicoll.library.wisc.edu/cgi-bin/FRUS /FRUS-idx?type=article&did=FRUS.FRUS1943CairoTehran.i0012&id=FRUS.FRUS 1943 CairoTehran&isize=M.

33. Leahy NHHC, "Unofficial Personal Notes . . . ," 27.
34. Ibid., 17.
35. Leahy NHHC, Tehran Conference Notes, November 28–December 1, 1943, 1.
36. Leahy, *I Was There*, 210–11.
37. Tripartite Political Meeting, December 1, 1943, 6:30 p.m. Bohlen Minutes. Accessible online at: http://digicoll.library.wisc.edu/cgi-bin/FRUS/FRUS-idx?type=article&did= FRUS.FRUS1943CairoTehran.i0012&id=FRUS.FRUS1943CairoTehran&isize=M.
38. Leahy Diary, November 30, 1943.
39. Charles Bohlen, *Witness to History: 1929–1969* (New York: Norton, 1973), 152.
40. Leahy Diary, December 5, 1943.
41. Leahy, *I Was There*, 212.
42. CCS, December 3, 1943, 2:30 p.m. Accessible online at: http://digicoll.library.wisc.edu/ cgi-bin/FRUS/FRUS-idx?type=article&did=FRUS.FRUS1943CairoTehran.i0012&id= FRUS.FRUS1943CairoTehran&isize=M.
43. Meeting of Combined Chiefs with Roosevelt and Churchill, December 4, 1943.
44. Leahy, *I Was There*, 213–14.
45. CCS 134th Meeting, December 4, 1943, 687. Leahy had an aside in this meeting that he thought of the Burma operation as "diversionary." It was a very odd thing for him to say, considering how much effort he put into it before and after Cairo. It might be that he was smarting from his first real grand-strategic setback and was trying to explain away his defeat.
46. Leahy NHHC, "Unofficial Personal Notes . . . ," 19.
47. Leahy, *I Was There*, 214–15.

Chapter 20: ACTING PRESIDENT

1. William Leahy, *I Was There* (New York: McGraw-Hill, 1950), 221.
2. Carl Vinson also attested to the fact that originally Roosevelt only wanted to promote Leahy. Henry A. Adams, *Witness to Power: The Life of Fleet Admiral William D. Leahy* (Annapolis: Naval Institute Press, 1985), 236.
3. Leahy Diary, January 10, 1944.
4. Ibid., December 31, 1943.
5. Leahy, *I Was There*, 220.
6. See: Stanley Weintraub, *Final Victory: FDR's Extraordinary World War II Presidential Campaign* (Philadelphia: Da Capo Press, 2012) for a discussion of McIntire's role in the suppression of the truth about Roosevelt's condition.
7. David Roll, *The Hopkins Touch: Harry Hopkins and the Forging of the Alliance to Defeat Hitler* (Oxford, UK: Oxford University Press, 2013), 331–34.
8. Leahy, *I Was There*, 220.
9. Leahy Diary, January 22, 1944.
10. Ibid., February 4, 1944.
11. Leahy Mss., NHHC, Smith to Leahy, March 9, 1944.
12. Leahy Diary, March 30, 1944.
13. Ibid., March 11, 1944.
14. Ibid., April 8, 1944.
15. Ibid., April 9, 1944.
16. For a good description of Roosevelt's medical condition during the stay in Hobcaw, see: Robert H. Ferrell, *The Dying President: Franklin D. Roosevelt, 1944–1945* (Columbia: University of Missouri Press, 1998), 69–73.
17. Leahy Diary, April 11, 1944.
18. "The Baroness of Hobcaw," *Charleston Magazine*, September 2013, accessible online at: http://charlestonmag.com/features/the_baroness_of_hobcaw.
19. Leahy Diary, August 30, 1944.
20. William Rigdon, *White House Sailor* (Garden City, NY: Doubleday, 1962), 100.
21. Leahy, *I Was There*, 234.
22. Ibid., 236–37.
23. Leahy NHHC, Leahy to Smith, April 18, 1944.

24. Joseph Persico, *Franklin and Lucy: Mrs. Rutherford and the Other Remarkable Women in Roosevelt's Life* (New York: Random House, 2009).
25. Jay Winik, *FDR and the Year that Changed History* (New York: Simon & Schuster, 2015), 156.
26. Elliott Roosevelt and James Brough, *Rendezvous with Destiny: The Roosevelts of the White House* (London: W. H. Allen, 1977), 371.
27. *Eleanor and Franklin: The Story of Their Relationship, Based on Eleanor Roosevelt's Private Papers* (New York: New American Library, 1971), 698.
28. Ward, *Closest Companion*, 294.
29. Ibid., 296.
30. Ibid.
31. Ibid., 339.
32. Leahy NHHC, Leahy to Smith, May 5, 1944.
33. Leahy Diary, May 6, 1944.
34. Leahy NHHC, Engagement book for May 8–9, 1944. Also see: Leahy Diary, May 8–9 1944.
35. Leahy Diary, May 15, 1944.
36. Ibid., July 12, 1944.
37. Leahy, *I Was There*, 247–48.
38. Leahy Diary, June 17, 1943.
39. Robert Sherwood, *Roosevelt and Hopkins: An Intimate History* (New York: Harper, 1948), 840–41.
40. Leahy JCS, See Memorandum for Leahy January 25, 1944, enclosing Lubin letter of January 25, 1944. This is a fascinating example of how the relationship had metamorphosed. Hopkins was refusing to commit himself either way on a question of how aid was distributed to the USSR. He clearly wanted Lubin to go to Leahy to bring it to the president first.
41. Leahy Diary, Baruch to Leahy, September 6, 1944.
42. Ibid., March 1, 1944.
43. Leahy Mss., Leahy to Sarnoff, November 24, 1944.
44. Ibid., Sarnoff to Leahy, November 24, 1944.
45. Leahy Diary, May 10–11, 1944. Also see: Leahy, *I Was There*, 237–38.
46. Leahy Diary, June 1 and 16, 1944.
47. Ibid., October 19, 1944.
48. Leahy JCS, Berle to Leahy, October 15, 1943, and Leahy to Berle, October 20, 1943.
49. Ibid., Matthews Memorandum for Leahy, October 17, 1944.
50. Ibid., Memorandum for file, August 26, 1944; see also: Freeman Memorandum for Leahy, August 26, 1944.
51. Cordell Hull, *The Memoirs of Cordell Hull* (New York: Macmillan, 1948), 1581.
52. Charles Bohlen, *Witness to History, 1929–1969* (New York: Norton, 1973), 166.
53. Ibid.
54. Ibid., 206.
55. Truman Oral, Charles Bohlen Interview, April 9, 1970, 320–21. Accessed online at: www.trumanlibrary.org/oralhist/elsey6.htm#320.
56. Leahy Diary, June 8, 1944.
57. "Marshall, Arnold and King in London," *New York Times*, June 10, 1944, 1. By this time it seems that since Leahy was White House staff, his daily briefings with Roosevelt were no longer recorded as individual meetings. For instance, in the *New York Times* report of Roosevelt's press conference on June 9, Leahy is described as being by Roosevelt's side, which makes sense, as the press conference took place in the morning, which meant right after the briefing. However, Leahy is not mentioned in the Roosevelt meeting diary that day.
58. Leahy Diary, May 10, 1944.
59. George Elsey, *An Unplanned Life: A Memoir by George McKee Elsey* (Columbia: University of Missouri Press, 2005), 75.

CHAPTER 21: LEAHY'S WAR

1. Leahy NHHC, "Discussion of Pacific Strategy, Joint Chiefs of Staff," 6–7.
2. Ibid.
3. JCS, 172nd Meeting, September 5, 1944, 2–4.

4. O'Brien, *How the War Was Won,* 198–215.
5. Ibid., 58–66.
6. Leahy Diary, March 21, 1943.
7. Ibid., March 28, 1943.
8. Henry A. Adams, *Witness to Power: The Life of Fleet Admiral William D. Leahy* (Annapolis: Naval Institute Press, 1985), 240.
9. JCS, 151st Meeting, March 11, 1944.
10. Ibid., 4.
11. Ibid., 3.
12. Leahy Diary, March 11, 1945.
13. FDR Mss, Online, Daily Calendar, March 11, 1944, accessible online at: http://www.fdrlibrary.marist.edu/daybyday/daylog/march-11th-1944/.
14. JCS 713/4, "Future Operations in the Pacific," March 12, 1944.
15. O'Brien, *How the War Was Won,* 212–13.
16. Leahy Diary, June 20, 1944.
17. Ibid., July 10, 1944.
18. Columbia Oral, Richard Conolly Interview, Naval History Project, 372.
19. In his memoirs Leahy made this point and emphasized it with italics, which is why I have done so here as well. William Leahy, *I Was There* (New York: McGraw-Hill, 1950), 245.
20. King Mss., Box 35, Notes, "Mr. Roosevelt Versus the Philippines and Formosa," 4.
21. Leahy NHHC, Leahy to Smith, July 21, 1944.
22. Leahy, *I Was There,* 250.
23. Leahy Diary, March 10, 1944.
24. Ibid., April 30, 1944.
25. Leahy, *I Was There,* 250.
26. JCS, 145th Meeting, February 8, 1944, 5.
27. Ibid.
28. Leahy Diary, July 29, 1944.
29. Ibid.
30. William Rigdon, *White House Sailor* (Garden City, NY: Doubleday, 1962), 128.
31. Leahy Diary, August 17, 1944.
32. This was on August 17, the day the president first returned to work in the White House.
33. Leahy Mss., NHHC, MacArthur to Leahy, August 7, 1944.
34. James Forrestal Papers, Princeton University Special Collections, James Forrestal Diary, September 26, 1944.
35. Leahy Diary, August 16, 1944.

CHAPTER 22: ATOMIC BOMBS AND ELECTIONS

1. FRUS, Quebec Conference, Preparatory Papers, Bohlen Memorandum, September 4, 1944. Also see: Leahy NHHC, Leahy Memorandum, September 22, 1944.
2. William Leahy, *I Was There* (New York: McGraw-Hill, 1950), 241.
3. Roosevelt Day by Day Diary, September 9, 1944. Roosevelt had met with Hopkins earlier that day, which made the decision to leave him behind even more of a slight.
4. Morgenthau Presidential Diary, September 15, 1944.
5. FRUS, Quebec Conference, Leahy-Churchill Conversation, September 11, 1944.
6. FRUS, Quebec Conference, CCS Meeting, September 14, 1944. See also, Mark A. Stoler, *Allies in War: Britain and America Against the Axis Powers, 1940–1945* (London: Hodder Arnold, 2005), 169–70.
7. Cunningham Mss. (British Library), Somerville to Cunningham, November 4, 1944.
8. Stephen Roskill, *The War at Sea, volume 3: The Offensive* (London, Naval and Military Press, 2009), 337–64.
9. FRUS, Quebec Volume, Roosevelt-Churchill dinner, September 13, 1944. White wrote a record of what supposedly transpired at the dinner, but as he was not in attendance, the only way he would have been able to do so was from a conversation with Morgenthau.
10. In his diary, Leahy was particularly banal, stating simply that the policy on the future of Germany was discussed at dinner. Leahy Diary, September 13, 1944.
11. Morgenthau Presidential Diary, September 15, 1944.
12. Ibid.

13. Doris Kearns Goodwin, *No Ordinary Time: Franklin and Eleanor Roosevelt—The Home Front in World War II* (New York: Simon & Schuster, 1994), 545.
14. George Elsey, *An Unplanned Life: A Memoir of George McKee Elsey* (Columbia: University of Missouri Press, 2005), 63.
15. Leahy Diary, September 18, 1944.
16. Ibid., September 19, 1944.
17. Ibid. Italics mine: the "PS" was actually written in by hand so that Leahy would not divulge the nature of the project.
18. While Leahy's opposition to the bomb has been mentioned in a number of works, his role in the debate and postwar US atomic policy has never been discussed. For mentions of his opposition to the bomb, see: Gar Alperovitz, *Atomic Diplomacy: Hiroshima and Potsdam, the Use of the Atomic Bomb and American Confrontation with Soviet Power* (New York: Pluto Press, 1994), 14–15.
19. Steven L. Rearden, *Council of War: A History of the Joint Chiefs of Staff, 1942–1991* (Washington, DC: Joint History Office, 2012), 47. Accessible online at: http://www.dtic.mil/doctrine/doctrine/history/councilofwar.pdf.
20. "Interview with General Marshall," Tape 14, February 11, 1957, 26–27; accessed through Marshall Foundation online, http://marshallfoundation.org/library/wp-content/uploads/sites/16/2014/05/Marshall_Interview_Tape14.pdf.
21. Leahy, *I Was There*, 245.
22. Frank Freidel, *Franklin D. Roosevelt: A Rendezvous with Destiny* (Boston: Little, Brown 1990), 553–54.
23. Leahy, *I Was There*, 439.
24. Ibid.
25. Ibid., 440.
26. JCS Minutes, February 8, 1945. There is a copy of these minutes in the *Foreign Relations of the United States* volume on Yalta, which is accessible online at: http://digicoll.library.wisc.edu/cgi-bin/FRUS/FRUS-idx?type=turn&entity=FRUS.FRUS1945.p0826&id=FRUS.FRUS1945&isize=M.
27. This comes from the H. Freeman Matthews oral history interview on the Truman Library website, http://www.trumanlibrary.org/oralhist/matthewh.htm, 6 (interview given June 6, 1973).
28. H. F. Matthews Papers, Princeton University Special Collections, Unpublished memoirs, 604.
29. FDR Mss., September 18, 1944, Aide-Mémoire of FDR-WSC conversations, Tube Alloys, 155. Accessed online: http://www.fdrlibrary.marist.edu/_resources/images/atomic/atomic_03.pdf
30. Leahy Diary, September 19, 1944.
31. Ibid., September 22, 1944.
32. Ibid., July 13, 1944.
33. Ibid., March 16, 1944.
34. Ibid., October 14, 1944.
35. George Marshall Mss., Marshall Library VMI, Lexington, VA, Marshall to Leahy, October 1944.
36. David Rooney, *Stilwell the Patriot: Vinegar Joe, the Brits and Chiang Kai-shek* (London: Greenhill Books, 2005), 234.
37. Leahy Diary, October 16, 1944. This meeting is listed in Roosevelt's day-by-day diary online. It started at 12:30 p.m. and lasted for approximately fifteen minutes.
38. Roll, *The Hopkins Touch*, 346.
39. Morgenthau Diary, October 19, 1944.
40. Leahy NHHC, Leahy to Stokes, July 16, 1956.
41. Morgenthau Diary, October 25, 1944.
42. Ibid., October 19, 1944.
43. Robert H. Ferrell, *The Dying President: Franklin D. Roosevelt, 1944–1945* (Columbia: University of Missouri Press, 1998), 91.
44. Leahy Diary, November 4, 1944.
45. Jim Bishop, *FDR's Last Year: April 1944–April 1945* (New York: Pocket Books, 1975), 257.
46. Ward, *Closest Companion*, 341.
47. Merle Miller, *Plain Speaking: An Oral Biography of Harry S. Truman* (New York: Berkley Publishing, 1973), 189.
48. Leahy Diary, November 9, 1944.

CHAPTER 23: YALTA AND DEATH

1. Harry S. Truman, *Memoirs: Volume 1, Year of Decisions* (Garden City, NY: Doubleday, 1955), 5.
2. John Crider, "Stone Gives Oath," *New York Times*, January 21, 1945, 1.
3. Fourth Inaugural Address of Franklin Roosevelt, January 20, 1945. Accessible online at: http://avalon.law.yale.edu/20th_century/froos4.asp.
4. William Leahy, *I Was There* (New York: McGraw-Hill, 1950), 290.
5. Morgenthau Papers, Morgenthau Diary, January 10, 1945.
6. Ibid., November 18, 1944.
7. Ibid.
8. Ibid.
9. Leahy Diary, November 21, 1944.
10. Leahy, *I Was There*, 280.
11. Morgenthau Papers, Morgenthau Diary, November 22, 1941. Meeting of American delegation.
12. Ibid., November 27, 1944.
13. Ibid.
14. Ibid.
15. Morgenthau Papers, Morgenthau Diary. Leahy wrote to Morgenthau on November 28, with a list of seven major changes.
16. Morgenthau Papers, Morgenthau Diary, transcript of call with Leahy, November 29, 1944.
17. John Crider, "Lend Lease Will Be Cut 43% When Reich Falls," *New York Times,* December 1, 1944, 1.
18. Constantine Brown, *The Coming of the Whirlwind, 1914–1952* (Chicago: Henry Regnery Co., 1964), 309.
19. Arnold was too unwell to make the trip to Yalta and was replaced by General Kuter.
20. Leahy, *I Was There*, 294.
21. NHHC Oral, J. V. Smith Interview, 117.
22. Eleanor Roosevelt, *This I Remember* (New York: Harper Brothers, 1949), 342.
23. What they wanted Roosevelt to do was to separate the Federal Loan Agency from the Department of Commerce. While serving as vice president, Wallace had been stripped of any influence over wartime military construction, and the Federal Loan Agency was responsible for making billions of dollars in loans to military producers. This move, it was hoped, would defang Wallace's critics by making it clear that he would have little influence over military production. See Charles R. Geisst, *Encyclopedia of American Business History* (New York: Facts on File, 2006), 358.
24. Leahy Diary, January 29, 1945.
25. NHHC Oral, J. V. Smith Interview, 130.
26. Columbia Oral, Anna Roosevelt Halsted Interview, 44.
27. NHHC Oral, J. V. Smith Interview, 144–45.
28. Anna Halstead Roosevelt Papers (FDR Library), Yalta Recollections, 22.
29. Leahy, *I Was There*, 297.
30. There are twenty-two pages devoted to the Yalta talks (1945, 12–34), starting with the flight into the Crimea and ending with the drive out.
31. NHHC Oral, J. V. Smith Interview, 136.
32. Leahy, *I Was There*, 298.
33. Frank Costigliola, "Broken Circle: The Isolation of Franklin D. Roosevelt in World War II," *Diplomatic History* 32, no. 5 (November 2008), 711–12.
34. Leahy Diary, February 8, 1945.
35. Brown, *Whirlwind*, 317.
36. Thomas M. Campbell and George C. Herring, eds., *The Diaries of Edward R. Stettinius, Jr., 1943–1946* (New York: New Viewpoints, 1975), 237.
37. Leahy Diary, February 12, 1945.
38. George Elsey, *An Unplanned Life: A Memoir by George McKee Elsey* (Columbia: University of Missouri Press, 2005), 67–68.
39. W. Averell Harriman and Elie Abel, *Special Envoy to Churchill and Stalin* (New York: Random House, 1975), 399.
40. Columbia Oral, Thomas Hart Interview, 1: 44.
41. Leahy Diary, February 8, 1945. There is also a copy of the Bohlen minutes of this Roosevelt-Stalin meeting in the online copy of FRUS devoted to Yalta. See http://

digicoll.library.wisc.edu/cgi-bin/FRUS/FRUS-idx?type=turn&entity=FRUS.FRUS1945
.p0862&id=FRUS.FRUS1945&isize=M.

42. Leahy, *I Was There*, 318.
43. FRUS, Yalta Volume, Conference Proceedings, Matthews Minutes of February 7, 1945, Plenary Meeting.
44. FRUS, Yalta Volume, Conference Proceedings, Letter from Roosevelt to Stalin, February 6, 1945.
45. Leahy Diary, February 12, 1945.
46. Brown, *Whirlwind*, 316.
47. Ibid.
48. Leahy, *I Was There*, 317–18.
49. Ibid., 315–16.
50. Leahy NHHC, Leahy undated Yalta Notes, 25.
51. Campbell and Herring, eds., *Edward R. Stettinius*, 238.
52. Leahy Diary, February 16, 1944. In *I Was There*, Leahy says this meeting happened on February 12, but the diary clearly has it on February 16.
53. Leahy Diary, July 8, 1944.
54. Leahy NHHC, "FDR Meets with Ibn Saud," William Eddy manuscript, 14.
55. Leahy, *I Was There*, 295.
56. Leahy NHHC, "FDR meets with Ibn Saud," 26–28.
57. Leahy NHHC, Leahy to Hull, April 26, 1943. This was a letter Leahy sent as chairman of the JCS to Hull, advising against the resettlement of European Jewish immigrants to North Africa. Leahy was clearly worried about its impact on Muslim opinion.
58. Leahy NHHC, "Memorandum Regarding Conversation Between President Roosevelt and the King of Saudi Arabia," August 1945.
59. Samuel Rosenman, *Working with Roosevelt* (New York: Harper and Brothers, 1952), 475–77.
60. Leahy Diary, March 17, 1945.
61. Leahy, *I Was There*, 342.
62. Truman Presidential Papers, PSF 194, "Atomic Bomb" memorandum, 4.
63. Leahy Diary, March 17, 1945.
64. Ibid., April 12, 1945.
65. Leahy, *I Was There*, 432; Leahy Diary, April 12, 1942.
66. Columbia Oral (online), Perkins Interview, accessible online at: (http://www.columbia.edu/cu/lweb/digital/collections/nny/perkinsf/transcripts/perkinsf_8_1_814.html), 814–16.
67. Leahy Diary, April 15, 1945. Here is his entire entry about the train ride down: "When the brief ceremonies were ended, we all returned to our trains at the Hyde Park Station and departed for Washington where we arrived at 3:30 P.M., bringing to an end a long day that was full of sad memories, and that also for me probably was the last visit to the home of my friend who will live in history as one of our greatest Presidents. He was a great gentleman and a true friend."
68. Leahy Diary, April 12, 1945.

CHAPTER 24: TRUMAN

1. Harry S. Truman, *Memoirs: Volume 1, Year of Decisions* (Garden City, NY: Doubleday, 1955), 4.
2. Ibid., 5.
3. "Truman Is Seventh Elevated by Death," *New York Times*, April 13, 1945, 3.
4. Wilson Brown, "Aide to Four Presidents," *American Heritage* 6 no. 2, 1955. Accessible online at: http://www.americanheritage.com/content/aide-four-presidents?page=show.
5. William Leahy, *I Was There* (New York: McGraw-Hill, 1950), 347.
6. Truman, *Memoirs*, 1: 18.
7. Leahy Diary, May 19, 1939.
8. Ibid., April 12, 1945.
9. David McCullough, *Truman* (New York: Simon & Schuster, 1992), 388.
10. There is a detailed book on the complex relationship between Truman and Pendergast: Robert H. Ferrell, *Truman and Pendergast* (Columbia: University of Missouri Press, 1999).

11. Truman Papers, Naval Aide to the President, Box 11. See the telegrams drafted by Leahy in June 1945.
12. George Elsey, *An Unplanned Life: A Memoir by George McKee Elsey* (Columbia: University of Missouri Press, 2005), 84.
13. Ibid., 85.
14. Leahy NHHC, Pinney to Connelly, May 18, 1945.
15. Truman Oral (online) Matthew J. Connelly Interview, November 30, 1967; http://www.trumanlibrary.org/oralhist/connly2.htm#231.
16. Forrestal Diary, April 23, 1945, Meeting at White House, 3.
17. Truman, *Memoirs*, 1: 78.
18. Ibid., 80.
19. Ibid., 82.
20. Leahy Diary, April 23, 1945.
21. Leahy, *I Was There*, 357.
22. Leahy NHHC, Eleanor Roosevelt to Leahy, August 14, 1945.
23. Leahy Diary, May 8, 1945.
24. Leahy NHHC, Leahy to Pétain, June 22, 1945.
25. Leahy Diary, October 1, 1946.
26. Truman, *Memoirs*, 1: 239–42.
27. Leahy Diary, June 7, 1945.
28. Leahy, *I Was There*, 373.
29. Truman, *Memoirs*, 1: 11.
30. Wilson D. Miscamble, *The Most Controversial Decision: Truman, the Atomic Bombs, and the Defeat of Japan* (Cambridge, UK: Cambridge University Press, 2011), 33.
31. Minutes of the Interim Committee, June 1, 1945. Accessed online at: https://www.trumanlibrary.org/whistlestop/study_collections/bomb/large/index.php.
32. Ibid., May 20, 1945.
33. Leahy Diary, June 4, 1945.
34. JCS Minutes, Argonaut Conference, February 7, 1945 (JCS, 189th Meeting), 3.
35. Henry A. Adams, *Witness to Power: The Life of Fleet Admiral William D. Leahy* (Annapolis: Naval Institute Press, 1985), 290.
36. Richard B. Frank, *Downfall: The End of the Imperial Japanese Empire* (New York: Penguin, 2001), 30.
37. Leahy NHHC, MacArthur to War Department, April 20, 1945.

CHAPTER 25: THE END OF THE WAR

1. There are only two historians who have sensibly discussed Leahy's intentions here: Richard B. Frank, *Downfall: The End of the Imperial Japanese Empire* (New York: Penguin, 2001), 143, 145; and D. M. Giangreco, *Hell to Pay: Operation Downfall and the Invasion of Japan* (Annapolis: Naval Institute Press, 2009), 58–59.
2. JCS Minutes, Minutes of Meeting Held at the White House, June 18, 1945, 1. As this was a special meeting called by the president, the meeting was not assigned a sequential number in the JCS meetings roster.
3. Wilson D. Miscamble, *The Most Controversial Decision: Truman, the Atomic Bombs, and the Defeat of Japan* (Cambridge, UK: Cambridge University Press, 2011), 49.
4. JCS Minutes, Minutes of Meeting Held at the White House, June 18, 1945, 4.
5. Marshall was certainly being told by army intelligence in mid-June that approximately 350,000 Japanese troops were in Kyushu. There is an excellent online source put up by the CIA that discloses what US estimates of Japanese troop numbers on Kyushu were at the time of the June 18 meeting, and how these estimates were steadily increased over the coming weeks: https://www.cia.gov/library/center-for-the-study-of-intelligence/csi-publications/books-and-monographs/the-final-months-of-the-war-with-japan-signals-intelligence-u-s-invasion-planning-and-the-a-bomb-decision/csi9810001.html#rtoc4.
6. Giangreco, *Hell to Pay*, 59.
7. JCS Minutes, Minutes of Meeting Held at the White House, June 18, 1945, 6.
8. Giangreco, *Hell to Pay*, 99.
9. William Leahy, *I Was There* (New York: McGraw-Hill, 1950), 385.
10. D. M. Giangreco, "Casualty Projections for the US Invasions of Japan, 1945–1946: Planning and Policy Implications," *Journal of Military History* 61 (July 1997), 569.

There is an accessible copy online of this article at: http://theamericanpresident.us /images/projections.pdf.

11. Douglas J. MacEachin, *The Final Months of the War Against Japan* (CIA Publications Online). See section IV, "Tracking the Japanese Build-up as Allied Leaders Met in Potsdam," accessible at: https://www.cia.gov/library/center-for-the-study-of-intelligence/csi -publications/books-and-monographs/the-final-months-of-the-war-with-japan-signals -intelligence-u-s-invasion-planning-and-the-a-bomb-decision/csi9810001.html#rtoc4.

12. Frank, *Downfall*, 245.

13. Leahy, *I Was There*, 385.

14. Truman Oral Online, Elsey Interview, April 9, 1970, 253–53. Accessible online at http:// www.trumanlibrary.org/oralhist/elsey6.htm#252.

15. Leahy, *I Was There*, 369.

16. Truman Mss., Truman to Bess, July 3, 1945, http://www.trumanlibrary.org/whis tlestop/study_collections/trumanpapers/fbpa/index.php?documentid=HST-FBP_14–78 _01&documentYear=1945&documentVersion=both.

17. This was Truman's idea, it seems, as Leahy said he was surprised when first told that Hopkins was going.

18. Leahy Diary, May 23, 1945.

19. Harry S. Truman, *Memoirs: Volume 1, Year of Decisions* (Garden City, NY: Doubleday, 1955), 335.

20. Leahy, *I Was There*, 386.

21. Leahy Diary, July 15, 1945.

22. Truman Oral Online, Collado Interview, July 11, 1974, 50–52, http://www.truman library.org/oralhist/collado2.htm#48.

23. William Rigdon, *White House Sailor* (Garden City, NY: Doubleday, 1962), 193. Also see: Truman Oral Online, Rigdon Interview, 22, http://www.trumanlibrary.org/oralhist /rigdon.htm

24. Robert Murphy, *Diplomat Among Warriors: The Unique World of a Foreign Service Expert* (New York: Doubleday, 1964), 330.

25. Truman, *Memoirs*, 1: 327.

26. Murphy, *Diplomat Among Warriors*, 331.

27. Leahy Diary, July 19, 1945.

28. Ibid., July 17, 1945.

29. Truman, *Memoirs*, 1: 351.

30. Typed draft of Truman memoirs, Truman archives online (this did not make it into the final draft). See http://www.trumanlibrary.org/whistlestop/study_collections/truman papers/psf/longhand/index.php?documentid=hst-psf_naid735373-02&documentYear =1954&documentVersion=both.

31. Truman Papers, Truman to Bess, July 20, 1945, http://www.trumanlibrary.org/whis tlestop/study_collections/trumanpapers/fbpa/index.php?documentid=HST-FBP_14 -83_01&documentVersion=both.

32. Henry A. Adams, *Witness to Power: The Life of Fleet Admiral William D. Leahy* (Annapolis: Naval Institute Press, 1985), 297.

33. Leahy Diary, July 26, 1945.

34. Francis Williams, *A Prime Minister Remembers: The War and Post-War Memoirs of the Rt. Hon. Earl Attlee* (London: William Heinemann, 1961), 161.

35. Leahy Diary, July 18, 1945.

36. Truman Papers, Truman to Bess, July 18, 1945, http://www.trumanlibrary.org/whis tlestop/study_collections/trumanpapers/fbpa/index.php?documentid=HST-FBP_14 -82_01&documentVersion=both.

37. The Soviet delegation, led by Molotov, asked Truman to make a public speech formally asking for the USSR to enter the war against Japan, to provide some diplomatic cover for the move. Leahy thought this was unnecessary and advised Truman against doing it. In the end, Truman provided the USSR with a bland written statement with no specific request for them to join the fighting. Leahy Diary, July 28, 1945.

38. The Truman Library has put copies of these notes and a collection of other very interesting primary source documents covering the atomic bomb decision-making process online. They can be accessed at: http://www.trumanlibrary.org/whistlestop/study _collections/bomb/large/.

39. Ibid. Specific copy of the original: http://www.trumanlibrary.org/whistlestop/study _collections/bomb/large/documents/pdfs/63.pdf#zoom=100.

40. Harry Truman, Notes on the Potsdam Conference, July 17, 1945, PSF. Accessible online at: http://www.trumanlibrary.org/whistlestop/study_collections/bomb/large/documents/pdfs/63.pdf#zoom=100.
41. For a description of why Hiroshima was thought to be an appropriate target, you could see the post-bombing report by Gen. Leslie Groves, the project director of the Manhattan Project. The Avalon Project maintains a copy online—targeting and Hiroshima are discussed in sections 5 and 6. See: http://avalon.law.yale.edu/subject_menus/mpmenu.asp.
42. This is a widely recalled story mentioned in most history books on the subject. See, for instance: Arnold A. Offner, *Another Such Victory: President Truman and the Cold War, 1945–1953* (Palo Alto: Stanford University Press, 2002), 92, for a particularly censorious description of Truman's elation. For another description of Truman's celebrations see: Rigdon, *White House Sailor*, 206–7.
43. Leahy Diary, August 8, 1945.
44. Forrestal Diary, August 10, 1945.
45. Leahy Diary, August 14, 1945.
46. Adams, *Witness to Power*, 299.

CHAPTER 26: TWO SPEECHES

1. Leahy Diary, September 3, 1945.
2. "Admiral Leahy Is Named Leading Eagle by Sioux," *New York Times*, September 4, 1945, 7.
3. Leahy Diary, September 6, 1945.
4. Leahy Diary, August 24, 1945.
5. "De Gaulle Urges US French Amity," *New York Times*, August 25, 1945, 1.
6. "Britain Decorates 4 Military Chiefs," *New York Times*, November 22, 1945, 21.
7. Leahy Diary, November 21, 1945.
8. George Elsey, *An Unplanned Life: A Memoir by George McKee Elsey* (Columbia: University of Missouri Press, 2005), 260.
9. Truman Oral Online, de Weldon Interview, January 22, 1969, 9, 11–12, https://www.trumanlibrary.org/oralhist/deweldon.htm#11.
10. Leahy Diary, September 26, 1945.
11. Ibid., October 19, November 6, December 20, 1945.
12. Ibid., November 23, 1945.
13. Robert H. Ferrell, ed. *Off the Record: The Private Papers of Harry S. Truman* (Columbia: University of Missouri Press, 1997), 11.
14. Elsey, *An Unplanned Life*, 96.
15. Henry A. Adams, *Witness to Power: The Life of Fleet Admiral William D. Leahy* (Annapolis: Naval Institute Press, 1985), 308.
16. Leahy Diary, August 5, 1950.
17. Leahy NHHC, Leahy to Tully, April 2, 1949.
18. Truman Oral Online, Samuel Rosenman Interview, 24–25, https://www.trumanlibrary.org/oralhist/rosenmn.htm#24.
19. Harry S. Truman, *Memoirs: Volume 1, Year of Decisions* (Garden City, NY: Doubleday, 1955), 537.
20. "The President's Navy Day Speech in Central Park . . . ," *New York Times*, October 28, 1945, 34. Leahy kept a copy of the twelve points in his JCS file. Leahy JCS, "President Harry Truman's Statement . . . ," October 27, 1945.
21. The Miller Center at the University of Virginia maintains an online copy of the address. Eight paragraphs of the speech are focused on atomic weapons, more than on any other single topic. See http://millercenter.org/president/truman/speeches/speech-3342.
22. Ibid.
23. Leahy Diary, October 27, 1945.
24. Ibid.
25. "City Warms to Him," *New York Times*, October 28, 1945, 1.
26. Ibid.
27. Leahy Diary, October 27, 1945.
28. Leahy NHHC, Foreign Policy Draft, December 1, 1945.
29. Leahy NHHC, Leahy memo for JSC, January 14, 1946.
30. "Warships and Peace," *New York Times*, October 28, 1945, E8.

31. "Congress Pleased by Truman's Talk," *New York Times*, October 29, 1945, 3.
32. Ibid.
33. Ibid.
34. Elizabeth Spalding, *The First Cold Warrior: Harry Truman, Containment and the Remaking of Liberal Internationalism* (Lexington: University Press of Kentucky, 2006), 27.
35. James Ramsden, "Mr. Churchill Goes to Fulton," in James W. Muller, *Churchill's "Iron Curtain" Speech Fifty Years Later* (Columbia: University of Missouri Press, 1999), 40.
36. Leahy JCS, US Embassy London to Leahy, November 24, 1945. Also see: Winant to Leahy, December 31, 1945.
37. Martin Gilbert, *"Never Despair": Winston S. Churchill, 1945–1965* (London: Heinemann, 1988), 180–82.
38. For a text of the address see: http://soviethistory.msu.edu/1947–2/cold-war/cold-war-texts/stalin-election-speech/.
39. Leahy Diary, February 10, 1946.
40. Robert A. Pollard, "The National Security State Reconsidered: Truman and Economic Containment, 1945–1950," in James Lacey, ed. *The Truman Presidency* (Cambridge, UK: Cambridge University Press, 1991), 210.
41. US Department of State, Office of the Historian, Kennan and Containment 1947, Accessible at: https://history.state.gov/milestones/1945–1952/kennan.
42. For a typical example of how the Long Telegram has been put on a pedestal, see: Denise M. Bostdorff, *Proclaiming the Truman Doctrine: The Cold War Call to Arms* (College Station: Texas A&M University Press, 2008), 23, 40–41.
43. Leahy Diary, May 6, 1947.
44. Elsey, *An Unplanned Life*, 137.
45. Clark Clifford Oral History, Truman Library online, April 13, 1970, 89, https://www.trumanlibrary.org/oralhist/cliford2.htm#89.
46. See Prologue.
47. Winston Churchill Papers, Chur 2/4, Churchill to Prime Minister, March 7, 1946.
48. Gilbert, *"Never Despair,"* 197.
49. Leahy Diary, March 5, 1946.
50. Ibid., March 3, 1946. This entry is a real problem. David Reynolds, an excellent historian, uses it to claim that Leahy did not suggest any changes. David Reynolds, *From World War to Cold War: Churchill, Roosevelt and the International History of the 1940s* (Oxford, UK: Oxford University Press, 2006), 262. Actually, what Leahy says was more subtle than that—the "find no fault" comment.
51. The Churchill Centre maintains an online copy of the Fulton Speech, which can be accessed here: http://www.winstonchurchill.org/resources/speeches/1946–1963-elder-statesman/120-the-sinews-of-peace. The mention of American military men occurs early in the speech in chapters 6 and 10.
52. Paul Addison, *Churchill: The Unexpected Hero* (Oxford, UK: Oxford University Press, 2005), 222.
53. David Dilks, *Churchill and Company: Allies and Rivals in War and Peace* (London: I. B. Tauris, 2012), 225.
54. Churchill Mss., Chur 2/4, Churchill to Prime Minister, March 7, 1946.
55. Leahy NHHC, WSC to Leahy, May 5, 1948. This letter was part of a series of letters that passed between Leahy and Churchill at this time, mostly about giving Churchill approval to discuss issues sensitive to the US government in one of his many books: Leahy JCS, Leahy to Truman, May 11, 1948.

Chapter 27: PERSONAL SNOOPER

1. Leahy Diary, January 14, 1946.
2. Ibid., June 27, 1946.
3. Eben A. Ayers and Robert H. Ferrell, *Truman in the White House: The Diary of Eben A. Ayers* (Columbia: University of Missouri Press, 1991), 123.
4. Leahy Diary, January 24, 1946.
5. CIA Records, Remarks of the President, November 21, 1952. Also see: https://www.trumanlibrary.org/publicpapers/index.php?pid=2232.
6. NHHC Oral, Admiral Arthur McCollum Interview, 760.
7. Leahy Diary, August 20, 1944.
8. Ibid., January 10, 1944.

9. Leahy NHHC, Memo for Marshall, King, and Arnold, March 25, 1944 (signed by Mc-Farland, authorized by Leahy).
10. Leahy JCS, Leahy for JCS to Roosevelt, August 28, 1944.
11. Ibid., Roosevelt to Leahy, May 10, 1944.
12. Ibid., Roosevelt to Leahy, March 29, 1945.
13. Leahy Diary, September 7, 1942.
14. Ibid., March 27, 1945.
15. Ibid., September 28, 1944.
16. Ibid., June 14, 1945.
17. Leahy JCS, Leahy to Truman, August 22, 1944.
18. Ibid. Kim Gu, as he is now called, was a leader in the Korean Independence movement who was nicknamed "the Assassin" He was tailor-made to work with Donovan. See: Hugh Dyson Walker, *East Asia: A New History* (Bloomington, IN: Author House, 2012), 605
19. The CIA maintains an online history, which amazingly mentions Leahy not at all. However, it is very clear on Truman's distaste toward Donovan and the OSS. See: https://www.cia.gov/library/center-for-the-study-of-intelligence/kent-csi/vol20no1/html/v20i1a02p_0001.htm.
20. CIA Records, Truman to Byrnes, September 20, 1945. Also see: http://www.presidency.ucsb.edu/ws/?pid=60673.
21. The JCS had been contemplating a new intelligence service plan for a while, from 1944.
22. Leahy NHHC, Leahy for JCS to Forrestal and Stimson, September 19, 1945.
23. CIA Records, Leahy for JCS to Forrestal and Stimson, September 19, 1945.
24. Dean Acheson, *Present at the Creation: My Years at the State Department* (New York: W. W. Norton, 1969), 160–61. Acheson was aware that the rejection of the State Department plan put Leahy in a uniquely powerful position over US intelligence.
25. Clark Clifford Mss., Box 12, Souers to Clifford, December 27, 1945.
26. Leahy NHHC, Leahy memo in regard to Harry Dexter White case, November 1953. This memorandum is an excellent example of just how controlled Leahy could be. The real details end in May 1945, after which Leahy started receiving regular reports of spying in the US government.
27. Bruce Craig, "A Matter of Espionage: Alger Hiss, Harry Dexter White and Igor Gouzenko—The Canadian Connection Reassessed," *Intelligence and National Security* 15, no 2, 213.
28. Ibid., 215.
29. Leahy Diary, November 28, 1945.
30. Ibid., January 1, 1946.
31. Ayers and Ferrell, *Truman in the White House*, 203.
32. Robert L. Messer, *The End of the Alliance: James F. Byrnes, Roosevelt, Truman and the Origins of the Cold War* (Chapel Hill: University of North Carolina Press, 1982), 119. Also see: Randall B. Woods and Howard Jones, *Dawning of the Cold War: The United States' Quest for Order* (Athens: University of Georgia Press, 1991), 87.
33. Byrnes was in London from September 4, 1945, until October 8, 1945, and then again from January 7, 1946, until January 25, 1946. He was in Moscow from December 12, 1945, until December 29, 1945.
34. Charles Bohlen, *Witness to History: 1929–1969* (New York: W. W. Norton, 1973), 250–51. See also H. F. Matthews Papers, Princeton University Special Collections, Unpublished Memoirs, 645.
35. Leahy Diary, September 21, 1945. Leahy kept a copy of the teletype conversation with Byrnes in his diary, one presumes because he was so unimpressed with the situation Byrnes has brought about.
36. Matthews, Unpublished Memoirs, 640–41.
37. Leahy Diary, December 11, 1945.
38. Ibid., December 12, 1945.
39. Robert H. Ferrell, ed. *Off the Record: The Private Papers of Harry S. Truman* (Columbia: University of Missouri Press, 1997), 75.
40. James Byrnes, *Speaking Frankly* (New York: Harper Brothers, 1947), 237.
41. Jonathan Daniels, *The Man from Independence* (London: Victor Gollancz, 1951), 310.
42. John Lewis Gaddis, *The United States and the Origins of the Cold War, 1941–1947* (New York: Columbia University Press, 2000), 287–88.
43. Truman Oral Online, Connelly Interview, November 28, 1967, 98. https://www.trumanlibrary.org/oralhist/connly1.htm#98.

44. Robert J. Donovan, *Conflict and Crisis: The Presidency of Harry Truman, 1945–1948* (Columbia: University of Missouri Press, 1996), 160.
45. Leahy Diary, December 29, 1945.
46. Ibid., January 30–31, 1946.
47. George Elsey, *An Unplanned Life: A Memoir by George McKee Elsey* (Columbia: University of Missouri Press, 2005), 136.
48. CIA Records, NIA minutes, February 5, 1946.
49. Ibid., 1.

CHAPTER 28: PRIORITIES

1. Drew Pearson, "The Washington Merry-Go-Round," *Washington Post*, February 12, 1946, 10.
2. Bert Andrews, "Leahy Denies War on Byrnes or His Policy," *New York Herald Tribune*, March 16, 1946.
3. The War and State Departments helped produce a joint statement at the beginning of the Marshall Mission. It didn't talk openly about the plan to bring the Communists into a coalition but spoke of the need for a Chinese unity government. Truman Mss., Box 151, "US Policy Towards China," undated but produced for the announcement of Marshall's departure to China.
4. Leahy Diary, March 15, 1946.
5. Jay Taylor, *The Generalissimo: Chiang Kai-shek and the Struggle for Modern China* (Cambridge, MA: Harvard University Press, 2009), 349–58.
6. Chao Hsiang-ke and Lin Hsiao-ting, "Beyond the Carrot and the Stick: The Political Economy of US Military Aid to China, 1945–1951," *Journal of Modern Chinese History* 5, no. 2 (2011), 203–4.
7. Leahy JCS, Marshall to Truman, August 17, 1946.
8. Sumner Welles, *Seven Decisions That Changed History* (New York: Harper, 1951), 208.
9. Leahy NHHC, Notes of China Timeline, August 11, 1946, 15.
10. Leahy Diary, February 16, 1946.
11. Ibid., April 1, 1946.
12. Elsey Mss., Box 1, Memorandum, November 30, 1945.
13. Leahy Diary, April 25, 1946
14. Ibid., October 10, 1946.
15. Truman Mss., Box 213, Souers to Leahy, May 7, 1946.
16. Leahy Diary, April 26, 1946. Eisenhower wrote to Truman the following day still arguing for Bonesteel.
17. Truman Mss., Box 213, Leahy Memo for Truman, May 9, 1946.
18. Leahy Diary, June 8, 1946.
19. NIA minutes, July 17, 1946, 3. Leahy did not want the CIA's budget to be publicly scrutinized as long as the NIA had the total oversight he expected for it. Also see: NIA Minutes, October 16, 1946, 2–3.
20. Ibid., 2. The intelligence advisory board was a new bureaucratic element within the CIA that Vandenberg was pressing to give the organization more overall control over US intelligence collection. It was to help centralize the activities of the intelligence efforts of the various government departments (State, War, Navy, etc.).
21. NIA minutes, October 16, 1946, 2–3.
22. Leahy JCS, Hoover to Leahy, August 23, 1946.
23. Ibid., Leahy to Hoover, September 4, 1946.
24. Vannevar Bush Mss., Box 59, Spaatz to Bush June 12, 1946; Patterson to Bush, June 20, 1946.
25. Leahy NHHC, Eisenhower to Leahy, Nimitz, and Spaatz, April 3, 1946.
26. Ibid., Leahy to Rosenman, December 14, 1945.
27. Ibid., Clifford to Truman, May 13, 1946.
28. Ibid., "Comment on the Majority Report of the 'Joint Chiefs of Staff Special Committee' on the Reorganization of the Departments Charged with the National Defense," October 1945.
29. Elsey Mss., Box 93, Handwritten notes, December 18, 1945.
30. Forrestal Diary, May 13, 1946.
31. Ibid. See also: Walter Mills, ed. *The Forrestal Diaries: The Inner History of the Cold War* (London, Cassel & Co., 1952), 164.

32. Leahy JCS, Draft Letter to President, included after October 22, 1945, Leahy/JCS memo for Secretaries of War and Navy.
33. Ibid., Leahy Memorandum for the President, October 23, 1945.
34. Leahy Diary, November 14, 1945. I think Leahy meant to write "Anglo-American" or "American-British" as opposed to the redundant "Anglo-British."
35. Leahy Diary, April 3, 1946.
36. For a copy of the Army Day Speech see: http://www.presidency.ucsb.edu/ws/?pid=12625.
37. Leahy Diary, January 12, 1946. Three pages of transcript were kept by Leahy.
38. Groves Memorandum, January 2, 1946, "Foreign Policy Aspects of United States Development of Atomic Energy." Available from FRUS online at: http://digital.library.wisc.edu/1711.dl/FRUS.FRUS1946v01.
39. NIA minutes, August 21, 1946, 3–4.
40. Leahy NHHC, Leahy to JCS Secretary, July 2, 1946.
41. NIA minutes, August 21, 1946, 3–4; Also see: NIA minutes, September 25, 1946, 2–3.

CHAPTER 29: COLD WAR

1. Arthur Krock, "His Ideas Stronger Since Byrnes Left, Believed a Factor in Foreign Policy," *New York Times*, March 26, 1947, 4.
2. Forrestal Diary, July 3, 1946.
3. Leahy Diary, May 28, 1946.
4. Ibid.
5. Ibid., May 21, 1946.
6. Clark Clifford, *Counsel to the President: A Memoir* (New York: Random House, 1991), 111. Byrnes, whose ego was much bigger than Leahy's, was much angrier that he had not been asked to write the report.
7. Ibid., 111–12.
8. George Elsey, *An Unplanned Life: A Memoir of George McKee Elsey* (Columbia: University of Missouri Press, 2005), 143.
9. Clifford Mss., Box 15, Clifford to Leahy, July 18, 1946 (formal letter asking for JCS report), and July 18, 1946 (formal letter asking for CIA response).
10. Elsey Mss., Box 63, "Recommended Military Policy to Be Followed by the United States with Respect to the Soviet Union," signed by Leahy for the JCS, undated.
11. Clifford Mss., Box 15, CIA report, *Soviet Foreign and Military Policy*, July 23, 1946.
12. Clifford Mss., Box 15, Patterson to Truman, July 27, 1946.
13. The only copy of the document that I was able to find was in Leahy Mss., NHHC. It is an undated piece, but in the file with the other papers he collected as part of the Clifford/Elsey memorandum.
14. Leahy NHHC, Undated Memorandum, "For Adm File."
15. Robert Pollard, "The National Security State Reconsidered," in Michael James Lacey, ed., *The Truman Presidency* (Cambridge, UK: Cambridge University Press, 1991), 212.
16. The copy of the report consulted for this chapter was in Leahy Mss., NHHC, Report by Special Counsel to the President, "American Relations with the Soviet Union," September 1946. Chapter 6 has the policy recommendations. Others have commented on the close connection between the rhetoric of the report and the later Truman Doctrine; see: Lawrence J. Hass, *Harry and Arthur: Truman, Vandenberg and the Partnership That Created the Free World* (Lincoln, NE: Potomac Books, 2016), 114–15.
17. Leahy Diary, July 29, 1946.
18. Columbia Oral, Henry Wallace Interview, 3539.
19. Truman Library, documents online: https://www.trumanlibrary.org/whistlestop/study_collections/trumanpapers/psf/longhand/index.php?documentVersion=both&documentid=hst-psf_naid735240-02.
20. Leahy Diary, September 18, 1946. Leahy says in his diary that he told Truman that the government could not keep both Byrnes and Wallace in the administration.
21. Truman Mss., Box 195, White House Statement, September 20, 1946.
22. Robert L. Messer, *The End of the Alliance: James F. Byrnes, Roosevelt, Truman and the Origins of the Cold War* (Chapel Hill: University of North Carolina Press, 1982), 215.
23. *United States News*, April 11, 1947, 64.
24. Harry S. Truman, *Memoirs, Volume 2: Years of Trial and Hope* (Garden City, NY: Doubleday, 1955), 100–1.

25. Melvyn Leffler, *A Preponderance of Power: National Security, the Truman Administration and the Cold War* (Stanford: Stanford University Press, 1992), 145; also see: Robert J. McMahon, *Dean Acheson and the Creation of the American World Order* (Dulles, VA: Potomac Books, 2009).
26. Truman Library Online, Description of February 27, 1947, meeting: https://www.truman library.org/whistlestop/study_collections/doctrine/large/documents/index.php?doc umentid=8–4&pagenumber=3.
27. Leahy was spot-on about Acheson, who, when China was falling, seemed relatively unconcerned. The undersecretary of state believed Japan as an industrialized power was far more important to the United States: John Lamberton Harper, *The Cold War* (Oxford, UK: Oxford University Press, 2011), 91.
28. Leahy Diary, February 27, 1947.
29. Ibid., March 6, 1947.
30. Ibid., March 7, 1947.
31. There is an online copy of minutes of the March 7, 1947, cabinet meeting available through the Truman Library. See: https://www.trumanlibrary.org/calendar/cabinet _minutes/index.php?date=1947-03-07.
32. Ibid.
33. Ibid.
34. Leahy Diary, March 10, 1947.
35. In this way, Leahy was actually closer to some Cold War revisionist historians. He never seemed particularly worried about Soviet intervention in the Greek Civil War on the side of the Communists, nor did he play down the ability of Turkey to be a military block to the USSR. For a discussion of the revisionist views on the Greece-Turkey question (from a critical angle), see: Robert Ferrell, *Harry S. Truman and the Cold War Revisionists* (Columbia: University of Missouri Press, 2006), 29–31.
36. Leahy NHHC, "The Military Situation in Greece and Turkey at the Present Time," April 1947.
37. Arthur Krock Mss., Box 1, Notes of Marshall and Leahy. There are two separate dates: one is March 1947 and the other is May–June 1947. It was probably March.
38. Ibid.
39. Ibid.
40. Leahy Diary, August 16, 1947.

CHAPTER 30: KEY WEST

1. There are copies of all of Truman's official travel logs, including the one describing this trip to Key West, at: https://www.trumanlibrary.org/calendar/travel_log/.
2. Leahy microfilm, NHHC, Atwood to Leahy, dated October 4 (no year given—but definitely post–World War II).
3. Truman Oral Online, John Steelman Interview, March 1, 1996, 130–31. https://www .trumanlibrary.org/oralhist/steelm2b.htm#130.
4. Ibid., 225.
5. Truman Oral Online, Louis Renfrow Interview, March 12, 1971, 63, https://www.truman library.org/oralhist/renfrow.htm.
6. Truman Oral Online, Phileo Nash Interview, 262–63, https://www.trumanlibrary .org/oralhist/nash6.htm#262.
7. Truman Library, online documents, Truman to Bess, November 22, 1946, https://www .trumanlibrary.org/whistlestop/study_collections/trumanpapers/fbpa/index.php?docu mentid=HST-FBP_15–57_01&documentYear=1946&documentVersion=both.
8. Truman Oral Online, William Rigdon Interview, July 16, 1970, 23, https://www.truman library.org/oralhist/rigdon.htm#23.
9. Leahy NHHC, Leahy to Powell, January 2, 1952.
10. Truman Oral Online, William Rigdon Interview, July 16, 1970, 23.
11. Leahy Diary, November 21, 1946.
12. Truman Oral Online, Eben Ayers Interview, May 16, 1967, 173, https://www.truman library.org/oralhist/ayers5.htm#172.
13. Letter from Harry Truman to Bess Truman, July 4, 1947, Truman Papers, Family, Business and Personal Affairs. Accessible online at: http://www.trumanlibrary.org/whis tlestop/study_collections/trumanpapers/fbpa/index.php?documentVersion=transcript& documentid=HST-FBP_15–76_01.

14. Truman Oral Online, Roger Tubby Interview, February 10, 1970, 98, https://www.tru manlibrary.org/oralhist/tubby.htm.
15. Truman Mss., online, Truman to Bess, September 26, 1947, https://www.trumanli brary.org/whistlestop/study_collections/trumanpapers/fbpa/index.php?documentid =HST-FBP_16-020_01&documentYear=1947&documentVersion=both.
16. NHHC Oral, Albert Murray Interview, 120–1.
17. Leahy NHHC, Hassett to Leahy, October 11, 1948.
18. Leahy NHHC, Rear Admiral Leland Lovette to Leahy, September 8, 1947.
19. Leahy NHHC, Wedemeyer to Leahy, April 28, 1947.
20. Leahy NHHC, Nimitz to Leahy, August 28, 1958.
21. Leahy Diary, October 5, 1946.
22. Columbia Oral, Braden Spruille Interview, vol. 3, part 2, 1253–55.
23. NHHC Oral, Adm. Charles K. Duncan Interview, 272.
24. Leahy described the trip in great detail, devoting ten pages of his diary to it.
25. Leahy NHHC, Videla to Leahy, May 30, 1947.
26. The most detailed description is in Henry A. Adams, *Witness to Power: The Life of Fleet Admiral William D. Leahy* (Annapolis: Naval Institute Press, 1985), 326–28.

CHAPTER 31: ON THE OUTSIDE

1. Harry S. Truman, *Memoirs, Volume 2: Years of Trial and Hope* (Garden City, NY: Doubleday, 1955), 58–59.
2. Clifford Mss., Box 11, "Draft: Directive."
3. NIA minutes, July 17, 1946, 2.
4. Jay Taylor, *The Generalissimo: Chiang Kai-shek and the Struggle for Modern China* (Cambridge, MA: Harvard University Press, 2009), 372–73.
5. Leahy Diary, July 7, 1947.
6. Taylor, *The Generalissimo*, 357.
7. Truman Mss., Box 151, Wedemeyer to Secretary of Army, August 8, 1947.
8. Leahy NHHC, "Notes of China," 15.
9. Leahy Diary, October 19, 1947; Truman Mss., Box 177, Wedemeyer to Forrestal, March 29, 1948.
10. Leahy NHHC, "Notes of China." The first entry is for March 1943 and the last for December 1947.
11. Tang Tsou, *America's Failure in China, 1941–1950* (Chicago: University of Chicago Press, 1963), 474–75.
12. Roger B. Jeans, *The Marshall Mission to China, 1945–1947: The Letters and Diary of Colonel John Hart Caughey* (Plymouth, MA: Rowman and Littlefield, 2011), 34.
13. Justin Hart, *Empire of Ideas: The Origins of Public Diplomacy and the Transformation of US Foreign Policy* (Oxford, UK: Oxford University Press, 2013), 149–50.
14. Chao Hsiang-ke and Lin Hsiao-ting, "Beyond the Carrot and the Stick: The Political Economy of US Military Aid to China, 1945–1951," *Journal of Modern Chinese History* 5, no. 2 (2011), 207.
15. Aiyaz Husain, *Mapping the End of Empire: American and British Visions of the Post-War World* (Cambridge, UK: Cambridge University Press, 2014), 268–69.
16. Leahy JCS, Leahy to Forrestal, October 10, 1947.
17. Ibid.
18. Leahy NHHC, Leahy for JCS to Forrestal, July 27, 1948. This document has just been declassified for this book.
19. Betty Beale, "Miss Leahy Bows to Society," *Washington Star,* December 31, 1947, B3.
20. Leahy Diary, April 17, 1948.
21. Ibid., March 14, 1948.
22. Truman Oral Online, Wilfrid McNeil Interview, June 19, 1972, 63, https://www.tru manlibrary.org/oralhist/mcneilwj.htm.
23. Leahy NHHC, "Notes for Friday, Opening for Meeting," March 11, 1948.
24. Leahy NHHC, Wedemeyer to Leahy, March 16, 1948.
25. Clifford Mss., Box 11. In the letter that Forrestal sent to Truman announcing the decision, Leahy was the only member of the JCS mentioned. Forrestal to Truman, March 27, 1948.
26. Clark Clifford, *Counsel to the President: A Memoir* (New York: Random House, 1991), 3–7.

27. In Clifford's memoirs there is no mention of Leahy being in the room and Leahy's diary makes no mention of him being there.
28. Leahy Diary, May 14, 1948.
29. "UMT Is Attacked by Einstein Group," *New York Times*, January 19, 1948.
30. Leahy Diary, January 29, 1948.
31. Ibid., January 19, 1948.
32. Leahy NHHC, Recommendation by Admiral Leahy, May 1947 (specific day is obscured by hole punch).
33. The FBI's website has a definition of WMDs according to US law (18 USC §2332 a). It is: "(A) any destructive device as defined in section 921 of this title (i.e., explosive device); (B) any weapon that is designed or intended to cause death or serious bodily injury through the release, dissemination, or impact of toxic or poisonous chemicals, or their precursors; (C) any weapon involving a biological agent, toxin, or vector (as those terms are defined in section 178 of this title); (D) any weapon that is designed to release radiation or radioactivity at a level dangerous to human life." See: https://www.fbi.gov/about-us/investigate/terrorism/wmd/wmd_faqs.
34. Leahy Diary, July 10, 1945.
35. David Rosenberg, "The Origins of Overkill: Nuclear Weapons and American Strategy, 1945–1960," in Lori Lyn Bogle, ed., *The Cold War* (New York: Routledge, 2001), 2: 53.
36. Leahy Diary, November 12, 1947.
37. Leahy NHHC, Leahy memo for JCS, "Control and Direction of Strategic Atomic Operations," March 26, 1948.
38. Leahy Diary, May 12, 1948.
39. Leahy NHHC, Leahy Memo for JCS, JCS 1844/4, May 13, 1948.
40. *FRUS*, Vol. 1, Part 2, 1948, Royall Memo, May 19, 1948, 572. Accessible online at: http://digicoll.library.wisc.edu/cgi-bin/FRUS/FRUS-idx?type=header&id=FRUS.FRUS1948v01p2.
41. For examples of statements that Halfmoon was an approval of atomic warfare, see: David Alan Rosenberg, "American Atomic Strategy and the Hydrogen Bomb Decision," *Journal of American History* 66, no. 1 (June 1979), 68; also, Harry Borowski, "A Narrow Victory: The Berlin Blockade and the American Military Response," *Air University Review*, July–August 1981. Accessible online at: http://www.airpower.maxwell.af.mil/airchronicles/aureview/1981/jul-aug/borowski.htm. For an example of the assumption that Truman was responsible for the conventional alternative in Halfmoon, see: S. David Broscious, "Longing for International Control, Banking on American Superiority: Harry S. Truman's Approach to Nuclear Weapons," in John Lewis Gaddis et al., eds., *Cold War Statesmen Confront the Bomb: Nuclear Diplomacy Since 1945* (Oxford, UK: Oxford University Press, 1999), 31.

CHAPTER 32: FADING AWAY

1. Truman Mss., PSF, Box 177, NSC minutes, 16th Meeting, July 22, 1948.
2. Leahy, JCS Chairman's Files, RG218, Landry to Leahy, July 16, 1948.
3. Leahy JCS, Hillenkoetter to Truman, June 30, 1948.
4. Kenneth Condit, *The Joint Chiefs of Staff and National Policy: Volume 2, 1947–1949* (Washington, DC: Joint History Office, 1996), 70–71. Available online: http://www.dtic.mil/doctrine/doctrine/jcs_nationalp.htm.
5. Leahy JCS, Memorandum of record, US and British chiefs of staff meeting, June 30, 1948.
6. Leahy Diary, June 30, 1948.
7. Leahy JCS, Memorandum of record, US and British chiefs of staff meeting, June 30, 1948, 1.
8. Ibid., 3.
9. Leahy Diary, October 21, 1948.
10. Leahy JCS, Hillenkoetter to Truman, July 6, 1948.
11. Forrestal Diary, July 28, 1948.
12. There is some real confusion on NSC-30. It has been argued that NSC-30 authorized a US first strike in case of war with the USSR. See: Gregg Herken, *The Winning Weapon: The Atomic Bomb in the Cold War, 1945–1950* (Princeton: Princeton University Press,

1988), 270–2. However, the final draft of the document did not say that, as the sections calling for a first strike were removed. The Office of the Historian, State Department, has digitized the FRUS section on NSC-30. While it is clear that the army and air force, supported by their civilian heads, were pushing for clear instructions, Truman in the end refused to give them. See: https://history.state.gov/historicaldocuments/frus1948v 01p2/d42#fn1.

13. Leahy Diary, October 4, 1948.
14. Truman Mss., Box 176, Gleason to Truman, October 23, 1952. The president was sent a memorandum about US atomic policy by the NSC on this date, which explicitly admitted that NSC-30 was not a first-strike doctrine.
15. Condit, *The Joint Chiefs of Staff and National Policy,* 158.
16. Leahy Diary, October 16, 1948.
17. Truman Mss., Box 177, Souers to Truman, June 2, 1948.
18. Truman Mss., Box 177, NSC Minutes, 13th Meeting, June 17, 1948, 1.
19. Richard Immerman and Timothy Sayle, "The CIA, Its Origin, Transformation and Crisis of Identity from Harry S. Truman to Barack Obama," in Mary Ann Heiss and Michael Hogan, eds., *Origins of the National Security State and the Legacy of Harry S. Truman* (Kirksville MO: Truman State University Press, 2015), 102–4.
20. Alvin Shuster, "CIA Circulates History of Itself," *New York Times,* July 9, 1961.
21. Leahy Diary, December 15, 1948.
22. Truman Mss., Box 266, Constantine Brown news clipping, "This Changing World."
23. Truman Mss., Box 266, Leahy to Truman, September 20, 1948.
24. There are copies of Leahy's letter to the president and Truman's reply, as well as Clifford's letters to Brown and Leahy, kept in the Leahy Diary between the entries September 23 and September 24, 1948.
25. Truman Mss., Box 266, Truman to Leahy, September 27, 1948.
26. Truman Mss., Box 266, Clifford to Leahy, September 23, 1948.
27. Truman Mss., Box 266, Clifford to Brown, September 23, 1948.
28. Pearson, "The Washington Merry-Go-Round," B15.
29. Leahy Diary, November 5, 1946.
30. Ibid., November 27, 1948.
31. Truman Oral Online, Louis Renfrow Interview, March 12, 1971, 63, https://www.tru manlibrary.org/oralhist/renfrow.htm.
32. Leahy Diary, December 14, 1948.
33. Leahy NHHC, Leahy to Powell, June 6, 1949.
34. Leahy Diary, December 28, 1948.

CHAPTER 33: THE FORGOTTEN MAN

1. Dave Zieman, "Admiral Leahy, Alone, Recalls Role in War," *Washington Star,* September 24, 1958, A27.
2. Ibid.
3. Jeffrey G. Barlow, *Revolt of the Admirals: The Fight for Naval Aviation, 1945–1950* (Washington, DC: Department of the Navy, 1994), 250–54.
4. Henry A. Adams, *Witness to Power: The Life of Fleet Admiral William D. Leahy* (Annapolis: Naval Institute Press, 1985), 339.
5. Barlow, *Revolt of the Admirals,* 269–70.
6. Leahy NHHC, Leahy to Powell, July 17, 1950.
7. Leahy NHHC, Leahy to Powell, January 2, 1952.
8. Leahy NHHC, Leahy to Hart, November 24, 1954.
9. Leahy NHHC, Leahy to Reece, November 23, 1951.
10. Adams, *Witness to Power,* 332.
11. Ferdinand Kuhn, "Leahy 'Notes' Reveal His Impact as 'Mystery Man' of White House," *Washington Post,* March 19, 1950, B6.
12. Orville Prescott, "Books of the Times," *New York Times,* March 20, 1950.
13. Leahy NHHC, Leahy to Brandt, September 24, 1954.
14. Leahy Diary, July 14, 1950.
15. Ibid., July 13 and 17, 1950.
16. Between 1951 and 1953, the US deployed on average between 200,000 and 250,000 army troops and the 1st Divison US Marine Corps in Korea. For army deployment, see: Office of the Chief of Military History, *Statistical Data on Strength and Casualties for*

Korean War and Vietnam, 1965, accessible online at: http://www.nj.gov/military/korea/stats.pdf; for Marine Corps see: Meid, Pat, *US Marine Operations in Korea 1950–1953: Vol V, Operation in West Korea* (Washington, DC: Historical Divison USMC, 1973), 573, accessible online at: https://www.marines.mil/Portals/59/Publications/U.S.%20Marine%20Operations%20in%20Korea%201950–1953%20Vol%205_Operations%20in%20West%20Korea%20%20PCN%2019000264000.pdf?ver=2017–04–26–105935–777.

17. Leahy Diary, June 26, 1950.
18. Leahy NHHC, Leahy to Powell, June 28, 1950.
19. Leahy Diary, September 12, 1950.
20. Dean Acheson Papers, Secretary of State Files, Memorandum of Conversation with the President, June 30, 1949. Available online at: https://www.trumanlibrary.org/whistlestop/study_collections/achesonmemos/view.php?documentid=65-4_42&documentYear=1949&documentVersion=both.
21. Leahy Diary, September 22, 1950.
22. The details of this trip are recorded in his diary entry for July 12, 1950.
23. Leahy NHHC, McCarthy to Leahy, July 5, 1951.
24. Adams, *Witness to Power*, 342.
25. Leahy Diary, August 1, 1952.
26. Ibid., August 11, 1951.
27. Ibid., August 19, 1951.
28. Leahy NHHC, Leahy to Sherwood, December 7, 1949.
29. Leahy NHHC, Leahy to Hassett, May 4, 1953.
30. Elsey Mss., Box 103, Elsey to Tannewald, June 27, 1951.
31. Leahy NHHC, "Notes on Yalta Conference"; Leahy, *Wisconsin Magazine of History* (Winter 1954–55).
32. Leahy NHHC, Leahy to Byrd, June 22, 1953.
33. Leahy Diary, November 12, 1952.
34. Leahy NHHC. There is a logbook of visitors to Leahy during the last year of his life. Truman came by with Harry Vaughan on May 3. After that, it was pretty quiet until early July. Then the news must have gotten out that Leahy was in extremis, as a few people came by each day, often family or former staff members. His last recorded visitor was at 5:30 p.m. on July 17, 1959.
35. "Fleet Admiral Leahy Dies at 84; President's Chief of Staff in War," *New York Times*, July 21, 1959.

EPILOGUE

1. "Fleet Admiral Leahy Dies at 84; President's Chief of Staff in War," *New York Times*, July 21, 1959.
2. "William D. Leahy," *Washington Post*, July 23, 1959, A18.
3. "Marshall Buried After Simple Rite," *New York Times*, October 21, 1959, 3.

Index

Note: Page numbers in *italics* refer to a table.

Abetz, Otto, 147
Acheson, Dean
  and China, 505n27
  and Greece, 404
  and intelligence operations, 502n24
  and lend-lease deal, 309, 311
  and Truman Doctrine, 408
African Americans, 9
Afrika Korps, 182, 211
aircraft carriers
  construction of, 88, 117, 283
  and Leahy's support of navy-run air
    wing, 97, 117
  modernization of, 116
  role of, in sea power, 115
  and war production strategies, 206, 207,
    209, 283
airpower, naval
  and air-defense weapons, 76
  and aviators' pay, 63, 67
  and battleships, 97
  development of, 62–63
  efficacy of, 63, 77
  and Guam base, 118–119, 477n32
  Leahy's attitudes toward, 76–77, 473n30
  Leahy's support of navy-run air wing, 76,
    97–98, 117–118, 422
  and naval buildup, 117–118
  and organization of US military, 422
  technological improvements in aircraft,
    76, 97, 117
  and war production strategies, 202, 203,
    204, 207, 209, *281*, 283
  See also aircraft carriers
Alanbrooke (formerly Sir Alan Brooke)
  and Cairo Conferences, 256, 263
  Leahy's impatience with, 227
  and Mediterranean theater, 237, 259
  and Operation Overlord, 259–260

  and Quebec Conference, 237–238,
    239–240
  and Tehran Conference, 259–260
  and Trident Conference, 226, 227–228
alcoholic beverages, consumption of, 42,
  63–64, 65, 72, 413–414
ambassador post of Leahy
  and anti-Semitism in Vichy France, 167
  and confidence in Allied victory, 162, 171
  and de Gaulle, 231
  and death of Leahy's wife, 175–176
  and embargo on oil shipments to Japan,
    155–156, 158
  and embassy staff members, 154
  and French Indochina, 148–149, 155,
    156–157, 158–160, 189
  Leahy appointed as, 143, 144, 145–147
  Leahy recalled, 172–173
  and Operation Barbarossa, 165–166
  and Pearl Harbor attack, 169–171
  and Vichy–Germany collaboration, 147–149,
    152–155, 157, 159, 162–165, 166–167,
    173–174
  and Weygand, 167–169
American Red Cross, 443
Andaman Islands, 255, 264
Annapolis. *See also* US Naval Academy
anti-Semitism, 167
Archambault, G. H., 149, 163
armed-robbery attempt, Leahy's escape
  from, 80
arms-control treaties, 61–62, 70, 71, 81, 114
Arnold, Henry "Hap"
  and Cairo Conferences, 253, 257
  and Casablanca Conference, 212, 216,
    218, 220
  and deployment on multiple fronts, 282
  end-of-war honors bestowed on, 360–361
  and FDR's inner circle, 194

Arnold, Henry "Hap" (*cont.*)
  health issues of, 361
  and Joint Chiefs of Staff, 188–189, 260
  Leahy's relationship with, 199–200
  light duty status of, 361
  and Operation Overlord, 278
  and Operation Torch (North Africa),
    190, 191
  and Pacific strategy, 290
  and plans to invade Japan, 344
  promotion of, 266
  strategic planning of, 182
  and war production strategies, 204, 205,
    206, 207
Arthur, Chester, 46
Ashland, Wisconsin, 6–7, 126, 469n3
atomic bombs
  bombing of Hiroshima and Nagasaki,
    357, 392
  and Churchill's "Iron Curtain"
    speech, 374
  and civilian casualties, 357, 358,
    359, 394
  FDR–Churchill meeting on, 296, 297, 299
  FDR's positions on, 324
  and first-strike doctrine, 392–393, 394,
    424–426, 430, 507n12, 508n14
  Interim Committee on, 341
  international prohibition on, 394
  Leahy's influence on US atomic policy,
    298, 300, 368, 424–426, 430–431,
    495n18
  Leahy's moral issues with, 298–299, 355,
    357–358, 426, 431
  Leahy's opposition to use of, 297–300,
    340–341, 343, 355, 392–393, 394, 423,
    495n18
  Leahy's reaction to Hiroshima, 358–359
  motives for dropping, 355–356
  and NSC-30, 430
  and plans to invade Japan, 347–348
  and Soviet Union, 355, 424, 425,
    426, 430
  study on fallout from, 393
  tests of, 348, 355
  Truman's enthusiasm for, 340–341,
    340n, 393
  and Truman's twelve points speech, 368,
    393, 455
  and United Nations, 381
Atomic Energy Commission, 394
Attlee, Clement, 354, 373, 393, 397
Austin, Bernard, 109–110
Australia, 20–21

Bad River Chippewa tribe, 126
Bailey, Josiah, 117
Bankhead, William, 116
banking system crisis of 1933, 82–83
Barker, A. W., 11
Barkley, Alben, 370
Barlin, Jorge, 22, 470n43

Baruch, Belle, 245, 269–270
Baruch, Bernard, 186, 209, 245,
  269, 274
battle force command, Leahy's assignment
  to, 93–94, 95, 96–97
Battle of El Alamein, 211
Battle of Iwo Jima, 342, 345
Battle of Okinawa, 294, 342, 345–346, 347
Battle of Santiago de Cuba, 14
Battle of Tsushima, 33
battleships
  and air control/supremacy, 121
  and aircraft, 97
  aircraft carriers' replacement of, 115
  buildup under Wilson, 55–56
  construction of, 70, 114–117
  dreadnoughts, 33, 55, 170
  gunnery ability of, 33, 114–115
  and Hughes' proposal (5-5-3 agreement),
    61–62
  Iowa class of, 116, 116n
  Leahy's focus on, 115, 116–117, 141, 206
  modernization of, 70
  and scout destroyers, 75–76
Bayard, Chevalier, 20
Ben-Gurion, David, 422
Benson, William, 45, 49, 55
Bentley, Elizabeth, 381
Berkner, Lloyd, 391
Berlin, Germany, 427–430
Bevin, Ernest, 397, 404
Bland, S. Otis, 117
Blandy, William, 394
Bohlen, Charles "Chip," 102, 263, 276
Bonesteel, Charles, 389–390, 503n16
Braden, Spruille, 415
Bradley, Omar, 421, 428, 430, 441
Brazil, 416
Bristol, Mark, 60, 60n, 76
Brooke, Sir Alan, 218. *See also* Alanbrooke
Brown, Constantine, 58, 118, 272, 321,
  432–433, 446
Brown, Wilson, 181, 330
Bullitt, William
  as ambassador to France, 144–145, 480n9
  FDR's relationship with, 269
  and Hopkins, 186
  and Truman's twelve points speech,
    366–367
  and Welles scandal, 242–245, 490n3
Bureau of Aeronautics, 91
Bureau of Navigation, chief of, 85,
  86–89, 91
Bureau of Ordnance, chief of, 68, 70–72, 76
Burma land route
  Britain's delays on, 215, 223, 224, 227, 228,
    231, 236–239, 255, 264
  and Cairo Conferences, 255
  postponement of operation, 264
  priority of, for Leahy, 215, 223, 228,
    492n45
  and Quebec Conference, 238, 239

and Roosevelt, 238, 255, 264
seized by Japan, 189
and Trident Conference, 227, 228, 236
Bush, Vannevar, 300, 340, 391
Butler, Smedley, 37
Byrd, Richard, 67
Byrnes, James
appointed secretary of state, 364
and atomic weapons, 341, 393, 394
and China, 387
and Churchill's "Iron Curtain" speech, 1, 2
FDR's relationship with, 106, 333
and intelligence operations, 380, 384
and Japan's surrender, 358
and Leahy, 366, 381–383, 384, 385,
386–387, 403, 502n35, 504n20
office of, 187n
and personnel controls committee, 209
and Potsdam Conference, 348, 350, 354
and presidential race of 1944, 273
and report on Soviet relations, 504n6
resignation of, 403
and Truman, 335
and Yalta Conference, 314

Cairo Conferences, 253–257, 263–264
Callaghan, Daniel, 127
Canada, 393
Caperton, William Banks, 44–45, 47
career of Leahy
diplomatic post (*see* ambassador post of
Leahy)
naval service (*see* naval career of Leahy)
political post (*see* Puerto Rico)
during World War II (*see* Chief of Staff
post)
See also political skills of Leahy
Caribbean, military base in, 140
Carney, Robert Bostwick, 109
Cary, G. H., 98
Casablanca Conference, 211–213,
216–220, 240
Central Intelligence Agency (CIA; initially
Central Intelligence Group)
and Berlin Crisis, 428
budget of, 390, 503n19
and Clifford Report, 400
and Cold War, 431
covert operations of, 431
directors of, 376, 380, 389–391 (*see also*
Souers, Sidney; Vandenberg, Hoyt)
and domestic surveillance, 391
Leahy's influence on, 376–377, 379–380,
417–418
Leahy's role in, 376–377, 384, 390, 431,
502n19
and National Intelligence Authority,
379–380, 384, 390–391
and Truman's briefings, 385
Chauvel, Jean, 155, 156–157
Chiang Kai-shek
and Axis advances into China, 301

and Cairo Conferences, 253, 255
correspondence of FDR with, 182
pressures placed on, 120
and Soviet relations, 319
and Stilwell's command, 301–302
and Truman administration, 406
undermined by US diplomats, 419
and US leadership, 387–388
and US's insistence on coalition
government, 387–388
chief of naval operations post of Leahy
(CNO), 100–130
and authority of Leahy, 109–110
and cabinet meetings of FDR, 106–107
and FDR–Leahy relationship, 104–106
and Guam base, 118–119, 477n32
and looming threat of war with
Germany, 121
and naval buildup, 114–118, 122–123, 141
and *Panay* crisis, 112–113, 115, 117–118
retirement from, 124, 129–130
and Second Sino-Japanese War, 106–109,
111–113, 119–120
and Soviet battleships, 103–104
and Tongue Point, Oregon, naval base,
104, 125
Chief of Staff to the Commander in Chief,
Army and Navy of the United States
appointment of, 178, 180
and atomic bombs (*see* atomic bombs)
authority of Leahy as, 220, 347, 352,
417–418
briefing FDR, 180–181, 183–184, 484n23,
493n57
briefing Truman, 329–330, 334, 364–365,
384–385, 411, 418, 420, 443
and Churchill's "Iron Curtain" speech,
1–3, 365, 371–374, 385, 501n50
and criticisms of Leahy, 423–424, 432
daily routine, 180–181
dual roles of, 178–180
and end of war, 358–359, 360–361
and FDR's correspondence, 220, 235, 272
and FDR's death, 324–327, 325n, 497n67
and FDR's health, 267, 268, 322n
and FDR's Map Room, 181, 181n, 194, 220
first week of, 182–183
influence in Roosevelt administration,
180, 195–196, 198, 200, 202, 220, 269,
274, 303–304, 308, 451n
influence in Truman administration, 386,
403, 410, 416, 417–418, 420, 423
intelligence (*see* intelligence operations)
and leadership style of Leahy,
196–197, 200
office of, 187
and organization of US military,
421–422
position discontinued by Leahy, 392
postwar role of, 364
power of Leahy as, 220, 222, 290, 308, 385
and praise of Leahy, 274

Chief of Staff (*cont.*)
  promotion to five-star fleet admiral, 266, 313, 492n2
  and proximity to FDR, 183–184
  and relative anonymity of Leahy, 278
  and respect for Leahy, 414–415
  retirement from post, 434 (*see also* retirement of Leahy)
  title, 179–180
  and Truman's Army Day address, 393
  and Truman's Navy Day address, 365, 367–371, 385
  Truman's relationship with, 334–335, 351–352, 375, 385
  and Truman's request for Leahy's continued service, 361–362
  See also specific historical events, including atomic bombs *and* World War II
Chile, 35, 415–416, 436
China
  aid needed by, 223, 227, 255, 387–388, 404–406, 418–419, 431, 442
  Boxer Rebellion, 18
  and Cairo Conferences, 255
  and Chinese Communist Party, 363, 387–388, 418, 431, 503n3
  and Four Policemen, 261
  government of (*see* Chinese Nationalist regime)
  and Japan's invasion of Manchuria, 77–78
  Japan's withdrawal from, 363
  Leahy's affection for, 33, 34–35, 36, 67
  Leahy's first trip to, 17–18
  and Leahy's wartime strategy, 215, 223
  and "Open Door" policy of US, 78
  and Operation Anakim, 223–225, 227–228, 236, 237–238, 239–240, 488n46
  road to (*see* Burma land route)
  and Second Sino-Japanese War, 106–109, 111–113, 119–120, 223
  Shanghai, 17, 18, 34, 107–109
  and Soviet support of Nationalists, 319
  and Stalin, 261
  and Stilwell, 301–303
  and Trident Conference, 225–228
  US relations with, 387–389
  Wedemeyer's ambassadorship, 418–419
Chinese Nationalist regime
  and Burmese road to China (*see* Burma land route)
  and Byrnes, 382
  and Chinese Communist Party, 363, 387, 418, 503n3
  collapse of, 431
  intelligence on, 120
  Leahy's support and sympathy for, 388, 405–406, 431
  Soviet support of, 319
  and Stilwell, 301–302
  and Trident Conference, 228

  and Truman administration, 406, 418–419, 503n3
  and US's arms embargo, 387–388, 418, 419, 442
  and US's insistence on coalition government, 387–389, 418
  vulnerability of, 120, 223–224, 419
  See also Chiang Kai-shek
Churchill, Winston
  and Allied strategic planning, 217, 487n16
  and Andaman Islands, 264
  and atomic bombs of US, 296, 297, 298, 299, 356
  and Cairo Conferences, 255, 256, 257, 263–264
  and Casablanca Conference, 212, 216, 217, 218
  and China, 224
  confidential telegrams to, 333
  and Edward, Duke of Windsor, 296
  FDR's correspondence with, 182
  and FDR's Map Room, 181
  and German surrender, 337–338
  health issues of, 398
  and Hopkins, 185
  "Iron Curtain" speech, 1–3, 365, 371–374, 385, 501n50
  and Italian naval assets, 268
  and Japan's surrender, 358
  language of, 259
  and Leahy, 296, 299–300, 353–354, 437
  and Mediterranean theater, 256, 261, 263
  and Morgenthau Plan, 294–296
  and Octagon Conference, 292–296
  and Operation Anakim, 236, 488n46
  and Operation Overlord, 260–261
  party honoring, 397–398
  and Potsdam Conference, 348–349, 353–354, 356, 358
  and Quebec Conference, 236, 238, 239
  removed from office, 354
  Rhodes invasion proposal of, 252
  on state of war in 1943, 230
  and Tehran Conference, 249, 262
  and Trident Conference, 225–229, 231
  and Truman's Navy Day address, 370–371
  and United Nations, 261, 319
  and Yalta Conference, 313, 315, 317, 318–321
civilian control of military, 91, 194, 302, 444
Clifford, Clark, 398–401, 409, 411, 423, 432, 433
Clifford Report, 398–401, 457–459
Cold War
  beginning of, 396–397, 403–404
  and Central Intelligence Agency, 431
  and Churchill's "Iron Curtain" speech, 1–3, 365, 371–372, 385
  and Clifford Report, 398–401, 457–459
  and containment policy, 372, 396, 401
  and Leahy's influence, 401–402, 408
  and "Long Telegram" of Kennan, 372

Index

and perceived vulnerability of Greece/
Turkey, 404–408, 505n35
rhetoric of, 365, 385
and Truman Doctrine, 396–397, 407–408
and Truman's twelve points speech, 367
Combined Chiefs of Staff
about, 188
and Berlin Crisis, 428–429
and British forces in Pacific theatre,
292–294
and Casablanca Conference, 217
first meeting of, 182
and Operation Torch (North Africa),
191–192
and Trident Conference, 225, 227, 228–229
and western front, 259
communism
capitalism's incompatibility with, 371,
401, 408
and Churchill's "Iron Curtain" speech, 373
and fears of Soviet threats, 404–408
in France, 165
Leahy's perspectives on, 58–59, 103n, 251,
363, 388, 401
and Truman Doctrine, 396–397, 407–408
Connelly, Matthew, 334, 383
Cunningham, Sir Andrew, 182, 192
Czechoslovakia, 121, 127–128

Daniels, Josephus, 42–43, 44, 46, 47, 64
Darlan, François
assassination of, 232–233
confidence in German victory, 152, 162
and embargo on oil shipments to Japan,
158–159
and Germany's Operation
Barbarossa, 166
Leahy's concerns about, 152–153
and Leahy's role in France, 152
and Leahy's warnings about
collaboration, 159, 173–174
and "Popeye" code name, 153, 481n31
and Protocols of Paris, 163–164
and Vichy collaboration policy, 152,
153–154, 157, 162–164, 166–167
D-Day. See Operation Overlord
de Gaulle, Charles
and Darlan's assassination, 232
and end of war, 339–340
French support for, 169, 483n39
and Giraud, 232–234
grandstanding of, 171–172
Joint Chiefs of Staff honored by, 360
Leahy's disdain for, 51, 169, 231–234, 276,
360, 437
in North Africa, 232–234
and Pétain, 169, 482n36
and Roosevelt, 218, 232
and Syrian agreement of Darlan, 164
Denfeld, Louis, 421, 428, 439
Dennison, Robert, 196–197
Dewey, George, 313n

Dewey, Thomas, 304–305, 432
Dill, Sir John, 182, 192
Donovan, William "Wild Bill," 182, 377,
378–379, 385
Dreyer, Frederic, 50
Dulles, Allen, 378, 431
Durham, R. C., 134–135

Eaker, Ira, 344, 346
Early, Stephen, 328
Eden, Anthony, 212, 325
Edison, Charles, 100–101, 109, 115
Egypt, 322, 397
Eighteenth Amendment to the US
Constitution, 63
Einstein, Albert, 297, 423–424, 432
Eisenhower, Dwight
and atomic bombs of US, 425
and CIA director, 389–390, 503n16
and civil administration of France, 268
and death of Marshall, 447–448
and German surrender, 337
and Joint Chiefs of Staff, 415
and Leahy's funeral, 447
Leahy's teasing of, 415
and Operation Overlord, 260, 277
postwar public reception of, 369
and presidential race of 1952, 445
and unification proposal, 392
and US policy toward France, 222
Elsey, George, 246, 276, 333–334, 398–400,
401, 446, 487n20
Emergency Banking Act (1933), 83
Estonia, 251

family of Leahy
birth of son, 30 (see also Leahy, William
Harrington)
and death of aunt, 94
family history composed for, 74–75
favors requested for, 274
grandchildren, 71, 126
homes of, 65, 69, 73, 183
parents, 5, 6, 7, 8, 24–25
and Patriot (dog), 65
and retirement of Leahy, 439–440
wife, 24–25 (see also Leahy, Louise
Harrington)
Fife, James, 196
finances of Leahy
bankruptcy, 79, 82, 126, 474n44
and Colusa County Bank stock, 68–69,
73–74, 79, 82, 83, 473n53
difficulties with, 73
and drop in home value, 73
and empathy for others, 79
finances of Leahy (con't)
and farm land in Colusa County, 68–69,
73, 79, 473n53
and financial security of military career, 8
and Great Depression, 73
at time of death, 5

Flynn, Edward J., 144, 314
Formosa, 279, 286, 288–289, 330, 451–452
Forrestal, James
    and atomic bombs of US, 425, 430
    and Berlin Crisis, 429
    and China, 419
    demands for Leahy's retirement, 432
    and Greece, 405
    influence of, 248, 490n30
    and intelligence operations, 379
    and Leahy's office in Pentagon, 438
    and Leahy's postwar role, 364
    Leahy's relationship with, 247–248
    and organization of US military, 422,
        506n25
    and plans to invade Japan, 344, 346
    Secretary of Defense post, 417, 421
    Secretary of the Navy post, 275
    strategic planning of, 184
    and Truman Doctrine, 408
    and Yalta Conference, 336
Four Policemen, 250, 261
France
    Allied invasion of (*see* Operation
        Overlord)
    and Allied strategic planning, 217, 218,
        225–226, 228
    "Appeasement" policy of, 127
    Bullitt's ambassadorship to, 144–145
    and Casablanca Conference, 218
    and despair of citizens, 151–152
    and French Communists, 165
    and German aggression, 130
    and Greco-Turkish War, 60
    imperialism of, 362–363
    Joint Chiefs of Staff honored by, 360
    Leahy's love of, 56–57
    Leahy's wartime role in (*see* ambassador
        post of Leahy)
    navy of, 148
    and Pétain's trial for treason, 338–339
    and Soviet relations, 319
    and Truman's Navy Day address, 370
    and US industrial production
        strategies, 207
    wartime government (*see* Vichy regime)
    and Washington Naval Conference, 61
    and World War I, 51
    See also de Gaulle, Charles
Franklin Roosevelt Memorial
    Foundation, 444
French Indochina, 148–149, 155, 156–157,
    158–160, 162, 189
French North Africa
    and Axis plans, 157
    and Cairo Conferences, 255
    and Casablanca Conference, 211–213
    and de Gaulle, 232–234
    FDR's concerns about, 148
    German advances on, 189
    and Giraud, 232–234
    and Joint Chiefs of Staff, 190–192

Leahy's position on invasion of, 223, *281*
    and Operation Torch, 182, 183, 190–192,
        198, 206, 211, 223, 231–232, 484n9
    surrender of German/Italian forces
        in, 225
    US aid sent to, 149, 168
    and Vichy–Germany collaboration, 158,
        159, 162–163
    vulnerability of, 149, 190–191
    and Weygand, 168–169
Fullam, William, 40

gambling, Leahy's, 64, 65, 412–413
Garner, John Nance, 106
General Board, 76–77, 91
Geneva Naval Conference of 1927, 70
George VI, King of Great Britain, 397
Germany
    atomic weapon development of, 297–298
    and Berlin Wall, 427
    and Czechoslovakia, 127–128
    destruction in, 350
    division of, 355, 427
    and foreign policy of FDR, 102
    and Morgenthau Plan, 294–296, 303–304,
        494n10
    and Nazis' rise to power, 120–121
    and Operation Barbarossa, 155, 165–166
    and Poland, 127, 128, 130, 166
    submarines of, 47, 189, 412
    surrender of, 337–338
    Versailles Treaty violations of, 121
    war declared on US, 170
    World War I, 51
    and Yalta Conference, 319
Giraud, Henri, 218, 232, 233–234, 489n11
Goodwin, Doris Kearns, 181n
Gorgas, William, 31
Gouzenko, Igor, 381, 384
Great Britain
    and Allied strategic planning, 215–217
    "Appeasement" policy of, 121, 127
    and arms-control treaties, 61–62, 71, 114
    and atomic weapons, 297, 393
    and Berlin Crisis, 428
    and Burma (*see* Burma land route)
    and Cairo Conferences, 253–257, 263–264
    and Casablanca Conference, 216–220,
        224, 240
    and Chinese Nationalist regime, 223–224
    and German aggression, 130
    and German surrender, 337–338
    and Germany-first strategy, 216, 224
    and Greco-Turkish War, 60
    imperialism of, 362–363, 397, 398
    and invasion of France, 240 (*see also*
        D-Day)
    Joint Chiefs of Staff honored by, 360–361
    Leahy's 1946 trip to, 397–398
    Leahy's perspectives on, 49, 50–51
    and Leahy's research of Royal Navy,
        49–50

and lend-lease deal of FDR, 140, 275, 308–312
and Mediterranean theater, 237, 240, 255, 256, 261, 263
and Morgenthau Plan, 294–296
naval dominance of, 47, 49
and Octagon Conference, 292–296, 303
and Operation Anakim, 224–225, 227–228, 236, 237–238, 239–240, 488n46
and Operation Overlord, 491n29
and Pacific theatre, 224–225, 236, 240, 292–294
and Quebec Conference, 236–240, 251
and Tehran Conference, 257–263
and Trident Conference, 222–229, 231, 234, 239, 251
and Truman's Navy Day address, 370
US's relationship with, 49–51
See also Churchill, Winston
Great Depression, 71–73, 75, 78–79, 81, 88, 94, 474n9
Greece
aid for, 396, 404, 405–406, 407, 420
Greco-Turkish War, 53, 54–55, 59–61
and threat of communism, 402, 404–408, 505n35
and Truman Doctrine, 396–397
Groves, Leslie, 300, 394
Guadalcanal campaign, 214–215, 230, 282
Guam, 15–16, 117–119, 285, 477n32

Haiti, 45
Halfmoon Joint Emergency War Plan, 425–426
Halsey, William "Bull," 76, 284
Harding, Warren, 80
Harriman, Averell, 247, 256, 272, 319, 403
Hart, Thomas, 10, 26, 43, 172, 440
Hartsfield, William B., 98
Hassett, William, 409, 414, 444–445, 446, 447
Hawaii, Pearl Harbor base in, 141–142, 155–156, 169–171, 451–453
health of Leahy
fainting spell, 414
kidney issues, 432, 435, 438
psychosomatic conditions, 66, 74
in retirement years, 437, 439, 446
yellow fever, 31
Hepburn, Arthur, 10
Hepburn Report, 478n5
Herring, Clyde, 106
Hillenkoetter, Roscoe, 154, 376, 416, 417, 418, 431
Himmler, Heinrich, 233
Hiss, Alger, 381
Hitler, Adolf
Czechoslovakia seized by, 127–128
death of, 337
and Germany's weakened state, 291

and Great Britain's Appeasement policy, 121
Leahy's perspectives on, 120–121
and Munich Conference, 121, 127
rise to prominence, 95, 103
and Russian front, 249
Stalin on fate of, 352
and Sudetenland, 121
Versailles Treaty violations of, 121
Holmes, Julius, 380
Holocaust, 167, 323
homosexuality, 241–245
Hoover, Herbert, 71–72, 79, 81, 82, 84, 473n4, 474n9
Hoover, J. Edgar, 381, 391
Hopkins, Harry
advising role of, 183
background of, 185, 186
and Cairo Conferences, 253, 254n, 255
and Casablanca Conference, 212, 213, 219, 220
and de Gaulle in North Africa, 233
and Edward, Duke of Windsor, 296
and FDR–Leahy relationship, 220–221, 241, 296
and FDR's Canadian vacation, 235
and FDR's correspondence, 193
and FDR's death, 325
and FDR's inner circle, 194
and FDR's Map Room, 181
and FDR's meeting with MacArthur and Nimitz, 287
FDR's relationship with, 101, 106, 186, 293, 315, 317, 494n3
FDR's trust in, 159–160
health issues of, 221, 245–246, 255, 267–268, 315, 325, 348
influence of, 185
and Leahy, 186–187, 220, 246, 273–274, 493n40
and lend-lease deal, 309, 311
and Marshall, 198
office of, 187
and personnel controls committee, 209
political ideology of, 185–186
and Potsdam Conference, 348
and presidential race of 1944, 273
and Soviet relations, 250, 263
strategic planning of, 184
and Tehran Conference, 257–258, 263
and travels to Britain, 182
and war production strategies, 204, 205, 486n6
Hopkins, Harry (con't)
and Welles, 102, 241–242, 245
and Yalta Conference, 313, 315, 317
House Naval Affairs Committee, 87–88, 90, 129
Hughes, Charles Evans, 61
Hughes, Howard, 122, 361

Hull, Cordell
  and Bullitt, 480n9
  and Casablanca Conference, 212
  and FDR's Map Room, 181
  FDR's relationship with, 101–102
  health issues of, 275–276
  and Japan's surrender, 358
  and Leahy, 112–113, 125, 246–247
  and looming threat of war with
    Germany, 128
  marginalization of, 247
  and Protocols of Paris, 163
  resignation of, 276
  and Second Sino-Japanese War, 107,
    112–113
  and "slaves" comment of Leahy, 103
  and Tehran Conference, 251
  understanding of strategic policy, 194
  and Vichy–Germany collaboration, 163
  and Welles, 102, 242, 243–245, 490n3
Hurley, Patrick, 301, 302, 445
Hutcheson, Joseph, Jr., 389
Hyland, John, 86–87

I Was There (Leahy), 440–441
Ibn Saud, 322–324
Ickes, Harold
  and embargo on oil shipments to
    Japan, 160
  and Hopkins, 186
  and Leahy's governorship of Puerto Rico,
    128, 132, 136, 144
  and naval buildup under FDR, 115–116
  and Second Sino-Japanese War, 107
  and war production strategies, 182, 205
  and Welles, 102
  and Winship's resignation, 131
India, 397, 398
intelligence operations
  and Clifford Report, 400
  and Japanese fishermen in Alaska, 119–120
  Leahy's influence on, 376–377, 379–380
  Leahy's role in, 119–120, 376–378, 383,
    384–385, 418
  National Intelligence Authority (NIA),
    379–380, 384
  Office of Strategic Services, 377–380,
    391, 431
  and Roosevelt, 119–120
  spies' infiltration of US government,
    380–381
  and State Department proposal, 380
  and Truman's briefings, 384–385
  See also Central Intelligence Agency;
    National Security Council
Ireland, 50, 398
"Iron Curtain" speech (Churchill), 1–3, 365,
    371–374, 385
isolationism
  isolationism of Leahy, 78, 95–96, 108, 136,
    216, 309, 363
  and rise of Nazi Germany, 121

Israel, 420, 422–423
Italy, 61, 128, 234–236, 238, 252, 489n11
Iwo Jima, battle of, 342, 345

James VII, King, 6
Japan
  and Allied strategic planning, 214, 215, 217
  Americans' perspectives on, 33
  and arms-control treaties, 61–62, 71, 114
  and atomic bombs of US, 356, 357,
    392–393
  Battle of Iwo Jima, 342, 345
  Battle of Okinawa, 294, 342, 345–346, 347
  as competitor of US Navy, 56
  and FDR's foreign policy, 102
  and FDR's oil embargo, 155–156, 158
  and French Indochina, 148–149, 155,
    156–157, 158–160, 189
  and Germany-first strategy of Allies, 214,
    215, 216, 224
  and Guadalcanal campaign, 214–215, 230
  and gun size, 115, 120
  intelligence on oil stockpiles, 120
  invasion of Manchuria, 77–78
  and Kyushu, 341, 342, 344–346, 347–348,
    498n5
  and Leahy's battle force, 96–97
  and Leahy's focus on Pacific war, 223,
    281–282
  Leahy's perspectives on, 33–34, 36, 96
  Pearl Harbor attack, 155–156, 169–171
  and Philippines campaign, 279–280
  plans to invade islands of, 286, 289, 320,
    341, 342–343, 344–348
  potential naval threat of, 95
  and Potsdam Conference, 348, 355–358
  and Russia, 33
  and Second Sino-Japanese War, 106–109,
    111–113, 119–120, 223
  ship construction of, 88
  and Stimson's inflammatory remarks,
    81–82
  surrender of, 358
  territories seized by, 189
  and Trident Conference, 225–226
  and USS *Panay* crisis, 112–113, 115, 117–118
  war manufacturing capabilities of,
    282–283
  withdrawal from China, 363
Jewish people, 167, 323–324, 389, 420
Johnson, Edwin, 106
Joint Chiefs of Staff
  and atomic bombs of US, 395, 425
  and Berlin Crisis, 428
  and Cairo Conferences, 253–254
  and Casablanca Conference, 211–213,
    216–220, 224
  and China policies, 224
  and Clifford Report, 400
  and deployment on multiple fronts, 282
  dysfunction in, 188–189, 216, 220
  and Eisenhower, 415

end-of-war honors bestowed on, 360–361
establishment of, 188, 484n1
and FDR's inner circle, 194
and intelligence operations, 379, 502n21
and Leahy's political skills, 196–200
and Leahy's retirement, 432, 438
Leahy's role as chairman of, 182, 192, 196, 485n27
Leahy's status as senior member of, 178, 193–194 (*see also* Chief of Staff post)
and Mediterranean theater, 236
meetings of, 191n
nearing war's end, 312–313
and Operation Overlord, 260, 264
and Operation Torch (North Africa), 190–192, 198
and Pacific theatre, 215, 283–286, 451–453
and Philippines campaign, 279, 280
and plans to invade Japan, 289, 347
proposed formalization of, 222
roles of chiefs, 192, 485n14
and Supreme Commander choice, 260
and Trident Conference, 222–229
and Truman, 330
and war production strategies, 204, 206–208
and weapons of mass destruction (WMDs), 424
and Yalta Conference, 313
See also Arnold, Henry "Hap"; King, Ernest; Marshall, George C.
Joint Research and Development Committee, 391

Kennan, George, 372
Key West, Florida, 396, 409–413, 421–422, 434, 438, 443
Keynes, John Maynard, 309–311
King, Ernest
and accidental torpedo launch, 254
anti-British order withdrawn, 274
and atomic bombs of US, 341
and British forces in Pacific theatre, 293, 294
and Cairo Conferences, 253, 254n, 257
and Casablanca Conference, 212, 216–220
as chief of naval operations and CINCUS, 172
and Churchill's Rhodes proposal, 252
and deployment on multiple fronts, 282
end-of-war honors bestowed on, 360–361
and FDR's inner circle, 194
and FDR's Map Room, 181, 181n
and Forrestal, 248
and Germany-first strategy, 281
and Joint Chiefs of Staff, 188–189, 260
Leahy's relationship with, 196, 199
and Leahy's roles as chief of staff, 178, 179
and navy–army tension in Pacific, 283–284

and Operation Overlord, 278
and Operation Torch (North Africa), 190, 191, 192, 206
and Pacific strategy, 285, 286–287, 288, 290
and Philippines campaign, 279
and plans to invade Japan, 344, 345–346
and Potsdam Conference, 348, 354
promotion of, 266
and recruitment of sailors, 208
retirement of, 361
and Standley's centralization plans, 91
strategic planning of, 182
and travels to Britain, 182
and war production strategies, 204, 205, 207
and Yalta Conference, 315
King, Mackenzie, 381, 384
King Neptune's court (initiation ritual), 12, 416
Knox, Frank
and Casablanca Conference, 212
death of, 271
and FDR's Map Room, 194
and Forrestal, 248
Leahy's relationship with, 182
limited influence of, 194, 195
secretary of the navy appointment, 129
Koo, Wellington, 223, 431
Korea, 379
Korean War, 441–442, 508n16
Krock, Arthur, 180, 243, 407
Krug, Julius, 405–406
Krulak, Victor "Brute," 86–87

Land, Emory, 117
Landry, R. B., 428
Larimer, E. B., 86
Latvia, 251
Laval, Pierre, 147, 152, 173–174
League of Nations, 165, 420
Leahy, Caroline (niece), 275
Leahy, Daniel (grandfather), 6
Leahy, Elizabeth Beale (daughter-in-law), 66, 71
Leahy, Louise Beale (granddaughter), 71, 126, 361, 420–421, 439–440
Leahy, Louise Harrington (wife)
birth of son, 30
and career of Leahy, 26
courtship and marriage, 25–26
death of, 175–176, 177, 365
European trip, 56, 482n20
gravesite of, 440, 447
influence on Leahy, 26
and Leahy's ambassadorship to France, 150
Leahy's mourning of, 365, 440
in Puerto Rico, 137
relocation to Washington, DC, 43
and retirement of Leahy, 124
social life, 27, 43–44, 126

Leahy, Mary Eagan (grandmother), 5–6
Leahy, Michael Arthur (father), 5–8, 24, 94, 443, 470n3
Leahy, Robert Beale (grandchild), 126
Leahy, Rose Mary Hamilton (mother), 5, 6, 24, 94, 443
Leahy, Stephen (brother), 66, 443
Leahy, William Daniel
  ancestry, 5–6, 75
  birth, 5, 6
  career (*see* career of Leahy)
  commitment to duty, 20
  death, 446, 447
  diary, 74, 129
  education, 7–10 (*see also* US Naval Academy)
  ethics (*see* morality of Leahy)
  family (*see* family of Leahy)
  finances (*see* finances of Leahy)
  funeral, 447
  marriage, 25–26 (*see also* Leahy, Louise Harrington)
  medals, 49, 129, 439, 483n10
  memoir, 440–441
  memorials, 448
  portraits and busts, 7, 361, 413–414
  religion (*see* religious outlook of Leahy)
  social skills and socialization, 43, 59–60, 365–366
  vices, 63–65, 412–414
  youth, 6–7, 94, 126
Leahy, William Harrington (son)
  at Annapolis, 65–66
  birth, 26, 30
  career choices, 74–75
  daughter, 71
  European trip, 56
  health issues, 66
  Leahy's first experience with, 32
  marriage, 66
  and parenting style of Leahy, 66
  and retirement of Leahy, 439–440
  youth, 66
LeMay, Curtis, 394
Life magazine, 180
Lippmann, Walter, 125
List, Eugene, 353
Lithuania, 251
London Naval Conference, 71
"Long Telegram" of Kennan, 372
Lovett, Robert, 309

MacArthur, Douglas
  appearance of, 288
  and Bonus Marchers, 79
  dismissed by Truman, 444
  FDR's meeting with, 287–289
  and Leahy, 288, 290, 435
  and navy–army tension in Pacific, 283–284
  and Pacific strategy, 287–289
  and Philippines campaign, 279–280, 286–287
  and plans to invade Japan, 342–343
  and presidential race of 1944, 286, 288
MacArthur, Douglas, II, 154, 288
Mahan, Alfred Thayer, 41, 97, 148, 203
Manhattan Project, 297–298, 298n, 300, 356, 384, 394. *See also* atomic bombs
Mao Tse-tung, 363, 363n, 387, 419, 431
Mariana Islands, 118, 284–286
Marín, Luis Muñoz, 135–136
Maritime Commission, 117
Marshall, George C.
  and atomic bombs of US, 298, 341, 425, 430
  authority and influence of, 197–198
  and Cairo Conferences, 253–254, 254n, 257
  and Casablanca Conference, 212, 216, 217, 218, 219, 220
  and casualties, 213, 345
  and China, 224, 300, 387–389, 418, 419, 442, 443
  and Churchill's Rhodes proposal, 252
  and Cold War, 403
  and conscription of civilian labor, 208–209, *281*
  cross-Channel invasion plan of, 188, 203, 213–214, 218 (*see also* Operation Overlord)
  death of, 447–448
  and deployment on multiple fronts, 282
  end-of-war honors bestowed on, 360–361
  FDR's correspondence with, 193
  and FDR's inner circle, 194
  and FDR's Map Room, 181, 181n
  FDR's relationship with, 139, 197, *281*, 290, 335
  and Germany-first strategy, 213, *281*
  and Greece, 405
  and Hopkins, 198
  and Israel, 422–423
  and Joint Chiefs of Staff, 188–189, 260, 485n33
  and Leahy's funeral, 447
  and Leahy's governorship of Puerto Rico, 133
  and Leahy's power/influence, 280, *281*
  Leahy's relationship with, 129, 196–199, 300, 433
  and Leahy's roles as chief of staff, 178, 179
  and Mediterranean theater, 234–235
  and Operation Overlord, 260, 264, 277–278, *281*, 491n29
  and Operation Torch (North Africa), 190, 191, 192, 198, 206, 484n6
  and Philippines campaign, 279
  and plans to invade Japan, 342, 344–347, 498n5
  and Potsdam Conference, 348, 354
  promotion of, 266
  and Quebec Conference, 236–237

and recruitment of troops, 208
retirement of, 361
Secretary of Defense appointment, 442
Secretary of State appointment, 403
and size of army, 203–204, 208, 209
and Stilwell, 301, 302–303
strategic planning of, 182, 213–214
and travels to Britain, 182
and Trident Conference, 226
and Truman, 335
and Truman Doctrine, 408
and Turkey, 405
and war production strategies, 202–203,
    205, 207, *281*
and Yalta Conference, 315, 336
Martha, Princess of Norway, 182, 229,
    244, 325
Martin, Joseph, 404
Matloff, Maurice, 304
Matthews, H. Freeman, 154, 170, 275, 299
Mayo, H. T., 32, 38, 39, 40, 49, 471n22
McCarthy, Joseph, 443–444
McCloy, John, 268, 344
McCollum, Arthur, 377
McCrea, John L., 181, 212
McCully, Newton, 62
McIntire, Ross, 127, 212, 216, 267, 272
McKinley, William, 12–13, 15, 21–22
McNarney, Joseph, 182, 302
McNary, Charles, 125
Mediterranean theater of World War II
    British support for, 237, 240, 255, 256,
        261, 263
    and Cairo Conferences, 255, 256
    and Casablanca Conference, 217, 218
    and German defense of Italy, 252
    and Italy's vulnerability, 234–235
    Leahy's concerns about, 222, 235–236
    and Quebec Conference, 237, 238
    and Stalin, 256, 258–259
    Supreme Commander for, 254
    and Tehran Conference, 259
    and Trident Conference, 225,
        226, 228
    waning support for, 236
memoir of Leahy, 440–441
Mena, Luis, 37
Mercer, Lucy, 271
merchant ships, 55, 117, 117n
Mexico, 30, 32, 405
Middle East
    and Clifford Report, 400
    decline of European influence in, 363
    and Israel, 422–423
    and Jewish immigration, 323–324,
        389, 420
    and talks with Ibn Saud, 322–324
    US policy toward, 269
Mitchell, William "Billy," 63
Molotov, Vyacheslav, 318, 336, 352, 382,
    499n37
Montgomery, Bernard, 211

morality of Leahy
    and atomic bombs of US, 298–299, 355,
        357–358, 426, 431
    and civilian targets, 298–299
    and cockfighting in Manila, 16–17
    and Greco-Turkish War, 53, 54–55, 59–61
    and Second Sino-Japanese War, 111
Morgenthau, Henry
    and FDR's death, 325n
    and Hopkins–FDR relationship, 293
    and Jewish population in Europe, 323
    Leahy's relationship with, 269, 275,
        303–304
    and lend-lease deal of FDR, 309–312
    and Octagon Conference, 294, 295, 494n9
    and presidential race of 1944, 304–305
    resignation of, 352
    and Wallace, 314
Morgenthau Plan, 294–296, 303–304,
    303n, 352
Munich Conference, 121, 127
Murphy, Robert, 352
Murray, Albert, 7, 413–414
Murville, Maurice Couve de, 155
Mussolini, Benito, 121, 128, 234

Nadal, Rafael Martínez, 133
Napoleon I, Emperor of the French, 56
Nash, Philleo, 411
National Defense Act of 1947, 194, 417,
    418, 421
National Intelligence Agency, 417
National Intelligence Authority (NIA),
    379–380, 384, 390–391
national security advisor role, 183, 364,
    418, 418n
National Security Council (NSC), 416,
    417–418, 426, 428, 430, 431
National Security Resources Board, 417
naval base construction, 61
naval career of Leahy
    and ability to kiss ass, 45–46
    assigned to personnel division, 39,
        40–41, 67
    assigned to study the Royal Navy, 49–50
    as assistant director of target practice,
        38–39
    as battle force commander, 93–94, 95,
        96–97
    as chief aide to Mayo, 39
    as chief of Bureau of Navigation, 85,
        86–89, 91
    as chief of Bureau of Ordnance, 68,
        70–72, 76
    as chief of staff to Caperton, 45
    command of minelaying flotilla, 62
    command of scout destroyers, 73, 75–76
    command of USS *Chattanooga*, 56
    command of USS *Dolphin*, 44–45, 46,
        47–48
    command of USS *New Mexico* battleship,
        67–68

naval career of Leahy (*cont.*)
  command of USS *Princess Matoika*, 48–49
  command of USS *Shawmut*, 62, 67
  command of USS *St. Louis*, 57
  and desire to see the world, 8
  and early combat experiences, 36, 37, 48
  and Greco-Turkish War, 53, 54–55, 59–61
  as gunnery director, 48–49, 55–56
  as gunnery officer, 32–33, 38, 55–56
  and gunnery training of sailors, 97
  and international outlook of Leahy, 35–36
  medals of Leahy, 129
  positions declined by Leahy, 56, 62
  promotion to captain, 52
  promotion to CNO, 95, 98, 99
  promotion to five-star fleet admiral, 266,
    313, 492n2
  promotion to rear admiral, 68
  promotion to vice admiral, 93–94
  and reputation of Leahy, 38
  retirement from, 124, 129
  serving on USS *California*, 32–36, 77
  serving on USS *Constellation*, 8–9, 74
  as special naval aide to Taft, 38
  two-year extension of active duty, 129
Naval Intelligence, 380
Naval War College in Newport, Rhode
    Island, 64
Nehru, Jawaharlal, 370
Nelson, Donald, 202, 205, 206–207
Netherlands, 435–436
New Deal
  and Hopkins, 185, 186
  influence on Leahy, 416
  and Leahy's governorship of Puerto Rico,
    132, 133
  Leahy's support for, 82–83, 98–99
  newspaper clippings on, 479n13
Niblack, Albert, 25, 35, 44, 60, 69, 473n30,
    473n53
Nicaragua, 36–38, 45
Niles, David K., 432
Nimitz, Chester
  and atomic bombs of US, 425
  as chief of Pacific Fleet, 172
  as commander in chief of Pacific
    Operating Area, 283
  and Eisenhower's ambitions, 415
  FDR's meeting with, 287–289
  and Leahy's crooked nose, 7
  and Leahy's teasing of Eisenhower, 415
  and MacArthur, 283–284, 288
  and navy–army tension in Pacific,
    283–284
  and Pacific strategy, 283–285, 287–289
Nordskov, 48, 472n20

Octagon Conference, 292–296, 303, 304
Office of Economic Stabilization, 205
Office of Strategic Services (OSS), 377–380,
    391, 431
Okinawa, fighting at, 294, 342, 345–346, 347

Operation Anakim, 223–225, 227–228, 236,
    237–238, 239–240, 488n46
Operation Bagration, 291
Operation Barbarossa, 155, 165–166
Operation Bolero, 190, 487n11
Operation Forager, 285, 285n
Operation Husky, 234
Operation Olympic, 344–348
Operation Overlord (invasion of France)
  British delays/objections, 217, 231, 237,
    256, 259–260, 263
  and Cairo Conferences, 256
  and Churchill, 225, 231
  FDR's negotiations for, 238
  initiation of invasion, 277
  Leahy's perspectives on, 215, 251–252, *281*
  Marshall's call for invasion, 188, 203,
    213–214, 218
  naval support of, 285, 285n
  preparations for, 277
  and Quebec Conference, 238
  Soviet support of, 256, 259, 260, 261
  Supreme Commander for, 254, 260–261,
    264, 491n29
  and Tehran Conference, 259–260
  and Trident Conference, 228, 231, 239
Operation Torch, 190–192, 198, 206, 223,
    231–232, 484n9

Pacific Fleet
  commanders of, 44, 87, 141, 172 (*see also*
    Nimitz, Chester)
  and evacuation of US citizens in
    Shanghai, 107
  and Guam base, 118
  and Japan's naval competition, 56
  Pearl Harbor attack, 155–156, 169–171
  Pearl Harbor base of, 141–142, 451–453
  in post–World War I period, 56
Pacific theater
  Allied forces dedicated to, *281*, 281–283
  and Allied strategic planning, 217,
    280–289, *281*, 451–453
  American sea/air power in, 205, 214–215
  Battle of Iwo Jima, 342, 345
  Battle of Okinawa, 294, 342, 345–346, 347
  blockades employed in, 117–118, 123, 280,
    286, 289
  command structure in, 283–284
  commanders in, 283–284 (*see also* Hart,
    Thomas; MacArthur, Douglas; Nimitz,
    Chester)
  FDR's negotiations for, 238
  and Germany-first strategy of Allies, 214,
    215, 216, 224, 281, 285
  and Great Britain, 224–225, 236, 240
  and Guadalcanal campaign, 214–215,
    230, 282
  Japanese dominance of, in 1942, 189
  Leahy's focus on, 223, 281–282
  Leahy's preparations for, 96–97
  and Mariana Islands, 118, 284–286

and Operation Anakim, 223–225,
227–228, 236, 237–238, 239–240,
488n46
and Pearl Harbor attack, 155–156, 169–171
and Philippines campaign, 279–280
and plans to invade Japan, 286, 289, 320,
341, 342–343, 344–348
and Quebec Conference, 237, 238
Soviet participation in, 320, 343, 355,
499n37
and Trident Conference, 225–226, 227
and Truman, 340
and war production strategies, 117, 206
Palestine, 323, 324, 389, 420, 423
Panama Canal, 31, 64
Paris, France, 51, 56–57
Patterson, Robert
and Berlin Crisis, 429
and China, 387
and Clifford Report, 400
forceful engagement of, 364
and Greece, 405
and lend-lease deal, 309
and Truman Doctrine, 408
and unification dispute, 391
Pearl Harbor attack, 155–156, 169–171
Pearl Harbor base, 141–142, 451–453
Pearson, Drew, 386, 433
Pehle, John, 323
Pendergast, Thomas, 332–333
Pepper, Claude, 106
Perkins, Frances, 129, 326
Pershing, John J., 145, 313n
personnel office of US Navy, 39, 40–41, 43, 67
Peru, 12, 67
Pétain, Marshal
anti-Semitic laws of regime, 167
and Darlan, 152
and de Gaulle, 169, 482n36
dictatorship of, 165
and embargo on oil shipments to Japan,
158–159
and Germany's stranglehold, 150
and Leahy's arrival in France, 151
and Leahy's role in France, 147
and Leahy's warning about collaboration,
157, 159, 162, 163
trial of, 338–339
and Vichy collaboration with Germany,
143, 162, 164–165, 172, 173
and Weygand, 168–169
Philippines
casualties in, 345
independence movement in, 11, 15, 136
Leahy's assignment to, 19–22
and Pacific strategy, 279–280, 284,
286–287, 288–289
and Philippine–American War, 15, 19
Pogue, Forrest, 298
Poland
and Donovan, 378
and German aggression, 127, 128, 130, 166

Leahy honored by, 360
and Potsdam Conference, 355
and Soviet Union, 263, 292, 320–322,
360, 362
and Stalin, 251, 262
and Truman, 336–337, 368
and Warsaw uprising, 292
and Yalta Conference, 318, 336
political ideology of Leahy, 21, 90,
98–99, 125
political skills of Leahy
and cabinet meetings of FDR, 106
as Chief of Staff, 196–200
and foresight of Leahy, 98
and King, 199
and life in Washington, 126
and Marshall, 196–199
and naval readiness in Pacific war, 117
and Pearl Harbor base, 141–142
and respect of colleagues for Leahy, 90
and Soviet relations, 103
and support base of Leahy, 92
and tensions with Standley, 92–93
and Tongue Point, Oregon, naval base, 125
and work with US Congress, 89–90
in youth, 10
Pompeii, 58n
Portal, Sir Charles, 218
Portugal, 56
Potsdam Conference, 333, 348–358
Pound, Sir Dudley, 218
Powell, Louis, 440
power and influence of Leahy
as chairman of Joint Chiefs of
Staff, 222
and MacArthur, 290
and promotion to five-star admiral, 266
in Roosevelt administration, 180,
195–196, 198, 200, 202, 220, 269, 274,
303–304, 308, 451n
in Truman administration, 385, 386, 403,
410, 416, 417–418, 420, 423
and US atomic policy, 298, 300, 368,
424–426, 430–431, 495n18
wielded in background, 3, 278, 387
Pratt, William, 72–73, 85, 474n11
press officer of Leahy, 109–110
Prohibition Era, 63, 72
Protocols of Paris, 163–164, 168
Puerto Rico
and governorship of Leahy, 127, 128, 129,
130, 131–137, 140, 479n13
Leahys' departure from, 143–144
Leahy's return to, 421, 422
naval base on, 139–140, 478n4
WPA projects in, 132, 133, 134, 137, 140

Quebec Conference (QUADRANT),
235–240, 251

race and racism in America, 22, 137–138
Rayburn, Sam, 106, 328, 329

receptions and parties required of Leahy, 59–60
Reeves, Joseph, 91
religious outlook of Leahy
  Catholic background of Leahy, 27
  Episcopalian affiliation of Leahy, 27, 65, 177–178
  and influence of Louise on Leahy, 26–27, 177
  and Leahy's ignorance of religion, 22, 65
  and sexuality propriety, 58n
Renfrow, Louis, 411, 434–435
respect for Leahy, 10, 90, 414–415
retirement of Leahy
  and connecting with friends, 440
  and Eisenhower's election, 445
  and family time, 439–440
  and final days of Leahy, 446
  and health issues, 437–438, 439, 446
  and hospitalization, 437, 446
  and influence over US policy, 445
  initiated by Leahy, 434
  and memoir, 440–441
  from naval career (1939), 124, 129–130
  time spent in Key West, 438, 443
  and trip to Wisconsin, 443
  and Truman, 434–435, 438, 442–443, 446
  and visitors, 437–438, 446, 509n34
Rhodes, Greece, 252
Ribbentrop, Joachim von, 156–157
Richardson, James O., 141–142
Rigdon, William, 96, 270
Ringquist, Dorothy, 358–359, 366, 446
RMS *Lusitania*, sinking of, 47
Robinson, Joseph, 98
Roman Catholic Church, 27
Rommel, Erwin, 182, 211, 227
Roosevelt, Anna, 314, 315, 316, 446
Roosevelt, Eleanor
  and Churchill, 297
  entertaining of, 43
  and FDR's death, 325, 329
  and FDR's failing health, 307
  and FDR's Hobcaw Barony retreat, 271
  FDR's relationship with, 184–185
  and German surrender, 338
  Leahy's relationship with, 184
  and Quebec Conference, 238
  and Wallace, 314
Roosevelt, Elliott, 271
Roosevelt, Franklin Delano (FDR)
  and accidental torpedo launch, 254
  and anti-Semitism in Vichy France, 167
  and arms-control treaties, 81, 474n38
  as assistant secretary of the US Navy, 40
  and atomic bombs of US, 296, 297, 298, 299, 324
  and Axis Unconditional Surrender doctrine, 218–219, 487n20
  background of, 41–42
  and banking system crisis, 82–83

battle force displayed for, 95
and Bullitt, 144–145, 244, 269, 480n9
and Burma land route, 264
cabinet of, 102, 106–107, 275
and Cairo Conferences, 253–257, 254n
Canadian vacation of, 235
Caribbean trip of, 126–127
and Casablanca Conference, 211–213, 218–219
on central importance of Navy, 41
and China policies, 224
and conscription of civilian labor, 208–209, *281*
correspondence of, 220, 235, 272
and de Gaulle, 172, 232
death of, 324–327, 328–329, 497n67
and deployment on multiple fronts, 282
and economic crisis, 84
embargo on oil shipments to Japan, 155–156, 158
entertaining of, 43
family of, 46–47
foreign policy of, 102, 105, 128
and Four Policemen, 250, 261
and German aggression, 127–128
and Germany-first strategy, *281*, 282
and Germany's Operation Barbarossa, 166
and Guam base, 119, 477n32
health issues of, 216, 267, 269, 270–272, 305, 307–308, 315, 317
and Hobcaw Barony retreat, 269–272
and Hull, 243–244
Hyde Park residence of, 107–108
inauguration of, 307–308
inner circle of, 101–102, 127, 179, 194, 212
and intelligence operations, 119–120, 378–379
and Japanese attack of USS *Panay*, 113, 115
Leahy trusted by, 42, 104, 105, 109, 128, 131–132, 208–209, 270, *281*
and Leahy's ambassadorship to France, 143, 144–147, 172–173
and Leahy's briefings, 180–181, 183–184, 484n23, 493n57
Leahy's loyalty to, 142, 300, 442, 444–445
and Leahy's promotion to CNO, 95, 98, 99
and Leahy's promotion to five-star fleet admiral, 266, 313, 492n2
Leahy's relationship with, 43, 47, 92, 94, 104–106, 109, 119, 126–127, 139, 161–162, 241, 290, 437–438
and Leahy's restraint, 65
and Leahy's retirement, 130
and Leahy's roles as chief of staff, 178–179, 193
Leahy's support of, 81–83, 99
lend-lease deal of, 140, 275, 308–312
and looming threat of war with Germany, 128–129, 130, 139

MacArthur and Nimitz's meeting with, 287–289
and Mahan's sea power theories, 41
Map Room of, 181–182, 194, 220
marriage of, 184–185
and Marshall, 197, *281*, 335
and Mediterranean theater, 254, 256
and military spending, 81, 84
and military strategy, 214
and Morgenthau Plan, 294–295, 303–304
naval buildup under, 88, 114–118
and naval policy, 105, 115
as nominee for vice president, 80
and Octagon Conference, 292–296
and Operation Anakim, 224
and Operation Overlord, 260, 261, 278, *281*
and Operation Torch (North Africa), 190
and Pacific theatre, 224, 285, 287–289
on Pearl Harbor attack, 170
and Pearl Harbor base, 141–142
and personnel office of US Navy, 39, 40–41
and Poland, 321–322
polio of, 80–81, 92
and Polish uprising, 292
and presidential race of 1932, 81, 82
and presidential race of 1936, 98
and presidential race of 1940, 134–135
and presidential race of 1944, 273, 287, 304–306
and Protocols of Paris, 163
and Puerto Rico governorship, 127, 128, 129, 130, 131–132
and Quebec Conference, 235–240
racial attitudes of, 138
reliance on Leahy, 139, 270
religious life of, 177–178
and Soviet relations, 103, 250–251, 250n
and Stalin, 257–258, 445
and Standley–Leahy tensions, 93–94
and Stilwell's service in China, 302–303
and Tehran Conference, 249–251, 257–263
and Trident Conference, 225–229
and Truman's twelve points speech, 368
and United Nations, 250, 261, 319
and USS *Dolphin*, 46
and Vichy–Germany collaboration, 147–149, 159–160, 163, 164, 172–173
and Vinson, 88
and Wallace, 314–315
and war production strategies, 202, 203, 204–205, 206–207, *281*
and Welles scandal, 241–242, 243–245, 476n7
and Weygand, 168–169
and Yalta Conference, 313, 317, 318, 326, 445
Roosevelt, Henry Latrobe, 85, 89, 100, 257
Roosevelt, Theodore, 14, 22, 38
Roosevelt Roads Naval Station, 140

Rosenman, Samuel
and Democratic National Convention, 287
Leahy's relationship with, 366
and medal of merit, 375
and personnel controls committee, 209
and Truman's Army Day address, 393
and Truman's twelve points speech, 367, 369
and unification dispute, 392
Royall, Kenneth, 426

San Francisco, California, 12, 27–29
Santiago, Chile, 35
Sarnoff, David, 274–275
Saudi Arabia, 360
scout destroyers, 73, 75–76
sea power, Mahan's theories on, 41, 97
Second Vinson Act (HR 9218), 116, 118
secretary of the navy
and chief naval officer (CNO), 91, 93
Daniels as, 42–47
and death of Swanson, 129
and health issues of Swanson, 100
Leahy as de facto, 103
and organizational system of US Navy, 85, 91
See also Forrestal, James; Knox, Frank; Swanson, Claude
Senate Naval Affairs Committee, 87, 118, 129
Shanghai, China, 17, 18, 34, 107–109
Sheppard, Morris, 106
ship construction, 70–72, 84, 88, 114–118, 202. See also arms-control treaties
shipyards, US, 103–104
Shoreham Hotel, Washington, DC, 44
Simpson, Wallis, 296
Smith, J. V., 271
Smith, Walter Bedell, 178, 431
Snyder, John, 383
Somervell, Brehon, 204
Soong, T. V., 223–224, 229
Souers, Sidney, 375–376, 377, 389, 416, 417, 418
South America, 35
Southerland, William, 38
Soviet Union
and aid, 274
and Allied strategic planning, 217
and atomic capabilities of US, 355, 424, 425, 426, 430
atomic weapons of, 430
Axis invasion of, 155, 211, 230
Axis repelled/captured by, 249, 291
and battleship construction, 103–104
and Berlin Crisis, 427–430
Bullitt's ambassadorship to, 144
and Chinese Nationalists, 319
and Churchill's "Iron Curtain" speech, 1–3, 372, 373, 374
and Clifford Report, 398–401, 457–459

Soviet Union (*cont.*)
 and eastern Europe, 362
 and France, 319
 and German surrender, 337–338
 intelligence agents in US government,
  379–380
 intelligence on oil stockpiles, 120
 and Japan, 33
 Leahy's perspectives on, 122, 250,
  262–263, 353, 400–401
 and "Long Telegram" of Kennan, 372
 naval capabilities of, 122
 and Operation Bagration, 291
 and Operation Barbarossa, 165–166
 and Operation Overlord, 226, 256, 259,
  260, 261
 and Pacific theatre, 320, 343, 355, 499n37
 perceived threat of, 396–408 (*see also*
  Cold War)
 and Poland, 292, 320–322, 360, 362
 and Potsdam Conference, 348, 355
 and "slaves" comment of Leahy, 103
 and Tehran Conference, 257–263
 and Truman's twelve points speech,
  367–368, 455
 and US military strategy, 215
 US policy toward, 397
 US relations with, 103, 250–251, 250n,
  336–337, 362, 363–364, 370, 372,
  398–401
 women émigrées from, 57–58
 and Yalta Conference, 313–321, 326, 336
Spaatz, Carl "Tooey," 391, 421
Spain, 12–14
Spanish-American War, 11, 15
SS *Borinquen*, 146
Stalin, Joseph
 appearance of, 258
 and atomic bombs of US, 356
 on capitalism vs. communism, 371, 401
 and China, 261
 confidential telegrams to, 333
 deterioration of relationships with, 348
 FDR's correspondence with, 182
 FDR's meeting with, 258
 and FDR's stay in compound of, 257–258
 and German surrender, 337–338
 on Hitler's fate, 352
 and Japan's surrender, 358
 Leahy's concerns about, 250–251, 262
 Leahy's impressions of, 259, 437
 and Mediterranean theater, 256,
  258–259
 and military parade on film, 122
 and Operation Overlord, 256, 259,
  260, 261
 and Pacific theatre, 320
 and Poland, 262, 292
 and Potsdam Conference, 348, 352–353,
  355, 356, 358
 and Quebec Conference, 235
 rise to prominence, 95

and Tehran Conference, 249–251,
 257–263
and Truman, 352–353, 355
and United Nations, 250, 319
and Yalta Conference, 308, 313, 317, 318,
 326, 445
Standley, W. H., 85, 91–94
Stark, Harold, 129
Steele, George W., 80
Stettinius, Edward, Jr., 269, 309, 311,
 315, 335
Stevenson, Adlai, 445
Stilwell, Joseph "Vinegar Joe,"
 301–303, 414
Stimson, Henry
 and atomic bombs of US, 324, 340n, 356
 and Casablanca Conference, 212
 and FDR's Map Room, 181, 194
 and intelligence operations, 379
 Leahy's antipathy for, 81–82, 194–195
 limited influence of, 194–195, 485n24
 and Morgenthau Plan, 303–304
 and Operation Torch (North Africa),
  190, 191
 and plans to invade Japan, 344, 346
 and Stilwell's service in China, 302
 strategic planning of, 182
 and Truman, *281*, 330
 and Yalta Conference, 336
Stokowski, Leopold, 134
Stone, Harlan, 329
Stuart, John Leighton, 419
submarines, 47, 55, 189, 412, 422
Suckley, Margaret, 244, 271–272
Sutherland, Richard, 284
Swanson, Claude
 death of, 129
 and FDR, 105
 health issues of, 100
 and Leahy's letter of commendation, 90
 and Leahy's promotion to CNO, 95, 98
 Leahy's relationship with, 89
 and naval buildup under FDR, 115
 as secretary of the navy, 85–86
 and Standley–Leahy tensions, 93
Syria, 159, 163–164, 333, 363

Taft, William Howard, 22, 38
"Tampico Incident," 32
tankers, 116, 117, 477n27
Tehran Conference, 249–250, 252–253,
 257–263
Tito, Josip Broz, 348
Tongue Point, Oregon, naval base, 104, 125
Trident Conference, 222–229, 231, 234, 239,
 251
Truman, Harry S.
 Army Day address of, 393
 and atomic bombs of US, 340–341, 340n,
  348, 355–357, 392–393, 426
 background of, 332–333
 and Berlin Crisis, 427–428, 429

and Byrnes, 382–383
cabinet of, 402–403
and China, 388–389, 419
and Churchill's "Iron Curtain" speech,
　1–3, 371–372
and Clifford Report, 398, 401
and Cold War, 396–397
communication style of, 336–337
and communism, 396–397, 405–408
correspondence of, 445
and de Gaulle, 339–340
and FDR's death, 325, 328–329
and FDR's failing health, 307
and German surrender, 337–338
and gold-plated revolver, 438, 446
and intelligence operations, 375–376, 379,
　383, 384–385, 390
and Israel, 423
and Japan's surrender, 358
and Joint Chiefs of Staff, 330
and Kennan's "Long Telegram," 372
in Key West, 396, 409–413, 434, 439, 443
and Korean War, 441–442
lack of international experience, 331–332
last days in office, 445–446
Leahy attacked in press, 432–433
Leahy trusted by, 397, 433
and Leahy's briefings, 329–330, 334,
　364–365, 384–385, 411, 418, 420, 443
and Leahy's final days, 446
and Leahy's funeral, 447
Leahy's influence with, 403, 410, 416,
　417–418, 420
Leahy's loyalty to, 434, 444
Leahy's perceptions of, 331–332, 334, 337
and Leahy's post-retirement job offers,
　442–443
and Leahy's postwar service, 361–362
Leahy's relationship with, 334–335,
　351–352, 375, 385, 410–413
and Leahy's retirement, 434–435, 438
and MacArthur, 444
and Marshall's funeral, 448
and McCarthy, 444
museum in hometown of, 446
musical interests of, 349, 353
Navy Day/twelve points address of, 365,
　367–371, 385, 393, 455
and Neptune's Court initiation, 416
and Palestine, 389
and plans to invade Japan, 344, 346–347
and Potsdam Conference, 348–358
preparedness for presidency, 332
and presidential race of 1944, 273, 287,
　305, 333
and presidential race of 1948, 432, 434
in Puerto Rico, 421
and restraint of Leahy, 65
and Soviet relations, 336–337
and Stalin, 352–353, 355
swearing in, as president, 329
traveling with, 373

and Truman Committee, 333
and Truman Doctrine, 396–397, 401,
　407–408
and unification of armed services,
　391, 392
on universal military training, 393–394
as Vice President, 314, 328, 333
Tubby, Roger, 413
Turkey
　aid for, 396, 404, 405–406, 407, 420
　Greco-Turkish War, 53, 54–55, 59–61
　and threat of communism, 402, 404–408,
　　505n35
　and Truman Doctrine, 396–397
　and World War II, 256, 263

unification of armed services, 391–392
United Kingdom. *See* Great Britain
United Nations
　and atomic weapons, 381
　and Churchill's "Iron Curtain"
　　speech, 374
　proposal for, 250, 261, 319
　and Security Council, 319
　and Truman's twelve points speech,
　　368, 455
United States
　and arms-control treaties, 61–62, 70, 71,
　　81, 114
　China's relations with, 78, 387–389
　and Germany's declaration of war, 170
　Great Britain's relationship with, 49–51
　interventionism of, 13–14, 18, 78, 111
　Pearl Harbor attack, 155–156, 169–171
　and Soviet relations, 103, 250–251, 250n,
　　336–337, 362, 363–364, 370, 372,
　　398–401
　as superpower, 3, 363
　*See also specific historical events and
　　institutions, including* atomic bombs
　　and World War II
US Air Force, 417, 421, 422, 425, 430
US Army
　chief of staff (*see* Marshall, George C.)
　and European war, 282
　recruitment of, 202, 207–208
　size of, 203–204, 208, 209
　and unification dispute, 391–392
　and war production strategies, 202–203,
　　283, 486n6
US Army Air Force, 77, 204, 207, 282,
　391–392. *See also* Arnold, Henry "Hap"
US Congress
　and Bureau of Navigation, 87, 89
　and FDR's naval expansion plans, 115–116
　and Guam base, 119, 477n32
　Leahy's lobbying of, 89
　Second Vinson Act (HR 9218), 116
　and Truman Doctrine, 396
US Department of Defense, 391, 392, 417
US Department of State
　and China, 107, 503n3

US Department of State *(cont.)*
    and FDR's inner circle, 101–102, 186
    and intelligence operations, 379, 380
    and Kennan's "Long Telegram," 372
    Leahy's concerns about, 381–382
    Leahy's connections in, 222, 275–277
    liaison of, 276
    and Second Sino-Japanese War, 112
    Soviet spies' penetration of, 380
    and Welles scandal, 241–245
    See also various secretaries of state,
        including: Byrnes, James; Hull, Cordell;
        Marshall, George C.; Stettinius,
        Edward, Jr.; Stimson, Henry
US Department of War, 289, 400, 417, 503n3
US Marine Corps, 214–215, 282
US Military Academy at West Point, 7–8
US Naval Academy, in Annapolis,
    Maryland, 8–10, 31, 32, 40, 86–87
US Navy
    and admirals' revolt, 439
    aircraft of (*see* airpower, naval)
    and alcohol consumption, 63–64
    ambitions of US for, 49, 61
    antiaircraft weapons of, 76
    and arms-control process, 81, 474n38
    budget cuts, 71–72, 76
    buildup under FDR, 41, 88, 114–118,
        122–123, 141
    buildup under Wilson, 55
    chief of naval operations and CINCUS
        (*see* King, Ernest)
    command opportunities in, 61
    competitions of 1927–1928, 67–68
    and court-martial of Steele, 80
    and Daniels' General Order 99, 42
    Daniels' post as secretary of the, 42–43
    fleet train concept of, 117, 117n
    and General Board discussions, 76–77
    and Great Depression, 71–72
    gun club of, 56, 115
    height requirements of, 86–87
    and Hoover administration, 71
    and Japan's competition, 56
    Leahy as face of, 124
    Leahy memorialized by, 448
    Leahy's career in (*see* naval career of
        Leahy)
    Leahy's impact on, 122–123
    and Marine Corps, 392, 422
    and Neptune's court, 12, 416
    and organization of US military, 422
    organizational system of, 85, 91, 93, 96,
        475n29 (*see also* secretary of the navy)
    and Pacific theatre, 282, 283
    and Panama Canal, 31
    pay cuts in, 79, 84
    promotional system of, 89
    ship construction, 70–72, 84, 88,
        114–118, 202
    and shipyards, 103–104
    and Soviet relations, 103

    torpedo launched accidentally, 254
    and unification dispute, 391–392
    and war production strategies, 202–203,
        205, *281*, 283
US Supreme Court, 99
USS *Augusta*, 349
USS *Boston*, 30, 32
USS *California*, 32–36, 77, 471n18
USS *Chattanooga*, 56
USS *Chicago*, 29
USS *Constellation*, 8–9, 74, 469n5
USS *Dolphin*, 44–45, 46, 47–48
USS *Enterprise*, 88
USS *Glacier*, 20
USS *Houston*, 95, 126–127
USS *Iowa*, 63, 116n, 253, 254, 265
USS *Leahy*, 448
USS *Leviathan*, 51–52
USS *Lexington*, 116, 124
USS *Maine*, 12–13
USS *Mariveles*, 19–20
USS *Missouri*, 116n, 369
USS *Murphy*, 323
USS *Nevada*, 15, 16, 48
USS *New Mexico*, 67–68, 440
USS *Oregon*, 11–13, 16, 26–27
USS *Panay*, Japanese attack of, 112–113, 115,
    117–118
USS *Pittsburgh*, 77
USS *Princess Matoika*, 48–49
USS *Quincy*, 314–315, 322, 324
USS *Ranger*, 97
USS *Renshaw*, 369
USS *Saratoga*, 80, 116
USS *Shawmut*, 62, 67
USS *St. Louis*, 53, 57, 59, 61
USS *Tacoma*, 30
USS *Wasp*, 88
USS *William D. Porter*, 254
USS *Wisconsin*, 116n, 415, 416
USS *Yorktown*, 88

Vandenberg, Arthur, 404
Vandenberg, Hoyt, 376, 389–391, 428
Vaughan, Harry, 383, 409, 413
Versailles Treaty, 121
Vichy regime
    anti-Semitic laws of, 167
    collaboration with Germany, 147–149,
        152–154, 157, 159–160, 162–165, 166–167,
        172–174
    as dictatorship, 165 (*see also* Pétain,
        Marshal)
    and *Dunkerque* battleship, 154, 481n35
    and French Indochina, 148–149, 155,
        156–157, 158–160, 162
    and Japan's Pearl Harbor attack, 170
    Leahy's role with (*see* ambassador post of
        Leahy)
    Leahy's warnings to, 162, 163, 173–174
    and Office of Strategic Services
        (OSS), 377

and Protocols of Paris, 163–164, 168
Vichy, France capital of, 150–151
and Weygand, 167–169
See also Darlan, François; French North
    Africa
Videla, Gabriel González, 415–416, 436
Vinson, Carl, 87–88, 90, 115–116, 266, 492n2
Vinson-Trammell Act, 88
Virgin Islands (previously known as the
    Danish West Indies), 47–48

Walker, John Cusworth, 440
Wallace, Henry, 194, 273, 314–315, 402–403,
    496n23, 504n20
Walsh, David, 121
War Manpower Commission, 205
War Production Board, 202, 204, 205
Warner Springs Spa, 74
Washington, DC, 43–44
Washington, George, 313
Washington Navel Conference treaties,
    61–62
Watson, Edwin "Pa," 127, 167, 271, 324
Wausau, Wisconsin, 6, 94, 443
Wavell, Archibald, 226–227
weapons of mass destruction (WMDs), 424,
    507n33
Wedemeyer, Albert, 414–415, 418–419
Weldon, Felix de, 361
Welles, Sumner
    and de Gaulle, 172
    and embargo on oil shipments to Japan,
        156, 158
    and FDR–Leahy communications,
        157–158
    and FDR's inner circle, 101–102, 186,
        476n7
    foreign-policy outlook of, 102
    and Japan in French Indochina, 159
    and Leahy's ambassadorship to France,
        145–146, 172
    and Leahy's commitment to China, 223
    Leahy's relationship with, 102, 125, 183
    scandal surrounding, 241–245, 490n3
    and strategy conferences, 222
Weygand, Maxime, 164, 167–169
Wheeler, Burton, 370
White, Harry Dexter, 295, 309, 381, 494n9
Willkie, Wendell, 135
Wilson, Henry Maitland "Jumbo," 256
Wilson, Hugh, 113
Wilson, Woodrow
    advisors of, 183
    and Daniels' cabinet post, 42
    Fourteen Points of, 367
    and Haiti, 45
    and League of Nations, 165
    Leahy's perceptions of administration, 47
    and naval buildup, 55–56
    racial attitudes of, 138
    and Roosevelt's assistant secretary
        appointment to US Navy, 40

and "Tampico Incident," 32
and World War I, 47
Winant, John, 354
Windsor, Edward, Duke of, 296
Winship, Blanton, 131
Woodring, Harry, 105, 112
Woodson, Walter, 110
Works Progress Administration (WPA),
    132, 133, 134, 137, 140, 185
World War I, 47–49, 55–56, 79, 472n20
World War II
    and Allied strategic planning, 211–213,
        216–220, 225–229
    and Axis Unconditional Surrender
        doctrine, 218–219, 346, 358, 487n20
    bombing of Hiroshima and Nagasaki, 357,
        358–359, 392
    and Cairo Conferences, 253–257, 263–264
    and Casablanca Conference, 211–213,
        216–220, 224
    and casualties, 213, 342, 342n
    and collaboration of France (*see* Vichy
        regime)
    and deployment on multiple fronts,
        281–282
    and embargo on oil shipments to Japan,
        155–156, 158
    end of, 358–359, 360
    and FDR–Leahy communications,
        157–158
    and FDR's death, 329
    German advances in, 162
    and German occupation of France,
        147–148
    and German surrender, 337–338
    and Germany-first strategy, 213–214, 215,
        216, 224, 225, *281*, 281–282, 285
    Germany's weakened state, 291
    and Guadalcanal campaign, 214–215, 230
    invasion of France (*see* Operation
        Overlord)
    Iwo Jima battle, 342, 342n, 345
    and Japan's surrender, 358 (*see also*
        Pacific theater)
    and Leahy's ambassadorship to France,
        143, 144, 145–150
    Leahy's anticipation of, 95–96
    Leahy's confidence in Allied victory,
        162, 171
    looming threat of, 121–122, 127–128,
        130, 139
    and Marshall, 448
    Mediterranean theater of, 217, 218
    and Morgenthau Plan, 294–296, 303–304
    and Octagon Conference, 292–296,
        303, 304
    Okinawa battle, 294, 342, 345–346, 347
    Pearl Harbor attack, 155–156, 169–171
    and Pétain's trial for treason, 338–339
    and plans to retrieve American
        citizens, 122
    and Potsdam Conference, 348–358

World War II *(cont.)*
  and Protocols of Paris, 163–164, 168
  role of sea power in, 147–148
  and Tehran Conference, 249–250,
    252–253, 257–261
  and Trident Conference,
    222–229, 231
  US's influence on outcome of, 3
  and war production strategies,
    202–208, 209–210, *281*,
    283, 486n6
  and Yalta Conference, 308
  See also Mediterranean theater of World
    War II
World Zionist Organization, 422
writing of Leahy, 54, 400–401,
    440–441

Yalta Conference, 308, 313–322,
    326, 336, 445
Yarnell, Harry, 10, 107, 108–109
Yugoslavia, 348